Political Violence under the Swastika

Political Violence under the Swastika

581 Early Nazis

Peter H. Merkl

Princeton University Press, New Jersey

To Theodore Abel

*whose intellectual imagination and
initiative made this possible.*

Acknowledgments

This study has been five years in the making and, during this period, inevitably developed something of a history of its own. Its continuation and eventual completion is owed to the generosity of a succession of grant-giving agencies and to the labor of many people other than the author. At the beginning, there was the republication of Theodore Abel's *Why Hitler Came to Power* (1938) by Atherton Press (1966), which alerted me to the availability of the Abel documents in the vault of the Hoover Library. I secured a grant from the National Endowment for the Humanities to spend a summer at Stanford reading the *vitae* and extracting the desired information from them. Professor Karl Kahrs assisted me with this task and contributed in particular from his knowledge of the German military terminology and social and political settings. Professors Heinz Eulau and Sidney Verba were among the first to whom I presented my tentative ideas of what I might do with the data. Professor Verba was particularly helpful and encouraging, although neither one of these two sophisticated methodologists should be held responsible in any way for my methodological flights of fancy. The staff of the Hoover Institution, especially Mrs. Petersen and Mrs. Paul, were patient and supportive to a fault. I also benefited immensely from discussing the history of the period in question with Professors Joachim Remak and Annelise Thimme of Santa Barbara, Henry C. Meyer of Irvine, and Otto von der Gablentz of Berlin.

Then came the years of struggle with the processing of the data. I had been under the mistaken assumption that computers would do the analysis much faster than any mortal could and had to learn the hard way that I was merely getting involved with a whole new set of problems whose solution was quite beyond my training and skills. After a number of false starts and breakdowns, the project finally began to get under way thanks to the unfailing generosity of the UCSB Committees on Research and on the Digital Computer and the patience and helpfulness of the UCSB Computer Center staff. A special debt of gratitude is owed to Anthony Shih, my programmer, and to the two coders, Magdalena Huwe and Dr. Georg Bahn.

When at last the end of the processing was in sight, I tried in vain to reapply to NEH and other foundations for funds to enable me to write up the results of the study. In the meantime, my original NEH grant had come under fire on the floor of Congress and in at least one popular newspaper column. James J. Kilpatrick may have expressed the opinion of many conservatives when he castigated my study of the motives of German fascists as a poor use of the taxpayers' money. In any event, neither NEH nor any other foundation seemed ready to support this research any further until I was finally rescued by the Ford Foundation, which made me a senior fellow for a period long enough to allow me to complete the write-up.

At that stage, I also benefited enormously from opportunities to present parts of the study to various learned audiences—the Conference Group on German Politics in 1969, the VIIIth World Congress of the International Political Science Association in Munich in 1970, the Los Angeles Psychiatric Institute in 1971, the Institute of International Studies at Berkeley late in 1971, and the annual meeting of the American Political Science Association in 1973. Having to present a topic and listening to the responses of a sophisticated audience is vital to the development of a work such as this. I also talked with many individuals and benefited from their comments and encouragement such as those of Professors Peter Loewenberg, James Diehl, James Rhodes, Martin Plax, Gerald Feldman, and Erwin Faul.

I am also indebted to Marge Rycek and Joan McGarry, who typed the manuscript with painstaking care. Last, but surely not least important, was the patient, supportive attitude of my wife, Elisa, and my children, Jackie and John, throughout this long period of gestation. No scholarly work of any magnitude can be carried on without such a setting of domestic peace and tranquillity. My family deserves a good part of the credit just as much as they had to endure a good part of the pain and inconvenience.

Preface

It is with a sense of feeling closer to the answers to questions that have long troubled me that I see this study appear in print. My life-long mystification about the motives of millions of ordinary rank-and-file Nazis had never been particularly assuaged by the facile discussions of Nazi ideology, the historical accounts of the move-ment and the regime, or even the biographic literature on the Nazi leadership. Anyone can understand the motives of a Nazi leader. But why did the little Nazis act as they did, and what could have been their motives long before Hitler won power?

Implicit in the answer to this question are also plausible explana-tions for broader historical questions about how it could happen. With all the concern about what flaws in the Weimar setting, or in German character and history, could have caused the rise of Hitler, we have tended to forget the obvious, central role of the movement itself, of the large number of ordinary men and women who flocked to his banner and fought for him at considerable risk to themselves. A leader cannot be a leader without willing followers. If it had not been for his legions of enthusiastically marching, fighting, and pros-elytizing followers, Hitler would never have had the bargaining power to become Reich Chancellor of Germany on that fateful day in January of 1933. It is the unique distinction of the Abel collec-tion not only to reveal the motives of the ordinary, pre-1933 Nazis, but to do so precisely at their moment of triumph. No post-1945 expression of Nazi sentiment, and perhaps not even statements col-ored by any experiences of the Third Reich, can be expected to ring as true.

There is also the question of human understanding, at a personal level, of the cataclysmic events of that age. Reading of ideological explanations or of the history of entire states and movements is somehow not as real to me as a first-person account, especially when it involves such momentous decisions and monstrous deeds as did the Nazi era. If we can understand one person, or a number of persons in their individual motivations, the arbitrary and drastic course of history becomes intelligible and a repetition of it, perhaps, avoidable. *Initiis obsta*, wrote the ancients, but also *nihil humanum me alienum*. There is a little of the Nazi in us all. Seen in their historical context, the lives of these early Nazis were commonplace and understandable indeed. There is very little to be found in them that seems sinister or ominous. And yet the consequences of their common foibles, errors, and delusions cost an estimated fifty million human lives and untold destruction and misery. And today, with the benefit of more than a quarter-century's hindsight, there is still not much evidence that mankind has learned much from the German catastrophe.

Contents

List of Tables[a]

[a] Frequency Distribution tables III, X, and XI in Appendix B.

Political Violence under the Swastika

Introduction

Nearly half a century has passed since the brownshirted storm-troopers were marching and battling in the streets and meeting-halls of the Weimar Republic on their way to power. It all began as a wild-eyed and rather violent movement of the extremist fringe, not unlike similar movements of the right or left in many other countries since. It ended with the slaughter and destruction of World War Two and with the slaughter of European Jews, not to mention the brutal suppression of political opponents and the establishment of totalitarian dictatorship in Germany. While few people will ever view the Third *Reich* with scientific detachment, perhaps the time has come to examine more carefully the nature of the Nazi movement prior to its ascent to power. Who were these men and women who fought for the brown utopia as if it were going to be the millennium? Was there something in their background or personalities that caused them to become extremists? What were their motives for joining the movement and what kind of satisfactions kept them in it, often in the face of considerable discouragement? What did they think and believe in, whether in harmony or in contrast with the official party ideology? Did some of them show particular character traits which made them more prone to violence than others? Can we learn anything from the character of the pre-1933 Nazi movement that would illuminate the internal dynamics of other extremist movements?

There is a large and still growing literature on National Socialism which includes a few speculations about the motives of the average party member, such as the literature on the "authoritarian personality." There are biographies of some of the more prominent party leaders of the period, such as Josef Goebbels and Hermann Goering, whose motivation, of course, is likely to differ somewhat from that of their followers.[1] There are even studies of the childhood and

---

[1] Joachim C. Fest, *The Face of the Third Reich*, New York: Pantheon, 1970 is particularly noteworthy in this respect among recent books.

adolescence of Adolf Hitler and Heinrich Himmler.[2] There are also, in addition to the wide-ranging literature on the fatal weakness of the republic before the Nazi onslaught, some excellent histories of the NSDAP during the "fighting years."[3] These histories tend to be on the macro-political level and rarely concern themselves with local situations and with the motivations of small local leaders and their followers. Despite their informative value, therefore, they still leave us with the impression that we do not really understand the rank-and-file Nazis as people.

To be sure, there are some accounts of local struggles that were published under the Nazi regime. The Munich *Institut fuer Zeitgeschichte* has a collection of such materials.[4] They tend to be unsystematic and highly subjective, as well as biased, but they can serve as valuable sources. Some of the local materials date from before 1933,[5] and there are now also a few current attempts to fathom the Nazi phenomenon at the local and personal level on the basis of police reports and local government records.

One of the most illuminating of these accounts and document

[2] Bradley F. Smith, *Adolf Hitler: His Family, Childhood and Youth*, and *Heinrich Himmler, A Nazi in the Making 1900-1926*, both Stanford: Hoover Institution, 1969 and 1971. See also Robert G. L. Waite, "Adolf Hitler's Guilt Feelings: A Problem in History and Psychology," *Journal of Interdisciplinary History*, I: 2 (Winter 1971), 229-249; and "Adolf Hitler's Anti-Semitism: A Study in History and Psychoanalysis," in Benjamin B. Wolman, ed., *The Psychoanalytic Interpretation of History*, New York: Basic Books, 1971, pp. 192-230.

[3] Most recently, Dieter Orlov, *The History of the Nazi Party, 1919-1933*, Pittsburgh: University of Pittsburgh Press, 1969. See also Georg Franz-Willing, *Die Hitlerbewegung: Der Ursprung 1919-1922*, Hamburg: Schenck, 1962; and Ulrich Lohalm, *Voelkischer Radikalismus*, Hamburg: Leibniz, 1970, on the early period and on the *voelkisch* antecedents of the NSDAP.

[4] For example, A. Gimbel, *So kaempften wir!* Schilderungen aus der Kampfzeit in Gau Hessen-Nassau, Frankfurt: NS Verlagsgesellschaft, 1941; R. Hochmuth, ed., *Koburg, Nationalsozialismus in der Praxis*, Berlin, 1932; Will Hermanns, *Stadt in Ketten, Geschichte der Besatzungs- und Separatistenzeit 1918-1929*, Aachen: J. A. Mayer, 1933; Friedrich Heiss, *Das Schlesienbuch*, Berlin: Volk and Reich, 1938; Wilfrid Bade, *SA erobert Berlin*, Munich: Knorr & Hirth, 1941, and many others.

[5] For example, Ernst Juenger, ed., *Der Kampf um das Reich*, Essen: Kamp, no date; and many of the materials published as documents by the *Forschungsstelle fuer die Geschichte des Nationalsozialismus* in Hamburg or discussed in appropriate publications of the *Kommission fuer die Geschichte des Parlamentarismus und der politischen Parteien* in Bonn.

collections deals with the efforts of local and regional agencies in the Mainz-Koblenz-Trier area to control the spreading brown poison. It relates, for example, an incident in December 1926 in Koblenz when the local NSDAP smuggled an unauthorized car carrying antisemitic slogans and calls for a boycott of Jewish stores into a parade of advertising floats of local merchants. The police removed the vehicle. Thereupon the Nazis prepared a demonstration for the following week with signs that read "Germans, buy *only* in Jewish stores." By that time, fortunately, the *Reichsbanner*, the republican paramilitary organization, threatened to hold a counter-demonstration which gave the police an excuse to refuse permits to both groups. Encounters of this sort allow us revealing glimpses of the motives and conduct of the "little Nazis." This collection abounds with examples of how the law enforcement efforts against the most vitriolic National Socialist agitation were time and again frustrated by the constitutional and judicial safeguards of freedom of speech and assembly. It also details Nazi protests on these grounds against arrests, searches, and seizures carried out against them.[6] Needless to say, once in power the Nazis had no such compunctions about their own lawless terror.

This book attempts to penetrate further into the minds and motivations of the rank-and-file members than some of the existing, generally non-empirical interpretations have done. We hope to probe, in particular, the internal dynamics between extremist thought and behavior as reported by the respondents themselves. In so doing, it will raise many questions that have never been raised before in the literature on the NSDAP or other extremist movements. We hope to encourage other students of extremism to carry out similar studies so that our understanding of these phenomena may be deepened and confirmed by comparison. The material we have used here is admittedly subjective and incomplete. The answers to the questions we have raised, therefore, must perforce be tentative and await confirmation by comparative evidence.

The Abel Collection

The principal material[7] used for this study was a collection of 581

---

[6] Franz J. Heyen, *Nationalsozialismus in Alltag*, Boppard: Boldt Verlag, 1967, pp. 5-7. There are also detailed accounts of Nazi agitation and propaganda in the villages and of violent clashes with the Communists (KPD).

[7] In addition to the literature on the period, the NSDAP membership files in the Berlin Document Center were also used to determine what careers, if any, the Abel respondents had made during the Third Reich.

autobiographical statements of early members of the NSDAP. These *vitae* were collected by means of an essay contest run in June 1934 by a Columbia University sociology professor, Theodore Abel, for "the best personal life history of an adherent of the Hitler movement." Respondents had to have been members or adherents prior to January 1, 1933, and were promised small cash prizes for "the most detailed and trustworthy accounts." They were asked to describe accurately and in detail "their personal lives, particularly after the World War . . . [their] family life, education, economic conditions, membership in associations, participation in the Hitler movement, and important experiences, thoughts, and feelings about events and ideas in the postwar world."[8] The contest was announced as having been "organized under the tutelage of the sociology department of Columbia University." The announcement was posted at all local NSDAP offices and carried in the party press and in releases of the *Reich* Ministry for Propaganda. In some localities it seems to have been particularly promoted by the party leadership, which may account for the uneven geographic distribution discussed below. Six hundred eighty-three respondents sent in their *vitae*, some typed, some handwritten, and varying in length from one to 80 pages.[9]

The Weak Points of the Material

Although this book is not addressed to the social science purist, its use of statistical methods suggests an extensive discussion of the weak points of the materials used and of their interpretation. To begin with, a collection of *vitae* solicited by an essay contest is most unlikely to yield a statistically representative sample. The people who respond are likely to select themselves because of motives that inevitably introduce a bias. An essay contest among members of a grassroots movement, for example, will very likely miss functional illiterates and people who lack confidence in their ability to express themselves in writing. The Abel *vitae* are by and large remarkably articulate and are frequently well-written. Conceivably, the rabidly anti-foreign attitudes of many Nazis could have kept them from

[8] Theodore Abel, *The Nazi Movement*, New York: Atherton, 1965, p. 3. Abel's account of his research first appeared under the title *Why Hitler Came to Power*, Englewood Cliffs, N.J.: Prentice Hall, 1938.

[9] The original number was reduced by about 100 cases in 1951 when the FBI confiscated the documents for unstated reasons, most probably for pending de-nazification trials. The missing cases were never returned and can be presumed to be lost. Also lost were 3000 Nazi *vitae* Abel acquired with a second essay contest in 1939.

writing *vitae*, too. Other kinds of bias emerge from the distribution of indices such as age, occupation, or geography, as will be shown below.

A major source of error might lie with the party agencies which helped to collect the *vitae*. Not only is there some evidence that some locals went out of their way to promote contributions, but there is also the danger of censorship. Since the NSDAP obviously wanted to impress the foreign sociologist and his American audience,[10] it conceivably could have handpicked respondents or quietly removed autobiographical accounts it considered embarrassing. A reading of the *vitae* suggests, however, that at least no effective censorship took place. The collection still includes many cases that any prudent censor would have wanted to remove because of their patent prejudice, the violent or hateful behavior they report, or their obvious lack of mental balance. The impression made by the Abel *vitae* is not exactly flattering to the NSDAP.

Ulterior Motives and Truthfulness

The respondents themselves sometimes candidly state their reasons for writing down the story of their lives. "It is not the prize or contest that induced me to turn in my *vita*," a school teacher (no. 31, born 1898) wrote, "but the fact that an American corporation of the stature of Columbia University is setting out to gain an impression of our National Socialist movement in this objective manner. Knowing furthermore that these contributions will be made available to a larger audience, I consider it a service to the German people to do my share for the enlightenment of foreign countries." Another respondent (no. 199, born 1897) is even more direct when he relates that his immediate reaction to reading about the contest was to write and "show the great American people (1) that the horror stories about my fatherland . . . are nothing but nasty lies, and (2) that Germany and Europe can be saved from Bolshevism only by National Socialism." While most writers simply tell their stories in a straightforward manner, there can be no question but that they were addressing themselves to this task of "enlightening foreign countries" about their movement even if their ideas of how to make the movement look good may fall short of deceiving a discerning observer.

[10] The announcement said, "The purpose of the contest is the collection of material on the history of National Socialism, so that the American public may be informed about it on the basis of factual, personal documents."

Another kind of ulterior motive of many Abel respondents, namely impressing the party with their past dedication, is less openly acknowledged. In 1934, a good many of the old fighters felt pushed aside by a flood of opportunists who had joined the party only recently in the scramble for privileges and offices. Thus, the old stalwarts had an obvious incentive for drawing the attention of their *Ortsgruppenleiter* (local chief) to their efforts and sacrifices during the fighting years or, at the very least, to gain approval by contributing their *vitae*. Some, in fact, hint that the party has forgotten them. Unlike the previous ulterior motive, this concern would have the effect of inducing respondents to exaggerate and to claim to have engaged in more extremist activity than they really had. It is also likely that the respondents minimized their involvement with the republic and republican parties for this reason. The fact that their *Ortsgruppenleiter* had probably been longer in the party than the respondent and could tell fact from fiction, on the other hand, may have curbed their imaginations.

Both of these concerns merge with the general question of whether such autobiographical statements by Nazi extremists can be taken to be "truthful" and "reliable" accounts of their political lives. Would they not be likely to hide all kinds of disagreeable things about themselves, such as their intense ethnic and other prejudices or their involvement in violence? The answer is, very simply, that the vast majority of the Abel respondents is astonishingly candid about both their hatreds and their violence. A few may indeed hide some things from us, but many more actually tell in considerable detail what we need to know. The respondents obviously felt very righteous about their prejudices and downright proud and heroic about their violent struggle. In 1934, they had won their battle for utopia and their hearts were filled with the urge to tell their stories exactly as they perceived them.[11]

Their perception, of course, is highly subjective and self-righteous, but it appears almost always to be quite honest and sincere.[12]

---

[11] Abel also stresses the fact that most of the respondents were enthusiastic converts to the cause and that they were ordinary, unsophisticated people who were not very likely to resort to deception and, we might add, whose little lies are easy to see through. *The Nazi Movement*, p. 7.

[12] On the question of the honesty and sincerity of extremists like the early Nazis, a psychological footnote seems in order. Most of us feel a rather exaggerated aversion from any extremism, which may well stem from a fear of recognizing certain tendencies in ourselves in the extremist image. Hence, we try not to look too closely or we prefer to believe that

Subjectivity is a built-in problem with all autobiographical materials, including memoirs and even scholarly biographies. The Abel *vitae* are no exception to the rule. The respondents obviously see themselves in a favorable light and rationalize or ignore whatever may not fit this image.

One of the respondents (Abel case no. 106, born 1899) puts it rather perceptively when he writes:

> When I go about trying to describe my life and path to the NSDAP, I am aware of the arrogance of this undertaking. Here I am presenting great and little events and assigning them importance by their very selection. Calling them trail-blazing or retarding in my development as a Nazi further increases the subjectivity of my presentation. . . . I may also have forgotten many a small incident which may well have had a more profound influence on me.
>
> Perhaps it would have been better for me to give the information about my life to another person, to have him put it together for the sake of objectivity. But then, can another person really appreciate how this event, that encounter, or that process affected me personally? Can another person set aside his own self enough to slip into my skin without adding his own subjectivity?

In a manner of speaking, our attempt to process the items of information about each respondent quantitatively indeed amounts to a more objective "putting it together" along lines beyond his subjective grasp or his own motivation. Many of our quantitative findings point up relationships the individual respondent could not have known about. But then again, the last sentence quoted makes an all-too-valid point. The interpretation of the *vitae* by the researchers adds a further subjective element which no scientific trimmings of coding, quantification, and computer processing should obscure. In working with the entire lives of people, there is a place for both subjective understanding and objective evaluation. We need not be afraid of the respondents' subjectivity so long as we can use our own subjective understanding as a corrective rather than relying exclusively on the mindless manipulations of a machine.

The most persuasive argument in favor of the credibility of the Abel *vitae*, next to their *prima facie* plausibility, concerns the nature of the information we have drawn from them for quantitative processing. The "hard" information about the respondent's age, occu-

---

the extremists in question are trying to deceive us, when, in fact, sincerity and self-righteousness are literally the hallmark of bigots of every stripe.

pation, social mobility, education, and location was unlikely to be falsified. Some of it, in fact, was confirmed by an external source, the NSDAP membership file in Berlin, which turned up few discrepancies.[13] The descriptions of the respondents' youth group memberships, other organizational affiliations and activities prior to joining the Nazi party, and the accounts of childhood, school environment, and economic conditions also were sufficiently neutral to be reliable and reasonably complete. There are, of course, limits of subjectivity and perception with regard to, say, an authoritarian childhood. A true authoritarian would probably fail to perceive and hence fail to describe the abnormality of the situation at home. The information supplied by the respondents about their own engagement in street violence, as indicated above, was so plentiful that we need not worry greatly about what little information may have been withheld. All items of belief or attitudes were drawn from the *vitae* by careful textual analysis and often involve dimensions of which the individual respondent could hardly have been aware. Here we undertook to record not "objective facts" but rather themes on the respondents' minds.

We were careful not to seek kinds of information the majority of the respondents was unlikely to supply. Our interest in political violence, for example, was limited to street-fighting and meeting-hall battles and did not extend to bombings or political assassinations, even though a few respondents admitted to having been involved in such crimes. Most of our information on service in the Gestapo or as concentration camp guards in the Third *Reich* came from the membership files in any case, even though several respondents describe their early service in Dachau or Oranienburg in their *vitae* (for example no. 25). It might have been interesting to know also which respondents had problems with alcohol, drugs, or morals, but none of them supplies this information. Some tell about their nervous breakdowns with a frankness we never expected from Nazis or from anybody in that period. Many respondents, on the other hand, fail to state whether or not they were married and had children. Sexual behavior, if we could get a record of it, would have been another test of certain psychological theories of National Socialism. Instead, we get only occasional glimpses such as of a sickly student

[13] A few respondents, especially women, omitted their date of birth. The occupational categories of the files sometimes differ from our own, especially if the respondent was older and underwent a change of career in connection with the economic crises of Weimar.

and veteran (no. 283, born 1888) who likes to think of how strong and healthy his body was before he was in the war, and writes:

> As soon as I had recovered somewhat from the hardships of war, I began to swim against the political current of the day. The initiative for this came from my far more massively-built friend, a rabid anti-semite. Our first scene of battle was the waiting-room of the railroad station Zoo. We sat there every night after the restaurant had closed down, adorned with a swastika and ready to pick a fight with the Jews and their lackeys who were lingering around there. Aside from our sharp tongues, our weapons were the surprisingly thick and heavy bouillon cups which we quickly emptied. In skilful hands they served us extremely well in the clash of opinions. Then we followed in the tracks of *Knueppelkunze* [an antisemitic demagogue] whose pretty little pictures of the lords of this world we bought in innumerable quantities and glued untiringly all over town, in the subway, on park benches, and in public toilets.

Once he was "caught" and beaten up soundly for defacing Social Democratic (SPD) posters at the time of the Kapp *putsch* of 1920. This was prior to a brief and evidently unsuccessful marriage. There is more than a hint of homosexuality in the tales of this unsavory character and his bully of a friend.

Unwittingly, many reveal psychological abnormalities; if it had been possible, it would certainly have been better to have an independent judgment of these, based on personal contact, from an authoritative source. Some show signs of paranoia, though again there is little objective evidence. Many more than say so may have gone around with a gun hidden on their persons. Because of the lack of possibilities for an objective analysis of their personalities, we abandoned an attempt to classify the Abel respondents as "types." Some day, better-qualified scholars will perhaps tackle this and other mysteries of the Abel collection. In any case, a differentiated approach to the different kinds of information in the Abel *vitae* obviates any blanket criticism of the overall veracity of the data. We may have been deceived in some details but hardly in the broad assessments.

The Sample: Age and Occupation

Although we conceded from the start that the Abel sample cannot by any stretch of the imagination be considered statistically representative, because of the manner of its collection, there is still some point in comparing its dimensions with those of the NSDAP. The next best thing to a representative sample is one whose bias or biases are known. To establish the distribution of various social indicators in the NSDAP, we shall use the official *Parteistatistik* of 1935,[14] which breaks down its information for party members who had joined prior to the 1930 landslide elections, those joining between that date and January 1933, and the figures for 1935. The age groups of the *Parteistatistik* are at ten-year intervals and not as closely related to meaningful generational experiences as our own, but we have matched them as closely as we could in Table 0-1.

Table 0-1: Age Distribution of the Abel Sample (in %)

Date of birth (Abel in parentheses)	Joined before 1930 elections		Joined 1930 to 1933		Total in 1933	
	Abel	NSDAP	Abel	NSDAP	Abel	NSDAP
1904-1916 (1902-1916)	41.2	36.8	29.8	43.4	26.2	42.7
1894-1903 (1895-1901)	28.2	31.4	25.0	26.9	37.8	27.2
1884-1893 (1885-1893)	16.4	17.6	24.2	17.1	20.7	17.2
1874-1883 (1878-1884)	6.8	9.7	12.1	9.2	10.4	9.3
-1873 (1860-1877)	7.4	4.5	8.9	3.4	4.9	3.6
Totals	100.0	100.0	100.0	100.0	100.0	100.0

At first glance, the totals in 1933 show the Abel collection to be rather far from the mark. It has far fewer respondents in their 20s and more in their 30s than did the NSDAP according to the *Parteistatistik*. A look at the figures for the pre-1930 joiners and those who joined between 1930 and 1933, however, suggests that the discrepancies between the sample and the party are due mostly to the interval between 1930 and 1933. The early joiners of the sample have an age distribution quite similar to that of the early joiners of the NSDAP. A further check of the relative share of pre-1930 joiners in the totals of 1933 shows our sample to have a heavy pre-1930 bias. The NSDAP total of 1933 includes only 15.3% who joined before the 1930 elections, all the rest having joined in a little more than two years. The Abel sample, by comparison, includes no less than 56.3% of pre-1930 joiners. Our sample, in other words, is representative mostly of the pre-1930 party when it was still clearly an extremist fringe group of a mere 130,000, and not of the landslide popular movement of 1933.

The Nazi party, even more than our total sample, was also a very young party, and we will devote special attention to the youth angle

[14] NSDAP, *Parteistatistik*, 2 vols., *Reichsorganisationsleiter*, 1935, printed as manuscript. These statistics may fall short of census standards today but are certainly the most authoritative source available.

below (part III). It was certainly much younger than the general population. In 1935, for instance, the party had 37.6% between the ages of 18 and 30 (vs. 31.1% of the general population) and 27.9% between 31 and 40 (vs. 22%). Only 14.9% of the Nazis were over 50 (vs. 29.8%).[15] The Communist party (KPD) was probably the only other mass party of comparable age. The SPD, unfortunately, was a far "older" party than the NSDAP or KPD, older even than the average of the general population.[16] The bourgeois parties were

Table 0-2: Age Distribution of NSDAP and SPD in 1930-1933 (in %)

	NSDAP 1933	Abel 1930	SPD 1930	Population 1933
18-30	42.7	41.2	18.1	31.1
31-40	27.2	37.5	26.5	22.0
41-50	17.2	13.9	27.3	17.1
50-60	9.3 ⎫		⎧ 19.6	14.5
over 60	3.6 ⎭	7.4	⎩ 8.5	15.3
Totals	100.0	100.0	100.0	100.0

not much different from the SPD. Polarized between the youthful extreme right and left and alienated from the "old men of Weimar," German youth set up the stormladders against the republic and helped one of its false alternatives, the Nazi party, to power.[17]

The occupational distribution of the Abel sample is not very different from that of the party in 1933 with the exception of an overrepresentation of civil servants and underrepresentation of business and professional people.[18] If we look at the earlier occupational com-

[15] Parteistatistik I, 155-162. Before 1930, it should be noted further, the party members over 50 tended to be most numerous in the southern Gaue, which also happened to be the older Gaue. The more youthful character of the northern Gaue was further accented by the influx of young people in the period between 1930 and 1933.

[16] The figures on the SPD in Table 0-2 are from Richard N. Hunt, German Social Democracy, 1918-1933, New Haven: Yale University Press, 1964, p. 107.

[17] See also the remarks of Robert Michels on the "political youth" of Weimar, its suspicion of education and scientific relativism, and its desire to wrest power from the economic gerontocracy, mostly born in the 1860s. Umschichtungen in den herrschenden Klassen nach dem Kriege, Stuttgart, Kohlhammer, 1934, pp. 100-101.

[18] These figures are from Parteistatistik I, 53 and 69-70. However, the general population figures list instead of "housewives, pensionists, and others" only "others." The same is true of the very last column. It is hard to imagine a society with only 6% housewives. See also the figures cited

position, some of the shifts within the party come to light as well, such as the increase in civil servants and in the blue-collar element (opposite to the trend of the sample) and the relative decline of white collar and farmers since 1930. The civil servants under the Weimar Republic were long forbidden to belong to the NSDAP, which may help to explain their late entry. The large number of civil servants in the Abel sample, including quite a few teachers, may be

Table 0-3: The Occupational Distribution of the Sample (in %)

	General population in 1933	Joined before 1930		1930-1933		Total in 1933	
		Abel	NSDAP	Abel	NSDAP	Abel	NSDAP
Workers	46.3	32.6	26.3	20.2	32.5	27.1	32.1
White-collar	12.4	17.0	24.0	20.6	20.6	18.7	20.6
Business and professions (incl. students)	9.6	14.1	19.9	13.2	18.5	13.6	20.2
Civil servants	4.8	16.1	7.7	25.2	6.5	19.9	13.0
Farmers	20.7	7.5	13.2	9.2	12.5	8.2	10.7
Housewives, pensionists, others	6.2	12.7	8.9	11.6	9.4	12.5	3.4
Totals	100.0	100.0	100.0	100.0	100.0	100.0	100.0

partly due to the greater willingness of this group to express itself in writing. In part it may stem from occupational categories geared to the prewar and wartime careers of many older respondents who had served in the imperial army and had been transferred to a civil service career (*Kapitulant*).

The business and professional group in the party statistics consists of two large blocs of artisans and small businessmen and a smaller group of professional persons. The independents of the Abel sample show a similar composition. If we compare the party to the general population, it becomes abundantly clear how the NSDAP tended to overrepresent this group along with white collar, civil servants, and teachers at the same time that it underrepresented farmers and workers.[19] The pre-1930 party had a high con-

by Hans H. Gerth, "The Nazi Party: Its Leadership and Composition," in Robert K. Merton et al., eds., *Reader in Bureaucracy*, Glencoe: Free Press, 1952, pp. 100-113.

[19] See also David Schoenbaum, *Hitler's Social Revolution; Class and Status in Nazi Germany 1933-1939*, Garden City, N.Y.: Doubleday, 1966, ch. 1. The SPD, according to the SPD *Jahrbuch 1930*, p. 194, had a composition of 64.1% workers (incl. 4.6% pensioners), 10% white-

centration of independents, civil servants, white collar and women in the south; and workers and peasants played a greater role in the north, and after 1930. After 1933, the party became rather concerned about the wave of civil servants and teachers who were jumping on the bandwagon.[20] But there is no evidence to suggest that the party very seriously pursued its desire to be a mirror image of the population at large.

The Geographic Distribution of Respondents

Since the local party agencies in some areas seem to have gone out of their way to encourage members to participate, it is not surprising to find considerable imbalances in the geographic distribution of the respondents as compared to the tabulations of the *Parteistatistik* of 1935. Before we can take a closer look at these patterns, however, a word of caution is in order. The *Parteistatistik* records the respondents' residences in 1934; we are more interested in where they were during the height of the struggle, 1929-1933. We are, moreover, dealing with a highly mobile population many members of which moved from city to city up to five times in these years. Such movements occurred especially in response to unemployment or bankruptcy during the Great Depression and frequently went back and forth between cities and rural areas, or from anywhere to Berlin and back. The vast majority of our (overrepresented) Berlin respondents had moved there rather recently. Many of the underrepresented areas are not underrepresented among previous residences of the respondents. For these reasons, any record of geographic distribution has to be viewed as at best a fleeting glance at a situation in flux.

---

collar, 4.2% self-employed, and 0.6% free professions, 4% civil servants and teachers, and 17.1% housewives. Except for the farmers, there is no denying that the SPD was much closer to the mainstream of German society than their brown antagonists were.

[20] The *Parteistatistik* II, 298, also gives a surprisingly high unemployment figure for party members as late as January 1, 1935, 8.7%, composed to nearly a third of pre-1933 members. They were particularly concentrated in the Rhineland, in Hamburg, and in Danzig. The Abel sample includes a good one-fifth of victims of the Great Depression. The KPD, according to Ossip K. Flechtheim, also began to be swamped by the unemployed beginning in 1929. Its chief strongholds were also in such areas as the Rhineland and Oppeln (Silesia), although much of its vote came from unincorporated areas and probably from the newer industries. *Die KPD in der Weimarer Republik*, Offenbach: Drott, 1948, pp. 209-213.

There are several meaningful ways of comparing the geographical distribution of the Abel sample with that of the party.[21] We can juxtapose, for example, the southern *Gaue* (including Hessen-Nassau and Koblenz-Trier) to those in the north. The significance of such a comparison lies in the fact that the NSDAP in the south was considerably older and still bore the earmarks of its pre-*putsch* character.[22] The northern party was largely the product of post-1924 expansion and development. The Abel sample rather over-represents the south with 29.7% southerners rather than the 17.1% indicated in the *Parteistatistik*. The difference can be explained in part with the substantial shift from the south to the north that occurred between the *Reichstag* elections of 1930 and the appointment of Hitler as *Reich* Chancellor in 1933. With the growth of the party in the north, for instance, two of the oldest *Gaue*, Muenchen-Oberbayern and Bayerische Ostmark, slipped from the eleventh place in size to the eighteenth and from the sixth to the sixteenth place, respectively. As the reader will recall, those who joined prior to 1930 are heavily overrepresented anyway.

The specific southern areas of which the sample has a share far in excess of the party of 1933 are the Saar-Pfalz (10.4%), Koblenz-Trier (4.6%), and Hessen-Nassau (10.7%), including Frankfurt, which have two to five times the percentage they have in the *Parteistatistik*. On the other hand, some southern *Gaue*, notably Baden (0.2%), Bayerische Ostmark (0.7%), and Nuernberg-Franken (0.2%) have only a fraction of what their share should be. Evidently the local party agencies in these areas were less zealous in promoting the essay contest than those in the first-mentioned *Gaue* around the Upper Rhine.

A second method of checking the geographic distribution is along the lines of religion, that is, as Catholicism and Protestantism were distributed in the Weimar Republic. To compare personal affiliation was not practical since two-thirds of the respondents gave no indication of their religious membership, which is in itself a remarkable feature, and since the *Parteistatistik* also supplies no statistics on

---

[21] The comparison is based on the distributions by party *Gau* given by the *Parteistatistik* I, pp. 19 and 21 for NSDAP membership in January 1933 (according to residence recorded in 1934-1935).

[22] For example, there was a much greater union of party offices and high stormtrooper (SA) ranks in the south, which gave the southern NSDAP more of a fascist character than could be found in the north. See below pp. 629, 706-707 and Wolfgang Schaefer, *NSDAP: Entwicklung und Struktur der Staatspartei des Dritten Reiches*, Hannover and Frankfurt: Goedel, 1957.

this point. The significance of the religious-geographical juxtaposition lies in the well-known fact that the Nazi landslides of 1930 and 1932 took place almost exclusively in Protestant areas. In the predominantly Catholic areas, the voters generally remained loyal to the church and the Center party. Twenty-one and nine-tenths percent of the Abel respondents, as compared to 24.7% of the party members of 1933, lived in Catholic areas. The religious-area balance of our sample, in other words, is not far from what it ought to be.

The third approach is based on points of political emphasis suggested by a reading of the Abel *vitae* and Weimar history. A great deal of subjective significance, for example, was attached by many respondents to the ethnic drama of the border clashes and the German exodus in post-1918 Poland and Czechoslovakia.[23] The ethnic tensions evidently aroused an aggressive nationalism in many of the people involved and led them directly into the arms of the NSDAP and its Austrian-born leader,[24] who was motivated by similar concerns of the German ethnic border in the east. The Nazi party, the reader will recall, started out as an international movement of affiliates in Bavaria, Austria, and Czechoslovakia where the roots of National Socialism go back to a pre-1914 anti-Socialist and anti-Czech German ethnic labor movement. The numerous anti-Polish "border Germans" in the Abel sample tended to end up in East Prussia, Silesia, or along the eastern fringes of the *Gaue* Kurmark and Pommern. Their disproportionate numbers within these *Gaue*, at least in the sample, give the Abel sample a distinct hue of the vengeful *Drang nach Osten* of the Third Reich. As a group, these *Gaue* are overrepresented (14.2% vs. 10.2% in the party of 1933) in the sample. Closer examination shows, however, that it is only the East Prussians and the eastern fringe of *Gau* Kurmark that are overrepresented. Silesia, the second largest *Gau*, and Pommern are grossly underrepresented.

Another area of considerable subjective importance are the territories, mostly on the left bank of the Rhine, which were occupied by the French and Belgians after World War One and in the course of the French invasion of 1923. Here too, friction with the occupation and, in many cases, punishment or expulsion to the unoccupied areas of the Weimar Republic so greatly aroused superpatriotic feelings in many respondents that they promptly found their way to the

[23] See below, pp. 105-110.

[24] There are also a number of former Austrians in the sample, namely nos. 47, 63, 69, 350, 400, 475, and 540.

NSDAP. The respondents from the occupied areas, too, are over-represented in the Abel sample (26.3% vs. 8.6% in the party of 1933) since the *Gaue* Saarpfalz and Koblenz-Trier are grossly overrepresented. The Rhein-Ruhr area and the *Gau* Koeln-Aachen are also somewhat overrepresented in the sample, and so are the western parts of Hessen-Nassau. Since many of the respondents who were in conflict with the occupation fled or were expelled and then encountered the NSDAP elsewhere in Germany, the problem is not strictly one of geographic overrepresentation but rather a matter of emphasis on this particular formative experience. It is also conceivable that these respondents from the occupied areas and those from the ethnic border felt a particular urge to "tell America" their life stories or that the party especially encouraged them to do so.

Table 0-4: The Geographic Distribution of the Sample

| | Abel sample | | NSDAP 1933 |
	Number	Per cent	(Per cent)
Ethnic border areas	83	14.2	10.4
Occupied areas	152	26.3	8.6
Berlin	180	30.9	6.5
Rest of Northern Germany	82	14.1	64.1
Rest of Southern Germany	85	14.5	10.4
Totals	582	100.0	100.0

The third area of emphasis and considerable overrepresentation is Berlin, the metropolitan locale of Goebbel's campaign for the conquest of the heart and soul of the republic.[25] The capital of the empire and the Weimar Republic attracted or provided a transit station for many millions, especially throughout northern Germany. As late as in the 1950s, one of every two West German adults was

[25] Police reports before the Prussian diet for 1930 give an inkling of the importance of Berlin in the Nazi struggle for power as well as of the general, intense level of political activity. In that year alone, the police had to be present at 23,946 open-air rallies and demonstrations involving about 25 million participants, and at 34,742 indoor meetings with 13.5 million participants in Prussia. Berlin accounted for 4.9 and 4.8 million participants, respectively, probably including many of the monster rallies of the NSDAP. The Nazis and Communists, in any case, were involved in nearly 90% of the rallies and demonstrations which required police intervention, and in all but 4% of the disruptions they were in fact the disrupters. The *Stahlhelm*, *Reichsbanner*, and *Jungdo* or *Wehrwolf* accounted for the rest. *Sammlung der Drucksachen des Preussischen Landtags*, 3. Wahlperiode (June 8, 1928), pp. 6053-6055.

found by the *Institut fuer Demoskopie* to have been in Berlin at some time of his (or her) life. No less than 30.9% of the Abel respondents (vs. 6.5% of the party of 1933) were in Berlin during the end phase of the Nazi struggle for power. But a very large part of these respondents appears to have used Berlin as a transit station or temporary abode rather than as permanent residence. Among them especially were people moving from city to city (21.7%), rural-urban migrants (23.8%) who might not stay, and people from the ethnic border, from foreign countries, or the German colonies (15.9%), for whom Berlin was a natural stopping-off point before they settled somewhere else. The big melting-pot and transit station thus represents a much larger area as well as the international relations of the whole country.

The upshot of the overrepresentation of Berlin, the occupied areas, and the eastern border is the corresponding underrepresentation of the rest of the north German territory. In particular, Saxony, Thuringia, Pomerania, but also the *Gaue* Westfalen-Nord, Hamburg-Schleswig-Holstein, and the Hannover area are woefully underrepresented as compared to the party statistics of 1933. The rest of the south, by comparison, is overrepresented only because it includes Hessen-Nassau, and especially Frankfurt, which on a smaller scale performed functions for south German mobility similar to those of Berlin in the north. In summary, the geographic distribution of the Abel sample appears to exhibit several obvious biases which are likely to give a disproportionate emphasis to experiences such as the impact of the border struggles and of the occupation experience, or of spatial mobility.

What Can We Learn from the Abel Data?

Given the nature of this sample, its pre-1930 emphasis and other biases, can we really expect it to tell us anything about the Nazi movement before 1933? The answer is both yes and no. We clearly can regard this sample as representative of the whole movement only with great caution. We cannot simply assume that its distributions will correspond to those of the entire party at the time. This is perhaps less true of the pre-1930 movement, both because the distortions seem much smaller and because we have as many as one out of every 400 pre-1930 Nazis in our collection (as compared to one of every 1500 pre-1933 Nazis). In any case, there is obviously no reason to derive great theoretical conclusions from a few percentage points here or there. On the other hand, again, there is the powerful argument that this is one of the very few empirical sources of insight into the mentality of the men and women who led Germany into the Third Reich, and that no one could produce a better sample today.

Our chief interest, in any case, is not with the distribution of various attributes in the Abel sample, but rather with how some variables and attributes relate to other variables and attributes in the respondents. We cannot make any well-founded statements about the Nazi party as such and especially not about how Nazis may have differed from non-Nazis in background, behavior, and attitudes. We have no external control-group data with which we could compare the Abel data. We can, however, attempt to get at the internal dynamics of being a Nazi activist by comparing groups within the sample, say the more active with the less active, and by relating their combined differences to interpretative theories of political behavior.

We shall discuss the contents of our measurements in greater detail below. Suffice it to say here that we started out by drawing variables such as the date of birth or the intensity of the reported involvement in violence, and attributes such as the dominant theme of a respondent's ideology, from each of the Abel *vitae* and put them on data sheets. They were then coded and put on cards for computer processing. With each of the 79 items we determined first of all the frequency distribution (FD) for the whole sample.[26] Then we grouped the items according to their bearing on selected topics, such as political socialization, and crosstabulated them in pairs with one another and with other variables and attributes. In the text, the discussion of each item begins with the distribution of this item (FD) throughout the sample. But these frequency distributions are meant to inform the reader about the basis of the particular inquiry and not necessarily to indicate the distribution of the same property among the party members of that time.

The crosstabulations produced several thousands of tables which for obvious reasons we chose not to include in this book.[27] Their significance, instead, is discussed in prose that should be intelligible to any reader regardless of his or her statistical background. As we indicated earlier, this book was not meant only for quantitatively-oriented social scientists but also for historians and for the general reader interested in the Nazi phenomenon. Even readers with slide rule in hand will have to accept on faith our report on the statistical

[26] A list of the items and the page number of where each frequency distribution is located can be found in the appendix.

[27] On request, the disks or the crosstabulations will be made available to scholars who would like to use them.

manipulations undertaken just as they would accept the historical research that may lie behind non-quantitative books. The validity of what we seek to demonstrate lies not in the fine percentage points, as mentioned above, but in the plausibility of the relationships we uncover.

An Example of a Crosstabulation

A brief explanation of the use made of the crosstabulation tables and of the language employed in the presentation is in order. To begin with, any effective crosstabulation requires a small number of categories, say between three and five of each item. The first item

Table 0-5: Example of a Crosstabulation Table

Rows = Functional membership			Columns = Membership in SA, SS			
	Not a member	Joined when joined NS	Joined SA later	Graduated from SA to SS	SUM	KEY
None	109	128	27	16	280	RAW
	(38.9%)	(45.7%)	(9.6%)	(5.7%)	(100.0%)	RPR
	(57.4%)	(75.7%)	(56.3%)	(80%)	(65.6%)	RPC
	(25.5%)	(30%)	(6.3%)	(3.7%)	(65.6%)	RPT
Women,	27	11	8	3	49	RAW
farmers,	(55.1%)	(22.4%)	(16.3%)	(6.1%)	(100.0%)	RPR
professional,	(14.2%)	(6.5%)	(16.7%)	(15%)	(11.5%)	RPC
students'	(6.3%)	(2.6%)	(1.9%)	(7%)	(11.5%)	RPT
associations						
NSBO	17	17	6	1	41	RAW
(Factory cell	(41.5%)	(41.5%)	(14.6%)	(2.4%)	(100.0%)	RPR
organization)	(8.9%)	(10.1%)	(12.5%)	(5%)	(9.6%)	RPC
	(4%)	(4%)	(1.4%)	(.2%)	(9.6%)	RPT
Civil	37	13	7	—	57	RAW
service	(64.9%)	(22.8%)	(12.3%)	—	(100.0%)	RPR
association	(19.5%)	(7.7%)	(14.6%)	—	(13.3%)	RPC
	(8.7%)	(3%)	(1.6%)	—	(13.3%)	RPT
Sums	190	169	48	20	427	RAW
	(44.5%)	(39.6%)	(11.2%)	(4.7%)	(100.0%)	RPR
	(100.0%)	(100.0%)	(100.0%)	(100.0%)	(100.0%)	RPC
	(44.5%)	(39.6%)	(11.2%)	(4.7%)	(100.0%)	RPT

Note: Markings (⌊_⌋) show significant relationships.

of our example, the membership of Abel respondents in various functional Nazi organizations, started out with eight categories to record all the different Nazi groups. The small numbers of organized Nazi women, farmers, professionals, and students in the sample suggested collapsing these categories into one in order to maintain a statistically significant number for crosstabulation. The Nazi civil servants and the NSBO (labor cells), on the other hand, were large enough for this purpose. The new combination column, of course, runs the danger of becoming so heterogeneous as to lose in general relevance what it may gain in statistical significance. The second item, stormtrooper membership, consisted of no more than four categories.

In the crosstabulation, each little box shows in the first line the absolute number of respondents who fit the appropriate categories of both items. One hundred nine persons in the first box had no functional membership and also never joined the stormtroopers. The second line gives percentage per row: these 109 cases amounted to 38.9% of all the respondents who were not in a functional group. The third line indicates percentage of column: 57.4% of all the non-stormtroopers also had no functional membership. And the fourth gives the percentage of the entire table: 109 is 25.5% of the table total (427) in the right bottom corner. This last-mentioned percentage (RPT) can indicate, depending on the total number of boxes in the table, which particular box contains the highest significant relationship. The last three boxes of the fourth column, for example, are not worth much except as an indication of a negative relationship: SS men generally did not bother with functional memberships.

At first glance, such a table appears to have many noteworthy dimensions that we could use for interpretation. There are, to begin with, the frequency distributions of both items along the right (RPC) and bottom (RPR) margins.[28] These determine the central tendencies of the table by showing where and how much the two items coincide in the same box. Each row and column also has its frequency distribution which more or less follows the distribution of the item concerned: the first row resembles the bottom margin in its distribution except for certain deviations. These deviations are another important indication of how the first item relates to the sec-

[28] Cases from which the relevant information for both items could not be extracted were not included in the table. In the presentation, below, the complete frequency distribution of the first item is always presented first. But that of the second item has to be looked up if desired by means of the list in the appendix.

ond item. They show us, for example, a distinct (10% or more)[29] tendency of respondents who are not in functional Nazi organizations to become stormtroopers immediately upon joining the party and eventually to "graduate" from the SA to the SS, the bodyguard elite in the Weimar years. The other rows, by the same token, show that members of Nazi civil servant, women, student, or farm groups, by comparison, became stormtroopers either not at all or only reluctantly, after having been in the party for a year or more. We can conclude, then, that there is a bifurcation in early Nazi careers between the violence-oriented stormtrooper and the person who would join, or hold office in functional organizations. The NSBO members, who rather resemble the functional non-members in stormtrooper membership, appear to be an exception to the rule.[30]

The Content of the Vitae

The first impression on reading the Abel *vitae* is one of tremendous variety. Each story appears to have its own rationale, and there are so many seemingly important angles that the researcher tends to get lost in a sea of particularities with few common meridians to guide him. Gradually, however, we began to discern major areas of concern that could form the backbone of a systematic analysis:

1. The dynamics of the social backgrounds of many Nazis;
2. The impact of the war, the "revolution," and the counter-revolution;
3. The political socialization of each Nazi and the youth angle;
4. The escalation of extremist involvement and of political violence;
5. The *Weltanschauung* and prejudices of the Nazis, viewed from an empirical angle; and
6. Life and individual careers within the Nazi party and its affiliates.

Each of these areas involved a number of very specific queries for information available in most of the *vitae*. Except for the basic in-

[29] If the deviation is 50% or more, we refer to it as "heavily tending" in that direction.

[30] Methodologically, we have thus shifted from the univariate distributions, which are a hazardous basis because of the flaws in the sample, to the relationships between two variables or attributes. Even if the sample is atypically distributed on each of the two dimensions, this procedure can give us a basically correct picture of their interrelationship within broad boundaries.

formation contained in the Nazi files, it was quite unlikely that, after the passage of 40 years and the denazification trials, we could supplement any significant amount of the personal recollections and attitudes laid down in the *vitae* by locating and reinterviewing surviving respondents.[31] We had to take the data as we found them and devise our questions in such a way as to stay very close to the material.

The rationale of quantitative processing suggested an emphasis on parameters such as age, or size of community of residence, which are continuous and could be found in nearly all the *vitae*. A careful reading, on the other hand, also suggested a large number of subgroups and attitude groupings worth a closer look in the light of the social experiences and issues of the historical period in question. Both of these aspects were taken into account in making up the final list of items for coding and statistical manipulation. Thus an awareness of the history, sociology, and social psychology of the fateful years of the Weimar Republic was programmed into the statistical analysis of the data, with an emphasis which at times created conflicts with the pure canons of social science research design. However, the special insights into the human and social motivation of early Nazi members to be gained thereby appeared well worth the sacrifice.

The most important of the universal parameters that describe major aspects of a respondent's life situation and motivation was age (item 1), or estimated age,[32] because the birth-dates of the respondents range from 1860 to 1916, a period of extraordinary social change in Germany. The autobiographical accounts of the older respondents, indeed, breathe a spirit rather different from those of people who grew up in the twentieth century. The oldest cohorts seemingly accepted their position and the limited opportunities in a stratified society and took a naive pleasure in social deference, military uniforms, and patriotic displays. The youngest sound dis-

---

[31] The average age of the Abel respondents would be about 80 today, which indicates a very small number of survivors and a considerable incidence of mental incapacity to answer such questions as we might wish to ask. The fall of the Third Reich and the disclosure of its misdeeds, moreover, is certain to make respondents fearful of inquiries about their past, not to mention the likely rationalizations and distortions we have to expect. Finally, the intervening war and postwar mobility and the desire of many respondents to hide from the past would make locating them rather difficult.

[32] In a few cases, including some of the female respondents, the exact age had to be estimated to a range of about 3-5 years.

tinctly modern in their social attitudes and expectations. In between is that unhappy war generation which had grown up in peace and was disoriented by the experience of the trenches.

There are other indicators, such as the size of the community of residence during the principal period of the Nazi struggle for power, 1929-1932 (item 3). According to most accounts of these fateful years, town and country, or the small and big cities, differed considerably in their reaction to the brown onslaught. Then there is a detailed record of the respondents' principal occupations (item 4) which allows us to put the more significant sociological hypotheses about the radicalization of various social and occupational groups to the test. White-collar respondents indeed have a very different story to tell than do businessmen or blue-collar workers. The farmers and women respondents, though small in number, could not be fitted smoothly into the occupational categories and were reserved for special attention. Of particular importance in the sample, moreover, were the many military and civil service respondents whose outlook on life seemed particularly homogeneous and, perhaps, more likely to get them involved with the early Nazi party than any other career group.

We coded also the level of education (item 11), a very important index in German society, the state of health (item 12), and religious affiliation (item 10) as far as this information was supplied. We also recorded the Protestant or Catholic majority or mixed character of the area of residence, which enabled us to look into such questions, for example, as whether a Protestant in a Catholic or mixed area would engage more in political violence or be more prone to certain ideological views than would a Protestant in a Protestant-majority area.

Socio-economic Dynamics

These basic dimensions are part of the changing social setting in which the Abel respondents were motivated to join the Nazi party when it was still regarded as an extremist fringe group. There are already several theories that explain fascism as an outgrowth of social tensions and experiences, although unfortunately they often contradict each other. Many of the respondents clearly indicate that some social causation may indeed have accounted for their personal political development. We undertook to record and code further social dimensions and attitudes which might permit broader generalizations about the social dynamics of the early Nazi recruits.

Since most respondents volunteered the relevant information, for example, we recorded whether the person had been born abroad or had lived for several years abroad, whether he or she had been in the German colonies or a participant in the "internal colonization" in the Alsace or in the province of Poznan at the invitation of the Reich government (item 2). We also recorded as particularly significant if a person was from the German border areas in the east or from the western areas occupied by the French or Belgians. If none of these "location experiences" applied, we recorded whether the respondent was a rural-urban migrant, was spatially immobile, or highly mobile from city to city.

In addition to the respondent's occupation, moreover, we noted the father's occupation (item 7) and any noticeable economic improvement or decline of the parents while the respondent was still a dependent (item 6). The respondent's own economic change (item 5) was likewise taken into account in order to examine the theories which connect Nazi recruitment with the economic troubles of the Weimar Republic. It became clear at an early point that the economic difficulties of the individual Nazi were highly related to the generation to which he belonged. The prewar generation had very little economic trouble. The war generation disproportionately suffered in the years before 1928, and the postwar generation was the hardest hit, during the Great Depression.

The comparison of occupation and education of fathers and sons or daughters, furthermore, made it possible to determine in most cases whether a respondent's family was upwardly mobile, socially declining, or maintaining its level (item 8). Upward mobility, or its opposite, decline, is a favorite plot of sociological theories of fascism and also of studies of other revolutionary movements. In the case of the Nazis, moreover, it was likely to be significant what attitudes they would express toward social class (item 9), since the party liked to parade the egalitarian slogan of the "community of the people (*Volksgemeinschaft*)." Many respondents emphatically linked their Nazism to their class feelings, which were often illustrated with bitter tales of social snubs and humiliations. Since imperial society was a rigid class society and classes began to disintegrate during its last decades and in the Weimar Republic, the significance of this element hardly requires elaboration.

Youthful Politicization

Weimar politics was racked by extremes of generational revolt. The Nazi movement was one of the spearheads of rebellious youth against the gerontocracy that ruled society and government. It is all the more welcome, consequently, that the Abel *vitae* are full of details about the political socialization and organized youth activities of the respondents. For our purposes, we defined the youthful phase as extending to the 25th year, and a youth group as any voluntary formal organization other than unions, the military, or economic organizations, in which the respondent actively participated. The vast majority of the groups covered were well-known youth groups, and in the rest some evidence of youthful group life with peers was present.

Thus we recorded the first youth group a respondent ever belonged to (item 13) and any change to other groups if present (item 14). The positive or negative feelings toward this first group were also recorded (items 15 and 16), since the autobiographies generally stated whether and why the person liked or left this first group. At this point, the strongly activist, even violent temper of our sample already emerged. A surprisingly large number of the respondents gloried early in physical battle, demonstrations, and ideological inspiration, and left their first youth group, if it did not satisfy the need for them, in favor of one that did.

We further kept a record of any youth group offices held by each respondent (item 17), and of the most extreme youthful activity in which he engaged (item 18). An attempt was also made to classify the character of his or her youthful political involvement on a scale running from "parochial-prepolitical" over "fully politicized" to "politically militarized" for those yearning to march and fight in uniforms (item 19). The respondent's reaction to his military service, if any, was also noted, on the theory that there may be a significant relationship between military and paramilitary enthusiasms (item 22).

Finally, we inquired into other socializing influences such as the home, the school, and early employment if any. The information on the childhood setting (item 25) of the respondents was rather sketchy, as we might expect. But the partisan color and involvement of the home (item 23) and the school or peer group environment (item 24) was often clearly set forth. For the most part the respondents also indicated whether they had been obliged to work at home or outside it at a tender age (item 26), and whether they had encountered any political friction at their place of employment as young adults (item 20). A great many did endure harassment and not only from Socialist or Communist fellow-workers but also from conservatives (DNVP), Liberals (DVP or DDP), or Centrists as bosses or colleagues. Political friction often served to bring out or to reinforce their extremist tendencies.

Militarizing Influences

A careful reading of the autobiographies reveals again and again the presence of a quasi-military urge to march and do battle, without much thought of goals or purpose. For all three generations, and especially for the war and postwar generations, the experiences of World War One, the "revolution" of 1918, and the ensuing counter-revolutionary upsurge seem to have been the most direct militarizing influences. To assess the exposure of the respondents to these stimuli, we recorded first of all their military service (item 21) and their reaction to it (item 22). Since about half of them never served at all, there is also a large contingent who were too young to be in the war but who, according to their own testimony, were vicariously socialized into the war experience by their fathers, older brothers or friends, or by the war enthusiasm in their schools. We dubbed them the "victory-watchers" because of the eagerness with which they observed the goings-on at the front.

Whether they served or not, nearly all expressed attitudes toward the war experience, ranging from enthusiastic "support to the bitter end" to disaffection and disillusionment toward the last years of the war (item 30). This attitude was obviously related to but not identical with the reactions to Germany's defeat (item 34), which for the most part amounted to an indication of who was to blame for it. The trauma of the unhappy ending of the war effort and, for the soldiers, of their return to a drastically changed scene at home expressed itself so vividly in the *vitae* that we classified it and recorded its themes of cultural shock (item 31). Since such a trauma is a highly subjective matter and not necessarily a reflection of external events, this index is essentially a measurement of the alienation of the respondents from their society.

We also ascertained the reaction of the respondents to the various left-wing uprisings, the "still-born revolution," as W. T. Angress has called it (item 35), which again boiled down mostly to recording who was being blamed for it. Despite some overlap with the responses to item 34, the reaction to the defeat, the respondents frequently separated the two events, regardless of the legend of the "stab in the back," and assigned the blame to different groups or agencies. Many just took defeat and revolution in stride. A limited but significant part of the sample reported conflict with the French or Belgian occupation after the war, and especially at the time of the French invasion of the Ruhr in 1923 (item 33). Their accounts range from reports of expulsion or punishment by the occupation to tales of active involvement in the anti-French and anti-separatist underground.

Finally, we recorded the involvement of the respondents in counter-revolutionary activities and organizations in 1919-1921 (item 32) and again in 1923 (item 36), the year of the beer-hall *putsch*, and other plans for a "march on Berlin." The word "counter-revolutionary" is not to imply that the legally elected republican governments constituted a revolution in Germany, but rather that the right-wing groups were originally and primarily formed to combat the attempts at a left-wing revolution. By 1923, of course, and in some instances before that, they had openly shifted their goal to an all-out attack against the legal government which makes them right-wing revolutionaries rather than counter-revolutionaries, strictly speaking. As our data will show, there was also a noticeable qualitative difference between the earlier Free Corps fighters and counter-revolutionaries and the right-wing revolutionary host of 1923, who had rather specific ideological goals.

The Escalation of Extremist Activity

One of the most absorbing topics in studying extremist movements is the process by which a person becomes an extremist and goes on to engagement in political violence. The Abel biographies generally permit an assessment of the distinct stages of this process in each case, although the stages may vary somewhat. For our purposes, we decided to posit four stages:

1. A prepolitical stage or apolitical state of mind, such as that of early youth or a certain civil service or military mentality (item 37).
2. A stage of paramilitary involvement with counter-revolutionary and veterans' organizations, generally during the early postwar era or around 1923 (item 38).
3. A stage of political involvement with Weimar political parties and elections (item 41).
4. The full-blown extremist stage as a Nazi stormtrooper or activist (item 45).

Some respondents went through only three stages, leaving out either stage two or stage three. Rather frequently, they entered stage two and found it wanting ideological direction. Or they entered stage three first and, after some time, were driven on by a thirst for militant action. Their arrival at stage four meant, in the words of one stormtrooper, that they had become "the political soldiers of Adolf Hitler," a phrase aptly summarizing the two elements sought, plus the charismatic appeal of the movement.

The unit of analysis of this phase of the project is the individual's progress toward ever greater involvement in extremist activities rather than the succession of historical stimuli in time. Their recruitment began when a respondent first entered either stage two or stage three and ended with stage four. The ages (items 39, 42 and 46), motives (items 40, 43 and 47), and most extreme activities (items 44 and 45) at each stage were recorded so that all kinds of generalizations are possible. At stage four, the full-fledged character of the movement emerges with appropriate emphasis on the two main activities, political violence and proselytizing. Nearly half the respondents were engaged in street and meeting-hall battles, a number overlapping with the two-fifths who were avidly converting new recruits to the cause. A total of three-fourths (again overlapping) of the sample was out marching and demonstrating for the cause, while only one-fourth contented themselves with non-militant membership activities, not counting a handful of secret proselytizers.

Joining the Early Nazi Party

Despite the large numbers that eventually became members, joining the early NSDAP was a momentous step. Why would the philistine burghers of a small town or village want to become active in such a notoriously violent and ostentatious movement when for the most part they loathed political parties and public demonstrations? One reason was their perception of the local political scene as dominated by disagreeable or threatening other forces. We recorded in each case the political color of the threat reported or imagined by the respondent, Communist, Socialist, Centrist, or "reactionary" (item 27). Whether the respondent joined when the local NSDAP was just a handful of men or only after the bandwagon had started to roll was also noted (item 28). A large number of the people who felt motivated enough to respond to Abel's essay contest claim to have been founders or co-founders of NSDAP local chapters.

About one-twelfth of the Abel respondents had joined the pre-1925 Nazi party (item 57). Nearly one-fourth joined in the years from 1925 to the 1928 elections. Another quarter joined between the 1928 and 1930 elections. One-third joined between 1930 and the presidential elections of 1932. The manner in which they were introduced to the Nazi party is also worth noting, if we bear in mind the Nazi devotion to propaganda and rallies (item 59). Nearly one-third was attracted primarily by reading literature and learning about the ideology and another third simply went to a public rally of the party.

Being a member often involved a person in personal friction with his employers or fellow-workers, and frequently with landlords, neighbors, or members of his own family (item 69). On the other hand, many respondents had other members of their families, especially spouses or children, in the NSDAP. An analysis of the members' attitudes toward their movement reveals the extent to which an extremist movement has to relate to personality needs (item 63). Of nearly half the cases it could be said that they experienced a sense of personal integration by their battle for utopia, while only about one-twelfth seem to have gotten personal integration by engaging in hatred and fighting *per se*. Nearly one-fourth cites the spirit of comradeship among the stormtroopers and about one-sixth were devotees of their leader above all. A small number even refers to the time of the bitterest struggle as "the best time of my life."

Over half the respondents held minor offices in the party (item 64). A similar number were stormtroopers, most of whom had joined the storm section (SA) when joining the party (item 65). Many belonged to functional auxiliaries of the party (item 29). Nearly half the stormtroopers held minor offices (item 65). This strong activist element explains the high involvement in political violence mentioned earlier (items 45 and 67). Their attitudes toward violence exhibit curious features which call for interpretation (item 68). About 40% accepted violence more or less realistically; over one-fourth of the respondents show a distinctly masochistic attitude toward the violence they were courting. They delighted in counting their own bruises and the casualties among their fellow troopers, possibly to rationalize their active involvement. Only about one-fifth could be classified as sadistic bullies in their feelings about violence. Suffering and persecution at the hands of the outside world, of course, are an important functional aspect of how an extremist movement retains solidarity and a sense of belonging among its members. The political enemy is characterized in terms ranging from vitriolic vituperation to a kind of sportsmanship (item 70). The particular enemy could be the police or the "reds" who reportedly dominated the political habitat of the majority of the Abel cases. At the same time, the extremist is torn between his desire to convert the enemy and the need to hate him. Many respondents felt a strong desire "to win them over," and one-twelfth expressed a liking for some of them. One-fifth, on the other hand, characterized them as "rodents," or subhuman, while one-fourth considered them as either traitors, immoral, or all-powerful.

An Ideological Crusade?

In his book *The Pursuit of the Millennium,* Norman Cohn describes some of the earlier quasi-religious movements which rose like a devastating sandstorm and died down again, having laid waste the lives of their own supporters and many others. How does such an ideological crusade gather followers and speed up until it becomes a cataclysm? We recorded, in addition to the personal escalation described above, the historical progression of the organizational memberships and political activities of the respondents in 1919-1921, 1922-1924, 1925-1928, 1929-1930, and 1931-1933 (items 48 to 55). This record of what political or paramilitary groups the respondents belonged to before joining the NSDAP not only documents their ideological search for salvation; it also constitutes an excellent historical reference point to which we can relate other indices by means of crosstabulation. We can also read from the record of memberships and political activities, as from a fever thermometer, the peaks and lows of political violence of the Weimar Republic.

As the movement increasingly reveals its character as an ideological crusade, we cannot help wondering about the nature of this virulent faith. There is indeed about the Abel biographies a pervasive enthusiasm and utopian fervor. More than half of the sample claim to have been among the first to join, in their localities or places of work, including one-fifth who were founders of their local. There is the implication that such early extremist initiative invariably drew ridicule or persecution from straight Weimar society. Their utopian consciousness also appears in many creditable accounts of the respondents' reaction to the radio announcement of Hitler's appointment as *Reich* Chancellor. They were stunned, having been convinced that the struggle for the millennium would last many more decades, if not centuries. Even in 1934, after a full year of the Nazi regime (including the Roehm purge), their expectations mirrored their utopian consciousness (item 74). Over half of the respondents looked forward to "a nation reborn" and free of "the system." One-sixth speaks of the "1000 years' *Reich*" or expresses the hope that their glorious leader may live long. About one-tenth voices hopes for national resurgence in the world or expansionistic policies. Only one-sixth thought of economic and social recovery and restitution, often in personal terms.

Their more specifically ideological preconceptions were particularly evident in their views of the unhappy Weimar Republic (item 56). Their responses range from calling it "Jewish-run" to dissatisfaction with the "red and black (SPD and Center) parties." A breakdown by dominant ideological theme (item 60) shows about one-third to be primarily preoccupied with the solidaristic *Volksgemeinschaft* and over one-fifth to be superpatriots. Nearly that many are devotees of Hitler's personal charisma. About one-seventh appears to be motivated mostly by their antisemitism. A preoccupation with German cultural pessimism, blood and soil, or Nordic purity is salient with only a few. Ranked by the chief object of their hostility, Abel's early Nazis by two-thirds turned out to be anti-Marxists (item 61). Only with one-eighth was antisemitism the most salient concern, as compared to one-seventh who vented their spleen most on liberals, capitalists, reactionaries, and Catholics. This is not to say that shadings of antisemitism (item 62) were not pervasive among as many as two-thirds of the biographies. Over one-fourth had evidently contracted a virulent case of it in reaction to the great shock of 1918 or to personal crises. Nearly that many had a more chronic version of prejudice with psychiatric symptoms, such as a paranoid fear of "the conspiracy." The rest are characterized by mild verbal projections.

Apart from antisemitism, the Nazi respondents also showed a good deal of ethnocentricity, as we would expect, viewing aliens and Catholics within Germany and the allies of World War One with equal hatred (item 71). We have already mentioned the record of their attitudes toward political enemies (item 70) and toward political violence (item 68). We also attempted to record their attitudes toward authority, with regard to government, police, and the leadership cult (item 72), although the full syndrome of authoritarianism is difficult to capture short of personal interviewing, if then. The evidence available was rather weak and inconclusive. An attempt to classify personality types was abandoned as impracticable with the available materials. Instead, we undertook three classifications to distinguish among personality types without entangling us too deeply in the thicket of personality theories.

One is a measurement of the level of political understanding according to how well-informed and differentiated a picture the respondent presents of Weimar politics (item 73). This index distinguishes not only highs and lows of political cognition but also the ideological from the more pragmatic visions. The second classification raises the question of what particular feature in each autobiographical account appears to be the most pathologically out of balance (item 77). The responses tend to stress such features as a high degree of paranoia or irrationality, extreme leadership cult, high personal insecurity or self-pity, or high cultural shock (alienation) from war or revolution. Third, we undertook to determine what in each case could be called the single most formative or influential experience of the reported lives of the respondents (item 76). Typically, the prewar generation would cite social snubs or class barriers, the war generation the experience of war and revolution, and the postwar generation experiences of comradeship in youth groups or not being able to find employment. Typically also, the members of this last generation would be far more politically oriented in the way they told their stories, concentrating on their political development rather than on their personal or the general historical circumstances (item 78).

Third Reich Career

Reading the accounts of the struggles and expectations of these early Nazis, we cannot help wondering what actually happened in Germany and in their lives after 1933 that would correspond to their utopian hopes. Since the *vitae* all end with the year 1933-1934, we thought of checking the card file of the NSDAP in the Berlin Document Center for information of what had happened to the respondents in the twelve years of the Third Reich. It turned out to be rather difficult to arrange for access to this carefully guarded membership catalog. But it was worth the trouble in spite of some minor disappointments such as the general absence of information about improvement in the economic status of the respondents. The entries in the party files, to the extent that the respondents could be identified (item 79), indicate about one-fourth who achieved an administrative, police, or party career, presumably because they were "old fighters." They also show another one in ten as having been concentration camp guards, or in the Gestapo, SS, SD, or RSHA. At this point the object of our study turns from the seemingly harmless "idealism" of an extremist fringe movement into the sinister instrument of totalitarianism. We are saving this transformation for the end of the book, where we also examine how these respondents differ from the rest.

Substantial numbers of the respondents showed no record of unusual advancement, and quite a few had died during the fateful twelve years. They may, of course, have benefited in other ways, such as by acquiring the expropriated property of Jews or political enemies of the regime. Some also dropped out of the party or were tried by the Supreme Party Tribunal and demoted or expelled. It would be a mistake, though, to seek signs of internal dissent or of moral revulsion behind these cases. They were mostly embezzlers, thieves, or morals offenders who were embarrassing to the party.

Method of Approach

These 79 variables and attributes, and the distinctions drawn in each of them, can be examined in the codes, a list of which is appended to this book. The significance of the responses to each item is described and compared at length in the chapters that follow. Grouped around major topics such as the "social dynamics" or political socialization of the early Nazis, the relevant items are discussed in some detail. The frequency distributions of each are set forth and compared with the responses to other items. The frequency distributions (FD) are also listed in the appendix so that interested readers can find each FD table and assess its relation to the codes. Each FD table also indicates with brackets how the categories of each item have been collapsed for purposes of crosstabulation.

Following the description and FD table of each item, there are various crosstabulations between the item concerned and other relevant items. If the reader should ever be in doubt about the other item of a crosstabulation, he can look up its code and frequency distribution. When we discuss the adult involvement of the respondents in political violence, for example, items 45 or 67 will be crosstabulated with the date of birth (item 1) in order to find out how violent different age groups were. Political violence as adults may also be fruitfully crosstabulated with youthful political violence (item 18) or earlier involvement in counter-revolutionary organizations (item 32). Crosstabulation can, in particular, serve to test some of the hypotheses advanced in the literature. The statistical presentation will be illustrated with direct quotations from the *vitae*, a particularly effective device with small, hard-to-compare subgroups such as the Nazi women of the sample. Occasional summaries will attempt to draw the gist from the more detailed discussion.

PART I

The Social Dynamics of the Nazi Movement

Over the last decade, the comparative study of fascist movements has made great strides in distilling out of the experiences and studies of many countries a common set of hypotheses. To be sure, no general model of fascist movements exists as yet, and there is reason to think that none can be found as long as we insist on attaching the label "fascism" to so many heterogeneous social movements in disparate settings. If we narrow our attention to the genesis of fascist movements in the more developed European countries, however, there are enough common elements to build a model and, of course, there has already been a variety of attempts at explanation. Theoretical constructs such as "social anomie" or social disintegration, the rise of a "mass society," the "authoritarian personality" of leaders and followers, and more or less sophisticated versions of a Marxist class analysis of fascism have been presented since the triumph of National Socialism in Germany. To the extent at least that these theories address themselves to the same subject as this study, they deserve to be briefly reviewed as background for the current investigation.

The limitation to the genesis of the movement makes it unnecessary to deal here with any "class analysis" or political assessment of the Third Reich itself, or of the social dynamics of the non-Nazi elements of Weimar society. We are concerned solely with the attempt to explain the social reasons for which the persons under consideration may have joined the NSDAP. Other aspects will be discussed whenever appropriate in later sections of this book.

The Marxist interpretation of fascist movements in industrialized societies takes a variety of forms. Social scientists such as Franz Neumann[1] have argued not only that the Nazi regime was a dic-

---

[1] *Behemoth, the Structure and Practice of National Socialism, 1933-1944,* New York: Oxford University Press, 1944. See also Robert A. Brady, *The Spirit and Structure of German Fascism,* London: Gollancz, 1937, Daniel Guerin, *Fascisme et Grand Capital,* Paris: Gallimard, 1936, and Maxine B. Sweezy, *The Structure of the Nazi Economy,* Cambridge: Harvard University Press, 1941.

tatorship of monopoly capital and great landowners over the workers, but also that the Nazi movement constituted a movement of class struggle *au rebourse*, that is, by the capitalists and their lackeys against the revolutionary labor movement. The bourgeoisie, the lower middle class and backward or demoralized parts of the proletariat presumably made up the "capitalist army" against the industrial workers. The lower middle classes also participated for fear of "proletarization" and the *Lumpenproletariat* for lack of proletarian class-consciousness. Since it failed to account for the prominent role of veterans, professional military men, civil servants, alienated youth, and peasants in the Nazi movement, a Marxist interpretation usually required additional non-Marxist hypotheses to give it plausibility. The charisma of the leader, the "uprootedness" of youth, soldiers, and peasants, or the "inborn resentments" of the lower middle class were often used to buttress this weak line of argument.[2] The work of Max Horkheimer and Theodore W. Adorno then de-emphasized the class angle while stressing the psychological nature of the new "authoritarianism" of fascist movements.[3] They defined authoritarianism as a sense of ambiguity or ambivalence toward authority figures resulting from the decline of traditional authority in family and society.

To this combination of class analysis and psychology should be added certain theories of social development, commonly known under the labels of "mass society" or *anomie*. The development of society from the familiar rural or small-town *Gemeinschaft* (community) to impersonal large cities in which only the cash nexus and centralized bureaucracy manipulate human interactions is said to have brought on social disorganization, a weakening of primary links, and individual alienation and disorientation. The atomized mass society of uncommunicative individuals without a sense of identity, then, is said to tend toward the formation of mobs and extremist movements.[4] The psychology of neo-authoritarianism and the alleged qualities of "mass man" can, of course, also be linked

[2] The writings of Franz Neumann, Max Scheler, Werner Sombart, and Erich Fromm, each in their own way, can serve as examples of the linkage between class and psychological analysis of fascism. Inasmuch as a strictly economic interpretation does violence to historical fact, especially before the arrival of the "economic society" of capitalist development, such a linkage constitutes of course a giant step toward realism.

[3] See Horkheimer's *Autoritaet und Familie*, Paris, no publisher, 1936, and Adorno, *The Authoritarian Personality*, New York: Harper, 1950.

[4] See especially William Kornhauser, *The Politics of Mass Society*, London: Routledge & Kegan Paul, 1960.

to one another to give the nebulous mass man more empirical substance. The relationship between the class interpretation and the mass-society analysis of fascism varies somewhat between two extremes. On the one hand there are writers like Ortega y Gassett with elitist fears of a "revolt of the masses" against traditional elites. Others, such as Hannah Arendt,[5] stress the *déclassé* nature of mass society and of fascist movements. In either case, class and status are swallowed up by the distinctionless mass and thus rendered less effective as factors of social motivation.

Toward a Theory of the Social Origins of National Socialism

In the case of Germany, these differences of interpretation become poignant indeed. Was the Nazi revolt really a class revolt, say of the bourgeoisie and its allies against the rising labor movement, and did it result in a dictatorship of the capitalist or bourgeois class? Was it an example of the revolt of the masses over traditional elites which resulted in a dictatorship of mass men over the homogenized mass society? Both of these hypotheses represent sweeping generalizations based on exceedingly slim evidence. Their very generality makes them implausible and unhistorical. How can these large abstractions be brought down to an empirical level suitable for our purposes? Much of the social dynamics of fascist movements may indeed be universal among industrialized societies. But what was it that made the Nazi movement so enormously attractive to vast numbers of Germans after the First World War, thereby sealing the fate of Germany's first try at parliamentary democracy with twelve years of totalitarian dictatorship, genocide, and an even more devastating world war?

The social drama of the Abel biographies opens upon the seemingly tranquil and stable stage of prewar imperial society. From his grand bourgeois vantage point, Walter Rathenau, the economic genius of the war and later Foreign Minister of the republic, painted a telling picture:[6]

> The Kaiser was surrounded by his self-effacing, adoring court which regarded matters of state as the family affairs of the Highest Family and kept all annoyance from him. The court was enclosed by the whole stratum of the landed, military, and bureaucratic aristocracy. They

[5] See especially Hannah Arendt, *The Origins of Totalitarianism*, new ed., New York: Harcourt, Brace, 1966.

[6] Quoted in Harry Graf Kessler, *Walter Rathenau, Sein Leben and Sein Werk*, Wiesbaden: Rheinische Verlagsanstalt, 1962, pp. 53-54.

owned Prussia which they had created and they were linked with the Crown by mutual interests. . . . This layer of society in turn was beseiged by the plutocratic bourgeoisie which craved admittance at any price and was ready to defend everything, accept responsibility for everything. . . .

Outside, however, there were the people: the rural populace, tenacious beyond comparison and devoted to the leadership of the country nobility, the church, the drill sergeant, and the local prefect [*Landrat*]; the urban populace, nimble, disrespectful and yet easily impressed, transported and consumed by the rush of making a living and enjoying life; on the sidelines, the resentful working-class, spiteful for being spited, living for the future and rejecting the present on principle.

There is more than a hint of social tensions in Rathenau's hierarchic picture of prewar society, especially in the pose of the working classes. But was it mostly or even primarily a clash of economic interests? We prefer to think of the "identifiable" social classes and status groups primarily as social communities of sorts which share social self-images and other attitudes and tend to pass them from generation to generation. Each such class or group undergoes its own process of modernization and social mobilization[7] including, possibly, its dissolution into a larger social community. Thus, the various groups of the German bourgeoisie formed at a certain point in history and underwent their own process of crises and evolutions during the period in question, including their great moral crises of 1918 and the early 1930s. The working-class groups were well-consolidated and conscious of their goals before their moral crisis of 1914 and the subsequent history of fateful splits and schisms. In the 1920s the German peasants and farmers had barely begun to develop a sense of identity after many years during which social mobilization among them was chiefly characterized by the departure of farm boys and girls from the countryside and from the social class and status of the peasantry to membership in the working and middle classes.[8]

[7] On the concept of "social mobilization" see Karl W. Deutsch, "Social Mobilization and Political Development," *American Political Science Review*, LV (June 1961), 493-514. The concept of social mobilization as currently used refers to the process by which immobile, particularly rural, populations are motivated to seek a better life elsewhere or to advance socially by means of political organization and action.

[8] On the social mobilization of the rural population, see especially Frieda Wunderlich, *Farm Labor in Germany, 1810-1945*, Princeton: Princeton University Press, 1961. On the development of a class consciousness, for example, see Alois Hundhammer, *Die Landwirtschaftliche*

The Nazi movement appears to have recruited itself from a variety of groups motivated by the social dynamics of prewar or postwar society. Their social crisis either stemmed from their unhappy in-between state between the major class communities, such as in the case of the new white-collar or the old handicraft groups who had not found their way into the bourgeoisie or the working-classes. Or the crisis was the result of the impact of the German defeat in World War One on military men, civil servants, and countless others affected by foreign occupation or the cession of their homeland to other countries. In the former case, such processes of change as rural-urban migration or upward social mobility or decline, as dimensions of social experience, become very important, inasmuch as they often involve being caught between the antagonistic major social classes. The non-commissioned professional military man whose career leaves him stranded between the classes;[9] the rural-urban migrant or upwardly mobile person who never really arrived and cannot go back again either; the person uprooted by expulsion from occupied or ceded territory; the middle-class daughter who takes employment and finds herself ostracized by the traditional prejudices of the bourgeoisie—these are typical examples of victims of the social dynamics which tended to drive many of the Abel respondents into the Nazi movement and may have motivated millions of others to vote for it in the landslide years 1930 to 1932. The chapters below, on frustrated upward mobility, on the Nazi women and other such topics will treat these subjects in great detail. Social mobility was the major avenue of social change open to these people in the Empire. Here we shall examine some of the broader dimensions of social mobility and also the effect of all kinds of social cleavages upon the process by which a person was prevented from finding a place in the existing social order and thus became "marginal" and "available" for Nazi recruitment.

Social and Spatial Mobility

Regarding social mobility, we must distinguish between spatial or geographic mobility, and vertical mobility among the social classes.

Berufsvertretung in Bayern, Munich: Pfeiffer, 1926, Karl Heller, *Der Bund der Landwirte (Landbund) und seine Politik*, unpublished doctoral dissertation, Wuerzburg University, 1936, or Wilhelm Mattes, *Die Bayerischen Bauernraete*, Stuttgart: Cotta, 1921.

[9] See for example the description by Konrad Heiden of the predicament of the small time officers in the Weimar Republic. *Der Fuehrer*, Boston: Houghton Mifflin, 1944, pp. 28-29.

It is significant to note, for example, that 47.2% of the Abel sample were spatially immobile: they never moved from where they were born, with the exception of temporary absences such as for education or military service. Twenty-two and one-tenth percent were rural-urban migrants as we would expect in an age of rapid urbanization, and the remaining 30.5% moved around the country or, in a few

Table I-1: Spatial and Social Mobility (FD 2 and 8)

	Spatially immobile	Rural-urban migrant	Mobile
No attempt to rise	60 (45.4%)	27 (35.1%)	44 (45.4%)
Upwardly mobile	44 (33.3%)	40 (51.9%)	30 (30.9%)
Decline	20 (15.1%)	7 (9.1%)	20 (20.6%)
Other	8 (6.2%)	3 (3.9%)	3 (3.1%)
Totals (100%)	132 (43.9%)	77 (24.4%)	97 (31.7%)

TOTAL 306

cases, could even be called drifters. When we cross spatial mobility with upward mobility, we find that the rural-urban migrants were considerably more upwardly mobile and less in social decline than either of the other groups. They were also somewhat older than the other two groups in the sample, over half of them having been born before 1895. The fathers of nearly three-fourths were farmers, artisans, or agricultural laborers. Their occupations tended to be the military or civil service, or business and the professions; the highly mobile in cities tended to be blue- or white-collar workers, and the immobile include disproportionate numbers of farmers, women, and civil servants. This conjures up a mental image of an older generation of Nazis whose life experience was based on the, at least initially, successful departure from their rural past. Many of them chose the public service or the "old middle-class" way of small entrepreneurship or professional skills as their road out of the countryside. A later generation of Nazis was made up of the "less successful" families, both the immobile and the perhaps aimlessly mobile. The reader may be reminded of the phrase that characterizes the social base of the Nazi movement as the "losers in the industrial revolution." However, most of them became obvious losers only when the defeat in World War One ushered in a long period of recession and stagnation.

The Impact of Economic Crises

The long era of prewar prosperity came precipitately to an end with the defeat and the losses of 1918. In the years of stagnation and recurrent economic crises of the Weimar Republic many people lost their livelihood, their jobs, savings, or businesses, or had to abandon their chosen careers. Historians give varying emphasis to these economic crises as aggravating factors of right-wing radicalization. Our three groups of the spatially mobile differ strikingly in the ways they were affected by these crises. The immobile group was the least badly injured, even though nearly a fourth of it suffered economic loss, slightly less than the average of the sample. The rural-urban migrants were harder hit and lost jobs or capital investment disproportionately in the years from 1914 to 1928. The respondents moving from city to city were by far the hardest hit, with over one-third economically ruined or unemployed in the depression years of 1929 to 1933.

If we take the economic life experiences as the independent variable, moreover, we find that those with normal economic careers tended to be older, those who were ruined in 1914-1928 were the war generation (born 1890-1901), and the victims of the Great Depression tended to be of the postwar generation. Further, the respondents of normal economic lives tended to be the best-educated and the victims of the earlier economic doldrums of the republic (i.e., the war generation) the least-educated. The latter group also was the most likely to have spent its childhood in poverty or as orphans, and to have had to work at an early age. In short, they appear to have had several strikes against them even before the war disrupted their lives. The ideological views of these groups show corresponding and predictable differences. The economically normal (prewar) group was characterized mostly by superpatriotism, revanchism, and law and order. The economic casualties of 1914-1928 were preoccupied with Nordic or German romanticism and with social solidarity, and the victims of the depression were for the most part antisemites or devotees of the personality cult of Hitler.

Ideology and Attitudes of Mobility Groups

The backgrounds and economic fates of the three mobility groups form a curious contrast with their ideological preoccupations after they joined the NSDAP. The spatially immobile tended to be revanchists, law-and-order-minded, intent on social solidarity among the classes (*Volksgemeinschaft*), and devotees of the Hitler cult. The rural-urban migrants were in disproportionate numbers antisemites, superpatriots, but also devoted to the *Volksgemein-*

schaft. The highly mobile tended to be Nordic or German romantics, antisemites and revanchists. The military, civil servants, and small businessmen of rural background often came to economic grief even before the final economic and political death throes of the republic. Their migration experience, or their economic undoing, is evidently related to their antisemitism and superpatriotism and most certainly to their concern for social solidarity. The sense of futility in the minds of the mobile white- and blue-collar workers who were frequently wiped out by the depression can be gauged from their autistic fantasies, which mix defensive themes of Nordic race and precious German culture with hatred for Jews and for the victors of World War One. It is not surprising that this group was already heavily involved in demonstrations and political violence in the years 1919 to 1924.

Organizational Behavior and Attitudes

Generally speaking, the immobile tended to be among the very first in their area to join the NSDAP, much in contrast to the other two groups. What was their attitude toward the Nazi party after they had joined? The immobile and the rural-urban migrants both stress the classlessness of the party and the joys of fighting for a utopian goal as the features that attracted them the most. The highly mobile, on the other hand, tend to describe the struggle itself as the aspect from which they derived exhilaration and a sense of integration of their personalities. We would expect them to be the most involved in violence but they are not. The immobile and the rural-urban migrants seem to have been the most involved in actual political violence, and the highly mobile tended more toward proselytizing and demonstrations.

Their attitudes toward their political antagonists also split the three groups. The immobile and the highly mobile tend to characterize their "red" enemies as "subhuman," venal, or immoral, or with epithets such as "rodents." The rural-urban migrants describe them more in terms of treason or conspiracy. The attitude of the immobile toward violence in many cases exhibits a certain self-pity or masochism manifested by emphasis on the beating or injuries received rather than those dealt, possibly a rationalization for breaking the social taboos against violence. The highly mobile, by contrast, tend to gloat over the violence they inflicted.

It appears that the extremism of the immobile, who are presumably well-rooted and at home in their environment, comes to an earlier and more self-confident expression than that of the other groups. Their split attitudes toward authority mirror the options left to a political dissenter, short of moving away: either he tries to use the police to control his antagonists or, failing this, he discredits the legitimate authorities altogether. The rural-urban migrants resemble the immobile in many respects, but seem to possess less self-confidence and a lower breaking-point, reflecting perhaps the trauma of their initial migration. The highly mobile are very different from both, as their exhilaration with the struggle itself suggests, for the other two need the utopian goal. The seeming paradox between this love of struggle and the fact of their actually lower involvement in political violence can be explained with a more detached attitude toward involvement. Their fundamental political orientation is introvert and directed toward the self rather than toward changing the community in which they happen to be living at the time. Identification with the struggle and non-violent participation in demonstrations, electioneering, or proselytizing is quite sufficient as a quasi-realistic backdrop for their self-images. They feel no great urge to grace the list of martyrs for some transient local cause. If "the system" becomes too unbearable or "the establishment" too repressive, they can always move on again. There are interesting parallels with the large numbers of transient youth in the American movements of revolutionary dissent of recent years, moving from one locale of confrontation to another. There is every likelihood that the myth of the violent "outside agitator" or "out-of-town crazy" might be exploded if social scientists would design a parallel study to compare the violent activities and attitudes of the immobile and the highly mobile of "the movement" in America.[10]

The Social Dynamics Behind the Early Nazi Movement

The great social drama of German society before and after the war, the chasm beneath Rathenau's stable hierarchy, was the class struggle between the capitalistic bourgeoisie and the mobilized masses

[10] The current American literature on revolutionary dissent has tended to concentrate on student and general-population samples because of their easy availability for drawing representative samples. There is, however, an illuminating section on riot participation in the *Report of the National Advisory Commission on Civil Disorders*, New York: Bantam Books, 1968, pp. 127-135, which also contradicts the myth of the rioters as "recent migrants" or social deviants. The profile of the typical rioter instead is "an unmarried man under 25, who is a lifelong resident of the riot-torn city. Only menially employed and frequently out of a job, he feels strongly that he deserves a better job and that he is barred from achieving it . . . because of discrimination by employers. . . . He takes great pride in his race and believes that in some respects Negroes are superior to whites. . . . This hostility (to whites and middle-class Negroes) is more apt to be a product of social and economic class than of race. . . ."

of the working class. When the power slipped from the hands of Kaiser, court, and the aristocratic elite in 1918, the class struggle broke out again more nakedly than ever between the two powerful camps. How did the Abel respondents and millions like them manage to end up in a side-show, as it were, between the two class camps? It was often a matter of cross-pressures within the home, irreconcilable differences between mother and father or with the social environment. As one respondent (no. 162) relates:

> My father was an enemy of the church. My brothers and sisters were christened secretly. Father was not supposed to know. When he found out there were confrontations I would rather not describe. . . . Mother and the children prayed though Father watched us so we *wouldn't*. I don't want to malign him now that he has passed away, but we did not understand him and he may not have realized the effect of these conflicts on children's souls.
>
> I was bound to notice the social conflicts . . . among the classes of the people. I experienced this with bitterness at school. We went to school barefoot, though with clean and well-mended clothes. The sons of the bourgeoisie wore collars and shoes. Thus they had an advantage that did not rest on their achievements or their ability.
>
> I thought more and more about it and slowly began to understand why my father was such a passionate Social Democrat. I could see with my own eyes how wage demands were often justified, how hard they had to be fought for, and how all too often honest working people were exploited by the capitalists. I felt immeasurably bitter about the inflated egos of the bourgeoisie toward its proletarian compatriots. . . . It wasn't the workers who invented the class struggle, but the bourgeoisie that created the conditions. . . . When Father returned from his construction job and we children sat around him, knocking the mortar spots out of his jacket, I resolved that some day I was going to do my share so a German man in Germany would be appreciated for his own sake and not according to his suit of clothes. . . .

The writer was born in 1886 and, after a restless apprenticeship, wanted to become a soldier. He applied to the Garde du Corps and was accepted. "When my father found out in which regiment I was going to serve there were unbelievable scenes. We said goodbye with words about 'my Kaiser' which I cannot repeat."

His first experiences in the Prussian military were brutal and he soon acquired the reputation of being "a red" because he rebelled against being manhandled by the older guards. Later on he made himself useful to his superiors by his phenomenal memory. Because his father had fallen ill and his support was needed, he re-enlisted after an interval of plans for emigration.

As I came to understand later, the officer corps was of the highest social classes. I often wondered how this feudalism would stand up if hard blows of fate were to hit the country. . . . I knew my own ability and saw what little others around me and above me could do. I felt how painful it was not to be allowed to become an officer no matter how fit and able. It hurt me to see the social chasm between these cavalry lieutenants and the infantry commission I later received on the battlefields of World War One. . . .

The social conflicts and divisions, which impressed themselves so painfully on the mind of this young man who later became a high-ranking SS leader are fairly typical. They are among the mechanisms separating people from both major social classes which are relevant to our examination of the social dynamics of the Nazi movement. Parents were split violently between religious devotion and anti-clericalism or between the prewar Social Democrats and a conservative party. Seething class consciousness and resentment of the snobbery of the upper classes often are part of the dynamic forces at work. Some of the respondents of the Abel collection even have a social split between their parents, as in the case of a proletarian father and a bourgeois mother. The son or daughter can neither accept his (her) working-class identity nor win acceptance among the bourgeoisie. In the rigidly stratified class society of the German empire, the Socialist bricklayer's son should have become a militant Socialist and trade unionist and have had no other ambitions. But for this his mother was too devout and he was too bright a student at school and in the Prussian military. His desire to emigrate, and his hopes for a military career, in themselves may have been an attempt to escape from the cross-pressures on his mind. It should also be noted how the motives of achievement and merit of a modern society clashed in his mind with the ascriptive nature of the bourgeois and aristocratic privileges that stood in his way.

By way of a psychological footnote, attention should also be drawn to the respondent's poor relationship with his father, who was too busy with SPD party work to spend much time with his children. As the current theories of hate groups and haters like to stress, a poor relationship to paternal authority often brings forth feelings of unworthiness and an uninhibited propensity to project this unworthiness on objects of hatred. A hate group and its leader, as a father substitute, then permits the hater to channel his feelings with the help of righteous rationalizations, and to feel group support in doing so. In identifying with Adolf Hitler, of course, these men and women had selected a man similarly consumed with resentment of the upper classes, not to mention his strained relationship with his father.[11]

The bricklayer's son was not alone in feeling thwarted in his career by class barriers. Another volunteer (no. 50), born in 1899, won many war decorations and an appointment as a stand-in officer:

> When I received my appointment as a *Feldwebel-Leutnant* [warrant officer] I shook my head in disgust. I was being treated as second-class in spite of my three years' record as a combat soldier. I was not considered worthy of becoming an officer in the regiment. Why, why not—again and again this "why" knocked around in my head. Although most of the regiment's officers met me with comradely feelings, there remained between me and some "gentlemen" an unbridgeable chasm.

The resentment and frustration was not limited to the military. On the contrary, the military was rather an avenue of social mobility as compared to many areas of private enterprise. The second son of a miller (no. 19), for example, became a journeyman in 1925 as his older brother took over the mill. After working in the Palatinate, Thuringia, Saxony, Mecklenburg, Luebeck, and in the Ruhr area, he reports bitterly:

> I thought I would get ahead with honest work. But when I realized how . . . insincerity, falsehood, and groveling bring you material advantages, I was revolted. The struggle of a young man for recognition and respect encounters only smiles of contempt. He is only a "proletarian," a "worker," and has no "connections"; he is only a cipher that one exploits to get the job done. . . . On the one hand there are the liberal entrepreneurs and their lackeys, who care only about the dividends. On the other hand, there are the Marxist workers and their representatives, for whom the wage-envelope is all that counts. Here contempt, there fraternal conflict.

The malaise of German society under the empire and later produced, among other things, the heterogeneous social motive forces of the Nazi movement. It created a whole crisis stratum in the military and public service. It raised ambitions of social advancement and then frustrated them when hard times followed the prosperous prewar era. It even produced among the Nazis and many others the trite slogan of the people's community (*Volksgemeinschaft*) to as-

[11] See, for example, Hitler's *Mein Kampf*, Boston: Houghton Mifflin, 1943, which is full of seething class resentments. Particularly revealing on young Hitler's relationship with his father is Bradley F. Smith's *Adolf Hitler, His Family, Childhood and Youth*, pp. 55-79.

sert national solidarity, rather than class struggle or religious or regional tensions. The latent malaise was basically that of a society in rapid transition from agriculture to industry and services, from rural majorities to metropolitan predominance, and from patriarchal family life to the emancipation of women and youth.[12] Obviously, not all the strains of transition worked in the direction of the neither quite proletarian nor quite bourgeois Nazi movement, nor did all the people who endured these strains become Nazis. Nevertheless, there are several aspects of the transition which turn up with surprising frequency among the autobiographical statements of the Abel collection. The following sections will take them up and examine them in some detail.

[12] On the consequences of the transition and the transition itself, see especially Theodor Geiger, *Die soziale Schichtung des deutschen Volkes*, Stuttgart: Enke, 1932, and David Schoenbaum, *Hitler's Social Revolution*, pp. 1-15.

ONE

A Time for Sergeants

It is not easy in this anti-militaristic age to imagine the aura surrounding even a minor professional military career in imperial Germany. Marlene Dietrich still sings the old marching song[1]

> Wenn die Soldaten durch die Stadt marschieren,
> oeffnen die Maedchen die Fenster und die Türen. . . .

Not only did uniforms and drums and fifes impress the girls, but also many a young fellow tired of his humdrum apprenticeship to a trade. One of the Abel respondents, a locksmith born in 1873 of working-class parents, relates how he re-enlisted after the draft (no. 27):

> The love for a soldier's calling made me become a professional military man. . . . After seven years I was promoted to sergeant and after nine to *Vizefeldwebel* [Staff Sergeant].
> . . . During these years I dutifully attended the first two grades of the school for non-commissioned officers and voluntarily went for further semesters of training.

Many respondents of that generation similarly went through years of sub-officer training without setting their sights any higher than this.

The staunchest pillars of the German empire, the armed forces and the civil service, embodied its stability and order in their dedication and sense of duty. They were possessed of an extraordinary *esprit de corps* and constituted the main link of continuity from the disintegrating empire to the Weimar Republic. The republic eagerly accepted their services to maintain the internal cohesion of the new state against the many centrifugal forces at hand. In so doing, the republican leaders were taking considerable risks. The military and

[1] "When the soldiers come marching through town, the girls open up their windows and doors."

civil service exhibited a good deal of hostility toward the republican institutions and seemed more inclined to turn from the old empire and authoritarianism to new imperial and authoritarian visions rather than to become the backbone of a parliamentary democracy. Military and civil service were linked in many ways besides their common frame of mind. It was not only the highest military officers who were frequently called upon to perform important roles in the civil administration of the *Reich* or the states. A person of the lowest social origins could enter the sub-officer training program. After twelve years of service up to the rank of non-commissioned officer, he was entitled to a civil service career at the low or medium levels. Many of our respondents followed this route and ended up as minor officials of the imperial railroads or the postal and telegraph service. Some became grade-school teachers and may have carried their drill sergeant's ways from one "school of the nation" into the other. Large numbers of military careers were ended by the defeat of 1918 and the limitations of size imposed on the German army by the Treaty of Versailles, which again encouraged transfer to the civil and particularly the police administration. The locksmith quoted earlier (no. 27) describes the process of transfer before World War One:

> After 12 years of service I was given a *Zivilversorgungsschein* [civil career certificate]. I applied for medium-level civil service with the post office, the Prussian-Hessian railroads, and various communal administrations, and furthermore for a position as a court secretary with the higher military judiciary. I passed all the preliminary tests given by these authorities. I followed the first call to the medium, non-technical railroad service and in 1906 was summoned to Bad Harzburg for training. . . .

After a year's training, at the age of 34, he passed another examination and entered the railroad service.

Military and Civil Service Occupations

It is easy to speak of a "militarist strain" in the genesis of the Nazi movement, but much more difficult to give statistical precision to this term, at least on the basis of autobiographical statements. One approach consists of defining the military-civil service element according to occupation, a method which ignores, however, the range of attitudes to be expected among professional military and civil servants attracted to the, for a proper *Offizier* or *Beamter*, rather scandalous early Nazi party. In other words, these are people who must have been rebelling against their background.[2] This core group of military and civil servants of all levels amounts to 23% of our sample. It was composed as follows:

FD-4: Military and Civil Service Occupations

	Number	Per cent
Officers	6	4.4
Military-civil servants	34	25.1
Higher and medium level civil servants (including reserve officers)	30	22.2
Low level civil service	30	22.2
Grade School teachers	16	12.1
Other public employees (white and blue collar)	19	14
	135	100.0

Many members of this group also were young and rather atypical soldier-civil servants. Hence another approach to the "militaristic" background might warrant a look at the occupation of the fathers of all the respondents. Seventy-one (15.2%) of the fathers were lower civil servants or professional military men, and another 24 (5.1%) were in the higher ranges of the imperial military or civil service at a time when the ethos of army and civil service was still unbroken. When we narrow the sample to the fathers of respondents in military-civil service occupations rather than the whole sample, the fathers' occupations are rather evenly spread over the different categories. Military-civil servant fathers, as we might expect, are more heavily (22.9%) represented, while relatively few (9.4%) respondents are the sons of independent businessmen. Thus, less than one-fourth of the military-civil servants actually grew up in a similar atmosphere. The fathers' occupations in general differ from the respondents' occupations in a manner reflecting the progress of urbanization and industrialization between two German generations of that period of rapid social change. The share of the military-civil servants increases in the second generation and the share of the farmers and blue-collar workers evidently shifts to white-collar occupations.

[2] Their break with the orderly ways of the military and civil service usually manifested itself in sudden political awakening and activism. One of them (no. 37) relates: "As a professional soldier I paid no attention to politics and parties. It was only after my release from the service that I became alert to the struggle of parties and classes and the indignities and conflict between occupational groups." See also no. 151.

Table I-2: Respondents' and Their Fathers' Occupations (FD 4 and 7)

	Milit.-civil servant (below lieuten.)	High milit.- civil servant	Worker and white-collar	Artisans (depend. and indep.)	Indep. and businessman	Farmer and farm laborer	Professional man, artist	Other	Total (n)
Resp.									
no.	124	11	162	100	37	49	22	62	567
%	(21.9)	(1.9)	(28.7)	(17.7)	(6.5)	(8.6)	(3.8)	(10.9)	(100)
Fathers									
no.	71	24	87	89	63	107	10	16	467
%	(15.2)	(5.1)	(18.7)	(19.1)	(13.4)	(23.0)	(2.1)	(3.4)	(100)

Reaction to Military Experiences

There appears to be less point in inquiring into the extent to which respondents were drafted into the military service. Nearly half were never in the service, chiefly for reasons of age, since the Nazi movement was a relatively young movement. Most of the others were swept up in the nearly universal wartime service. More to the point are their subjective reactions to their military service or non-service. Their attitudes were broken down as follows:

FD-22: Reaction to Military Experience

	Number	Per cent
No military experience (no attitude indicated)	179	31.0
No service, but vicarious enthusiasm (victory-watcher)	76	13.1
Service with no hint of attitude	73	12.6
Enthusiastic combat soldier	159	27.3
Non-combatant service	48	8.2
War invalids	33	5.6
Disaffected after initial enthusiasm	13	2.2
	581	100.0

The vicarious enthusiasts of the second category are particularly significant, because they were generally too young to serve in World War One and yet intensely involved in and influenced by it. They often had fathers, uncles, older brothers, or friends in the war with whose imagined exploits they tended to identify, quite likely following the official war propaganda with rapt attention and perhaps marking the great battles on maps on the walls of their classrooms. One respondent describes his attitude (no. 15):

I was 13 when the war broke out. My 18-year-old brother volunteered and had to report to Friedrichsfeld for training. The following Sunday I walked the 16 miles to Friedrichsfeld with friends of my own age to visit him and become acquainted with a soldier's life. . . . We used to gobble up the war news in the paper and celebrate solemnly all the victories, as there was no school on days of major victories. At school everybody strove to get mail from soldiers at the front and so we often wrote to all our friends and relatives at the front and asked for war souvenirs. . . . I always hoped that the war would last so long that I would be old enough to fight.

Three years later, however, this respondent showed strong signs of disaffection and resentment toward the government, especially when he heard that "they used the draft to punish people," e.g., by drafting malcontents.

The enthusiastic combat soldiers varied in the focus of their enthusiasm and in the manner they expressed their commitment. One out of five specifically mentioned the egalitarian experience of comradeship in the trenches which set aside all class and status distinctions in the face of death. The others vary between those eloquently relating their *Fronterlebnis* (front-line experience), the experience of death and gore in the great patriotic struggle against hostile encirclement and those whose commitment is mute and to be sensed only between the lines. The *Fronterlebnis* obviously left a deep imprint on their lives and characters, marking them off as "the front generation" from both younger and older generations, including respondents who had served in the war only in their mature years. As one Catholic respondent put it (no. 8):

My old world broke asunder in my experiences. The world of the trenches instead opened itself to me. Had I once been a loner, here I found brothers. Germany's sons stood shoulder to shoulder in heated battles aiming their rifles at the common enemy. We lay together in the bunkers, exchanging our life stories, sharing our possessions. We got to understand one another. . . . In battle we tied up each others' wounds. Who would ever question authentic German-ness (*Volkstum*), or how much education you had, or whether you were a Protestant or a Catholic?

The overwhelming nature of the events seemed to obscure all the petty divisions of German society. It should be noted, however, that the Nazi party certainly had no monopoly on the *Fronterlebnis*, which patterned men of all German parties at the time. By 1933, in fact, the NSDAP, together with the Communists (KPD), probably had more than its share of the generation too young to have served in World War One. But, probably unlike the KPD, the Nazis had many victory-watchers among their younger members.

Most of the noncombatant soldiers were rather happy with their lot, as we would expect. About one-third, however, found the military life unpleasant. They may have been aware of the hatred of the front soldiers for the *Etappenhengst* (behind-the-lines stallion). The war invalids, finally, bore perhaps the heaviest cross of all the bitter survivors of the lost war, for they had the effect of their commitment to the national cause indelibly branded onto their bodies. When the same sacrifices that had once been called patriotic or even heroic began to encounter scorn and derision after the war, they must have found it psychologically impossible to retreat from their national commitment. Long-term prisoners of war sometimes showed similar attitudes. One respondent who was both wounded and for four years a prisoner of the Allies, described his fury upon his return a few days before the armistice (no. 32): "In the streets of Hamburg, the mutineers tore the uniform piece by piece off my back. In vain we volunteered to wipe out the traitors to the German army who came from Hamburg and Berlin. The red traitors to the people, Ebert, Scheidemann, Erzberger, and their accomplices forbade us to shoot at the mutineers who had been freed from the jails and prisons."

Social Profile of Military-Civil Servants

A closer examination of the military-civil servant group reveals its social profile. More than any other occupational group of the collection, its members were born in 1894 and earlier (70.8%). Thus they were already going on 30 in 1923 and 40 in 1933, which further underscores their rigid and conventional set of mind. They include disproportionate numbers of rural-urban migrants, Germans of foreign background, and persons who never left their area of origin. Nearly two-thirds of them resided in Berlin during the last years of the republic. Four-fifths suffered no particular economic setbacks during those years, nor were their parents hit by economic disaster during their years of growing up. They include the largest number (40.7%) of people with a secondary (*Mittlere Reife*) or higher education of any occupational group, and also the largest group (15.5%) reporting an authoritarian or military-disciplined home environment. Their perception of where they fit into the German class society is well-represented by a young teacher of no military background although he calls his father "a genuine Prussian civil servant" (no. 22): "The philistine German bourgeoisie, segregated from the people by its snobbery and pride of class, looked down at me as a 'worker.' The real German worker regarded me as a 'reactionary' because of my education."

The war must have been the climax of their lives, with zenith and nadir of their feelings often but a year or less apart. Their wartime experiences place particular stress on the *Fronterlebnis*—the egalitarianism of the trenches and their common hostility to the enemy. They excelled in their sustained enthusiasm for the war, and in earning decorations and promotions (50.5%). They also had more than their share of invalids and prisoners of war. Upon their return, they felt a distinct sense of shock when they became aware of the sharp difference between the realities of postwar Germany and the idealized picture of the *Heimat* they had formed in their minds. As one battle-field-commissioned lieutenant put it (no. 162):

> We sat in our bunkers and heard about the mess behind the lines, about the dry rot setting in back home. . . . We felt that Frenchmen and Tommies were no longer our worst enemy, that there was worse coming, real poison being brewed in the witches' cauldron at home. . . . The march home was my most bitter experience. . . . I was a broken man who could no longer find God and who was about to lose himself. . . . With fear and courage, storm, enthusiasm, and spite, from blood, muck, and misery, we returned. But when we glimpsed Germany, the ground under our feet began to sink. We front soldiers strode off into the night, parting with a last handshake, into the bottomless night where "the others" would not even recognize us any more.

They were particularly shocked by the disparagement of military honor in the form of physical attacks on the flag, the uniform, or on officers' insignia by hostile mobs. They simply could not understand the vast wave of internationalism and pacifism which was sweeping the land. The ignominious flight of the Kaiser, the downfall of the monarchy and of the traditional institutions of the German empire left their sense of legitimacy deeply shaken. The new rulers of Weimar society and politics, the red (Socialist), black (Catholic Center), and Democratic (DDP) politicians, and the aggressive world of Weimar business and the press, all frequently seen as representing the takeover of Jews and Catholics, were not accepted as legitimate authority. Germany's defeat in the war appeared to them to be the result of a "stab in the back" by the "Marxists" and the Spartakus movement. They also tended to blame the inept leadership of the Kaiser and his high command, the weakness of the civilians, and the trickery of President Wilson and his allies. The revolution, on the other hand, was attributed mostly to the new Weimar parties (SPD, DDP, and Center), the "red revolutionaries," to an unspecified rabble in the streets, or to foreign interests, such as those of France.

Organizational Behavior

Did the military-civil servant group play a particularly prominent role among the paramilitary elements of the immediate postwar era, perhaps in the manner suggested by Waite's book about the Free Corps, *Vanguard of National Socialism*? The answer is yes indeed, but not only in the Free Corps. More than half (56.8%) of the respondents of this group had considered themselves to be "unpolitical military men" or "unpolitical civil servants" before the breakdown of 1918. Another one-fifth was a part of traditionally unpolitical farming or bourgeois elements of German society. The great collapse of the power structure they had served so "unpolitically" (i.e., in a nonpartisan sense) aroused them to enroll *en masse* in numerous paramilitary organizations. More than any other occupational group except for the farmers, they joined vigilante groups such as the *Einwohnerwehr*, *Buergerwehr*, and Free Corps units, to suppress domestic insurgents and their isolated strongholds. Large numbers of them later entered the *Stahlhelm* or other militant veterans' groups which provided military drill and training with weapons. They also stood out among the occupational groups in their membership in more or less illegal military organizations fighting foreign enemies such as the Poles or the French occupation in Free Corps, *Zeitfreiwillige*, Black *Reichswehr*, or *Grenzschutz* units. Finally, they were prominent, along with the white-collar employees, in early *voelkisch* action groups such as the *Schutz- und-Trutzbund*, the *Deutschvoelkische Freiheitspartei*, and in the pre-1924 Nazi party or its fronts. They played a lesser role in such *voelkisch* paramilitary troops as *Oberland*, *Wehrwolf*, or *Stahlhelm-Westkueste*.

Table I-3: Military-Civil Servants in Paramilitary Organizations

	Number	Per cent
Free Corps, etc. (anti-insurgents)	12	9.8
Stahlhelm, veterans	14	11.4
Free Corps, etc. (anti-foreign troops)	17	13.8
Voelkisch action groups	18	14.6
Wehrwolf, etc.	5	4.1
Others	3	2.4
Not a member	54	43.9
	123	100.0

The motives of half of them for joining were shock at the "revolution" of 1918-1919 and desire to oppose the "red" revolutionaries. Another one-third cites the defeat in war and the cession or occupation of German territory as the motive for their militarization.

The year of crisis, 1923, found the military-civil servants of the Abel sample predominantly in the innumerable militant veterans' groups which had armed themselves and kept up their military training in readiness for the resumption of a "war of liberation." Disproportionate numbers also were in militant *voelkisch* action groups such as General Ludendorff's *Deutschvoelkische Freiheitsbewegung* or the *Deutschsoziale Partei* of Richard Kunze (*Kneuppelkunze*), a rabidly antisemitic demagogue. One out of five participated in or reports great sympathy with Adolf Hitler's beer-hall *putsch* in Munich. Even in the quiet years of 1925 to 1928, they were heavily represented in the conservative parties, in the rising Nazi movement, and in the *Stahlhelm* veterans organization, in this order. Many of them joined the NSDAP in their neighborhoods when it was still a mere nucleus of no more than half a dozen men. A significant number, however, stuck with their regional conservative party, with the *Jungdeutscher Orden* (Jungdo), or with the German Nationalists (DNVP) until the last big landslide of 1931-1932.

Their political involvement during these years begins with cautious reserve during the first five years of the republic, as compared to other occupational groups, with the exception of some electioneering, or with political violence in counter-revolutionary organizations such as the Free Corps or the *Einwohnerwehr* vigilantes. From this early point on, the relative share of persons engaged in political violence declines sharply and recovers only during the last two years. Two other activities show a more consistent increase over the entire period, demonstrations and proselytizing, the typical

Table I-4: Political Activities Reported by Military-Civil Servants (in %)

	Shopping around	Following public events	Campaigning only	Campaigns and demonstrations	Campaigns, demonstr. & pol. violence	Campaigns, demonstr. & proselytizing	Totals (n)
1919-24	27.1	25.4	1.7	10.2	21.2	14.4	118 (100)
1925-28	19.4	26.6	8.9	10.5	12.9	21.8	124 (100)
1929-30	13.7	16.4	8.2	17.1	12.3	32.2	146 (100)
1931-32	0.6	4.2	4.8	25.1	18.6	46.7	167 (100)

activities of an ideological crusade. In 1931 and 1932 nearly half of the military-civil servants were engaged in converting new recruits to the cause, 90.4% were marching for it in the streets, and 95.2% were campaigning for it in the brown election campaigns.

Ideologies and Attitudes

How do the political attitudes of the military-civil servants compare with other groups in the early Nazi party? They tended to view the Weimar Republic predominantly (35.8%) as the *Judenrepublik*, a system run by Jews, alien elements, and un-German trends of culture. Another one-fourth of the group criticized in it the "liberal-Marxist element" often associated with internationalism and with the Young Plan of German reparations, which "mortgaged the future of three generations of Germans" to Allied and international interests. This conservative stance of the military-civil service group differs quite noticeably from the attitude of the working-class and farmer groups, which stressed opposition to capitalism, high finance, and monopoly, or scored the Weimar establishment for the economic disorders. Blue-collar and white-collar groups both also compared the "red and black Weimar government" invidiously with the glory and unity of the empire and with the Third Reich that is yet to come.

The main ideological themes of the military-civil servants are revanchism, dreams of a German military renaissance, and authoritarianism. There are also more superpatriots, German nationalists, and haters of the French occupation among them than in any other occupational group save business and the professions. Finally, they have a disproportionate share of the relatively few persons (5%) motivated by romantic visions of Nordic heritage, German culture, or "blood and soil," though no more than the blue- and white-collar groups. By contrast they were only half as engrossed in the personality cult of Hitler as the women or working-class Nazis and not nearly as motivated by antisemitism (as a main theme) as were the business and professional or the white-collar groups.

Nevertheless, a breakdown according to what constitutes the chief object of the respondents' hostility shows the military-civil servants nearly as likely as business and the professions to name the Jews, often in connection with the Socialists or Communists. Both military-civil and business-professional respondents also tended to turn their hatred on Catholics, "liberals," and "reactionaries" though less so than the white-collar group, for example.

The attitudes toward the Jews deserve more precise exploration, since the range of the prejudicial attitudes is central to an understanding of the dynamics of the Hitler movement. The military-civil service group was highest in manifestations of the so-called *Juden-koller*, a sudden outbreak of antisemitic mania in response to personal trauma such as the cultural shock experienced in 1918, unemployment, or divorce—of course with no objective connection to "the Jews" except in the eyes of the beholder. Thirty-five and two-tenths percent of the military-civil servants in the sample report such a sudden outbreak and another 13.2% reveal more chronic anti-semitic bias with stories of probable and improbable personal experiences about Jews, often with sexual overtones. The same percentage, in fact, cite this or experiences with aliens as the "formative experience of their lives." It is perhaps typical of the social climate of the imperial military and civil service that this group otherwise ranks lowest in the milder sort of verbal projections of antisemitism, which play a prominent role in the autobiographical accounts of the salesmen and secretaries among the respondents of the white-collar group. This kind of pornography of social status and human relations was evidently not encouraged in the proper circles of the public service.

The Satisfactions of Nazi Membership

An understanding of the membership of any social movement usually requires some insight into the nature of the satisfactions, tangible or spiritual, which a person derives from membership. What did the military-civil servants get out of belonging to this extremist fringe group? They stand out from the average in two ways. More than half of them exude the conviction that the eventual victory of the Hitler movement would set all the present ills of society right. Their personality is integrated by the vision of utopia, so to speak. And another one-tenth looked forward to or had already received tangible rewards, such as jobs or promotions, for their loyalty, an expectation they shared also with business and professional Nazis and with the farmers of the sample. By contrast, they did not share the stress of working-class respondents on the satisfactions of the struggle itself nor the emphasis on the absence of class divisions in the Nazi party expressed by blue- and white-collar workers and farmers. Possibly due to their higher age, the military-civil service group did not join the stormtroopers in numbers comparable to the working-class (57.5%), farmer (48.8%), or business and professional respondents (45.8%), which might account for less involvement with the violent struggle for power. Only about one-fourth participated in the political violence perpetrated by the Nazis.

The attitudes they express toward political violence also show surprisingly little of the sadism or masochism characteristic, for example, of the working-class group. We would expect people of military background to show little squeamishness about addressing violence to a well-defined foe. But the military-civil servant group expresses more regret over or loathing of violence than any other group save the women. Their tendency to glory in the physical defeat of their enemies (sadism) is slightly below the average and not so high as among the farmers and the blue-collar and white-collar respondents. More typically, they rarely show the curiously self-pitying, endless descriptions of wounds suffered and lumps received which characterize over one-third of the blue-collar Nazis and nearly as many of the business and professional group. Instead, the military-civil servants appear to have taken the violence in stride, without lengthy descriptions, and to accept it rather realistically as the price of political victory. Similarly, in their attitude toward political enemies in general, they tend to show some understanding of, and even a liking for, them and often express the desire to win them over to their own side. This attitude forms a sharp contrast to that of the blue-collar Nazis, who tend to view their enemies as traitors or as members of a faceless, hidden conspiracy, and even more to the white-collar and business and professional groups, who emphasize such venomous labels for their political enemies as "subhuman criminals," "rodents," "murderers" and insist on calling them "venal," "paid," "immoral cheats," and using terms of personal uncleanliness.

This is not to say that the military-civil servants were free of the authoritarian syndrome of being obsessed with cleanliness and law and order. They typically criticize the police for not maintaining order, while workers or farmers just show hostility toward the police. They also show a high degree of ethnocentricity with regard to such issues as the "encirclement" of Germany by hostile, greedy neighbors, and the "moral inferiority" and other great failings of alien nations, particularly the French occupiers of the Rhineland. They exhibit far less of the obsession of the white-collar and business groups with subversive foreigners, Catholics, and other "international conspiracies" in Germany. As compared to the business and worker groups, the military-civil servants are also notably less ideological in their view of society and politics.

It should be mentioned that at least the civil servants and police officers among them had some reason to feel persecuted and repressed. Until the very end, the state of Prussia did not allow them to join or to be active in the party of their choice. Nearly half of them report friction at their job over their political convictions. Many tell about their secret burrowing in the bureaucratic ant-hill which made proselytizing as easy as it was risky for the secret party member. A few report having been fired for their political views. Still, we may wonder how a civil servant who is deliberately violating laws and subverting the state from within can manage at the same time to be an advocate of law and order. For any setback in his career, suffered in consequence of his political activities, there is also the obverse, the concrete expectation of jobs, promotions or other concrete rewards of which the military-civil servants reaped more than their share by 1934, nearly as much as the business and professional group.

Concluding Remarks

In conclusion, we can characterize the military-civil service group as probably the most prominent element of social and behavioral continuity between Wilhelminian Germany and the emerging Nazi movement. This generalization receives further confirmation from a comparison of the different groups with regard to what seems to have been the most influential or formative experience of their lives. Half of the respondents of this group describe with special emphasis the momentous events of 1918 or the *Fronterlebnis* of World War One, which makes it by far the most war-influenced group of the collection. When we compare the groups with an eye to ascertaining the degree and kind of alienation from society they experienced, the military-civil servants stand out as the group which experienced the most intense cultural shock at the end of the war. Thus the picture emerges of an entire social stratum of the old empire which was forcibly severed from its most meaningful relationship, its public service to the old order, and which therefore strove to reconstitute the essentials of the *status quo ante* as best it understood them.

To this we should add the social significance of the public service. On the one hand it was an inviting avenue of social mobility in a rigidly stratified society. But it also was a mobility trap because of its pre-1918 class barriers and the termination of many military and civil careers resulting from the loss of territories and the limitations placed upon the Weimar army. Despite some class distinctions, the public services also cannot be fitted into either one of the two major class camps; this has a bearing on the many professional military men and some parts of the civil service who had to return to the private sector after 1918 or who had to change their training in midstream, say, from officer cadet or primary school teacher to something else. The something else invariably landed them in the middle of the bourgeois-proletarian class tensions, though many tried to escape into gentleman-farming or into right-wing political careers.

TWO

Frustrated Upward Mobility

Seymour M. Lipset cites with approval a host of sociological writings which picture the Nazi movement as "the extremism of the center . . . [in ideology] similar to liberalism in its opposition to big business, trade unions, and the socialist state."[1] An independent, small-property-owning class consisting of merchants, independent craftsmen and farmers, and white-collar and professional persons aspiring to similar independence is said to be at the basis of the socio-economic revolt of the lower middle class. The enemy is on the one hand the overbearing economic activity of the upper middle class, and on the other hand the economic and political pressure of the organized working classes. The image is one of a clearly identifiable, static social class desperately defending its position against the encroachment of more active classes both above and below it. The questions to be raised, then, are: (1) to what extent are the cases of the Abel collection really of this description? (2) is this lower middle class really a static condition? and (3) was the suggested socio-economic motivation really typical of many of our cases? Explanations of fascism as the ideology of upper-class families in social decline or, like other revolutionary movements, as the ideology of frustrated upward mobility should also be considered as alternative theories.

To answer the first question, it may be appropriate to take a look at the original breakdown made by Theodore Abel of his 600 cases (after elimination of women and cases of insufficient information). He does not explain the criteria of his classification. We can assume that they were the standard definitions based on estimated levels of income and a list of occupations, although the remaining autobiographical statements of the collection are often vague with regard to this type of information:[2]

[1] *Political Man*, Garden City, N.Y.: Anchor, 1960, p. 129. For a broader assessment, see esp. Herman Lebovics, *Social Conservatism and the Middle Classes, 1914-1933*, Princeton: Princeton University Press, 1969, pp. 3-48, and 205-220.

[2] *The Nazi Movement*, New York: Atherton Press, 1965, p. 5. The

Table I-5: Abel's Breakdown of Class Affiliation

	Number	Per cent
Workers skilled or unskilled	209	35
Lower middle class	304	51
Upper middle class and aristocracy	45	7
Peasants	42	7
	600	100.0

The Occupational Composition of the Sample

Our tally with a somewhat different collection (with the women but without the cases confiscated by the FBI) arrived at somewhat different conclusions. To begin with, we separated the military-civil servant group as basically outside the class structure,[3] although they include six officers and five higher civil servants Abel may have counted among his upper middle class as well as large numbers of low and medium-level civil servants he may have counted as "lower middle class." Since they were not directly subject to the economic forces of industrial society and had little reason to resent the state as interventor and regulator, however, their sharing of the socio-economic motivation of the private sector cannot be taken for granted.

Table I-6: Social Class and Status of the Sample (FD-4)

	Number	Per cent
Military-civil servants	125	21.3
Workers, skilled and unskilled	169	28.8
Middle class, old and new	189	32.2
Agriculture	49	8.3
Women	39	6.6
NA, other	16	2.8
	587*	100.0

* Note: Multiple entries.

According to our count, nearly one-half of the workers are dependent artisans in smaller shops (46), skilled workers in larger factories (24) and foremen (9). The rest are unskilled (19), miners (3), taxicab drivers, or domestic servants (5), appren-

---

breakdown was made after the elimination of a considerable number of cases with insufficient information and of 48 women.

[3] There is at least subjective justification for this exclusion in many of the autobiographical statements that the respondent was not aware of the bitter social antagonisms until he left the service.

tices or family helpers of minor age (4), unemployed (33), or working-class of undeterminable occupation (12). We look almost in vain for the "proletarian masses" of the "NS German Workers Party," even if it is granted that the blue-collar workers may be less likely to participate in an essay contest. There is much living misery and the flotsam of a disintegrating class society, such as an aristocrat driving a taxicab. But the dominant element is a kind of labor aristocracy of foremen, skilled workers, and artisans. These dependent artisans may have been considered lower middle-class by Abel. Without further information, there is also the problem of classifying persons unemployed, as well as the question of which phase of a varying career should be counted.[4]

The middle-class respondents are perhaps the most interesting of the sample, even though our count accords them a far more modest role than the 51% of Abel's count. The dominant group is the white-collar group, which is composed of secretarial (49) and qualified or managerial (32) employees and sales or shipping clerks (20).[5] In this context the civil servants without prior military career

Table I-7: Middle-class Respondents (Male) [FD 4 (20-29)]

	Number	Per cent
Independent business	35	18.6
Independent handicraft	26	13.7
White-collar	101	53.9
Professions and students	25	12.8
NA	2	1.0
	189	100.0

[4] Wherever possible long-range occupational plans rather than makeshift arrangements or temporary unemployment were recorded. In the Stanford study of the Nazi elite, oddly enough, artisan and peasant respondents and sons of artisans or peasants were considered "marginal" or deviant from the majority, with the implication that this contributed to their tendency to become Nazi notables. Harold D. Lasswell and Daniel Lerner, eds., *World Revolutionary Elites*, Cambridge: MIT Press, 1965, pp. 288-300, 304.

[5] Robert Michels relates the social demotion of sales clerks in the feudalization of the bourgeoisie since the 1870s. Helping the customers simply became socially unacceptable for the bourgeois shopkeeper, who thus began to delegate this responsibility to the sales clerks, thereby stressing their social inferiority. *Umschichtungen*, p. 103. The increasing employment of women, finally, led to the growth of a large, anti-feminist, and antisemitic Retail Clerks Union (DHV) which aligned itself in the republic with the *voelkisch* wing of the DNVP.

of record[6] would indeed be germane except for the points raised earlier. The independent businessmen and craftsmen generally have rather small shops and businesses. Together with the professions and students at the secondary or university level, they constitute the old middle classes which Lipset and others see at the basis of fascist socio-economic motivation.

Then there is also the underrepresented agricultural sector, which is discussed in greater detail below. Medium-size farm ownership characterizes only a relative minority (15). The bulk are dependent farmers (21), especially family helpers, as well as farm laborers (8), who appear to be Abel's "peasants." There are also a few agricultural managers on estates or apprentice managers (5), such as Heinrich Himmler was in his student days. It is a matter of general knowledge that despite Nazi propaganda about "blood and soil," farmers in the NSDAP were hard to find. They were also less likely to respond to an essay contest.

We can conclude then, that the present sample and probably the whole Nazi party *at the time* were not dominated so heavily by clearly identifiable lower middle-class interests as to be characterized as part of the "revolt of the lower middle class."[7] There is

Table I-8: Class and Occupations of Nazi Party and Abel Sample Compared (FD-4) (in %)

	Party	Abel Sample
Workers	31.5	28.8
White collar	21.1	17.2
Independents	17.6	15.0
Civil service	6.7	21.3
Farmers	12.6	8.3
Miscellany	10.5	9.4
	100.0	100.0

a curious circularity in the arguments presented by advocates of the "lower middle-class revolt" thesis who are often content to compare the Nazi statistics with those of the Social Democrats or, at the most, with those liberal (DDP and DVP) or regional parties whose voters the NSDAP seems to have inherited toward the end of the

[6] Fewer than 40 (30%) respondents of the military-civil servant group fall into this bracket if we exclude all who held a military rank or attended officers' training prior to becoming a civil servant.

[7] See the comparison of the occupational structure of the sample with that of the party, above, p. 14, and NSDAP, *Parteistatistik*, I, 1935, p. 185. The data are for the period immediately prior to the ascent to power.

Weimar Republic. But there were also other strong bourgeois parties, the Catholic Center Party and the Protestant German Nationalists (DNVP), who survived more or less intact until mid-1933.[8] The relatively high bourgeois or lower middle-class component of the NSDAP proves little as long as there are still these other bourgeois parties present. If the "lower middle-class revolt" is relegated to a less central role as a motivating force—there is no intention of denying its significance altogether—only then can the curious ambivalence of the Nazi movement between Hitler's conservative tendencies and the socialist note of the Strasser brothers and the NSBO cell organization be properly appreciated.

Social Class and Economic Change

To proceed to our second question, is the point of departure, the socio-economic dynamic of the Abel sample, really as static as the thesis of the defense of the lower middle class suggests? It may be a mistake to attribute social class to the respondents only on the basis of their current occupations or employment status during the economic crises of the main years of the Nazi rise. The respondents themselves frequently underwent such decisive changes in their economic career and employment as to make their class and status uncertain in the extreme. If a person's livelihood or career is destroyed, what social class does he belong to then?

FD-5: Respondents' Economic Change

	Number	Per cent
Normal progress or stagnation	285	48.8
Pre-war loss, decline	49	8.5
Unemployed, career disrupted, loss of business 1914-1928	94	16.0
Unemployed 1928-1933	93	15.9
Bankrupt, economic loss, 1928-1933	39	6.7
Career disrupted 1928-1933	15	2.6
Other economic trouble	9	1.5
	584	100.0

It may not be entirely clear what constitutes normality in economic fortune in an industrial society. Perhaps instances of gradual decline or an occasional business failure or loss of a job such as occurred in the "good old times" before the Great War are par for the

[8] The DNVP lost a part of its vote to the NSDAP in the final stretch of the electoral battles of 1931-1933; the losses of the Center and the SPD were negligible.

course. There is a surprising number of economic drifters (23) in the sample. Some respondents lost their business or their job several times during the 14 years of the republic. There are many who were unemployed (47) for some period before 1928, who lost their business in the great inflation of 1923 (15), or whose intended career came to an involuntary end, forcing them to change to a different calling (30). A good example of the last-mentioned category were respondents in teacher training colleges who never managed to land their first teaching jobs because the few available positions were all given to German refugee teachers from annexed territories of the empire.

The statistics of the economic troubles 1928 to 1933 speak for themselves. As we pointed out earlier, nearly half of the economic casualties of the Great Depression were among those born too late to be drafted. They may well have included many young workers who, according to Theodor Geiger, were the saddest victims of the crisis, the last to be hired and the first to be let go.[9]

Did the economic hardship drive them not only into the Nazi party, but also into political violence? Half of the economic casualties of 1928-1933 joined the stormtroopers (SA) directly upon entering the party, and another one-sixth joined the SA a year or two later and another one-tenth went on from the SA to the SS. The failures of the years between 1914 and 1928 are far less involved, although half of them also joined the SA right away. Both groups engaged heavily (47-48%) in street-fighting, meeting-hall brawls, demonstrations and electioneering during the dying years of the republic. Many of them in those days fought literally "day and night," according to their own accounts. Since they tended to be unemployed, young, and single, the party put them up and fed them in special stormtrooper dormitories (*SA-Heime*) in exchange for their paramilitary services. Inasmuch as they often claimed to have been fired or boycotted because of their political convictions, they also expected and often received jobs or other economic rewards from the movement after it became successful. Respondents of normal economic background participated significantly less in the stormtroopers and in political violence.

Early Socio-Economic Tracking

Even if we disregard what may be a temporary derailment from the tracks of a person's career, more attention should be paid to his antecedents. In imperial Germany even more than in most contem-

[9] Geiger, *Die soziale Schichtung*, pp. 96-97.

porary societies, the tracks of a socio-economic career began very early in life and major switches in direction had to be deliberately engineered by the parents. The father's occupation and economic change may be a truer indication of the social class of a respondent than his own. On this point, the Abel autobiographies are not always as informative as they are on the respondent's occupation, although about four-fifths name their fathers' occupations, albeit without much further information. The comparison between fathers

FD-7: Occupation of Respondents' Fathers

	Number	Per cent
Military-civil servants	95	20.3
Independent businessmen	63	13.6
Professions, artists, students	10	2.1
Artisans, dependent or independent	89	19.1
Workers, skilled or unskilled	87	18.6
White-collar employees	—	—
Farmers	98	21.0
Farm laborers, domestic servants	9	1.9
Others	16	3.4
	467	100.0

and sons shows both the difference between an older German society and that of Weimar, and the generational shifts within this group bound for right-wing extremism. The most notable changes are the decline of farmers, independent business, and artisans,[10] a shift of nearly one-third from more or less independent fathers to economically dependent sons. There are more sons in the professions, to be sure, but there are also more workers and an entirely new social class, white-collar employees, no less than 17.2%.

These changes are not untypical of the society at large, but the question still arises whether this is a story of social decline of these families or not. The loss of independent ownership of a farm or shop sounds grim at first, but appearances can be deceptive. The romantic vision of "blood and soil" aside, life on many German farms at the end of the nineteenth century was anything but idyllic.[11] The large exodus from the farms to the city was motivated mostly by an expanding population in grinding poverty with very hard

[10] The scant information on fathers' occupations did not permit distinction according to dependence or independence, but it is likely that the decline occurred chiefly among the independents.

[11] See also Frieda Wunderlich, *Farm Labor in Germany 1810-1945*, Princeton: Princeton University Press, 1961, pp. 22-27.

work and little chance of individual betterment. A farm boy with many older brothers and sisters on a marginal farm could hardly do worse in the city, even if his education in a rural one-room school was very limited. Ownership of a shop or business might have been more attractive, although there, too, large families and economically marginal operations would limit the opportunities at hand.

About two-thirds of the Abel cases contain some information about the economic fortunes of the respondents' parents during the years that the respondents were still at home. Over one-fourth evidently came from homes deprived of the father or economically deprived during the years in which the son could have started on a better economic career. For whatever it may be worth to the psychological imagination of some readers, it should be mentioned that these sons, especially the orphans, also figure prominently among

FD-6: Parents' Economic Change

	Number	Per cent
No notable change	286	72.8
Notable improvement	5	1.3
⌐ Father died before respondent 10 years old	37	9.4
∟ Father died when respondent 10-17	18	4.6
⌐ Loss of job, business when respondent under 18	11	2.8
Respondent had to stop education, go to work (as a result of crises such ∟ as the above)	15	3.8
Both parents worked when respondent under 14	21	5.3
	393	100.0

the economic failures of 1914-1927 and 1928-1933. There is also a breakdown according to childhood setting which the respondents describe as follows:

FD-25: Childhood Settings of Respondents

	Number	Per cent
Economically secure and freewheeling	113	25.8
Economically secure and sheltered	86	19.6
Authoritarian, strict	41	9.3
Orphan, personally deprived	55	12.5
⌐ Large family (over 4 children) in poverty	49	11.2
⊢ Farm childhood	47	10.7
∟ Hard times, others	48	10.9
	439	100.0

From this it would appear that poverty and deprivation were even greater than we could gather from the previous table, possibly around 40% or more of the sample. We also have a tally of work under the age of 18. The normal career at the time would have been for a child to go to the *Volksschule* or its equivalent until age 14 and then to learn a trade, or, for the more privileged, not to have to go to work until age 17 or later. One out of five did not have the

FD-26: Early Work Experience of Respondents

	Number	Per cent
Normal apprenticeship	294	54.7
Not working until 17 or later	112	20.8
Worked outside home before age 14	17	3.2
Worked at home before age 14 (family farm, shops)	36	6.7
Unskilled labor at 14 to 17	54	10.1
Other	24	4.5
	537	100.0

privilege of a normal economic start. Again, these respondents make up a disproportionate share of the economic casualties of the Weimar years. There is obviously a substantial element of poverty here.

Upward Mobility, Stagnation, or Decline

The answer to the question of whether the family fortunes of the Abel sample declined from one generation to the next obviously requires some differentiation. Given the rapid urban-industrial transformation of the country, a farm boy or farm laborer's son, for example, might aspire to learning a marketable trade or acquiring a shop in a less rural setting. Sons of the undifferentiated urban working class might strive to become skilled workers or artisans, to acquire a shop or business, or to climb to the middle-class level by acquiring a better education than their fathers had. By comparing the fathers' occupation with the careers of the sons, we arrived at the following tabulation. There are four distinct groups here that are worth investigating further, the static plurality, families in decline, aspiring farm boys, and urban climbers. They should all be viewed against the curve of rising prewar prosperity followed by economic crises and stagnation in the 1920s and early 1930s.

The static group was born mostly after 1890 (except for a strong cohort of 1860-1877),[12] so that it came of age in the Great War or

[12] According to Michels, the generation of the leading business and industrial executives of the republic was also of this cohort, with isolated

FD-8: Upward Mobility of Respondents

	Number	Per cent
No attempt to rise	206	44.0
Declining families	62	13.3
Farmer, farmworker to artisan, small businessman, white-collar worker	71	15.3
┌ Unskilled worker to artisan, skilled │ worker, businessman	8	1.7
└ Workers to middle class via education	99	21.2
Other	21	4.5
	467	100.0

in the economic stagnation of the Weimar years, a fate shared also by the families in decline. The farm climbers, by comparison, were born mostly (53.5%) before 1890 and evidently grew up when the rural exodus was in full swing. The city climbers, on the other hand, were born generally (58.9%) after the turn of the century and probably represent the second generation, the sons of rural migrants, who were setting their sights higher even though further migration from the countryside had now dwindled to a mere trickle. The static group also was located mostly in rural areas and in towns up to 100,000 and suffered no disproportionate economic strictures after 1914. The decliners, by comparison, lived mostly in Berlin and other metropolitan areas and fell victim to the economic troubles of the Weimar Republic far more often than the other groups. The farm climbers, as we would expect, were heavily concentrated in small towns under 10,000, but also in Berlin, and did not suffer economically after 1914. The social climbers of the city did suffer and are heavily represented in all the urban areas save the capital. The economic troubles as a significant motive were evidently a crisis of the cities more than of the countryside.

As for their occupations, the static group consists mostly of farmers (14.2%), middle class (14.7%), and urban working class (32.7%), so that it falls considerably short of the idea of the static middle class and its "fascism of the center." The scions of declining families are predominantly women (12.9%), workers (41.9%), and white-collar employees (24.2%). The farm boys on the make are mainly military-civil servants (47.9%) or old middle class

exceptions in banking and trade who often had made a career exploiting the war. The generation born just before or after 1870 tended to identify strongly with the glory of the empire and to be quite out of step with the needs of Weimar society and politics, Michels, *Umschichtungen*, pp. 99-100.

(16.4%), typical representatives of an earlier era in Germany. The city climbers are heavily white-collar (28.6%), business and professions (17.1%), or military-civil servants (24.8%). If we take the occupations as the independent variable, the picture becomes clearer yet. The military and civil service was evidently a favorite route of advancement for social climbers, especially from the countryside. The old middle class of business and professions is equally divided between the upwardly mobile and the static and presumably defensive of the stereotype. Farmers tended to be static (66.7%) and Nazi women were typically in social decline. White-collar work, it appears, was both a way-station for city boys on the make and a reservoir of social decliners. The Nazi worker, on the other hand, was either in social decline (21.1%) or static (56.1%). The differentiated picture, in other words, shows a bewildering variety of social motivations rather than a clear and dominant pattern such as a "fascism of the center" or a fascism motivated chiefly by social decline.

Political Views and Social Mobility

How did the static and mobile groups differ in their political views? The political ideology of the socially static Nazis, the largest mobility group, especially stands out as revanchist and as stressing classless solidarity (*Volksgemeinschaft*). Their hostility was aimed especially at the Communists, the Socialists, and the Jews. Although some of them give no expression of antisemitism in their *vitae*, disproportionate numbers of them indicate belief in "the conspiracy," drop threatening hints, or tell personal antisemitic stories. Their ethnocentricity also manifests itself in fears of the hostility of foreign nations, especially of the "Allied encirclement of Germany," and in viewing alien nations as inferior. They show disproportionate preoccupation with authority, cleanliness, and order in private life as well as in the government, objecting particularly to the multi-party regime of Weimar. Their authoritarianism also comes to light in a high degree of social conformity. In 1934, their expectations culminated in two visions, one of the economic recovery and social restoration of the nation, and the other of the glories of the 1000 years' Reich, which might, of course, require extensive ideological brainwashing and purges among the citizenry to make it a reality.

The declining Nazis, by contrast, rate highest with ideologies of Nordic or Germanic romanticism, with revanchism and for the fetish they make of Adolf Hitler. Social decline and elitist or messianic yearnings are easy to relate to one another. They also see their chief enemy in the Jews or in various Marxist parties; their

Table I-9: Upward Mobility and Occupation (FD 8 and 4)[a]

	Military-civil servants	Working-class, urban	Business, professions, univ. students	Sales, secy., white-collar	Farmers	Women	Other males	Sum
No attempt to rise	31 (14.7%) (31.6%)	69 (32.7%) (56.1%)	31 (14.7%) (47.7%)	31 (14.7%) (35.2%)	30 (14.2%) (66.7%)	3 (1.4%) (9.7%)	16 (7.6%) (72.7%)	211 RAW (100.0%) (44.7%)
Farmer to lower middle, middle class	35 (47.9%) (35.7%)	9 (12.3%) (7.3%)	12 (16.4%) (18.5%)	10 (13.7%) (11.4%)	4 (5.5%) (8.9%)	— —	3 (4.1%) (13.6%)	73 (100.0%) (15.5%)
Urban working to middle class	26 (24.8%) (26.5%)	18 (17.1%) (14.6%)	18 (17.1%) (27.7%)	30 (28.6%) (34.1%)	8 (7.6%) (17.8%)	3 (2.9%) (9.7%)	2 (1.9%) (9.1%)	105 RAW (100.0%) (22.2%)
Declining families	5 (8.1%) (5.1%)	26 (41.9%) (21.1%)	4 (6.5%) (6.2%)	15 (24.2%) (17.0%)	3 (4.8%) (6.7%)	8 (12.9%) (25.8%)	1 (1.6%) (4.5%)	62 RAW (100.0%) (13.1%)
Other	1 (4.8%) (1%)	1 (4.8%) (.8%)	— —	2 (9.5%) (2.3%)	— —	17 (81%) (54.8%)	— —	21 RAW (100.0%) (4.4%)
Sums	98 (20.8%) (100.0%)	123 (26.1%) (100.0%)	65 (13.8%) (100.0%)	88 (18.6%) (100.0%)	45 (9.5%) (100.0%)	31 (6.6%) (100.0%)	22 (4.7%) (100.0%)	472 RAW (100.0%) (100.0%)

[a] This is a standard crosstabulation table with table percentages omitted. The percentages on each second line add up horizontally, those on the third line vertically. Percentages of table totals have been omitted. Hitherto and elsewhere in this book, the crosstabulations have only been quoted rather than directly presented because they are rather confusing to most readers. Highly related entries are marked ⌐__⌐.

antisemitism, however, is pronounced and inclines particularly toward the sudden *Judenkoller* outbreaks as well as toward the "conspiracy," complete with perceived threats and counterthreats. Otherwise, the decliners rank low in ethnocentricity and show instead a corrosive hatred and contempt for the Weimar police and the government. Their perception of political reality is noticeably more ideological than that of other groups even though they include nearly as large a share of politically naive, poorly informed persons as does the static group. The decliners also exhibit a higher degree of personal insecurity and a masochistic attitude about political violence than any other group. Examined as to what formative experience seems to have shaped their minds, they resemble the static group in the frequency with which they describe a social snub or humiliation and in their stress on the experience of comradeship in a youth organization. Instead of the stress of the static Nazis on the *Fronterlebnis* of World War One and the impact of defeat and revolution, however, they emphasize the influence of educational experiences in school or on reading a book.[13] There is an air of introspection, preciousness, and of feeling unloved about the declining Nazis. But this did not keep them from expectations of considerable individual gain or of visions of an externally aggressive, national resurgence in 1934.

As for the two upwardly mobile groups, there is a tell-tale difference in formal education to begin with. The farm boys on the rise had at best a completed vocational education following the primary school; no fewer than three-fourths of the urban mobile had completed six years of secondary education (*mittlere Reife*), or even the coveted *Abitur*. Their ideologies, consequently, differ sharply. To begin with, the upward-bound city boys were more ideological and perceptive. The farm climbers resemble the static group in their heavy emphasis on revanchist ideology, authoritarianism, and superpatriotism. The city climbers instead stress the Nordic or Germanic romanticism and antisemitism fashionable among the intelligentsia in those days. They also stress the slogans of classless solidarity, perhaps in order to atone for their upward scramble. Both groups also exhibit hostility toward the established "reactionaries," the Catholics, and the Liberals, in poignant contrast to the static and declining groups. The better-educated urban

[13] Their formal education considerably exceeds that of the static group. Sixteen and one-tenth percent of them have the *Abitur* and often some university study (7.6% of the static), another 16.1% the *mittlere Reife* (9.6%), and 16.1% some secondary schooling and a trade school behind them (7.1%).

mobiles are particularly encompassing in their hatred for all groups on the National Socialist hate-list. This is evidently the major fault line between the anti-establishment and the establishmentarian forces in the Nazi movement.

The farm climbers are also particularly antisemitic and especially inclined to the manic *Judenkoller*. The city climbers incline more toward mild verbal projections and toward the conspiracy theme with perceived threat and counter-threat. The other ethnocentric themes also show sharp differences between the farmers' relative unconcern about the outside world together with some nationalism and the city Nazis' stress on the inferiority of other nations and hatred of aliens, Catholics, and other "international enemies of the people" in Germany. In their attitudes toward authority, likewise, the rural mobile incline more toward authoritarianism and the leadership cult, while the urban mobile are more concerned with the messy multi-party system and the hostile police of some Weimar *Laender*, notably Prussia.

Both allege episodic encounters with Jews or aliens to have been the formative experiences of their lives. But the rural mobile, like the static group, also stress the formative impact of war and defeat on their lives, while the urban mobile, being younger, mention instead the experience of comradeship in a youth organization as well as educational influences. Their expectations in 1934, finally, were mainly the social, economic, and political recovery of the nation, although the farm climbers also had in mind more concrete rewards for their loyalty. Their upward mobility gave them a special interest in social restoration. Both groups, and especially the farmers, being older, had suffered a particularly intense cultural shock in 1918. The city respondents, by contrast, rate higher in their propensity toward a cult of leadership and in a pronounced tendency toward paranoia and irrationality.

Conclusions

To sum up the implications of this section, there are several basic flaws in many of the existing theories of how class and status may relate to the genesis of National Socialism. The biggest mistake is to take the "lower middle class" as an undifferentiated and unchanging entity rather than as a collection of persons who are either on their way up or down, or static.[14] The second source of error lies

[14] See especially Geiger, *Die soziale Schichtung*, pp. 108-109, who comments on "the complex and confusing middle whose sophisticated analysis increases the impression of complexity, especially when we attempt to summarize its mental and ideological state." Geiger also ques-

in the definition of this class or any other groups as the mainstays of the fascist upheaval. The complex maze of social status or class motivations of the Nazis is no easier to analyze if they are lumped together under a generic social label. Instead, the more differentiated the occupational analysis, the more reliable the generalizations that can be drawn from it. The social starting point, the early tracking, and any later derailment of each individual career are further indications of the socio-economic dynamics behind the rise of the Nazi movement. By dividing the sample into the upwardly mobile, the stagnant, and the socially declining families, finally, we can arrive at a differentiated picture of each major occupational group: the mobile military-civil servant from the countryside, the woman in social decline, the rising or stagnant old middle class or static farm respondent, the white-collar employee who is either moving up or sinking, and the static or declining urban worker—these are typical images of the social careers of early Nazis. Their political views differ accordingly, down to the cleavage of anti-establishment and establishmentarian attitudes.

---

tions the internal cohesion of the middle-class elements in the rising Nazi vote.

The Myth of Blood and Soil

The ideal of the family farm and of the German farmer was the epitome of the anti-urban currents not only in the Nazi party, but throughout much of German literature and the conservative-bourgeois ideologies during the years of the great shift of German society away from its rural antecedents.[1] Motives such as a yearning for farming as an authentic way of life close to nature were mixed with the ethnopolitical struggle against Czech and Polish minorities in the eastern border areas. In spite of the long-smoldering farm crisis of the empire and the Weimar Republic, however, the farmers were notably hesitant to cast their lot with the Nazis until the declining years of the republic. They were by nature rather reluctant to become involved in political organizations of any sort,[2] and their loyalties were nearly monopolized by the Catholic Center, or Bavarian People's Party (BVP), and the mostly Protestant DNVP. The accelerating economic crisis of north German farmers finally led to a flare-up of protest movements, demonstrations, and terrorist bombings which Hans Fallada described in his novel *Bauern, Bonzen und Bomben*.[3] The collapse of the farm protest movement allowed the Nazis to move in and take away much of the substantial farm following of the DNVP.[4]

[1] See, for example, George L. Mosse, *The Crisis of German Ideology*, New York: Grosset and Dunlap, 1964, pp. 24-27, or Fritz Stern, *The Politics of Cultural Despair*, Garden City, New York: Anchor Books, pp. 189-191. See also R. Walther Darré, *Das Bauerntum als Lebensquell der nordischen Rasse* and *Neuadel aus Blut und Boden*, Muenchen: J. F. Lehmann, 1929 and 1930 for the National Socialist position.

[2] Wilhelm Mattes, *Die Bayerischen Bauernraete*, pp. 28-31 gives a revealing picture of the suspicion and political awkwardness of Bavarian peasants before World War One and of the situational obstacles to effective, labor-union-style farm organization among farmers.

[3] First written in 1931 à propos of the *Landvolk* trial of 1929 in Neumuenster, it was reissued by Rowohlt, Hamburg in 1964.

[4] Rudolf Heberle describes the rural landslide in Schleswig-Holstein in exhaustive detail in *From Democracy to Nazism*, Baton Rouge: Louisiana

The Sample of Nazi Farmers

The 49 respondents with farm occupations in the Abel collection are a somewhat smaller proportion (8.4%) than the 12.6% indicated by the *Parteistatistik* for 1933. Nevertheless, there appears to be ample representation of most of the significant groups. We could examine them according to their occupational groupings: 15 independent farmers, 21 dependent farmers and family helpers, eight farm workers, and five agricultural managers and apprentice managers. But since farm politics tends to be geographically determined, it seems more important to look at the regional groups, after a few basic statistics.

In age, the farmers of the sample are quite a bit younger than the rest of the Nazis of the collection. Only 6.1% were over 40 at the outset of the Depression, and the rest were divided evenly between the war generation (born 1890-1901) and the postwar generation. Thus, they are mostly "young peasants" rather than the older farm generation. Nearly one-fourth were from the border areas and a like number from occupied territory. Three-fourths of them were living in rural areas and another one-eighth in small towns (2,000-10,000) at the time of the survey. Four out of five were the sons of farmers. Two-thirds (33) had only a primary education, often (14) with some vocational training in a trade. Their parents suffered fewer economic or personal crises during their childhoods than the other respondents. The farm respondents themselves, with only seven economic casualties of the years 1914 to 1928 and another ten of the depression among them were less harshly afflicted than any other group in our sample save the military-civil servants.

East Prussian Farm Respondents

A large number of the farm respondents came from East Prussia. One Protestant farmer (no. 511), born in 1872, tells how he volunteered for military service and attended sub-officer training in 1892-1895. He then returned and took over his father's farm in 1900 at the age of 28. He volunteered once more to serve in the war and won decorations and the rank of sergeant. After the war he joined the DNVP until he became involved with the farm protest

---

State University Press, 1945, which has been updated and translated into German. Similar landslides were taking place in many parts of northeast Germany, especially in East Prussia, and also in Protestant areas of the south.

movement. In 1929, at the very first NSDAP rally in the area, he joined the party.[5]

Many other East Prussian farmers have similar stories. Some carried on a trade along with the farm. A farmer-blacksmith (no. 499), born in 1893, learned the trade from his father before volunteering for military service in 1912 and becoming a blacksmith in the artillery. He proudly relates having fought in fifty-two battles and being injured by a motor vehicle. He returned, took over the family farm, and was elected communal mayor. In 1930 he joined the party.[6] Another Protestant farmer (no. 236), born in 1911, worked on his father's farm and oil mill. He joined the *Stahlhelm* in 1926 "because I had been raised along DNVP lines." In 1930 he joined the party and a year later the SS; he was deputized as an auxiliary policeman in early 1933 "to protect, along with the regular police, the elections against Communist disturbances." There are other respondents who worked on their parents' or an older brother's farm (nos. 507 and 504) and also joined the party in 1930.

Many of the farmers' *vitae* are rather short and give little attitudinal information. One of the few who are more eloquent is a young East Prussian born 1909 (no. 168), who relates the arrival of Russian troops on his father's farm and, later, how he got to know the Russian prisoners of war working there. After the war, at school in Tilsit, he experienced the border struggles.

> One day we children had to collect signatures on [self-determination] petitions for West Prussia and Danzig. We did not mind and I realized for the first time that we children had kept the faith our fathers had in 1914. One day people said that East Prussia would be lost also, and I cried bitterly in bed and prayed to the Lord that we be allowed to remain Germans. Then the rumor became fact that the area beyond the Memel would have to be ceded, although only Germans lived there. The French occupied the country. It was hard to bear the shame. . . .

Barely a teenager, the boy joined a militant *voelkisch* youth group (Ammonites) marching and brawling in the streets. By the time he had to break off his secondary education and return to the debt-ridden farm, he was obviously well on his way toward the Nazi

[5] See the similar story of a prisoner of war born 1896 (no. 505).

[6] See also the story of a farmer-innkeeper's son with *Abitur* who became a forestry official and joined in 1932 (no. 358). He had held a rank in the artillery and became involved with the *voelkisch* wing of the DNVP after the war.

party. He describes the downward path of the farm from debts to bankruptcy, blaming "Jewish creditors" and the German reparations.

> The greater the crisis, the more the farmer clung to his soil. Everyone knew that when they drove him from the soil, his life was destroyed, [he was] rootless, and he was drifting to his end. There emerged peasant leagues to take up the battle against the system; they stopped foreclosures by force and boycotted tax auctions. Any means to defend the soil was self-defense and had at least the semblance of right. They strove to form a peasants' front which hoped to get superior numbers in the representative assemblies.

The respondent did not agree with these efforts against the system because they were aiming at "a narrow agrarian dictatorship in which the conservative owners of the estates would never make concessions to the workers." In 1931 he left home after an argument with his father and became a laborer himself. He joined the party in 1931, feeling that "peasant sons and farm laborers made . . . the best Nazis . . . and, conversely, the wealthiest are often the greatest traitors of the people." The Nazi peasants and laborers "grasped national socialism not intellectually, but with their emotions, not from books but with their blood, their natural instincts which drove them into the movement. They were seeking the way to the people, just like myself, by dropping all consciousness of class and seeing in every German just a comrade."

Another East Prussian (no. 517), born in 1902, claims descent from "a line of peasant families that goes back to the 16th century." He also experienced the Russian invasion of East Prussia. The family was evacuated from there at one point and settled in the province of Hannover, where they were homesick and could hardly understand the local dialect. On their return they found their farm destroyed and the whole area turned into a battlefield. About the end of the war he says: "It hurt my soul to hear that our undefeated army which had fought so bravely was to be dissolved for I had yearned with body and soul to become a soldier. When the war ended, they tried to enroll us youths among the Marxists, but I joined the *Wehrwolf* instead until the movement of our *Fuehrer* appeared in this village in 1930." This respondent's simple, rustic mind was overwhelmed when he first saw a big railroad bridge and even more when he saw Berlin at the age of 12.[7] Others show no

---

[7] See also no. 360, another family helper born 1910 who also joined in 1930. The *Wehrwolf* organization was a militant, youthful, nationalist

less bewilderment at the complexities of Weimar politics. One respondent who grew up under the Polish government in Poznan (no. 525) expresses his disdain for "the party mess," for in Pilsudski's Poland he had apparently not been exposed to political parties. The same attitude can also be found in the autobiographies of Nazis who grew up in Tsarist Russia.

The East Prussian respondents who were agricultural laborers differ from the farmers and family helpers in that they were usually exposed to the SPD, Independent Socialist (USPD), or Communist efforts at recruitment and did not share the economic anguish of the farm crisis. It is interesting to observe why they were not persuaded by this exposure to join the other side. A laborer born in 1898 relates how he attended an SPD meeting while still in the service. "Upon my return, a new world opened up which I at first did not understand. I had paid no attention to politics up until then, and hardly ever heard the word politics. Together with other comrades I was invited to one of the ongoing meetings of the SPD. My ideas about the state, the church, and the school were pulled into the dirt and knocked about. Everyone was supposed to get rid of such backward ballast." At home he immediately "had to join a union," but became suspicious when he learned that his trade union secretary had denounced veterans who were hiding army rifles to the Allied Control Commission. Nevertheless he stayed in the union for another five years until he lost his job as a result of a strike and could not find another for three months. Eventually he was indoctrinated by the Nazis and joined them in 1928.

Another laborer (no. 501), a miller born in 1885 and the father of 16 children, was a local SPD official (*Bezirksleiter*) and chief of the local district of the German Farm Labor Union in 1919. Two years later he dropped out of the SPD "because I realized that this government was not for Germany but international." In the late twenties he finally joined the NSDAP, though obviously not for the same reasons as the agrarian protesters did. Another East Prussian, born in 1890 (no. 362), saw the SPD strictly from the perspective of a man out of a job. "In 1927 I went to an SPD meeting where all kinds of promises were made to the workers, but none kept." The "contempt shown the worker everywhere" and the rising unemployment figures in 1928 caused him to vote for the NSDAP, which he joined four years later. To his mind the proof of the pudding was in the relative decline of unemployment at the time of the essay

---

action group somewhat like *Oberland—voelkisch*, anti-capitalistic, and authoritarian.

contest.[8] "Everything is different now and I am no longer treated as a second-class citizen."

One of the few Catholics among the farmers (no. 515) "found no place at home" after the war and for this reason became a miner in the Ruhr area. There he experienced the Communist uprising of 1920 when machine guns and hand grenades inside the mine stopped him from going to work and he nearly joined the Free Corps, which put the insurgents down. According to his own account he was almost thrown down a 120-foot mine shaft during a political argument with Communist fellow workers underground. Upon losing his job in 1926, he returned to East Prussia and became a forestry worker, having brought along the Nazi gospel he had learned in the west. He joined the party in 1929 and was excommunicated by the church two years later. There were confrontations, he lost a law suit, and people called him a "heathen" in the street.

Agricultural laborers were not the only ones to get acquainted with the sorrows of the proletariat. An agricultural official and manager (no. 516), born 1901, the son of an attorney, became acquainted with the workers and their "Marxist indoctrination" and "subversion of military morale" while volunteering his labor in 1917-1918. "I came to brood over the inability and unwillingness of the various layers of the German people to understand each other. . . ." Traveling through East Prussia as an agricultural official later, he "realized increasingly that a system of irresponsibility, selfishness, and the struggle of all against all would never allow the fatherland to recover." In 1923 he lost the savings set aside by his late father for his university education in the inflation for which he promptly blamed "the system." He joined the *Stahlhelm* in 1923 and gradually became interested in *voelkisch* groups and the NSDAP, which, together with a brother, he joined in 1931.

Another agricultural official, the son of a family which elected to stay in Poznan (no. 361), opted for Germany when he was faced with being drafted to fight the Soviets. He had already been in the German army in 1917 and in the border protection squads against the Poles after the war. He wandered through a *voelkisch* group and then joined the *Stahlhelm* and held the office of treasurer, although he considered this organization "only nationalistic, but not socialistic enough" in this time of great social needs. In 1930 he joined the Nazi party and soon became a local chairman in it.[9]

[8] For other unemployed farm workers, see nos. 469, 484, and 497.

[9] See also the similar cases of an agricultural official expelled from Polish West Prussia, no. 508, and of a young forestry manager, no. 509.

Rare among the salient concerns on the minds of the respondents is a case such as one "hereditary farmer (Erbhofbauer)," born in 1901, the oldest son of "an old East German, Protestant farming family" that could afford a private school for him.

> From the very beginning my wish and goal for the future was to be a farmer like my forefathers, an independent farmer on his own sod. I . . . married a farmer's daughter from the West Prussian territory ceded to Poland who, like me, is from an old farming family. In 1928 I bought my 1400-acre (289 *morgen*) farm in Posilge, which has now been declared a "hereditary farm" thanks to the present government. Thus I and my offspring can work as independent farmers for the German people, free from capitalistic greed.

The respondent does not really explain what attracted him to the NSDAP, aside from Walther Darré's phrases. He professes to have been interested in it when most farmers in his area were still loyal to the DNVP. Perhaps his wealth helped him to have the courage of his convictions. He joined only in 1932, but carried the flag in demonstrations and got himself elected to the communal council in 1933.

As we move from East Prussia to other regions, there is often a remainder such as an agricultural apprentice manager, born 1907 (no. 488), whose whole family was expelled in 1923 from the occupied Rhineland. He describes his parents as "descended from old Westphalian peasant families of which the father's side can be traced back to 1230 and the mother's side back to the Thirty Years' War." He went to school in Kassel and eventually did his apprenticeship in East Prussia, all the while deeply involved in *voelkisch* action groups such as the *Jungsturm* and hardly representative of any area. No more typical is another young (born 1908) agricultural apprentice who moved freely around Silesia, Saxony, and Pomerania (no. 374). The son of a Prussian civil servant and Free Conservative deputy in the Prussian diet who, as a Prussian lieutenant, was killed in battle in 1915, he also had a great-uncle whose estate the family inherited in 1911. The boy grew up in painful awareness of the social chasm between his village playmates of the lower classes and his own family and private-school environment. From 1924 on, at the age of 16, he became involved in *voelkisch* groups including the *Frontbann*, a cover-up for the outlawed NSDAP. His family eventually became alarmed about their "incorrigible brawler." His fiancée called him a "beast of a bully (*wuester Schlaeger*)" when he failed his *Abitur*. In 1928, the family shipped him from Goebbels' Berlin to where "no one has ever heard of the NSDAP," to Catholic Silesia and other apprenticeship locations in the northeast, but he promptly went on proselytizing "among the Catholic laborers and Center papists."

North Central Germany

Another group of farm respondents is from north central Germany. One agricultural manager near Braunschweig (no. 78), born in 1900 to a farmer with a brick factory, aspired to a naval officer's career but was rejected for "insufficient chest measurements." After an agricultural apprenticeship and a year of military service in the war, he returned to take over the farm. In 1928 he began to be interested in the NSDAP upon reading *Mein Kampf*. But the resistance of his family, whose loyalty belonged to the three republican parties (SPD, DDP, and Center), and the absence of a Nazi organization still held him back until 1930, when he and others formed an SA troop and began to campaign in earnest.

Another farmer's son, born in 1903 and well-trained in agriculture, relates his early interest in politics and political news.

> While managing my father's farm, I learned to think in economic terms and realized that it was completely impossible to get out of the hole, especially during the deflation (1924). I soon came to sense that the economic crisis was political in origin, and that our current government and the people they duped were not interested in saving German agriculture, not to mention the German peasant.
>
> They scorned the national values while they carried on their international politics. Although the farmers were just as poor as the workers, the former were made out to be capitalists by the latter. It was clear to me from the beginning that it was the Democratic [DDP], Social Democratic, and Communist leaders who were leading the workers astray and thus wanted to use them. The thing to do was to persuade the workers of the importance of other social elements [*Staende*].

The respondent consequently joined the Young German Order (*Jungdo*), an oppositional, conservative-bourgeois group which "advocated solidarity among the classes" (*Volksgemeinschaft*) and had some *voelkisch*, Russophile, and agrarian overtones. He stayed with *Jungdo* for five years until the group allied itself with the declining DDP. He and his father had voted all along for the DNVP and its *voelkisch* offspring but at last became disenchanted with their "purely economic thinking."

> The development was inexorable as the so-called bourgeoisie disintegrated from election to election. In my confusion I once even voted for the Christian National Peasant and *Landvolk* party. Communism grew

by leaps and bounds, pitting proletariat against capitalism. My economic activity, I think, had taught me to recognize the disproportion between the factors labor and capital. I sensed that a new economic order was dawning . . . socialism.

At this point the Nazi party made its appearance and the respondent joined it in 1931.

For every clear case of the farm revolt there are many that do not fit the pattern. Another farmer's son and helper, born in 1895 (no. 77), was more a frustrated professional soldier than a farmer. He volunteered for the service in 1912 and stayed throughout the war, typically blaming the Jews and the Marxists for demoralizing the German army. After the war he joined the police until 1922, and comments approvingly on the "soldierly spirit" which caused many policemen to volunteer for the units suppressing "Communist stirrings." When he finally returned to the farm, he also joined the *Stahlhelm* and never missed a *Stahlhelm* demonstration until he discovered the stormtroopers in 1930. He immediately joined them because "there was a very different revolutionary spirit among these young people as compared to the *Stahlhelm*." He delightedly involved himself in the street fighting of the SA against the Communists.

More typical of the farm crisis is a lumberjack born in 1902 whose mother had to lease the family farm and cattle after his father's death in 1911 (no. 98). Instead of pursuing his hopes for a secondary education, the respondent had to work as a farm hand. A bright student, by the age of eleven he began to read socialist and antisemitic tracts, which gave him the ideological mixture typical of national socialism. Working in a sawmill with many "Marxist rascals," he got into so many arguments that he had to quit and become a lumberjack.

> The signing of the shameful Treaty of Versailles and especially the recognition of the lying clause about our war guilt triggered great bitterness in me against the government we had then. I decided to become politically active. My struggle was directed first of all against the reactionaries, for they were the true origin of the November [1918] takeover. I was convinced it was they whose hostility to the workers gave the Jews the weapons to stir up the workers against everything German. I had felt on my own body how the worker was treated like a second-class human being.

On other forestry jobs he encountered more friction with "Communist fellow employees" who again forced him to quit. He joined the *Stahlhelm* but withdrew the same night in disgust over the drunken singing of the national anthem at the initiation meeting. He returned to farming when the farm lease expired and struggled on with some success. His political attitudes met with little understanding among the other farmers because of his "red tinge." In 1927 he began to campaign in earnest for the NSDAP.

Northern Hesse

Another group of farmers is from northern Hesse and they appear to be rather more politicized throughout the Weimar era than the East Prussians. One calls himself "a simple peasant from a remote little village" (no. 131) and then proceeds to demonstrate that he is neither simple nor remote.

> I can recall how as a schoolboy I was already aware of the heavily emphasized social contrasts between the farmers and their "inferiors," meaning the workers. I could not stand these distinctions and always used to side with these underdogs in the brawls among the boys, regardless of who was in the right. Since that time I still find it impossible to use the deprecatory word "inferiors" in conversation for those who are economically worse off than the farmers. Even then I could not understand why even the most competent German worker should not be every bit as good as persons of other occupational status.

The respondent, who was born in 1896, simply attributes this attitude to the influence of his mother, without further explanation. It may be a fair guess that she was of proletarian origin herself. Her son voted SPD in 1919 and then, appalled at the "undignified attitude of this party toward the dictate of Versailles," joined a conservative veterans group (*Kriegerverein*) in search of "the comradeship I had experienced during the war years at the front." He voted DNVP and was somewhat disappointed with both, the veterans and the DNVP. It was the name of the National Socialist Workers Party which really attracted him, the combination of nationalism and socialism. He joined in 1929 when the Nazis came to his village and was delighted to find in the party the "old front comradeship."

Another Hessian (no. 581), a farmer born in 1899, joined the *Landjugendbund* of the Hessian Peasant League, a Democratic (DDP) organization whose "thinking turned out not to correspond to my feelings about society." He became actively involved with the Nazis in 1929 and joined two years later. Another respondent of the same age (no. 455) reports having voted for the *Landbund* in 1923 and being disappointed with its sole concentration on concrete interests. Only after he "married into a farm" does his active interest awaken in politics. After considerable friction with his family and other farmers, he joins the party in 1929 and even helps to found a local organization.

A third Hessian (no. 127) assures the reader that his "descent is purely Aryan and his forefathers, all peasants who often headed this commune, can be traced back to 1710." He was born in 1905 and in 1923 joined the Young German Order (*Jungdo*) of Arthur Mahraun, an ex-officer and Free Corps leader in Hesse who had been in the prewar Youth Movement. The respondent simply attributes the defeat in World War One to "the treason of the SPD and felt henceforth an instinctive aversion, even rage toward the Marxist ideology." *Jungdo* appeared to him as "the strongest wall against the SPD," although he left the organization after four years because of "the democratic liberalism" underlying Mahraun's abstruse nationalist philosophy. While he was among DNVP and *Landvolk* sympathizers at the university in 1929-1930, an East Prussian estate-owner's son indoctrinated him about the NSDAP. The respondent and his friend particularly and somewhat implausibly like the ideas of social solidarity and of dividing up large estates among the peasants, although his real emphasis appears to be on revanchism and Versailles. His nationalistic feelings are echoed by another Hessian, born in 1899, who also joined *Jungdo* in 1923. This respondent became a fully involved stormtrooper in 1930.[10]

The last respondent of this group (no. 128) is an older waterworker (born 1888) who was a French prisoner of war until 1920. Upon his return he inclined toward Marxism "until I saw how the leaders of this party [presumably the SPD] were humiliating Germany and pulling it into the dirt." He was "always revolted by its preaching of class hatred and of hatred among the German compatriots." Its internationalism did not impress him because he had found the French workers anything but brotherly during his confinement. The prevailing economic misery while he tried to support eight people with his tiny farm did its share to motivate him toward the NSDAP after "I found the bourgeois parties' thinking also to be disagreeable." He joined in 1932, another example of a man who fit neither the working-class nor the bourgeois camp.

The Catholic Rhineland

The next group of farm respondents is from the Rhineland and mostly Catholic. A young vintner from the Moselle area, born in

---

[10] See also another young nationalist family helper (no. 126) who cried when he first heard Hitler speak.

1906 (no. 266), for example, relates how he braved the resistance of his family and the whole Catholic town by proselytizing for the Nazi party at Center party meetings, using the popular technique for getting attention by arguing with the speaker at another party's rally. The church and the Center party then persuaded members of his family to put pressure on him and attempted to prosecute him on various charges in court. He joined a neighboring Nazi local in 1931, because "in this black [i.e., Catholic] town we simply could not organize until after the seizure of power, because our adherents were so afraid of the other side, even though we had a majority of the vote long before that time."

Another Rhinelander (no. 331), born 1901, spent the war years working behind the lines and in an ammunition factory where he witnessed corruption, unrest, and anti-war propaganda to the bitter end:

> Back home, red socialism had won out. Why? The owners of the quarries, our only industry, used to be nationalists but only as far as their pocketbooks would permit them to go. They ignored the human side of the worker, who was only a chattel to them like everything else. These fine gentlemen never even thought it necessary to say a greeting . . . and thus Marxism was already spreading here in the 1880s. The Social Democrats were the second-strongest party in the Center-dominated city of Mayen, but their Marxism was more an opposition to bourgeois liberalism than a "revolutionary movement."

The foreign occupation caused the respondent and other young men to hoist a black, white, and red flag on the top of a mountain, which caused quite a stir among the local populace. His stepfather's farm and transport business suffered greatly in the inflation of 1923, which, together with domestic arguments, drove the respondent away from home. As he writes, "my youthful experiences produced a revolutionary consciousness in me and I began to look for like-minded comrades." Instead of joining a "red" trade union while working in a Duisburg mine ("where I came from you just did not do that"), he became a street fighter against the separatists and ended up in prison. With this background, it was natural for him to join the stormtroopers as soon as they came to his area.

Another Mayener, born in 1893 (no. 342), worked from an early age to supplement the meager farm income and was never able to learn a trade until he became a miner at the age of 20. At the end of his wartime service he was "tired of war and was greatly allured by the promises of freedom and dignity the Marxists misleadingly presented." But they could not bring him salvation and he positively resented their implication that it would be impossible for him ever to be independent.

> I remembered the life of my youth and returned on father's request to take over . . . the tiny farm left after the other four surviving children had received their share. It was too little to subsist on. . . . I succeeded with much effort, work, and sacrifice in getting ahead by buying more land. But this meant cumulative debts from year to year which threatened to ruin me with the interest going up all the time, and the markets poor, and industrial prices rising too.

At this point, of course, the reader may well say to himself, "Why didn't he remain a miner rather than returning to this marginal existence?" The respondent continues:

> I began to show my fighting spirit toward the outside. Having thrown aside the Marxist idea long ago, I thought and thought. I wanted in the future an equal right to a living. I did not like the "interest parties" but professed to be above parties. In 1928-1929 I read and heard about Adolf Hitler and his words went right to my marrow. Since the Catholic clergy always warned us against him, I thought at first that my conscience would not permit me to follow him. But the worsening economic situation once more threatened to ruin my laboriously built-up livelihood and I began to worry about the future of my four sons.

In 1930 he decided to join, but the clergy put so much pressure on his wife and family that he grudgingly put it off for two years. When he finally did join, he reports, the church withheld the sacraments from him notwithstanding an appeal to the bishop. His boys were beaten up at school for shouting "Heil Hitler," and he was told that he would lose his communal office. He reacted with stubborn fury and "envied the fighters in the city who could openly combat the SPD or KPD (Communists). My spiritual struggle with the clergy tore wounds that are still bleeding today."

Another respondent, from the Moselle area, was a day-laborer in the wineries (no. 346). He was born in 1903, the son of a bricklayer who died the same year, leaving the family in penury. The respondent was unemployed in 1923 and 1924, and again from 1928 on. He was deeply dissatisfied with "the system" which "in 1918 promised us a life of freedom, beauty, and dignity." When the Nazis came to his area, he was immediately taken in by their radical, anti-system tirades and, in 1929, became a stormtrooper.

The last of the Rhenish respondents is a Protestant from a village close to the Belgian border (no. 144). He was the only son of a well-to-do farmer, for whom he worked after leaving school. In

1923, he fought the Belgian occupation and became involved in a series of *voelkisch* action groups beginning with the *Voelkisch-soziale Block* and ending with the NSDAP in 1928 "because all the other parties had ideologies invented by Jews and were subordinated to the supranational powers," meaning the Catholic church, Bolshevism, and international finance.

Rhine-Hesse and the Palatinate

The last group of farm respondents is from the Palatinate and Rhenish Hesse. Due to underrepresentation of the southeast and extreme north there are none from Upper or Lower Bavaria, Franconia, or Schleswig-Holstein. The Palatinatian *vitae* are much like those of the Rhineland except that the respondents often heard of the Hitler movement earlier, since the Palatinate was a part of Bavaria. One vintner's son, born in 1891 (no. 444), relates his postwar experiences when "the powerful Social Democrats not only drove away Kaiser and kings but scored all *voelkisch* thinking and replaced it with liberal-capitalistic ideology." He belonged to the DNVP and was very deeply dissatisfied with the repression of the Nazi party by "Marxist-Jesuitic" influence and by the French occupation. He encountered the NSDAP in 1928 and found its program and principles to be "nothing new, but old German doctrines which our undistorted good peasant sense would certainly welcome and which are in our blood." He lost his winery because of political boycotts and circumstances, and then openly joined the NSDAP in 1930. In 1931 he entered the SS, where he soon advanced to higher office.[11]

Another respondent of the same age (no. 571), but from southern Hesse, was a farmer and innkeeper who acquired military rank during his service before and during the war. After the war he first belonged to the Peasant League (*Bauernbund*) which participated in the Munich revolution of 1919 on the "red" side, but he became disenchanted for lack of militant action. Then he went through a bewildering variety of sports and target-practice groups which were the cover-ups of outlawed militant veterans groups. His urge for action led him to join the NSDAP in 1928 as soon as it came to town, whereupon the same Peasant League along with the "Marxists" boycotted him. A second Rhine-Hessian, born in 1887 (no. 580), blames the French occupation, with the support of the separatists and the Jews, for holding back the Nazi development in his area by jailing the Nazi leadership. He joined late in 1928 when the NSDAP began to organize rural Hesse. A third Rhine-Hessian farmer's son

[11] See no. 441 for another Palatinatian vintner of *voelkisch* persuasion.

was born in 1903 and became heavily involved with militant veterans groups in 1922-1923 although he had never served in his life. He may well have been a "victory-watcher"; he says that in 1923 he guarded a large arms cache until the regular army took it over. After a few years he became tired of playing soldier and instead looked for "a movement of liberation composed of German-thinking men of all strata, classes, and occupations in order to overcome the split of the German people into parties, interest groups and classes." He joined the party in 1929.

Organizational Behavior of Nazi Farmers

How do the attitudes of the farm respondents compare with those of the other occupational groups of the Nazi sample? The reader will recall their relative youthfulness. They show a high enough degree of involvement in youth groups, especially agricultural or Catholic ones, *Jungdo*, and militant veterans groups, not to mention youthful membership in the Nazi party, that we may characterize their mobilization as a farm youth revolt. What they liked best about their first youth organization was usually the ideology and the military training. If they disliked something about it, by the same token, it tended to be the ideological overtones or the leadership. Their youthful activities in such organizations disproportionately tended toward political violence against insurgents or foreign soldiers, and toward demonstrations. We can characterize their youthful involvement as fully politicized or even politically militarized, to a degree rivalled only by the young blue- and white-collar employees. Their parents' politics tended to be conservative (DNVP or Center) or *voelkisch*, and this is also the description they give of their school influences.

Their attitude toward the war stands out as particularly positive, although not a few of them ended up with major injuries or languished for years in POW camps. Nevertheless, they tended to accept the defeat and to show less cultural shock upon their return than the other groups. Regarding the ongoing revolution, however, they often blamed the republican parties for the revolution and served in disproportionate numbers in militant veteran or anti-occupation organizations. In 1923, a surprising number of the farm respondents claims to have been aware of and sympathetic to Hitler's beer-hall *putsch* in Munich. Many were in other political parties. During the relatively peaceful years from 1925 to 1928 quite a few were with the *Stahlhelm*, with various conservative or agrarian groups, and, increasingly, with the NSDAP. They continued this in 1929 and 1930, and reached their peak in joining the party in 1930. Because of their remote locations more than half of them, they say, founded or co-founded their local Nazi organization. Even at this late date there were many among them who were merely following public events, but others threw themselves into electioneering, demonstrations, and political street violence. In 1931 and 1932, the farm respondents still stand out among the other groups in these three activities. They have the second-highest rate, next to the urban workers, of joining the SA and the SS. And they encountered a lot of friction because of their political beliefs, most of all in the family, at school, and in their neighborhood—a reflection of the differences between rural and urban life.

Attitudes and Ideologies of Farm Respondents

Their ideological views differed from the other groups in a predictable fashion. Their criticisms of the Weimar Republic stress traditional objections to Marxism, capitalism, and to the multi-party state. Their dominant ideological themes, after they had joined the party, tended to be revanchism and the *Volksgemeinschaft* among the classes, a telltale sign of their feelings about the old class society. It is interesting that the farm respondents are far behind all the other occupational Nazi groups in their stress on Nordic or German romanticism, including the *voelkisch* myth of blood and soil, even though many of our respondents were aware of it.

Their hate lists generally include all the objects of the national socialist demonology—Jews, Marxists, reactionaries, and the clergy —although they were less ethnocentric toward the outside than other groups. Their attitude toward political enemies within, however, tended to be physically aggressive. They had indeed a disproportionate number of bullies among them, and no hesitation to describe their enjoyment of brawls in fulsome, rustic detail. In their attitude toward authority they exhibit notably more hostility toward the police and the government than do those in most other occupations. The formative influence or experience in their lives tended to be either a sense of social snub or humiliation or the experiences of the *Fronterlebnis* and the defeat. The theme of social humiliation also characterizes their attitude toward the Nazi movement. What they praise most is its classlessness, a boon to the outcast, and hopes for social and economic betterment for the individual peasant or for the whole country.

Points of Emphasis

By way of a summary, several points about the Nazi farmers of the sample should be repeated and emphasized. These points may also characterize the Nazi farmers in the party at large and, to a degree, even the Nazi farm vote of the last years of the republic. The farmers, farm laborers, and other agricultural respondents who rallied to the NSDAP represent chiefly the political mobilization of the younger rural generations. Their mobilizing catalyst tended to be either the experiences of war, defeat, and foreign occupation, or the economic crisis of German agriculture. As with other varieties of youth revolt, of course, this is not to suggest a simple causative effect of these events and circumstances on the young respondents. It was rather the general disruption of the rural way of life which caused the normal socialization processes of farm families and communities to fail in their customary function of turning farm youths into conforming adults. It is quite plausible, therefore, that in many cases a person turned extremist even before the economic crisis caught up with him. There are many examples of such general disruptive influences, such as fathers absent in the war, the effect of wartime military experiences on a young man, or economic crises of whole families, that could be cited.

There are also other mediating factors such as the timing of Nazi recruitment efforts, or of the local availability of a Nazi organization, or the differences between a Protestant and a Catholic environment. The Catholic church typically and rather effectively met the Nazi challenge through family and community pressures. There is no Protestant equivalent to this in the entire Abel collection except for the sad story of a prominent Berlin pastor (not a respondent) who had the courage to tell Joseph Goebbels after a speech before a huge audience that Goebbels did not look much like a Germanic youth. The minister was roughed up and thrown out of the rally and in response the Nazi party was silenced by municipal decree for a year. But in the end the good pastor is rumored to have joined the movement too. The Catholics had a better hold over their flock also because the proportion of believers and practicing parishioners was so much greater than among the Protestants. It is a matter of general knowledge by now that, in the Catholic areas of Germany[12] and among Center party or BVP voters, there was no landslide between 1928 and 1933 in favor of the Nazis. Since the rural Protestants were more likely to be devout than urban Protestants, it is all the more surprising that not one of them in the sample voiced any scruples of conscience about joining the NSDAP comparable to those expressed by several of the Catholics. Quite apart from the

[12] See Heinrich Striefler, *Deutsche Wahlen in Bildern und Zahlen*, Duesseldorf: Wende, 1946, pp. 49-55. The Bavarian offshoot of the Center party was called the Bavarian People's Party (BVP).

bad example given by certain Protestant ministers (and later by Catholic dignitaries), in failing to rise to the Nazi challenge, the acceptance of national socialism appears to have been a function of the decay of the Protestant faith in Germany. Nazism was a substitute religion for Protestants who had lost their faith.

In spite of the siren song about blood and soil, moreover, there appears to have been little genuine identification among Nazi farmers with the substance of the Nazi slogan. Even those who speak about their peasant ancestry and about blood and instinct tended to do so as if they had just looked up the appropriate phrases in a book by Walther Darré. There was, however, in many of the farm lives an exposure to *voelkisch* groups and propaganda, especially of the action-oriented postwar variety. In other words, young farmers tended to be preoccupied not so much with their precious *voelkisch* soul as with a desire for militant *voelkisch* action, such as demonstrations, proselytizing, and political violence against the French or Belgian occupation, the Communists or Socialists, or the Poles. On an ideological-pragmatic attitude scale, also, the farmers were considerably more pragmatic than the other occupational groups.

The last point of emphasis, finally, and also the main reason why the section on the farmers appears in this context, is the attitude of the farm respondents toward their class and status in German society. There are, of course, great differences between upper-class farmers and agricultural managers on the one hand and the marginal farmers, family help, and laborers on the other hand. But for varying reasons even the upper-class respondents appear to have felt a great desire to opt out of their upper-class or bourgeois circles, a change which was always implied in switching from the DNVP or *Stahlhelm*, not to mention the other bourgeois parties, to the vulgar NSDAP. The typical mixture of ideological elements necessary to produce national socialism was DNVP, *Stahlhelm*, or *voelkisch* conservative nationalism with a touch of socialism, or concern for the laboring masses. The farm respondents, at least of the lower and middle classes, typically wanted to be regarded neither as part of the capitalistic bourgeoisie nor as proletarians, no matter how poor and ill-educated they might be. Their autobiographies are full of stories of social humiliation and anti-bourgeois sentiments, as well as of stories of dissociation from organized labor and the Marxist parties along with expressions of affection for the workers themselves. Like the military-civil servants, the upwardly mobile and socially declining groups, the artisans, and white-collar employees, the farm respondents found themselves unhappily caught in the crossfire between the two antagonistic camps of the class struggle. And for this reason the Nazi slogan of the social solidarity among the classes and interests of the nation (*Volksgemeinschaft*) was very attractive to them.[13]

[13] The argument that *Volksgemeinschaft* would symbolically reestablish the homogeneous village community, has also been advanced to explain its attraction to farmers. However, rural society in most parts of Germany was never communitarian to begin with and in areas with large estates and a rural proletariat such as in East Prussia, the social contrasts were so extreme as to make this a ludicrous, if not self-serving, explanation.

FOUR

Solidarity Among the Classes

No other Nazi slogan was as popular among the Abel respondents as that of the *Volksgemeinschaft* (solidary community of the people), although its meaning remained rather vague. It has long been customary among historians and social scientists to speak condescendingly of the "vague, verbal invocation" of socialism by the Nazi program and leadership.[1] It is indeed true that the Nazi leadership was stridently anti-Marxist and yet at the same time liked to invoke a "national" or "German socialism," just as it was anti-capitalistic (at least prior to 1935) and at the same time wooed German capitalists like Thyssen. The Nazi leadership cynically played fast and loose with many such issues, for example, the question of economic reorganization, the role of the nobility, federalism, church and state, and even the claims of youth against the "old ones" of Weimar. However, we are not concerned here with the intentions of the Nazi leaders or the shoddy quality of Nazi philosophizing as compared to the compelling logic of Marxist socialism. Our sole purpose here is to find out why the rather untutored, rank-and-file Nazi members were attracted by the idea and what they saw in it. And our thesis is precisely that many of the Nazi followers fit neither in the capitalistic bourgeoisie nor in the existing labor movement.

Attracted they were indeed. All the social yearning for comradeship, for fraternal acceptance, and for community, engendered by the social tensions of the class society of the empire and the republic, seemed to culminate in the call for the *Volksgemeinschaft*. The fear of disunity, of divisive issues of class or economic interest, of freely contending parties and interest groups likewise pointed in this direction, as did the related Nazi slogan *Gemeinnutz geht vor Eigen-*

[1] See, for example, Karl D. Bracher, *The German Dictatorship*, New York: Praeger, 1970, pp. 145-148 for a discussion of many of these intentional ambiguities. See also Theodor Geiger's excursion *op. cit.*, pp. 109-122, and the discussion of the theories of Othmar Spann in Lebovics, *Social Conservatism and the Middle Classes*, pp. 109-138.

nutz (the common good is more important than self-interest). To be sure, solidarism is an idea as old as Aristotle and Thomas Aquinas. The nineteenth-century neo-Thomists had already thought of applying it to the social cleavages created by industrialization, and the Center party's Adam Stegerwald proclaimed it at the time of the Weimar Republic. It was given lip-service support by the DNVP and on occasion even by the People's party (DVP) and the Democrats (DDP). It was an idea particularly dear to all the *voelkisch* groups which first rivalled and eventually merged with the NSDAP. However, none of these other parties and groups ever sold the *Volksgemeinschaft* as aggressively and persuasively as did Hitler himself, the "drummer" of the nationalistic right wing. It takes salesmanship, not necessarily good faith, to persuade the masses of what they really need.

As with many political slogans, moreover, many subjective meanings were hidden in the word and it may well have been its very ambiguity which made it acceptable to so many kinds of people. To understand what the early Nazi followers meant when they used the term, we first need to distinguish among the solidaristic desires expressed by persons of upper-, middle-, or lower-class background, at least *as defined subjectively by themselves*. A self-styled upper-class person crying for *Volksgemeinschaft* may generally have felt guilty about his status. His solidarism signified a desire to be accepted by the lower classes. Other upper-class members who were not solidaristic typically would express their resentment of lower-class hostility toward themselves. All the Nazis, of course, rejected the advocacy of class struggle by Socialists or Communists. A middle-class solidarist was usually a man in the middle trying to bridge the rigid class barriers above as well as below him. A lower-class advocate of *Volksgemeinschaft* wanted most of all to be accepted or not to be snubbed by the middle and upper classes. This group frequently included persons of a socially split parentage such as a proletarian father and a bourgeois mother, or families who had declined from a higher class to a more or less proletarian status.[2] The typical lower-class person who was not a solidarist was likely to complain about social snubs or about the snobbery (*Klassenduenkel*) of the higher classes.

There is also a concept of solidarism which has to do less with the class distinctions than with national solidarity toward other na-

[2] Our meaning of social decline here is the same as in the preceding sections and not just the declining living standards of many strata in the 1920s.

tions. One variety of this national solidarity was the stress on the egalitarian *Fronterlebnis* of World War One. Another strain was the solidarism of people who were born abroad or who have resided abroad, and who were motivated by an enormous desire to merge again with their own co-nationals. This kind of solidarism from without often involves stories of snubs or discrimination abroad. We

FD-9: Class Feelings

	Number	Per cent
Solidarism from above	12	2.6
Solidarism from the middle	141	30.0
Solidarism from below	73	15.5
Solidarism of *Fronterlebnis*	27	5.7
Solidarism from abroad	17	3.6
Resentment of lower-class hostility	36	7.7
Resentment of upper-class snobbery	38	8.1
Strong class consciousness	16	3.4
No class feelings	110	23.4
	470	100.0

shall come back to these two groups later. Finally, there are also respondents who exhibit a lively class consciousness, even snobbism, and those who never even mention the class distinctions still so deeply ingrained in German society at the time.

The Social Background of Solidarity Groupings

These categories were regrouped for purposes of crosstabulation in such a manner as to combine the upper-class solidarists with upper-class respondents who resented lower-class hostility, the two kinds of solidarism toward the outside, and the two typical attitudes of the old class society, strong class consciousness and resentment of upper-class snobbery. If we cross these groups with the static or socially mobile groups of the preceding section, for example, some interesting patterns emerge. The upper-class solidarists and non-solidarists belong in disproportionate numbers to the static and declining groups. Middle solidarism was championed mostly by the upwardly mobile in city and countryside. Solidarism from below was a pose assumed mainly by the static and the farm climbers, two groups of predominantly rural and small-town origins. Solidarism toward the outside world again seems most typical of the city climbers and decliners, who also figure prominently among respondents showing strong class feelings and among those exhibiting no class feelings at all. It would appear then that the *Volksgemeinschaft* slogan was a kind of free currency which could bind together the static or declining upper classes with the upwardly mobile thrust of middle-class elements, and especially respondents from the rural and small town settings. Urban settings were subject to conflicting motives of class feelings, often overshadowed by an awareness of the hostile outside world around Germany.

Leaving aside for the moment the idea of national solidarity against the outside world, there are significant generational differences among the groups that desired to bridge the class barriers of German society. The men in the middle, as in Aristotle's flattering vision of middle-class mentality, were evidently the first to discover the good sense of solidarity among the classes rather than the opposites of class struggle from below (socialism) or class domination from above (conservatism and liberalism). Three-fourths of them were born before the turn of the century. The solidarists from below are noticeably younger, with only half born before 1900. The defensive upper-class Nazis, finally, are the youngest, with 54% too young to have been drafted in World War One. We can speculate that after the development of middle solidarism, it was the progress of the socialist labor movement which first mobilized lower-class solidarists and then frightened upper-class Germans into pleading for their own acceptance. Many of the youngest respondents show no class feelings at all.

These relationships become clearer after we find out more about the character of the various solidarist groups. When they are crossed with the breakdown of occupations, for example, "upper-class solidarism" and resentment of lower-class hostility turn out to be held most strongly by members of the labor aristocracy, nominally working-class themselves, and by farmers, both of whom are also prominent among the lower-class advocates of *Volksgemeinschaft*. The men in the middle are over one-third military-civil servants and one-fifth each white-collar employees or independent business and professional men. They are also considerably more urban than both the other groups. This is the character of this upwardly mobile group of middle solidarists.

Substantial numbers of white-collar employees also show up among both the strongly class-conscious and those innocent of class feelings. Other occupational groups prominent among those without class feelings are women, business or professional men, and members of the urban working class. Further corroborating evidence comes from crossing the class feelings with the occupation of the respondents' fathers. Here the "upper-class" respondents turn out in disproportionate numbers to have high-ranking military or professional and artisan fathers, very likely of traditional anti-socialist views. The lower-class solidarists are descended especially from workers and farm laborers, farmers, and artisans. The soli-darists from the middle had mostly military-civil servants, business-men, and farmers as fathers. The background of small business and handicrafts of a transitional society can of course be ideologically very ambiguous, as the roles of these elements in the 1848 revolu-tion and in the following century have demonstrated. Businessmen and artisans as fathers also play a prominent role among the strong-ly class-conscious and the non-class-conscious groups. These cross-tabulations suggest that the slogan of the *Volksgemeinschaft* had a strongly political, anti-socialist tenor and that we should not over-emphasize the desire for social acceptance or a rationalization of upward mobility in a rigidly stratified society.

Solidarism and Economic Crises

The changes in economic fortune reported by these groups also give food for thought. The advocates of *Volksgemeinschaft* of all varie-ties, with the exception of the men of the middle, report more eco-nomic hardship in their childhoods and again during the Weimar days than do the non-solidaristic Nazis. Well over one-third of the lower-class solidarists lost their fathers or the family livelihoods, or had both parents away at work during their tender years. Nearly one-third of them fell victim to the great crisis of 1929-1932 and another 19% suffered great economic loss between 1914 and 1928. Thus their idea of solidarity among the classes may well have been nourished by personal experiences of hardship and helplessness, if it did not indeed originate there. The level of education, which is such an important index of social class in most European countries, also divides the solidarists from below, and those without class feel-ings from the better-educated two-fifths of the sample, leaving soli-darists on both sides.

Another potential source could have been religion, especially Catholicism, which also advocates a solidaristic social philosophy. Respondents indicating their religion (about one-third) indeed are more likely to profess the *Volksgemeinschaft* than those who do not. Among the Catholics it is especially the lower- and "upper-class" solidarists and also the respondents innocent of class feelings who stand out. Among the Protestants, it is the men in the middle, the upper-class respondents, and persons of strong class-conscious-ness who are overrepresented, all recognizable groups of Weimar Protestant society.

Ideology and Views

There remains the question of how the various versions of *Volksgemeinschaft* relate to other views and attitudes. The respondents' image of the Weimar Republic is a good example. Here the solidarists from above tend to characterize the ill-fated republic with traditional objections such as criticisms of rampant capitalism and the multi-party state of Weimar, which are also the chief objections of the solidarists from below. The solidarists of the middle, by contrast, prefer to call the republic a "liberal-Marxist system," a criticism shared by the solidarists from below and again a confirmation of the anti-socialist and anti-liberal nature of the slogan of the *Volksgemeinschaft*. It is worth noting that both the strongly class-conscious and those exhibiting no class feelings instead stress images of the "Marxist-run" and "Jewish-run" republic, images that evidently were ambiguous in their class implications.

A breakdown according to the dominant theme of the respondent while he was a member of the party shows that *Volksgemeinschaft* among the classes was indeed very important to the solidarists from the middle and from below, but clearly secondary to the solidarists from above. Themes emphasized by both the upper and the middle solidarists are revanchism, authoritarianism, and antisemitism. The solidarists from above also stress Nordic or German romanticism and the Hitler cult, motives they hold in common with both the strongly class-conscious and those without class feelings. Nearly one-third of the last-mentioned group, finally, stand out for their superpatriotism, a motive shared only by the solidarists toward the outside world. Solidarity among the classes was a key concept of the party members, it appears, but certainly not the only or most dominant theme for many of them except for the solidarists of the middle and from below who seem to constitute a kind of (upwardly mobile) mainstream of the social dynamics of the movement.

In-group Solidarity and Prejudice for Out-groups

Pursuing this inquiry further, we can cross the solidarist groups with the hate lists of phobias and objects of hostility typical of extremist movements. The favorite collection of scapegoats of the Nazi solidarists from above and from below are Communists, Socialists, and Marxists in general, a phobia they share with respondents of no class feelings. The solidarists of the middle, together with respondents of strong class-consciousness, prefer to pillory the Catholic, Liberal, or reactionary establishment instead. The middle solidarists also favor a combination of Jews and Marxists as their dominant

Table I-10: Class Feelings and NS Ideology

	None worth noting	Anti-semite	Nordic-Germ. romantic	Revanchist, authorit.	Super-patriot	Social Volks-gemeinschaft	Hitler cult	Sum
Upper solidarism (or resents lower-class hostility)	1 (1.4%) (10%)	9 (13%) (11.1%)	6 (8.7%) (15%)	6 (8.7%) (17.6%)	14 (20.3%) (10.8%)	16 (23.2%) (7%)	17 (24.6%) (12.7%)	69 RAW (100.0%) (10.5%)
Middle solidarism	— —	31 (15%) (38.3%)	12 (5.8%) (30%)	13 (6.3%) (38.2%)	28 (13.5%) (21.5%)	92 (44.4%) (40.4%)	31 (15%) (23.1%)	207 RAW (100.0%) (31.5%)
Solidarism from below	1 (1%) (10%)	8 (8%) (9.9%)	2 (2%) (5%)	— —	17 (17%) (13.1%)	52 (52%) (22.8%)	20 (20%) (14.9%)	100 RAW (100.0%) (15.2%)
Solidarism from outside, Fronterlebnis	— —	5 (7%) (6.2%)	4 (5.6%) (10%)	7 (9.9%) (20.6%)	21 (29.6%) (16.2%)	17 (23.9%) (7.5%)	17 (23.9%) (12.7%)	71 RAW (100.0%) (10.8%)
Strong class consciousness	1 (1.4%) (10%)	12 (16.2%) (14.8%)	7 (9.5%) (17.5%)	2 (2.7%) (5.9%)	9 (12.2%) (6.9%)	24 (32.4%) (10.5%)	19 (25.7%) (14.2%)	74 RAW (100.0%) (11.3%)
No class consciousness	7 (5.1%) (70%)	16 (11.8%) (19.8%)	9 (6.6%) (22.5%)	6 (4.4%) (17.6%)	41 (30.1%) (31.5%)	27 (19.9%) (11.8%)	30 (22.1%) (22.4%)	136 RAW (100.0%) (20.7%)
Sums	10 (1.5%) (100.0%)	81 (12.3%) (100.0%)	40 (6.1%) (100.0%)	34 (5.2%) (100.0%)	130 (19.8%) (100.0%)	228 (34.7%) (100.0%)	134 (20.4%) (100.0%)	657 RAW (100.0%) (100.0%)

object of hostility—a preference related to their upward ambitions.

On the antisemitism scale, indeed, the solidarists from the middle and from below rate quite high, with mild verbal antisemitic projections and with the sudden onset of *Judenkoller*. The advocates of *Volksgemeinschaft* from above, on the other hand, to nearly one-half give no indication of prejudice, possibly in part out of upper-class scruples against open vulgarity. Yet they have one out of five, more than any other group, who are engrossed with the conspiracy theme or speak of threat and counter-threats in veiled hints of aggression and persecution. This seems to confirm the link found between social decline and prejudice in other studies. It is worth noting also that the group with the strongest antagonistic class feelings is also the most antisemitic, with the highest indices of verbal projections, *Judenkoller*, and personal stories about Jews. The group innocent of class feelings appears to be lowest in antisemitism. It is easy to draw the conclusion that the disintegrating class structure of German imperial society was a chief source of the fatal hostility directed against the Jews.

Other ethnocentric phobias and foibles round out the picture. Of the solidarists, only the middle group shows pronounced hostility toward "inferior nations," aliens in Germany, Catholics, and others vaguely referred to as "international enemies of the people." The strongly class-conscious respondents mildly share the same phobias, while those without class feelings seem very low in ethnocentricity aside from the not unrealistic perception of hostile countries surrounding the Weimar Republic. On a scale distinguishing ideological from pragmatic political thinking, also, the middle solidarists and the strongly class-conscious appear as more pragmatic; the upper and lower solidarists and respondents without class feelings appear as more ideological. The motives get intertwined, but the direction remains constant.

For nearly a third of the solidarists from below, the formative experience of their lives was either a social snub or the experience of classless comradeship in a youth organization. For more than a third of the solidarists from above, it was an "educational experience" such as a teacher or a book, or a reported episode with aliens or Jews. Nearly half of the respondents innocent of class feelings also report youth group comradeship, educational experiences, or projective episodes as their formative experiences. This evidently characterizes their more ideological bent of mind in contrast to the pragmatic middle solidarists, whose outstanding formative experience was the shock of the defeat and revolution of 1918. This cultural shock was indeed very high for this group when measured with other indicators. Its expectations in 1934 stress a renaissance of the nation which is to make up for the lost self-esteem. The solidarists from above dreamed instead of social restitution, economic recovery, and of external revenge when the thousand-year *Reich* would renew the struggle. The lower class advocates of *Volksgemeinschaft* were content with individual economic rewards and pay-offs, which had not exactly been the idea behind the slogan either.

National Solidarity against the Outside World

We have separated the nationalistic meaning of *Volksgemeinschaft* from the class feelings as much as possible because it represents an entirely different set of attitudes, even though the two sometimes intersect. The 44 respondents who praise the *Volksgemeinschaft* because of their painful foreign experiences or the *Fronterlebnis* in the trenches also meant to connote social solidarity or at least to reject class struggle or other socially divisive doctrines. But they are motivated less by their place in the disintegrating class structure than by their encounter with other nations abroad.

They generally belonged to the war generation, half of them having been born between 1890 and 1901, and another one-fourth during the preceding decade. They lived mainly in small to large cities outside of the capital and were made up most of white- and blue-collar workers and business and professional people, not unlike the middle solidarists. Disproportionate numbers of them not only had extensive foreign experience, but had been in the German colonies, or in German resettlement programs[3] among populations whose loyalty to Germany was doubtful for ethnic or political reasons. Some also were among the large numbers of respondents who lived in fought-over German border areas in the east and often, after bitter paramilitary and political struggles, had to leave them to another nation designated by the Treaty of Versailles, such as Poland, and not a few of them lived in French- or Belgian-occupied areas and experienced friction with the occupation forces. Many, in fact, were punished or expelled by the occupiers, especially in 1923, and their nationalistic indignation led them more or less directly into the superpatriotic arms of the NSDAP.

[3] The German imperial government had facilitated migration to the Prussian province of Posen (Poznan) in the east and the newly acquired federal territories of Alsace-Lorraine in the hope of increasing the German ethnic base among Poles and Frenchmen or Alsatians. Such internal colonials, of course, tended to be rather patriotic in attitude.

Foreign Origins or Experiences

There are many notable examples of Nazi leaders who were born abroad or had substantial foreign experience, such as Rudolf Hess, Walther Darré, Alfred Rosenberg, or Joachim Ribbentrop—so many, in fact, that social scientists have repeatedly drawn attention to this

FD-2: Respondents of Foreign Contact Experience

	Number	Per cent
Born or resided abroad	19	3.2
Colonial in German colonies	7	1.2
Internal colonial	5	0.8
Border-area resident	61	10.1
Occupied area resident (in conflict)	132	21.9
Other solidarists toward outside	17	2.8
No foreign experience (other than in war)	362	60.0
	603*	100.0

* Note: Due to multiple entries, total exceeds 581.

fact as a possible explanation of Nazi character.[4] Our rank-and-file sample has many examples which show the link between foreign experience and superpatriotism.

Typical examples are two German-Russian aristocrats (nos. 90 and 123) who first came to feel that they were outsiders in Russia when war broke out between the Kaiser and the Tsar, and who ended up fighting with the Whites against the Red Army. Reduced to the lonely life of Russian refugees lecturing to German rightwing groups about Bolshevism, they finally discovered Adolf Hitler and were swept off their feet by his charisma. One of them relates his first experience of hearing Hitler speak in 1926 (no. 123):

> In Prussia they had forbidden Hitler to speak and so . . . our whole group went as one man to Schwerin (Mecklenburg) to hear him.
>
> My heart pounding with curiosity and anticipation, I was awaiting the appearance of our Hitler from my seat in the crowded auditorium. A storm of jubilation rising from afar, from the street and moving into the lobby, announced the coming of the *Fuehrer*. And then suddenly

[4] The Nazi elite study of Daniel Lerner, Ithiel de Sola Pool, and George K. Schueller pinpointed half of the "propagandists" and a fourth of the "administrators" drawn from the *Fuehrerlexikon* of 1934 as persons of foreign contacts, including 7% and 4.6% respectively, who had been born abroad. Lasswell and Lerner, *World Revolutionary Elites*, pp. 220-221.

the auditorium went wild, as he strode resolutely, in his rain coat and without a hat, to the rostrum. When the speech came to an end, I could not see out of my eyes any more. There were tears in my eyes, my throat was all tight from crying. A liberating scream of the purest enthusiasm discharged the unbearable tension as the auditorium rocked with applause.

I looked around discreetly and noticed that others, too, men and women and young fellows, were as deeply moved as I. They also wiped tears from their eyes. Deafened and with a sense of enormous joy I stormed into the street. At last I was no longer alone. There were people around me who felt the same as I, who were looking at each other in joyful rapture, as if they were all one family or a brotherhood (*Bund*), or a new, firm, and happy community where everyone could read in the others' eyes a solemn oath of loyalty. . . . This experience I had again and again during the course of the following years, and my feeling became ever stronger and deeper.

It is worth noting that this enthusiastic description contains not a word about the content of the speech. The personal isolation and the momentous confrontations of the Russian revolution and civil war eased the way from militant anti-Bolshevism in Moscow or Riga to militant anti-Marxism in Berlin or Halberstadt.

No less typical are two Germans, both born in 1886 (nos. 70 and 161), who went abroad to get ahead, one as a teacher to Adrianople, Turkey, the other as a university assistant to St. Petersburg. The first fled from the incipient Russian revolution into what looked superficially like its German counterpart. When the Nazis held their first rally in his Communist-dominated area, he fell for them. The other man bravely overcame his homesickness in Turkish Bulgaria by making a fetish of the smallest mementoes from home. His encounter with the national pride of the restive peoples of the Balkans reinforced his own ideas of blood and race and brought out a swashbuckling militarism. Expelled from Bulgaria at the end of the war, he settled down in West Prussia, only to be expelled once more as the Poles took over. Passing through the DNVP and the *Stahlhelm*, neither of whom was mindful enough of the true *Volksgemeinschaft* for him, he eventually became a Nazi.[5]

Another respondent spent half his life in various European countries and during the war was busy in Spain organizing a German propaganda campaign against French influence (no. 528). A Swiss-German respondent (no. 381) who fought in the German army found himself and his family humiliated, detained, and boycotted when he returned to Switzerland in 1919. He came to hold office

[5] See also nos. 355 and 531.

in a German Protective Association there and eventually returned to Germany a superpatriot. There are also some who resided for a while in the United States (nos. 366, 539, and 557), including one who founded a Nazi group in New Jersey in the early thirties. His reaction to America is worth quoting since it mirrors the attitudes which can make a foreign sojourn a nationalistic experience. Obviously, not every *Auslandsdeutscher* reacts as he did:

> Here I glimpsed a different world. Things we already scorned as old and inadequate, such as the Bismarckian social security system, had not even arrived in New York, and the masses were not even talking about it. I was also disturbed about the attitude of the Americans toward us Germans. Whereas we looked at them as the honorable, soldierly enemy of the war, they regarded us as pariahs. Well-schooled as I was, I came to feel sorry for the Americans, for they had been brainwashed by *alien elements* (italics in original). . . . They learned to see everything through spectacles of arrogance, "from above" as it were . . . an arrogance which stems from alien inoculation. . . . I also suffered from the degeneration of German-American circles I had approached unsuccessfully—the same "democratic" arrogance—and behind it the grinning face from Syria. Life was made intolerable for me and my German wife. . . . I traveled to many countries and peoples but none could compare with the civilization we were struggling for back home.

He returned late in 1932.

German Colonists Abroad and in Border Areas

Quite a few of the colonials in the sample were born in the early 1880s and volunteered to serve in Southwest Africa against the uprising of Herreros and Hottentots (nos. 304, 320, 368, and 388). They served under the same General von Epp who in 1919 led the Free Corps that bloodily put down the Soldiers and Workers Council of Munich and later played a major role in the Nazi government of Bavaria.[6] Their swashbuckling, adventurous attitudes led them directly into *voelkisch* action groups such as the *Schutz-und-Trutzbund* or to the early Nazi party. They viewed the victorious British as "destroyers of our peaceful homeland" and the French occupiers as "black beasts raping German girls." Their "indelible hatred" for the enemy nations of the war was easily transferred to the Weimar leaders, the "parliamentary clique of criminals," not to mention the Socialists and Communists. Some of the colonials, a dozen years older, were high military officers in Tsin-tao (China) or Africa

---

[6] See the account in Edward N. Peterson, *The Limits of Hitler's Power*, Princeton: Princeton University Press, 1969, pp. 158-162 and *passim*.

(nos. 132 and 235). They reacted with the same vituperation toward all the enemies of the Kaiser's regime, foreign and domestic, with the further reinforcement of old pre-war hatreds and phobias. What attracted them to the Nazis was their aggressive antisemitism and outraged hostility to the Weimar government: "In my heart of hearts I was bent on high treason." Having learned to hate *early* in life, these men are among the most hostile of the sample.

The internal colonials were generally too young to have served in World War One (nos. 313, 407, 414, 427, and 436). It was their fathers who followed the governmental encouragement to move to Metz, France, or Poznan. The sons grew up just as the fruit of the labors of the parents was wiped out by the end of the war and by the families' expulsion from areas that were no longer German. Their youth was often spent with ethnic friction or distrust of the "politically unreliable" natives. The expulsion was brutal and often preceded by violent clashes. Many immediately joined Border Protection (*Grenzschutz*) units in the east, fought the French occupation, or joined *voelkisch* action groups or the Nazi party while still teenagers. A typical case is that of a young Berliner (no. 525) whose father bought a farm in the Poznan area in 1902, when the respondent was a year old. The father was in the war and died in 1918, leaving the farm to his son to manage. The son relates:

> After the unfortunate end of the war, the road of suffering began for me and our homeland. In the winter of 1918-1919 the Polish uprising started and my homeland was occupied by so-called Polish soldiers. We vainly hoped that it was only temporary; the Versailles Treaty of Peace determined that we were Polish and thus lost to the fatherland.
>
> Since the newly established Poland intended to eliminate everything German by and by, chiefly the German settlers, they refused to give me legal title to my father's farm. To dodge the draft of the Polish army, I opted for Germany and was asked in July, 1925, to leave Poland.

His savings were lost in the great inflation and he had difficulty finding a job in Berlin "without belonging to the SPD." He tried to get to know the SPD and other left-wing parties better, but they seem to have been incompatible with his loyalty to Kaiser and Reich. In Poland he had never had anything to do with political parties. "Former countrymen who had been in Berlin for some time, and had jobs, used to tell me that they would get me a job but I would have to join an organization. I always replied, if anything I would join the *Stahlhelm*. And so they laughed at me of course." He finally left Berlin for the countryside and found a farm job with a widow. "Now I really learned the difference between being an employer or a worker. I only wish all employers could get a sampling of this, it would be a blessing for their social attitudes." Not a veteran himself, he joined the *Stahlhelm* anyway and liked its cult of military traditions and target practice, though some of the war stories of heroics struck even him as "rather fantastic." He was less happy with its snobbery and lack of a feeling of community, which "put down those of lesser means" such as he was. He also criticized the empty eloquence and the obsession of the *Stahlhelm* with the past. "I began to doubt that the *Stahlhelm* could bring about the resurrection of the German people." In 1928 he encountered the NSDAP and decided that "only Adolf Hitler and his movement will be in a position to save Germany." He left the *Stahlhelm* before they could expel him, and joined the NSDAP.

Germans from the Ethnic Border and Austria

The border-area Germans are mostly from the east and comparable in age to the internal colonials of the sample. To understand their motivation, we have to delve into the dynamics of ethnic friction in Austria, Czechoslovakia, and Poland at that time. As one respondent with a subtle sense of class, sex, and ethnicity (no. 47) relates: "In Graz it was always considered a shame for a Christian girl to dance with a Jewish boy, or for a university-educated man to be caught with a Jewess." The respondent interprets this as a defense of the Germans in Austria against the intermingling of the "races." He came to the Nazis not for ideological reasons, however, but because his father involved him in vigilante military training of the *Einwohnerwehr* from the age of eleven and because of a freely admitted "lust for brawling." Other Austrians and Sudeten Germans grew up with a burning desire to join the German *Volksgemeinschaft*, to them the epitome of a desirable identity among many flawed choices. (Adolf Hitler himself was born in Austria and became a German citizen only in 1931.) Many were well aware of Austrian antisemites such as Mayor Lueger or Schoenerer, or became involved with the German National Socialist Workers Association of Czechoslovakia (nos. 33 and 69). Others were temporarily in the Communist, Independent Socialist, or Social Democratic parties at the same time that they expressed bitterness about "the alien Czechs taking over our homeland" and joined Sudeten German defensive organizations (nos. 400 and 475). One older Austrian, born 1873, spent his life organizing anti-socialist (yellow) restaurant unions and never lost his hatred for the unpatriotic Marxists and "brutal Communists" (no. 350).

The Polish border-area respondents are more articulate about the ethnic dynamics of their situation.[7] They sometimes begin their tales with sincere expressions of the belief that they were surrounded almost only by loyal Germans until the unrest of 1918 taught them how many Poles all around were awaiting self-determination. Then the politicking began with a wave of distrust and hatred for anyone, such as the Catholic church, who sympathized even moderately with Polish demands or who set out to divide the German *Volksgemeinschaft* with Marxist slogans of class struggle. Even public officials who cooperated with the decreed plebiscites and cessions of territories such as the Weimar government or local officials (nos. 63, 65, 165, 168, and 258) were vilified. The intensity of these anti-republican feelings may well account for the early wave of the Nazi vote along the borders of East Prussia and Lower Silesia in 1930.

Most of the eastern border-area respondents are of the postwar generation, but one older (born 1888) school teacher from Upper Silesia (no. 63) perceptively analyzed his situation and motives. In Upper Silesia, he states, "foreign agents" skilfully turned the "socialist-bolshevik wave" of 1917-1918 into Polish nationalist feelings by pointing at the "German exploiters" in business, the civil service, and land ownership. The government in Weimar and later in Berlin did not really understand the ethnic border problems, nor those of the Germans born abroad. The hypocritical Center party and the Catholic clergy were actually encouraging the Poles. The respondent was finally exiled after the third Polish uprising there. Back in the Reich he shopped around among *voelkisch* groups and the DNVP until he settled upon the Nazis. What attracted him were his "border-area experiences," for "the Nazi party was anchored in Germandom, in the German mission": "We cannot stem the Slavic flood unless we stick together."

Organizational Behavior of Foreign Contact Groups

The struggle against the French or Belgian occupation and against German separatists collaborating with it similarly tended to empha-

[7] See also Karl Hoefler, *Oberschlesien in der Aufstandszeit 1918-1921*, Erinnerungen und Dokumente, Berlin: Mittler & Sons, 1938. The author was a *Grenzschutz* leader in 1918-1920 and describes the organization of the militia, the plebiscite, and its aftermath in considerable detail. See also Reinhold Weigel, *Schicksalsweg des oberschlesischen Volkes*, Berlin: Zentralverlag, 1931.

size national solidarity at the expense of class feeling, but we shall come back to this in more detail in the next chapter. In the meantime, let us crosstabulate the following combined categories with other variables. One category will combine the respondents with foreign contacts and the external and internal colonials. A second group will be the border-area people, and a third those who lived in and painfully experienced the occupation in the west. We can also take an occasional look at the group of advocates of *Volksgemeinschaft* toward the outside world, which strongly overlaps with these three groups.

When we compare the groups by age, the foreign and colonial types are by far the oldest, with over one-half born before 1890. In a sense they represent social-imperialist trends of the empire. The occupation fighters are the youngest, with nearly one-half born after 1901, and were last called into wartime military service. Their adolescent period of storm and stress often coincided with the 1923 occupation of the Ruhr area. The border-area people are rather evenly distributed over the entire age range; they also tend to be more from rural or small-town areas and to include more farmers' sons than the other two groups. The foreign and colonial respondents came predominantly either from workers' families or from those of independent businessmen or high-ranking military or professional families.

The foreign-colonials and the anti-occupation respondents were among the most heavily involved in Hitler's beer-hall putsch in 1923, or at least they had heard of his subsequent trial and were sympathetic to his attempted coup. The border-area respondents tended to be in other political parties or in military organizations. As we can see from Table I-11, the rates at which the three groups turned into Nazis are quite closely comparable in the three storm-and-stress periods of Weimar history. The relative lagging behind of the respondents from the occupied areas can be explained with their age. In 1929-1930, at any rate, they joined faster than the other groups which still clung to conservative and bourgeois opposition parties such as *Jungdo*. It is also of interest to note the heavy involvement of all the groups in 1919 and 1923 in militant veterans' and other conservative action groups. At a time when nearly half of them were not members of any group, half of those that were belonged to the groups threatening the republic. Over 40% of the foreign colonials and of the occupation fighters and a good third of the border area group were in fact engaged in demonstrations and/or organized political violence in 1923, the year the Weimar Republic stood at the brink of a right-wing takeover.

Table I-11: Foreign Contacts and Organizational Memberships (in %)

	Foreign/ Colonial	Border area	Occupied area	Average of sample (Row percentages)
NS, voelkisch				
1919-1921	|12.5|	|13.6|	9.3	10.1
1922-1924	|24.2|	|25.0|	18.6	21.3
1929-1930	88.0	91.7	|97.4|	93.5
Bourgeois, conservative, regional parties				
1919-1921	|9.4|	|8.5|	1.7	5.8
1922-1924	|15.2|	7.1	6.8	8.5
1929-1930	|12.0|	|8.3|	1.7	5.4
Conservative-military anti-occupational groups				
1919-1921	|25.0|	18.6	17.8	20.3
1922-1924	12.1	|19.6|	|19.5|	17.4
1929-1930	—	—	—	—
Left and republican organizations				
1919-1921	6.3	6.8	|8.5|	6.7
1922-1924	6.1	|8.9|	5.9	5.6
1929-1930	—	—	0.9	1.1
None				
1919-1921	46.8	52.5	62.7	57.1
1922-1924	42.4	39.3	49.2	47.2
1929-1930	—	—	—	—
All Totals	100.0	100.0	100.0	100.0

Political Views and Attitudes

How do the various foreign-contact experiences relate to the views and attitudes of these respondents? The foreign and colonial types tended to have revanchism, antisemitism, and superpatriotism as their dominant motive. Those from the border areas were often Nordic or Germanic romantics and devotees of Hitler's personality cult, with revanchism and the *Volksgemeinschaft* running a close second in relevance. The respondents from the occupied areas were superpatriotic and Hitler cultists, terms which describe well over half of them. The solidarists toward the outside, it will be remembered from Table I-10 above, also stood out for their revanchism, superpatriotism, and their Hitler cult.

Among the chief objects of the hostility of these groups, also, the Catholic-liberal-reactionary combination is the strongest with all three, a timely reminder of their anti-establishmentarian character. On the antisemitism scale, the anti-occupation group rates the lowest of all, although it includes a good one-fourth who report a sudden outbreak of *Judenkoller*, conceivably in reaction to the feeling of helplessness under the occupation. This is true as well of similar proportions of the other two groups, which also exhibit mild verbal projections and tell personal antisemitic anecdotes. The solidarists from without likewise report a great frequency of *Judenkoller*. With other kinds of ethnocentricity, the occupation fighters have a very high rating, with special emphasis on hatred of aliens and the Catholic church, and on allegations of the inferiority of foreign nations. The border-area respondents echo this sentiment more feebly and presumably substitute Poles, Czechs, and Italians for the French and Belgians of the west. The foreign and colonial respondents, by contrast, concentrate on the perceived hostility of the foreign powers "encircling Germany," a reaction shared also by the anti-occupation group, as a result of their special experiences.

Authoritarianism and Political Acumen

All the foreign-contact experiences involve a strong sense of ambivalence about, perhaps even a rejection of, the legitimate authorities in the area. How authoritarian are these groups? There is a high degree of leadership cult in all three groups, especially those from border and occupation areas, as compared to the total sample. The foreign-colonial and anti-occupation respondents are particularly obsessed with law and order and the police. The border area people, on the other hand, are more apt to complain about the multiparty state of Weimar and its leadership. The experiences of the border areas were obviously not to be remedied by local police action alone.

All three groups score surprisingly high on political acumen, especially the foreign-colonial and anti-occupation respondents. But the latter also stand out as particularly inclined to ideological reasoning of a low caliber, which may well have been the only way they could grope their way through the confused alliance of extreme right and extreme left against the occupation.[8] Evidently their intensity of

---

[8] See the account of Jean-Claude Favez, *Le Reich devant l'occupation francobelge de la Ruhr en 1923*, Geneva: Droz, 1969, ch. 5. The Communists and *voelkisch* groups were in the forefront of the sabotage and violence against the occupation while the conservative right limited itself to verbal bombast and plans for a coup against the republic. The moderate parties vacillated from passive resistance to accommodation.

leadership cult, conformity, and a certain self-pitying masochism contributed to their inclination toward ideology. The outstanding formative experiences of the anti-occupation respondents were alleged episodes with aliens or Jews and educational or literary experiences. These two kinds of experience are also cited by respondents of foreign or colonial experience, but along with strong reactions to the defeat of 1918 or to social snubs and humiliations. The formative experiences of respondents from the border area were the comradeship in youth groups, the defeat in war and its consequences, and alleged episodes with aliens or Jews. Thus, intense prejudice tended to combine with the experience of defeat and typical socializing experiences to mobilize these victims of geographical accident in the Nazi direction.

In the Nazi Party

Were the foreign-contact experiences a spur to immediate enrollment in the Nazi party and to intense involvement in its activities? One-third and more of the border- and occupation-area respondents claim to have been the very first in their localities to join, and two-thirds of the foreign and colonial Nazis claim to have been among the first nuclei of half a dozen people in their areas. Once in the party, what did their membership mean to them? For both the foreign-colonials and the anti-occupation respondents, a sense of personality integration as a result of the common quest for utopia was the dominant motive, with the satisfactions of identifying with the great leader running a close second. To the border-area men, who were evidently yearning for a sense of community, it was the classless comradeship of the Hitler movement, again with the personality cult second in importance. As to their most extreme activity while in the party, all three groups are above the average in engaging in electioneering, demonstrations, and acts of individual provocation. For the anti-occupation respondents, however, political violence was more important. They were in fact the most violent group of the whole sample, while the border area and the foreign and colonial respondents remain considerably below the average. The last-mentioned group also stands out for its proselytizing, a very important activity for the Nazi movement.

The attitude of the respondents toward the use of violence is also worth examining. Here the anti-occupation people stand out again in their curious combination of high involvement in violence and a self-pitying masochism which counts the lumps received and punishments suffered as if they had not expected violent clashes. This group also has a share of sadists who gloried in the violence they inflicted upon others. Together the sadists and masochists make up two-thirds of this group. By comparison, the border-area respondents were more likely to limit themselves to verbal abuse or to express regrets about the political violence. The people with foreign or colonial experience shrank the most from the violence, or perhaps they were less candid about it. They appear to have accepted it more or less realistically as the price of Nazi victory.

The attitudes shown toward political enemies round out the picture. More than half of the anti-occupation respondents engage in the strongest vituperation, referring to their political enemies either as a conspiracy of traitors, or, in the gutter language of the *outré*, as "immoral," "subhuman," or unclean "murderers," or "rodents." The two other groups, and on a weaker level even the anti-occupation people, instead, express a liking for many of the political enemies except for their leadership: "they have been led astray." They often say they want to win them over. The violent involvement and attitudes among the respondents affected by the occupation may well reflect the basic nature and lack of legitimacy of such a foreign military dictatorship. It rules by sheer force and therefore its presence calls forth equally reckless and chaotic forces of violence from volatile minds. The French and Belgian occupation was said to be particularly harsh and brutal.

Conclusions

In an age characterized by intense nationalistic passions and prejudices throughout the Western world, the momentous emotions aroused by the First World War and its aftermath often produced strong yearnings for national solidarity against the outside world. It did so with particular intensity among Germans born or residing abroad, German colonists in the colonies abroad or settlers among Poles or Alsatians, residents of the ceded or embattled ethnic border areas of prewar Prussia or Austria, and respondents in conflict with the Franco-Belgian occupation. Not all the many people of this description, of course, reacted in this fashion or became Nazis. Willy Brandt became an *Auslandsdeutscher*; Julius Leber from Alsace, and Konrad Adenauer in the occupied Rhineland reacted very differently. Evidently it takes a certain personality and perhaps also instances of personal friction to turn foreign contacts into a source of superpatriotism rather than fraternization. Once a person becomes antagonistic to his foreign contacts, of course, they are likely to respond in kind and provide him with ample cause to feel persecuted. Frequently, the group setting for ethnic hostility was already there as a result of the war or the nationality struggles in

Eastern and Central Europe, giving an individual little choice but to take sides.

The Stanford elite study of the *Fuehrerlexikon* of 1934 also deals with some of the categories we have considered, such as foreign birth or sojourn, but often in a dubious fashion hinging on the use of the term "marginality." Lerner, Pool, and Schueller mention the "lost eastern territories," the Austrian Hitler, and the ethnic Germans, though they offer no tabulations. They also consider origin in Bavaria,[9] Alsace, Saar, and the Rhineland as "marginal" without, however, mentioning in any way that the latter, at least, included the bulk of the occupied areas. Our anti-occupation group, moreover, was not selected by birth in occupied areas but by whether the respondent lived there at the time of the occupation and reports hostile feelings or actions against it. Hence we can say with confidence that the occupation experience was very important to his political development. The Stanford study does not actually state why Bavaria and the Rhineland were considered marginal except for a brief mention of its predominant Catholicism,[10] which also happens to be on its list of "marginal attributes." But if this indeed was the criterion, why were not other Catholic areas of birth such as Baden or Westphalia and the appropriate parts of Hanover, East Prussia, and Silesia treated in the same fashion? And why pick on Catholicism in the first place, the religion of more than a third of the Germans in 1919?

The concept of marginality of the Stanford study is defined as "an accumulation of statistically non-predominant or deviant attributes," such as being an artisan, Catholic, or Bavarian, or having a farmer for a father, or having married earlier or later than most people in Germany. The idea behind this argument, quite apart from the preposterous choice of indices, is evidently that there is something, or a lot of somethings, wrong with the background of most Nazi leaders and followers. This idea has at least subjectively some *prima facie* merit. It is a matter of common knowledge that Hitler had a peculiar relationship to women, that Goering used hard drugs, that Goebbels had a deformed foot, and so forth. We could

[9] Lasswell and Lerner, *World Revolutionary Elites*, pp. 289-90. Their curious explanation of Bavarian "marginality" is that "it had been a major problem since the triumph of Hohenzollern over Wittelsbach and the integration of *Grossdeutschland* under predominant Prussia." Since the NSDAP got its start in Bavaria, moreover, such a theory would make the oldest members the most "marginal."

[10] Lasswell and Lerner, *World Revolutionary Elites*, p. 297. Catholics made up a good third of the entire Weimar population.

supply further examples from the little Nazis of the Abel collection, such as a medical doctor (no. 552) who describes his deformed backbone and shortness of face on the left side as a result of a childhood bout with tuberculosis. Most of the respondents, of course, were neither willing nor able to tell us about their deformities or shortcomings, of which all their friends may have been aware and to which some of these friends might even have attributed, in a non-scientific manner, the respondents' joining the NSDAP.

Nevertheless, the marginality approach used by the Stanford researchers is statistically unsound and highly questionable in terms of the values of the Lasswellian policy sciences to which the authors specifically refer. It is statistically unsound in a social science sense because "predominant" attributes of a given population cannot be determined in a value-neutral manner without first making some evaluative judgments which have to supply the merits of the whole operation. Daniel Lerner and his co-authors gloss over this crucial point with the example that "in a society predominantly Moslem, Christians are marginal with respect to religion" and then forget to follow through with the limitation indicated with the phrase "with respect to religion." *Only* with respect to religion, indeed, in this case; and religious marginality can be related to other attributes only insofar as a good case can be made for such a relationship. No such case has been presented for Catholicism or artisans and farmers in the Stanford study. Furthermore, most statistical indicators (including religion) are either continuous or multi-dimensional and not just dichotomous as in the Moslem-Christian example. A continuous age distribution, for example, can be broken down many ways and not even the median of a normal curve can indicate "normality" without well-reasoned explanations. If we wanted to relate age to joining the storm troopers, for example, we could just as easily ask why a grown man beyond the folly of youth and well short of senility would want to do anything so foolish as assume that there is a "normal age" for putting on a brown shirt. There is no self-evident nexus between statistical central tendencies and significance in social science analysis.

The policy sciences to which the authors refer,[11] moreover, tend to place theories which infer that one kind of deviancy (Nazi leadership) comes from other kinds of deviancy in an illiberal light. To come back to the individual deformities and shortcomings mentioned earlier, it is entirely possible that everybody, if examined carefully enough, can be found to be deviant from the majority, or

[11] Lasswell and Lerner, pp. 299-300.

deformed in some rather important way. A policy science bent on combating totalitarian movements that are dedicated to investigating the warts on other people's noses, or the non-Aryan grandmothers in their ancestry, must be very careful not to slip into similar approaches. This is not to deny that the idea of "marginal men" in fascist movements may have merit if carefully defined. A déclassé in a class society may well be such a marginal man and fascist prototype if he can be shown to be gravely concerned about his status. A border-area German may well be similarly marginal, not because of the area of his birth, but because of his experiences and reactions at the time of nationality struggles or his expulsion, and because of his difficulties of settling down in the rump nation. A woman who joined the early Nazi party may well turn out to be marginal too, but surely not because women were in the minority in the Weimar Republic (they were not), nor even because they formed a small minority of politically active adults. We will have to dig deeper to come up with what may indeed have motivated them.

FIVE

Nazi Women

The role of women in the Nazi party is surrounded by profound historical, political and psychological paradoxes. They lived in a setting of rapid social change, if not always emancipation, from the gilded cage of the nineteenth century bourgeois home and the pariah position of the proletarian scrubwoman or rural help. Some of the indices of change were in the labor statistics of the 1907 census. Almost nine and one-half million, or 30.6%, of German women were gainfully employed then, nearly double the figure of 1895 and probably the highest percentage of any country in the world at that time. Half of these women were employed in agriculture at a time when men had migrated to the cities. Nearly one-fourth worked in industry. Of the unmarried women over sixteen, 87% were no longer at home but working, carried on the unemployment rolls, or in occupational training of some sort. Twenty-eight percent of the married women were also gainfully employed.[1] After centuries of economic restrictions, this development seemed to correspond at long last to the call of Luise Otto, the founder of the General German Women's Association (1865) for the "emancipation of women's work."

But, as in other aspects of German industrial development, social relations lagged far behind the industrial expansion. The feminist movement made only minor progress in persuading women to its views or improving their position until about the turn of the century. It was only in 1901, after decades of controversy about women's secondary education, that Heidelberg and Freiburg Universities first opened their doors to women. During the First World War, women rose from about 6% to 35% of the students at all German universities, which led to some restrictions and a lot of predictions of

[1] Quoted by Katherine Anthony, *Feminism in Germany and Scandinavia*, New York: Holt, 1915, ch. vii. These percentages rose slightly by 1933 and, after a temporary reduction decreed by the Nazi government, rose further after 1936.

dire consequences.[2] The access to professions and managerial positions was uncertain and even the choice of white-collar occupations was bedeviled by bourgeois prejudices against women working outside the home and by anti-feminist organizations such as the *voelkisch* Retail Clerks Union (DHV). As late as 1918, this writer's mother found herself pointedly snubbed by bourgeois schoolmates for going to work as a secretary. Nice girls from bourgeois homes were not supposed to do that. At the same time, the husband- and fatherless state of German society during World War One was an enormous boost for women's role in business, the professions, and public life. Necessity often brought an incisive change of social relationships as women found the courage and self-confidence to assert themselves in ways the patriarchal prewar society had not permitted. Would they once again settle for subordinate roles after they had tasted autonomy?

The development of the political role of German women was the final paradox. The cause of the working woman had found effective spokesmen among Social Democratic leaders such as August Bebel (*Woman and Socialism*). The SPD increasingly became a party in which women such as Clara Zetkin could achieve important positions, and also the one party which came out strongly for women's suffrage before 1918.[3] But the women's suffrage and feminist movement had not really spread beyond small circles. When women were given the vote for the National Constituent Assembly of 1919, in any case, the bulk of them were not by any stretch of the imagination ready for this important new responsibility. They turned out to vote in large numbers, but their votes tended to favor mostly those who had been most hostile to women's suffrage rather than their friends. A heavy share of the women's votes, far more than male votes, went to the Center party and to the DNVP, the successor of the Conservative party which had been downright vituperative toward them. *Voelkisch* politicians in the DNVP and outside, who later switched to the Nazis, also drew a bigger share of women voters than of men. The feminist SPD and Communists (KPD), and incidentally also the Nazis until the great landslides of 1930 and 1932, drew far more male voters than women.[4] There is plausi-

[2] Hugh Wiley Puckett, *Germany's Women Go Forward*, New York: Columbia University Press, 1930, pp. 200-201.

[3] For details, see Puckett, *Germany's Women Go Forward*, chs. 9 and 10. As early as 1911, over 300,000 working women were organized in various trade unions, a sign of their growing political strength.

[4] See esp. Gabriele Bremme, *Die politische Rolle der Frau in Deutschland*, Goettingen: Vandenhoeck & Rupprecht, 1956, pp. 10, 68-77. The

bility, perhaps, in the rejection of the new female roles and free-doms advocated by SPD and KPD by traditionally oriented German women voters. But why would any woman want to join the Nazi party, which was not only the epitome of "male chauvinism" but also so prone to vulgar crudities, expressions of hatred, and violence as to offend any traditional mind?

The Social Profile of the Women Respondents

There are 36 women in the Abel collection who were not analyzed in Abel's book because they did not fit many of his categories and he wanted to save them for a later article that never got written. They are hardly a representative sample,[5] but a few basic statistics may help to bring them into focus. In age they ranged from 17 to 73 in 1933, with a particular concentration of women of 50 or more, and another one of the war generation (born 1895-1898) whose lives were probably disrupted by fiancés' or husbands' being killed or other effects of the war. Nearly half of the women never moved from where they were born. Some were rural-urban migrants, some moved all over the country. Nearly three-fourths lived in metropolitan areas.

Over one-third fell victim to the economic crises of Weimar, which is less than the average for the sample. Their parents, how-ever, to a disproportionate degree were visited by misfortunes which must have had a deep effect on the women's childhood and outlook on life. About one-fourth of the fathers or mothers died before the girl had reached 18, including many who died before the child was 10 years old. The absence of the father is particularly significant in the light of psychological theories, such as those of Adorno or Bruno Bettelheim, which relate political hatred or a propensity for extremism to a disturbed authority relationship between father and child. The *vitae* are not likely to tell us very much about dis-turbed relations, but a father's absence is certainly conclusive evi-dence. With another one-sixth, the parents either lost their liveli-hood or were both working during the daughter's childhood and

---

Democrats (DDP) also came to champion women's rights after a rather ambiguous beginning under their pre-1918 predecessors, the Progres-sives. The early Nazi party, by contrast, solemnly resolved with the con-currence of several women in attendance that no woman could ever be the leader or a member of the executive board of the organization.

[5] Women are, however, somewhat overrepresented in this collection. They make up 6.2% as compared to the 3% of women in the NSDAP in 1932, when half the Nazi voters were women.

adolescence, which often meant that the girl had to work, too. Their fathers were predominantly high-ranking military, or professional, or business people. Some were military-civil servants. Their daughters, however, tended to be in social decline, relatively speaking. Nearly half the women were married, often with children, or widowed. One-fourth, all single, were employed or in training for a vocation, including a number of nurses. Some were students at the time of the essay contest. As to education, half of them have only primary level (*Volksschule*) and another one-third went to commercial or trade schools. Five went as far as the *Abitur* or enrollment in a university.

In his brilliant study of the lives of ordinary Nazis, *They Thought They Were Free*, Milton Mayer sums up much of their motivation with a telling chapter title, "The lives men lead." We can change this phrase to "the lives women led in those days" as we take a closer look at the stories told by the women respondents. Since the rapidly changing social context appears to be of prime importance, they will be discussed primarily grouped by age with allowance given to other relevant factors.[6]

Older Nazi Women

The oldest respondent was born in Duesseldorf in 1860 and in 1934 clearly recalled the patriotic enthusiasm surrounding Bismarck's founding of the empire (no. 30). Her mother died when she was four and she was raised by a maiden aunt. She married in 1885, was left a widow with two children in 1893, and took over the direction of her late husband's successful wholesale business. She tells with deep distaste about the red Soldiers Councils of 1918: "Impossible characters in uniform in the streets, and of course with women on their arms." She also relates the Communist uprising of 1920 in the Ruhr, its suppression by Free Corps units, and the subsequent French occupation, when French soldiers "habitually pushed the civilians off the sidewalk" into the street. The inflation of 1923 and later crises by 1930 had ruined the family business which had passed under her son's direction. Totally defeated and broken down, the old lady moved in with her daughter in Hannover. Why did she become a Nazi? In her own words: "Adjusting to Hannover was very hard for me; I had not come to die. So I remembered my attendance in 1925 at an astrologers' school in Dortmund where at a lecture they talked about the coming turning-point of the world, the

[6] The women frequently neglected to indicate their age or date of birth. Lacking the male index of the draft age, we could not always make a reliable estimate within a few years of the mark.

dying Age of Pisces and the dawning of the Age of Aquarius. There were going to be new life styles, new people. The beginning . . . dated at least from the World War and it might last until 1940." She contrasts the mismanaged, "torn-up Germany" with "this *one man* (italics in original) with his infinite faith in the rise of Germany" and his ability to mobilize tens of thousands with his faith, mission, and will. Crisis and fall of the family business and of the German empire, in her mind, had evidently become one. The savior of the country might also rekindle a new life identity in her old bones.

There are several women in their 50s and 60s (nos. 456, 347, 141, and 297) whose careers tended to become the vehicle that eventually carried them into the Nazi movement. Particular attention should be drawn to their hatreds and fears, including their identification with the hostilities of the war, which constitute a major projective release of the feelings of unworthiness typical of members of extremist movements or hate groups.

One was the daughter of the owner of a debt-ridden estate near Danzig, one of seven children (no. 456). The parents died early and the respondent became a nurse and social worker, a career which brought her to the African colonies and into service behind the front in World War One: "I shall never forget the horror of the war in which so many hopeful young lives were destroyed by the murderous fire of enemy artillery." Identifying with the war effort and glorying in every report of victory, she obviously enjoyed being with the wounded soldiers and ministering to their needs. Transferred to an epidemic hospital in France, she describes her anguish at "seeing their strong young bodies waste away and turn to skeletons even before they died." She also complains bitterly about the allied hunger blockade and about "the traitors within, the forces from the lower depths, and the Jewish influence" which she claims brought on the revolution. As a social worker she knew the depths of poverty and deprivation until her early retirement in 1923. Her account does not reveal whether she had paid much attention to political movements before, but suddenly she was deeply involved in the nationalist agitation for the overthrow of the government and sympathetically aware of Hitler's abortive beer-hall *putsch* in Munich. Late in 1923 she once more went back to work, setting up a children's home which was temporarily used also by refugees and expellees from the occupied Rhineland whose fate stirred her emotions. Struck down by ill health again, she repeatedly tried to find re-employment as a nurse, until her final retirement in 1927 in Berlin. With more time on her hands, she learned a lot more about Hitler's fight "for the liberation of the German fatherland from alien destroyers." "I heard about the courage to face sacrifice and death of Hitler's storm-troopers and just could not but join the movement." In 1928, aged 57, she began to care for the "unemployed fighters of Hitler," to collect money to proselytize "even among the Communists," and to propagandize for the coming of the Third Reich.

The attraction of caring for the stormtroopers was not always the major motive. Another side of the role of women in the Nazi party is revealed by a stormtrooper's account of a pitched battle between the SA and Communists in 1930 in Pirmasens (no. 408). The young tough adds to his story: "To this I would like to say a word which will tell you something about the National Socialist spirit of our women. We were not allowed to carry weapons, and when the police showed up, they could not find any on our bodies. The weapons had all fallen under the skirts of the women present. My mother alone had six of those things dangling inside her clothes." Another orphaned respondent of comparable age but of proletarian background (no. 347), a nursemaid, cook, and concierge in Berlin, was in the prewar SPD prior to being lured away by a movement of political antisemites.[7] In the early twenties she was active on the board of a parents' and teachers' organization in a campaign against secular education. In 1926 she fell under the spell of the great leader.

Another onetime nurse (no. 141), a professor's daughter, tells how she secretly volunteered her services to a hospital and how this experience enabled her to meet the lower classes and to develop a sympathetic. interest in them. She had to struggle every step of the way with her disapproving parents to get her training, until she married at the age of 32. They also broke up an early romance with a "proletarian" when she was only 17. Her friction with her parents combined oddly with intense ethnic prejudice against Jewish classmates to make up what she calls "a national socialist character since I was 17." Nationalism came naturally and socialism from her broken romance. Eventually she married a judge who had the academic education her parents insisted on. When he died after two decades, she felt free to join the Nazi party and induced her teenage son to join the Hitler Youth and later the SS.

Another respondent, a governess (no. 298) with a French family in Rio de Janeiro at the turn of the century, was motivated mostly by homesickness. Whenever she saw a European ship leave or enter

[7] For another prewar political antisemite, see no. 365, a woman born in 1867 in Tilsit who marched and proselytized for *voelkisch* groups and, since 1925, for the Nazis.

Guanabara Bay, she would gather her charges at the window and they would sing *Die Wacht am Rhein* or *Deutschland, Deutschland ueber alles* together to stanch her yearning. She returned after four years, only to be plagued by a longing for faraway places. She married an older man who escaped the draft in the war but rendered military auxiliary services at home. The signing of the "shameful so-called peace treaty of Versailles" motivated both to shop around among the many political postwar parties. Repelled by personal encounters with an anti-religious Social Democratic neighbor and a Jewish woman doctor, they first identified with the *Deutschvoelkische Freiheitspartei* and then switched their votes to the NSDAP. Attendance at the Berlin rallies eventually brought her, her husband, and two grown children into the fold.

The foreign background may also have been a factor with another older respondent (no. 175) who was born in Singapore and raised by a maiden aunt in Hamburg for the first six years of her lonesome life. The family fortune was confiscated by the British in Singapore when the war broke out and the respondent went to work as a secretary to support her mother. Her whole life finally centered on a patriotic science professor for whom she did typing and through whose eyes she experienced the tragedy of defeat and revolution. Whereas her professor wisely refrained from political activity, she became involved, first with the DNVP and soon with the Nazis: "Every moment, day or night, I am ready even to lay down my life in order to do for this Fuehrer whatever he requires of me. May every moment of his life be blessed, this Fuehrer who has risen for us Germans!" The role of leadership cult, according to the psychological theories, is both as a father substitute and as the liberator and channeler of the urge to hate somebody.

Another respondent who had to support her mother, because her father died when she was seven, was a nursemaid and tailor (no. 547). She married late and her husband was immediately drafted and eventually captured by the British, who kept him until late in 1919. In the meantime she experienced the outbreak of the revolution in Berlin in particularly vehement form and was recruited by a *voelkisch* student for a group founded by the *voelkisch Reichstag* deputy Wulle (DNVP):

So I entered the Herold group and began to be interested in politics. After all, since we women were given the right to vote, we had to try and develop some understanding for it. Then came the election and I had to stand with a DNVP poster around my neck. . . . I felt as if I had been put into the pillory and had to struggle to suppress the feeling of being exposed. Passers-by accosted and insulted me. And when the votes were counted that night, the party had received only seven votes. For that we had stood all day, and taken insults like "club of the prayer-ladies."

She went from there with her husband to the *Deutsch-Soziale Partei* (*Kunze*), the *Deutschvoelkische Freiheitspartei*, and the *Schutz-und-Trutzbund*, and in 1926 to the Nazis.[8]

The War Generation Among the Women

The next group of women respondents were in their thirties and forties at the time Hitler came to power. Their lives generally bear the harsh marks of World War One, although there are also other elements, such as strong antisemitic influences at home. A Prussian civil servant's daughter and commercial secretary born in 1887 (no. 574), for example, reports that her father was "a German national-ist and severe antisemite, as loyal German civil servants were bound to be" and goes on:

As a young girl and very young woman I never busied myself with politics which in those days . . . was reserved exclusively to the men. I did notice as a growing girl and later in my secretarial calling that Jewish men were paying particular attention to me, probably because of my delicate blondness (*zarte Blondheit*). This observation caused me to play the unapproachable, but to no avail. It made me even more exciting (*es reizte nur noch mehr*). Then I began to feel disgust and revulsion at everything Jewish.

The projective comment on the civil service and the curious inter-twining of public, political themes with the most private motives is rather typical of a racist mind. Her "delicate blondness" eventually led to a proposal and very brief unsuccessful marriage which ended in divorce, a rather unusual step at the time. She mentions marriage, divorce, and going back to work to support her child (born 1914) all in a single sentence without a word about the identity of her hus-band or the cause of her divorce. Her personal difficulties were fur-ther aggravated by her work among civil servants, judges, and lawyers who identified with the SPD, the Catholic Center, or with "an alien race," all of whom differed from her initial description of

[8] See also the antisemitic and anti-Masonic tirades in no. 582, the daughter of a local official. This case also contains extensive descrip-tions of the confrontations between the Nazis and the police or the Com-munists in Berlin.

German civil servants. Her brother-in-law introduced her to the NSDAP and she eventually got fired from her job for joining and wearing the party insignia at work in defiance of specific rules to the contrary. In the end, she delivered the *Voelkischer Beobachter* for the party, together with her stormtrooper son, until her reinstatement by the victorious Nazis. The frequency with which Nazi women drew their off-spring and other family members into the party is worth noting.

There are also other civil service cases such as a local judge's wife (no. 453) whose conservative husband and Nazi sympathizer son were restless under the civil service restrictions on political activity. The death of her husband in 1928 threw the family into crisis. A year later the slaying of her son at a Nazi party rally in Nuremberg "turned her into a National Socialist." Her second son then became a stormtrooper and was shot in the chest by "the reds." Nevertheless, she gloried even in her tragedy: "Whenever a party comrade falls, hundreds, even thousands rise to take his place. I experienced it in our town with the death of my son Erich and with Werner's injury. . . . How wonderful these fighting years were—I would not have missed them for anything, the wonderful development, the rallies, and the demonstrations!"

Another case mixes the border-area syndrome with economic motives (no. 353). A daughter and wife of conservative factory owners in Poznan and West Prussia relates her early concern about the class snobbery of her circles "which is bound sooner or later to divide the German people." This "socialism" and her patriotism, she says, naturally added up to national socialism. The real story she tells suggests quite a different motivation. Her entrepreneur husband organized his own workers' council until "the Jews came" and spoiled his experiment in *Volksgemeinschaft*-building. During the upheaval of the border plebiscites, in which Poznan was lost but her West Prussian area retained by Germany, her husband organized and dominated the local *Stahlhelm* and *Wehrwolf* groups. The respondent joined the NSDAP a short time before the declining family business broke down completely and her husband had a nervous collapse. To join the Nazis meant a painful but long-desired break with her conservative circles.

Often there are social motives, such as the need to overcome the loneliness and fear of aging, which moved a woman into involvement with the Nazis. A trained flowershop girl, born 1887 the daughter of a gardener, married a widower whose wife had died in childbirth with twins. He already had a child and she, a seventh child herself, bore him another seven children he could hardly support on a telegraph assistant's salary. Her interest in the Nazi party was aroused by the prohibition of such membership in the civil service and the hostility of the Social Democratic colleagues of her husband. Partly paralyzed and with a weak heart from her last confinement, she delayed enrollment for a while because of her health and her children. Her eldest, in fact, joined first and held secret Hitler Youth meetings in his room. She ended up feeding and mothering up to 28 boys and 20 Nazi girls in their modest abode. "Muttchen" (mother) felt amply rewarded by their gratitude for small favors.

Another woman, a Silesian weaver's daughter and one of eleven children (no. 339), recalled how her mother used to be up the day after each birth preparing the family's meals and working back at the loom within a week. Six of the eleven died in infancy under circumstances of abject poverty and she herself was not strong. She had to go to the textile factory as soon as she finished the limited rural primary school. Nevertheless, as a young girl she dreamed of having twelve children. She married an older engineer in Berlin who had been in the war, and later joined a Free Corps and then the *Frontbann*, a cover organization for the NSDAP and other *voelkisch* action groups. She and her husband and her sister avidly attended every Nazi rally in Berlin. Her husband joined in 1925 and she followed three years later. After he lost his job in 1930, they leased a restaurant in Moabit which became a stormtrooper hangout, *Tante Klara's*. Klara had already enjoyed ministering to them with little gifts and celebrations at Christmas time, and now she gave them free beer since they were for the most part unemployed and impecunious. After a year and a half, predictably, the restaurant failed and they eked out a living on a dole of 52 marks a month for three persons, spending the winter with her sick father in a friend's summer cottage, somewhat as Hans Fallada has described it in his novel *Kleiner Mann Was Nun?*

A third woman respondent of similar motivation and age was a nurse whose father was a bourgeois ducal court official very intent on class distinctions, who discouraged her social contacts with the lower classes. Her mother was an aristocrat who had died when the girl was only six. The respondent married a wounded officer who died after a year and a half. She seems to have suffered a breakdown as a result of her nursing service during the war, for she had to go to a dietary sanitarium at the age of 27. There and in her service she developed a sudden violent aversion to Jews and especially to "married Jews who take their blond mistresses to their apartments," a *Judenkoller* which was probably another symptom of her breakdown. The short period of her marriage appears to have coincided with her illness. She made enough of a recovery to raise a son, but only by clinging to extremist views and engaging in bizarre acts and confrontations, such as physical clashes with "Communist neighbors," flying a Nazi flag from her working-class apartment, and making her boy a laughingstock at school. For a touch of moral rearmament, the boy had a motto hanging over his bed: "What would the Fuehrer say to that?" The boy soon joined the Hitler Youth and his mother the party. Her strong hatreds were generously disbursed to the upper classes, "un-German culture," the *Stahlhelm*, the Prussian police, and the Communists or, interchangeably, the Jews. She would have loved to send all young aristocrats into a kind of job corps (*Arbeitsdienst*) to teach them something. She also liked to play Santa Claus to poor Nazi children in Berlin tenement houses, wearing stormtrooper riding boots. On one occasion, in fact, she had to give a lecture on dietetics in this costume because she could not get the boots off by herself.

Many of the less bizarre stories center around the dramatic involvement of women with the "great patriotic war." One writes (no. 36): "As the child of a soldier and peasant I always had the mission in my blood to serve and sacrifice for the fatherland. I gave my fiancé to it in the war and, after his heroic death, put myself in its service." She established a home for officers and men in Flanders and returned with the troops in 1918 to experience the revolution. From its early beginnings in 1920 in Munich she followed the Hitler movement and maintained close contact with it, but actually joined only in 1931.

Many women envied their brothers or male friends in 1914 and wished that they were boys and could go out and fight in the great patriotic struggle, such as one woman (no. 44) whose case otherwise stands out mostly with its phrase-making.[9] This respondent became a political activist with the People's Party (DVP) and ended up as what must have been the only woman *Ortsgruppenleiter* (Dortmund) of the NSDAP. Her political career is seemingly a function of her personal life: She attributes her antisemitism to wartime experiences during volunteer services with the railroads. Her four years of canvassing for the DVP in the Rhineland are described as a struggle for the loyalty of the working classes there, "for their German soul." She became disenchanted with the exclu-

[9] See also the extravagant praise of Hitler in nos. 116, 160, 195 and 532. Often the Hitler cult seems to go together with a virulent antisemitism, as with nos. 193 and 459.

sively economic interests of the DVP, withdrew, and married a farmer who eventually ran away to Africa, leaving her stranded with the children.

She went back to the Rhineland to live with her mother and found herself greatly attracted by what she describes as the "unjustly maligned" stormtroopers. She became a super-activist again because "our unconditional commitment made even us female fellow-fighters into a kind of soldiers." She did all kinds of auxiliary service work for the party and SA, went to nightly rallies, and steeped herself in racist and Nordic-cult literature, which to her constituted the content of her "deepest religion" and patriotic loyalty. As with most of the single, divorced, or widowed women in the sample, the respondent was an ardent devotee of Hitler. Others relate to the war through borderland experiences, such as one respondent (no. 177) who as a young girl witnessed the passing through of the Russian army. She describes hiding with other women in boats. She also lost two brothers in the war. Another respondent (no. 305) was forced by the Poles to serve as a nurse on the battle line and writes: "The war and these Polish experiences caused me to take an interest in politics much earlier than women usually do."

Another woman (no. 207) painfully tore herself from her native Alsace where she had personally experienced the hostilities and rendered volunteer services of various sorts. Her husband, a professional soldier, fought with a Free Corps to suppress the short-lived Soviet Republic of Munich and then became a police official in Darmstadt. The respondent felt so antagonistic to the upper classes that to her husband's horror she nearly joined the Communists. Other Alsatians then acquainted her with the NSDAP, and from 1929 she became so active that her husband twice had to endure punitive transfers for her notorious actions. She saved every penny for propaganda materials for proselytizing and engaged also in bizarre acts of confrontation, such as wearing a home-made brown shirt to market and physical clashes of all kinds. She evokes the Protestant ethic as she relates: "At night in bed I always went over the day's work for the movement. And if I found I could have done more, I did it on the double the very next day." She had her own theories about the role of women in the Nazi revolution: "We want to wake up Germany from its sleeping-beauty slumber and that is a calling also fit for a woman. My children should not have to say, one fine day, 'and where were you, Mother, when the ruin of Germany threatened?'" She made appearances at rural Nazi rallies, together with other city women, in order to encourage the more timid country women to venture forth: "This was my purpose for participating in rallies in the countryside. I had often had the experience that, if the wife could be converted to our cause, eventually we would get the husband as well." To protest against her husband's first punitive transfer, she made a fifteen-foot swastika flag and displayed it on the street where the SPD minister of the interior, Leuschner, was living.

In some cases, the subjective perception of history is so distorted that events become unrecognizable. One aristocratic respondent (no. 212) relates: "While my husband [a captain with the general staff] was in the Red Cross hospital in Munich, alien, uncanny elements made a revolution. They spoke only broken German, and appeared in the disguise of sailors, a uniform hardly ever seen in Munich." Her husband longed to become a farmer since his army career had come to an end. He seriously pursued this intention and eventually acquired a run-down farm in an area of Bavaria where many other former professional soldiers had gone rural. From there they sympathetically watched the early Hitler movement and vented their spleen against big cities, un-German culture, capitalism, and Marxism. The aristocratic respondent saw life strictly through the eyes of her husband and his friends.

Politicized Nazi Youth

The last group of Nazi women were in their twenties or younger in 1933 and had joined while they were still very young. Unlike the previous groups, who were the products of imperial society and of the war, these women represent the new wave of politicized youth which beat against the fragile buttresses of the Weimar Republic. Their social origins and religion threw only a passing shadow on their political lives as they were swept along by the new passion for unreflected action. The youngest of them was only 16½ when Hitler came to power (no. 107). She tells of her awakening to politics as a 13-year-old lyceum student during a summer vacation on a farm owned by her uncle, a secret Nazi. She badgered her uncle for more information about Hitler, which he supplied with evident enthusiasm: "Every night before going to sleep he had to tell me about Adolf Hitler and his struggle. He had given me a little picture of him which I kept like a shrine to which I could look up in adoration. I enclosed him in my little heart and was determined not to rest until I had finally grasped the meaning of his idea and struggle." A clash between stormtroopers and the "Moscow bandits" of the Red Front, in which her uncle was injured,[10] gave reality to her

[10] An account of this clash in which seven stormtroopers were injured appears in Friedrich A. Beck, *Kampf und Sieg, Geschichte der NSDAP im Gau Westfalen-Süd*, Dortmund: Westfalenverlag, 1938, p. 459.

hero-worship, and she began to propagandize at school and stuck with it in spite of ridicule and hostility from some quarters. Her ostentation soon "brought out among the other students the party loyalties of their parents or other people who had influenced them," which led to loud arguments and the hostility of three Jewish girls in her class. When she was not quite 16, she and four other girls founded the National Socialist School Girls' League, a predecessor of the BDM, the girls' Hitler Youth, and recruited forty members in her school. It is remarkable that her account up to this point omits all mention of her parents and talks only about her uncle, her hero, and her peer group. Then the parents appear; it turns out that they were quite unaware of her activities and especially her frequent attendance at Nazi rallies where "there were always injuries, broken chairs, and flying window-glass." When the parents finally found out they were worried about their only child rather than disapproving. Aunts and grandmothers berated her for getting involved in politics, not for being a Nazi.

A pair of sisters, born 1913 and 1915, relate their early political interest in a Catholic school at the time of the 1925 presidential elections (nos. 41 and 42). They also bitterly recalled the words of a "red" in their village: "Those who were in the war should all be beaten up because they must have been crazy; and those who died there had it coming." Their father, an officer, was a casualty in 1915. Their conservative (DNVP) or liberal (DVP) family and the Center-party-oriented teachers made feeble efforts to persuade them otherwise, but from their first encounter with Nazi activity in 1929 on they became active propagandists for the NSDAP. They passed out leaflets, sold party newspapers, and contributed what little money they had. In December 1930, they were admitted to membership in the party and two years later they persuaded their mother to follow suit. In 1931 and 1932 they were right in the thick of violent big-city campaigning in Kassel while their mother, a midwife, was losing most of her "red" clientele. They were busy "mothering and consoling many a poor stormtrooper who had been driven from his home."

Another girl shows some of the heritage of the past before the activism of the present engulfed her thinking (no. 363). She was born in 1913 in the Polish border areas and nostalgically remembered the time before the exodus from there in 1921. She also recalled political discussions in school when she defended the Kaiser and monarchy. In 1929 she became interested in the Hitler movement and "almost daily I cycled five miles of bad road into town to listen to a Nazi speech, and then home again alone, for there was no one but Centrists, SPD, and Communists in my village." The rallies often became violent and Nazis were assaulted and injured. She also had to avoid being dismissed from school for her involvement. In 1931 she joined and worked full-time, collecting money and propagandizing door-to-door, and putting up election posters. She also helped to get supplies for, and spent two evenings a week at, the local SA home where the young stormtroopers lived who had no job and had been thrown out by their fathers. In 1932, her sick parents lost their farm and moved back to a city where she got a job in a factory, "the kind of treadmill where our German girls are made unsuitable for their real calling, that of housewife and mother." She was fired for proselytizing among her fellow-workers and moved on to another job and more passionate proselytizing.

The rest of the young women are about six to eight years older, which is to say that their political maturation did not coincide so directly with the great Nazi campaigns as to make them the brown "teenage crazies." Instead, there were more specific influences at work to direct them toward the Hitler movement. One woman (no. 145), born in 1908, the daughter of a *voelkisch* nurseryman, claims to have encountered some Communist and even "Freudian ideas" among certain lyceum classmates. She also came across H.F.K. Guenther's racist theories, which impressed upon her "the necessity of racial hygiene and of Nordic thought." She matriculated at Bonn University but found her courses and student life there so totally irrelevant to her life that she transferred to Munich where another racist was teaching and where, as she knew, Hitler was holding forth. She ended up with the National Socialist Student Association, for which she did a good deal of propagandizing. She also read more racist literature, such as Rosenberg's *Myth of the 20th Century.* "Our greatest enemy was student apathy," but there were also conflicts over wearing party insignia in class or putting up posters on the university grounds. The academic establishment was not very cooperative. Fellow students thought she was crazy, always trying to sell tickets to meetings or lending Nazi literature to perfect strangers who often failed to return it. The annual student government elections were the high point of her political activity. Eventually she returned to Bonn where she organized another Nazi student group and worked also for the party, especially in the 1930 parliamentary elections. Upon graduation in 1932 she worked for the National Socialist Women's Union (*Frauenschaft*) in the Rhineland.

Another young woman (no. 457) was born in poverty in 1906 and, at the age of five, lost her mother. Her father, a parson, was not well enough to be drafted, but an older brother served in the navy and, after the war, in a Free Corps. She worked as a maid from 1921 and later became a trained Protestant hospital nurse in Danzig, 1929 to 1930. In this capacity

> I really got to know the spirit of the times. Even in the children's section you were received with cries of "Hail Moscow" and "Red Front." The men's section was soon filled by wounded men of various political parties. I often overheard little political discussions which seemed harmless at first. But they had a way of degenerating into heated arguments. The nurse often had to stop the argument by moving some men to another room.

In this fashion she became interested in partisan politics, and by 1930 the NSDAP had particularly impressed her. She went to Vienna and stayed there from 1931 to 1933, attending Austrian Nazi meetings and joining the party there. She returned to Germany after Hitler had come to power.

Politics makes strange bedfellows, judging from two other cases, one with Communist and the other with Catholic antecedents (nos. 390 and 244). In 1926 the first married a man who earlier (1921-1923) had been deeply involved with the Communist party, but had sworn off politics and concentrated on holding down a job. Suddenly he brought home Nazi literature, and she feared a relapse into a consuming political involvement in radical politics even though she did not object to the content of the literature. The Nazi proselytizer who had given him the literature was persistent. "He was the founder of the N.S. local here at Giessen and he was stronger than I. He did not cease or rest until he had convinced my husband of the absolute necessity to fight for the party." A year later she learned by accident that her husband had already joined the stormtroopers. In 1929, she followed him into the party and regularly helped to carry the stormtrooper flag home from rallies so that her standard-bearer husband could defend himself against the "red assailants" waiting outside. She also had three brothers-in-law in the movement and worried many a night whether they would get home unharmed from all the rallies they had to guard. Nazi students often came to protect her husband along his way and he helped them run their student government campaigns. And after she heard Hitler speak, the wife also believed in the victory of the brown insurrection.

The Catholic woman was the oldest child of a small Rhenish peasant; she first worked at home and later as a maid in Saarbruecken and Cologne. At the age of 19, she expressed deep shock when she learned that her younger brother believed in National Socialism, since she and her parents were loyal to the Catholic associations and the Center party. Three years later her brother and his Nazi friends began to meet at her parents' house. "Stimulated by the Center campaign against the first Nazi rally in this town, I considered it my sacred duty to inveigh with all my strength against the doctrines of National Socialism. The racism and the Jewish question, in particular, struck me as un-Christian and unjust. Jewishness to me was just a religion." But the brother won out and she learned to hate the "Marxists" for dividing the people and the Center for its "hypocrisy." Even the relatives began to avoid her family, as she and a second brother became actively involved.

Ideologies and Organizational Behavior

How did the political views of the Nazi women compare with the official Nazi ideology, particularly having to do with women and their role in society? Since the women's motives were so often deeply personal or derived from their social predicaments, did they really share the antifeminism of the NSDAP, which David Schoenbaum with good reason has called "a kind of secondary racism?"[11] Or is it not more likely that the issues really important to them were other matters which tended to overshadow the antifeminist nonsense of official Nazi speeches and remarks? In all our cases, there was only one pertinent comment, the statement quoted above about how the factory treadmill made girls unsuitable for their true calling of motherhood. It was made by a very young girl and suggests her boredom with the factory routine, rather than deep conviction. The evidence of later Nazi policies toward women suggests that Nazi women leaders had no intention of turning their following into mere birth machines and homemakers for the Third Reich. An American sociologist, Clifford Kirkpatrick, likewise concluded, after a year's study, that the Nazis had not had the courage of their convictions on the role of women but had settled for a halfway solution between the emancipated woman of the 1920's and their own petty-bourgeois ideal.[12]

There is little reason, then, to expect a pronounced antifeminism in the women's views. On the contrary, their activism and militancy suggest a leaning toward greater participation in the social and po-

[11] *Hitler's Social Revolution*, pp. 187 and 189-190. Schoenbaum quotes Hitler to the effect that "equal rights for women means that they experience the esteem that they deserve in the areas for which nature has intended them," meaning "motherhood, the home," and "womanly work."

[12] *Nazi Germany: Its Women and Family Life*, Indianapolis: Bobbs-Merrill, 1938, ch. xi; and Schoenbaum, *Hitler's Social Revolution*, ch. 6.

litical decisions of the nation rather than the opposite. In any case, it is worth comparing the political views of the Nazi women with those of the men.

A first difference, possibly due to the large number of older women, is the far lower proportion of the women who had been in youth groups. Only one-third, as compared to nearly three-fourths of the men, report such memberships. Their home environments were more often *voelkisch* or unpolitical than those of the boys. They also more frequently report having been at odds with Jewish classmates in school. They were significantly more often upset about the dissoluteness and "moral disintegration of society," that allegedly set in in 1918. They also tended more often to have been in *voelkisch* groups or to have sympathized with the beer-hall *putsch* of 1923 than the men. Finally, they report more often that they encountered political friction in the neighborhood, in the family, or at school. It may be appropriate to suggest that their behavior patterns and also their accessibility as women at home and in the family differ significantly from the males.

As for their views, there are many differences. They include disproportionate numbers of Nordic or Germanic romantics and Hitler cultists. Their hostility was focused considerably more on the Jews and Communists than with the men. Their antisemitism frequently had a sex angle and they liked to think of alien nations as inferior. Their venom against political enemies disproportionately addressed itself to the "traitors," "the conspirators," or resorts to engaging names such as "subhumans" or "rodents." The Nazi women tended to be highly ideological and not well-informed. The leadership cult of Hitler was to them the most important feature of the movement. Their outstanding activities while in the movement were electioneering and proselytizing. They tended to deplore violence far more than the men. They also tended to emphasize their personal experiences, such as social snubs, and the circumstances of the Weimar Republic at, the expense of the story of their own political development. In 1934, their expectations disproportionately ran in the direction of the totalitarian utopia of the thousand-year *Reich* laced with undertones of revenge on their enemies and detractors.

It is difficult to draw any generalizations from this collection of women's lives. The striking differences among the age groups do not obscure what nearly all these women had in common, the syndrome of projective hatreds and the cult of Hitler. At first glance, the Nazi women seem to have had it more clearly and to exhibit more bizarre actions per autobiographical page than the men. But then we have to remember that Nazi men could easily discharge their hatreds in physical violence. The Nazi women for the most part express regret about the violence, or at the most lead a reader to sense their secret pleasure at the expectation of *Klopperei* (brawls) at the rallies. And what could be more bizarre than Nazi stormtroopers and Communist Red Fronters beating each other up because, in the last analysis, perhaps their fathers were absent or neglected them as children?

PART II

War, Revolution, and Counter-revolution

There is a striking analogy between the mass mobilization of modern war and the mass mobilization of extremist movements such as the NSDAP. It is no coincidence that totalitarian mass movements and regimes like to borrow military terms such as battle, militia, fronts, or flanking maneuvers, and that they are fond of uniforms, flags, and quasi-military titles for their party organization. Large modern wars such as World War One can create an almost totalitarian unity of purpose even in a divided and stratified society such as imperial Germany, a unity which tends to bring together people from all classes, religions, and regional origins in one encompassing feeling of community.

But the purpose of this social unity is to fight and kill the enemy for the ultimate survival or triumph of one's own nation. For the young man drafted at an age when he still has not yet been able to rein in and domesticate his own hostilities, being at war makes an enormous difference in his socialization. Adults, instead of telling him that he must learn to get along with others and resolve his disagreements without resort to violence, tell him now that it is all right to hate and kill as long as he directs his hostility only against the Tommies, the Ivans, and the poilus: "Jeder Stoss ein Franzos, jeder Schuss ein Russ (every blow a Frenchman, every shot a Russian)." German soldiers as young as a very young 17 were thus indoctrinated in World War One. Mentally and physically, being 17 in those days perhaps compares with being 14 today. Older men and women also learned that it was praiseworthy and patriotic to hate and destroy, but they had already been broken in to the nonviolent ways of a civilized society for a few years before 1914, and were more easily able to shift back and forth between atavistic aggression and domestication. Younger boys and girls also learned to hate and kill vicariously through their fathers, uncles, and older brothers in the trenches.

Where does all this legitimated hatred and violence go when the war ends and everybody has to go back to a humdrum job and family life, or worse, to unemployment, lack of purpose, and loneliness?

What happens to the young men warped in the war at the end of the fool's-paradise world of war in which domestic suicides and homicides are almost unknown while the slaughter goes on abroad? Will they be able to domesticate their hostility when their boss or family frustrates them or when they do not get their way in politics? Will they be able to endure the privatization and loneliness of everyday life after years of brotherly comradeship in the trenches, in the wolves' pack of licensed killers? How great an attraction must the militant veterans' organization or the Free Corps be to them, since it allows them to continue enjoying the comradeship, the common hatreds and reminiscences, and perhaps even demonstrations and licensed violence against enemies foreign or domestic? World War One threw a long shadow over the first five years of the republic, a field-gray shadow of uniforms and warlike behavior in domestic politics which nearly overthrew the Weimar Republic in 1920 and again in 1923.

There is a revealing portrait of this "lost generation" in Joachim C. Fest's description of the Free Corps and veterans' backgrounds of the stormtroopers.[1] He speaks of "their incapacity for civilian life" and "extremist adventurism and criminality masquerading as nationalism":

> Active unrest, readiness to take risks, belief in force and irresponsibility were the essential psychological elements that lay behind the organized nihilism of those whose formative experience had been the war, with its underlying sense of the decline of a culture, and whose heroic myth was the spirit of the front-line soldier. Agents of a permanent revolution without any revolutionary idea of the future, they had no goal . . . only a wish to eternalize the values of the trenches. They fought on and marched on beyond the Armistice and the end of the war . . . because the world appeared to them a battlefront and their rhythm was that of marching feet. "Marching is the most meaningful form of our profession of faith."

The *vitae* of the Abel collection largely present the war, the defeat, or the "revolution" of 1918 as the formative experience of many respondents' lives. If we consider the central experience or influence of each autobiographical statement, we find nearly one-half under the spell of war, revolution, or foreign occupation. The other half, the postwar generation, are dominated by youthful comradeship, schooling, or unemployment. The experiences of social

[1] *The Face of the Third Reich*, New York: Pantheon, 1970, pp. 136-138. See also the descriptions of Free Corps life in Ernst von Salomon, *Die Geaechteten*, Guetersloh: Bertelsmann, 1930.

FD-76: Formative or Influential Experience

	Number	Per cent
Fronterlebnis, war	101	13.8
Defeat, revolution	175	23.8
Social snub, humiliation	29	4.0
Alleged episode with Jews	37	5.0
Alleged encounter with aliens (including occupation)	55	7.5
Comradeship in youth organization	75	10.2
Educational, literary influence	131	17.8
Unemployment, economic crisis	43	5.9
Other experiences	88	12.0
	734*	100.0

* Note: Multiple entries add up to more than 581.

snubs or humiliation with which we dealt in Part I, and even the impact of unemployment or personal economic crisis appear to have played a minor role.

The Free Corps, patriotic vigilantes, and militant veterans' organizations are one telling outgrowth of the war experience, emphasizing military life-styles, rituals, and symbols. But there was also another outgrowth which placed greater stress on ideological direction and totalitarian unity of political will. Alongside and often inseparably mixed with the quasi-military organizations and actions were extremist parties of the right and left for those who found the *Stahlhelm* parades and fantasies of military coups too dull and pointless. In the Independent Socialist and Communist waves of 1918-1920, it *was* possible to march and fight against the feudal-capitalistic establishment and to strive for a glowing utopia of proletarian democracy, peace, and human liberation. The Red Soldiers League founded by the Spartakists in 1918 and, in 1923-1924, the Proletarian Hundreds and Red Front Fighters League[2] provided the red militant with his own ideological army in which to indulge his "noble hatred for the exploiters."[3]

[2] The Proletarian Hundreds of Central Germany and Berlin were organized in May 1923 and numbered about 800 members by October. The Red Front Fighters League (RFB) was formed in 1924 and headed by Ernst Thaelmann. The local organization had no cells and often up to three-fourths of their members belonged to no political party. At the 1926 *Reich* rally, 100,000 RFB men were said to be in attendance. They were meant to be an unarmed electioneering organization. Hermann Duenow, *Der Rote Frontkaempferbund*, East Berlin: MNV, no date, pp. 20-37, 65.

[3] The phrase is that of Lothar Berthold in *Das Programm der KPD zur nationalen und sozialen Befreiung des deutschen Volkes vom August*

The right wing had a plethora of groups ranging from the military-tradition-minded *Stahlhelm* and other veterans and anti-revolutionary vigilante organizations over the more ideological, *voelkisch*-oriented *Oberland* and *Wehrwolf* groups to the NSDAP and its many *voelkisch* predecessors.[4] In all these organizations, a person could cultivate his hatreds amid like-minded haters with whom he experienced a *Fronterlebnis*-like ideological comradeship and community. Most of the groups catered especially to youth, from the Communist Youth and Young Red Front to the right-wing *Jungstahlhelm*, *Jungdo*, and the Hitler Youth, not to mention the largely youthful action groups themselves. Here the experience of youthful community shaded into the primary, irrational experiences and concerns of the Youth Movement and youth revolt of the Weimar Republic and the preceding decade. The politicized or politically channeled hatreds which made the climate of the extremist organizations resemble the psychological effects of war are, as in Orwell's *Nineteen Eighty-Four*, only the other side of the coin of the highly prized homo-erotic comradeship in the fighting groups. The Nazi party, and particularly the stormtroopers, had a reputation for comradely love and community in direct proportion to their aggressive brutality toward the political enemy. A very hostile youth could indulge his aggressions against the designated enemy and at the same time feel the warm, friendly support of his group whether its commonality was a matter of military style and ritual or of utopian ideology.

1930, Berlin: Dietz, 1956, pp. 26-27. Berthold names "monopolists, militarists, imperialists" as well as the "bourgeois agents in the Communist party (such as Levi, Brandler, Thalheimer, Fischer, Maslow, and Ewert)" and of course the SPD and the free trade unions as the chief objects of Communist hostility.

[4] For a brief list of the more important militant right-wing organizations, see for example Karl D. Bracher, *Die Aufloesung der Weimarer Republik*, 4th ed., Villingen: Ring Verlag, 1959, p. 138, fn. 43 and the discussion there, pp. 128-142.

ONE

Three Early Nazi Generations

There are probably many ways of periodizing the politically active generations between 1918 and 1945. The momentous impact of the war on contemporary lives offers a convenient and plausible criterion at least for the era of political struggle of the early Nazi movement, until 1933. Most of the early Nazi leaders fit into the mold of the prewar or war generations even if, like Josef Goebbels, they never served in the military. While the postwar generation of Nazis was slugging it out in the streets and meeting-halls of the Weimar Republic, moreover, there were further generations of Germans growing up. One grew up just in time to be brainwashed in the schools and then sent out to kill and be killed in World War Two. Another generation, including this writer, came to political awareness in the years of defeat and Allied occupation when the mass graves and concentration camps were opened to reveal the extent of the carnage the Nazi generations had visited upon the world.

Military Service

It may be remembered from our discussion of the military-civil servants that not all the Abel respondents had spent time in the military service. Nearly half of them, in fact, had not served at all. Many had been too young or perhaps in ill health;[1] some had two years of peacetime service but were not in the war. Altogether only 14.5% served a peacetime stint, a figure to which we should perhaps add many of the professional soldiers, because they frequently started their career by volunteering for the peacetime service. Only 11.3% volunteered in World War One; 11.1% served a year or two and another 20.6% served three years or longer.

Peacetime or wartime volunteering may well denote a certain attitude, though attitudes may change. Just being drafted or being recalled from the reserves at a time of war, regardless of the length of service, is less easy to interpret. The shorter length of service can be due to having come of draft age later or being considered over-

[1] Thirty-five percent of the sample were born in 1902 or later—i.e., in the age cohorts that missed the last wartime draft.

FD-21: Military Service

	Number	Per cent
No military service	263	47.0
Two years peacetime (TPT) only	13	2.3
TPT plus 1-2 years in war	9	1.6
TPT plus 3-4 years in war	48	8.6
TPT plus volunteer in 1914-1915	11	2.0
Volunteer in war without TPT	52	9.3
1-2 years in war without TPT	53	9.5
3-4 years in war without TPT	67	12.0
Professional soldier, or other service	43	7.7
	559	100.0

age until the last desperate year of the war. It could also denote a service prematurely interrupted by injury or illness. Only the cross-tabulations are capable of shedding more light on the subject.

When we cross the service categories with age, for example, 75.7% of the respondents who never served were indeed born in 1902 or later. Yet another 15.2% were of the prime military age for World War One, having been born between 1895 and 1901. In fact, as many as 41% of the Nazi respondents born from 1899 to 1901, who were called after the optimism of the first two years had given way to glum forebodings and dogged persistence amid hunger and discouragement at home, evidently managed to avoid conscription. They could not all have been ill, unfit, or so badly needed at home that they would escape the last scraping of the bottom of the barrel. Meet the Nazi draft-dodgers in "the hour of the nation's greatest need."

The volunteers with or without previous peacetime service again are concentrated among the group born 1895-1898 and in the ten years prior to 1895 rather than among those due for service in the last two years of the war. In other words, they were mostly volunteers of that great wave of patriotic enthusiasm which engulfed Germany in 1914-1915. Adolf Hitler himself (born 1889) it may be recalled, was such an early volunteer, although he himself left little doubt that his motives were other than that of patriotic enthusiasm.[2] He had already dodged the Austrian draft for three years of his aimless youth when he fled to Munich and volunteered in August 1914:[3] "To me, those times were like a deliverance from the vexing emotions of my youth . . . overcome by passionate enthusiasm, I fell to my knees and thanked heaven from an overflow-

[2] See Smith, *Adolf Hitler*, p. 150 and Bracher, *The German Dictatorship*, pp. 64-66.

[3] *Mein Kampf*, p. 177.

ing heart." Finally he had found something to do with his misspent life and he proceeded to do it with an abandon that presaged his later obsessions. This was not the enthusiastic idealism which drew hundreds of thousands of young Germans and most of the Nazi volunteers to the murderous battlefields of World War One.

It is worth noting also that the respondents serving in peacetime are generally older, with nearly half born before 1885; 85.5% of those drafted or recalled from the reserves were born between 1885 and 1901. The latter is the true war generation, broadly defined, while some of the older Nazis with prewar military service may well have been old imperial swashbucklers who could not resist marching with the stormtroopers. The professional military group is also concentrated among the age cohorts born before 1890.

How do these groups compare otherwise? Those with no military service were more likely to have come to grief economically in the years 1928 to 1933, and tended to be either in social decline or urban climbers. Their fathers were mostly artisans, military-civil servants, or small businessmen, in contrast, for example, to the peacetime soldiers whose parents were mostly farmers. As for their social mobility, the volunteers of 1914 stand out as the most upwardly mobile. The peacetime soldiers instead were farm climbers or socially static. So far there is a strong impression that the differences among these groups were mostly the generational differences between older and younger age cohorts.

When we consider their childhood influences, we find that these differences are more specifically indicative of what led the different generations into the Nazi party. Disproportionate numbers of the older respondents with peacetime service had a militaristic or authoritarian father or one of conservative or liberal party loyalty. Many also suffered poverty during childhood. The volunteers often came from militaristic homes, although they were generally better educated than the rest. The postwar generation and other Nazis who never served, by contrast, tended to be from *voelkisch* or antisemitic homes and to report a *voelkisch* political climate in their school environment. We can assume, then, that the political socialization patterns in the Nazi party shifted significantly from the prewar militaristic strain to a *voelkisch* wave among the younger generation.

Reaction to War and Defeat

How did these groups react to their war experiences? As many as one-third of the Nazis with no military service report a change from initial enthusiasm to disaffection as hunger and deprivation grew at home. Nearly another one-third of them resolved to stick it out to the bitter end. Their slogan *Durchhalten* (sticking it out) was often laced with vituperation toward draft-dodgers, subversives, or Jews. The volunteers, by contrast, were preoccupied with egalitarian comradeship, *Fronterlebnis*, and hostility against the enemy nations. They maintained their enthusiasm and often earned decorations or promotions in rank throughout the war. As a matter of fact, if we scale the length of military service from one or two to three or four and over four years, sustained war enthusiasm and performance actually seems to grow with the length of service.

It is this differential between the war experiences at the front and demoralization at home which often produced so great a jolt among the returning soldiers in 1918 that we can speak of a cultural shock. The longer they served, the greater the shock at coming home to a society very different from the one they remembered having left. Among the volunteers, the cultural shock mostly took the form of objections to the "moral and social disintegration" of society, or to "dissolute women," beatniks, Communists, and to the new Weimar leadership in politics, business, and the press, a sentiment shared by most of the draftees in the war. The respondents who had already served two years before the war were particularly upset about the disparagement of military honor and symbolism, the fall of the monarchies, and the wave of internationalism and pacifism. They also criticized the new leadership and the "absence of order and discipline" in German postwar society.

How did these groups react to the defeat? Whom did they blame the most? The respondents with no military service show the greatest display of unfocused emotion—rage, sadness, or grudging—evidently because of their youth. The professional soldiers, by contrast, directed their wrath at the Marxists or the Spartakists, which along with simple acceptance of the defeat was the attitude of most of the sample. The volunteers, whose high hopes were dashed, tended to blame the defeat on the Kaiser, the weakness of the civilians, or the trickery of President Wilson, views shared particularly by the respondents who had already served in peacetime. There was an obvious sense of disappointment in the old order and the people back home.

Reaction to the Revolutionaries

There is still a good deal of controversy regarding the question of whether a revolution ever took place in 1918-1919 in Germany.[4]

[4] Annelise Thimme explains the conservative insistence that there was indeed a revolution with complex psychological motivations. See her book

Right-wing opinion has always insisted that there was a revolution and that it "stabbed the military effort in the back." German Liberals and Socialists, not to mention Communists, relegate the perception of an accomplished revolution to the realm of wishful thinking. In any case, there can be little doubt that there were indeed revolutionaries present who made every effort to overthrow the government by force. Thus, the question arises as to how the various military service groups reacted to the revolutionaries and what they were doing.

The Nazi respondents without military service typically identified the revolution with the Spartakists, the Independent Socialists, and the mutineers, as most respondents tend to do. But they also disproportionately blamed the Kaiser and the old order, the Western allies, or insurgent national minorities, as well as unspecified "rabble." The volunteers, by comparison, tended to identify the revolution with the Weimar parties (SPD, DDP, and Center) or with the "international Bolshevik conspiracy." The peacetime enlistees also blamed international Bolshevism and the mutineers and extreme leftists, and the draftees of World War One tended to single out the Weimar parties and the Jews as the perpetrators of the "revolution." A typical response reads like this (no. 35): "When in 1918 the Marxist revolution broke out . . . the Spartakists, dressed as sailors, raged and destroyed everything they could lay their hands on. They were headed by Jews. . . ."

To what extent did their reactions toward the "revolutionaries" induce these groups to engage in counter-revolutionary activities? Nazis of no military service, probably for reasons of age, became the least involved, only to one-third; more than half of the volunteers were involved in one way or another. The respondents with no military past frequently joined *voelkisch* or conservative-liberal opposition groups instead, but they stand out only among those who strongly sympathized with the Free Corps or expressed hatred for the domestic insurgents. Some of them, in fact, joined or sympathized with the insurgents. The volunteers of World War One, by comparison, fought with the Free Corps against both domestic and foreign enemies (Poles), or joined the vigilantes of the *Einwohnerwehr* and various militant veterans' or *voelkisch* action groups, in disproportionate numbers.

These paramilitary involvements are also typical of the draftees who were furthermore often part of or at least in sympathy with the

Flucht in den Mythos: die deutschnationale Volkspartei und die Niederlage von 1918, Goettingen: Vandenhoeck & Ruprecht, 1969.

Kapp *putsch* of 1920. They were heavily involved in political violence and included nearly a dozen who, at the time, belonged to the
left-wing side. The respondent quoted above (no. 35), a draftee,
relates how in Halle the whole non-commissioned officer corps, to
which he belonged, "demonstrated against the terror of the Spartakists and Independent Socialists." They were received "with machine guns" by the Spartakists and with fists by the workers in the
street, and ended up having to defend their barracks and weapons
depots against Spartakist assaults. Respondents with peacetime military service were less involved in action, probably again for reasons of age, except for expressing sympathy for the Free Corps and
hatred for the insurgents. They did belong to many militant veterans'
or *voelkisch* action groups, though.

Half a decade later, in the crisis of 1923, when nearly half of the
respondents became involved, how did the different military service
groups react? The Nazis without military service tended to be in
other legitimate parties or in the anti-occupation underground; the
war volunteers were more likely to be found in militant veterans'
groups or *voelkisch* organizations. The peacetime soldiers also
tended to belong to veterans' and *voelkisch* groups, and the draftees
of World War One stand out for their membership in the NSDAP
and sympathy with the beer-hall *putsch* in Munich. The chief support for the Nazi and *voelkisch* movements of the first five years of
the Weimar Republic evidently came from the prewar and war generations rather than from those born in 1902 or later. The merging
of the Nazi upsurge with the youth revolt occurred much later.

As Table II-1 shows, there were striking differences in the organizational behavior of the three groups between 1918 and 1932.
Their rate of involvement, for example, increased from a low level
for the no-service group, and from an intermediate one for the
peacetime soldiers to about the same two-thirds in 1929-1930. The
draftees and volunteers, on the other hand, began at a high level and
fought right through the years of the Nazi build-up. At the same
time, the peacetime and wartime soldiers, and particularly the latter, were more heavily involved with militant veterans' groups such
as the *Stahlhelm*, and the no-service group even in 1923 stands out
for its membership in the conservative and bourgeois opposition,
such as in *Jungdo*, or the DNVP. The rate of enlistment in the Nazi
party in the "quiet years" 1925-1928 shows a noticeable increase
among the no-service and a slighter one for the war generation. We
have the impression that the prewar soldiers took longer to become
mobilized even though they started out with a certain militaristic
and prewar-*voelkisch* legacy. The war generation was evidently the

Table II-1: Organizational Memberships of Military Service Groups

		None	NS-voelkisch	Conserv. oppos.	Militant veterans	Left wing	Total (n)
Peacetime service or professional military	1919-1921	43 (58.1%)	8 (10.8%)	4 (5.4%)	15 (20.3%)	4 (5.4%)	74 (100%)
	1922-1924	36 (45.6%)	20 (25.3%)	5 (6.3%)	14 (17.7%)	4 (5.1%)	79 (100%)
	1925-1928	35 (43.7%)	24 (29.1%)	9 (11.1%)	9 (11.1%)	4 (5.0%)	81 (100%)
	1929-1930	28 (33.7%)	50 (60.3%)	4 (4.8%)	—	1 (1.2%)	83 (100%)
	1931-1932	—	81 (100%)	—	—	—	81 (100%)
Draftees and volunteers	1919-1921	78 (47.6%)	14 (8.5%)	11 (6.7%)	50 (30.5%)	11 (6.7%)	164 (100%)
	1922-1924	70 (44.6%)	34 (21.7%)	13 (8.3%)	30 (19.1%)	10 (6.4%)	157 (100%)
	1925-1928	60 (41.2%)	55 (37.6%)	15 (10.3%)	11 (7.5%)	5 (3.4%)	146 (100%)
	1929-1930	70 (36.4%)	115 (59.8%)	6 (3.2%)	—	1 (0.5%)	192 (100%)
	1931-1932	—	193 (100%)	—	—	—	193 (100%)
No military service	1919-1921	178 (70.6%)	25 (9.9%)	16 (6.3%)	24 (9.5%)	9 (3.6%)	252 (100%)
	1922-1924	129 (50.8%)	51 (20.1%)	25 (9.8%)	37 (14.6%)	12 (4.7%)	154 (100%)
	1925-1928	110 (41.9%)	112 (42.6%)	20 (7.6%)	18 (6.8%)	3 (1.1%)	263 (100%)
	1929-1930	111 (35.2%)	194 (61.7%)	7 (2.2%)	—	3 (0.9%)	315 (100%)
	1931-1932	—	323 (100%)	—	—	—	323 (100%)

one most mobilized by the war experience itself even though it did much of its earlier demonstrating and fighting in the Free Corps or *Stahlhelm*.

The postwar generation began mainly in 1923 in the conservative-bourgeois opposition and was then roped in by the NSDAP build-up during the years 1925 to 1928. Broken down by the exact dates of joining, in fact, the figures show that half of the peacetime and professional soldiers joined only after July 1930. The same is true of the war generation except for a large contingent which joined before 1925. One-third of the postwar generation, however, joined before 1927, and another third by July 1930. For these latter years, they report far heavier involvement in Nazi electioneering, demonstrations, and political violence than do any of the other groups. In 1929 and 1930, again, their involvement in demonstrations and physical violence was by far the heaviest; the draftees and volunteers of World War One were more often engaged in demonstrations and electioneering. Both the war generation and the peacetime and professional soldiers also participated more heavily in proselytizing, the other quintessential activity of the Nazi movement. In 1931 and 1932, the postwar generation of Nazis was still the main force in street demonstrations and violence. Substantially greater numbers of them were also in the SA and SS, while the others engaged more in electioneering, demonstrations and proselytizing. However, the war generation more often held higher offices in the SA or SS than those without military service. Anyone with a military rank was most welcome as an SA leader.

The Political Views of the Three Groups

How did the three military service groups differ in their political views? The postwar generation tended to call the Weimar Republic a Marxist-run republic or to look forward to the replacement of its "red" and "black" rulers and its pluralistic system by the Third Reich. The peacetime and professional soldiers also objected to the red-and-black leadership and to the alleged dominance of Jews, aliens, and "un-German culture." The war generation tended to raise, besides the Jewish, un-German argument, traditional criticisms of the "liberal-Marxist system," or of capitalism, and unfavorable comparisons to the glories of the empire.

Their dominant ideological themes, after they had joined the party, again show the difference between the two older generations and those without military service. The former tended toward revanchism, superpatriotism and antisemitism, especially among the peacetime and professional soldiers. The war generation also opted strongly for the *Volksgemeinschaft* among the classes. The postwar generation had as their dominant themes the personality cult of Hitler, Nordic or German romanticism, or the *Volksgemeinschaft*.

The postwar generation also differed from the others in that its evidently politically more active members tended to be introduced to the party mostly through relatives, friends, or groups. The more passive earlier two generations instead tended to read about the NSDAP or to be attracted by its ideology and propaganda before joining, a difference resembling David Riesman's concept of inner- versus other-directedness. Their attitude toward the party and what it could do for them varied accordingly. The war and prewar generations felt uplifted and personally integrated by their ideological vision of utopia, the Third Reich. They also hoped for jobs or party careers, which many of them achieved. The postwar generation, by contrast, felt integrated by the struggle itself, by the classlessness of the party, and by the Hitler cult.

Last but not least important, there were differences in their less rational underlying attitudes. The chief objects of hostility for the respondents without any military service were the Communists and Socialists. The peacetime and professional soldiers show hostility to Jews and Marxists, as do the war generation. The latter, however, also show an anti-establishment streak, in their pronounced hostility against "reactionaries," Liberals, and the Catholic church and its political representatives.

Their ethnocentricity toward other nations and international forces varies in inverse proportion with their age. The prewar and professional military respondents, for example, express much more hostility toward the foreign nations who "encircle Germany" and even toward aliens, Catholics, or other "international enemies" within Germany than do the respondents without military service. Even the war generation still had a disproportionate number of these responses. Those with no military service instead tended to think that alien nations were inferior to their own and otherwise simply showed less ethnocentricity. It appears that even then national ethnocentricity was already slowly beginning to decline, a trend which has continued to this day.

The pattern of attitudes toward authority also changed visibly from the earlier to the youngest generations. The attitudes of peacetime and professional soldiers tended toward complaints about the "pluralistic disintegration" of the Weimar state, or toward blaming its allegedly Marxist or Jewish leaders. They also expressed an obsession with order, or criticize the government and the police for not maintaining it. The youths with no military service, on the other hand, stressed the leadership principle or expressed uninhibited vituperation against all police authority.

Their attitudes toward violence and toward their political enemies again set the postwar generation off from the two earlier
groups. The most prominent difference in their attitudes toward violence was in the pronounced self-pitying masochism of the respondents with no military service. Although the war and prewar generations were less actively involved in physical violence, they tended
to take a straightforward approach and show little inhibition about
inflicting violence on the enemy. Perhaps the *frisch-froehliche Krieg*
(merry war) taught them to channel their aggressions in this fashion. The respondents without military experience, by contrast, were
mostly preoccupied with the blows they received rather than those
they dealt the Communists or the police, an obvious rationalizing
maneuver to make up for the violation of the social taboos against
violence. Their masochism and self-pity are very reminiscent of
some of the contemporary student rebels and all the more surprising, since they were far more heavily involved in political violence
than the two older generations of Nazis. How can a person fling
himself into violent political action and yet dissolve with self-pity
about what his antagonists or the police may on occasion do to him
and his fellow-fighters?[5]

Their images of the political enemy are less sharply distinguishable. The peacetime and professional soldiers mostly refer to their
political enemies as traitors, a sinister conspiracy, or as "subhuman," "rodents," venal, or immoral, in the language of the *outré*.
The war and postwar generations, by comparison, often exhibit a certain liking for their antagonists or say they would like to win them
over. The draftees and volunteers of the war also liked to view their
political antagonists as a traitorous conspiracy, and the respondents
without military service also use the gutter language of the *outré*,
though neither of them as frequently as the prewar generation of
Nazis.

The military service generations also differ in their reactions to
their social environment. Nearly all the respondents report some
political friction but there are telling differences in the locale of this
friction. The two older generations suffered friction as a result of
their political views mostly at their job or business. Many of them,
in fact, were boycotted or fired because of their politics. The respondents with no military service, on the other hand, more often
experienced friction at school, in the family, and in their neighbor-

[5] A possible interpretation appears below, pp. 542-543. In a nutshell,
the explanation derives from our earlier thesis that growing up in a world
at peace involves the acquisition of considerable inhibitions against violence which are overcome only by masochistic or ideological rationalization.

hood, a clear reflection of their age, for these are the locations of authority over the lives of young people.

There are other indications of these differences in the respondents' lives. On a pragmatic-ideological scale, the postwar generation was far more ideological than its elders. It also numbered a good many more "dimwits" and people of little political understanding, often with romantic or heroic ideas about their own political role. On the other hand, it was also the generation with a clear idea about its own, personal political development, and a deeply politicized generation. The others tend to tell their life stories more in terms of their personal or general social and economic circumstances rather than, as Abel had requested, their political development. The formative experiences in the lives of the prewar, wartime, and professional soldiers tend to be their *Fronterlebnis*, and the impact of war and defeat. The draftees and volunteers also tend to stress stories of social snubs and humiliation. It is hardly surprising that the two earlier generations included as many as one-fourth of respondents who experienced a particularly intense cultural shock when they returned from the war. The postwar generation, by comparison, tended to have as their formative influences such things as the experience of comradeship in a youth organization, educational experiences at school or from reading a book, and alleged encounters with aliens or Jews. This is indeed "the political youth generation," as the German sociologist Helmut Schelsky has called them in retrospect—an unprecedented, intense political youth culture appearing on the German scene of the 1920s.

To sum up, these three Nazi generations present a vivid picture of the generational elements that made up the pre-1933 party. One such element was the peacetime and professional soldiers who tended to come from peasant stock and frequently grew up in poverty and in patriotic, militaristic, or authoritarian homes of the empire. Nothing shocked these respondents more at the end of the war than the disparagement of military honors and symbols and the fall of the old monarchic institutions. They tended to blame defeat and revolution on international Bolshevism and to flock to the Nazi party and similar *voelkisch* groups in the early years of the republic. Their bulk, however, did not get into the NSDAP until after about 1930 when the bandwagon was well under way. Their ideological views stressed especially antisemitism, revanchism and chauvinism, and law and order. The draftees and volunteers of World War One, by comparison, were by and large an upwardly mobile and better-educated lot than the other two groups. The egalitarian *Fronterlebnis* was their formative experience, and enthusiastic, long-term service their distinction. When the war ended in defeat, they blamed the Kaiser and the weakness of the civilians, and complained about the moral and social disintegration they found on returning from the war. The revolution, however, they blamed on the Weimar coalition of SPD, DDP, and the Center, and on the Jews. Hence they joined the Free Corps, vigilantes, and veterans' groups in large numbers, fought domestic insurgents and Poles, and sympathized with the Kapp *putsch* against the new Weimar government. They played no particular role in the pre-1924 NSDAP, but began to join it and the *Stahlhelm* veterans in increasing numbers after 1925. They were especially in the SA and held many SA ranks, which enabled them to keep on marching and fighting through the republican era. Their political views emphasized the *Volksgemeinschaft*, revanchism, superpatriotism, and antisemitism, as well as comparisons between the glories of the empire they hardly knew and the "liberalistic-Marxist" republic.

Fundamentally different from both of these was the postwar generation, which never saw any military service although it included many a "victory-watcher." Frequently from *voelkisch* or antisemitic homes, it also included quite a few who became disaffected with the war effort, as well as others who wanted to stick it out to the bitter end and blamed draft-dodgers and subversives for the final defeat. There were even a handful of former left-wing insurgents among them, although they otherwise abstained from any violent involvement in the early years of the republic, apart from encounters with the Allied occupation. Instead they appear to have been mostly in youth groups and in conservative-bourgeois opposition groups such as *Jungdo*. After 1925, however, attracted by the struggle, the classless comradeship, and the Hitler cult, they became heavily and violently involved with the party and especially with the SA, typically being introduced to the party by a friend or relative. The older generations were attracted by Nazi ideology and propaganda. The postwar Nazis were also far more ideological (in a stereotyped way) and political-minded than their elders, and were truly politicized youths who enountered friction at school and in the family because of their political involvement. They were anti-Communist, less ethnocentric than their elders, and neo-authoritarians: hostile to police and other authority, utterly dedicated to their leader, and masochistic in the sense we have explained earlier. Their formative experiences clearly insulated them against the effects of defeat and *Fronterlebnis* on their elders; they were formed by youthful comradeship experiences, educational experiences, and alleged encounters with aliens or Jews.

TWO

The Impact of War and Defeat

Many of the Abel respondents eloquently describe the impact of World War One on their lives and on German society. "The experience at the front . . . gave me a great deal for my whole life," wrote a schoolteacher born in 1884 (no. 210). "I took it for granted that I had to fulfill my duty as a man, convinced then and for all time of the justice of our sacred cause. We had been attacked and had fought for our most sacred goods."

"The war of 1914 and the events of 1917 marked the great divide in modern history," Hans Kohn wrote in *The Mind of Germany*.[1] It was a watershed for German history in particular, and not only because the central powers lost. Long before the collapse of the German war effort, the inner credibility of imperial society and government was shot to pieces in the trenches and on the battlefields of the war. Many respondents remark on the critical failings of the old regime, which prepared the country for defeat and revolution. "That the German people could sink so low was purely the consequence of the hard-nosed policies of our old rulers who did not care about the state of the lower classes" (no. 274).

The effect of the gigantic struggle was heightened by the wave of early enthusiasm and patriotic displays of solidarity above the deep fissures of prewar society. By the fateful year of 1917, if not earlier, it had become abundantly clear that after the war it would no longer be possible to send the workers back to their menial positions, the agricultural laborers back to their feudal estates, or the women back to the hearth, without major readjustments or open battle or both. In 1917, the parliamentary majority in the *Reichstag* resolutely expressed its disagreement with the Kaiser and his chancellor, and labor unrest broke out in war-related industries, while the long shadow of the Russian Revolution fell over Germany. All the social and political underdogs of prewar Germany, all the continuing

[1] New York: Harper Torchbooks, 1965, p. 290. The "events of 1917" centered on the famous Peace Resolution of SPD, Progressives, and Center party who later became the "Weimar coalition."

grievances and social injustices resurfaced despite the deceptive *Burgfrieden* (solidarity) proclaimed by the Kaiser in 1914. They clamored for attention and refused to wait until the end of the war. Yet, at the same time, there was also a patriotic establishment which identified with the war effort and saw only one way out of the dilemma, namely to charge forward and win the war. Greatly exaggerated expectations of glory and gains and feelings of loyalty and patriotism were mixed inseparably with fears of internal reform or revolution. The patriots and patriotic associations knew that they had a great deal more to lose than the war. Hence, their slogan, *Durchhalten*, at any price. And this was also the reason for their strong hostility for anyone who opposed or failed to support the war effort to the bitter end.

Stormtrooper Captain Roehm, descended from a line of Bavarian military-civil servants, constitutes an archetype of the bitter-ender. As Fest describes him, he simply could not conceive of those in the opposing civilian camp as being anything but "draft-dodgers, deserters and profiteers." As late as 1933, Roehm said to a British diplomat that he "would reach an understanding more easily with an enemy soldier than with a German civilian; because the latter is a swine, and I don't understand his language."[2] This total suspicion of the civilian environment colors the reaction of the bitter-enders toward the war, the German defeat, and the revolution. And it frequently defines their outsiders' sentiments while they belonged to Free Corps, veterans, or vigilante groups as well.

War Experience and Youthful Attitudes

The respondents of the Abel collection overwhelmingly, if not exclusively, belonged to the part of the population that did not lose its enthusiasm for the war. Nevertheless, their reactions vary and are less polarized than those of right-wing politicians and voters at home. In spite of their *Fronterlebnis* and their proximity to the slaughter, the soldiers at the front tended to be relatively sheltered from the effects of the peace movement and from the social and political antagonisms breaking out at home. They often felt so overwhelmed by their own fate that they did not reflect on it.

We have two measurements of the attitudes and reactions to the war. One attempted to record the changing attitudes toward the

[2] Fest, *The Face of the Third Reich*, p. 140. Fest also comments on Roehm's strong aversion in his book to the words "prudent (*besonnen*), compromise, objective, intellectual, bourgeois" and his predilection for "fresh, untroubled, strapping, honest, daredevil, ruthless, and faithful" in his remarkable portrait of this military freebooter. *Ibid.*, pp. 139 and 347.

early and later phases of the war, especially in terms of the enthusi-
asm-disaffection dichotomy and of the hostilities expressed, but
without regard to whether the respondents actually served in the
war or in the military. The breakdown (FD-30) includes nearly
two-thirds of the sample. The responses fall into fairly clear categories, nearly half striking a positive pose of sustained enthusiasm
and performance throughout the war effort. A small percentage,
about one-twelfth of those responding, became disaffected or disillusioned during the last year or two of the war. The two disaffected categories have been combined for the crosstabulations.
Also combined were the bitter-enders, whose *Durchhalten* was invariably coupled with nasty suspicions about people who might be
less committed to the war effort. A fourth combination are the respondents to whom the *Fronterlebnis* became an experience that
changed their whole lives.

FD-30: War Experience (dominant theme)

	Number	Per cent
No information	236	40.3
Sustained enthusiasm, decorations, promotions	167	28.3
Bitter-enders, hostility toward draft dodgers, back-of-front staff	15	2.5
Bitter-enders, hostility for civilians, Jews, subversives	49	8.3
Hostility toward enemy nations	12	2.0
Camaraderie, egalitarian *Fronterlebnis*	36	6.1
Early enthusiasm, then disillusionment	26	4.4
Disaffected from suffering, death	19	3.2
POW, invalid	29	4.9
	590	100.0

The other breakdown (FD-22) was originally meant as a measurement of the attitudes toward the service of soldiers up to 25
years of age, within the framework of the study of political socialization processes. It makes clear the reaction to the war also, but
with reference to whether the respondents actually served. Here too
we have a sizeable number of enthusiastic young soldiers, but they
have been combined with other categories committed to the war
effort, namely those who stress comradeship, and the invalids and
prisoners of war. There also are those who disliked their military
service, combat or non-combat, and those who became disaffected
in the war, a youthful disaffected group. Also, there is the important
pro-military group of the victory-watchers during the war who did

not serve at all and the respondents who were enthusiastic about their non-combatant military service before or during the war. Finally, there are non-attitude categories for those who served and those who never served in the military.

The two measurements overlap, of course, and are complementary in spite of the age limitation, since most soldiers served when

FD-22: Reaction to Military Experience (25 or younger)

	Number	Per cent
Enthusiastic soldier in war	126	21.7
Stresses comradeship in war	33	5.6
POW or war invalid	33	5.6
Enthusiastic, then disaffected	13	2.2
Unpleasant military experience (non-combat)	14	2.4
Enthusiastic victory-watcher (no service)	76	13.1
Enthusiastic non-combat soldier	34	5.8
Service (no attitude reported)	73	12.6
No service (no attitude reported)	179	31.0
	581	100.0

they were no older than 25. There are some moments of subjectivity in coding dominant themes or interpreting autobiographical comments which can account for small discrepancies even in the count of war invalids. There are degrees of war disability and they can vary over the periods in question.

When we crosstabulate the two variables with military service (FD-21) and with each other, their meaning and relationships become clear. Regarding the war experience table, for example, half of all the bitter-enders who express great hostility toward draft-dodgers and subversives, as it turns out, were not in the service themselves or only in non-combat service, but evidently watched the military action in the war with vicarious enthusiasm. This circumstance, of course, makes their expressed hostility a matter of superpatriotic political opinion rather than feelings that personal risk and sacrifice are not properly shared and appreciated. One-fourth of those who sustained their enthusiasm throughout the war also were either in non-combatant service or not in the service at all. They were victory-watchers of less than the draft age, or what we earlier called the Nazi draft-dodgers. The respondents who stress comradeship in the trenches are generally the same people in the two tables.

As for the youthful military attitude table, one-third of the respondents who served without indicating their attitude, and the enthusiastic soldiers, invalids, and those stressing the camaraderie of the trenches, had served already prior to 1914. The majority of those who loved their non-combat service also were prewar enlistees. The victory-watchers, as will be recalled, were juveniles who strongly but vicariously identified with the war effort. One of them, born in 1905 (no. 66), describes the onset of the war: "A terrific time began for us boys. Everyone turned soldier and we plundered kitchen and cellar in order to give presents to the departing troops. Then came the first victories. One victory celebration followed the other. But gradually things calmed down. Young as we were, we realized that war was not a game of soldiers. Air raids day and night brought the war closer and closer. . . . Then came the collapse. For us boys who had been soldiers with body and soul, a great deal collapsed."

Comparing the two tables directly, we must remind ourselves that the attitude toward the service itself is not necessarily identical with the attitude toward the war. The sustained enthusiasts of the war experience table naturally coincide in their majority (60.7%) with the enthusiastic young soldiers, etc., of the youthful military table, as do the respondents who stress the *Fronterlebnis* (71.2%). The disaffected in their war experience, however, are only in part (39.1%) identical with the youthful disaffected, the rest being scattered over the other youthful categories, especially those who never served. Disaffection was typically a youthful phenomenon. The bitter-enders are about as strongly represented among the victory-watchers (30.2%) as among the enthusiastic young soldiers (33.3%). Thus, the categories of the two tables have an existence of their own which should be recognized.

Let us take a closer look at both measurements and their cross-tabulations with combinations of other variables. Among the war experience groups the disillusioned and disaffected tend to be among the younger respondents, which is not true of the respondents who disliked their youthful non-combat service or became disaffected on the other table. The oldest war experience group is the one of sustained enthusiasm. More than half of its respondents were born before 1894 and grew up in time of peace under the empire. Among the youthful military groups the oldest is the one which served without giving any hint of its attitude toward the service, which probably reflects the importance this generation tended to attach to opinions or attitudes toward military service. In those days, they took it for granted that a man would do his duty regardless of feelings and circumstances. However, they were also a highly mobile lot which includes many of foreign sojourn or origin. The prime war generation, born between 1890 and 1901, stands out especially for its egalitarian *Fronterlebnis*, the stress on camaraderie, and hostility toward the enemy nations as well as toward draft-dodgers and subversives. They were evidently the chief apostles of *Durchhalten* and other hostile attitudes, which they passed on to the right-wing opposition movements of the early Weimar Republic.

Social Dimensions of the Groups

The war experience group which became disaffected tended to make up, together with those hostile toward draft-dodgers and subversives, namely the bitter-enders, a disproportionate share of the economic casualties of the Great Depression in Germany. The somewhat older respondents who stress the *Fronterlebnis*, and the POWs and war invalids, more often were financially ruined or lost their jobs prior to 1928. It is also worth noting that nearly half of the respondents who disliked their youthful non-combat service or became disaffected had lost their fathers during their childhood. Early loss of the father may well produce the kind of ambiguity toward paternal authority which may drive a young man into the peace-time army in search of authority but may still leave him deeply rebellious and hostile toward his superiors there. There are shades here of Lee Harvey Oswald and the U.S. Marine Corps.

Relating the war experience groups to upward mobility, we find revealing connections with the generations. The (oldest) group with sustained war enthusiasm was mostly static or rising from rural antecedents. The most hostile toward draft-dodgers and subversives were static or rising from an urban setting. The respondents who stress their *Fronterlebnis* and those who became disaffected include a disproportionate number in decline and urban climbers. The urban background of most decliners and the urban mobile, in other words, seems related to the fear of failure and hostility toward others. On the other hand, those who watched the military action with great enthusiasm tended to be static or also urban climbers. The enthusiastic young soldiers as well as those who indicate no feelings for or against the service were static or farm climbers.

Reaction to Defeat and Revolution

The military defeat and the minor revolutionary changes at home met the returning soldiers in the form of harassment and humiliation by mobs or organized groups of the extreme left. "Everything sacrosanct to a German soldier was stepped upon. I still remember painfully the day they took away my sabre and insignia," an officer reports (no. 274). "I was amazed at how the leading circles allowed themselves without a fight to be thrown out of the saddle. . . .

Everything in the fatherland had begun to stagger. I was particularly demoralized when General Groener told the Kaiser that the oath of loyalty sworn by all the soldiers and civil servants was a mere idea. This cost me my innermost countenance." The respondent promptly joined a Free Corps and went to fight in Upper Silesia.

How did these military attitude groups react to the defeat and its momentous consequences? Of the war experience groups, the sustained enthusiasts and the disaffected tended toward diffuse displays of rage or sadness. Many of them simply accepted the defeat. The bitter-enders and those of the *Fronterlebnis* instead blamed either the Marxists or Spartakists or the weakness of the Kaiser and the civilians. The same reaction is characteristic of the victory-watchers and those who loved their non-combat service. The enthusiastic young soldiers, by contrast, only stand out for placing the blame on the Kaiser and the civilians. The respondents of no youthful military service tended either to accept the defeat or to show emotion. By this time, the extra-punitive, projective reaction of the bitter-enders, the *Fronterlebnis* respondents, and the victory-watchers and non-combat military has become quite clear.

When the soldiers came home, most of them experienced a deep cultural shock. As one returnee from a prison camp put it (no. 325): "Everything had changed. I simply could not adjust to the new relationships." The respondent suddenly turned antisemitic. What we are measuring here, in other words, are themes of shock to the respondents' minds and not necessarily external events. Even among the respondents of no youthful military service, only half indicate an absence of cultural shock. The rest express their shock at the "moral disintegration of society," the new rulers of Weimar society, and the institutional changes. The sustained enthusiasts, on the other hand, show the least cultural shock and complain mainly about the absence of order and discipline, a reaction shared by the disaffected and disillusioned. The bitter-enders and those stressing *Fronterlebnis* have the highest number (88-90%) reporting cultural shock. The two groups stress such themes as (1) the moral and social disintegration in postwar Germany, dissolute women, and immoral Communists, (2) the new Weimar leaders in government, business, and in the press, especially the real or alleged Jews among them, and (3) the disparagement of military honor, insignia, and symbols; internationalism and pacifism; and the shocking fall of the monarchy and its replacement by the multi-party state.

These reactions are also typical of the enthusiastic young soldiers of the youthful military experience table. The happy non-combat soldiers and the victory-watchers complain mostly about the absence of order and discipline, and about the institutional changes, such as the disparagement of military symbols. With the young victory-watchers in particular, we may assume that their vicarious enthusiasm for the war effort involved a process by which they must have absorbed many of the deeply treasured prewar values of the prewar and war generations. On this subject, evidently the very opposite of the generation gap visible in other matters occurred. The young took over the sense of shattered values from their elders without really having lived by them. It may also be true that in the psychological limbo of the fatherless families of young sons of soldiers in the war, this form of identification with the distant, idealized, and yet personally threatening father was the only possible identification under the circumstances.[3]

Their attitudes toward the revolutionaries and their attempted "revolution" separated the war experience groups along the same lines as did the defeat. As a university-educated teacher in Wiesbaden, born in 1880 (no. 186) puts it: "Even though I never was a monarchist, the revolution of 1918 hurt me terribly in my heart of hearts. I witnessed the corruption of the workers' and soldiers' councils, people who called themselves socialists . . . a pack of thieves. . . . I also witnessed the Spartakist uprising, often in danger of death, and saw its many acts of violence, even murders." How did the military experience groups react to these events? The sustained enthusiasts and the disaffected tend to accept the revolution. Others blame the Kaiser, the old order and its stubborn resistance to change, the economic interests of Western powers, the national minorities within Germany; or they rage about unspecified rabble or scoundrels. Respondents without any youthful military service show the same response. The bitter-enders and the *Fronterlebnis* respondents, by comparison, tend to blame the Jews, international Bolshevism, or the mutineers and Spartakists. The youthful victory-watchers also tend to blame the Spartakists or the Jews.

Counterrevolutionary Involvement

From these views and reactions sprang specific actions and involvement in counter-revolutionary activities. Of the youthful military groupings, for example, the victory-watchers and non-combat sol-

[3] See, for example, the hypotheses presented by Peter Loewenberg at the International Political Science Congress of 1970 at Munich and published as "The Psycho-Historical Origins of the Nazi Youth Cohort," *American Historical Review*, vol. 76 (Dec. 1971), 1457-1502, and the sources cited there, especially Ernst Glaeser, *Jahrgang 1902*, Berlin: Kiepenheuer, 1931.

diers were the most highly involved (59.2%) though they stand out mostly for their strong expressions of hatred of the insurgents (28.6%) and for a few (13.3%) who participated in Free Corps or vigilante defense organizations. A handful (4%) actually was on the side of the revolutionaries. Those Nazis who disliked their youthful non-combat service or became disenchanted there show the same reactions. The enthusiastic young soldiers participated less heavily (50%), but they show up frequently in the action categories such as with the Free Corps against the Poles (12.2%), with the vigilantes against domestic insurgents (14.6%), or in sympathy with the Kapp *putsch* (8.5%) of 1920 which temporarily toppled the Weimar government. The group which served without indicating their attitude toward their youthful military experience now gives us an inkling of it. They were either too old or felt so little identification with their military experience that only 35% of them became involved with the drama of revolution and counter-revolution. Only the Nazis with no youthful experience were less involved than this—only 21%—having been too young at the time.

The war experience groups behave somewhat differently from what we might expect. Now it is the sustained enthusiasts of the war who show up heavily in the action groups, with 13.2% in the Free Corps against the Poles, 17% in Free Corps and vigilantes against the domestic insurgents, and 6.9% with the Kapp *putsch*. The disaffected more often express hatred for the insurgents, and a few of them (3) were revolutionaries themselves. The bitter-enders were the most heavily involved (67.7%), but their involvement consisted mostly in expressions of hatred for the insurgents (38.7%) and in siding with the Kapp *putsch* (8.1%). The Nazis who stress their *Fronterlebnis* fought the insurgents via Free Corps and vigilantes (20%), hated them (22%), and again a few (3) belonged to them.[4]

Reaction to the Occupation

The occupation of German territory immediately after the war and again in 1923 must have seemed, to many who had identified with the war effort or their military experience, one more aggression of the wartime enemy. If it had been all right to hate that enemy from 1914 to 1918, why not keep on hating him and, perhaps, sabotage or attack him when he was in the vulnerable situation of a military

---

[4] Of the NSDAP and *voelkisch* groups of 1919-1921, the sustained war enthusiasts make up more than half. The veterans, vigilante, and anti-occupation groups of that period have the war enthusiasts and the *Fronterlebnis* groups as their dominant elements.

occupier trying to make up by brute force what authority he lacked. The occupation situation also tended to invite the tried methods of terrorist agitation: Attacking the military occupation could provoke it to lash out in blind retaliation at the civilian population, thereby kindling in broader circles the hatred and outraged superpatriotism felt by the terrorist himself.

One young respondent whose brother volunteered and was killed at the front in 1916 (no. 488) brings out the warlike attitudes against the occupation:

> The French invasion of the Ruhr in January 1923 in violation of international law was of great significance for my life. There has never been such a brutal act of violence without any justification whatsoever against a highly cultured people such as the Germans.
>
> It should not have surprised the French that they were met with a wave of rage and hatred—not a raging fire, but an icy, grim silence of the deepest contempt and annihilation. Shops closed down, the railroads stopped running, and telephone connections were cut off. Passive resistance started. The cruelty of the French even invaded the house of my parents. A very young lieutenant was quartered there who ordered us around just as he pleased and refused to allow the maid to wait on him. This monster insisted that my mother, an old lady, wait on him and he treated her in the most inconsiderate way.
>
> The brutal, uninhibited conduct of the French invaders soon brought me around to the desire to join an organization which would turn the passive into an active resistance. Friends introduced me to circles of this basic tendency and I also stayed in touch with the Schlageter group. I had a lot of free time on my hands because the schoolhouse had been turned over to the soldiers and we had no school. I did not join these groups in search of wild adventures but in order to work quietly and help the fatherland.

As the respondent explains, the French soon discovered that the telephone lines past his house had been severed and arrested first his father and then him. He was in jail for three months and finally released because he was only sixteen. Then the entire family, including the maid, was expelled on two hours' notice from the occupied area. He calls this "the climax of French arbitrary rule" but makes no comment about his own childish prank which got the whole family into trouble.

"All this kindled a searing hatred for France in me. Even today it is my ardent desire to take revenge some day for all we had to take from the blackguards of Poincaré in the midst of peacetime." In this fashion, the occupation of 1923 or earlier may well have been the equivalent of the *Fronterlebnis* for many younger Nazis.

The French and the Belgians helped them to externalize their hostility and self-hatred, and the underground solidarity taught them the thrills of comradeship and sticking together in mock battle. Bearing in mind that no more than one out of five respondents resided in an occupied area and could respond, we find that the war experience groups reacted to the occupation as follows: About three-fourths of the respondents of sustained war enthusiasm, as well as those who became disaffected, express strong hatred of the occupation or report having participated in the passive resistance[5] or in rallies in memory of the captured and executed Free Corps officer Schlageter, or having been fined, jailed, expelled, or tried and condemned by the occupation. The bitter-enders evidently continued to blame others, such as the Weimar government, for "weakness" or even collusion with the occupation, or the "red revolutionaries" who in actual fact were also fighting the occupation. The bitter-enders also participated in non-violent action and frequently suffered expulsion for it. The *Fronterlebnis* respondents for their part stand out for participation in violent resistance activity such as bombings and shooting incidents involving occupation soldiers or Rhenish separatists. They also suffered fines, jail, and expulsion. Of the youthful military groups, the victory-watchers stress their part in non-violent resistance, their hatred of the occupation, and the responsibility of the Weimar government. The enthusiastic young soldiers show the same syndrome, but they also stand out for bombings and assaults and were frequently punished or expelled.

The occupation experiences of 1923 were not the only involvements common that year among the Nazi respondents. The bitter-enders, for example, were heavily involved (70%), especially in sympathizing with or taking part in the Hitler *putsch* in Munich (36.7%), or belonging to other political parties (15%). The less involved *Fronterlebnis* group had one out of five in a militant veterans group such as *Stahlhelm*. The sustained war enthusiasts had a disproportionate number in various *voelkisch* action groups (12%) and in the early NSDAP or in the beer-hall *putsch* (17.1%).

We can also turn the question the other way and ask what groups stand out among the rebels of 1923. The answer for the NSDAP *putsch*ists is the bitter-enders and sustained war enthusiasts. For the other *voelkisch* groups it is also the war enthusiasts, and for the

---

[5] After the Franco-Belgian occupation of the Ruhr area in 1923, the Weimar government at first declared a policy of passive resistance and non-cooperation for all federal employees, especially of the railroads. The occupation responded by expelling the resisters from the occupied area.

Stahlhelm those who stress the *Fronterlebnis* and the war enthusiasts. For anti-occupation activities, the dominant elements are the bitter-enders, the disaffected, and the war enthusiasts, evidently the largest and most active group in the whole sample. As for the youthful military groups, the victory-watchers and the enthusiastic young soldiers, in this order, make up the Nazi sympathizers and *putsch*ists. The enthusiastic young soldiers and those who served without indicating an attitude dominate the *voelkisch* groups. The anti-occupation respondents include many who never served and also many of the victory-watchers who also never served. The Nazis from republican and left-wing groups, finally, both in 1919-1921 and 1922-1924 have as their main elements the respondents disaffected from the war effort, the POWs and war invalids, and the bitter-enders. It is easy to imagine the political volatility of a bitter-ender who joins the left wing and, on the rebound, becomes a Nazi.

War and Political Violence

What role did the war experiences and attitudes play in the Nazi surge? Which of these groups was most likely to become involved in political violence? Are not the attitudes toward war activities likely to carry over into the political confrontations of the postwar period? Of the war experience groups, the respondents who sustained their enthusiasm through the war make up nearly two-thirds of those who were personally involved in physical violence between 1919 and 1924. The demonstrators and marchers for various causes of those years also had many of the disaffected and prisoners of war among them. During the quiet years of the republic from 1925 to 1928, the sustained war enthusiasts continue to dominate (57.1%) the violent among the Nazi respondents, although bitter-enders and the disaffected play an increasing role among the violent as well as among the demonstrators.

Toward the final fighting years, however, the proportion of war enthusiasts drops in relation to these two other groups. Among the youthful military groups the trend is even more obvious. The violent of the early years 1919 to 1924 are found chiefly among respondents without military service and among the enthusiastic young soldiers. The demonstrators were chiefly from among the victory-watchers and those who never served. In 1925-1928, the young soldiers' role in political violence had already dropped far below that of any other group, and the non-soldiers played the dominant role. This continued to be true during the final phases as well. There can be little doubt but that the wartime attitudes toward violence carried over among the Nazi respondents only during the first five years and after that became increasingly irrelevant as a clue to political behavior.

Nazi Ideology and Military Experiences

Since the war and military experience categories are in large part attitudinal dimensions rather than a record of what happened to the early Nazis in the war, they are bound to be related in some fashion to other facets of their political ideologies. Comparing the war experience groups with regard to their ideology after entering the party, we are not much surprised to find the bitter-enders and invalids or POWs among those with whom antisemitism was dominant. The bitter-enders' projective hostility against draft-dodgers and subversives indicated a tendency toward strong prejudice. As for the POWs, an example will throw some light on typical attitudes. A schoolteacher born 1884 (no. 210) reports his *Fronterlebnis* in east and west, and his eventual capture by the French who mistreated him. He goes on to describe his feelings:

> The way the war ended we simply could not understand. I was resigned to the disloyalty of the Poles (which I had encountered during the war) but could never grasp how Germans could let us down. Today I know better. There were people who once called themselves Germans and now pledge loyalty to another people if necessary. They taught our German brothers lies and hatred. They stabbed our soldiers in the back. The German Siegfried found his murderer.

He describes his return from the prison camp early in 1920:

> Captivity is death and freedom means life, or so I thought in those days. But I soon noticed the chains slung around our poor people and recognized our slave-masters. The first official to meet me at home was a Jew who talked very fast and praised the blessings of the revolution. I replied with hard and bitter words but was not yet completely aware of the role of the Jews. Years of observation and, at last, reading my *Fuehrer's* book *Mein Kampf* fully opened my understanding for the fateful mole-like activity of these corrupters of the earth.

He goes on in the same vein and puts some blame also on the. Freemasons. Another respondent (no. 199) tells of the bitter struggles in Flanders: "We fought for months for every inch of soil. Every day we risked our lives in the solemn knowledge that a single life has value only if the fatherland is saved." He was wounded twice and lost his left leg.

I lingered over the description of my experiences at the front in some detail for good reason. The hour of birth of National Socialism was in the *Fronterlebnis* and only by understanding the *Fronterlebnis* can one understand National Socialism. . . . When the revolution broke out on November 9, 1918, I was in the hospital in Trier. I still thank my stars for sparing me the experience of witnessing the shame and humiliation inflicted in the streets upon wounded comrades by these subhuman animals (*vertiertes Untermenschentum*). I shall never forget the scene when a comrade without an arm came into the room and threw himself on his bed crying. The red rabble, which had never heard a bullet whistle, had assaulted him and torn off all his insignia and medals. We screamed with rage. For this kind of Germany we had sacrificed our blood and our health, and braved all the torments of hell and of a world of enemies for years.

The sense of outrage of the war invalid who carries the marks of his patriotic sacrifice on his body for the rest of his life soon brought him into the *Stahlhelm* and into conflict with the Weimar leadership. He especially disliked the left-wing parties,

> because they failed to accord the front soldier, and especially the war invalid the respect and honor which are unquestionably their due, for they are the first citizens of the state. It was solely the fault of the SPD that a large part of the populace even came to despise the war invalids. You often got the answer thrown into your face: If you hadn't been so stupid and stayed home like me, man, you would still have your leg today. The Socialists even gave me dirty looks because I always wore the ribbon of my Iron Cross in the lapel . . .

There can be little doubt about the central importance of his injury to this man's political development and views.

As for the other ideological themes, the Nordic and German romantics occur most often among respondents stressing the *Fronterlebnis* and those who became disillusioned with the war, but also among the young victory-watchers of the youthful military experience groups. Revanchism as a dominant theme is found most heavily among the *Fronterlebnis* group and the sustained war enthusiasts, who also show up strongly, along with the war invalids and POWs, among the superpatriots. The *Volksgemeinschaft* as the dominant theme is found often among respondents stressing the *Fronterlebnis*, the disaffected, the bitter-enders, and the sustained war enthusiasts, in this order. The cult of Adolf Hitler, finally, was most heavily represented among the disaffected, the bitter-enders, and the sustained war enthusiasts.

The most significant youthful military groups fit in as follows. The victory-watchers and those who loved their non-combat service were made up mostly of revanchists, Nordic-German romantics, and advocates of *Volksgemeinschaft*. The enthusiastic young soldiers were mostly revanchists, superpatriots and, to a lesser degree, antisemites and solidarists. By contrast, the older respondents giving no hint of how they liked their military service have many antisemites among them. Respondents who never served score highest on the Hitler cult, and next highest on the Nordic-German mania and on antisemitism as their dominant motives.

The Impact of the Defeat

Because of the consistent barrage of the German war propaganda and the determined readiness of the hard-liners to believe in a German victory, the sudden death of the German war effort came as rather a surprise. The military collapse had first taken place in faraway Bulgaria and had been preceded by a seemingly vigorous German offensive in the west. And there were enough political rumblings going on in Austro-Hungary and in connection with last-minute constitutional reforms in Germany to obscure the signs of military collapse from the view of the common people at home and at the front. Right-wing politicians and military men, including many who knew better, desperately seized upon the legend that the "victorious" German armies had lost only because they had been "stabbed in the back" by the red revolutionaries or by traitors in high places. Some also claimed that Allied promises of an equitable peace, and especially President Wilson's "just peace," had tricked the German army into laying down arms. "In our faith in Wilson's fourteen points, we German soldiers of the front allowed the most horrible treason of the history of the world to be perpetrated on the people" (no. 32). There had indeed been last-minute calls for a desperate *levée en masse* to defend the fatherland rather than to capitulate completely, but the military command itself at least initially shied away from such a suicidal undertaking.[6] In the long run, and viewed with the benefit of hindsight, a *levée en masse* would probably have cleared the air and might have been, in spite of its undoubted cost in blood and destruction, better than the legacy of an "unfinished war" that led to the Third Reich and on to World War II.

Two-thirds of the Nazis of the Abel collection indicate their feel-

[6] See the account in Werner Conze, *Die Zeit Wilhelms II und die Weimarer Republik*, Tuebingen: Wunderlich, 1964, pp. 112-125.

FD-34: Reaction to German Defeat

	Number	Per cent
Accepts defeat, more or less	125	32.7
Sad, resigned (no further specifics)	57	14.9
Rage at defeat (no specifics)	9	2.3
Blames Kaiser, bad leadership •	12	3.1
Blames weakness of civilians, hunger	4	1.0
Blames trickery by Wilson, Allies	14	3.7
Blames Marxists, Spartakists, other "treason"	138	36.0
Other, such as blames Jews, Freemasons	24	6.3
	383	100.0

ings about the German defeat. One out of three more or less accepted the German defeat or at least failed to argue with it. Another one-third blamed it on "treasonous" forces on the left. A typical response (no. 263) was the following:

Unfortunately, the struggle came to a different end than our soldiers' hearts had dreamt of. Ruthless elements had long prepared to undermine this iron front, to rob it of its faith in the fatherland, and to make it tired of the war. They sold out their own fatherland with their treason. Thus, we returned humiliated but undefeated. . . . Until the last minute, we had hoped that our military leader von Hindenburg, whom we trusted and loved, would succeed after all, but this turned out to be an illusion.

The respondent decided to blame the Jews and the Freemasons with a "sudden, enormous hatred."

The respondents who display strong and diffuse emotion such as sadness or rage, without designating a target, tended to be somewhat younger than the rest. Those who blamed the weakness of the civilians or the old leadership were considerably older than the other groups. Evidently, criticism of the old regime required not so much youthfulness as experience. This group tended to have artisan fathers while the fathers of the emotional respondents were mostly military-civil servants with whom they probably shared a deep sense of discouragement. Respondents who simply accepted the defeat were often farmers' sons and lived in rural areas, where nationalism was not closely associated with social status or class struggle. The group which blamed the "stab in the back" by Marxists was interestingly composed mostly of the sons of workers and businessmen, the two embattled camps of the class struggle. For them, the defeat was just one more nasty trick of the Marxists against the ruling classes. The respondent quoted above (no. 263), although he does not indicate his father's occupation, lived in proletarian poverty while aspiring to a bourgeois life. He wanted to become a physician and later tried just as unsuccessfully to learn agriculture. In this fashion, the impact of war and defeat was closely linked to the social dynamics of the movement.

War, Defeat, and Revolution

Did the attitudes toward the war condition the reactions to defeat and revolution? To begin with, about one-half of both the anti-Marxists and the emotionally diffuse had not served in the military at all. The same is true of a good one-third of those who accepted the defeat. Those who blame the old leadership for the defeat, conversely, had one-third already in the prewar military and more than half among the draftees and volunteers of World War One. Hence, they were hardly representative of the anti-militaristic movement that swept the country in 1917-1918. On the other hand, the deep discouragement and demoralization of the defeat also expressed itself in an extraordinary amount of hatred and suspicion directed against everyone. The anti-Marxists and those who blame the old leadership for the defeat, for example, also stand out together among the bitter-enders who were hostile toward draft-dodgers and subversives, as well as among those who stressed their *Fronterlebnis*. As for the young victory-watchers and non-combat military, over one-half of them blamed the Marxists and Spartakists for the defeat and some tended to blame the old leadership and the civilians. With such an excess of hatred being freely dispensed, who could escape it?

The attitudes toward the revolutionaries follow predictable patterns. Two-thirds of those who accepted the defeat also more or less accepted the alleged revolution. Similar numbers of the respondents who blamed the Marxists, Spartakists, and mutineers for the defeat also blamed them for the revolution. About one-fourth of those who blamed the defeat on the old leadership, the weakness of the civilians, and Wilson's or Allied trickery, also blamed the Kaiser and the old order, the Western powers, and unspecified street rabble for the revolution. Substantial numbers of this group put the blame on the Jews and on the parties of the Weimar government coalition (SPD, DDP and the Center). The emotional respondents, again, tended to stress the responsibility of the Marxists, and of the Kaiser, the West, and the street rabble for the revolution. To significant numbers of the Nazi respondents, the causes of defeat and revolution were the same, the same fatal *junctim* (linkage) which Prince Max von Baden had hoped to avoid in October 1918 when he tried unsuccessfully to keep separate the introduction of parliamentary democracy and General Ludendorff's insistent request for an immediate ceasefire.

To what extent did their feelings toward defeat and revolution induce these attitudinal groups to engage in counterrevolutionary activities? The most involved group were the anti-Marxists, who often enlisted in conservative-bourgeois organizations, or in the Free Corps and various vigilante organizations fighting domestic enemies and who, of course, display great hostility to the "red" insurgents. They were also the most involved in physical violence and thus constituted a kind of class-struggle troop against the Marxist revolt. The least involved were respondents who accepted the defeat —probably because of their youth or rural background—and the emotional respondents who also may have been too young to get involved. To the extent that they became involved, the former tended to be in *voelkisch* action groups or in Free Corps action against the Poles, while the latter often belonged to republican or left-wing groups, or identified with the Kapp *putsch*. The respondents who blamed the old leadership tended to be in the Free Corps or the vigilantes, or to be involved in the Kapp *putsch*.

What was their reaction to the multiple challenges of the crisis year of 1923? Again the anti-Marxists were the most involved group and a good third of them were either in a *voelkisch* action group such as the early NSDAP or sympathetic to the Hitler *putsch*. They, together with the emotional group, were also the most involved in political violence. Those who blamed the old leadership for the German defeat had a similar record except that they also had a few men in conservative parties and militant veterans groups like *Stahlhelm*. The respondents who accepted the defeat of 1918 were the least involved in 1923. Their involvement tended to be with various legitimate political parties, republican, conservative, and *voelkisch*. The emotionally diffuse responses of 1918 belong to the less involved of 1923, of whom the largest contingent claims to have been sympathetic to the beer-hall *putsch* or involved in fighting the occupation. The prominent role in the early *voelkisch* and Nazi movements of those who blamed the German defeat on Marxists and Spartakists faded away in the reconstituted NSDAP of 1925 and later, as did that of the war enthusiasts in Nazi political violence.

Defeat and Nazi Ideology

Even though the effects of war and defeat appear to slacken off after 1923, the question still remains whether the attitudes toward the

German defeat are related to the main ideological themes of the respondents after they joined the NSDAP. In other words, to what extent was the Nazi rank and file motivated by revanchism rather than by other preoccupations? To begin with, revanchism constituted the dominant theme for only 5.6% of all the respondents. Another 21.3% were superpatriots, the only other theme we could relate to the shock of the military defeat. Together they make up 26.9%, which is considerably exceeded, for example, by the respondents who blamed the old leadership. Revanchism alone accounts for 11.9% of this group, and represents its most prominent motive. The other groups are close to the average of revanchism and superpatriotism. But among the anti-Marxists, for example, there was a greater disproportion of Nordic or German romantics as well as many Hitler cultists and advocates of the *Volksgemeinschaft*. Among those who simply accepted the defeat there were proportionally more antisemites and solidarists and among the emotional respondents, there was a greater share of devotees of Hitler's cult of personality. It would appear, then, that revanchism, and even superpatriotism, was not all that important to the Nazi rank and file. The anti-Marxist strain seems to have been a more reliable link from the reactions to defeat and revolution to the early Nazi party.

Cultural Shock and Alienation

Returning home we no longer found an honest German people, but a mob stirred up by its lowest instincts. Whatever virtues were once found among the Germans seemed to have sunk once and for all into the muddy flood. . . . Promiscuity, shamelessness, and corruption ruled supreme. German women seemed to have forgotten their German ways. German men seemed to have forgotten their sense of honor and honesty. Jewish writers and the Jewish press could "go to town" with impunity dragging everything into the dirt. They stopped not even before our most sacred feelings and dared to mock our crucified Lord in public exhibitions. While criminals and Jewish "big-time operators" were wallowing in feasts and traitors were floating in champagne, the poorest of the poor hungered and suffered the most dire need.

The writer of this purple prose was a retired officer (no. 43), born in 1878, who clearly mirrors some of the symptoms of the "cultural shock" experienced by many soldiers and some others on their first encounters with postwar society. Although much of the verbiage has political intent or may merely repeat phrases heard elsewhere, there are certain authentic elements that deserve attention. One of them is the reference to sexual dissoluteness, another the stress on dishonesty or a lack of a sense of honor. There are also the frequent mentions of indecent feasts, drunken orgies, or other debauches of the "beatnik" revolutionaries or Communists which tell more about the critic than about his target (see nos. 23, 24, 30 and 39). Another obvious manifestation are phrases such as "chaos without discipline and order." Another element are references to unusual clothes or hair styles, often connected to outrages against uniforms, officer's insignia, and other symbols of old. The criticism of literature and the press in itself also reflects cultural discontents because these had been neither so prominent nor so "socially corrosive" in their content before the war. The antisemitic note not only is to be expected of a Nazi sample, but mirrors also the linking of cultural defensiveness with the more prominent Jewish role in these professions after the war. Similarly, the objections to internationalism, parliamentary democracy, and the multi-party state not only

FD-31: The Cultural Shock of 1918-1919

	Number	Per cent
No shock experiences	176	30.2
⎡ "Moral, social disintegration"	35	6.0
⎣ Reference to beatniks, dissolute women,		
immoral Communists	23	3.9
"Absence of order, discipline," honesty	107	18.4
⎡ Shock at the disparagement of military		
honor, symbols, flags	55	9.4
⎢ Shock at internationalism, pacifism	31	5.3
⎣ Shock at institutional changes, end of		
monarchy, multi-partyism	46	7.9
⎡ Shock at new elites (politicians, the		
⎢ press, Jews, etc.)	93	16.0
⎣ Several of these, other response	17	2.9
	583	100.0

are political, but include strong cultural reactions to the demise of authoritarian monarchy and its replacement by presumably alien, un-German ways of politics.

The examination of the intensity and kind of cultural shock reported is essentially a measurement of the sense of alienation which overcame the respondents face to face with postwar society. The most intense alienation is represented by the themes of "social disintegration" such as immorality and sexual dissoluteness, since they unravel the web of primary relationships formed in the most basic processes of childhood socialization. Next in intensity is "order and discipline" which constitutes over one-fourth of the cultural shock responses and represents more external aspects of primary socialization. The traditional attachment to the symbols, rituals, beliefs, and institutions of the old order after it has passed implies a relatively mild degree of alienation, although it does relate to the individual and collective sense of identity of the respondent. To a military-civil servant whose whole life was built around them, their disparagement or destruction was, of course, a shattering experience, more so than to a Wilhelminian civilian. A civilian of normal mental ability, in fact, could hardly have observed the imperial military and bureaucratic scene and the foibles of the Kaiser without some mental reservations.

Many of the older Nazi respondents, it will be recalled, viewed the old leadership and the social order of the empire with considerable misgivings and were quite ready to blame it for the German defeat and the "revolution" of 1918. The "shock at the new Weimar elites" in politics, business, and the press consequently was an ambiguous kind of cultural shock. It may have been mere political or personal distaste for the indecorous behavior of proletarian or lower middle-class careerists and newly-rich *parvenus*. But it could also reek of a prejudice against Jews, aliens, or intellectuals that goes far deeper into primary socialization processes. The political assassinations of Erzberger and Rathenau which evoked grisly expressions of sympathy in some of the respondents testify to the depth of the emotions stirred. The cult of the leader-savior, on the one hand, and murderous hatred for incumbent leaders are the simplistic recourse in any crisis of very disturbed minds. Their disturbance, moreover, very likely grew from a disturbed childhood.

These categories of FD-31 were regrouped for purposes of cross-tabulation by combining the groups complaining about moral disintegration and the beatniks, etc., under the new label of *social disintegration*. Furthermore, we collapsed all the traditional complaints about the disparagement of symbols, internationalism, and the institutional changes into one category and, finally, combined the last two categories into one.

Social Profiles of Cultural Shock Groups

It stands to reason that the group which reports no cultural shock should be heavily weighted with persons too young to have served in World War One. However, there are significant numbers who were older but report no cultural shock, especially among older respondents who never served in the war. And, still more important, a considerable share of those too young to have served strongly express the themes of cultural shock, especially the traditional shock at the demise of the old rituals and institutions and, frequently, the authoritarian complaint about the "lack of order and discipline." There is a twofold explanation for this phenomenon. We have seen the extraordinary extent to which youngsters during World War One were socialized into enthusiastic identification with the war effort and the social forces behind it. Thus it is plausible that they would pick up these concerns from their elders. Furthermore, the alienation of rebellious youth from their own society is naturally similar to the original meaning of cultural shock. They feel like strangers in their own country, contrasting its flaws to the imagined ideal ways of a utopia, or of the supposedly good old times.

The ages of the cultural shock groups, then, differ considerably between the youngest, who are concentrated among those reporting no shock, and the oldest group, which complains about the various themes of social disintegration, often with a sex angle. Half of the former were born after the turn of the century and half of the latter

before 1893. The complaint about the new leaders of Weimar society is also a relatively "old" one, leaving only the traditional and
authoritarian reactions which also enjoyed some popularity among
the postwar generation, as will be recalled.

There are also hidden relationships between religion and a propensity for certain kinds of cultural shock. The rise of the Nazi
movement has often been connected with the disintegration of German Protestantism, and the majority of the Abel respondents who
indicate their religion (only one-third do) were Protestants. But it
is among the Catholic Nazis that the traditional themes about the
end of monarchy, etc., are sounded most often, perhaps because
Catholics are more conscious of institutions, symbols, and rituals.
The Protestant Nazis, on the other hand, have the edge in the
themes of social or moral disintegration, perhaps a topic dear to
the Protestant conscience. Respondents who failed to state their religion deplore the absence of discipline and order and the new Weimar leadership. Going one step further and contrasting a person's
religion with the predominant religion of his chief area of residence,
we find that cultural shock seems to be highly related to religious
dissensus or the presence of different ways of life. Both Protestants
and Catholics in areas dominated by their own coreligionists show
far less cultural shock than Protestants or Catholics in the minority
or in evenly mixed areas or, for that matter, than persons who failed
to indicate their affiliation. Evidently religious minority status, or
conflict, or relative secularism increases a person's vulnerability to
cultural shock of this sort. The respondents in mixed areas, particularly, stand out with themes of shock about social disintegration and
the new leadership, while the religious-minority Nazi was rattled
more by the institutional changes. The authoritarian response was
more typical of Nazis who failed to indicate their religion.

These reactions overlap also with those conditioned by the respondents' location. Respondents from the border areas show the
least cultural shock, and those of foreign background or experience
show the most. Respondents from the occupied areas complain particularly about social disintegration and also about the new Weimar
elites and the institutional changes including the internationalism
and pacifism of Weimar. Spatial mobility appears to increase cultural shock in proportion to the distances traversed. Respondents
reporting no cultural shock tend to have been living in the same
small town or rural community where they were born; rural-urban
migrants predominate in all the other groups save one, the authoritarian advocates of discipline and order who tend to be highly
mobile among cities.

As for their location at the time of the depression, the respondents with traditional themes of cultural shock were nearly as rural and small-town-based as those of no cultural shock. The fall of monarchy and the disparagement of traditional symbols and rituals was felt more painfully in these tradition-bound regions than in the big city. The occupations of the fathers of the different groups further confirm this impression. Farmer and artisan fathers tend to have been typical of the traditional and the no-shock groups. Military-civil servant fathers were concentrated among the social-disintegration, the traditional, and the authoritarian groups. And businessmen and worker fathers are found mostly among the authoritarians and the group shocked at the new Weimar elites. It is remarkable that this double-barrelled authoritarianism, a concern with law and order and with the "right leadership," should occur along this major fault-line of the imperial society.

As for their social mobility, the respondents who express shock at the Weimar leadership and those reporting no cultural shock at all were the least mobile. Families in social decline were frequent among respondents with themes of social disintegration or among the authoritarians. The social disintegrationists interestingly were by far the least upwardly mobile, and they also had little taste for the *Volksgemeinschaft* except for solidarity toward the outside. Evidently, this kind of alienation affects most tellingly those who can hardly hold their own in the social pecking order. The most mobile were the traditionals and respondents reporting no cultural shock, who stand out for urban upward mobility. Probably because of their age, large numbers of the latter either show no class-consciousness at all or argue for solidarity from below. The respondents with traditional responses, and also the authoritarians, stress the *Volksgemeinschaft* from the middle. The traditional and law-and-order kinds of alienation are evidently not very severe, but closely related to social change and adaptability.

Reactions to Defeat, Revolution, Occupation

Over fourth-fifths of the young who report no shock simply accepted the defeat. In nearly the same numbers, they also accepted the "revolution" of 1918. The traditionalists, however, blamed the revolution on the Spartakists, on the old order, or international Bolshevism, and on the Weimar parties. The respondents who were upset about the new leadership of Weimar society set exactly the same accents, except that they blamed the Jews rather than the Bolsheviks. The authoritarians tended to put the blame on international Bolshevism or on the Kaiser, Western intrigues, or on the "rabble."

The respondents concerned about social disintegration again blamed the Jews and the Bolsheviks for the revolution.

What actions resulted from these feelings? Law-and-order turns out to be a mobilizing, even a militarizing kind of alienation. The authoritarians in disproportionate numbers enlisted in the Free Corps and in vigilante organizations to fight against insurgents and foreign enemies. An artisan's son born in 1902 (no. 426) who throughout the war had been dreaming of enlisting and becoming a hero describes his despair at the "red treason," the criticisms of the empire, and the public indifference.

> Quietly I was hoping the old soldiers' spirit would come through and chase the enemy out of the country. Nothing happened and I turned to my studies in disappointment. Then suddenly, in the midst of my [polytechnic] studies, they were looking for volunteers. Upper Silesia is in danger! The enemy is inside already! No sooner had I read the poster than I stood in the office to enlist. With hundreds of others I went to Upper Silesia. There my urge to become a soldier finally could take effect.

Quite a few of the authoritarians also participated in the Kapp *putsch* of 1920. The traditionals mostly express strong hatred for the insurgents and participated or sympathized with Kapp. Some were with the Free Corps. The respondents complaining about the social disintegration of postwar society express anti-insurgent feelings, joined organizations where they would receive military training, or participated in the Kapp affair. The respondents who are shocked by the new Weimar elites mostly vent anti-insurgent feelings. Some were in the Free Corps or in vigilante groups. It is interesting to note that the few respondents who participated or sympathized with the insurgents are concentrated among those who experienced no cultural shock, only half of whom participated in any counter-revolutionary activity at all.

Only a little more than a third of the respondents were in conflict with the forces occupying German territory. The group that experienced no cultural shock also was the least involved with the occupation. The traditionals have relatively the largest number of persons who participated in the passive resistance or in violent acts and who often were fined, jailed, or expelled from the occupied area. The authoritarians and those who were shocked by the new Weimar leadership were the least involved in these experiences, although they express a strong hatred of the occupation and like to link it with the Weimar government or the left-wing movements. In 1923, the traditionalists, the authoritarians, and the respondents shocked by "social disintegration" tended to be in *voelkisch* action groups, including the early NSDAP, or to sympathize with Hitler's *putsch*. Traditionals, authoritarians, and respondents shocked by the new leadership were also well-represented in militant veterans' groups such as the *Stahlhelm*.

National Socialism and Political Violence

In fact, we can observe the changing nature of the membership of the rising NSDAP during the main periods of the republic. In 1919-1921, the *voelkisch* groups, including the NSDAP, drew most of their support from respondents complaining about social disintegration and from the authoritarians, although the latter patronized the veterans and conservative organizations far more heavily than they did the *voelkisch* groups. In the period 1922-1924, however, the *voelkisch* and NSDAP membership dramatically began to outstrip the conservative and militant veterans' groups among all cultural shock groups except for only one, the authoritarians, who still had strong ties to the militant veterans' organizations. Over a fourth of the other three groups who report cultural shock were in *voelkisch* or Nazi organizations. By 1925-1928 the Nazi/*voelkisch* element was already two-thirds in all groups, including the respondents reporting no cultural shock. Only the traditionals were somewhat lower because now it was they who still had substantial numbers in the *Stahlhelm* and in the conservative parties. By the end of 1929, the membership avalanche was in full progress, with the authoritarians in the forefront (74.7%) and the traditionals trailing (62.2%) in party membership. Between 1925 and 1929 many authoritarians in our sample had evidently given up on the militant veterans' groups and discovered the NSDAP. The peak year of 1930 nearly evened out all the shares with the exception of the traditionals, who were still trailing.

An even more consistent picture of the varying political activism of these groups emerges from an examination of their active involvement in political violence and demonstrations in the first five years, 1919 to 1924. It is the authoritarians who indeed seem to have turned their complaint of lack of "order and discipline" into direct action in all kinds of organizations. They came closest perhaps to Waite's "vanguard" or Sauer's "military desperadoes."[1]

[1] Wolfgang Sauer makes the point in his article on National Socialism that historians have not so far paid enough attention to the role of military desperadoes in the early NSDAP. "National Socialism: Totalitarianism or Fascism?" *American Historical Review*, vol. 72 (July 1967), 411.

But the traditionals were not far behind. In later years the leading role in violence was less with these groups than with the youngest group which did not report any cultural shock. It is the latter who belonged in the largest numbers to the SA. The respondents sounding the social disintegration themes of cultural shock were the least violent through 1929-1930 and later as well, although they made up for this by demonstrating, electioneering, and proselytizing for the cause. Apart from their age, the intense alienation of this group evidently did not lend itself to violent aggression in the same way "discipline and order" concerns do.

Cultural Shock and Ideology

Since cultural shock is a measurement less of an external event than of an underlying propensity to react in certain ways, its significance is more likely to be "lasting" than is the effect of war and defeat. The relationship between cultural shock and later ideological attitudes, therefore, is significant and pronounced. The dominant ideological themes of the respondents after they joined the Nazi party were distributed over the cultural-shock groups as follows. The group without shock stands out with antisemitism and *Volksgemeinschaft* as their main themes. The authoritarians show disproportionate interest in revanchism, authoritarianism, and the Hitler cult as dominant themes. Respondents who deplore the "social disintegration" of postwar society include large numbers of antisemites, revanchists, and Hitler cultists. The traditional shock group is particularly strong on Nordic or German cultural romanticism, as well as on the Hitler cult and the *Volksgemeinschaft*. The chief motifs of the respondents shocked by the new Weimar elites, finally, turn out to be superpatriotism and antisemitism. In this fashion the underlying preoccupations tended to match and form patterns, "discipline and order" with revanchism and authoritarianism, fear of "social disintegration" with antisemitism and the leader cult, the shock of the end of monarchy and the disparagement of symbols and rituals with cultural romanticism, leader cult, and solidarism, and the objections to Weimar leaders with antisemitism and strident nationalism.[2]

The perception of the Weimar Republic is similarly colored. The traditionals, for example, see the republic as a "liberalistic-Marxist system" or through similarly traditional, anti-capitalist spectacles. They also pick out the "multi-party state" as a chief flaw, evidently

---

[2] On a pragmatic-ideological scale, the authoritarians and traditionalists are more often pragmatic and the other three groups ideological.

comparing the republic with its predecessor. The authoritarians stress the same criticisms of the republic, though probably from a different point of view. The respondents who emphasize themes of social disintegration, on the other hand, stress that the republic is run by Jews, or run in an "un-German manner," as well as that its leaders are Marxists, or the "red" and "black" (clerical) parties. These criticisms, together with the traditional anti-liberal ones, are shared by those who objected to the new Weimar elites to begin with.

Respondents who report some kind of cultural shock also show a good deal more ethnocentricity, other than antisemitism, than those who experienced no such shock. The authoritarians and those who object to the new Weimar elites, in particular, are preoccupied with their aversion to the "encirclement of Germany" and other foreign intrigues as well as with aliens or "the supranational forces," i.e, the Catholic church and international finance. The traditionalists and the social disintegrationists, by comparison, are more concerned with the aliens and supranational forces, or they aver the "inferiority" of all other nationalities. Here as before, the generational differences account for much of the changing outlook.

Underlying Attitudes

It is with their underlying attitudes even more than with overt ideological rationalizations that the patterns begin to match. In their attitude toward authority, for example, the authoritarian shock group turns out to have been most hostile to the pluralistic "party state" of Weimar (59.8%) and not particularly partial to the extremes of the leadership cult. Respondents shocked about "social disintegration" in 1918 show a similar reaction. Those who suffered no shock, on the other hand, are most obsessed with order, even to the point of criticizing the police for not maintaining order. Since they were the youngest Nazis and the call for "discipline and order" in 1918 was also popular among the youngest cohorts, it may well be true that this was an age-related preoccupation typical of young right-wing extremists and growing, perhaps, from their adolescent difficulties in establishing a stable relationship to paternal authority or its substitutes. The traditional respondents, by contrast, tend to express considerable hostility toward police and government and to make an extraordinary fetish of their leader cult. Respondents who were shocked by the new Weimar elites share the same sentiments, especially the extreme leadership cult.

The particular objects of the respondents' hostility vary from group to group. The traditionalists concentrated their hatred on the

Marxists of various shadings, a preference shared, along with anti-semitism, by respondents shocked by the new Weimar leaders. The authoritarians and respondents who report no shock in dispropor-tionate numbers express hostility toward conservative or liberal reactionaries and the Catholic church. Respondents without shock and those who complain about social disintegration instead focus their hostility upon Jews and Marxists or upon a list of hate objects encompassing all these and more.

Among those displaying different shadings of antisemitism, the authoritarians show the least and the respondents shocked by social disintegration the most overt prejudice. The traditionalists and au-thoritarians stand out with mild verbal projections. The sudden out-break of *Judenkoller* tends to occur most often among respondents complaining about the new Weimar leaders or about social disin-tegration in 1918. The latter two as well as respondents reporting no shock also like to tell of alleged personal encounters with Jews. The full-fledged aggressive syndrome, in the form of perceived threatening conspiracies and hints of counterthreats is heaviest among respondents shocked by social disintegration or reporting no cultural shock at all. The complaint of social disintegration is evidently most highly related to antisemitic prejudice.

The prominent role of the respondents who complain of "moral and social disintegration" or allude to sexual dissoluteness suggests a closer look at some of these respondents to gain more insight into their personal histories. One of them, an older civil servant turned innkeeper, born in Potsdam in 1868 (no. 156), vents his bitter scorn against the Kaiser and the Prussian aristocracy while ac-knowledging "the low point of public morals" and the deep sense of German humiliation in 1918. He joined the SPD temporarily and even held a local office in it until his virulent antisemitism drove him on to the DSP and the Nazis. Another respondent born the same year (no. 132) was a colonial officer and Prussian aristocrat who as a young officer encountered Social Democratic recruits for the first time in 1893. "There were Hamburg dockworkers, Halle in-dustrial workers, and Berliners, often subhuman types, pimps, and other sinister elements. The rolls had special marks next to the names of Social Democratic agitators and Social Democrats. In class, their skeptical cold eyes instead of the usual, loyally trusting glances were on me." After his colonial and war-time experience, he witnessed "the moral disintegration at home and . . . the human meanness, cowardice, and cravenness" of the change-over from the old society to the new to the point "that I can still feel nausea rising in me today when I think of it." He does not reveal any antisemitic or any other ignoble prejudice except between the lines when he relates his varied colonial experiences or the encounter with Social Democrats, but perhaps officers and aristocrats were above that sort of thing.

Another Prussian civil servant, born in 1885 (no. 28), tells how as an officer he was ready for the call to the last resistance with pistol and hand grenade in September 1918. When no such call was issued, he took his "regular (*ordnungsmaessige*) vacation" in East Prussia, but was back in time for the fateful day when "mobs with Jewish-looking girls tore off the insignia on officers' uniforms." Physically aggressive against Marxist workers and allegedly Jewish strangers, he was also in close touch with the military unit that murdered Karl Liebknecht and Rosa Luxemburg, with the Kapp *putsch*, and with Ludendorff and Hitler in 1923. His constant burrowing in the bureaucratic molehills of the Weimar Republic was evidently supported by the DNVP, and by militant veterans', and patriotic civil service groups. His rabid antisemitism was nearly matched by his venom against the Catholic church and the Marxist leaders.

A very popular phrase descriptive of the allegedly gypsy-like appearance of red demonstrators in 1918 is that they "ambled along with the music of shawms, accompanied by girls with red scarves, singing away." The respondent from whose *vita* this phrase is quoted was a disciple of the fired school principal Ahlwardt, who had founded an antisemitic association before the war.[3] After the war the respondent made the rounds of *voelkisch* action groups and was involved in the vigilante *Einwohnerwehr* and the Kapp *putsch*. His violent antisemitism was matched by his aggressiveness toward alleged Communists. He reports having once "poured water on a demonstration of Communist women in the dark [outside his window] in order to sober them up." Another frequent image of the "red gypsy caravan" is an Antonioniesque vision of shouting or singing young people in the back of speeding trucks festooned with red banners, dragging the imperial flag through the dust.[4] Another

[3] See also the account of Ahlwardt's career in Peter G. J. Pulzer, *The Rise of Political Anti-Semitism in Germany and Austria*, New York: Wiley, 1964, pp. 112-116 and the sources quoted there.

[4] A variation on the theme is "Liebknecht, the Jew, riding on the running board of a cab with the red flag, shouting, gesticulating, and preaching hatred. . . . Red soldiers, drunk and with red armbands, looting," which was offered as a Berlin scene of disgust in November 1918 (no. 24). The writer is an antisemitic clerk who in 1933 briefly ran the concentration camp Oranienburg for political prisoners. He also adds to his de-

image is that of the returning soldiers dancing in drunken intoxication or the people in revelry, forgetful of the fatherland (no. 133).

The front generation is well-represented with a building contractor's son from Munich, born in 1893 (no. 55), who served throughout the war and sustained major injuries. He reports on his return in 1918: "The sad pictures of red rule which we saw while marching back deeply depressed us front-line soldiers. We just could not and would not understand that this was the upshot of four and a half years of our struggle. . . . The homeland had become so alien and un-German to me and I felt a longing and desire for a new order which, on the basis of the *Fronterlebnis*, would resurrect the tormented fatherland in better and wonderful ways." His feelings led him into the early NSDAP in Munich, although he is rather cryptic about the extent of his involvement and gives no hint of prejudice.

The complaint of social disintegration is harder to find among the postwar generation. There is a baker's son from a small Odenwald village, born in 1901 (no. 197), who tells of his conflict of conscience in 1918 after his erstwhile buddies boasted to him how they had mistreated officers and looted the barracks in town. "A hard inner struggle began for me. Should I go along with this new tendency to blaspheme all that is German and sacrosanct or not? Many good people became Social Democrats and told us what wonderful times were ahead." His family and a former teacher of his decided to buck the trend and found themselves isolated in the village. His antisemitism soon turned him into a militant anti-Marxist and led him into various militant patriotic groups and to the DNVP, until the Nazis came along.

The respondents' attitudes toward their political enemies are another measure of their subjective orientations toward Weimar politics. Nearly half, and more with the traditionals and those without cultural shock, express a liking for their political enemies and often say that they would have liked to win them over. The traditionalists otherwise tend to view them as an abstract conspiracy or as traitors who "sold out Germany," a view that smacks of the reactions to defeat and revolution and is also popular with the authoritarians. Respondents who were shocked by social disintegration or by the new Weimar leaders viewed their political enemies as subhuman criminals, rodents, or as immoral or unclean. The complaint of social

---

scription of postwar decadence a lot of ex-convicts and fraudulent, corrupt deals, innocents being murdered, and big-time operators feasting. "Honest work was punished and the corrupt became rich. Cafés with whores as waitresses appeared everywhere."

disintegration thus is linked once more to *outré* attitudes expressed in the language of the gutter.

The attitudes of the cultural-shock groups toward violence round out the picture. Half of the traditionalists, for example, more or less accepted violence as the price of victory. Those who were shocked by social disintegration, and the authoritarians, tend either to glory in their physical involvement in political violence or to express regret about it. The young respondents without any shock also tend to show either an aggressive sadism or the curious masochism of chiefly counting their own injuries from street violence. This masochism is strong also among the traditionalists and those who expressed shock at the new Weimar leaders.

In the Nazi Party

The respondents without cultural shock by reason of their youth were most heavily (60.7%) enrolled in the stormtrooper (SA) movement or the SS. They were the privates of the movement, so to speak. Those shocked by social disintegration actually were the least (41.2%) involved in SA and SS and even less in actual violence, possibly for reasons of age. Higher stormtrooper offices were held chiefly by the authoritarian and the traditional groups, many of whom held military ranks or titles from the war. The most violent while in the Nazi movement were evidently the "order-and-discipline" people and respondents without cultural shock. The traditionalists and those shocked by the Weimar elites were mostly content with electioneering and demonstrations.

What was the great attraction of the Nazi movement for them? Those who objected to the Weimar leadership often tended to get a sense of personal integration out of fighting for the Nazi vision of utopia. Sometimes they were expecting concrete personal gains such as jobs or careers. The traditionalists were mostly attracted by the Hitler cult and the relative classlessness of the NSDAP, a view shared by the authoritarians except for one additional feature. The authoritarians, respondents without shock, and those shocked at social disintegration seem to have felt a sense of personal integration from the struggle itself. Presumably, political struggle, just like war itself, can relieve inner tensions and channel hostility. The last-mentioned group also was rather attracted by the Hitler cult.

As a result of active party membership, many respondents had to endure various kinds of personal friction in the different social settings. The youngest group, the one without any cultural shock, typically met political friction mainly in the schools or the family or in the neighborhood. The other four groups encountered it more on the job or in the form of being fired or boycotted for their political views.

Their expectations in 1934 mirror some of these economic predicaments. Especially the young and those shocked about the new Weimar elites expected tangible economic benefits or payoffs for themselves. The respondents with themes of social disintegration stress more the theme of German national resurgence in Europe and of social and economic recovery of the country. The authoritarians dreamed of the one thousand-year Reich, of the nation reborn (the most frequent response), and of socio-economic recovery. National rebirth was a theme that also attracted many of those who had not expressed any cultural shock. The dream of the one thousand-year Reich, laced with visions of internal purges and revenge on the political adversary, also motivated disproportionate numbers of traditionalists. The respondents who expressed objections to the new Weimar leaders also tended to stress national resurgence.

Personality and Cultural Shock

The attitudinal dimensions need certain final touches in order to become profiles of personality. One such touch is the question of the kind and quality of political acumen which each of these groups displays. There are some notable differences in their formal education. The best-educated are the traditionalists with one-third, and the authoritarians with 30.4%, who completed at least a secondary education (*mittlere Reife*). The least-educated are the respondents who sound themes of social disintegration and those who are shocked about the new Weimar leaders, with around one-fourth at the secondary level. Thus it may not be surprising to find about one-third of the traditionalists and authoritarians among those who show high or medium political acumen, of a pragmatic or ideological sort.

Of the groups of lower political acumen, however, the respondents critical of the new Weimar elites and those complaining about social disintegration are the least-educated and also the most anti-semitic, as the reader may recall. Nearly half of their number is in the large "low, ideological" category, which appropriately marks typical minions of a totalitarian party. After all, it is the purpose of totalitarian ideology to supply guidance beyond the reach of a man's natural intelligence, especially when the latter is hampered by certain obsessive concerns. The social disintegration respondents, furthermore, are almost absent from another low acumen category, "low, pragmatic (narrow)," in which the authoritarians and respondents without any cultural shock are prominent. This category is probably a haven for many a Nazi military-civil servant or for youthful, action-oriented respondents of comparable narrowness. There is one more low-acumen category which combines outright stupidity with a kind of romantic, or quixotic, blurry vision of politics such as may characterize some rather young extremists. In this category there are indeed many respondents without cultural shock, but also a disproportionate number of those who were shocked at social disintegration.

We can ask ourselves what was the chief formative or most influential experience in each respondent's life, bearing in mind that we are dealing with subjectively projected themes rather than with reliable assessments of the impact of external events. Since the psychodrama of individual lives can never be completely separated from the external events, however, the latter show up of necessity if they happened to coincide with important formative periods in the respondent's life. Up to one-half of the respondents, for example, relate the war, the *Fronterlebnis*, or the defeat or "revolution" of 1918 as the central event in their lives. These events stand out for 52% of the social disintegration group and 46-50% of the other groups save the young respondents without cultural shock, of whom only 26.9% give them such a central position. The latter group instead accords the central role to the experiences of comradeship in youth organizations (19.6%), being unemployed (11.1%), or educational or literary influences (19%). This dichotomy between the impact of the war and defeat and the different life experiences of Weimar youth appears to be a watershed in the motivational topography of the rising Nazi movement.

If we take the groups one by one, the relative prominence of these formative or influential experiences is as follows. For the respondents complaining about social disintegration, the events of 1918 and alleged encounters or episodes with Jews or aliens were still more important than the war itself, while the experience of comradeship in a youth organization, which was so important to the postwar generation, plays no role at all. To the traditionalists, by comparison, it is educational or literary experiences or social snubs which were important, though not so much as the experiences of war and defeat. The authoritarians are the only group outside the no-shock respondents who accord about as much importance to youth-group comradeship as to war or defeat. As may be recalled, they include a number of younger respondents without military service. To the respondents who expressed shock at the new Weimar leaders, the events of 1918, alleged encounters with Jews or aliens, and social snubs all came before the impact of the war itself.

For the respondents without cultural shock, finally, the priority of formative experiences runs from youthful comradeship to educational influences, joblessness, and alleged encounters. The euphoria of youths coming together, bad books and teachers, unemployment and antisemitism evidently led this generation to join the brown herd of lemmings.

There is an alternative way to judge personality types by raising the question of pathology: What in each case seemed to be the most obvious abnormality about the attitudinal posture presented by the respondent? Unlike the previous question, this one could be answered for only not quite two-thirds of the respondents, although the group profiles are fairly clear. Thus the authoritarians, for example, include a high percentage of persons suffering from intense cultural shock (37.9%) and of extreme devotees of the leadership cult (21.3%). The respondents complaining about social disintegration include a disproportionate number (25.5%) of accounts characterized by paranoia, irrationality, incoherence, or a gross lack of balance. They also have more than their share of intense culture shock (31.4%). The traditionalists show a large share (30.9%) of excessive, self-effacing group conformity, to the point where the life of the individual appears to have been swallowed up by the life of the movement. They also have their share (30.9%) of the highly culturally shocked. Those shocked by the new Weimar elites include many paranoid or irrational persons (18.3%), respondents of high cultural shock (36.6%), and people characterized by a high degree of personal insecurity, masochism, or self-pity (12.7%). Those without any cultural shock, finally, stand out for high group conformity (41.9%), high personal insecurity and self-pity (16.1%), and extreme Hitler cult (27.4%). This of course is the psychological profile of the postwar generation in contrast to the other, older groups.

FOUR

Foreign Occupation: School of Violence

It will be remembered what a profound and unsettling influence involvement in the postwar border area struggles had on some respondents. Being uprooted and driven off because their home areas were ceded to another country was often an important reason why some persons developed an outraged superpatriotism which eventually led them into the Nazi party. It may also account for the early Nazi landslides in certain border areas of East Prussia, north of Breslau (Wroclaw), and east of Frankfurt an der Oder. But its effect was short-lived and local as compared to that of the occupation in the west, which affected large areas normally dominated by the Catholic Center party and therefore relatively immune to the brown virus. In the areas west of the Rhine such as the Palatinate,[1] the foreign occupation began with the end of the war and lasted for nearly the duration of the unhappy republic. The occupation of the Ruhr area to the east of the Rhine river began in January 1923 and lasted for about two years. The late historian Koppel S. Pinson described the German reaction: "German public opinion was only united all the more in an orgy of nationalistic frenzy. . . . A flood of propaganda was let loose, both in Germany and throughout the world, charging the French with carrying out a policy of terror, brutality, rape, destruction, abuse of justice, sadism, and willful creation of starvation and disease."[2] Much of this right-wing propa-

---

[1] The Treaty of Versailles had provided also for four bridgeheads, Cologne, Koblenz, Mainz, and Kehl, to be occupied, presumably in order to secure France and Belgium from German aggression. See also the exaggerated account of Gauleiter Josef Grohe, *Der politische Kampf im Rheinland nach den ersten Weltkrieg*, Bonn: Universitaetsdruckerei, 1941, or the book by Hans Spethmann, *Der Ruhrkampf 1923-1925*, Berlin: Hobbing, 1933, which has on its cover a picture of a greedy French capitalist in coat-tails and a proletarian German Michel standing on top of the Ruhr industrial area.

[2] *Modern Germany, Its History and Civilization*, 2nd ed., New York: Macmillan, 1966, pp. 430-431. See also, P. Wentzke, *Ruhrkampf, Einbruch und Abwehr im rheinisch-westfaelischen* Industriegebiet, 2 vols.,

ganda campaign may have exaggerated French harshness and the deeds of the patriotic underground. Nevertheless, the actual conflict and the emotions generated on the German side seem to have played a major motivating role in the progress of many of the Abel respondents toward the Nazi movement. In this, the anti-occupation struggle bears some resemblance to the uses of the Young Plan campaign of 1929 by which the right wing succeeded in mobilizing hundreds of thousands who later joined the Nazi surge into power.

One out of four of the respondents of the Abel collection was in conflict with the occupation or expressed strong sentiments toward it. Very few Nazis of the collection who were living in the occupied areas fail to accord their feelings toward the occupation major importance in their account of their political development. These cate-

FD-33: Anti-Occupation Attitude or Experience

	Number	Per cent
Expresses hatred for occupation	64	40.5
In passive resistance, non-violent encounters, demonstrations	27	17.1
In violent underground activity	19	12.0
Jailed, fined, or tried by the occupation	14	9.0
Expelled by the occupation	16	10.0
Accuses Weimar leaders (or the extreme left) of collaboration with occupation	18	11.4
	158	100.0

gories overlap to some degree, since punishment or expulsion by the occupation was usually related to passive or violent resistance. They were coded differently whenever the respondent chose to stress the one at the expense of the other. Examples and quotations will throw more light on the nature of the experiences and feelings.

Occupation and Patriotism

The most immediate effect of the hostile foreign occupation was to spur political interest and patriotic feelings. "The invasion [of the Ruhr] mobilized my political instincts," writes a judge (no. 89)

Berlin 1930-1932. More recently, an East German literature on the Ruhr invasion has been added to the large existing literature which stresses the Communist fight against the mineowners and other collaborators with the French occupation. See, for example, Heinz Koeller, *Kampfbuendnis an der Seine, Ruhr, und Spree*, der gemeinsame Kampf der KPF und KPD gegen die Ruhrbesetzung 1923, Berlin: Ruetten & Loening, 1963, or Manfred Uhlemann, *Arbeiterjugend gegen Cuno und Poincaré, das Jahr 1923*, Berlin: Neues Leben, 1960.

who was only 16 then. A shoemaker and pacifistic Socialist, born in 1888 (no. 114), relates, "I came to feel the rifle butt of the French and became patriotic again."[3] "The separatists [who were encouraged by the French] and the occupation really taught me a patriotic outlook," reports a young itinerant artist (no. 424), who was 15 in 1923. A schoolteacher, born in 1880 (no. 186), who lived in the area west of the Rhine, comments on the misbehavior of American troops in Koblenz and of the French elsewhere long before 1923:

I was saying already then that we should build a monument to the French, particularly to Clemenceau and Poincaré, and to their allies for their chicanery, for they managed with their torments to make genuine Germans out of us, just Germans and no longer Prussians, Bavarians, Hessians, etc. Even people of Socialist or Communist persuasion agreed with me on that.

A sales clerk in Neuwied, born in 1904 (no. 240), vents his feelings about the separatists and their support by the occupation:

Then the foreign occupation stood at the Rhine and I often felt a holy rage rising when I saw how our freedom-loving people had to suffer the alien rule. Not to be allowed to sing our German patriotic songs in our own country alone seemed intolerable. And this was not all. Now a separatist movement appeared which aimed at the secession of the Rhineland from Germany.

The respondent claimed that Marxist leaders in German government were "glad to deepen the rifts opening up among the people."

A grocer's son born in 1910 in Muehlheim-Ruhr (no. 4) describes the popular mood in 1923 and later:

I shall never forget the disconsolate mood of the people. The enemy in our country! When the first shock wore off, young and old in public places began to sing *Deutschland ueber alles* and the *Wacht am Rhein*, songs which had to fall silent for years of an unjust occupation. I never felt more at one with my people than in that era. Do you blame

[3] See also nos. 306 and 10. The latter adds after a lengthy description of brutal actions and general repression by the occupation: "The martyrdom suffered by hundreds of thousands of Germans surely did not fail to leave an impression on them. It has ever been thus in history that a people suffering such brutal repression gains inner strength from it. With me, likewise, these events led to early political awareness and maturity." Hans Ostwald, in his *Sittengeschichte der Inflation*, Berlin: Henius, 1931 claims that even the prostitutes began to have nationalistic compunctions then.

me for cheering every successful assault on the taken-over railroads and occupation troops? I would have loved to participate myself. . . . Schlageter was the hero to us boys.

The respondent, "like all red-blooded German boys," felt motivated by this experience to resist such brutal usurpation and, with many others, joined a militant veterans organization.

Other young men who joined the Young Stahlhelm (no. 298) or the Navy Youth (no. 61) proceeded to demand military action against the occupiers. "Why didn't the republic attack the French rather than make compromises with them?" Often the call for action follows a description of a particular outrage by the occupation. But it should also be noted that there are quite a few accounts (nos. 184, 389, 409, 450, 451, and 580) of how the occupation hampered the development of Nazi organization and activity. Especially in the Palatinate and in Rhine-Hesse, there are reports of occupation interference with the party as well as arrests and deportation of local Nazi leaders.[4] The occupation also outlawed certain other extreme right-wing and militant veterans' organizations and forbade patriotic demonstrations and observances.

The Interpretation of Horror Stories

Needless to stress, many respondents tell horror stories of French or allied brutality and incidents of thieving or assault on innocent civilians. Most of these stories have probably a kernel of truth in them although there is no reason to regard them as any more objective than any other episodes told with great emotion in the Abel documents; many of the incidents also report only one side of continuing conflicts carried out with or without violence. The choice of themes, in any case, deserves attention.

A popular cause for complaint is the liberties which occupation soldiers were said to have taken with people's baggage on the railroads or packages in the mails (no. 186). A related theme is theft and confiscation of private belongings in connection with billeting troops in houses or apartments (no. 17). Others complain about the harsh management by the French of railroads or mines taken over by the victors. A Saar miner, born in 1879 (no. 334), relates his visceral reaction to the French take-over of his place of employment:[5]

[4] On the Palatinate, see especially *Die Pfalz unter franzoesischer Besatzung von 1918 bis 1930*, Muenchen: Sueddeutsche Monatshefte, 1930.

[5] See also no. 429, a bank clerk born in 1896 who speaks of "a nightmare off my soul" when he finally is able to leave the occupied zone.

We miners had to suffer particularly from the coming of the French to the Saar because all the mines passed into their direct ownership. The French mining officials expressed their Germanophobia and desire for revenge from the war toward us mine workers. Hatred and bitterness built up in me day after day against these alien elements and drove me physically and mentally to the end of endurance. I just could not bear the thought that these creatures were laying hands on our things and bodies. I could not go on letting these alien tyrants dominate me and decided to leave the mine.

He soon fell sick and had to be pensioned off to the little forest village where he was born. Another popular complaint is the restrictions the occupation placed on the wearing of insignia of patriotic organizations, such as black-white-red ribbons or the swastika of Captain Ehrhardt's Navy Brigade.

Finally, there are unabashed racial animosities and fears. "The yellow and black hordes of France were raging through our Palatinate," writes a young miner from the Saar (no. 448). Another respondent relates how "Siamese, Senegalese, and Arabs made themselves the masters of our homeland." He tells luridly of a brother who suffered a knife-wound while defending his wife against assault (no. 183). A young civil engineer (no. 198), born in 1906, discusses the coming of the French to the town of Langen on the heels of the German retreat with a sharp eye for French prejudice as well:[6]

> The last German troops had not been gone for half a day, when French officers rode into town and marked the occupation boundaries. Shortly thereafter our town was heavily occupied. All private houses had to accept billets. Blacks, Moroccans, and Arabs were put up in schools and public buildings. . . . We had our fun with the colored colonial troops. They were so stupid you could show them an old newspaper in place of a valid pass at the checkpoints. But it was dangerous at night for women and girls. Rape and miscegenation were unfortunately frequent.

Passive Resistance and Punishment

Many of the respondents expelled by the occupation fall into one of two categories. Either they participated in the passive-resistance policy proclaimed by the Weimar government as its first reaction to the Ruhr invasion, as particularly did railroad officials of all ranks and their families, or they engaged in various hostile actions, often of a personal, spiteful sort or committed with political intent.

[6] See also nos. 24, 30, 54, 57, 111, 335, 384, and 415.

Sometimes the political and the personal elements are hard to separate. One bank clerk and *voelkisch* activist, born in 1897 (no.
438), was expelled with his family for a "violation of respect" toward a French captain. Little imagination is required to guess that
his disrespectful action, which he fails to identify, probably grew
from his strong beliefs and activist temper. He may also have acquired a reputation with the occupation as a political trouble-maker
and may have been deliberately provoked into a confrontation. Another respondent (no. 443), born in 1902, reports somewhat naive-
ly how he had "a physical collision" with a French occupation
soldier "who insulted my honor." He ran all the way to Saxony to
escape the consequences of this confrontation. Another respondent
of about the same age (no. 265) relates: "On the very first day the
French came I got involved in an incident with them and was punished. This oppression and terror and the constant insults of the
occupation troops together with the meanness and vulgarity of the
party politicians motivated me to fight back and caused my early
interest in politics." He directed his energy into fighting the SPD,
which he had already hated from the days before 1918. The immediate appearance of the French occupation upon his return from
the war "really made obvious the treason of November 9, 1918, and
from that day on I wanted nothing more than some day to take revenge on the traitors."

More typical was the fate of railroad officials, who as their part
of the passive resistance campaign refused to work under the
French. "Since my father naturally declined working for the French
railroad administration, he was expelled across the Rhine and his
family had to follow. Our furniture was confiscated by the occupation authorities." The respondent (no. 439) writing this was only
twelve at the time but calls this "the time of my political awakening." A railroad worker, born in 1898 (no. 248), reports from the
Moselle area:

> Then came the worst and most humiliating time for our homeland
> with the terror regime of the separatists under the protection of the
> occupation. The patriotic population fought with all means possible
> against these vagabonds.
> Then there followed the time of the passive resistance when the
> loyal railroad officials refused to work for the alien occupation. I too
> was out of work again. They proceeded against the loyal civil servants
> and workers with all kinds of chicanery. Almost every day there were
> ten expulsions. I was constantly living with the excitement and wonder-
> ing when they would get around to me. One had to be ready any
> moment to be expelled with wife and children from one's homeland like

a criminal. Thus we were to give up the homeland that we had defended with our goods and blood for all those years. This time was even worse than being in the trenches. It is impossible to write down everything just as it happened. We were completely cut off from the rest of Germany.

For good measure, the respondent also throws in a non-sequitur, or two. He developed a kind of Bolshevik or anti-Communist choler:

At that time I began to hate Bolshevism from the depth of my German heart. For here we saw how under the protection of alien bayonets this rabble established itself and what would have been our fate if we had not resisted the alien influences with our fanatical love of the fatherland. Our patriotism and readiness for action won out. The separatists were beaten decisively and scattered in all directions. The bonds of blood and the ties to our native soil were stronger than weapons and alien bayonets.

The respondent bears a deep grudge for the "November usurpers," for "I experienced the first consequences of the dictate of Versailles on my own body." But he hated even more the exploitation of his labor by the "money people and stockholders who 'live it up' on the *Reichsbahn* dividends and at the expense of the sweat of workingmen." He was evidently as ill-informed about the operation of the *Reichsbahn* as about the links between the separatists and the Bolsheviks or, for that matter, the Weimar government.[7]

A former officer, born in 1885 (no. 182), relates his experiences after he became a railroad official:

As a consequence of the Ruhr invasion, all civil servants, employees, and workers of the *Reichsbahn* who refused to work for the French railroad administration were driven out of their offices and places of work by French soldiers with bayonets on their rifles. It was on March 3, 1923. Denounced by very mean, traitorous persons, most of them were expelled. I cannot begin to describe the humiliations and chicanery we suffered from that day until November. Our wages and salaries were smuggled across the Rhine and by the time we received the money, the run-away inflation had reduced its purchasing power to very little. Anyone caught distributing the salaries was severely punished and often beaten up by the occupation.

The hardest day of my life was the day our red government ordered me to report back to the French railroad administration. If you refused they cut off their support.

[7] See also the railroad cases nos. 122, 200, 242, 567, and 568.

The stiff back of this military-civil servant was bent still further when his war injuries caused prolonged illness and, after eight months, the French cut off his pay while the various German agencies gave him the bureaucratic run-around. Finally pensioned off, he joined the NSDAP and was immediately made head of the party local and of the local SA detachment. There is also a case of a railroad worker, born in 1893 (no. 567), who was a war invalid but still working until he was dismissed and expelled with his wife and children for making a speech at a monument for the casualties of World War One. Then there was a customs official, a former sergeant, also born in 1893 (no. 122), who was one of the first officials arrested and expelled when he would not cooperate with the French soldiers.

Passive resistance of the railroad officials had its counterpart among the civilian population. A teacher (no. 199) tells how he had his pupils turn their backs on the French troops marching by. He had a way of finding out who was still using the French-administered railroads and sent threatening, presumably anonymous letters to these unpatriotic souls. In the summer of 1923 he was expelled, together with his family. A son of a hotel and vineyard owner, who was only 12 in 1923 (no. 206), claims that the French administration of the railroads led to many accidents resulting from carelessness, and goes on to say:

> Naturally, none of us 13- to 16-year-old schoolboys ever used that so-called *Regiebahn*, especially after the government had called for passive resistance. Consequently, my younger brothers and sisters and I walked every day for nearly a year from Assmannshausen to Geisenheim, which took us about four hours. As you can imagine, this did not increase our love for the French, and certainly not for the separatists, those traitors on the German side.[8]

Another youth, then only 14 (no. 66), describes other facets of the youthful reaction to the coming of the French in 1918: "At school we received instructions on how to conduct ourselves. But we knew from the start that we were never going to greet a French officer. We would run into a strange house rather than take off our caps."

Of Boys' Games and Resistance

Even without the inclination toward patriotic indignation, which most of the younger respondents obviously had, the presence of the

---

[8] There is also another case of a young man who reports having walked from *Karlsruhe* to *Landau* in order not to use the railroads at the time the expulsions were taking place (no. 419).

occupation was likely to invite youthful pranks and games. Boys' games were not always meant to be political from the outset, but they would easily pass over the invisible line between playfulness and serious involvement. One young man, born in 1908 (no. 250), tells of his and his friends' reaction to the occupation armies immediately after the retreat of the German troops. He describes his way to school past occupation quarters, and muses:

> Our favorite literature then was books about German heroes and descriptions of great men of other nations, and particularly the Nibelungen saga. On the way to school we often talked about them and felt sad that the proud times and all the beauty of olden times were gone. During the war years, even Easter, Pentecost, and Christmas could not be celebrated well. We hoped and believed that Germany would soon rise again and shake off the chains and the occupation. And we did not want to stand aside idle in the liberation but be useful as spies, etc. Three of us formed a secret club and made up a secret code and language.

Another respondent, born in 1907 (no. 1), joined a militant organization, the *Wehrvolk Deutscher Aar* (German Eagle Militants) and, barely 16 in 1923, undertook to spy on the invading French: "We tried to count as well as possible the numbers and strength of the French occupation forces, their armaments, rifles, tanks, etc." This *voelkisch* action group put on patriotic plays and showed the old imperial flag as an act of defiance against the republic and its symbols. The respondent often had to defend flag and stage bodily against "Marxists and Communists." An even younger respondent, born in 1912 (no. 379), tells about the boys' games at his Latin school at the time of the Ruhr invasion:

> Since my friends and I so often heard older boys at school talk about boycotts and passive resistance, we wanted to find out about these things too. We could not have understood too much of it, but one thing was clear: It was against the French and you had to watch out for spies! So about six or eight of us boys got together to help in our own way. Our activities consisted in distributing forbidden handbills, putting up posters, and cutting off the hair of girls who were shamelessly consorting with the French. These were all more or less activities the dangers of which we could understand only much later.[9]

[9] See also nos. 413, another young *voelkisch* activist, and 340, a respondent born in 1902 who relates how he and another young man, who also later became a Nazi, "sat down at night to write tirades against the French which we glued on walls."

Given strong feelings, a youthful hankering for action, and a ready-made target, it was only a short step to violence. Boys' games had a way of suddenly turning into bitter confrontations. One high-school student, born in 1905, tells how he and some other 14-year-olds broke several windows at the home of an SPD leader in order to "get even for the Marxist revolution." He goes on (no. 181):

> At that time the French moved into my homeland. They tried to win us over with chocolate, white bread, etc. But I had already drilled my friends so well that they proudly declined everything. I wanted to tie them to me even more and in a carpenter's shop I founded a *Jungdeutschlandbund* after the one founded by von der Goltz. My father had to lead it and we secretly began our work, the physical training of our youth by sports, games, and hiking. . . . In 1922 my father was tried by the French military court in Kaiserslautern and punished rather hard.

Later the respondent was wounded in a violent encounter with the separatists and arrested by the French, who took away his passport and henceforth opened his mail. Like so many young respondents, he went from these anti-occupation antecedents directly to the NSDAP. Another young man, born in 1901 (no. 178), tells of his fight against the separatists' movement in the Palatinate:

> With several classmates I went to demonstrate together with the workers, who had by and large been the only support of the defense movement against these traitors. We demonstrated against the French whose presence alone enabled the separatist movement to flourish here. We threw rotten apples and other things at various French units and even managed to disarm one unit. Only the appearance of French armored cars and tanks broke up the demonstration, which cost the lives of two young Germans who were shot by the French soldiers.

Organized Active Resistance

From these instances of less and less playful activities, we get to cases of substantial political involvement. One respondent relates how the good-natured American occupation suddenly became tough, when he and his friends hoisted the imperial flag on a hill. A Pirmasens locksmith, born in 1903 (no. 410), wandered from the Socialist Workers Youth (SAJ) and the "red" Metal Workers Union to the Nazi stormtroopers, with a brief interlude as an irregular volunteer (*Zeitfreiwilliger*) in the army. He claims to have suffered political persecution from the beginning, without indicating why. Early in 1924 he had to flee the occupied zone in order to escape arrest by the occupation. He fled to Munich, where he first encountered and joined the SA. On his return to his home town, he founded and headed a local stormtrooper organization and endured a series of occupation fines and jail sentences: 40 marks and 4 days of incarceration for use of flags during the presidential elections of 1925; 500 marks and 41 days of preliminary detention in connection with a Schlageter commemoration; and 300 marks and 25 days in jail for illegal assembly after he became chief of the regional Hitler youth.

Many others received fines, jail sentences, or expulsion orders for participation in right-wing political activity, or Schlageter rallies,[10] or for displaying flags or insignia of patriotic organizations. The occupation had understandably outlawed many organizations and activities. One respondent, born in 1911 (no. 149), was arrested for participation in a torchlight parade to celebrate the "liberation" of his home town from the separatists. There are many others who got shot at by the occupation while fighting the separatists (no. 50), or jailed and expelled (nos. 180, 185, 417, and 442). There are also stories of arrest and mistreatment (nos. 22 and 118), often without a full statement of the charge or reason for the arrest (nos. 434, 486). The occupation had its eye particularly on former officers or Free Corps members (no. 423), as well as on members of *voelkisch* action groups. In some cases, returning officers were warned beforehand and avoided the occupied areas. In others, the urge to serve in a Free Corps and to engage in military action was so strong that young men from the occupied area went to join Free Corps action in the east (nos. 406, 426).[11] One respondent even went from the anti-occupation struggle by way of the militant *Wikingbund* and the Nazi stormtroopers to the French Foreign Legion (no. 226). For these violent elements, it stands to reason, it was hardly the ideology which led to violent actions but rather the other way around. At the very least, they can be said to have found the perfect symbiosis between their yearning for violent action and ideological rationalizations.

Less military and more political were careers such as that of an elementary school teacher born in 1902 (no. 413), who joined the

[10] See, for example, nos. 3, 29, and 201.

[11] See also nos. 182 and especially 245, a frequently unemployed Free Corps graduate who together with his father was quite involved in the anti-occupation struggle.

militant *Bund Oberland* and reports briefly and concisely the nature of his involvement:

> During my years [at the teacher-training college] in Kaiserslautern I was active in the defense organization (*Selbstschutz*). I joined *Bund Oberland*. I participated actively in the liberation from separatist rule. . . . In 1927 I shared with two comrades, who are today also in the SA, in the propaganda work accompanying the French fall maneuvers in the Hunsrueck mountains. . . . At the same time I was part of the bombing squad "Keller" which worked against the occupation in the Germersheim district.

Another respondent born in 1902 (no. 411) tells a confused tale of violence and involvement worthy of dramatic fiction:

> In March 1919 I had the opportunity of saving a girl who had been attacked by a French soldier. The next day I was going to give this sex maniac something to remember me by and I wounded him while he was standing guard. But a Frenchman-lover betrayed me and I was arrested at work. Fortunately, a friend of mine . . . went to the other [unoccupied] side of the Rhine and wrote from there to the French *gendarmerie* claiming he had done it. So they let me go but I had to report three times daily to the *gendarmerie* for the next eight weeks.

In 1923, the respondent joined the anti-revolutionary *Buergerwehr* "to stop the looting by the red guards" and the Anti-Separatist Intelligence (*Separatistenabwehr*), which used him to infiltrate and spy among the separatists. He was eventually arrested and managed to flee, still under a death sentence imposed by the separatist government. He temporarily returned to his home town, Pirmasens, when the "separatists and red guards" were ousted, and collected many more fines and jail sentences from the French and German courts for further violence against the separatists and the "reds," and for attending a Schlageter commemoration. He also went directly from the anti-occupation struggle to the NSDAP, evidently sensing a certain psychological or ideological kinship with the stormtroopers.

A military-civil servant born in 1890 (no. 14) describes his activities with a *voelkisch* action group:

> As professional soldiers we had no chance to concern ourselves with the politics of the country. It was only after my entry into civilian life [as a municipal official] that I realized the chaos into which the revolt of 1918 had plunged Germany. Having for years known only discipline

and orders, I simply could not find my way any more in postwar Germany. In 1921 I joined the *voelkisch Schutz-und-Trutzbund*. The entry of the occupation troops into Duisburg really brought the misery of the German people before our eyes. Ruthless elements and criminals did not hesitate to collaborate with the occupation troops right before the eyes of the German population. For a Judas' reward they betrayed the German fatherland. It was our task to fight these people. We enlightened the population about these scoundrels by distributing handbills and putting up posters.

The respondent and some of his friends were surprised by separatists one night while putting up posters. There was a violent clash and the separatists' police captured him. Some loyal German policemen permitted him to escape and were promptly arrested themselves the next day by the occupation. The escapee soon joined the NSDAP.

The last case that is germane to this subject is that of another elementary-school teacher born in 1895 (no. 404) who served in the Free Corps Epp during the "liberation" of Munich from the workers'-and-soldiers' councils. In 1920 he obtained his first teaching job in the Palatinate under the French occupation:

Following my innermost urge, I joined the *Organisation Consul*,[12] which fought actively against both domestic and foreign enemies and which participated in particular in the overthrow of separatist rule in the Palatinate. At that time I also heard for the first time about the ideas of the front-line soldier Adolf Hitler, who was speaking to big rallies in Munich. He said the things I had always felt without being able to express them. With just a few men of like mind, about fifteen in number, we founded the first NSDAP local in the Palatinate in October of 1924.

The School of Violence

It is remarkable that the literature on the early Nazi party gives so little indication of the significance of the anti-occupation struggle in the west. The struggle against the occupation and the separatists appears to have been a major recruiting vehicle for the NSDAP in the areas concerned, just as the *Deutsch-Soziale Partei* (DSP) and various militant organizations such as *Oberland* and *Wehrwolf*, or the so-called Black *Reichswehr*, a conglomerate of militant and vet-

---

[12] A notorious right-wing underground organization linked with political murders on a systematic scale. See also Howard Stern, "The Organization Consul," *Journal of Modern History*, vol. 35 (March 1963), 20-32.

erans' organizations in eastern and central Germany[13] that in their respective territories became primary recruiting vehicles in those crucial years. Only the beer-hall *putsch* debacle seems to have retarded the coming together of a potent nationwide Nazi movement in the mid-1920s. With the benefit of hindsight, of course, we can say that it might have been much better for German democracy had the brown wave crested during the years of relative prosperity rather than in the trough of the Great Depression.

How do the anti-occupation and anti-separatist respondents differ from the rest of the Abel sample of early Nazis? For one thing they appear to have been less well-educated and younger by about four to five years on the average. In particular, the more involved respondents who either participated in passive resistance, or underground, or were punished or expelled by the occupation tended to be of the postwar generation. This circumstance further corroborates the impression that the stimuli of occupation, invasion, and separatism tended to strike a particularly responsive chord among respondents in generational revolt, the political youth of the 1920s.

The occupations of the respondents' fathers also differ in certain ways. There are considerably more military-civil servants and, because of the small-town structure of much of the occupied area and perhaps also of the anti-occupation movement, more independent businessmen and artisans among the fathers of the anti-occupation respondents than among the whole sample. The small-town character of this movement also emerges from its patterns of social mobility. A greater percentage of the respondents were socially immobile, especially among those who engaged in violence. On the other hand, the anti-occupation group has fewer ambitious farm boys and more of the upwardly mobile in an urban environment than is true of the entire Nazi sample. As we would expect, also, the

---

[13] Among the Black *Reichswehr* men in the sample is a former Prussian cadet, born in 1903 (no. 351), who reports having helped to organize "*Stahlhelm, deutsch-nationaler Jugendbund, Bismarckjugend, Junglandbund, Jungdo, Wehrwolf* . . . all able-bodied Germans" into a basis for the Black *Reichswehr* of Major Ernst Buchrucker. This group attempted an abortive *coup d'état* from Kuestrin about ten days prior to the beer-hall *putsch* in Munich. Another respondent (no. 73) was in the *deutsch-nationaler Jugendbund* and *Wehrwolf* prior to getting involved in the Black *Reichswehr* adventure. *Wehrwolf*, he says, was dominated by real "soldiers, Free Corps men, and border area fighters." He went on from the *Wehrwolf* to the *Stahlhelm* which soon tired him with its flag rituals and beer busts. Returning in 1929 to his home town, he found that most of his old *Wehrwolf* friends had become SA stormtroopers.

anti-occupation groups has a much larger number of respondents who advocate a *Volksgemeinschaft* against the "outside enemies of the people."

Did respondents affected by the occupation show different patterns of joining the party than did the rest of the Abel sample? Yes, they were significantly more often among the first to join the first small nucleus of the NSDAP in their area. This fact answers the questions arising from the repression of nationalistic activities by the occupation. Far from being an effective curb on extremist development, this policy evidently had the effect of intensifying the feelings of the would-be Nazi and of causing him to found or cofound a Nazi local, if there was none in the area.

The anti-occupation group quite generally followed the sound of different drummers throughout the republican era. In the first postwar years, 1919 to 1921, in spite of its youth it was already rather more involved in *voelkisch* action groups, including the NSDAP— probably as a response to the occupation and separatist experience. Conservative opposition and militant veterans' organizations, Free Corps and impromptu anti-occupation or anti-separatist groups with names such as *Landesschutz* or *Abwehr* claim disproportionate numbers in 1919-1921 and especially in 1922-1924, at the time of the Ruhr invasion. The extent to which anti-occupation Nazis engaged in political violence in the years from 1919 to 1924 is nearly twice that of the entire sample, again despite their relative youth. It amounts to 34.1% of the anti-occupation group, which has another one-fourth engaged in demonstrations and propaganda.

After that time of intense nationalistic stimulation came the obvious response. Thirty-seven percent of the anti-occupation group (as compared to only a fourth of the entire sample) joined the NSDAP in the years up to 1927, when the scattered and demoralized movement badly needed recruits. Another 19.1% of the anti-occupation respondents joined in 1928, a year when many who had participated in the passive resistance campaign joined the party. Table II-2 shows how the occupation experience caused respondents to join earlier, until the 1930 *Reichstag* elections, when the brunt of foreign occupation had passed. The proportion of anti-occupation respondents engaged in political violence (two thirds) was still substantially higher in 1925-1928 than the small (12.8%) proportion of violent men in the general sample. The anti-occupation respondents who had participated in violent action against the occupation and the separatists played a prominent role among the violent of these years and they maintained this commanding lead in political violence in 1929-1930 and even into the final battles of

Table II-2: Date of Anti-Occupation Respondents Joining NSDAP (in %)

Date of joining:	1924 or earlier	1925 to 1927	1928 to mid-1929	Aug. '29 June '30	July '30 May '31	June '31 Mar. '32	April '32 or later
anti-occupation respondents	10.8	26.1	19.1	16.6	12.7	5.7	7.6
general sample	7.2	17.9	14.3	15.0	21.1	13.5	10.8

% joined

30

25

20

15

10

5

0

Legend: - - - anti-occupation respondents ——— general sample

1931 and 1932. There is ample evidence, then, that the occupation experience was indeed a school for political violence and for the Nazi movement itself in its reconstruction from 1925 until the ascent to power.

Occupation, Separatism, and Ideology

The question should now be raised whether the ideology and attitudes of the anti-occupation group were significantly influenced by this experience. To begin with, it is noteworthy that the anti-occupation respondents became acquainted with the NSDAP not so much through hearing of its ideology, seeing its literature or going to rallies, but through the introduction of friends or colleagues or through the youth groups, which simply went *en bloc* into the party. The circumstances of an occupation hostile to nationalistic agitation, of course, play a considerable role.

As for the ideology of the respondents after they joined the party, the one outstanding feature which distinguished the anti-occupation group from the rest of the sample is superpatriotism. Nearly one-third of the anti-occupation respondents, in other words, saw in the Nazi party primarily the answer to their patriotic indignation. They also indulged more than the other Nazis in the personality cult of Hitler, whom they viewed as "the savior in the hour of the deepest humiliation of the fatherland." As for the chief objects of their hostility, they were more prone to include the entire catalog of hate-images than the rest of the sample—possibly an indication of the intensity of their outraged feelings.

In their attitudes toward the Nazi movement, similarly, the anti-occupation group differs from the entire sample. They were considerably more beholden to the Hitler cult and they also tended to be more dependent on the struggle itself to integrate their probably not very well-balanced personalities. Personal integration by merging with a fighting movement was particularly pronounced among respondents engaged in violent resistance, or those jailed or expelled for passive resistance. Membership in the stormtroopers and the SS was again much higher than in the general sample, especially among the categories mentioned. More anti-occupation respondents, consequently, held offices of leadership in the SA and SS. In their attitudes toward violence, the high involvement of the anti-occupation group brings out their postwar syndrome. They show disproportionately many cases characterized by the self-pity and masochism that seem to have been typical of the violent youth of that day.

They express their attitude toward political enemies, especially among those more intensely involved with the occupation and the separatists, in the gutter language of the *outré*. They call them "subhuman," "rodents," "venal," "immoral," etc.—another indication of the intensity of the outrage felt. It is hardly surprising that their ethnocentricity apart from antisemitism is far higher than that of the rest of the collection. Their venom is directed especially at aliens, the Catholic church, and the foreign interests that had the country over a barrel during the occupation. Their attitude toward authority is characterized by strong hostility toward the police and the government and, of course, by their Hitler cult. This aspect, too, is probably related to their propensity for violence. The less trust in the conventional wielders of violence, the greater the tendency to rely on one's own physical force.

Finally, there are relationships between violence and a propensity toward ideological rather than pragmatic thinking which characterizes the anti-occupation group as compared to the whole sample. The thrust of this ideological commitment, at least as measured by their expectations in 1934, went in the utopian direction of a "one thousand-year Reich," laced with visions of internal purges within and national resurgence among the European powers.

The formative influences or experiences of the anti-occupation groups are the typical ones for the postwar generation, educational experiences and the camaraderie in youth groups, with one exception. Disproportionate numbers relate alleged episodes with aliens, Jews, and occupation personnel. But it is worth noting that the experiences of war and defeat, and the social snubs or unemployment important to previous generations made little impression on the anti-occupation respondents. Instead, they display the faults of their own generation: An extreme degree of leader worship, a sense of personal insecurity and self-pitying masochism, and a touch of irrational paranoia. This was the contribution of the occupation to the Nazi movement.

FIVE

Revolution and Counter-revolution

Was there a genuine revolution in Germany in 1918? Many historians answer this question in the negative or are at pains to point out the unrevolutionary character of the changes that actually occurred beginning in October 1918.[1] To conservatives and right-wing radicals, however, there was a great need to assert that a revolution had indeed taken place in order to motivate their venom and militancy against the legitimate government of Weimar. To play the role of patriotic counter-revolutionaries, they had to exaggerate the presence of revolutionaries and to insist that there had indeed been a dreadful conspiracy which led to the German defeat and to a revolution-like seizure of power in Berlin. The role of the counter-revolutionaries or of the "military desperadoes," on the other hand, also should not, without careful examination, be seen in an exaggerated fashion as the "vanguard of Nazism," even though the two had important personal and ideological links, as we shall see.

> In the streets of Harburg, the mutineers tore the uniform off my body. In vain we volunteered to wipe out the traitors to the German army on their way from Kiel and Hamburg. The red traitors to the people, Ebert, Scheidemann, Erzberger and their comrades, forbade any shooting at the mutineers let out of the jails and prisons. Believing in the fourteen points of President Wilson, we front-line soldiers then allowed the most terrible treason of world history to take place. The Jewish leaders of the International who attained leadership over the German workers during the war sold out our people and signed the treaty of Versailles.

This typical mixture of motives and explanations of the defeat and the "revolution" is from the pen of a commercial employee, born

---

[1] See for example, Pinson, *Modern Germany*, ch. 14, or the cautious formulations of Werner Conze, *Die Zeit Wilhelms II und die Weimarer Republik*, pp. 115-125, but also the contrary presentation in Charles B. Burdick and Ralph H. Lutz, eds., *The Political Institutions of the German Revolution 1918-1919*, New York: Praeger, 1966, for the Hoover Institution, pp. 1-15.

in 1894 (no. 32), who had spent most of the war as a French prisoner of war. He obviously identified the "red revolutionaries" with
the provisional government of Ebert, Scheidemann, and Erzberger
and blamed them for the defeat, the signing of the Treaty of Versailles, and the alleged revolution. Later on he strongly identified
himself with the Kapp *putsch* of 1920 and described the fate of an
army detachment loyal to Kapp in his area: [2]

> The red rulers of Harburg and Hamburg armed the rabble of the Polish
> harbor quarters of these towns and permitted them, contrary to their
> own word of honor, to shoot down and murder the troops of Captain
> Berthold. Under the kicks and knife-wounds of animal-like women and
> criminals Captain Berthold, one of the best flying officers of the Ger-
> man army, bled to death, and so did other soldiers, before we could
> intervene. A young officer, who had been stabbed many times and was
> to be hanged from a tree, managed to escape, clinging to a horse-drawn
> ambulance, so we could take him to a hospital.

The respondent, who already headed the local *voelkisch* Retail
Clerks Union (DHV), was moved to join a counter-revolutionary
group, *Organisation Escherich*, and to organize the illegal supply
of weapons and ammunition from Hamburg to the Free Corps in
Upper Silesia and central Germany.

Another respondent, born in 1903 (no. 174), relates his feelings
at the end of the war:

> The war was over. . . . Our troops came home, but the sights they saw
> were disgusting. Very young boys, degenerate deserters, and prostitutes
> tore the insignia off our best front line soldiers and spat on their field-
> grey uniforms, shouting something about liberty, equality, and fra-
> ternity. . . . In Berlin, violent battles raged around the imperial build-
> ings. . . . Defenseless people and wounded soldiers were bestially
> murdered. That was the liberty these heroes from behind the lines
> were talking about. . . . For the first time a searing hatred rose in me
> against these subhumans who were stepping on everything pure and
> clean with their feet. Well, at least I knew I did not want to have any-
> thing to do with those people, even though I was still rather young.

This young man strikes all the themes of shock at the defeat and
the "revolution" without really having witnessed much of anything.
However, we are only measuring themes on the respondents' minds

[2] See also Richard A. Comfort, *Revolutionary Hamburg*, Stanford:
Stanford University Press, 1966, pp. 79-81 for the background of the
political shifts in Hamburg at the time. There is no mention of the events
related here.

and how these themes may relate to other beliefs or become the causes of specific actions. Therefore, we need not be greatly disturbed about the frequent failure of the respondents to distinguish the defeat from the "revolution" or to keep apart fact and fiction. It is quite enough to ascertain a respondent's feelings about the "revolutionaries," however he may identify them, and about the changes in government which he attributes to them. Thus, there is also no need to determine whether a "revolution" did indeed take place and, if it did, what if anything it accomplished. By the same token, we need not have established that there was a revolution in order to discuss the "counter-revolutionaries," the men and groups who attempted to oppose whomever they regarded as revolutionaries.

Reaction to the Revolution

What were the feelings of the respondents toward the ongoing process by which revolutionaries attempted local coups and by which the old forces of society, the military, and the civil service, intermittently lost control to the rather unrevolutionary new leaders of the republic just when they were most anxious to wield it? A few

FD-35: Reaction to Revolutionary Processes

	Number	*Per cent*
Blames Kaiser, old order	8	1.9
Blames Western interests, insurgent minorities	4	1.0
Blames unspecified rabble	18	4.3
Blames international Bolshevism	51	12.3
Blames the Jews	50	12.0
Blames and opposes the Weimar leaders, parties	45	10.8
Blames and opposes the Spartakists, mutineers	138	33.2
Other response (accepts "revolution")	102	24.5
	416	100.0

respondents blame the stubborn resistance to change or mismanagement by the old order. Others somehow pin the "revolution" on Western interests, especially those of France, or on street rabble or mobs not further identified. To blame a Bolshevik conspiracy on the progressive new Weimar leaders was not as farfetched as it may appear today. After all, the Bolshevik take-over in Russia was still fresh in people's minds, and there were not only many links and surface similarities between the workers'-and-soldiers' councils of

1918 and those in Russia a year earlier, but also many personal and organizational links with the extreme left in Germany and abroad. The new Weimar leadership was the same that had insisted on the 1917 Peace Resolution in the *Reichstag* and had pressed for liberalization and constitutional reforms in 1918. Worse yet in the eyes of suspicious hard-liners, the Weimar leaders of SPD, Center party, and DDP (Democrats) reluctantly signed the Treaty of Versailles in the face of intense popular indignation. To blame the Spartakists and mutineers of 1918 for the "revolution" was perhaps flattering, but not far from the mark since they were trying their best to accomplish just that, whereas putting the blame on "the Jews," of course, signifies pronounced prejudice.

How do these groups compare, after we have collapsed the first three into one? The new group of respondents who blame the Kaiser and the rabble turn out to be the youngest and probably the ones with the least first-hand acquaintance with it, followed by those who believe in the Bolshevik conspiracy and those who simply accept the "revolution." The oldest and also the most small-town and rural group is the one which blames the Weimar leaders, evidently remembering all too well the defamation of the SPD and the Center party as "enemies of the state" long before the war. The fathers of this group are often farmers. The antisemites are the next oldest group and also the most metropolitan, with about 70% living in cities over 100,000 inhabitants. Their fathers tend to be military-civil servants or artisans. Respondents who blame and oppose the Spartakists are generally from an urban environment and their fathers tend to be businessmen, artisans, or workers—in other words, close to the impact of the class struggle. The antisemites are generally socially immobile or in decline, and so are the anti-Spartakists. The anti-Bolsheviks and those who blame the Kaiser or the rabble are urban climbers. And the anti-Weimar respondents as well as those who accept the "revolution" have come up from the farm.

War, Defeat, and Revolution

How did these opinion groups react to the war and to the defeat? The most likely relationship between attitude toward the war and attitude toward the revolution would be that respondents most supportive of the war effort would be the most vindictive toward anyone they suspect of having "stabbed the army in the back." The reality turns out to be rather more complicated. Those who blame the Kaiser or the rabble for the revolution tend to have been enthusiastic soldiers to the bitter end, and they blame the Kaiser and the civilians' lack of stamina for the German defeat. The anti-Bolsheviks are more likely to show a good deal of hostility toward draft-dodgers and subversives, and to stress the *Fronterlebnis*, a reaction also typical of those who blame the revolution on the Jews. In their reactions to defeat, however, the anti-Bolsheviks either show great, diffuse emotion or they blame it on Marxists and Spartakists; the antisemites are more critical toward the old regime and its military leadership. Those who blame the "revolution" on the Spartakists were mostly hostile toward draft-dodgers and subversives during the war, or they were enthusiastic soldiers. The German defeat they lay at the door of the Marxists and Spartakists. The old anti-Weimar respondents tended to stress the *Fronterlebnis* and, indeed, often were POWs or invalids as a result of the war. They tended to react to the defeat with a show of emotion or to blame the Kaiser and the civilians back home. The respondents who simply accept the "revolution," finally, tend to have been enthusiastic soldiers though many became disaffected in the worst years of the war. The great majority accepted the German defeat just as they had in many cases evidently rolled with the punches toward the end of the war and in the "revolution."

How did the feelings toward the revolutionaries and their "revolution" translate themselves into activities and membership in "counter-revolutionary" organizations? The vast majority of respondents who simply accept the "revolution" or take it in stride engaged in no counter-revolutionary activity at all. Quite a few of them (18.4%), in fact, were in republican organizations, and some even participated in insurgent activities.

It would be tempting to take a closer look at these cases, but they tend to be not very informative, either because their authors are still rather confused or because they would rather not go into details of their earlier revolutionary enthusiasm. One of the better accounts is by an unemployed militant worker born in 1894 (no. 125) who had been in the SPD and the Free Trade Unions since 1911. "I welcomed the ninth of November, 1918, in the belief that the German worker had won out. Only weeks later in Berlin I saw that the contrary had occurred. I witnessed how the workers and comrades were bashing in each other's heads while SPD, USPD, and Spartakus were wrangling over jobs." He left the SPD in protest and had briefly joined the KPD (Communists) when he encountered an officer friend of his on his way to join a Free Corps in the east. The respondent also signed up and joined the Iron Brigade in the Baltic area. On his return in 1922 he married a girl who voted for the DNVP while he was still voting for the Independent Socialists

(USPD). Henceforth he spurned the parties of the left and instead gravitated to the red flag with the swastika, an action that may well have satisfied his need to overcome the political ambiguities in his life. He proudly reports that after spending five years as the only Nazi among 200 Marxists, his fellow-workers almost unanimously elected him works councillor in 1933.

Another respondent of this description was an enthusiastic victory-watcher born in 1901 (no. 15) who had received a Christian up-bringing from his mother. His father, a skilled worker, died early. Toward the end of the war, he became disaffected but not enough not to resent the armistice conditions and the indignities visited upon the returning troops. The respondent joined a Communist union to which most of his fellow-workers belonged and quickly became involved in the civil war tensions of 1920.

> The constant strikes and unrest caused the police to be reinforced with very young and nervous *Reichswehr* soldiers. They tended to view any larger group of workers coming out of the mines or waiting at the intersections or streetcar stops as trouble-makers and brutally drove them apart. Thus hatred awoke for the *Reichswehr* and it was intensi-fied by means of leaflets to great heat. Hence, when the Ruhr uprising broke out, nearly all the workers participated and armed themselves. The first step was disarming the police.

The following clashes with Free Corps units, the red snipers and the robbing of the dead and mistreatment of captured Free Corps fighters changed his mind: "Then I had enough of Communism and its struggle for human rights, for I saw how the decent worker was fighting in Lippe while the rabble behind the lines and in town terrorized the people. That was also where the leaders and functionaries of the KPD were playing the big man." With many others, the respondent then left the Communists for the SPD. It took years for him to overcome his aversion to the NSDAP.[3]

[3] There were other political wanderers between the two worlds such as no. 148, a worker born in 1900 who had difficulty holding down a job after the war and ended up with the Duesseldorf police. The Ruhr uprising must have been hard on him, too, for he writes: "I was so disillusioned by the doings of our rulers that I resigned in November, 1920. I would rather be a miner than to be punished in place of the November crim-inals. And," he continues incredibly, "since all parties I knew in 1921 except the KPD were for the shameful peace of Versailles, I joined the KPD. In the summer of 1931, however, I realized that Communism and its ideas were the greatest crime against the German people." He still worked for a while against the KPD from within, until the party forced

The anti-Spartakists are the most deeply involved in counter-revolutionary activity. They not only express strong feelings toward the insurgents, but joined the Kapp *putsch* and various Free Corps and vigilante organizations to fight the insurgents from the extreme left. Their reaction is shared by the respondents who blame the "revolution" on the Jews. The latter group, however, tends to belong to *voelkisch* action groups including the early Nazi party, while the anti-Spartakists heavily belong to militant veterans, anti-occupation groups, and conservative opposition groups ranging from the anti-Communist *Jungdo* to the DNVP. The anti-Bolsheviks were also quite involved in the counter-revolution. They joined in particular *voelkisch* action and militant veterans groups and fought with the Free Corps against domestic insurgents and the Poles.

The respondents who blame and oppose the new Weimar leaders were less involved and belonged mostly to conservative opposition groups and militant veterans, including those that fought the Poles in the east. The respondents who blamed the Kaiser, Western interests, and the rabble for the "revolution" were less involved, but contain their share of Kapp *putsch* participants or sympathizers and Free Corps fighters. The anti-Bolsheviks and anti-Spartakists, it appears, were, at the time, the most aggressive and, as it turns out, the most violent of the opinion groups on the alleged revolution. We shall come back to the subject of counter-revolutionary activities at a later point.

Ideology and the Revolution

The attitudes toward the revolutionary events, we can assume, bear a close relationship to how the respondents came to view the Weimar Republic, even though there may have been some changes of mind after the immediate postwar period. In their perception of the Weimar Republic, it is worth noting, that of the 30 respondents who actually belonged to republican organizations in 1919-1921 only two said they liked the republic. Two-thirds of the antisemites, not surprisingly, regarded it as a Jewish-run republic. The anti-Bolsheviks rejected it not only because it was run by Marxists or by the "red and black" parties, but also because they regarded it as a "liberal-Marxist system," an objection they share with the anti-Spartakists and with those who blamed and opposed the Weimar leaders.

---

him to resign. See also no. 399, a truck driver who claims to have joined the KPD in 1929 because his wife was deceiving him with other men and because he had encountered injustice at work and hypocrisy in the SPD.

The latter also criticized Weimar for its multi-party and multi-interest system, an argument mentioned by those who accepted the "revolution" and by the anti-Spartakists, too. The respondents who took the revolution in stride raised the traditional objections to capitalism and scored the republic for its Marxist leadership.

As for their dominant ideological themes years later, when they were in the NSDAP, nearly one-third of those who blamed the "revolution" on the Jews turn out to have been primarily antisemitic, ideologically. Those who blamed the Kaiser or the rabble tended to be devotees of the Hitler cult in evident preoccupation with leaders and followers. The anti-Bolsheviks stand out for their Nordic or Germanic romanticism and for revanchism. The anti-Spartakists were mostly revanchists and superpatriots. The latter theme was the second most frequently mentioned by all the respondents, and played a particularly important role among respondents who blamed and opposed the new Weimar parties. Respondents who accepted the "revolution," finally, tended to endorse antisemitism or the *Volksgemeinschaft*, the most frequent response (33.8%) given by all the respondents of the sample.

The Counter-Revolution Begins

"At war's end we returned in a march of 28 days to Duesseldorf," writes a shell-shocked soldier (no. 21).

> Here the first red gangs were going to assault and rob me and my comrades. They did not overcome our resistance and we went on to Remscheid where we were stopped once more. The red guards demanded our pistols and luggage. An old frontline fighter . . . took out his army pistol and knocked off a red guard. We were with another four comrades who also fired some shots. I hit one of the red scoundrels over the head with my crutch and he collapsed right away. We abandoned our things and jumped on the moving train going back to Duesseldorf. There was no thinking now of going home.

The young respondent (born in 1900) instead returned to his unit and soon joined a Free Corps operation in the demilitarized Ruhr area against the insurgents of the extreme left. Battles raged with artillery on both sides, and he relates:

> We took lots of prisoners whom we at first brought to Wesel to lock them up in the citadel. But soon we began to shoot them directly after their capture because there were too many enemies and we could not spare any of our men. They were miserable, accursed scoundrels; traitors who wanted nothing but cowardly to stab the fatherland in the back and to build a new *Reich* like the one in the Soviet Union.

The respondent goes on to tell of a night-time assault by the insurgents which cost his troops eighteen dead and many wounded, and of their "bloody revenge" the next day. There can be little doubt that to a battle-hardened soldier, this fratricide was not much different from shooting at Tommies, poilus, or Ivans. And, as the egregious rationalizations seem to indicate, he may have hated the insurgents even more than his wartime enemies.

Substantial numbers of the Abel respondents were involved in specific counter-revolutionary activities or sympathized with them. Many joined a Free Corps, served as volunteers (*Zeitfreiwillige*) in irregular *Reichswehr* units, or were in vigilante organizations such as the *Einwohnerwehr* or various defense or protective leagues fighting against left-wing insurgents of various kinds. Some participated in 1919 in the conquest of Munich from the workers'-and-soldiers' councils. Others fought against Polish irregulars at the

FD-32: Counter-revolutionary Activity, 1919-1921

	Number	Per cent
┌ Participates in Kapp putsch	14	6.7
└ Sympathizes with Kapp	13	6.2
┌ Participates in Free Corps or vigilantes (against insurgents)	48	22.9
└ Sympathizes with Free Corps, hates insurgents	71	33.9
In Free Corps, defense leagues (against Poles)	28	13.4
Belongs to vigilantes, militant veterans' group (but no action)	25	11.9
Participates with or sympathethic to insurgent activity	10	5.0
	209	100.0

eastern borders. Much of this activity was directly supported and countenanced by the new Weimar government, which believed that it had to use the Free Corps to protect the border and put down by force the insurgents threatening its precarious stability from the extreme left. The Free Corps and other units, however, often felt a disloyal impatience with what more than one of the Abel respondents called the "false front of fighting for Noske," the SPD *Reichswehr* minister in control of their operations.[4] In March 1920, there-

[4] One victory-watcher who was in the Free Corps von Loewenfeldt for a year (no. 423) resigned, among other reasons "because I could not make up my mind to serve under the Noskeregime. The façade game (*Kulissenspiel*) of these people was no secret among the Free Corps men." On his return he was fined and locked up by the occupation for having

fore, Kapp, a Prussian civil servant, and General von Luettwitz staged a quick *coup d'état* which sent the Weimar government packing until it was restored by a general strike.[5] Many of the Abel respondents participated in or sympathized with this action.

Immediately following the Kapp *putsch*, a major uprising of the left occurred in the demilitarized Ruhr area and was put down by Free Corps action in defiance of the demilitarization provisions. Shortly thereafter, the June elections to the *Reichstag* shattered the early strength of the Weimar coalition of SPD, Center party, and DDP. The SPD lost much of its support to the Independent Socialists (USPD), largely in response to the forceful suppression of the extreme left. The Center party lost its conservative Bavarian wing (BVP), and the DDP lost much of its support to the right-wing People's party (DVP), both in part because they had signed the Treaty of Versailles. Deprived of the support of a popular majority for the three republican parties, the Weimar Republic was off on its tottering course of unstable government, barely surviving from crisis to crisis and without the power to solve its mounting problems, until the final batch of crises of 1929-1932 made it ready for the usurper.

A Social Profile of the Counter-Revolutionary Groups

How did the various counter-revolutionary groups differ in their social profiles? Beginning with age, it seems that the Kapp *putsch*ists and their sympathizers were the oldest group, evidently reflecting the hopes of the prewar generation. The youngest group were the members of militant groups who had received military drill but seen no action. Even the respondents who sympathized with the Free Corps or express strong hatred of the insurgents were somewhat younger than the other groups although their age spectrum is very broad and rather heavy with cases at both ends. We can guess that many respondents who were too young or too old to fight fall into this category. The actual civil war combat troops of Free Corps

---

been in the Free Corps. Worse yet, he could not easily find work or keep jobs for long without being persecuted by his co-workers, as a "murderer of workers." Another young worker who served as a *Zeitfreiwilliger* had to leave his job and the town when his fellow-workers discovered that he was "a Noske" (no. 120). Another Free Corps fighter against the Bolsheviks in the Baltic area (no. 143) complains that "our government ridiculed our effort and eventually made us abandon it."

[5] See also Johannes Erger, *Der Kapp-Luettwitz Putsch*, Duesseldorf: Droste, 1967, p. 63 where the disappointment of the Baltic Free Corps is mentioned.

and vigilantes cluster in the range of birth dates between 1890 and
1901. In other words, they were the war generation. In fact, the
median age of all the counter-revolutionary groups appears to fall
close to the middle of this range, which makes the counter-revolutionaries a generation different, say, from the anti-occupation
groups who were generally of the postwar generation.

It is noteworthy that the Free Corps and vigilante groups fighting
the insurgents tended to be either spatially immobile or quite mobile
between cities (i.e., no rural-urban migrants). They also tended to
be from the occupied areas, whereas the anti-Polish Free Corps
fighters naturally were often from the eastern border areas, as were
the militants with no action and the Kapp *putsch*ists. There was also
a disproportionate number of Free Corps sympathizers from the
occupied areas, including the Ruhr, where they may well have
learned to hate the insurgents during the great 1920 uprising. Many
tell about the battles in their neighborhood. Finally, there were
quite a few rural-urban migrants both among the Free Corps sympathizers and among the Kapp *putsch*ists, which somehow suggests
a psychological link between the experience of moving to the city
and the reaction to the crumbling of the empire. Like the old lady
quoted earlier,[6] they may have confused their life's work and
achievement with the rise and fall of the Second *Reich*. Comparing
the counter-revolutionary groups with the entire sample, moreover,
we see that the counter-revolutionaries of 1919-1921 were considerably more urban, even metropolitan, than the rest of the Abel
collection.

What were the chief occupations of the counter-revolutionary
groups? As compared to the rest of the sample, they tended to be
military-civil servants or white-collar employees. Military-civil servants stand out particularly among the Kapp *putsch*ists and the Free
Corps and vigilante fighters against insurgents and the Poles. White
collar occupations played an important role among the militants without action, the Free Corps and vigilante fighters against insurgents
and Poles, and among their sympathizers. The only other occupational groups worth mentioning are urban workers and businessmen
and professionals (probably mostly university students) among the
Free Corps and vigilante fighters. The prominent role of military-
civil servants is hardly surprising, but that of white-collar workers
calls for an explanation. There were several strong white-collar
groups such as the *voelkisch* Retail Clerks Union (DHV), which
appears in many a counter-revolutionary *vita*. And then there is the

---

[6] *Supra*, pp. 122-123.

psychological situation of the white-collar respondents in a world of open class struggle between the bourgeoisie and the proletariat, which was easily identified with the "red" insurgents. Not quite accepted by the old bourgeoisie and, in dependency and income, close to the proletariat, white-collar employees may well have felt a call to demonstrate by eager militancy where they wanted to belong.[7]

Among the occupations of their fathers, as among the sons, farming plays a negligible role. Military-civil servants are more prominent among the fathers of Kapp *putsch*ists and militants who saw no action. The Free Corps and vigilante fighters against domestic insurgents often had high military or professional, worker, or artisan fathers. The fathers of the anti-Polish fighters tended to be businessmen or military-civil servants. Workers, artisans, and businessmen fathers also stand out among the Free Corps sympathizers, and artisans and businessmen along with the military among the militants without action. Apart from the predominance of the military and civil service and the absence of farmers, no particularly strong trend appears to be discernible.

Were the counter-revolutionaries upwardly mobile? Yes, and especially in an urban context. The Kapp *putsch*ists militants without action, and Free Corps sympathizers all tended to be urban climbers. The Free Corps and vigilante fighters against Poles and domestic insurgents, by contrast, were often up from the farm or in social decline. There are some other statistical odds and ends that deserve mention. The counter-revolutionaries, for example, were not as interested in *Volksgemeinschaft* as the rest of the sample nor did they share its unconcern about class distinctions. The Kapp *putsch*ists, the militants without action, and the Free Corps and vigilante fighters all showed strong class consciousness, as did of course the insurgents themselves, though with the opposite meaning. The Free Corps and vigilante fighters against the Poles and the "reds" stand out more for solidarism toward the outside than among the classes. Only the Free Corps sympathizers and the anti-Polish fighters show a little of the solidarism of the middle which we would expect to find among so many military-civil servants and white-collar employees. In this respect, too, the counter-revolutionaries were a product of the war.

Another item is that of religion. Given the heavy preponderance of Protestants among the Nazis and also among these counter-revolutionaries, it is worth mentioning that the Kapp *putsch*ists and the

---

[7] On this point, see esp. Siegfried Kracauer, *Die Angestellten aus dem neuesten Deutschland*, Frankfurt: Frankfurter Societaetsdruckerei, 1930.

anti-Polish fighters were even more Protestant, Prussians to the core. The Free Corps sympathizers and the militants without action, by comparison, had relatively more Catholics among them, since the Ruhr uprising was salient to many of them. The Free Corps and vigilante fighters, finally, tended not to state their religion—an omission from which we can infer a less religious frame of mind. Whatever they thought they were defending from "atheistic Bolshevism," it was probably not their faith. The plot thickens further when we control the factor of religious area along with the respondent's faith. As compared to the whole sample, now, the counter-revolutionaries tend either to be from mixed Protestant-Catholic areas or to live in areas in which their own faith is in the minority. Again we note that religious dissension appears to play a hidden role in increasing the propensity for violence.

To mention one more miscellaneous piece of information, there is also a breakdown according to state of health. The counter-revolutionaries, it appears, were considerably more prone to nervous and especially to physical breakdowns, as far as we can tell from the information volunteered.[8] At more than twice the rate of the rest of the sample, they broke down physically as a result of their strenuous efforts in the Nazi party during the fighting years of 1929 to 1933. If we consider political violence the expression of an extreme state of tension within a person and between him and his social environment, as we so far have assumed it to be, then this health statistic must be a measurement of that tension as analogous as suicide is to homicide. A person must be an extremist indeed to work himself into the hospital or into a physical breakdown for the sake of the cause.

Youth and the Counter-Revolution

Our measurement of youthful involvement accounts for any organizational memberships (save in unions or the regular army) entered below the age of 25 and the respondent's feeling about these memberships. Even though they belonged to the war generation, the

---

[8] The breakdown is rather limited, because of scanty information. FD-12: State of Health: Nervous breakdown 1914-1918 8 (3.7%); nervous breakdown from friction encountered during Weimar Republic 3 (1.4%); nervous breakdown from struggle 1931-1932 4 (1.9%); nervous breakdown suspected 6 (2.8%); physical breakdown from struggle 2 (.9%); hospitalized from struggle injuries 22 (10.3%); poor health from childhood 9 (4.2%); poor health from war 32 (15%); good health reported 129 (60.3%); total 214. The rest gave no indication of their state of health.

counter-revolutionary groups had such experiences more often than did the whole Nazi sample. This is particularly true of military training groups such as were appended to many militant veterans' or patriotic organizations, or the Free Corps, given the proper age level. But there are also quite a few who belonged to youth groups of the DNVP (*Bismarckjugend*), the DHV, or certain nationalistic or *voelkisch* athletic groups, the DVP youth (*Hindenburgjugend*), *Jungdo*, and unpolitical Youth Movement groups such as *Wandervogel*. Hardly anyone except for a few Free Corps sympathizers was in the Nazi party prior to engaging in counter-revolutionary activities. Not only was the incipient Nazi movement rather small and localized in those days, but it was set off as a political fringe-group from the more respectable and predominantly military counter-revolution. Given the separation between patriotic-military goals and the political and ideological zealotry of the early Nazis, Hitler was lucky indeed to win the public support of renowned soldiers such as General Ludendorff, Captain Roehm, and Hermann Goering in those days.

What did the counter-revolutionaries like best about their first youthful association? In comparison to the entire sample, they liked best (1) the violence or physical attacks, (2) the "comradeship experience," and (3) military training, strikes, or demonstrations. The first two preferences are particularly pronounced among the Kapp *putsch*ists and Free Corps and vigilante fighters against domestic insurgents and the Poles. The militants without action instead liked military training and ideological direction best, and the Free Corps sympathizers liked military training, comradeship, and sports. It would appear that the thrust of youthful interest among the counter-revolutionary groups went overwhelmingly in the paramilitary direction. It may even be fair to say that they stood so much under the militarizing shadow of the Great War that even their emphasis on youthful comradeship was based on a desire to recreate the *Fronterlebnis* rather than the wish to create a youth culture. It is no coincidence that well over three-fourths of the counter-revolutionary fighters were in the war. Most of the rest were victory-watchers eager to be old enough to enlist.

The most extreme activities the counter-revolutionaries engaged in before they turned 25 accordingly differ from the general sample. They stand out spectacularly for organized violence such as the Free Corps and vigilantes waged, but are far below par in such political activities as partisan street-fighting, electioneering, proselytizing, propaganda, and demonstrations. Their style of political violence was evidently quasi-military. This is not by any means to say that they were lacking in militancy or aggressiveness, but rather in political-ideological direction. We have a range of characteristic forms of youthful political involvement which brings out this factor. This measurement has five types of youth postures of which only two are more often found among the counter-revolutionaries than in the general Nazi sample, namely "aggressive, hostile militant" and "authoritarian, leadership cultist." Both denote insufficient politicization and are quite pronounced among all counter-revolutionaries, but most of all among the Free Corps and vigilante fighters. We can surmise that these were people whose natural aggressive tendencies were fixated by the war at the point where they simply lacked all inhibitions against violence toward a designated enemy. The other postures are "prepolitical, parochial," and "fully politicized," of which the Free Corps sympathizers and Kapp *putsch*ists have more than their share. Then there is the posture of being "politically militarized," a synthesis of the paramilitary urge with political-ideological fervor, rather typical of full-fledged storm-troopers. Only the young militants of the "political youth" who saw no action have a goodly share of respondents of this description. Again it is no coincidence that half of this group and an even larger part of the young Free Corps sympathizers were never in the military service, while the Free Corps and vigilante fighters and the Kapp *putsch*ists in large numbers were enthusiastic soldiers.

The military rather than political emphasis continues also when we look at the political home environment of the counter-revolutionaries. Their fathers tend to be more often nationalistic, military-authoritarian, or unpolitical than the fathers of the entire sample, a condition also typical of the fathers of the war generation, as will be recalled. The *voelkisch* element among the fathers of the postwar generation and, with the exception of the Kapp *putsch*ists, conservative, liberal, or Center party fathers is rare. The same appears to be true of the political color of their peers and school environment. Their teachers and friends tend to be nationalistic rather than *voelkisch* or reflecting other prewar parties. In school and at home, incidentally, a disproportionate number of counter-revolutionaries of all groups report intense conflict between them and the school, classmates, or parents. This may well be a sign of their indomitable aggressiveness and lack of social adjustment. Their childhood experiences rarely were stories of the poverty (except for the Free Corps sympathizers) or personal deprivation that often occurs among the other Nazis. Instead they report economically secure and rather sheltered upbringings and strict disciplinarian homes. Conflict between father and son and parental discipline, of course, are very likely to reinforce one another.

War and the Counter-Revolutionaries

As we mentioned above, the Free Corps and vigilante fighters tended to be enthusiastic soldiers to the bitter end. But in general comparison with the entire Nazi sample, hostile reactions toward draft-dodgers and subversives, or the *Fronterlebnis*, were more frequent among the counter-revolutionaries, especially among the Free Corps sympathizers. Their reaction to the German defeat was to blame either the Marxists and Spartakists, or the Kaiser and the civilians. Their sense of cultural shock, moreover, tended to dwell on themes such as social disintegration, the absence of order and discipline, institutional changes, and the disparagement of the rituals and symbols of the old order. The "revolution," as will be recalled, they mostly attributed to the Spartakists, the Jews, or the Bolsheviks. The Kapp *putsch*ists and Free Corps and vigilante fighters against domestic insurgents, however, also tended to blame the rabble, but the anti-Polish fighters pinned some of the responsibility on the Weimar leaders.

Even though the counter-revolutionaries were not very likely to go from the Nazi party into counter-revolutionary activity in the years from 1919 to 1921, quite a few travelled the opposite route. Especially among the militants who never saw action and the Free Corps sympathizers, disproportionate numbers joined the NSDAP or other *voelkisch* action groups before 1922. Far more of them, however, remained with their Free Corps, vigilante, or conservative opposition groups or simply dropped out without joining any other group. When the designated target of their legitimate aggression was beaten, they either kept on ostentatiously marching with the *Stahlhelm* or simply abandoned the militant pursuits until much later. It is not easy to disentangle the multiple group memberships and foci of counter-revolutionary action, as Table II-3 demonstrates. The ages at which the respondents entered these groups average out as follows. The Kapp *putsch*ists were about 26, the Free Corps and vigilante fighters 22, the anti-Polish fighters 24, and the militants without action and Free Corps sympathizers 22 at the time.

1923: The Second Counter Revolution

In the years following the immediate postwar period the militant right by no means went to sleep. In a process of escalation helped along by the instability of the Weimar government and mounting

Table II-3: Organizational Memberships of Counter-revolutionaries, 1919-1921

	Stahl-helm	Anti-foreign group	Anti-insurg. group	Wehr-wolf	Voel-kisch or NSDAP	Jungdo or other	Totals
Kapp putschists	2	8	6	1	3	–	20
Free Corps, vigilantes against insurgents	2	26	13	4	4	–	49
Anti-Polish action	–	21	1	1	3	–	26
Militant groups (but no action)	2	1	8	5	8	–	24
Free Corps sympathizers	11	3	1	3	10	9	37
Insurgents or sympathizers	1	–	–	–	2	5	8
Totals	18	59	29	14	30	14	164

inflation, nationalist, anti-republican propaganda outdid itself. Political assassinations were committed on the republican leaders Matthias Erzberger and Walther Rathenau, and on minor figures. The Ruhr invasion by the French finally heated up right-wing ferment to the point of plans and attempts at a military or political *coup d'état* which was to take away the helm of state from the republican leaders. There are many questions arising from this second counter-revolutionary movement. Were the same people involved in both counter-revolutions, or was there an entirely new alignment? Was this a less military and more political revolt than the earlier one? The involvement of respondents in 1923 was distributed as follows:

FD-36: Involvement in 1923

	Number	Per cent
In other political parties, groups	54	21.9
Participates or sympathizes with Hitler putsch (or in NSDAP)	95	38.4
Anti-occupation activity, group	24	9.6
⌈Stahlhelm, Jungstahlhelm	16	6.4
⌊Other militant veterans' groups	17	6.8
⌈Deutschvoelkisch Freedom Movement	29	11.7
⌊Other voelkisch groups (Schutz-und-Trutzbund until 1922, DSP)	13	5.2
	248	100.0

Let us first of all examine the question of how the counter-revolutionaries of 1919-1921 overlap with those of 1923. As much as 46% of the Kapp *putsch*ists and of the militants without action are now in the Nazi party, or in other *voelkisch* action groups, or they express sympathy with the Hitler *putsch* in Munich. These two groups are the most involved (73%) in 1923. The Free Corps and vigilante fighters are somewhat less involved (65.1%), although many of them (27.3%) are in the NSDAP or in sympathy with the beerhall *putsch*. Quite a few are fighting the occupation or the separatists, or are in militant veterans groups such as *Stahlhelm*. Only a little more than half of the anti-Polish fighters and Free Corps sympathizers are active in 1923, the former mainly in *voelkisch* groups and the latter in the NSDAP or in a militant veterans' organization. We can conclude that not quite two-thirds of the counter-revolutionaries of 1919-1921 and 1923 are the same people and that the extent of this identity is more complete with some of the counter-revolutionary groups than with others.

However, the character of their groups and the nature of their activities have changed rather substantially. The Nazi party and its *putsch* as well as the other *voelkisch* groups which eventually lost most of their members to the NSDAP account for the lion's share of the second counter-revolutionary wave. And there were no more Free Corps or vigilante groups waging organized violence against domestic insurgents or the Poles, but only the strutting demonstration marches of the *Stahlhelm*, and clandestine anti-occupation or anti-separatist activity. Five years from the end of the Great War was too long a time for confused veterans not to get used to peacetime society. Anyone still involved in paramilitary marching and fighting now was likely to have political motives. The overlap of the 1923 activists with the total anti-occupation involvement, incidentally, is greater than it appears in the 1923 breakdown. Fifty-seven and two-tenths percent of the 152 persons involved with the occupation were fighting it in 1923. Quite a few of the anti-occupation respondents belonged to *voelkisch* action groups including the NSDAP, or to militant veterans' groups, or to other legitimate parties and were counted there in the 1923 breakdown.

The 1923 Activists

Unlike the counter-revolutionaries of 1919-1921, those of 1923 are clustered in age about the cohorts born between 1895 and 1905—in other words a mixture of war and postwar generations. In addition to this mix, the Nazis and Hitler *putsch* sympathizers also included some of the oldest age cohorts while the other *voelkisch* action groups are almost exclusively made up of the war and prewar generations. The militant veterans and anti-occupation groups were the youngest of the lot. Like the first counter-revolutionaries, the activists of 1923 tended to be rather urban, which was particularly true of the *voelkisch* and Nazi groups. These two groups also had a sizeable share of people who failed financially or became unemployed in the period prior to the great depression.

The 1923 group, and especially the *voelkisch* and Nazi respondents, tended to come from military-civil service, or artisans' and businessmen's homes. The militant veterans' groups, by contrast, often had high-ranking military men or professionals or farmers as fathers. Workers' sons or daughters are conspicuous by their absence among the Nazi and *voelkisch* samples of 1923, a time when the NSDAP and some other *voelkisch* groups were believed still to be somewhat "socialistic." The two *voelkisch* groups exhibit some upwardly mobile trend though only in urban settings. On the other hand, the Nazis and also the *Stahlhelm* respondents of 1923 include a good many persons in social decline. The much-touted *Volksgemeinschaft* finds warm endorsement from all 1923 groups save the militant veterans, a fact that casts considerable doubt on the special Nazi appeal of this *voelkisch* slogan. The military veterans and members of other parties show the most rigid class-consciousness.

Two Counter-Revolutions and the NSDAP

It has been suggested from various quarters that the Free Corps and vigilante organizations were a "vanguard of National Socialism." The term "vanguard" is, unfortunately, so imprecise as to leave in doubt what relationship other than one of preceding the main army in time might be suggested by it. Let us try to put different meanings of "vanguard" to the test. First of all, there is the meaning that the vanguard and main army are of the same kind and composition. The differences between the counter-revolutionary groups of 1919-1921, including the Free Corps and vigilantes, and those of 1923 have already been established. The first counter-revolution was quite different in social composition and military character from that of 1923, which bore at least some resemblance to the entire Nazi sample in this respect. There is a second kind of resemblance, similar ideological outlook, which we shall discuss in the next section.

Another meaning of vanguard might be that the counter-revolutionary experiences, like the anti-occupation and anti-separatist struggle, may have predisposed the people involved to enter the party earlier than others or even to found or co-found locals in their missionary zeal. In this respect, the record of the first counter-revolutionary groups is rather negative. As a whole, they played the role of founders or co-founders of locals far less often than did the rest of the Nazi sample. The Free Corps and vigilante fighters against domestic insurgents and the Kapp *putsch*ists, in particular, tended to join the NSDAP only after it had become at least a substantial minority in their areas or waited until the bandwagon was well in motion. The counter-revolutionaries of 1919-1921 indeed contributed greatly to the growth of the Nazi movement before its dissolution in 1924. But they did not join again in great numbers after the movement was revived in 1925 and therefore their contribution to the over-all growth of the Nazi party was actually lagging behind the rest of the sample as late as 1929.

The activists of 1923, by comparison, include disproportionate numbers of founders or co-founders of NSDAP locals, especially among those involved or in sympathy with the Hitler *putsch* and members of *voelkisch* or other parties. They also boosted the party's enrollment not only in the pre-1924 period, but also during the reconstruction era from 1925 to 1927. In this respect, then, the counter-revolutionary currents of 1923, rather than the Free Corps and vigilantes of 1919-1921, were indeed a kind of vanguard which contributed greatly to the strength and resurgence of the NSDAP in the second half of the 1920s.

There is a third meaning of "vanguard" which comes to mind in this context. Did the counter-revolutionaries of 1919-1921 or those of 1923 lay down a lasting pattern of political violence for the Nazi party to follow in the years of the great push, from 1929 to 1933? We have already seen that the earlier counter-revolutionaries tended to turn to *Stahlhelm* demonstrations or to stop indulging in political violence altogether once the warlike patterns of organized violence against domestic insurgents or the Poles had lost their point. In sheer numbers, there are 90 respondents of the early counter-revolutionaries who report having been engaged in political violence in the years 1919 to 1924, including 68 Kapp *putsch*ists and Free Corps or vigilante fighters. The activists of 1923 include only 61 who report having been engaged in political violence in 1919-1924—23 Hitler *putsch* sympathizers or Nazis, 17 anti-occupation fighters, 7 *voelkisch* and 9 other party members, and 5 militant veterans. The data do not permit sorting out the 1919-1921 counter-revolutionaries from the 1923 activists in the development sketched here.[9]

[9] The data for the counter-revolutionaries of 1919-1921 permit our approximation, though, if we leave aside the change from violence to demonstrations or the like. The Kapp *putsch*ists report 14 violently engaged in 1919-1924, 3 in 1925-1928, 5 in 1929-1930, and 9 in 1931-

Of the violent of 1919-1924, only 35 were still violently engaged in 1925-1928, while comparable numbers either withdrew completely or limited themselves to electioneering, demonstrations, and proselytizing. In the years 1929-1930 the number of violent fighters among the original group of 1919-1924 increased to 38, while many others shifted to proselytizing, another vital activity of the Nazi movement. During the final fighting years, the number of the violent from the original group climbed to 54 with another 44 proselytizing. By that time, of course, another 118 violent men who had not been politically violent in 1919-1924 had stepped alongside them. The originally violent group, in any case, maintained a disproportionate role as habitual purveyors of violence throughout the three periods following the first measurement.

It is a fair guess that the violent activists of 1923 did not slump as much in their engagement in political violence in 1925-1928 as did the earlier counter-revolutionaries for the simple reason that their kind of partisan street violence was more in line with the Nazi style of the years to follow. In any case, it appears to be true that both counter-revolutions of 1919-1921 and 1923 were indeed a vanguard of the violent style of politics that followed, although each in its own way.[10] And, though it may seem difficult to imagine, there was a sizeable panel of right-wing *Schlaeger* (sluggers) who literally pummeled their way through the entire duration of the Weimar Republic.

Counter-Revolutionary Ideologies and Attitudes

How do the two counter-revolutionary hosts compare ideologically after they joined the party? The counter-revolutionaries of 1919-1921 stand out with their emphasis on revanchism, a particularly strong tendency among the Free Corps and vigilante fighters and the Kapp *putsch*ists. Less prominent is Nordic or German romanticism, which characterizes a disproportionate number of Free Corps fighters and sympathizers and militants without action. There is also a good deal of Hitler cult among the Free Corps fighters. The *Volksgemeinschaft*, otherwise the theme most frequently named by

---

1932, with relatively constant totals. The Free Corps and vigilantes against Poles and insurgents report 64 in 1919-1924, 15 in 1925-1928, 19 in 1929-1930 and 36 in 1931-1932.

[10] Of 247 activists of 1923, 148 (59.2%) joined the stormtroopers, while of the 209 earlier counter-revolutionaries, 118 (56.2%) became stormtroopers. Considering the change in the style of violence and the passage of time, the latter figures are remarkably high.

all the Nazis, elicits a strong response only from the Free Corps sympathizers. Superpatriotism, the second most frequent choice, finds favor among Kapp *putsch*ists, Free Corps fighters, and militants who saw no action.

The activists of 1923 stand out from the general sample mostly with revanchism and Nordic-German romanticism. These two themes are disproportionately represented among all the 1923 groups, revanchism being strongest among militant veterans, and romanticism among the Hitler *putsch* sympathizers. Less prominent are the themes of antisemitism and superpatriotism, in which the members of *voelkisch*, anti-occupation, and militant veterans' groups excel. We may receive the impression that the NSDAP and the beerhall *putsch* sympathizers of 1923 were not so much preoccupied with antisemitism as with Nordic-German romanticism, revanchism, and the Hitler cult, in this order. The *Volksgemein-schaft* once more is underrepresented as a theme except among the members of other political parties.

The perception of the Weimar Republic by the two counter-revolutions differs in minor, but significant, ways. Both tend to see the republic more as "the system," run by the Jews or by the "red and black parties," than does the rest of the sample. To the Kapp *putsch*ists of 1920, these two are indeed the points of emphasis, along with accusing the republic of being "run by Marxists." The Nazis and Hitler *putsch*ists as well as the anti-occupation fighters of 1923 also place great stress on this "black-red-and-yellow republic," and to a lesser degree so do all the other groups. The differences appear with the traditional, anti-capitalistic objections to Weimar. Among the counter-revolutionaries, the Free Corps and vigilante fighters, their sympathizers, and also the militants who saw no action, raise these traditional criticisms against the "liberal-Marxist system" and the "multi-party state" of Weimar. In 1923, the militant veterans echo the charge, and there is a strong undercurrent of it also among the *voelkisch* and Nazi groups. This presumably constitutes the fault-line between anti-modernism and modernism in the two counter-revolutions.

A second such fault-line is the one which delimits the anti-establishmentarian sentiments in the two counter-revolutions. If we take the lists of chief phobias for both groups, the counter-revolutionaries of 1919-1921, much more than those of 1923, emphasize the Catholic, liberal, and reactionary establishment as an object of their hostility. This tendency is particularly pronounced among the Free Corps and vigilante fighters. In 1923, it also occurs among militant veterans and among the Hitler *putsch* participants, and sympathizers. However, the anti-establishmentarian strain in both counter-revolutions is only about one-fourth of the anti-Socialist, anti-Communist response, the largest response given. And it is not as strong as the combination of antisemitism with anti-Marxism, which was particularly favored by the Kapp *putsch*ists and Free Corps sympathizers of 1919-1921 and the members of *voelkisch* and militant veterans groups in 1923.

Let us take a closer look at the patterns of antisemitism in both counter-revolutions. The variation among the various groups of 1919-1921 are considerable. The Free Corps and vigilante fighters against domestic insurgents, with 56%, are the least antisemitic, while the militants without action (85.7%), the Kapp *putsch*ists (83.3%), the Free Corps sympathizers (76.6%), and anti-Polish fighters (76.2%) are all far above the average of the entire sample. Nevertheless, the Free Corps and vigilante fighters together with the Kapp *putsch*ists, have the highest proportion (19.5-20.8%) of respondents who speak of threatening conspiracies, the telltale sign of readiness for extreme prejudicial action. The Free Corps sympathizers are not far behind (16.7%). The counter-revolutionaries of 1919-1921 relatively less often tell of alleged personal encounters with Jews, nor do they seem to have experienced as much of the sudden *Judenkoller*, probably for the same reasons that they far less often report having suffered cultural shock than did the whole sample. They acted out their shock, so to speak, by becoming politically active. Many Kapp *putsch*ists and Free Corps sympathizers, however, give evidence of both strong cultural shock and *Judenkoller* as well as a propensity to tell antisemitic personal anecdotes. Finally, the counter-revolutionaries of 1919-1921 disproportionately tend toward the milder sort of prejudiced verbiage. Such verbal projections are especially frequent among the anti-Polish fighters and the militants who saw no action. The small number of insurgents and their sympathizers, incidentally, include a very high proportion of antisemites, which is probably the main reason they defected from the extreme left and eventually joined the Nazis. Perhaps the surprisingly high numbers of antisemitic early counterrevolutionaries and militant veterans in this collection of Nazis can be similarly explained.

The activists of 1923 turn out to be relatively less prejudiced than those of 1919-1921. The *voelkisch* members (91.8%) and the Hitler *putsch* participants and sympathizers (74.7%) lead the pack, but the other groups are only to about two-thirds overtly prejudiced. The *voelkisch* (27.3%), Hitler *putsch*ist (17.3%), and anti-occupation respondents (27.7%) have the largest numbers of persons who speak of threat and counter-threat. There is a smaller proportion of the milder verbal projections and more prominent clusters of persons with the *Judenkoller* among the *voelkisch* (39.4%) and early Nazi (33.3%) respondents. The over-all impression of the patterns of antisemitism among the counter-revolutionaries of both periods is, of course, modified by the fact that they all eventually joined the Nazi party, whether they were with the Free Corps, the *Stahlhelm*, or the early NSDAP at that time. Nevertheless it is remarkable that intense prejudice was just as often and sometimes more often found in these other organizations than in the early Nazi party. Far from being an alibi for the Nazis, this is an indictment of the climate of opinion in these other right-wing groups.

PART THREE

Weimar Youth Culture and the Young Nazis

Almost seamless is the web of youth organizations of the most varied kind in the Weimar Republic. Although we can, of course, draw lines of distinction, the protean nature of the youth culture was forever evolving new groups, merging or splitting old groups, and changing the names and nature of any and all established groups. Youngsters grew into the youth culture age, or rather they awakened to it at the light touch of the magic wand of Peter Pan. For youngsters the youth culture was a long moratorium between childhood and adulthood, a time for spontaneity, roaming on endless hikes and tours, for discovering their independence and competence away from home, an in-between state when they sought their identity by merging the self with the group or with a close friend and rediscovering their identity upon re-emerging from the cocoon of group life. The group for a while became their identity and therefore they often had to wander from group to group to find the right kind.

Politics had little to do with it, at least not in the early stages of a youth group career. Only gradually, as the young people became a little older and under the pressure of victimizing events, did political identifications and heroes emerge. If there had been no heroes and persecutions, they would have had to be invented, for they were needed for personality growth. We may wish that the early Peter Pan stage had never ended and the young person had never had to grow up. For, quite subtly, the carefree wanderings became political crusades, the occasional frictions turned into partisan street battles, and Peter Pan emerged a mindless stormtrooper slugging his way into the Third Reich.

Weimar Youth Culture

A sensitive account of the search for the right youth group interwoven with coming of age politically is given by a worker's son born in 1908 (no. 250) who was prevented from getting a *Gymnasium* education by financial reasons and his father's remarriage. He was quite taken by the war effort and used to play soldiers with his friends. He would not go into agriculture and his father would not let him go to sea. Instead, at 14, he became a technician's apprentice for four years in a large company:

> A short time after I started working there, I noticed a young man in strange clothes who one Saturday noon walked past us with a military knapsack. I could not resist asking him about it the following week. He was pleased to tell me that he was in a wandering group and that they went on hikes Sundays, or even Saturdays, and set up tents, and cooked in the woods. I was immediately enthusiastic and asked to be allowed to come along. . . .
>
> I got to know the group, several youths between 15 and 18. They did not smoke or drink alcohol and rejected so-called good manners and the conventional life-style.

In an aside the respondent distinguishes three kinds of youth groups, the "purely pacifistic" (Socialist or Communist),[1] Christian (Protestant or Catholic), and *voelkisch*-nationalistic youth movements, and continues:

> The group I was in was purely pacifistic. The brother of my hiking comrade belong to a *voelkisch*-nationalist group, the Journeymen of the DHV, with headquarters in Solingen. I did not like the pacifism of my group, but preferred the romantic and the military aspects and hence we split off after a short time and joined the Journeymen in Duesseldorf. Our leader was an older fellow who had been a soldier in the war. He was a nationalist and during our hikes always drew our attention to the beautiful sights of the fatherland. He told us of his experiences in the war and organized our group in a somewhat military manner. Thus we received our first political education.

The respondent also learned about the *voelkisch* movement, attended a Nazi rally addressed by Ludendorff after a 20-mile hike and met stormtroopers in the youth hostel.

> The youth movement was split three ways, as I explained, but because of our common interests the groups of right and left often cooperated. We had our common song fests when we rehearsed and sang old German folk songs. We had our common sports evenings . . .

[1] The Socialist *Arbeiterjugend* was founded in 1904 in competition with the Christian Social (Stoecker) and Christian Young Men's associations and at first concerned itself mostly with the exploitation and physical abuse of apprentices. In 1917 the *Freie Sozialistische Jugend* was founded; it soon developed a Youth-Movement-like style. See Wolfgang Arlt, ed. *Deutschlands Junge Garde*, Berlin: Neues Leben, 1959.

and, while hiking, we always met other groups in the hostels or elsewhere and got to know everyone. I used to go with my hiking comrade
several times to the "nest evenings" of a pacifist group and had great
discussions there. For hours we talked about one affair which we ourselves considered downright dishonorable. This group wanted to send
their members to France and Belgium in their love of mankind in
order to help rebuild what our fathers and the hostile troops had had
to destroy there.

These youth groups, invincible though they seem, had an obvious
weakness which contained the seeds of their destruction: the attraction of the opposite sex.

> Our group, the Journeymen, was not working out anymore, be-
> cause the leader wanted to get married and no longer had enough time
> for us. So we were looking for another youth group and I met this
> comrade in vocational school who belonged to the German Boy Scouts.
> He told me that the French occupation of Duesseldorf had outlawed the
> Boy Scouts. . . .
> I liked the whole approach of Scouting better than the purely
> *buendisch* (Youth Movement)[2] affairs earlier. Here we had literature
> and guidance on the meaning of Scouting and how to organize the
> hikes and encampments. In the earlier groups there had been such a
> search for something new and no one had a clear picture before his
> eyes. Here there was a goal and the work was laid out in a program,
> so to speak. There followed wonderful "nest evenings" and hikes and
> we also tried to recruit by all means one or another classmate or other
> acquaintances. In this fashion we got one fellow, who is still my friend,
> but who is now a high-up stormtrooper leader. . . .

On one occasion, the respondent again met one of the pacifists
who had meanwhile joined the *Nerother Bund*, a right-wing group
of university and secondary-school students. They agreed to bicycle
together to a *Stahlhelm* meeting outside the occupied area which
was also attended by *Jungdo* and the stormtroopers, all in uniforms
and with flags. On the way, they also met a group of the *voelkisch
Wikingbund* who had been expelled by the French and told stories
about skirmishes with Communists. The *Stahlhelm* rally left "an
enormous impression," all these "nationalist-thinking men" with
their uniforms, insignia, and various flags. The former pacifist was

---

[2] For a description of the *voelkisch*, conservative-revolutionary leanings
of the German Boy Scouts, see Curt Hotzel, ed. *Deutscher Aufstand: die
Revolution des Nachkriegs*, Stuttgart: Kohlhammer, 1934, pp. 239 ff.
This book also relates the takeover of the initially unpolitical Youth Movement by Free Corps officers. *Ibid.*, pp. 228 ff.

sorely tempted to join one of these organizations, but could not make up his mind, and in the meantime the respondent recruited him for his Boy Scouts. The group prospered and grew and subtly became more involved in politics.

> We *experienced* the death of Schlageter. We knew somehow that he was shot as a freedom fighter and not just as an adventurer. We understood his deed. We *experienced* how Willi Schwarz threw a hand grenade into a French patrol and was subsequently tortured in French jails to the edge of insanity. We *experienced* how even the Youth Movement leaders were arrested; how our houses were searched for military items like regulation knapsacks; and there were occasional small clashes with the occupation troops. And we *experienced* the passive resistance [italics supplied] . . . in a hidden water-mill near Duisburg where the activists of the passive resistance had found a hiding place. . . . A big iron swastika was outside the door. Every Saturday young people from Duisburg, Essen, Duesseldorf, etc. gathered here to tell each other of the new deeds of the Ruhr fighters. An old officer from the World War read from his war diary and told us a little war adventure. Monday morning we would be back at work with renewed strength, the heart full of resistance against the oppressors and of faith in Germany's future.

The respondent then tells of the frequent need to change the name of his Boy Scouts in order to elude their prohibition, and told of physical skirmishes with Socialist or Communist youth and, later, with the *Reichsbanner*. The group became more and more committed to *voelkisch* principles. The respondent, now 18, finally finished his apprenticeship and went with a hiking comrade on a three months' trip through Bavaria and Austria. After a series of sporadic jobs interspersed with further roaming, he finally began to lose interest in youth group activities because he had acquired a girl friend.

> The group life and hiking declined more and more. Various members got too old, some had already joined the NSDAP, others like me had girl friends, and some were too busy with their jobs. . . . I had been approached now and then to join the NSDAP, the *Stahlhelm*, or some other organization. I always declined because I felt too young to be a party member and would not permit myself a definite political opinion. I did not like the *Stahlhelm* anyway because there was no spirit of comradeship . . . and there were class distinctions there.

But soon he began to go to Nazi rallies and became "strongly enthusiastic." He joined in March 1930. At first, he was not inclined to become a stormtrooper, because their evening schedule would have interfered with his love life. But, witnessing a white-shirted SA demonstration at the time the brown-shirts were outlawed, he marched along and, having received his share of hateful "red" insults and attacks, he joined the SA as well.

The Political Youth of Weimar

The generation of German youth which came of age during and soon after World War One was dubbed "the political youth generation" by the German sociologist Helmut Schelsky in contrast to both the preceding and following generations. Prewar youth had been the setting of the romantic but not very political Youth Movement, a spontaneous hiking and guitar-playing, all-male youth culture movement of protest against the sterile urban and industrial world of their middle-class elders.[3] The youth generation of World War Two and the years after that war is called the "skeptical generation" because of its disillusionment with ideology and political causes and its preoccupation with private pursuits and accomplishments.[4] The "political youth generation" was politicized in part by the First World War and its postwar experiences. The absence of the fathers and the changing role of the mothers, together with the visible collapse of many prewar social norms, may explain the new attitude of youth. There are many testimonials to the generation gap in the Abel biographies by young respondents who contrast their own early interest in politics with the apolitical frame of mind of their *bourgeois* parents.

A typical response of this sort comes from a vintner's son, born 1911 (no. 206) to a socially respectable family, who preferred to be in a brawling "workers' party." As he puts it, "we young ones had more direct access to politics than the older generation. They

[3] There is a growing literature on the prewar Youth Movement. See, for example, Walter Z. Laqueur, *Young Germany*, New York: Basic Books, 1962, or Harry Pross, *Eros und Politik*, Bern: Scherz, 1964.

[4] See Helmut Schelsky, *Die skeptische Generation*, Duesseldorf: Diederich, 1960, and, for an overview, Werner Klose, *Lebensformen deutscher Jugend, Vom Wandervogel zur Popgeneration*, Muenchen-Wien: Olzog, 1970. Arthur Dix, in *Die deutschen Reichstagswahlen 1871-1930 und die Wandlungen der Volksgliederung*, Tuebingen: Mohr, 1930, describes the young generation as "frequently having a liking for playing war, for sports, discipline, and right- and left-wing radicalism, but in part also totally turned away from politics" (p. 35). See also Herbert Moller, "Youth as a Force in the Modern World," *Comparative Studies in Society and History*, vol. 10 (Oct./July 1967-68), 237-260.

were still told that politics is bad for the character, when in fact it is the bad characters that ruin politics." The "old aunties in my family," he relates, were deeply shocked about his political involvements and recurrent troubles with the law. Frequently, respondents mention that they began to read political tracts and partisan literature in their late teens, or even as early as at the age of fourteen or fifteen.

Another example is a clerk born in 1911 (no. 96), who at the age of 12 already founded a *Deutsch-voelkisch* Students' Association:

> One often hears the question why it was that youth spontaneously rallied to Hitler. But the experiences of war, revolution, and inflation supply an explanation. We were not spared anything. We knew and felt the worries in the house. The shadow of necessity never left our table and made us silent. *We were rudely pushed out of our childhood and not shown the right path.* The struggle for life got to us early. Misery, shame, hatred, lies, and civil war imprinted themselves on our souls and made us mature early. So we searched and found Adolf Hitler. What attracted us like a magnet was precisely the fact that he only made demands of us and promised us nothing. He demanded of every person a total commitment to his movement and therefore to Germany [italics supplied].

ONE

The Broad Range of Youth Organizations

One of the important differences between Weimar youth culture and contemporary parallels is that Weimar youth was highly organized in groups, however spontaneous their group life. The extent to which the Abel respondents belonged to youth organizations or to the youth sections of political movements is astounding. For the purpose of our measurement, we defined youth membership as membership before the age of 26 in any youth-oriented voluntary social group with the exception of trade unions, professional organizations, and the military. Seventy per cent (362) of the Abel respondents who gave a record of their affiliations (517) reported membership in such a group, including many who belonged to two or more groups in succession. The large proportion of organized youth is a measure of the extent to which the political youth of Weimar had emancipated itself from the age-heterogeneous family life and come into its own as organized peer groups. The respondents' first youth group memberships are distributed as follows:

The distribution shows that only a small proportion of these young people were immediately swept into the Nazi party and its youth groups. The common assumption that the typical early recruit to the National Socialists was a naive newcomer to politics and organizational life applies at best only to the 11.8% whose first youth organization was National Socialist. The others had all tasted other youth group settings before gravitating toward the Nazi party. The quasi-military groups make up about one-third of the memberships. Among them, the groups specifically related to the war, such as the *Jugendwehr* auxiliaries, or the postwar vigilantes and Free Corps, are a negligible portion. Far more prominent are the *Stahlhelm* and *Jungstahlhelm* veterans' organizations, which also accepted young non-veterans yearning to carry on the military traditions,[5] the *voelkisch Wehrwolf* and *Wikingbund*, which were also

---

[5] See the description of the *Jungstahlhelm* program for 17-24-year-olds in Hotzel, *Deutscher Aufstand*, pp. 222 ff. The author also describes the breakdown of "our beautiful faith in the fatherland" at the time of the

FD-13: First Youth Group Membership

	Number	Per cent
Quasi-military youth:		
Stahlhelm, Jungstahlhelm	11	2.1
Wehrwolf, Wikingbund, Oberland,		
anti-occupation group	27	5.2
Vigilantes	15	2.9
World War I auxiliaries		
(e.g., Jugendwehr)	23	4.4
Other military training groups	18	3.5
Stahlhelm after groups 2-5	8	1.5
Free Corps, border protection	17	3.3
All quasi-military	119	22.9
Youth-Movement-related groups:		
Jungdeutscher Orden (Jungdo)	12	2.3
Wandervogel, Buendisch Youth	23	4.4
voelkisch youth groups	27	5.2
Hindenburg Youth (DVP)	2	.4
Other bourgeois youth	2	.4
Bismarckjugend (DNVP)	17	3.3
DHV youth	13	2.5
National athletics clubs		
(Turnerbund etc.)	9	1.7
Religious, agricultural youth	11	2.2
All Youth-Movement related	116	22.4
Nazi Youth, Hitler Youth (first)	61	11.8
Other youth groups:		
Unpolitical sports clubs	12	2.3
Socialist, trade union youth	32	6.2
Communist youth, Red Front	10	1.9
Non-socialist unions	2	.4
Cultural groups	10	1.9
All other groups	66	12.7
No youthful group association	155	30.2
Grand total	517	100.0

clandestinely active in the occupied areas, and other organizations offering military training to youths anxious to play soldier.

A typical career of this sort was that of a minister's son, born 1904 (no. 97), who during the war volunteered for the *Jungmanns-organisation*, an auxiliary, and was after the war a *Zeitfreiwilliger*[6]

"revolution" and the unpolitical motives that drove many students into the Free Corps.

[6] The *Zeitfreiwillige* units were emergency units attached temporarily to Free Corps or the *Reichswehr*. See Erwin Koennemann, *Einwohner-wehren und Zeitfreiwilligenverbaende*, Berlin: Militaerverlag, 1969.

involved in the Kapp *putsch*. At the same time he belonged to the *Koernerbund*, joined the Boy Scouts, and then the *voelkisch Schutz-und-Trutzbund*, where he experienced his first meeting-hall brawl. Then he changed over to *Jungdo* and finally to the *Jungdeutsche* (*Jakobskoetter*) before ending up in the SA in 1924. He rejoined in 1931 after years of political inactivity.

The original Youth Movement was a purely bourgeois phenomenon even though by the turn of the century the growth of youth and hiking groups had spread into the Socialist and the Catholic proletarian masses. The SPD, in particular, had discovered the new needs of youth, especially of apprentices, and of children in the decade before the war. The Bismarck Youth of the DNVP, according to the respondents' descriptions, fit less well because it lacked the spirit of opposition against the establishment of the old order. The youth of the *voelkisch* Retail Clerks Union (DHV) which was allied to the DNVP, on the other hand, had all these qualifications and used to engage in hiking, too. But there is some doubt as to whether its membership can be considered all bourgeois.

The *Deutscher Turnerbund* and other national athletic groups harked back to the Napoleonic days of *Turnvater* Jahn, a nationalistic demagogue, and perhaps should not be considered an authentic part of the Youth Movement either. The sample also includes three members of agricultural youth and four each of Protestant and Catholic youth groups such as the *Windthorstbund*, whose traditional or religious cast may speak against its other Youth Movement characteristics. We have cross tabulated the agricultural-religious groups and the conservative groups (*Bismarckjugend*, DHV, and *Turnerbund*) separately so as not to dilute the more typical groups, although the small numbers may not allow much statistical inference in any case.

As for the rest, the Socialist and trade union youth shared some of the Youth Movement outlook and practices such as hiking and a love of nature and folklore. Yet working-class youth of necessity had a different perspective on youth group activity since it generally had to go to work from the age of fourteen, while middle-class youth would still be in school. Leisure-time activities for working-class youth, consequently, were less characterized by a personal need to demonstrate independence from home. They were less footloose and, in particular, less prone to the building of castles in the sky. It is hard to imagine a working-class organization with a name like the *Jungdeutscher Orden* (*Jungdo*), with its connotations of medieval knights and crusades. A young apprentice or worker was more likely to want to belong to a *Arbeitersportverein* or to the

Friends of Nature. The Socialist Workers' Youth (SAJ) was a more integral youth culture group and quite noticeably less politicized and militarized than Communist youth (KJ). Just as we may consider most Youth Movement groups to have been still in a relatively unpolitical limbo, the typical SAJ member did not yet consider himself a full-fledged Socialist fighter in a manner comparable to the young Red Fronter or SA stormtrooper. In the political life cycle, so to speak, Youth-Movement-type group memberships were still a part of the moratorium of youth culture halfway between the political innocence of childhood and adult involvement. Communist and Nazi youth, however, strove directly for the political adult role.

Age and Social Background

How do these groups differ in the cross tabulations with age, social background, and other variables? Broken down according to their dates of birth, those reporting no youthful association turn out to be by far the oldest group, with more than half born before 1890 and 91% born earlier than the postwar generation (1902). Evidently youth groups were not yet a mass phenomenon. The quasi-military youth groups are made up to 42.2% of the war generation (1895-1901) and another one-half born 1902 and later. Thus they evidently include a good many who joined their youth groups just before, during, or right after the war as well as later. The conservative and religious youth groups resemble them in their age distribution and so do the Socialist and Communist youth, of whom a good third was a part of that immediate postwar generation (born 1902 to 1905) which "broke without having been shelled by the cannons." By far the youngest group are those who directly joined the stormtroopers (SA) or Hitler Youth (HJ). Over one-half of them were born after 1908, and 82% after 1905. With the growth of the movement it stands to reason that SA and HJ were more available to these late age cohorts than to the earlier ones. *Jungdo*, the Youth Movement, and *voelkisch* youth are the next youngest with one-third born after 1905 and nearly two-thirds in the postwar generation. Prewar Youth Movement membership, it would appear, was less likely to produce Nazis than was that of the Weimar Republic.

As for their chief location, those reporting no youth group membership often live in Berlin, the residue perhaps of earlier rural-urban migrations. Respondents who immediately joined the SA or HJ are to over one-half from rural or small-town areas under 10,000. Altogether, over three-fourths of them live in non-metropolitan areas where political activism was probably more of a novelty in their day. The quasi-military youth group members are next in rural and small-town background, and the Socialist-Communist youth, the bourgeois Youth Movement and the conservative youth groups are nearly two-thirds metropolitan. The differential between huge, modern metropoles and the smaller towns and cities evidently mirrors major differences in Weimar youth cultures. Perhaps one has to live in a highly urbanized environment to feel the urge to run away from it. Their economic fates in the depression, however, show up those who immediately joined the stormtroopers, the quasi-military youth groups, and the Socialist-Communist youth members with the highest rates of victims of the depression. This may well represent a causal relationship between youthful unemployment and right-wing radicalization. This impression is deepened by the fact that 20-30% of these three groups in the same order report that their fathers died when they were under 18 years of age. The economic and psychological marginality of fatherless families may well have sent them on the way to look for a new father figure.

As to their fathers' occupations, the conservatives, the Youth Movement, and the young stormtroopers tended to have military-civil servants for fathers, another sign of the significance of this milieu. The quasi-military groups more often had rather non-military artisans, businessmen, or farmers as fathers. The young stormtroopers also tended to have artisan fathers; the fathers of more than half of the Socialist and Communist youth were, naturally, workers. The Youth Movement group members frequently had risen to middle-class status only in the last generation, though from an urban working-class background. In other words, their social-climbing parents may well have pushed their children into alienation. The same is true of the quasi-military group, which furthermore includes many in social decline. The recent upward mobility faintly reminds us of the complaint of young radicals in this country that their parents care only about the economic rat-race. The young stormtroopers, along with the conservatives and the agricultural and religious groups, tend to be socially static, a condition to which we shall come back again later.

Regarding their religious affiliation, close to three-fourths of the Socialists and Communists, the young stormtroopers, and the Youth Movement members fail to state their religion—an indication of their secularism. Their educational level also varies considerably. The bourgeois Youth Movement groups rank highest, followed by the young stormtroopers and the quasi-military groups. The Communists and Socialists have the least formal education, and just above them stand the older respondents who were never in a youth group. As for their military service, only the older group without youthful affiliation had seen peacetime service; it also shows the heaviest and most dedicated service in the war. More than half of the quasi-military, conservative, and agricultural-religious groups had no service at all, which is also true of two-thirds of the Socialist-Communist and Youth Movement groups, and of all the young stormtroopers. A good one-fourth of the quasi-military and Youth Movement groups were what we have called vicarious victory-watchers, a fact that may explain their subsequent urge to play soldier. Thus the effect or after-effects of the war constitute only a transition to the pure youth rebellion of the HJ and SA youth.

Reaction to War and Revolution

The reaction of the different groups to war and revolution varies according to their age and military service. Only a few of the young stormtroopers had any recollection of that time. To most of them the great war and the German defeat was an irrelevant piece of ancient history. The conservatives and the Youth Movement groups show a good deal of hostility toward civilians and draft-dodgers. Half of the same two groups and also of the quasi-military groups were enthusiastic soldiers who often won decorations or promotions. The attitude of the Communist and Socialist groups (and also of the older groups) to the defeat is one of acceptance. Many of them had also expressed their increasing disaffection with the war itself and accepted the "revolution" with equanimity. The Youth Movement groups, and to a lesser degree the quasi-military groups, tended to blame the Marxists or Spartakists for the German defeat. The Spartakus movement and the mutineers were also blamed by the older group, the Youth Movement, and the quasi-military groups for the revolution. The conservatives instead tended to blame it on the Jews or on the street rabble.

The themes of cultural shock upon the encounter with postwar society are also very revealing. The conservatives inclined toward the complaint of moral disintegration of society, while the quasi-military youth groups, naturally, were more concerned about the "absence of order and discipline." The Youth Movement groups, interestingly, stress the institutional changes and their shock at the new leadership of Weimar just as much as do the much older groups who never belonged to a youth organization. Here the sincere nostalgia of their elders is evidently mirrored in the ideology of the bourgeois youth counter-culture. Another group high in shock at the new leadership of Weimar are the Socialists and Communists.

This may also be a likely manifestation of the antisemitism which probably drove many of them into the Nazi camp.

Counter-revolutionary involvements and attitudes are naturally high with the quasi-military groups, which were heavily involved in the vigilantes and Free Corps or belonged to military training groups in the years from 1919 to 1922. The Youth Movement groups differ only by degree. But whereas the conservatives were quite involved in the vigilantes and the Kapp *putsch*, the Communists and Socialists stand out for their sympathy with or participation in the revolutionary activities of the insurgents. The young stormtroopers, and also the older respondents who never belonged to a youth group, were the least involved in the counter-revolution of 1919-1922. In the anti-occupation struggle, on the other hand, one-half to two-thirds of the young stormtroopers (n=15), the conservatives, and the quasi-military groups suffered expulsion and other penalties, another indication of the significance of the occupation. In 1923, the young stormtroopers were otherwise only minimally involved. The Socialists and Communists were mostly in other legitimate parties. The quasi-military groups were active in the *Ruhrkampf* and marched with militant veterans groups, or with *voelkisch* action groups, or sympathized with the Hitler *putsch*. The conservative and Youth Movement groups were mostly with other parties including *voelkisch* action groups.

How did the various youth group members become involved in adult political activity during the Weimar Republic? In the period from 1919 to 1924, the quasi-military groups, with two-thirds engaged in demonstrations and physical violence, were far out in front, followed at some distance by the Youth Movement, which at an early point seems to have suffered substantial defections to *voelkish* action groups and the Free Corps. The Socialist and Communist youth rank even higher in physical violence, though not in demonstrations. In the "quiet period" from 1925 to 1928, the young stormtroopers suddenly come to the top of the violence scale and, together with the Reds of past or present, report more engagements in physical violence than do the quasi-military groups, although the latter still report far more participation in demonstrations than any other group. In the years 1929 through 1932, when the political climate was becoming feverish, nearly half of the young stormtroopers and formerly Communist and Socialist youth were engaged in political violence, while another 35 to 45% of these groups and of the Youth Movement, the quasi-military youth groups, and older respondents were demonstrating and proselytizing.

Whether the youth organizations played a role in introducing the respondents to the Nazi party is not easy to say. The most frequent modes of introduction to the party were (1) through a friend or fellow-worker, (2) by attending Nazi rallies, and (3) by becoming aware of Nazi ideology from the press or literature. The first two could equally involve the intermediary role of a youth group. The Youth Movement groups, for example, were most often introduced to the party through a friend or fellow-worker, a popular route also for the young stormtroopers and the Socialists and Communists. Awareness of the Nazi ideology, on the other hand, was a more important attraction for the quasi-military groups and older respondents who had never been in a youth group. The relationship between the group memberships and the ideological points of emphasis after they had joined is also worth noting. There is a strong tendency for the quasi-military groups and the older respondents to emphasize revanchism and superpatriotism as their dominant themes. The conservative and Youth Movement groups, by contrast, stress Nordic romanticism and antisemitism most heavily. The Socialists and Communists emphasize the *Volksgemeinschaft*, and the young stormtroopers are notable mostly for their Hitler cult.

Change of Youth Organization

When a young person joins an organized group, we can assume that his (or her) choice may often be determined by imperfect knowledge of the available options. Once in the organization, however, the new member soon finds out how well the particular groups and his peers in it suit him. If he dislikes it strongly enough or learns of a group more suitable, he can simply change to another group. Since many of the respondents changed groups before they turned 26, we recorded the nature of these changes (item 14). About one-sixth of the respondents joined the stormtroopers or Hitler Youth (HJ) after having been in one of the quasi-military youth group settings. One-eighth dropped out of their first group without joining any other groups within the age limit. Between 4 and 5% each changed to the SA or HJ from the Socialist-Communist camp, the bourgeois Youth Movement, and the DHV or *voelkisch* youth. One out of 13 joined the *Wehrwolf* or another *voelkisch* youth group as his second group. About one-half of the respondents stayed with their first group. A comparison of the ratios between the original membership and the change to the SA or HJ reveals some interesting relationships even though the numbers are rather small. Evidently, there are several kinds of youth organizational careers here. One simply begins with immediate membership in SA or HJ, involving 59 respondents. Another career, including this first one, and also those who never joined a youth group (106), involves no change prior to the age of 26 and accounts for nearly half of the respondents. A third type of career led the respondents from their first group on to the *Wehrwolf* or another *voelkisch* group. This career applies to 52 respondents and seems to have been the only real competition to the SA or HJ for the early Nazis. A fourth career, finally, led from various first youth group memberships on to SA or HJ and involves 123 respondents (Table III-1).

Motivations for Change

Changing group affiliations is mostly a process of seeking out the most suitable features. What was it that the young people changing their youth organizations had liked best about them? For those who changed from quasi-military groups to the SA or HJ, what they had liked best about their first group were marching, rallies, uniforms, flags, military training, and violent battles. The Youth Movement-related groups, by contrast, liked the emphasis on hiking, cultural appreciation, and the spirit of comradeship best. The Socialists and Communists preferred the combination of demonstrations with the ideology of their youth groups. Those who switched to a *voelkisch* action group, the chief competitor to the attraction of the NSDAP to German youth, valued the experience of proselytizing and the emphasis on hiking and cultural appreciation.

By way of contrast, what the groups liked the least in connection with their first youth organizations pinpoints the reasons why they left them. The quasi-military members mention in particular a lack of political direction and also of political violence. They also disliked the ideological overtones of their group or rival groups, especially if they were "unnational," pacifist, or internationalistic. The former Communists and Socialists also disliked aspects of ideology and often objected in particular to the advocacy of class struggle and labor militancy—which makes one wonder about their socialism or communism. The Youth Movement-related groups and also those who changed to *voelkisch* groups stressed the lack of political direction and of political violence as the features they most disliked in their first youth group. For the recruits to *voelkisch* organizations as well as for SA and HJ, a sense of direction and real action were evidently the great attractions.

A check on the most extreme activities that respondents were engaged in before the age of 26 reveals that those who changed to the SA and HJ indeed included a heavy share of the most violent core. Forty to 50% of them engaged in partisan street fighting and

Table III-1: Change from First Youth Organization

First Group	SA or HJ after: Quasi-Mil.	Youth Movement	Comm.-Soc.	Voelkisch after anything	No change	Dropped out	Totals (n)
Quasi-military groups	53 (50%)	1 (.9%)	4 (3.8%)	15 (14.2%)	11 (10.4%)	11 (20.8%)	106 (100%)
Youth-Movement-related groups	19[a] (17.6%)	23 (21.3%)	2 (1.9%)	31 (28.7%)	20 (18.5%)	13 (12%)	108[a] (100%)
Communist-Socialist groups	—	1 (2.8%)	16 (44.4%)	5 (13.9%)	4 (11.1%)	10 (27.8%)	36 (100%)
Others, unpolitical groups	1 (4.8%)	3 (14.3%)	— —	1 (4.8%)	6 (28.6%)	10 (47.6%)	21 (100%)
SA or HJ first	—	—	—	—	59 (100%)	—	59 (100%)
No Youth Group	—	—	—	—	106 (100%)	—	106 (100%)
Totals	73 (16.9%)	28 (6.4%)	22 (5%)	52 (11.9%)	206 (47.1%)	55 (12.6%)	436 (100%)

[a] Includes certain conservative youth groups.

another 10 to 20% in the organized violence of Free Corps or vigilantes. By contrast, as many as half of the *voelkisch* converts seem to have engaged in no more than demonstrations and proselytizing. This is apparently an important difference between these two groups.[7]

[7] This difference corresponds closely to the main thesis of Martin Broszat, *German National Socialism, 1919-1945*, where the *voelkisch* organizations are characterized as relatively harmless debating societies in contrast to the determined political activism of the NSDAP. It should be noted, however, that there were some *voelkisch* action groups, such as the *Schutz-und-Trutzbund* which rather resembled the character of the Nazi party they preceded.

TWO

Youthful Likes and Dislikes

Young people are prone to strong likes and dislikes, and the Abel respondents are no exception. As they tell their experiences with youth organizations, their likes and dislikes at that stage in their lives are freely expressed, albeit with the possible distortion of the passage of time. A good example may be a very young retail clerk, born 1910 (no. 4), who considered joining the *Stahlhelm* but found it "not revolutionary enough" and who found *Jungdo* lacking in the spirit of youthful comradeship he yearned for. Another young respondent, born 1905 (no. 20), started out with the SPD in 1919 until his antisemitism caused him to quit. He tried the *Bismarck-jugend* of the DNVP in 1922 but found it wanting for lack of a social conscience. In 1926 he finally homed in on the NSDAP. Another respondent, born 1908 in Austria (no. 47), admits candidly that he liked the stormtroopers because of his "lust for brawling . . . and I absorbed the Nazi ideology only gradually."

FD-15: Positive Attitude Toward First Youth Group

Respondent liked most	Number	Per cent
Spirit of comradeship	40	12.3
Hiking, sports, nature	30	9.2
Cultural, historical, ethnic appreciation	18	5.5
Marching, rallies, uniforms, military training, flags	51	15.7
Violent battles, physical attack on foes	32	9.8
Ideology (world view) of group	106	32.7
Several of these, especially marching and ideology	20	6.2
Other features, especially proselytizing	28	8.6
	325	100.0

Age and Location Experiences

The different likes and dislikes are an indication of the motivations and underlying attitudes of the youth group members, as we shall see. As simple a device as a breakdown by age, for example, clearly separates the attitude groups in two or more camps. Of the positive attitude groups, for example, those who liked comradeship and political violence best more often turn out to be of the war generation than younger. Those who liked hiking and cultural appreciation or marching best (including marching and ideology) tend to be pre-

FD-16: Negative Attitude Toward First Youth Group

Respondent disliked most	Number	Per cent
Class distinction, prejudice	16	10.1
Lack of social concern, especially toward labor	20	12.6
Advocacy of class struggle, Socialist militancy	23	14.5
"Un-national views," internationalism, separatism, pacifism	36	22.6
Leadership, certain leadership decisions	22	13.8
Lack of political direction and of violent action	30	18.9
Other features	12	7.5
Totals	159	100.0

dominantly of the postwar generation. Comradeship and violence, of course, are the war syndrome of the *Fronterlebnis* while the other propensities are more the province of the politicized youth of Weimar, a search for political or ideological direction. The negative attitude groups fit a similar pattern. The respondents critical about the leadership and the lack of political direction tend to be of the postwar generation. Those who object to the advocacy of class struggle and to "unnational views" are more often of the war generation or older.

Another aspect comes out when we compare the positive groups with respect to their location experience. The urge to march with an ideological purpose, for example, is particularly frequent among the border-area respondents and among those from the occupied areas. The latter also have a particular liking for political violence in their youth group. We have already seen the significance of border-area origin or foreign occupation as a source of Nazi recruitment. Evidently the border struggles and the occupation were politically mobilizing and militarizing factors of particular impact on youth.

The urge to march and rally with flags and uniforms was also particularly prevalent among rural-urban migrants. The appreciation of German folk culture and of a spirit of comradeship, on the other hand, is more typical of those who still live in the community where they were born. Respondents who are highly mobile among cities exhibit far more enjoyment of political violence than the immobile, though not quite as much of the urge to march and demonstrate. To characterize the orientations of the location experience groups, the immobile appear to indulge in group life and to make a cult of ethnic and local traditions. Once mobilized, however, they are exceeded in their urge to march only by the rural-urban migrants. The highly mobile, by contrast, incline toward political violence, and somewhat less toward sports, German culture, and youthful comradeship.

As for the negative attitudes, the immobile are most dissatisfied with their group leadership and with the class prejudices or lack of social concern in their first youth group. The rural-urban migrants, by way of contrast, are most shocked by the "unnational views" and by socialist militancy, an attitude that indicates the subtle link between social mobilization and the growth of nationalism. The abhorrence of "unnational views" is shared emphatically by respondents from the border areas or from abroad, while the resistance to socialist militancy is shared by those from the occupied areas, especially from the Rhineland. The highly mobile, by comparison, complain most about a lack of political direction and action. The negative attitudes tend to complement the positive ones.

This inquiry into the social background of the youthful attitude groups acquires further depth when we consider where these young people fit into the picture of social mobility of their age. The children of families in social decline, for example, were most enamored with marching, rallies, ideology, and political violence in their youth groups. At the same time they deplored a lack of social conscience and of political direction and action. Those whose families never attempted to rise socially shared their concern about a social conscience and, like the spatially immobile, complain about the leadership of their groups. On the positive side, they follow the averages except for a strong appreciation of comradeship. The upwardly mobile from a rural background liked marching, ideological direction, and political violence the best.[1] The upwardly mobile in the city were evidently most eager for an appreciation of ethnic and cultural traditions and also for marching with an ideological purpose. Their strongest dislike was for advocacy of the class struggle, followed by "unnational views" and a lack of political direction and action. Their attitudes are plausibly related to their social situations.

[1] The negative attitudes of this group are too weakly represented (n=6) to permit statistical inferences.

The nature of the attitudes expressed may also suggest differences in the educational careers and levels of the different groups. Respondents with the most limited education (*Volksschule* only), indeed, turn out to have been the most enamored with political violence. But they were also the most concerned about a lack of social conscience, or conversely, about the advocacy of class struggle—which of course mirrors their proletarian environment and exposure to Socialist agitation. They also complain most about their group leadership. The best-educated (*Mittlere Reife* or better) liked marching with a purpose best (especially the university students) and complained most about the lack of political direction. They also criticized their group leaders, a common problem with intellectuals in organizations, and were particularly appreciative of youthful comradeship and of ethnic and cultural traditions in their youth group.

Youth and Violence

Crosstabulating the positive with the negative attitudes, we would expect to find a good deal of clustering along the lines suggested. However, the attitudes are rather evenly scattered. Those critical of "unnational views," probably especially the quasi-military youth, showed a decided preference for political violence (15.2%) and for marching with a purpose (48.5%). Those who complained about the lack of a social conscience strongly shared both of these views and, furthermore, were highly appreciative of youthful comradeship. By contrast, the respondents who wanted more political direction and action, such as the Youth Movement groups, disproportionately expressed a liking for marching, rallies, and German cultural appreciation.

A more striking relationship exists between the attitudes expressed and the nature of the activities engaged in during a person's youthful affiliation. The most extreme youthful activity of those expressing a liking for political violence tended indeed to be partisan street-fighting (30.3%) and organized violence (57.6%) such as with a Free Corps. Those who liked the combination of marching with an ideological sense of purpose were even more involved in youthful street-fighting (33.9%), but not in organized violence. They were evidently political activists and heavily engaged in electioneering and proselytizing (26.7%). Respondents with a liking for German cultural appreciation shared their high involvement in street fights (35.1%), with military training (13.5%), and in demonstrations (29.7%). Demonstrations were also the most prevalent activity of those who liked marching and rallies best. The least violent among the positive attitude groups, though only by a small degree, were the respondents who liked comradeship best in their youth group. As for the negative attitudes, the most violent were those critical of their leadership (47.1%) and of a lack of social conscience (44.8%). The least violent (18.8%) among the negative attitude groups were those who expressed shock at the advocacy of class struggle and who engaged heavily in demonstrations instead. The respondents critical of their leaders also stood out for demonstrations and political provocations. Those who complained about a lack of political direction and action were very violent (41.7%) as well as engrossed in proselytizing and electioneering (27.1%).

We can also attempt to classify basic postures of youthful involvement (item 19) along a continuum which runs from the *prepolitical parochial*, involvement for personal, nonpolitical reasons, to the full syndrome of *political militarization*, the urge to march, fight, and proselytize. Between these extremes there are waystations, such as the *hostile militant* youth who is not really politicized, but is mobilized by the violence of war or revolution and who carries his deep-seated hostility into the political arena; or the *authoritarian* and leadership cultist whose posture is likewise not truly political but rather derived from the father-son relationship. Before the extreme stage of *political militarization*, there is also still the stage of the *fully-politicized* individual who is eager to participate in politics but does not display the quasi-military features of political militarization.[2] Crosstabulating these types with the attitude groups, we obtain a deeper insight into the motivations of the respondents. The postures bring out the entirety of their attitudes toward political life, so to speak, and relate it to their likes and dislikes in youth group activities.

It hardly comes as a surprise, for example, that the *politically militarized* heavily express a liking for rallies and flags (20.9%), and marching with an ideological purpose (41%). Many of them also cite youthful comradeship as the aspect they liked best. Nearly two-thirds of those who liked political violence and physical attack best about their youth group, by contrast, turn out to be *hostile militants*, perhaps the Weimar equivalent of the "teenage crazies" of today. Those who liked marching with a purpose best, in addition to numbering many of the politically militarized (42.5%), also

[2] More details and a statistical breakdown of these postures will be presented in the next section below, pp. 270ff and especially pp. 274-276.

have a disproportionate share of the *fully politicized* (23.1%) and of the *prepolitical parochials* (11.9%) who are evidently caught up in the action without knowing why. Respondents who liked the stress on ethnic and cultural traditions best tend to be prepolitical parochials. As for the negative attitudes, the politically militarized number many who deplore the lack of political direction (37.5%) or criticize their leadership (17.9%); that latter category also figures large among the fully politicized. The hostile militants were particularly upset about "unnational views" (30.3%), evidently their favorite projection, and about a lack of social conscience (24.2%). The prepolitical parochials, finally, objected to unnational views and to the advocacy of the class struggle (28.6% each). It would appear, then, that the great liking for violent action is a function of youthful hostility rather than of political mobilization or militarization.

Was this liking for violence inspired by war and revolution? There is little evidence that it was caused by the war. The violence-minded were vicarious victory-watchers less often than the less violent attitude groups and only slightly more often served with enthusiasm in the war. During the war, they showed a good deal more extra-punitive hostility toward civilians and draft-dodgers than the others. They tended to blame the Kaiser, the civilians and, less strongly, the Marxists for the German defeat. They were also more often expelled, jailed, or otherwise punished by the occupation than the other groups, though probably mostly in consequence of their unruly behavior. A more plausible spur to their violent attitudes was the revolution. About half of them were in Free Corps action especially against the Poles, and against domestic insurgents, and many sympathized with the Kapp *putsch*. In 1923 they were disproportionately involved in anti-occupation activity, sympathizing with the Hitler *putsch* or members of *voelkisch* action groups.

Their organizational memberships during the successive periods of the Weimar Republic show their heavy representation among militant veterans' groups and the Free Corps in the years from 1919 to 1924. Then two-thirds of them abruptly switched to the NSDAP of the years from 1925 to 1928, more than from any other attitude group. By 1929, 80% of them were already in the party. Their political activities were violent from the first period (76.5%), with a little lapse in the middle years, to the last years (47.1%). They evidently represent a wave of relatively unpolitical postwar violence which carried over into the final struggle of the Nazi party for power.

Nazi Ideology and Youthful Likes and Dislikes

Did the likes and dislikes expressed by the youth group members relate to important points of Nazi ideology which the respondent later developed? Revanchism as a dominant theme was disproportionately frequent among those who complained about unnational views and advocacy of the class struggle, and those who liked violence or rallies and flags best. The latter were also frequently superpatriots and so were the enemies of the class struggle. Nordic romanticism was more popular with those who liked hiking and cultural appreciation in their youth groups and who complained about the lack of political direction. The devotees of the Hitler cult tend to be respondents who criticized the lack of a social conscience and unnational views, and who liked to march with an ideological purpose. The social *Volksgemeinschaft* found most support among the violence-minded and the marchers with a purpose, and among those who complained about a lack of social conscience and bad leadership in their group. The people who liked demonstrations and rallies, or marching with a purpose, also disproportionately had antisemitism as their dominant ideological theme, a prejudice they shared with those who deplored the lack of political direction and action. There is plenty of continuity between the preferences of the respondents as youths and as adult Nazis.

Significant differences between the attitude groups also appear with regard to the hate-lists so typical of extremist movements. The anti-Marxist line (anti-Socialist and anti-Communist) popular with two-thirds of the sample enjoyed less support among the violence-minded and among those who liked hiking and cultural appreciation best. These groups preferred to add the Jews to their anti-Marxism. Those who liked marching, rallies, and flags, and the friends of hiking and German culture also vented their spleen on the political establishment of "Catholics, liberals, and reactionaries," while the violent often preferred an all-inclusive hate-list regardless of creed or race. Of the negative attitude groups, those critical of their leadership and of unnational views were overwhelmingly anti-Marxist. But the sworn foes of unnational sentiments and, oddly enough, those opposed to the class-struggle argument also tended to pillory the Catholic-liberal-reactionary establishment as a convenient scapegoat. Respondents who complain about a lack of social conscience liked the all-inclusive hate-lists. And those who deplore the lack of political direction displayed a marked antisemitism.

On the subject of antisemitism, the reader will recall, we have a scale which ranges from one-third who exhibit no prejudice over mild verbal projections and the sudden *Judenkoller* to more permanent forms of prejudice, in particular fears of "the conspiracy" and veiled threats of aggression against "them." Of the positive attitude groups, the ones stressing youthful comradeship and rallies and flags are the least prejudiced, while those with emphasis on German culture exhibit the most frequent expressions of bias, especially of the milder, verbal sort. Yet this last-mentioned group also disproportionately tells personal antisemitic anecdotes and sounds the sinister themes of conspiracy and threat. Of the negative attitude groups, it is those complaining about a lack of political direction who answer the same description, followed by those calling for a social conscience. It is quite characteristic of "political antisemites" that they link prejudice with political motivation. The critics of unnational views are the least prejudiced, although they too include their share of people with paranoid fantasies. *Judenkoller* is most prevalent with respondents who either call for more social conscience or express shock at the advocacy of class struggle—in other words, respondents with some contact with the Socialist movement, perhaps even ex-Socialists. Those fond of rallies and flags, and of marching with a purpose, also tend to have *Judenkoller*, a sudden outbreak of severe prejudice, and quite possibly a concomitant to their itching feet and activist temper. Although the disease seems to take a number of distinctive forms, there is no evidence linking antisemitism with an early propensity for violence. But this is not to say that later prejudiced attitudes are not highly related to a respondent's youthful (non-prejudiced) political attitudes and activities.

The attitudes toward violence in general also differentiate our attitude groups. As the reader will recall, one of the important differences in this respect is between those who engage in violence with a curious masochism and self-pity and those who glory sadistically in the violence they inflict, not to mention respondents who shy away from violent engagements. Fifty-nine and three-tenths percent of the violence-minded of our sample tended to present the type of the sadistic bully, far more than in the next group, those who gloried in marching and rallies (29.2%). These young people evidently lacked the normal inhibitions against violence. The largest number of youthful masochists, by comparison, was among those who liked to march with an ideological purpose (47.5%) which apparently served to hide their violent tendencies from themselves. Among the negative attitude groups, the most sadistic were respondents who objected to the advocacy of class struggle (29.4%) and those who complained about the lack of political direction

(28.6%). But the latter also supply a disproportionate number of masochists (37.1%), as do those who were concerned about a lack of social conscience. The groups not mentioned in this connection, such as those who stressed German folk culture in their youth group, were not necessarily against violence, but rather tended to take a more pragmatic view of it. They often accepted it as the price of political victory without any indication of abnormal sentiments about it.

The attitudes expressed toward the respondent's political enemies add to the portrait to be sketched here. Enmity after all can be presented in many guises. The respondents who stressed cultural appreciation in their youth group, and those who complained of unnational views or lacking social concern, for example, tended to express a certain liking for their political enemies. The violence-minded, and those who deplore socialist militancy or a lack of political direction mostly speak of them as subhuman, rodents, or immoral, and sometimes hint at physical aggression toward them. Perhaps the propensity toward violence requires that the enemy be stripped of his human qualities. The groups who liked youthful comradeship or marching with a purpose best differ from them by only a small degree. The marchers with a purpose and the good comrades, however, also liked to refer to their enemies as traitors or as a faceless conspiracy, and so did those critical of their youth group leadership and of "unnational views." The language of the *outré* generally goes together with the unruly emotions either of violence or of extreme prejudice.

Yet another attitudinal dimension is ethnocentricity aside from antisemitism. The most ethnocentric are the respondents shocked at socialist militancy and the violence-minded, a fact that brings to mind the latter's heavy involvement in anti-Polish Free Corps action and anti-occupation activities. Superpatriotism and a horror of the slogan of class struggle go hand in hand. The least ethnocentric are, oddly enough, those who loved marching, rallies, flags, and uniforms and those critical of their leaders. Those who liked to march with an ideological purpose (such as the politically militarized) and respondents who deplore the lack of political direction are particularly hostile to aliens in Germany and even to the "ultramontane" Catholic church. This xenophobia, we shall see later, is a hallmark of the most virulent militants. Respondents who loved hiking and the stress on German culture are the most aware of hostile foreign nations, as are those who express shock at the advocacy of class struggle. There really must have been a strong inner conflict between chauvinism and militant socialism in the minds of some of these people.

The Moment of Truth

Some observers of the contemporary college and youth revolt in the United States have professed to see parallels between the jack-booted young stormtroopers of the 1920s and the American student radicals of today. On the face of it, such a comparison raises some obvious problems, for the young Nazis could hardly be called members of a movement for peace and ethnic or racial equality. But this objection would also apply to a comparison with Weimar Communist youth, which would be fascinating if we had the material for it. On the other hand, there are some persuasive parallels, and they go far beyond the infatuation with violence shared by the American New Left and the stormtroopers of forty or fifty years ago. The common elements relate mostly to phases of youthful development and to the process of becoming a radical, but they have to be viewed against a background of significant differences in settings. The German parents of Weimar days had a far more close-knit and authoritarian relation to their children than can be found, say, in the families of American student radicals studied by Kenneth Keniston.[3] Except for the probably significant fatherless lapse of the wartime years, in particular, German fathers then were unlikely to leave to their wives a dominant role in child-rearing and in the family in general.

Furthermore, even for organized youth the role of peer groups among Weimar youth was not as strong compared to that of the integral family as in the United States. Generally speaking, in European middle-class settings of that era, the crisis of early adolescence, or coping with the onrush of sexuality, was not absorbed by immersion in the teenage culture of peer groups. There are many instances among the Abel biographies, it should be noted, however, where youth group membership was kept hidden from the family as a kind of secret world away from it. There were many others who left home and roamed around like a good part of American youth today, truly breaking away from the parents.

Then there is also the difference in the age of maturing. Weimar youth may have matured earlier than their elders, but was far behind contemporary American and German youth in their rate of

[3] *Young Radicals, Notes on Committed Youth*, New York: Harcourt, Brace and World, 1968.

psychosexual development. This difference emerges especially from the often-mentioned homo-eroticism of the Youth Movement and the *Maennerbund* culture of so much of Weimar organizational life, which puts them on the level of the early adolescent crisis that is more or less sublimated into a group or political context. The contemporary New Left, by comparison, is rather heterosexual, even if unevenly integrated and frequently unequal. It would seem to relate therefore to a much later stage of psychosexual development.

The similarities lie in such areas as the strong antimaterialistic feelings which were already typical of the Youth Movement. There is also the cult of youthful comradeship, the emotional solidarity of the group, and the sense of belonging it imparts to the young member. Like Keniston's young American radicals, the young storm-troopers considered themselves highly idealistic and guided by the highest moral principles. They felt self-righteous and "absolutely right" to the point of arrogance. They liked to parade their principles before the tawdry world of social prejudice, selfishness, and compromise of their elders, and they often presented their youthful lives as examples of the conflict between their principles and "the system." Catchwords such as "the system" or the defiant "right on" (*nun erst recht*) also give an appearance of commonality.

On a deeper personal level, the young Nazis frequently showed a desire in word and deed to break out of their social class and to commune with and take the side of working-class youths, as we have seen in our discussion of the subjective meanings of *Volksgemeinschaft*. Like the radical scions of the American upper middle class, they often mixed social guilt feelings toward the lower classes with a sincere desire to want to communicate and be friends with them on a personal level. They also shared to an amazing degree the sense of being special and different as individuals that Keniston talks so much about.[4] While they obviously lacked the sophisticated psychological knack for self-analysis, the young Nazis hinted in many cases at a sense of social isolation. Some were exceptionally good students and may well have experienced isolation and resentment among their less gifted peers. They also tended to be in many cases rather bookish and, more broadly speaking, extremely literal in the way they expected stated ideals and principles to be realized in the world. Their precious conceptions of themselves, in many cases, tended to throw into stark relief their social and economic misfortunes in the depression and before. This was how "the system" was treating its most precious youths and denying them a viable future. Their poor chances in the German depression setting,

[4] Keniston, *Young Radicals*, pp. 70-74.

of course, cannot compare with the options of affluent adulthood which American radicals turned down in the late sixties. But there is an element of such rejection in the way many of the young Nazis deliberately ruined their chances of a career or livelihood by provoking political conflicts or proselytizing at their place of work.

It seems that the process by which a young person finds out that he is a right-wing extremist among many of the opposite faith or the middle-of-the-road is somewhat analogous to the various forms of social deviancy. There is a first moment of truth, often in a conflict situation in which the young person becomes involved by accident or force of circumstances. At this moment the deviant label is painfully and publicly attached to him. His personality henceforth develops a kind of fixation on the discriminatory label and on the strong social and political disapproval he has encountered. We could almost say he enjoys being known as a notorious troublemaker or disputatious radical because he has discovered his identity. At least he continues to engage in public activities that are sure to provoke conflict and to fix his extremist image further in the minds of his environment. To be sure, it is next to impossible to separate the external "hassling" of the young Nazis from conflicts caused or maintained by their own exhibitionism, as long as we can judge the cases only by their own self-serving accounts. Nevertheless, it is illuminating to conceive of political extremism in terms of a deviant's style of self-presentation and to look in the Abel cases for supporting evidence.

A good case in point is a contractor's son from Muehlheim an der Ruhr, born 1907 (no. 1), whose older brother went into the war. A second brother broke off his apprenticeship to volunteer. The young respondent became a vicarious victory-watcher, or at least he presents himself as one in justification of his later development: "The enthusiasm for the fatherland seized me, too. I helped carry the soldiers' rifles to the railroad station. Whenever the army reported a new German victory, I ran to the (Catholic) church in my enthusiasm and helped to ring the bells. The reports of my brothers when they came home on furlough always left a deep impression on me." His older brother and two cousins fell in battle. He remembers all too well the defeat and the "revolution," in particular "the shame of seeing the red revolutionaries tear off officers' insignia before our eyes at school." As soon as he was old enough to be an apprentice at the Thyssen works, he met his moment of truth.

Here I got to know the class struggle that the Marxists teach. On the very first day they tore the black-white-and-red ribbon from my windbreaker and tried to force me to join a syndicalist union. I joined the Metal Workers Union as an apprentice, since I had no choice . . . and dropped out again in 1923, having entered the *Wehrvolk Deutscher Aar* (a *voelkisch* youth group). Now I encountered hostility from all sides at work. I got beaten up for my German thinking at every wildcat strike, but they could not distract me from my chosen path.

Eventually, he was fired for his views, or so he says. Actually, it was because he missed work one day, because he was too tired from the political exploits of the previous night to get up in the morning. Now he became even more involved in provocative activities such as staging patriotic plays which drew Socialist and Communist raiders. At the age of 18, in 1925, he joined the NSDAP local which Josef Goebbels had just founded in his area. The personal isolation of this extremist is barely concealed by the thin veneer of righteous pretense that almost everyone thinks as he does, or at least they ought to. Underneath is the posture of the martyr who struggles on regardless of persecution. He longs to find others like himself and to merge with them in one *corpus mysticum*, the movement.[5] And there is that curious, masochistic attitude toward the political violence in which he engages which suggests an urge to verbalize his guilt feelings nearly as strong as the urge to commit mayhem in the first place.

Day and night we were persecuted, dubbed day-dreamers, and called Nazi punks and heathens by the Center party. . . . We were outlawed as a party and had to take off the brown shirts. If we showed up in white shirts to protect the meeting-hall, the police would pummel us out of the hall with their truncheons; also, if we were all wearing blue caps or black ties, they considered us subversive. The Communists knocked us down, the police put us in jail, some of our comrades were shot from the back: none of this stopped us in our redoubled will to make Adolf Hitler's idea prevail among the German people. . . . The Center party fought us the hardest [the respondent is a Catholic]. The clergy refused our dead comrades a regular funeral and we were not allowed to enter the church in uniform, although we National Socialists stand on Christian principles.

Poor stormtrooper! He may have done a lot to feel guilty about. The conflict situation at work in any case is a very common reinforcement mechanism even though it may be obscure in this case. A better example is an antisemitic miller's son born 1904 (no. 19), whose fixation on the label of the *"Nazischweinehund"* was so strong

[5] See also the remarks and examples of Keniston, *Young Radicals*, pp. 25-33.

that he put it in the mouth of the Communists long before he even joined the party. He claimed, for instance, that they mysteriously knew about his identity and followed his change of job to a town 25 miles away from his earlier employment. "Dirtying up my place of work, sabotage, unfounded charges, denouncing me with the boss, attacks with chairs and benches in our common room were daily occurrences. [Finally] . . . I signed my name to our leaflets and my place of work became hell for me." When he was late for work, his boss hollered: "Leave politics alone. I am going to fire you if you are late again." The respondent comments: "What can you expect of the reactionaries?"

Of the nearly two-thirds of the respondents who supply information on this subject, less than one in five describes his work environment as politically friendly; over one-third describe it as distinctly unfriendly and often tell of being fired or economically threatened for political reasons. As the breakdown further shows, their political job troubles were not limited to a hostile Socialist or Communist work environment but included also bourgeois settings where the employer or fellow employees strongly objected to the disreputable affiliation of the youthful respondent with a right-wing (not always Nazi) action group. On the other hand, the friendly work environments also included a considerable number of Socialist or Communist settings, which however may have been congenial only because the youthful respondent was either not yet a Nazi or still a leftwinger. We left out cases of security of employment in spite of political friction among the hostile environments because of the implication that the respondent acted with some prudence and reserve. There were also other points of emphasis, such as that a presumably sheltered middle-class youth became aware of the miseries of lower-class life only when he first took a job, or the tales of respondents proselytizing fellow-workers or customers on the job.

Work Environment and Friction

If we compare the factor of political friction at work among the different youth group memberships, it develops that by far the greatest concentration of respondents with a friendly work environment was among the older respondents who never belonged to any youth group. In other words, they grew up in a world relatively free from the generation gaps of postwar society, requiring neither the escape from the family to a youth group nor endangering their jobs. The largest number of cases where respondents were fired or economically ruined for political reasons before they turned 26 occurs among those who directly joined the Hitler Youth or the storm-

FD-20: Youthful Work Environment

	Number	Per cent
Friendly environment		
Nationalistic, patriotic	32	8.8
Catholic	5	1.4
Socialist, Communist	25	6.9
Voelkisch, Nazi	5	1.4
Liberal	1	.3
	68	18.8
Unfriendly environment		
Fired or bankrupt for political reasons	43	11.8
Nationalistic, conservative	2	.6
Socialist	25	6.9
Communist, Independent Socialist	24	6.6
Catholic	6	1.7
"Forced" into union	14	3.9
Liberal	4	1.1
Jewish	11	3.0
	129	35.6
Other		
Unpolitical, civil service, teaching	80	22.1
Unemployment, job troubles	40	11.0
Secure position despite friction	9	2.5
Respondent learns of lower class misery at work	22	6.1
Respondent uses job to proselytize for NSDAP	14	3.9
Grand total	362	100.0

troopers. As many as one-half of the members of the Socialist or Communist youth and of the bourgeois, Youth Movement-related groups complain about a politically unfriendly work environment. These groups and the young stormtroopers average 65-70% who complain about political friction ranging from hostility to firings. The friction, of course, is at least as likely to be the result of the respondent's militant behavior and his fixation on being politically deviant as of the "unfriendly environment."

If our suspicion that the friction originates largely from the respondent's state of mind is correct, there may be additional evidence in the extremist activities engaged in by the respondents before the age of 26. Those who report a friendly work environment, indeed, tend to be highly involved only in military training and in organized violence of the Free Corps or vigilante type. The more political kinds of activity, by contrast, tend to attract up to two-thirds of those reporting an unfriendly work environment or having been fired for political reasons. Forty-two and one-half percent of those who engaged in partisan street-fighting report having been fired or ruined, and another 30.1% report an unfriendly work environment. Nearly as large a share of those who participated in demonstrations, provocations, or proselytizing also report political friction on the job, though with a smaller share being fired or ruined. In the majority of these cases, it would seem unlikely that the respondents were victimized by their environment. Rather, we are dealing here with a highly politicized generation of social misfits who, like Jerry Rubin, were bent on "doing it" regardless of the consequences to themselves or anyone else. The greater their political activism, the greater their urge to polarize their immediate environment.

This is also how the work environment groups show up among our categories of the forms of youthful political involvement. The prepolitical, parochial youths tend to report a friendly work environment. As we go up the scale from there toward the politically militarized, the percentage of those reporting political friction at work rises steadily: 38.9% of the parochial youths, 56.3% of the hostile militants, 60% of the authoritarian youths, 61.1% of the fully politicized, and 74.3% of the politically militarized young respondents. The included proportion of those who report having been fired or ruined for political reasons similarly goes up from one out of seven parochials to two-fifths of the politically militarized youths. Thus the degree of political mobilization runs parallel to the reports of political friction, or, to put it another way, the reports of political friction on the job are another aspect of the pervasive masochism we have noted among the young militants. The respondent stirs up friction or gets himself fired and then complains about political persecution.[6]

The role of political friction, of course, goes beyond the youthful work environment, whose relevance to the developing radical lies chiefly in the fact that it constitutes one of the first settings where his self-willed personality collides with the constraints of an adult role. Other settings, such as the school or the neighborhood or his own family, are perhaps less fraught with role conflicts, but nevertheless are suitable for developing the deviant posture. Many respondents tell bizarre tales about neighborhood confrontations they sought out by insisting on hoisting swastika flags in a "red" neighborhood. Others tell of political clashes among their peers at school

[6] There are many contemporary parallels, such as the obsession of the New Left today with political persecution everywhere. See also Keniston's discussion of the refusal of his young radicals at the "end of the line," to enter into adult roles. *Young Radicals*, pp. 98-105.

or with teachers which led to disciplinary measures against them. And the tenuous family relationships, which usually could survive differences between Liberals and Conservatives or Socialists by the simple device of avoiding the discussion of politics, frequently exploded in dissension over the respondent's Nazi extremism. The NSDAP and its youth groups were not "just another party." This kind of political deviancy constituted an unignorable challenge to the entire adult establishment. Parents, grandparents, even uncles and aunts unfailingly got into the act of attempting to dissuade the young stormtrooper from his shocking involvement.

FD-69: Adult Political Friction Reported (by chief setting of friction)

	Number	Per cent
Friction at job, business	112	22.4
⌐ Political boycott	41	8.2
∟ Fired for political reasons	69	13.8
⌐ Friction in family	26	5.2
⊢ Friction at school	12	2.4
Friction in neighborhood	135	27.0
∟ Friction at job, family, and neighborhood	38	7.6
Friction sought out, provocation	25	5.0
No friction encountered	42	8.4
	500	100.0

We can compare the reported youthful frictions with the more comprehensive adult experience. Our statistical breakdown of the chief settings of political friction reported by all the respondents regardless of age shows the wide distribution of the settings. Nearly as many respondents chose the neighborhood as the place for showing off their political deviancy as report economic friction. We need not assume that a certain amount of partisan controversy and conflict was unnatural in the course of everyday life and in all kinds of settings, such as in a bowling club (no. 50), in order to pick out the pathology of friction. And we need to separate as carefully as possible the normal conflicts of the political arena which may be incurred during rallies, demonstrations, or canvassing, from the confrontations occurring in normally non-political settings, such as the family, the neighborhood, or the place of work. In a pluralistic society where political functions are normally separated from family, home, and economic pursuits, it is highly irregular for either side of the political contest to carry the conflict into these other settings.

For whatever it may contribute to the separation of internal and external factors of friction, it is worth looking at some crosstabulations. If we cross the locale of the reported adult friction with what the respondent claims was the dominant local political force prior to the Nazi landslide, for example, one dimension of external reality makes its presence known: 64.5% of those reporting friction in their neighborhood lived in an area dominated by Communists and Socialists, as compared to 67.8% of those who obviously sought out confrontations; 61.9% of those reporting friction at their job or business; 56.4% of those who report having been boycotted or fired for political reasons; and only 38.7% of those reporting friction in their family or at school.

Of the last-mentioned group, instead, nearly two-thirds lived in an area in which Liberals, the Center party, or the DNVP were an important part of the dominant local political forces. The implication is that these bourgeois elements also were the cause of the political friction in the family and at school, and that this kind of friction involves more of a process of disassociation from an otherwise homogeneous social environment. Political provocation, neighborhood friction, and friction at job or business (short of economic suicide), on the other hand, involves more of a process of displacement of hostility on an outgroup, the reds.

Another angle emerges from pairing the locale of friction with the date the respondents joined the NSDAP. We would assume that one had to have been a member for a while before friction was likely to occur and also that the public and private atmosphere of the Weimar Republic became most sharply politicized after 1929. As it turns out, however, the economic suicides were concentrated among the early joiners and took place long before the Depression. They are followed by those reporting political friction in the family or at school. Two-thirds of the latter had joined by June 1930; 84% by May 1931. Evidently, this was the moment of truth for the German bourgeoisie. Reports of neighborhood friction are only slightly behind, although they probably resulted mostly from what many respondents describe as "the fury of the reds when they could no longer ridicule us as an inconsequential group." The last to join were those reporting friction at the job and the provocateurs. Thus, economic suicide appears to have been mostly at the initiative of the respondent while the other forms of friction may have involved some external causes.

Then there is also the manner in which the respondents became introduced to the NSDAP. Those who report friction in their neighborhood tend to have been recruited by a relative, probably a sign of a certain personal isolation or at least of a poverty of non-family contacts. Those complaining about friction in their families or at school report having been introduced mostly by a friend or colleague, the most prevalent introduction among Nazi activists. Those reporting friction at the job and in the neighborhood stand out among those who first became aware of and were attracted by the Nazi ideology, while the economic suicides tended to catch fire just from attending a public rally or watching Nazi demonstrations. If the manner of introduction is at all indicative of personality traits, then indeed the friction at the job or in the neighborhood was unusually concentrated among introverted ideologues who may well have used these locales as a stage for their self-presentation. But the economic suicides again stand out with their propensity for extreme behavior.

Finally, it is interesting to compare the locales of reported friction with the incidence of membership in the SA or the SS, which in those days was Hitler's special guard. We can assume that if the friction were externally caused the respondent would be somewhat less likely to have become a stormtrooper. Non-membership ranges from a mere 11.5% of the provocateurs to a good half of those who report friction at their job or business. By contrast, the provocateurs and those reporting friction in the neighborhood or in family and school heavily tended to join the SA at the same time they joined the NSDAP. The provocateurs also in disproportionate numbers "graduated" from the SA to the SS.

It may be appropriate at this point to describe in some detail what we mean by a provocateur. This term is used for a Nazi who goes out of his way to bring about a major personal confrontation with political enemies for no recognizable end other than to exhibit his Nazi militancy. This is usually accomplished by venturing into meetings or areas of the enemy, usually the reds, to exhibit one's uniform or flag there.[7] The typical provocateur is often a raving antisemite whose mania drives him into the lion's den. A good example is a Berlin shopkeeper born about 1896 (no. 255) who was very active in the *Schutz-und-Trutzbund* and later in the *Deutsch-voelkische Freiheitspartei*. He was full of paranoid fears regarding what the Communists or others might do to him and his family, even though he had 10-15 brawny activists in his apartment preparing leaflets around the clock. At the time of the Presidential elections of 1925, he flew a seven-foot swastika flag out the window and kept it there all day against "Communist attempts to remove it." By nightfall "thousands of workers had gathered and I was forced to

---

[7] A variety of this conduct was to appear at work or in church in a Nazi uniform, in the full knowledge that such an exhibition would not be tolerated. This was how some respondents lost their jobs.

pull in the flag to save the window glass. The police cleared the streets."[8] The demonstrative hoisting of the flag or wearing of the Nazi uniform in the face of certain assault by the provoked enemy or the police, at least in the context of Weimar Germany,[9] takes on the air of an exhibitionist act of a deviant who gets his thrills from causing a sense of outrage or from getting arrested.

To come back to the younger cases reporting political friction, let us examine a few cases more closely. A local party treasurer who had to go around collecting the dues in a "red" neighborhood relates for example (no. 34):

> Collecting the dues, I won a real insight into the lives of the members and their families. There were wives who were not supposed to know that their husbands were party members. In other families, it was the parents who were not to learn that their children, especially their sons, were in the SA. Of course, this made it difficult to collect the dues since the member himself was often not at home. And in those times, it often happened that families were divided among themselves into various parties. One can imagine how family life declined and arguments, even brawls were the order of the day in these families.

The respondent, who was born in 1900, goes on to describe some of the conflict he encountered himself after joining the SA: "Old acquaintances looked at me from the side but did not have the courage to say hello. I could read contempt in their eyes at how low I had sunk. Only a few would make small talk or ask me what on earth we really wanted." His Communist neighborhood eventually laid siege to his apartment whenever he came home at night from his political activities as an SA *Truppfuehrer* (Corporal). According to his own report, he tried to avoid them by choosing different routes home and often ended up making his way "through a mob" with an open pocket-knife in his hand "firmly resolved to take along two assailants if I was ever assaulted." But he never was, and we have no way of checking whether his fears had any basis in reality.

Another respondent, born 1903 (no. 53) tells of his experiences in a family of divided loyalties.

> When I was with the *Stahlhelm*, there already was trouble with parents and brothers. My parents and one brother were with the Center party, four other brothers were with the *Reichsbanner* [a republican paramilitary group]. Since I was a drum major for the *Stahlhelm*, and

---

[8] See also no. 112.

[9] In the civil libertarian tradition of British or American society, such conduct may well deserve a different interpretation.

later for the NSDAP, and one of my brothers was a drum major for the *Reichsbanner*, the black-white-and-red insignia leaned in one corner of my parents' home and the black-red-and-gold ones in another corner. Yet my brown shirt and his *Reichsbanner* jacket hung peacefully side by side in the closet. With such contrasting political views, it was not always peaceful in my parents' home. Sometimes physical clashes were unavoidable because I was not about to give up my Nazi membership since I believed Hitler to be Germany's salvation. This circumstance made me unhappy at home since I realized I could never convert my parents and brothers to my view. They were reinforced in their opinion by a large number of relatives, all of the opposite camp.

Eventually, his family threw him out and even his company would give him no more work unless he gave up politicking. His reply was, "Even if you let me work only an hour a week or I become unemployed, I shall remain true to my opinions." A Nazi chieftain and former *Stahlhelm* leader finally took him in and converted him to the NSDAP.

The genuine reluctance to admit his own isolation and uniqueness is well-demonstrated by a respondent born 1904 (no. 59) who had been enrolled by his devout mother in a Catholic Young Men's Association. He went to a rally of the *voelkisch-sozialer Block*, was greatly taken by the antisemitic rantings of the speaker, and became annoyed at some "red" hecklers in the audience. As he relates,

> I was amazed to see that these hecklers were strongly applauded by most of the audience. After the rally I went to a meeting of the Young Men's Association to tell them of the incident, fully expecting the brothers and their president to be indignant about the reds and the Jews. To my great astonishment the contrary happened. I got into a big argument with some of the brothers, tore up my membership card, and left the group for good.

This respondent also tells of the special ordeal of picking up his unemployment check during the Depression, being the only unemployed stormtrooper among mobs of unemployed Communists. "It was like having to run the gauntlet." Another unemployed respondent (no. 67), a young worker, confirms this experience. His father, an old Social Democrat and innkeeper, threw him out the first time he came home bloody from a stormtrooper engagement. The respondent shows a surprising amount of understanding for his father's decision not to have him around for fear of risking his business, and even for Nazi employers who would not hire him for similar reasons. He was evidently not terribly unhappy with his lot.

Another respondent, a farmer's son born 1900 (no. 78), reports that the local Socialist Workers Youth (SAJ) liked to serenade him with shots, shouting, and curses under his bedroom window whenever he was out late, to the terror of his wife. A threatening letter of his to the SPD resulted in arson at his farm, he claims, and he rebuilt the burnt-down barn with seven-foot swastikas in each gable wall. The local SPD paper reportedly commented on this architectural event with a little verse:

> Von der Ostsee bis zur Schweiz,
> ein jedes Rindvieh hat sein Hakenkreuz.
> (From the Baltic Sea to Switzerland,
> every ox gets his swastika.)

It is not always easy to separate political purpose from the sheer exhibitionism of the extremist. One respondent, born 1903 (no. 81), tells how he decided that his group of villages really ought to have more Nazis in his local organization. "And so, all of a sudden in the middle of 1932, there was a swastika flag flying from the roof of my apartment house. This was too much for the enemy to bear. One day I received a letter from the owner of the house . . . demanding I remove that swastika flag from the roof and sending a roofing company out to repair the allegedly damaged roof at my expense." The roofing company found no damage. The flag kept on flying and, pretty soon, a few other members began flying swastikas on the roofs of their houses as well.

THREE

Portraits of Involved Youth

What kind of person is a "politically militarized" youth? To give an example, respondent no. 82 was born 1909 in Halle an der Saale, the son of a bank clerk. After a medium-level education, he was apprenticed for three years as a retail clerk in Hamburg and then returned to Halle, where his father supported him while he fought his battles as a stormtrooper. "We stormtroopers had no other goal but to make Germany National Socialist. Questions of a profession or private concerns did not exist for us." He tells the story of how he became involved with the SA in the happy-go-lucky style typical of many of the younger politically militarized youths:

> I got into the NSDAP in an unusual way. We were nine apprentices at work . . . and we often argued about politics. I was not interested in politics, and only went in for sports in my free time. One of the apprentices was with the *Stahlhelm* and one with SA, the rest unpolitical. The stormtrooper had always said to me that my opinions were pure National Socialism and that I ought to come along to one of his rallies some time. Misled by the newspapers, I objected that the Nazis were known as brawlers and, although I would not walk away from a fight, I was appalled at attacking people with a knife who did not agree with me. He tried to convince me that the contrary was the case.

Then the respondent witnessed an assault "by five Communists on two Nazis" in the street. He jumped into the fray together with a friend and the assailants fled. He relates: "The Nazis didn't even say thank you. One of them snarled at me: 'How come you're not with us yet? If you don't show up tonight and sign up, we'll work you over.'" The tone of address must have been exactly right, for the respondent went to the meeting, signed on the dotted line, and immediately began to proselytize among the other apprentices and to bully his older fellow-workers. Some six or seven Nazi apprentices between 18 and 22 soon made a point of marching into the office in the morning and after lunch shouting their "Heil Hitlers" at everyone. When a fellow-worker laughed and began to make disparaging remarks, "One of us—we were all strong young fellows who had been in sports for years—would ask him to step out into the cloak room or toilet if he had the guts. None of them ever did, and so we held the upper hand and henceforth teased them again and again about their cowardice." The young savages also laid out their propaganda newspapers in the toilet for the older fellow-workers to read. When they noticed that the newspapers began to be spirited away, they checked the toilet after each user. When they had caught one and he claimed to be taking the material home to read, they forced him to buy it "to raise a few marks for our hard-up newspapers." During election campaigns they also covered up the absence of Nazi comrades busy canvassing and putting up posters. Back in his home town, the respondent joined the SA there and experienced its "everchanging life": "Street and house-to-house propaganda, meeting-hall protection in city and countryside, breaking up Marxist rallies, demonstrations, battles in the street and in meeting-halls, persecution by the police, in short all the joys and sufferings all stormtroopers go through." It is noteworthy, though not entirely representative of his group, that the respondent never gives an inkling of his ideology or political views, if he had any. Notwithstanding the large literature on the "German ideology" from Luther to Nietzsche, he evidently went in for pure action unencumbered with the pale cast of thought.

To be *fully politicized*, by contrast, does involve exposure to ideas and ideological influences of various sorts. A good example is a worker's son born in 1901 (no. 15) and brought up in poverty and without a father after the age of 3. His devout mother taught him religious observances and the value of money "which was so rare and had to be earned the hard way." He was a good student in school, very bookish, and loved to read about history, travel, and adventure. He worshipped the Kaiser and was an ardent victory-watcher while his older brother was in the war. But his enthusiasm turned to disappointment in the last years of the war and was shattered when the Kaiser fled to Holland. In 1919-1920 the respondent became involved with the Communists "because of their reckless demands," until the excesses of the Ruhr uprising sobered him. Then he gravitated toward the SPD and prominent pacifists. In the mid-twenties he became aware of the NSDAP, which his younger brother, a former *Marinejugend* member, had already joined by then. He disliked it strongly until, in 1926, he was seized by a voracious interest in antisemitic literature. This *Judenkoller* brought about his break with socialism and democracy and led him to join the brown hordes. He found it difficult at first to change his political identity

in the midst of old Social Democrats who refused to take his rantings seriously, but soon he became an ardent and rather successful
proselytizer and organizer of the Nazi union, the NSBO. It is rather
typical that he never engaged in political violence. And again, at
least in this case, the "German ideology" was hardly the cause of
his corruption, although he was something of an ideologue and a
utopian to boot:

> When in January 1933, Field Marshall von Hindenburg entrusted
> the leadership of Germany to the Fuehrer, thus ending our hard battle
> with a victory, my old comrades and I could hardly believe it at first.
> We had not considered the possibility that we would live to see the
> victory of our movement. We had fought thinking of the next genera-
> tion. At work, the (SPD) fellow workers greeted me by saying "You
> were right after all," and they too were glad of it!

We have already sketched the portraits of some of the other types
of youthful posture. They are all less specifically political, although
there may be differences of degree. There are also the pre-political
parochials who are still too much caught up in their personal problems of growing up to pay much attention to politics.

There are, for example, the anti-political *Schwaermer* (romantics) of the Youth Movement and other cults. A good example of
a *Schwaermer* is a brick factory owner's son born 1900 (no. 133),
who expresses many contradictory feelings. He communed with
nature and life in the country and enjoyed himself as a youth whenever he was with the migratory brickyard workers of his father's
yard. He ate with them and went fishing with them, and yet, after
1918, he complained that "nobody wants to be a poor worker any
more . . . on Sundays you can't tell any more who is a worker and
who is not." He was also a fervent patriot and waxed enthusiastic
about the national heroes of German history. But when he had to
move a short distance from one small town to another, he was
homesick for years and claimed that "there's another race of people
living here." From the time he was a small boy, he had wanted to
wear a uniform and be a soldier in maneuvers but by the time he
could volunteer the war was over. The returning soldiers, as he relates it, were losing themselves in drinking and revelry. "The old
Germany is dead; everybody thinks only of himself and no longer
cares about the great fatherland."

He suddenly became antisemitic and also began to express hopes
for a great leader to come along and to rally people away from their
amusements and material pursuits. He decided to join a sports club
and then *Jungdo*, and voted for the DVP and later for the DNVP.

He also liked the militaristic antics of the *Stahlhelm* but would not join it, because it was lacking in social concern and unlikely to be attractive to the workers. The decline of his father's business and his increasing involvement in political campaigns finally made him reckless. He founded a Nazi local in his town. His views were still a woolly mixture of patriotic romanticism, leadership cult, and entrepreneurism. In the end he was quite active in proselytizing and electioneering, but got involved in street fighting only once, in 1933, when the NSDAP was already taking over his depressed little town.

Then there are the hostile militants whose personal hostility only happens to be taken out on politics without a serious engagement with or penetration of political matters. Most of them reflect the violence of the war and the counter-revolution in their lives. Even the physically aggressive among them—and many are only verbally aggressive—seem to have a curious kernel of fear and vulnerability from which they lash out at the world. They engage in political violence rather as a slum child might attack a teacher, or a man his rival for the affections of a girl. Most accounts of hostile militants are sparsely told stories of violent action in the war, in the Free Corps, or in the vigilantes. They have little to say about their feelings and mostly give a record of organizations and the locales of battles. A slightly different case is a charcoal worker's son, born 1894 (no. 125), who at 17 joined the SPD and the free trade unions. He relates, "I participated actively as a Social Democrat and hated anyone who was not with the SPD. I often got into arguments at my place of work and finally had to leave my job because of that." He then was drafted and served at many different fronts, all the while reading his SPD newspapers and expecting November 1918 to bring the victory of the German working class. He was deeply disillusioned when instead he witnessed the great schisms and hostilities among the different Socialist parties and the scramble for offices and sinecures of his SPD leaders. He was unemployed and strongly attracted by the KPD, he claims, when a former officer friend talked him into enlisting with the Iron Brigade, a Free Corps fighting in Kurland on the Baltic. Eventually he returned and married a conservative (DNVP) girl, although he himself voted for the Independent Socialists. The NSDAP must have helped to overcome the unresolvable conflicts in his life, for he was trying to join it in 1923 when it was dissolved. Finally having joined up in 1925, he relates that for five long years he was the only Nazi among 200 Marxist workers and also the only one in his community. He proudly mentions that his fellow-workers, who always used to call him a "traitor to the working-class," elected him their representative in 1934.

A more typical hostile militant is a Saxonian boiler-maker's son, born 1900 (no. 120), who joined the *Jugendwehr*, a military auxiliary in 1914, in spite of the ridicule of fellow-workers. He too was very anxious to volunteer for the war but did not succeed until the very last year. Nevertheless, he filled page after page with reminiscences from the war and, in fact, has the dubious distinction of having written by far the longest of the Abel *vitae*. More significant, he became a *Zeitfreiwilliger* after the war and acquired the reputation of having been a "Noske"—a reference to the SPD Minister of the Interior Gustav Noske, who had ordered the repression of uprisings of the extreme left wing by Free Corps and the like. He lost two jobs because of this matter and for several years withdrew from any political involvement. The NSDAP, through friends of his, lured him out of his shell, even though he learned of its ideology and goals only after joining. "What a wonderful popular movement," he thought, and his adventurer's heart became fully integrated with the violent struggle for power. He took pride in the beatings he received, including one "by 30 *Reichsbanner* men" that left him unconcious and unable to work.

Finally, there are the authoritarians and the leadership cultists. The former often come from military-civil servant homes or report a very strict or harsh upbringing which taught them to see the world in terms of discipline and order, and to fear nothing more than chaos. The leadership cultists are searching for a leader, perhaps a substitute father for the one who died when many of them were still small.

FD-19: Forms of Youthful Involvement

	Number	Per cent
Pre-political, parochial	48	8.9
Schwaermer, romantic-diffuse	23	4.3
Hostile militant	63	11.7
Authoritarian, leadership cult	38	7.0
Fully politicized	58	10.8
Politically militarized	132	24.5
Other forms	177	32.8
	539	100.0

Social Background of Youth Postures

The different forms of youthful involvement are highly related to generational cohorts. By far the youngest, with over three-fourths in the postwar generation, are the politically militarized youths. They are followed by the fully politicized, with 60.3% born after

1901. The hostile militants straddle the war and postwar generations; most of them were influenced by the combination of the outer
violence and inner fears of war, victory-watching, and revolution
or counter-revolution. The pre-political parochials and *Schwaermer*
are more of the war and prewar generations, just as the Youth
Movement was really more a prewar than a Weimar phenomenon.
The oldest of the groups, except for the residual "other forms," are
the authoritarians and leadership cultists, of whom 42.2% were
born before 1895, and 63.3% before 1899. They may fairly be
said to represent the authoritarian and militaristic strains of Wilhelminian Germany.

This periodization is complemented by the location experiences
of the different groups. The pre-political groups tend to be rural-
urban migrants or highly mobile among cities. At any rate they are
highly urban, with more than half living in metropolitan centers.
The hostile militants also are highly mobile among cities, but live
more often in communities under 100,000 inhabitants. The fully
politicized tend to live where they were born, mostly in metropolitan or large city areas. The politically militarized also often live
where they were born, especially in the occupied areas, though there
are also many of the highly mobile type. In any case, it is worth
emphasizing how large a portion of the last two groups, the most active, agitate in their own communities rather than being the proverbial "outside agitators." Their economic fate during the Depression further confirms the periodization. The fully politicized and politically
militarized frequently failed financially during the Depression, while
the pre-political youths and the hostile militants tended to become
economic casualties before the year 1928. The reader may recall
that the latter fate was typical of the war generation, the former of
the postwar generation.

In regard to the home background of these groups, a different
alignment comes to light. The fully politicized (44%) and the pre-
political youths (38.3%) tend to have fathers who were military-
civil servants or even high-ranking military or professional people.
We can surmise that the same mobilizing background in different
generations produced these different results. The authoritarians, as
expected, also have more than their share of military-civil servant
fathers. The politically militarized, by contrast, have disproportionately many (40.7%) fathers who are artisans or independent
businessmen. This, in other words, *is* the petit-bourgeoisie, though
on a youthful level that could hardly be caused by economics. The
hostile militants, finally, have a disproportionate number (28%)
of workers as fathers, a fact that conjures up the image of the pa-

triotic working-class Tory, who feels particularly hostile to the Socialist working-class movement.

With regard to upward mobility, in fact, the hostile militants tend to be stagnant or in decline. More than half of the politically militarized (51.5%) are also stagnant, and the upwardly mobile among them tend to be so mostly in an urban context. The authoritarians are similarly stagnant, while the fully politicized have the highest percentage of upwardly mobile families (42%). The pre-political youths are the next most upwardly mobile (36.6%) but they also have the largest number of families in social decline (23.3%). The evidence is so mixed as to discourage any single theory linking social mobility with radicalism, except perhaps among the upwardly mobile in the city. Rural-urban-migration is evidently not a cause of radicalization, which otherwise seems to occur mostly in a socially and spatially rather immobile setting.

Religion plays a negative role in political radicalization. Three-fourths of the politically militarized, the fully politicized, and the hostile militants fail to indicate their religious affiliation. As for their formal education, the fully politicized and the pre-political youth have the highest ratings, while the hostile militants and the politically militarized tend to have the least education.

To come back to the home, it is remarkable that nearly one out of four of the politically militarized and about one out of five of the authoritarians and the hostile militants had lost their fathers before they had grown up, some even before they had reached the age of ten. Especially with the latter, the loss of the father must have had a significant impact on their socialization amidst changing family roles. One out of six of both the politically militarized and the fully politicized grew up as an orphan or with foster parents, and an additional 28.7% and 19.6%, respectively, grew up in dire poverty. One out of four authoritarians emphasizes the strictness and discipline of his upbringing. Nevertheless, none of these groups appears disproportionately to have had to work early in life, except for the hostile militants, 17.5% of whom had to work as unskilled teenaged laborers while others could acquire an education or job training. These background data appear to supply psychological cues rather than motives of social or economic discontent.

Socialization in Partisanship

The political preferences of the parents seem to have had a fair amount to do with the youthful postures adopted. Nearly a fourth of the authoritarians indicate that their fathers had militaristic or authoritarian views. A disproportionate 21.3% of the politically militarized and 15.2% of the fully politicized describe their father's politics as *voelkisch* or antisemitic. Disproportionate numbers of the fathers of the pre-political and the hostile militants were, according to their sons, quite apolitical. What were the rest of the fathers? The largest number of fathers, especially of the pre-political and authoritarian youths, were conservative nationalists. The fathers of 21.2% of the fully politicized and 15% of the politically militarized were identified with the conservative, liberal, or Center parties, which also were sources of the landslide in favor of the National Socialists in the elections of the early thirties. Electoral landslides often result from generational shifts of opinion.

At school and with their peer groups, an astonishing 50% of the fully politicized report having had a *voelkisch* or Nazi teacher or conflict with Jewish fellow-students. The percentages are much lower with the other groups, such as the politically militarized (18.9%) or the hostile militants (24.1%). The other groups generally report having had nationalistic, patriotic, and anti-republican teachers (55-65%), except for the fully politicized, of whom nearly a third tells of Liberal, Catholic, or Marxist teachers. Attributing political color to one's education is obviously a highly subjective affair, considering the large number of teachers, their political reticence in a German classroom, and the relative lack of political perceptiveness of the students. Perhaps being fully politicized made these respondents more selective, more perceptive and, with respect to Jewish fellow-students, more wilful and aggressive.

The military as an opinion-forming environment applies to some respondents more than to others. Eighty-six and two-tenths percent of the politically militarized and 73.7% of the fully politicized saw no military service at all. Nevertheless, the violent emotions of the war left their imprint on nearly a fourth of the politically militarized and even more of the hostile militants who say that they were ardent victory-watchers. Surprisingly, one out of seven of the fully politicized and the authoritarians became disaffected toward the end of the war or reports his military service as a very unpleasant experience. These two groups also show particular hostility toward civilians and draft-dodgers during the war.

The cultural shock as a measure of alienation was the strongest emotional legacy of the end of the war. The callow youths who constitute the politically militarized, however, tend not to have experienced this cultural shock at all. The authoritarians, on the other hand, who are also older, frequently stress themes of social and moral disintegration. The hostile militants and pre-political youth, both of the war generation, tend to complain most about the absence of order and discipline or about the institutional changes of 1918. In reaction to the "revolutionary" activities, consequently, they tend to blame the Weimar parties, the Spartakists, and international Marxism. The authoritarians and the fully politicized, by contrast, more often blame the Jews or the "street rabble" for the revolution.

Demonstrations and Violence

To what extent do youthful attitudinal postures reflect the engagement in agitation and violent activities? There is a good deal of correspondence, especially in certain spots of our breakdown, according to the most extreme activity of the respondent before the age of 26. Fifty and nine-tenths percent of the politically militarized were engaged in partisan street fighting and, in fact, make up 73% of all the youthful street fighters. Another 31.6% of the politically militarized participated in organized violence of the Free Corps type. The fully politicized, by contrast, were heavily engaged in demonstrations (22.2%), proselytizing and electioneering (24.4% each) and much less in violence (24.4%). The hostile militants, by comparison, were heavily engaged in organized violence (46.3%) and less in partisan street fighting (22.4%). Looking more closely at their involvement in the "counter-revolution" of the first four years, we notice that their violence had not yet unfolded in its specific form. As late as 1923, the politically militarized were mostly in militant veterans' groups or in legitimate parties. Only the hostile militants were somewhat more involved in anti-occupation activity or in *voelkisch* action groups, or sympathetic to Hitler's beerhall *putsch*.

Later on, when they had joined the NSDAP, the pre-political (61.4%) and the authoritarian youths (53.3%) tended never to become stormtroopers, while all but 8.3% of the politically militarized, all but 25% of the hostile militants, and all but 35.8% of the fully politicized became stormtroopers. The role of the (older) hostile militants amid the political youth shows the meshing of the generations in the SA. Nearly two-thirds of the politically militarized and over half of the hostile militants and the fully politicized, moreover, joined the SA immediately, as if being a stormtrooper was the most important thing to them about the party. Once in it, 59.9% of the politically militarized indeed engaged in street fighting, including 16.9% who kept going "day and night" during the election campaigns of 1932. The hostile militants, with 48.7%, are next, followed by the fully politicized 36.9% engaged in street violence. The other groups were involved to no more than about one-fourth, but engaged more in proselytizing, demonstrations, and electioneering.

Once they were involved, how did these groups view their violent roles? Characteristically, the politically militarized tended to exhibit the curious self-pity (45.4%) repeatedly commented on far more than a bullying, sadistic attitude (24.7%). The second most violent group, the hostile militants of the war generation, by contrast, have more sadistic (33.3%) than masochistic (25.9%) responses. The fully politicized and the older authoritarians, again, show more self-pity though they were substantially less actively engaged in violence. The legacy of war and counter-revolution evidently gives the hostile militants fewer scruples about engaging in political violence, while the postwar and prewar generations feel that they have to present violent involvement as something the respondents suffered rather than initiated. This also comes out in their attitude toward the satisfactions of membership in the party. Both the politically militarized and the hostile militants tended to derive a sense of personal integration from the struggle itself, regardless of self-pitying rationalizations. The enjoyment of the classless comradeship of the party, which they share with the fully politicized, received only secondary emphasis. So did, among the politically militarized, the Hitler cult, which was far more important to the authoritarians, the fully politicized, and pre-political youths, in this order.

Ideology and Youthful Posture

Speaking of the Hitler cult brings to mind the probable relationships between youthful postures and various kinds of attitudes and ideological views. How do these postures, for example, relate to the dominant ideological themes of the full-fledged Nazi member? Not surprisingly, we find that the politically militarized have the highest percentage of people with no ideology worth noting (4.3%), while the fully politicized have none. Otherwise, the Hitler cult and super-patriotism are the favorite themes of the politically militarized—not exactly a distinctive ideology. The fully politicized, and also the pre-political youth, on the other hand, stand out for their Nordic-German romanticism, the social *Volksgemeinschaft*, and the Hitler cult. Of these three, the pre-political youth is particularly partial to the Nordic-German cult, a propensity shared also with the authoritarians. The authoritarians and the hostile militants emphasize revanchism, a sure link to the war effort, and also the Hitler cult. The hostile militants, by the way, are the only group with a strong emphasis on antisemitism as a dominant ideological theme. The same antisemitic note also comes out in their perception of the Weimar Republic. The older authoritarian group is the next most anti-semitic in its view of Weimar, although its traditional anti-capitalistic objections and dislike of pluralism have a higher priority.

On our scale of the shades of antisemitism, the politically militarized, with 43.2%, surprisingly have the largest number of respondents who exhibit no sign of prejudice. Given their youth and directness, they probably did not conceal their bias, if they had any. Their phobias seem to run more to anti-Communism, anti-Socialism, or to the orthodox, all-inclusive hate-list. The heaviest and most aggressive prejudice is found among the hostile militants, of whom no fewer than a good fourth show the paranoid syndrome of seeing conspiracies and threatening counteraction. The authoritarians are next with this syndrome (18.2%), and they also tend to tell personal anecdotes, often with a sexual angle. The fully politicized, oddly enough, have the highest incidence of *Judenkoller* (31.8%), perhaps an indication of the inner tensions that are working themselves out under all this politicization and that are apt to lead to sudden breakdowns of judgment. Otherwise, this group is also mostly anti-Communist and anti-Socialist. The pre-political youth, finally, incline toward the telling of antisemitic anecdotes and milder verbal projections. And they stress "reactionaries," liberals, and Catholics as their objects of hostility.

The not-so-subtle differences between these groups also color their choice of words when referring to their political enemies. Typically, the pre-political youth has the largest (65.4%), and the politically militarized (29.4%) and hostile militants (35.4%) the smallest, percentage of respondents who express a liking or sense of understanding toward some of their political enemies. Instead, the politically militarized and the hostile militants tend to refer to them in the gutter language of the *outré* as "subhuman," immoral, or rodents. The fully politicized are not far behind in the use of this language. The politically militarized and the authoritarians also like to call their enemies traitors or to speak of them as a faceless conspiracy. One is reminded of George Orwell's *Nineteen Eighty-Four*, where love and hatred—love Big Brother and hate Goldstein—are projected with similar vehemence. Evidently aggressive action has to be accompanied with the attempt to strip the antagonist of his human qualities.

The ethnocentric attitudes other than antisemitism are similarly indicative of the generations and their state of mind. The younger groups, the politically militarized and fully politicized, show significantly less ethnocentric prejudice than, say, the hostile militants, whose hatred lies equally on aliens in Germany and on the Allied nations abroad. The authoritarians and pre-political youth are more concerned with asserting the basic inferiority of alien nations as compared to their own nationality.

Were the attitudes toward authority of the most mobilized groups deferential and submissive, as theories of authoritarianism like to suggest? The answer is far more complex. Both the politically militarized and the hostile militants tend to show an intense hostility toward police and governmental authority. The fully politicized and the pre-political youth tend to be preoccupied with the "pluralistic disintegration of state authority" by the multi-party system of Weimar. And even the authoritarians were more preoccupied with the leadership cult of Hitler than with law and order for their own sake.

Finally, to round out the picture, there are our two measurements of the respondents' "formative experiences" and the pathological question of what appears to be the most abnormal feature of each case. As the reader may recall, the formative experiences tend to place strong generational accents on groups, which in this case will summarize much of what has been said before. There is, for example, the experience of the social snub or humiliation which turns up frequently among the pre-political youth, an experience typical of imperial society. Then there is the impact of World War One, or in particular the *Fronterlebnis*, which, along with the experience of the German defeat, is the formative experience of nearly half the hostile militants. The defeat also left a deep imprint on over one-fourth of the authoritarians and nearly as many pre-political youths, evidently the core of the war generation, including those vicariously socialized by the war effort. Then there were the experiences more typical of postwar youth. The experience of comradeship in a youth organization was frequently the formative influence among the politically militarized and the hostile militants. The stress on a formative educational or literary experience was popular among the politically militarized and the fully politicized. When the respondent relates an incident or experience as his formative influence, we have of course no way of checking the truth or accuracy of his account. However, we are more interested in what it meant to him and what he is trying to communicate about himself rather than what "really happened" or who might be to blame. This is particularly true of the alleged episodes with Jews or aliens about which many of the politically militarized, the authoritarians, and the fully politicized tell. We are making no attempt here to determine why a respondent may be prejudiced, but only what he places in a central position of his self-presentation.

As for the most prominent abnormal feature, we have a range of kinds of attitude or reported behavior in which it is the excess of an attribute which makes the case odd. We are not trying to assign all the early Nazis to abnormal psychology, but are attempting to describe and catalogue personality types that seem to occur frequently among them. Two-thirds of the authoritarians, for example, exhibit either a high degree of cultural shock or an extreme version of the leadership cult. The pre-political youths stand out with cultural shock (32.5%) and with a high degree of irrational or paranoid behavior (20%). The hostile militants and the fully politicized are quite high in leadership cult and in irrationality. And the politically militarized, finally, tend to exhibit an extreme degree of identification and conformity with the movement (54.1%) and of masochism and personal insecurity (16.5%). These two features are evidently very typical of the spirit of the movement and of its most mobilized members. They follow their urge to merge their individuality with it and yet they continue to be quite insecure and to wallow in self-pity amid the violence they unleash upon their enemies.

FOUR

Violence and Offices: Styles of Youthful Conduct

With organized youth groups, there is a wide range of individual conduct which might have a bearing on later conduct in the Nazi party. One of the most obvious is the holding of group offices, presumably a sign of maturity and of advanced integration with the group. It is worth noting, for example, that the respondents with the lowest number of youth offices or organizational service come from the Socialist or Communist youth; this may well denote their insufficient involvement there. The highest number of office-holders, by contrast, is among those whose first youth organization was the HJ or SA, where over one-half of the respondents report having held an office. The quasi-military groups and the conservatives, on the other hand, for reasons of their own are rather low in the offices held. Most of the offices held, of course, are those in relatively small groups or local founding activities.

FD-17: Youth Organization Office Held

	Number	Per cent
Small group leadership	37	11.9
Founded, co-founded local	37	11.9
Proselytizing, recruitment	18	5.8
Propaganda, speaker	11	3.6
Higher level leadership	14	4.5
No office held	193	62.3
	310	100.0

There is a curious bifurcation, moreover, between office-holding and engagement in violence. Respondents who liked violence best held the lowest percentage of youth group offices (70%). In particular they fall below the average in local group-founding activities, an area in which especially those who liked marching and rallies seem to excel. The violence-minded were also below par in proselytizing and propaganda, compared for example to those who liked comradeship or hiking and cultural appreciation. The office-holding respondents evidently are not the type to wallow in violence. Their satisfactions seem to lie in manipulation and in maintaining a group and its members. Nor do the violence-minded with minor exception hold youth group offices, since their personality needs require the group only as a supportive setting for violent, aggressive expression.

A Social Profile of Youth Office Holders

If we assume for the moment that holding a youth group office is a sign of maturity and adjustment, we need to ask all the more urgently: What kind of early Nazis tend to hold a youth office? A sketch of relevant social indices may give us at least a partial answer.

The leaders of small groups and the local founders tended to be very young, with more than half born after 1905. They were evidently part and parcel of the rising activist youth of the 1920s, and are either among the spatially immobile or in the occupied areas. By occupation of the respondent as well as of his father, military-civil servants were the least likely to strive for office, while workers, farmers, and businessmen and their sons play a prominent role. Respondents who lost their livelihood before the Depression also rarely held youth office except as small group leaders. A considerably higher percentage of the local founders, proselytizers, and higher leadership figures lost their livelihood during the Depression. The same three groups also tended to be socially immobile, having made no significant move toward upward mobility. Regarding their level of education, the least- and the best-educated respondents were least likely to hold a group office, presumably on the quasi-American premise that the former were not intelligent enough and the latter over-educated. In this respect, incidentally, they resemble the young street fighters, who also came chiefly from the middle range of the educational levels.

As to their youthful posture, however, more than half of the small group leaders and local group founders are among the politically militarized. The hostile militants claim another one-fourth of the small group leaders. The fully politicized, by contrast, have a lion's share of the proselytizers and the higher-level leadership. More than half of the small group leaders and local group founders, indeed, later engaged in street or organized violence. This record, nevertheless, is matched by those who held no youth group office. Thus, we are forced to concede that violence-mindedness and actual engagement in violence do not always coincide. It is also possible that group leaders may tend not to express their actual liking for violence very openly. Perhaps our further analysis will resolve this contradiction.

The small group leaders also tend to come from an economically secure childhood. The respondents from a strict authoritarian up-bringing play a respectable role among the local group founders, proselytizers, and higher leadership levels, which contradicts the presumable effects of authoritarianism on political participation. Respondents from a deprived background, on the other hand, are unlikely to hold youth office.

Youth Office and Party Office

Did the holding of youth offices denote a propensity to hold office in the NSDAP or its auxiliary organizations? First of all, non-holders at the youth level tended to join the party only when it was a matter of jumping on a rather crowded bandwagon. The small group leaders often joined when there was as yet only a small nu-cleus of the movement present. The local group founders and the proselytizers, by comparison, also tended to be founders or co-founders of a Nazi local in their respective areas. As for holding a party office, 72.4% of youthful non-holders of office also held none in the NSDAP. The local youth group founders tended to become organizers or speakers in the party, and the small youth group lead-er often became a functional organization leader or a minor local officer. As for the SA, both the small group leaders and the local group founders stand out for having joined it right away, and also for holding offices in it. Yet, even though they played a role in "day-and-night" fighting, they engaged in political violence as adults a good deal less, for example, than those who never held a youth office. Perhaps holding an office did denote a more integrated per-sonality than we expected.

A propensity for holding office in a group, of course, also has implications of seeking a sinecure. In 1933-1934, when the auto-biographies were written, the percentages of the small group lead-ers, the proselytizers, and the higher-level youth leaders whose ex-pectations of the Third Reich stressed a job or other economic pay-off for themselves, rather than the grandiloquent formulas of na-tional rebirth, were markedly larger than with the other groups. After 1934, moreover, holding party office and making a career of the party became the obvious route to follow. A disproportionate num-ber of the youthful proselytizers (40.0%), local founders (21.3%), and small group leaders (17.9%) indeed ended up with a full-time party career. Once a group leader, the tendency seems to have been, always a group leader.

Most Extreme Youthful Activity

The alternative to holding a youth group office appears to have been involvement for the personal satisfactions of extremist behavior. We have recorded the most extreme youthful activity reported by each respondent before he reached the age of 26. The breakdown and the subsequent crosstabulations show the extent to which the Nazi revolt was indeed a youth rebellion whose political-behavioral patterns were already present before the brown onslaught really got under way. There is no need to repeat here some of the descriptions of the rapid involvement in and escalation of extremist activities by the most mobilized youths. Instead, we shall concentrate on a social profile and on the relationship between youthful and adult involvement.

FD-18: Most Extreme Youthful Political Activity

	Number	Per cent
Partisan political violence (street fighting, meeting-hall)	104	28.3
Violence against occupation, separatists, Polish irregulars	30	8.1
Violence in Free Corps, vigilantes against insurgents	24	6.5
Provocation (in political enemies' area, meetings)	10	2.7
Demonstrations, marching, rallies	55	14.9
Proselytizing among friends, fellow-workers, relatives	28	7.6
Proselytizing, propaganda house-to-house	14	3.8
Electioneering	26	7.0
Other (e.g., military training)	78	21.1
	369	100.0

A Social Profile of Youth Activity Groups

A breakdown by age already divides the different activity groups in a significant way. Those engaged in partisan street violence are to two-thirds concentrated in the age cohorts born after 1905. Two-thirds of the brown street fighters, in other words, were between 15 and 25 years old in 1930, when the decisive struggle for power set in. The next youngest groups were those engaged in demonstrations and in electioneering, both with over three-fourths born in the postwar generation (1902 and later). All three groups, including the street fighters, evidently include nearly a third of victory-watchers each. Those who engaged in violence in a Free Corps or against the occupation or the Poles (hereafter all referred to as organized violence), by comparison, are concentrated in the chief age cohorts of the war generation, with 60.8% born between 1890 and 1901. They also include a good third of the victory-watcher cohorts (1902-1905). The proselytizers straddle the war and postwar generations. They evidently include diverse elements, especially of the cohorts of 1898-1901 and 1906-1916. Those engaged in "other" activities in their youth are mostly of the prewar generation.

Regarding their location experience, we meet the same three groups, the street fighters, marchers, and electioneers, again disproportionately represented among respondents who never moved from the area of their origin. This is evidently the youth rebellion of the "inside agitators." The street fighters and marchers also figure disproportionately among the border-area cases, which once more demonstrates the effect of the border struggles on youthful mobilization, though perhaps not on electioneering. The reader may recall how unaccustomed some of the borderland and foreign-origin respondents were to parties and elections. Those engaged in organized violence and proselytizing, by contrast, were more likely to be highly mobile among cities. The proselytizers even include rural-urban migrants, and those in organized violence naturally include large numbers in the occupied areas.

The street fighters and those engaged in organized violence tended to live in towns between 2,000 and 100,000 inhabitants, rather than in rural or metropolitan areas. The marchers, by contrast, were at home mostly in the countryside and in metropolitan areas other than Berlin. The proselytizers, oddly enough, lived mostly in small towns and in the countryside, perhaps a reminder of the rural and small-town roots of German antisemitism. During the Depression, the economic casualty rate was highest among the three groups—the street fighters, marchers, and electioneers. The organized violent and the proselytizers, by comparison, tended to be in economic trouble more often before 1929. The reader may recall that this was the typical economic crisis period of the war generation.

The patterns of the occupations of the fathers of the respondents were more complex. The fathers of the street fighters and electioneers tended to be artisans, military-civil servants, and (the street fighters only) businessmen. Moreover, one-fourth of the fathers died while the respondents were still under 18, clearly an unusual percentage for any group. The marchers were more often the sons of workers or military-civil servants. The proselytizers tended to be the sons of farmers, military-civil servants, or businessmen. And those in organized violence often had businessmen or workers for fathers. A glance at the patterns of upward mobility sheds more light on the situation. Substantial numbers of the street fighters (33.3%), marchers (32.7%), and electioneers (47.8%), were upwardly mobile from the urban working class to a middle-class status. Many had made no attempt to rise. If we combine this with their spatial immobility, we see that they may well have been second-generation urbanites, like the young black rioters of the United States in the 1960s, the sons of rural-urban migrants. The street fighters and the organized violent also include a disproportionate share of socially declining families. The proselytizers often were upwardly mobile in an urban context, conjuring up a mental image of how a little education in receptive minds may lead to dramatic consequences. The proselytizers, along with the electioneers, in fact, were among the better-educated groups.

Even in their religious affiliation or failure to state any, the groups differ notably from one another. The young street fighters and those in organized violence are considerably more likely not to state their religion than the non-violent groups. The latter tend to be Catholics. The violent also live mostly in areas that are religiously mixed or in which their own religion constitutes a minority. Violence may thus be related to secularization, and other kinds of extremist activity also seem to be stimulated by this kind of religious dissension, which in Germany has a long history. As one respondent (no. 234) put it, for example, "for us Protestants in the [Catholic] Rhineland, it was a constant battle with the Catholics . . . a Catholic to me is the same as a Social Democrat." This is an echo of the historic persecution of Catholics and Socialists under Bismarck.

Early and Later Involvement

The degrees of youthful extremist activity undoubtedly represent also degrees of readiness to become involved with the grown-up extremism of the NSDAP. When we compare the local progress made by the party at the time the respondent joined, for instance, the street fighters were far and away the most zealous. Forty-two and one-half percent of them report having been the first to join or having founded or helped to found the party local. Another 16.1% claim to have been among the first half-dozen or so to join. They also stand out in the choice of their chief object of hostility, the Communists and Socialists (76.9%), far ahead of any other group, and in the relative absence of antisemitism (42% show none).

All but a tiny percentage of the street fighters (4.4%) later were in the SA or SS. A good two-thirds, in fact, joined the SA the day they joined the NSDAP. This contrasts with half of the proselytizers and one-fourth of the marchers and electioneers who never joined either the SA or the SS. By the same token, it is hardly surprising to find 70.8% of the street fighters involved in the political violence and "day-and-night" campaigning of the party during its main fighting years. Only 51.5% of the electioneers, 46.4% of the organized violent, 41.3% of the marchers, and 32.8% of the proselytizers follow in their footsteps. The youthful proselytizers are heavily (48.3%) involved in adult proselytizing, more than any other group. The youthful demonstrators are still leading in adult demonstrations (20.5%), but barely more so than the other groups. Being in a demonstration appears to be less of an intrinsically symbolic activity than, say, violence or proselytizing. The youthful electioneers, upon closer analysis, also are the most involved in the "day-and-night" campaigning of 1932, but evidently less in the broader categories of violence.

There can be little question but that the youthful patterns of activity are broadly indicative of what the adult Nazi would do. Partisan street violence seems to be the most convincing case of this continuity. But we have to bear in mind that the youthful patterns of many of the street fighters may be identical with the adult patterns not because of such behavioral continuity but because they still had not passed their 25th year of age by the end of the Nazi struggle for power. In other words, we may have measured their conduct twice. With the electioneers, where the pattern is weaker, the same may be the case. Only the proselytizers were old enough to minimize the overlap in time. On the other hand, the implicit bias of recording only the most extreme political activity in both cases also means that continuity, say, in the case of a youthful electioneer will be demonstrated only to the extent that he does not report any involvement in a physical clash with the enemy. An indefatigable electioneer who reported even one clash or instance of proselytizing, demonstrating, or provocation, would not have been recorded again under his less extreme main activity, electioneering.

Nevertheless, the patterns of continuity in violence, proselytizing, demonstrations, and, not to forget, office-holding are pervasive and persistent. Perhaps even more than in matters of ideology, the behavioral patterns of mobilized youth tend to show what their behavioral patterns will be when they are adults. In this sense and in that of the overlap in time of youth and adult patterns, National Socialism indeed received its virulence from the youth rebellion of the Weimar Republic. And whatever other aspects of the brown triumph can be blamed on Weimar Germany, this youth rebellion was not one of the failed responsibilities of the unhappy republic. No government or social or economic establishment can be said to have "caused" this wave of youthful mobilization. Was it their parents, the older generation, their schools? The evidence is limited, but let us take a look at the home and school environments of the young Nazis.

FIVE

The Influence of Home and School

"Tall oaks from little acorns grow," wrote the poet and there is, probably, almost universal agreement that tall Nazi stormtroopers also may have grown from little problem children rather than from certain trends in German literature and philosophy. However, given the objective of finding out what the childhood of the Abel respondents was like, it is by no means easy to learn the answers from their own accounts or from the statistical tabulations we based on them. What can an untrained, conceivably rather anti-psychological mind be expected to tell us about his or her own childhood? Occasionally, to be sure, there are startling glimpses, such as when we learn that respondents who had reported a particularly strict, disciplinarian upbringing also happen to be most deeply engaged in the political violence of the Nazi party. But the visions of battered children growing up to be bruisers in the brown uniform were premature. Except for a few more transparent autobiographical statements, the relevant information in most cases is too meager to pursue such an inquiry. Instead, we had to content ourselves more with subjects such as the political color of home and school, on which the Abel autobiographies are more explicit.

Childhood Settings

Nevertheless, we can look at the distribution of some of the other observable characteristics over our sample and, briefly, examine them. The breakdown which contains the disciplinarian category was a broad classification of themes suggested by the respondents in describing their childhood. To the extent that a given respondent may have omitted mention of parental abuse and instead stressed his growing up in poverty, this is all we can know about him or her. A popular motif is that of the freewheeling childhood in an affluent home, roaming through the countryside with one's peers as the proverbial *Lausbuben*, a living contradiction of certain stereotypes about the making of the authoritarian mind, and also of the nature of the German family. We have juxtaposed this to a sheltered childhood which might conceivably have inculcated a sense of social distrust or of inability to cope with the social environment. The death or partial absence of the parents, of course, is very significant. The rest are settings of deprivation distinguished only by rather impersonal causes such as whether poverty was due to family size or rural setting. There were also a few cases of sickly, pampered children

FD-25: Childhood Settings

	Number	Per cent
Economically secure, freewheeling	113	25.8
Economically secure, sheltered	86	19.6
Strict, disciplinarian	41	9.3
Orphan, or personally deprived	55	12.5
⌐ Large family in poverty	49	11.2
⊢ Farm childhood, poor	47	10.7
∟ Hard times, other deprivation	48	10.9
	439	100.0

reminiscent of the role of illness in Himmler's and in Hitler's childhood, but not enough to warrant statistical inferences. Like the battered child who may turn into a stormtrooper, they must remain a foil for the imagination only.

A curious but not untypical mixture of strict upbringing and poverty is a poor farmer's son, born in 1879 (no. 202). His father was a drill sergeant in the war of 1870-1871 and drilled his five boys mercilessly for the military service. As a small boy, the respondent was locked into the house with three siblings while the parents worked the fields. At the age of nine, the respondent had to work on the farm, too, and at the age of fifteen he was sent to work on an estate. At sixteen, he lost his father, who had had stomach ailments all along, and had to help support the family. He finally became a professional soldier, as his father would have wanted him to, and he even compares his captain to "a strict but just father." After a wartime military career, he is off with the *voelkisch* movement and enjoys in particular the swashbuckling militarism of the *Stahlhelm*. His knowledge of Weimar politics is dim but his love of demonstrations—the bigger the better—and political violence, all the greater. He likes to describe his battles in a masochistic manner: being shot at, assaulted, and encircled. We cannot help wondering whether his father was physically abusive.

Social Background of Childhood Settings

Let us take a cursory look at how these groups appear to differ from each other. In terms of age, the disciplinarian childhoods are mostly from the earlier age cohorts, while the orphans or near-orphans are the youngest, often having suffered the loss of the father or temporary absence of both parents as a result of the war. As for the location experience, the combined backgrounds of poverty tend to be mostly with rural-urban migrants and with colonial or foreign backgrounds. The poverty may well have been a cause of the migration and the awareness of deprivation the result. The other three—freewheeling, strict, and orphaned childhoods—all tend to be among the highly mobile. The sheltered childhood, interestingly, takes place more often among spatially immobile families. The orphaned and personally deprived, incidentally, are composed of 68.8% who lost their fathers, and the rest were raised by relatives or strangers for other reasons.

The occupations of their fathers show little variation except for the prevalence of military-civil servant fathers of disciplinarian homes and the prominence of farmer and worker fathers among the poverty childhoods. For every disciplinarian military-civil servant father, by the way, there were nearly two military-civil servants who reportedly gave their children a freewheeling youth. The economically secure homes, whether sheltered or freewheeling, tended to be headed by businessmen, artisans, and military-civil servants. The orphans were often the children of workers or of highly placed military-civil servants or professional people. The latter also show up heavily among the families in social decline.

Was a disciplinarian upbringing the result of upward social mobility, of the upward scramble of those who are sometimes called the "bicyclist types" in Germany, because they bend their backs toward the forces higher up while viciously trampling those who are under their feet? Forty-one and seven-tenths percent of the disciplinarian homes are upwardly mobile, especially in the city, a number exceeded only by the poverty families, although the freewheeling ones are close behind. The rest of the disciplinarian homes tend to be in social decline or to have made no attempt to rise.

We also recorded whether a respondent had to work as a child or whether he could pursue his education or vocational training. For a working-class or lower middle-class boy it was the normal course in those days to go to school until the age of 14 and then to be apprenticed in a trade. Middle-class children might begin working at the age of 17 or later. If a boy had to work as an unskilled laborer from the age of 14, this meant that he would probably never be able to rise to a qualified job in his lifetime. As the statistical breakdown shows, only about one-fifth of the sample was condemned to child labor or subproletarian careers, a number well below the national average.

FD-26: Early Economic Involvement

	Number	Per cent
Worked from age 14 as apprentice	294	54.7
Worked from age 17-18 only	57	10.6
Worked from age 19-20 only	55	10.2
┌ Worked outside home before age 14	16	3.0
├ Worked at home (farm, shop) before 14	30	5.6
└ Worked before age 14 because of war		
(father drafted)	7	1.3
Worked from age 14 as unskilled laborer	54	10.1
Other	24	4.5
	537	100.0

This measurement quickly divides our childhood-setting groups into two social classes. The economically secure childhoods, whether sheltered or freewheeling, tend almost without exception to lead to normal careers, beginning either with an apprenticeship or with work at the age of 17 or later after some secondary or commercial training. Among the orphaned, however, 18.2% had to work before they were 14 and another 12.7% were unskilled teenage laborers. Among the poor childhoods, the figures are 23.1% and 19.6%, respectively. These were evidently the real "have-nots" of the Nazi party. Did this fact influence their participation in right-wing organizations? Not really. The economically secure and freewheeling group is the first to join the very early Nazi party and *voelkisch* groups, while the poverty and orphan groups tend to be in left-wing or republican organizations. Even during the crisis of 1923, and in the following quieter years, the "haves" continue to be more heavily represented in the brown movement. In 1929, still, it is the disciplinarians and people from a sheltered, economically secure childhood who have the highest percentage in the Nazi party, and only in 1930 do the "have-nots" catch up.

But while their membership seemed to be lagging behind, their involvement in political violence was not. In the years 1919 to 1924, for example, the respondents from a poverty background were just as frequently engaged in political violence as those from an economically secure background. And the orphans are as often involved in demonstrations and more often in electioneering and propaganda than the economically secure. In the years 1925 to 1928, this continues to be true. During the fighting years from 1929 to 1932, finally, the violence of the "have-nots" clearly rises above that of the "haves." The orphans and the respondents from disciplinarian homes also have a higher percentage of stormtroopers among them. And the disciplinarians, as mentioned above, now are the most involved in fighting, often "day and night," for the movement.

Childhood Settings and Ideology

The different childhood settings, we might think, might also color ideological outlooks. They do indeed, but sometimes in unpredictable ways. It is hardly surprising that respondents from a poverty background lay great stress on the *Volksgemeinschaft*, but so do those from a secure and freewheeling childhood. Neither does it come as a great revelation to find the orphans opting disproportionately for the Hitler cult. They have found their father figure. What is surprising is that the respondents from an economically secure and freewheeling childhood turn out most frequently to have antisemitism as their dominant ideological theme. There is no hint of this in the literature on the dynamics of prejudice, except perhaps the knowledge that some of the European nations with more familistic and restrictive childrearing practices, such as the French and Italians, have been considerably less prone to ethnic prejudices, even though the sense of social distrust resulting from these practices may have other deleterious effects. The sheltered childhood, at least among our respondents, is not free of prejudice either, although its main emphasis, as with the disciplinarian upbringing, is on revanchism, revenge perhaps for the broken walls of the nation's home.

To pursue this theme a little further, how do these groups differ with regard to the shadings of antisemitism? The respondents with a sheltered childhood, and also those from a poverty background, indeed show far less prejudice than the other groups. But the antisemitism of the respondents with a freewheeling childhood stresses mostly their *Judenkoller*, which is generally a sign of emotional instability. They also exhibit such verbal projections and anecdote-telling as may well fit their socially integrated, freewheeling personalities. It is the orphans and the strictly raised who show the greatest tendency toward perceiving conspiracies and hinting their own threats. Aggressive paranoia in adulthood may well be causally related to parental discipline or premature death.

The Abel respondents often mention their mother's influence as well as that of their father. But whether it is due to the nature of the unpolitical roles mothers actually played in imperial Germany or to the way their roles were perceived by their children, the mother is always credited with relatively unpolitical contributions. She teaches the children religious devotion, honesty, thrift, and cleanliness, and sometimes even a faintly patriotic appreciation of German culture or history. The father, on the other hand, has known partisan preferences and, not infrequently, a record of political participation which leaves a deep imprint on the children's formation of political opinions. The influence is not necessarily in the same direction, as will be remembered from the case of the son of an anticlerical, militant Social Democrat[1] whose mother secretly gave a religious upbringing to the children, but even in purely reactive impulses a political message has been received and digested. Where appropriate we also counted influential father substitutes such as uncles or male friends of the family, if the father had died or was in effect absent during a significant phase. In the latter case, boys often identified visibly with the paternal substitute and gave serious consideration to his politics.

FD-23: Father's Politics

Father's identification:	Number	Per cent
Nationalist, patriotic	148	45.4
Militarist, authoritarian	35	10.7
Voelkisch, politically antisemitic	40	12.2
⌐ Conservative	7	2.1
⊢ Liberal	7	2.1
⊢ Center party	15	4.6
⌐ SPD, Marxist	17	5.2
Acute conflict between father and son	8	2.4
Unpolitical home environment	50	15.3
	327	100.0

A typical example of conflict between father and son and of a paternal substitute is a farmer's son born 1909 (no. 168) who leaves his job on his father's farm after a quarrel in order "to sub-

[1] See above, p. 45. Another good illustration of the distribution of political influence between mother and father appears in one account (no. 265) where the respondent points out that his father was so busy that he had to leave raising the children to the mother. Then he wastes not another word on his mother, but proceeds at great length to describe Sunday walks with his farmer father in woods and fields during which the father inculcated in him an appreciation for German history and patriotism, and the father's strong National Liberal convictions, or at least the "national" part of them. After 1918, the respondent promptly joined the DVP, the equivalent of the prewar National Liberals.

merge myself among the people, to be a worker among workers."
He has a foster father and school headmaster, "a German patriot
through and through," whom he greatly admires. Another example
is a young bricklayer, born 1905 (no. 205), who at eighteen leaves
home and wanders on foot all over Germany. His father is an unsuccessful sculptor and the two simply could not get along. Not unlike some young Americans today, the son is a romantic wanderer
who above all wants to be dependent on no one, not even the employment office or an employer.

An example of the influence of both parents on a respondent is
the account of a steelworker's son, born 1902 (no. 13), who describes his father's views as a mixture of non-Marxist socialism and
patriotism. The father instilled in him an appreciation for "the quiet
heroism of the German worker," his longing for a better education
and a more interesting life, and his pride in the company's product
and reputation. The mother is depicted as a "good, honest German
Hausfrau," who believed in God, worked hard all day, and objected
to the boy's Marxist indoctrination by fellow-workers.

Another respondent, a gardener's son born 1908 (no. 5), relates
his father's "extremely nationalist" views: "We were raised this way
from infancy. National holidays such as the Kaiser's birthday were
celebrated like the greatest holidays." The war broke out just as the
respondent entered first grade. "Thus my earliest recollections are
closely tied in with the outbreak of war when my father was overcome by a boundless enthusiasm which gave way to disillusionment
only when the military service rejected him." The father tried to
serve the cause in other ways, by taking up collections and render-
ing services to the wounded. He impressed on the children how
much better off they were, even with their scarce food, than the
poor soldiers. The respondent plainly sees the world through his
father's eyes and with his father's feelings:

> Meanwhile the shameful ending of the war came closer. I shall never
> forget the day when father came home with the horrible news that
> parts of the army were in revolt. The big, strong man was in tears.
> This was the one and only time I ever saw him cry. We children of
> course felt helpless in the face of this emotional outbreak although I
> as the oldest of six had an inkling of the magnitude of the goings-on.
>
> There came the time when the red hordes roamed the streets, when
> Ebert, Scheidemann, and who knows who else promised us mountains
> of gold, and when we received in place of our old flag the black-red-
> gold colors. My father was bitterer than ever and expressed his con-
> tempt whenever he saw these colors. This hatred was inculcated in us
> children, too. I would never have thought of playing with a child from
> our neighborhood because I shared his hatred of "everything red."

The son promptly continued in this direction after his father's death regardless of friction at work or in the streets where he was electioneering for the DNVP.

Another respondent, born 1884 (no. 259), offers a kind of familial theory of the origin of his National Socialism. His father, a farmer and carriage maker born in 1850, "during his journeyman's years became acquainted with the socialism of Bebel's school and identified with this idea from the bottom of his heart to the end of his life. Nevertheless he was also devout and feared God." The mother came from small and poor circumstances. "After leaving school she was a domestic servant, also in Jewish households where she had some bad experiences. Hence she became antisemitic-*voelkisch* in her views. She was a very smart woman." The son became a *Kapitulant* (military-civil servant), and joined an antisemitic group, the *Hammerbund*, in 1910. At the end of the war he even got himself elected a workers'-and-soldiers' councillor in a German military hospital in 1918 "in order to allow patriotic elements a guiding role." He gives an amusing description of the outbreak of anarchy in his hospital and prison camp. The soldiers no longer wanted to do guard duty or clean up their rooms, and began to sell off food, horses, and military equipment for their private gain. Russian and Roumanian POWs began to raid neighboring villages and to take up residence there. At this point, the British POWs offered their services as guards and police units. The Workers' and Soldiers' Council gratefully accepted the offer and reestablished order with Draconian edicts.

The respondents are often quite perceptive, as children, of the significance of events and conflicts. One respondent, born 1886, the son of an artisan (no. 280), recalls Bismarck's death "which moved me deeply" and a local speech of the SPD leader Karl Liebknecht which caused great excitement among the children because it was closed to the public and guarded by the Prussian police. His father was a devout Protestant who held a position with the church. The Christian devotion of the parents and the father's patriotic convictions "frustrated all attempts to pull him into the camp of the then mightily growing SPD." The son was enthusiastic about a soldier's profession and "anything soldierly and heroic," and took pride in the fact that his home-town was the site of an historic battle connected with the rise of Prussia. He promptly enlisted and, despite his shortsightedness, became a military-civil servant.

Another respondent, born in 1892, the son of a silversmith, involved in many strikes and lockouts (no. 284), likes to recall how "my father, who like all workers of the discriminated fourth estate was forced into the arms of subversive, international Marxism by

the reckless exploitations of the liberalistic system . . . in his nationalistic enthusiasm nevertheless acquired a large map of the war, on
which to mark with little flags the state of the war." The respondent
himself floundered similarly between right and left at the end of the
war. Half-buried under his pompous phrase-making, we can
glimpse his immediate attraction to, and disillusionment with,
Marxism. Together with two prominent defectors from the SPD,
Unger and Kloth, he read the periodical *Deutscher Vorwaerts*, and
joined the Association of Nationalistic Workers after a confused interlude with the antisemitic Knueppel-Kunze movement and other
groups of the right. He also went to lectures at a shortlived National
Workers' School in Berlin until he was swept up by Josef Goebbels'
campaign in that city.

There are other examples of conflicting influences. Another artisan's son, born in 1893 (no. 285), reports how his uncle, a carpenter, "brainwashed" him with stories of Karl Marx and Ferdi-
nand Lassalle. The uncle had been in jail under the anti-Socialist
decrees of 1878 and still had an embroidered cloth hanging on the
wall of his house calling on the proletarians of all countries to unite.
The respondent's father, however, tried to inculcate him with his
own worship of great military figures like Roon and Moltke, and his
cult of Bismarck.

Sometimes also, the filial tail seems to be wagging the parental
dog as in the case of a printer's son born 1903 (no. 298) who obviously belongs to the brash postwar generation. His father wanted
the boy to have a better life and sent him to a *Gymnasium* so that
he might acquire all the advantages of a stiff collar and a reserve
officer status. Yet the son is already impatient with him when he is
barely ten years old. The war made the son consider only soldiers
as "human beings of value." "I almost felt like a second-class person when my father did not enlist right away, but only in 1916.
Four generations in our family had already served the fatherland
with arms in Prussian regiments." The respondent, in addition to
working to support the family, also served in youth auxiliaries and
in the *Jugendwehr* to acquire military training. He believed in the
war effort without being in the least attached to the Kaiser and the
old order. The sight of the red mutineers in army uniform, not anything his father did or said, made him a bitter enemy of the Weimar
Republic. "In the midst of this cauldron of treason and meanness,
the soldiers returned to their jobs. My father came home, too, sick
and mentally tired, unable to make any plans or to have any formative influence on me." The son, then 15, had grown up without his
father. Instead, the respondent and his buddies attached themselves
to Free Corps veterans and "adopted them as teachers." They fol-

lowed their heroic deeds such as the Kapp *putsch*, the respondent explains. He joined the *Jungstahlhelm*, where he met "front soldiers who regarded the new state as a betrayal of their sacrifices of blood, and youths who were ready to accept their legacy." He soon became what we have earlier called a politically militarized youth, ever ready to march and do battle.

A Social Profile of Parental Politics

Let us take a look at the social dimensions of the different political home environments. The age differences alone are striking in that they hint at the changing political environment in the empire from which National Socialism sprang. Each age cohort, let us assume, had been patterned by the trends in vogue among the parents when the respondent was between 5 and 15 years old. The oldest group is the one from a militaristic home. Half of its members were born before 1895. The nationalistic, conventional political (i.e., identifying with the existing imperial parties such as the Liberals or the Center), and unpolitical home environments form a middle layer close to the average. The *voelkisch* home environments are the youngest, with more than half of the respondents born after 1905, and 85% born later than 1895. We can estimate the *voelkisch* influence to have been most effective on our respondents during the years from about 1900 to at least 1915 and probably longer, since the cut-off date is dependent on the minimum age of the Abel respondents. Nineteen hundred to 1940, including the Nazi period, may be more accurate as the historical limits of the *voelkisch* mass movement, not counting the more isolated antecedents.[2]

In their location experience, the *voelkisch* home environments tended to be spatially immobile, or home-grown. They were apparently not particularly related to the rural-urban migration which shows up heavily among the nationalistic and the unpolitical environments. The *voelkisch* environment also tends to be more rural in location. By the father's occupation, it was concentrated among businessmen, artisans, and military-civil servants, while the conventional parties, for example, have most of their following among workers and farmers. The *voelkisch* families tend to be upwardly mobile in the city. Their sons and daughters have the highest rate (81.6%) of respondents who do not consider their religion significant enough to mention it in their *vitae*.[3] They also tend to live in religiously mixed areas or in an area in which they constitute the

[2] For a survey, see especially Pulzer, *The Rise of Political Anti-Semitism in Germany and Austria.*

[3] By comparison, only 37.8% of the sons and daughters of adherents to the conventional parties fail to state their religion.

religious minority, often historic areas of antisemitic agitation in the empire.

Respondents from a *voelkisch* home also tend to be far better educated than the rest, one-fourth having the *Abitur* and another good fourth the *mittlere Reife*. As for the political color of their school environment, several of the groups show an unmistakably strong tendency to fit the school environment to that at home. Forty-two and nine-tenths percent of those from a *voelkisch* home claim to have had a *voelkisch* teacher. Fifty percent of the sons of adherents of conventional parties found teachers who belonged to them also, and 67.7% of the nationalistically raised report that their school tended to be nationalistic as well. Obviously, these statements tend to select from a wide variety of manifestations whatever is most agreeable, or sometimes also what offends the most.

How did the political home environments affect the behavior of the respondents during the first 25 years of their lives? The first youth organization joined by respondents from a *voelkisch* home tended to be a Nazi organization such as the SA or HJ, or *Jungdo*, the DVP or DDP, or bourgeois Youth Movement-related groups. Those from a nationalistic home often joined no youth group, while the children of militaristic fathers tended to join military training groups, the Free Corps, or conservative groups (DNVP, DHV). Children of parents who identified with the conventional prewar parties frequently joined either Socialist or Communist youth groups or likewise the conservative groups. Respondents from an unpolitical environment, finally, mostly joined no youth group, or a military training group or a Free Corps. It would seem that the political environment of the home had a highly predictive relation not only to the kind of youth group a person would enter but also to whether or not he would enter any at all.

When we look at the change of youth organization, moreover, where the reader will recall a block of *voelkisch* youth groups which were a serious rival to the HJ and SA, we can tell who their clientele tends to be. It is chiefly the respondents who come from parental *voelkisch* influences who switch from their first youth group to these *voelkisch* groups, rather than the Nazis. This raises once more the question how the two differed from each other. As Martin Broszat has cogently argued, the *voelkisch* groups tended to be discussion clubs rather than of the unbourgeois, "goon-squad" character of the SA.[4] Nevertheless, the political mobilization of youth undoubtedly did not stop at the bourgeois aversion of their *voelkisch* parents to the stormtrooper approach.

[4] See his *German National Socialism: 1919-1945*.

What did the home environment groups like best about their first youth group, and what did they like the least? The respondents from a *voelkisch* background liked best a combination of marching and ideological direction which was also popular among respondents whose fathers identified with the conventional parties. The *voelkisch* group also liked hiking and cultural appreciation. What they disliked most was a lack of political direction and action. The children from militaristic homes liked political violence best about their group and were most critical of "un-national views" and of socialist militancy. The products of nationalistic homes preferred hiking and cultural appreciation, marching, and political violence, and disliked class barriers or a lack of social conscience. The respondents with unpolitical fathers, finally, liked the (unpolitical) spirit of youthful comradeship best, and, furthermore, demonstrations and violence. They objected most to a lack of political direction in their first youth group. Again, the likes and dislikes seem to follow rather clearly from the political environment at home.

As for the youthful posture and most extreme behavior, the *voelkisch* background generation tended to become politically militarized (43.6%), and to a lesser extent fully politicized (12.8%) or hostile militants (12.8%). The scions of conventionally involved families were the next most mobilized, with 25.5% politically militarized and 14.9% fully politicized. These two were evidently the most capable of extremist escalation. The children of militaristic parents tended to be authoritarians, or leadership cultists, and hostile militants. The offspring of nationalistic homes were most often pre-political parochials or also authoritarians, while those with an unpolitical father tended to be pre-political or hostile militants. It may be well to remember that in those days it was quite common for a person under 26 to be rather parochial or pre-political, even though he might still turn into a political extremist in his later years.

The most extreme behavior the respondents engaged in before they were 26 further confirms the impression of the *voelkisch* and conventional political backgrounds as breeding grounds of political extremism. These two groups have the highest rates of involvement in partisan street fights (a good third) and in proselytizing and demonstrations. The offspring from nationalistic and from unpolitical homes, oddly enough, are the most involved in Free Corps-style violence even though they are, relatively speaking, political innocents.

School and Peer Group Environment

The school environment, as we have seen, curiously parallels the parental influence. Since no one can pick his own parents, as he might pick out a teacher, for identification or friction, we have assumed that the home background is the deeper-lying cause and the choice of a teacher a somewhat dependent variable. The political socialization literature has always assumed that the earlier family socialization may go deeper than anything that happens later. The same can be said about the priority of family over the influence of literature, which is frequently cited by the respondents. Given a certain slant by the parents, the youngster tends to select further influences that converge with the original direction. Nevertheless, there is a good deal of non-convergence evident outside of the statistical trends we have cited. The process of personal development often involves conflicts and new anti-parent identifications which may well give school or literary influences a significant role.

We have classified the political influences of school, literature, and peers in a manner analogous to that of the home environment and strictly according to what the respondent has considered most worth mentioning in his *vita*.

FD-24: School, Literary, and Peer-group Influences

	Number	*Per cent*
Nationalistic, patriotic	121	53.5
Catholic	30	13.3
Liberal, conservative, anti-Marxist	6	2.7
Marxist, socialist	12	5.3
Voelkisch, antisemitic	31	13.7
Conflict with Jewish students, teachers	9	4.0
Other school troubles	17	7.5
	226	100.0

The respondents frequently comment on their school years. Especially the postwar generation often stresses the influence of books or of a particular teacher which may, among other things, reflect the expansion and intensification of education. The immediate prewar period was an age when the working classes and even the rural population felt a great yearning for culture and knowledge, the *Bildungshunger*, and the labor movement developed its *Arbeiterbildungsvereine* and *Arbeiterhochschulen*. The postwar generation, on the other hand, felt a great impatience with the schools and universities, which at times produced statements that could have been made by American radical students in 1970.

A few examples may suffice. A commerical apprentice born in 1911 (no. 61) ran away from home when he was younger. He returned and, on a vacation job, met "all kinds of rabble" as well as some Communist organizers who talked him into joining the KPD.

"We thought of ourselves as noble," he comments, although he never quite felt ready to communicate with a blue-collar worker. He read Ernst Toller's *Maschinenstuermer* and *Massenmensch*. His father was a nationalist who had encouraged him, at the age of 15, to join the *Marinejugend*. His teachers, according to the respondent, were Social Democrats: "They taught us to think, but never to make a serious commitment."

Another respondent, born 1884 (no. 210), was the son of a Hessian admirer of Bismarck who regretted only the exclusion of Austria from Bismarck's empire. The father disapproved of Wilhelm II's rule, and "this atmosphere influenced me all my life." The son became an elementary school teacher and comments on his training: "In the teachers' college we were indoctrinated with monarchism in every way. But as I think back, it was rather overdone. It was by no means a political education, and although we young people were to educate children, we ourselves remained strangers to life." Today, such education would be called "irrelevant." The respondent joined the nationalistic *Deutsche Turnerschaft* and *Jungdo* after the war.

Another respondent, born 1903 (no. 144), the son of a farmer, relates how he learned political understanding from his young athletics teacher who was the only one to explain to the students the meaning of the war effort. "He may well have been the one who awakened my later political involvement in me. This teacher had the gift to make clear to us boys the actual meaning of history and of the World War. This formed a strong contrast to everything else that was taught in school." More irrelevant education. The teacher was eventually drafted, which ended the informal political discussions, but from then on, the respondent followed the political developments in the local newspaper and read books on German history and antiquity. He often clashed with other teachers "because from childhood I have hated slavish submissiveness." At the age of 18 he attended an agricultural college where an older student successfully indoctrinated him about "the Jewish question." But what he liked best were the ideological discussions in class between the instructors and certain students. "The classes in *Staatspolitik* (government) were my favorite because there I frequently had the opportunity to enlighten my teacher, which is not to say that he was no good. He was one of the best." The expansive ego of rebellious youth could not pass up the opportunity to "enlighten" one of his best teachers to show his own superiority. For "the main law of nature is that the stronger push out the weaker. And this natural law, in fact all biological laws, form the basis of *voelkisch* ideology." The respondent began to propagandize this political faith by word of mouth and by passing out the leaflets and selling the literature of the rabidly antisemitic *Hammer* publishers. The respondent also reports having been in the resistance movement against the occupation and to have received a head injury from a Belgian occupation soldier. After the occupation, he formally entered the *voelkisch-sozialer Block*. When the latter dissolved into the Nazi movement, he worked for the *voelkisch Tannenbergbund* for a while and eventually (1928) joined the NSDAP.

A fourth respondent, born 1908 (no. 173), was so precociously politically militarized that he was thrown out of nearly every upper grade of the *Gymnasium* and out of every college. At the age of 13 he joined *Jungdo*, at 16 the *Wikingbund*, and shortly thereafter the *Jungstahlhelm*, in the service of which he was injured during the presidential elections of 1925. For "being against Marxism and Jewry, ever since I began to think politics," he reports, he was punished repeatedly. In 1923, 1925, and 1926, his *Gymnasium* suggested he leave because of his "formal insults" to Jewish fellow-citizens. Upon graduation there and enrollment at the University of Marburg, he joined a student corporation only in order to learn fencing "which had outstanding educational value for me, for I had always felt bitter hatred for those corporation brothers who would only recognize university-educated people and officers as persons of value." It is not clear what use he was planning to make of his fencing skills against the corporation brothers.

While a university student, he joined the NSDAP and began to be a speaker at rallies. The public prosecutor went after him, presumably because of what he said in those speeches, and he was arrested. He also complains about assaults by Socialists and Communists and about injuries he sustained as a stormtrooper. The University of Goettingen, where he enrolled in 1929, soon threw him out for "political crimes," and the University of Koenigsberg, a hotbed of Nazi student radicalism, did likewise a year later, after which he was barred from all German universities. The public prosecutor also followed up on some more rallies held in East Prussia, and before long, the respondent could boast of no fewer than 26 separate "political prosecutions" in progress against him. He was arrested again and had to raise 10,000 marks of bail. The Weimar Republic evidently used similar means of political suppression, as many an American radical of today can testify, including exorbitant bail.

Other accounts tend to stress the varied influences more than conflicts with the school authorities. One respondent, born 1906, the son of a Poznan postal official (no. 216), started out with the typical borderland nationalism, reinforced by his father's Prussian liberalism. Polish pressure drove them to Berlin, where the respondent, barely 14 years old, went to the nationalistic *Deutsche Jugend* and then to the Bismarckjugend (DNVP), fervently hoping that the Kapp *putsch* or the murder of Rathenau (1922) would bring about a radical change. "When everything remained the same and Germany's situation just got worse, I began to expect salvation only from the other side. I was influenced by a friend and by a Jewish teacher in ways that led me more and more into the pacifist and Marxist camp." He began to read the appropriate literature and, in his last years of *Gymnasium*, "I was regarded at school as a convinced Communist." At the university, the student colors and fencing at first struck him as "a romantic and reactionary affair," but after witnessing his first duel, he joined a nationalistic student corporation, *Germania*. Nevertheless, he felt ill at ease among the conservatives because of their lack of understanding of "socialism" and their "feudalistic attitude toward the workers." He began to rally a little core of oppositional spirits in his fraternity and undertook to drive the feudalistic spirit out of *Germania*. A year later (1929) he was in the National Socialist Student Federation (NS St.B) in Marburg, probably involved in the Nazi student drive to capture student self-government throughout Germany.[5] Through all this, the intense desire for "radical change" was constant in this young man.

Some respondents describe school settings of internal conflict. A vintner's son born 1911 (no. 206) tells of an old teacher and former soldier in his *Gymnasium* who preached patriotism and worship of the black-white-red imperial flag in spite of "Marxist and Catholic attempts to suppress him" and to snoop on his teaching. The other teachers and the principal, the respondent claims, were pro-French, pacifistic, Democrats (DDP), or Centrist. The respondent was in the *voelkisch Kyffhaeuserbund*, when he was 14 or 15, and once was spanked by the principal for beating up the son of a separatist. The school principal also forbade him to wear the Nazi emblem he picked up at the age of 16 and locked him up three

---

[5] This drive, which is sometimes cited as evidence of the parallels between recent American student radicals and the Nazi students of that time, chalked up its first successes as early as 1929, when the Universities of Greifswald and Erlangen were "captured." See especially Bracher, *The German Dictatorship*, pp. 164-166. The accusation of "irrelevance" logically led to student demands to institute chairs of "racial research" at all universities, as well as to a witch-hunt against "racially" or politically undesirable professors and fellow-students.

times for undisclosed reasons. He boasts of having been in court ten times for disturbing the public order. "Oh well," he comments, "boys will fight and somebody must lose the fight. So we're fanatics and radicals, so what!" He joined the NSDAP in 1928 because he was impressed by their physical courage in street fighting. Needless to add, we classified him as a politically militarized youth.

Another respondent (born 1905, no. 205) tells of a popular teacher, a wounded war veteran who gave his 13-year-old charges some revolutionary ideas: War is terrible, the monarchy rotten, and capitalism the country's ruin. The students were so impressed that they broke the emperor's picture on the wall. But the influence of this Social Democratic teacher soon found its antidote in a Jack Armstrong-like Boy Scout leader who brought the boys back from the SPD into the patriotic fold. A Scout Jamboree did the rest to indoctrinate the respondent with *voelkisch* and antisemitic ideas. From there, the respondent went to *Jungoberland* and the *Schutz-und-Trutzbund* with dramatic results at school. "At school we were now the outcasts." This called for acts of spitefulness, of course, and soon the respondent and his friend were arrested and expelled from school. It should be clear in all these accounts that the influence of the school is of a piece with peer-group influences in the school setting. These youths would rarely act in this rebellious fashion without at least one close buddy or a whole, eagerly recruited youth group agreeing with them.

Voelkisch Educational Influences

There are many accounts of *voelkisch* or antisemitic influences. One commercial employee, born 1883 (no. 230), tells of an antisemitic elementary teacher who taught his charges an early awareness of "alien races that were lazy, less gifted, and treacherous." It is not clear whether this was the cause of the respondent's phobia or whether his selection of this one teacher was an indication of an already established pattern. Of his father, we only know that he was a minor railroad official and died when the respondent was 14 years old. The boy joined a sports club "of German color"; no mere athletics club would do. A Christian Apprentice Association seems to have had no effect on him, but the *voelkisch* Retail Clerks Union (DHV) he joined in 1906 was the right setting.

Another respondent, a farmer born 1896 (no. 229), tells of his father who was with the prewar *Deutscher Antisemitenbund* and his religious grandfather who had known the court pastor Stoecker and who in 1920 was still active in the *Deutsch-Soziale Partei* of Kunze. His well-to-do parents subscribed to antisemitic periodicals such as the *Staatsbuergerzeitung*, Kunze's *Deutsches Wochenblatt*, and similar books, such as the forged *Protocols of the Elders of Zion*. The respondent doted on this and anti-Masonic trash with predictable results. In the absence of other information—the respondent describes his youth as "very pleasant"—we must assume that youth easily inclines toward prejudice and phobias for reasons of normal psychological development. In the absence of parental discouragement, or under positive encouragement toward projective prejudices, it tends to use displacement as a shortcut toward growing up.

Other respondents report their acquaintance with Paul de Lagarde, Houston Stewart Chamberlain (e.g., no. 101), with the anti-semitic outpourings of Theodor Fritsch (nos. 19 and 235), or with Alfred Rosenberg or Nazi periodicals (no. 149), and appreciation for their German and Nordic heritage. Others again report having had active Nazis as teachers (nos. 86 and 149). And there are curious human twists, such as the son of a princely family (no. 260) who claims: "With sadistic pleasure, the red system forced me into a public school directly under its influence in order to work on me there. . . . The result was the exact opposite . . . getting involved in National Socialist rallies . . . organizing . . . the harder they rode me the more I reacted."

Then there was a boy (born 1912, no. 267) who was losing his eyesight and wouldn't play with other children until, at the age of ten, he underwent several operations. In the meantime he was completely dependent on his sister, who read and wrote for him, and was very lonesome whenever she was absent. He tells of fearful clashes at home when he felt compelled to side with his mother and older sister against the alleged physical abuse of an older brother. He fought with his brother over everything except politics, for the brother was already a Nazi and once brought him a swastika which the respondent displayed at school. The father, a monarchist and patriot, was not allowed to see these emblems, and his teacher did not approve of their display.

His uncle once pulled him away from a stormtrooper demonstration, with an expression of revulsion. "Those are Hitler people!" The respondent also got into fights with Jewish fellow-students and sought the company of an older Nazi student. After graduation, he entered a commercial college and quickly became politically militarized in demonstrations and proselytizing activities. He challenged his teachers in class, ventured with his Nazi pin into a well-known KPD "hangout," and fought with the "red Falcons" (SAJ). Neither his father nor his teachers could pressure him to stay out of politics.

The Social Background of School Environment Groups

Let us take a look at the social profiles of these school and peer environment groups. The youngest group are again the respondents who report a *voelkisch* or antisemitic school environment. Seventy and nine-tenths percent of them are of the postwar generation. We must assume that most of the *voelkisch* teaching must have occurred during and after World War One. The oldest group are those from a nationalistic, anti-republican school environment, whose average period of schooling lies about a decade earlier. Nearly half of the respondents reporting conflict with Jewish fellow-students were born after 1905 and evidently grew up when school discipline was no longer a match for the new wave of young barbarians. Again, the *voelkisch* school settings tend to occur where the respondents were born and are still residing, mostly in small-town settings.

What about the level of education? Again the respondents from a *voelkisch* school environment tend to be far better educated than anyone else. Over a third of them had the *Abitur* and nearly as many achieved the *mittlere Reife*. Nevertheless, on a measure of political knowledge they rank conspicuously below the other school environment groups, often substituting ideological stereotypes for an awareness of basic political realities.

What about their Nazi ideology? After joining the NSDAP, the respondents from a *voelkisch* school environment tend to have antisemitism or Nordic-German cultural romanticism as their dominant themes. Half of those who tangled with Jewish fellow-students also are principally antisemites. By contrast, those reporting nationalistic school environments tend to be revanchists, superpatriots, or devotees of the social *Volksgemeinschaft*. It should be noted that this differs from the home environment groups where the *voelkisch* groups tend to be antisemites and Hitler cultists and the nationalists Nordic romantics and revanchists. Both the school environment and home environment groups referring to the conventional parties tend to be superpatriots which may explain why the sons and daughters abandoned the parties of their parents.

We might think from the ideological thrust of the *voelkisch* school environment groups that this group was attracted to the NSDAP by hearing about its ideology, but this is not so. Nearly half of them got into the party through a friend, relative, or fellow-worker, or because a group of which they were a part joined *in toto*. This again emphasizes the role of certain youth groups as conveyor belts to the party, not to mention its *voelkisch* forerunners and tributaries. Respondents with a nationalistic school environment, by contrast, are the ones who first became aware of the Nazi ideology or saw rallies or demonstrations before joining.

The hate-lists of the school environment groups present significant differences in emphasis. The *voelkisch* group disproportionately picks on Jews and Marxists, while the nationalists and those of conventional party settings tend to single out reactionaries and the old parties. Nevertheless, the *voelkisch* group does not rate very strongly on the antisemitism scale. While there is only one out of six among them who gives no evidence of prejudice, their rantings tend to be limited to mild verbal projections and anecdotes. Their ideology, it seems, was learnt by rote and often held without much affect. The nationalists who have many cases of *Judenkoller*, number just as many respondents with delusions of conspiracy (14.3%), as the *voelkisch* group. In their references to political enemies, on the other hand, the *voelkisch* group is as vitriolic as any *outré*, calling them subhuman, immoral, or rodents. And in their ethnocentric feelings other than antisemitism, the *voelkisch* group tends to be far more hostile to the aliens within the country than, as the nationalists, to the foreign nations outside. Theirs was mostly an integral nationalism.

Violence and the School Background

The *voelkisch* school environment group has a substantially larger percentage in the SA and the early SS than anyone else. They also participated a great deal more in political violence while in the party, and generally with sadistic overtones. They did not usually hold the more prominent party offices such as that of a legislative deputy, speaker, or *Ortsgruppenleiter*. These offices were reserved, it appears, for prominent old nationalists or defectors from the old parties. Instead they often held minor local offices or played a leading role in functional Nazi organizations such as NSBO or NS St.B, a sign of their relatively low or non-establishment status. In their attitude toward authority, also, they stand out for their hostility to police and government. We are reminded of their high educational level together with their low, ideologically stereotypical, political understanding. They are social and political outsiders pushing their way into power.

What were the formative experiences of these school environment groups and what seem to be their most glaring abnormalities? The nationalistic group was formed mostly by the *Fronterlebnis* of World War One, and by the experience of comradeship in a youth group. The *voelkisch* group cites alleged episodes with Jews or aliens, educational or literary experiences, or social snubs as their formative moments. The latter two are also prominent among those from old-party environments. As for the pathological question, the old-parties group suffers most from extremes of the leadership cult and of group conformity, an urge to merge with the movement. The nationalists exhibit high cultural shock and personal insecurity and self-pity. The *voelkisch* school environment group shows a high degree of irrationality and paranoia as well as personal insecurity and self-pity. In a manner of speaking, they embodied politically the often-mentioned wave of irrationality washing over the embankments of the bourgeois civilization of Weimar and sweeping it off to its doom.

PART IV

The Escalation of Political Violence

ONE

To Be a Political Soldier of Adolf Hitler

The systematic study of political violence is one of the most interesting of innovations of the social sciences today. Urban riots and civil disorders in the advanced countries no less than the revolts and revolutions of developing countries have been a potent spur toward systematic investigation.[1] But the political violence of the Nazi movement prior to the seizure of power, for lack of quantifiable material and because of the lapse of time, has not as yet been studied systematically, aside from historical investigations and the grim recollections of eyewitnesses. The Abel collection fills a gap in this respect, and we hope to shed some light on the motivations of the individual Nazi as we record his gradual advance on the road to extremism and political violence.

One of the most absorbing topics in the study of extremist movements is the step-by-step process by which a person becomes a full-fledged extremist. It is not easy to plumb the subjective depths of the individual lives with quantitative means. Even separate analysis of the social-class angle or the perspectives of political socialization can never quite recreate the immediacy of one account of "the ambiguous mixture of emotions" experienced when the respondent for the first time put on a stormtrooper (SA) uniform. He was acutely conscious of the decisive step of "stripping away [his] bourgeois habit once and for all in order to be a political soldier of Adolf Hitler." Ostensibly, of course, there was a real need to have men of physical courage ready to protect the rallies and propaganda activities of the party. But stormtrooper violence meant far more than

[1] For a survey, see for example, Ted Gurr, *Why Men Rebel*, Princeton: Princeton University Press, 1970, especially chapter 1. Gurr's theory of motivation for violence also posits several stages: the development of discontent in the sense of relative deprivation, the politicization of this discontent, and the actualization of violent action against political objects and actors. Our inquiry into the social dynamics fits his theory well, if inconclusively, but the examination of the effects of war and revolution less so. And there appears to be no way to account for the rise of the violent youth cohort of 1906-1915, which we examined in Part Three.

that—an outlet of inner tensions, a chance to march and fight for a cause, a good excuse for barbarous aggressions against victims "who had it coming."

The phrase "political soldier" is particularly suited to shedding light on the historical process as well as the psychology involved. Historically, the Nazi recruit more often than not went through two combined processes, one of militarization and one of politicization. The impact of World War I, the German struggle and defeat, and his opposition to the "red" revolutionaries or to the French occupation tended to militarize him if he was of a likely age cohort. There were numerous respondents too young though very eager to have served in the war. After 1918, they came in droves to join veterans' organizations and to ask them to provide military drill and training in the use of weapons. Many joined the Free Corps to fight and live in a quasi-military manner. They also exhibited their militarization in their great urge to march, to demonstrate, and to engage in organized violence in some of the youth groups they joined prior to the NSDAP. Politicization came more naturally with age and growing involvement in party politics.

Psychologically, too, large numbers of respondents appear to have striven to be both politicized *and* militarized. Soldiering alone, or the mindless posturing of veterans in military parades left them with a great desire for ideological, political purpose. Active participation in constitutional parties such as the DNVP, DVP, or the *voelkisch* parties left them crying for militant action. Thus, many wandered in and out of several military and party organizations until they finally came to a satisfactory combination of the two in the Nazi party.

The Stages of Mobilization

The Abel biographies generally permit an assessment of the distinct stages of this process, although the stages and their sequence may vary somewhat. For our purposes, we decided to posit four stages of recruitment based on how respondents described their own progress.

The first stage is a pre-political stage as broken down in FD-37. It includes not only non-involvement for reasons of youth or parochial attitudes, but also such typical German phenomena as the "unpolitical bourgeois" or military-civil servant of the empire and relatively unpolitical youth organizations.[2] It also includes any membership

[2] This group includes 22 of the bourgeois Youth Movement (3.9%) as well as 18 of the Socialist (SAJ), or Catholic, and Trade Union Youth

FD-37: Mobilization Stage One: Prepolitical Status

	Number	Per cent
Early youth, or other kinds of parochial attitudes for personal reasons	203	35.4
Traditional unpolitical attitudes such as the "unpolitical" bourgeois or farmer respondents	174	30.5
"Unpolitical" military men or civil servants	109	19.1
Membership in pre-political youth organizations, such as that of the Youth Movement, pre-political partisan youth, trade union, or sports clubs	47	8.3
Membership in pre-1914 parties of various kinds	38	6.7
	571	100.0

in political parties before World War One,[3] since we are interested only in their postwar progress toward the NSDAP. Stage one ends with the onset of stage two, three, or four.

The second stage is one of quasi-military involvement with violent counter-revolutionary or veterans' organizations, mostly during the early postwar years, or around the fateful year 1923. Military service in World War I, or professional military service, was not considered a symptom of militarization in this connection. Slightly more than half of the respondents went through stage two. Of these the largest groups belonged to the NSDAP and *voelkisch* action groups before the party was reconstructed in 1925[4] and to the Free Corps and militant veterans' groups of various sorts (FD-38). The median age at which the respondents went into stage two was 22 years.

Stage three is one of political involvement in the party politics and elections of the Weimar Republic, a stage also undergone by slightly more than half of the respondents. It includes such marginal involvement as expressions of distrust for the "old parties" so strong that they amount to a critique. We also included respondents who report having voted in, sympathized with, or otherwise participated in the normal electoral activities of the NSDAP or *voelkisch* parties

---

(3.2%), and members of a wartime military youth auxiliary, the *Jugendwehr*.

[3] Eight of the Catholic Center and SPD (1.4%), 18 of prewar *voelkisch* and antisemitic groups (3.2%), and Conservative and Liberal parties (2.1%).

[4] *Deutsch-voelkische Freiheitsbewegung* and *Schutz-und-Trutzbund*, primarily. On the significance of the latter for the early NSDAP, see Uwe Lohalm, *Voelkischer Radikalismus*, chapters 19-21.

FD-38: Mobilization Stage Two: Militarization

	Number	Per cent
Pre-1925 NSDAP and various *voelkisch* action groups	73	25.0
Buergerwehr or other vigilante groups directed against domestic insurgents	33	11.2
Free Corps, border defense groups, and other irregular units fighting foreign troops, including the French occupation	65	22.4
Stahlhelm and *Jungstahlhelm*	53	18.2
Wehrwolf, Oberland, and other *voelkisch* veterans' groups	35	11.9
⌈Militant bourgeois opposition groups such as *Jungdo* and others	25	8.5
⌊Communist Red Front, Red Hundreds, or militant trade unionists	8	2.8
	292	100.0

before the collapse of 1924. This is different from the marching and street-fighting of the early NSDAP and *voelkisch* action groups recorded in stage two, although in some cases the distinction was difficult to draw. The median age at entry into stage three was 26. Stage four, finally, consists in joining the resurrected, post-1924 NSDAP. This stage was entered at a median age of 30 by the entire sample, of which over one-half also joined the stormtroopers. Some respondents entered stage four directly or after skipping either stage two or three.

Can the respondents really be expected to be candid about their involvement in violence? With no other subject, perhaps, does the likelihood seem so great that they might wish to hide all or at least some of their physical involvement. Generally speaking, however,

FD-41: Mobilization Stage Three: Politicization

	Number	Per cent
Expresses strong distrust of all parties	60	20.0
Shopping around among parties	53	17.9
Joins or sympathetic to DNVP or other conservative group	47	15.8
⌈Joins or sympathetic to DVP, DDP, or kindred group	15	5.0
Joins or sympathetic to SPD, USPD, or KPD	32	10.7
⊢Joins or sympathetic to Center party	4	1.4
⌊Active in local politics	7	2.3
Votes or participates in the pre-1925 NSDAP, or *voelkisch* parties	80	26.9
	298	100.0

a large number of them do tell about it, not always in detail, but they give enough information to allow their involvement to be coded. A typical case of such codeable concealment is a goldsmith's son, born 1899 (no. 463), from Spandau who casually mentions having been fired from many jobs throughout the republican period because of his Nazi membership. He omits all mention of what acts he committed, but his record speaks volumes. Immediately after his discharge from the army he joined the *Einwohnerwehr* vigilantes and participated in the Kapp *putsch*. Following this, he had to leave town and was a *Zeitfreiwilliger* for six or eight weeks. He returned and joined the DSP of Kunze, then the Black *Reichswehr* of Major Buchrucker, and soon the *Frontbann*, which turned into the NSDAP and SA of his area. He became a stormtrooper in 1926 and eventually an SS officer. Although he refrains from the first-person descriptions of violence common among the younger recruits, he supplies a long list of the major rallies, demonstrations, and meeting-hall battles in which he "took part." Naturally, we coded him as a marcher *and fighter*.

A Few Examples of the Process

A few examples will illustrate the progress from stage to stage. One respondent who self-consciously went through all four stages was an "unpolitical" professional soldier, born 1889 (no. 302). A big Garde du Corps man, he returned injured from the war, a competent sergeant but evidently quite innocent of political developments.

> The crime of November 9, 1918, took me by complete surprise. In 1919 I joined the volunteer regiment Potsdam and took part in quelling the Spartakus uprising. On January 11, 1919, I helped to storm the building of the *Vorwaerts* (the SPD newspaper).
>
> Ignorant of politics like any soldier, I was now surprised by the elections to the National Constituent Assembly. The cavalry captain at the discharge office of the Garde du Corps ostentatiously tried to advertise the German National People's Party (DNVP). I liked the name, and so did my roommate, but soon doubts arose in our minds. For we had often seen the excesses of *Junkerdom*. Many officers believed—and in the Garde du Corps they were mostly high nobility—that only they were human beings. We sensed this and, unable to go with the left-wing scoundrels, the traitors of the Republican Sergeants Association, we voted for the golden middle way, the Democrats (DDP).

The respondent later regretted his decision for this "Jewish party," and speculated that the large DDP wave of 1919 may well have resulted from a similar mistake of other innocents like himself.[5] He subsequently entered a municipal service career and eventually became a secret Nazi who distinguished himself by getting unemployed Nazis short-term municipal jobs which henceforth would entitle them to unemployment benefits.

Another respondent, also a professional soldier and later civil servant born 1877 (no. 301) skipped stage two. He reports: "Before the revolution of 1918 I was unpolitical, although my interest in social policy got me to join the Tenants' Association of Greater Berlin, beginning in 1910. After the revolution I joined the Communal Civil Service Association of Prussia and the DNVP as well as the DNVP Civil Servants Federation. The latter I soon quit, however, because it was too monarchistic for my taste." For a year (1925-1926) he also belonged to Kunze's *Deutsch-Soziale Partei* (DSP), at least until its banking venture failed, when he rejoined the DNVP. In 1931 he ran for a "truly nationalistic" civil service representation list and soon (1932) joined a National Socialist Civil Servants' Group while burrowing as a secret Nazi in the bureaucratic warrens of the Berlin welfare administration. At the time he wrote his *vita*, he also prided himself on membership in the Reich Federation of Former Professional Soldiers, the Reich Federation of Fireworkers, the Nazi Welfare Association (NSV), the Reich Air Federation, the Reich Tenants' Association, the German Christian Faith Movement, and two military associations. His wife was also in the NSV and in the Nazi Women's League, and his son in the Hitler Youth (HJ).

A third respondent, born 1904 (no. 306), skipped stage three on his way to stage four. The son of a Thuringian blacksmith, he had to break off his education after passing the *Abitur* because the inflation of 1923 wiped out the family savings. After two years of training at a bank, he was dismissed "because of the report of a Jewish auditor" and remained unemployed for the next five years (1926-1930), no small accomplishment prior to the depression.

> In this period [of graduation] occurred my first political awakening. The Ruhr occupation by the French in January 1923 had touched off a strong wave of national feeling throughout the Reich, a sign of determined resistance to the French act of violence. Ever new nationalistic groups shot up like mushrooms from the ground. Next to *Stahlhelm* and *Jungdo*, a local group of *Wehrwolf* was established in my home-

[5] There is a ten-year gap in his account of his political development from 1919 to 1930, during which he may well have continued to vote DDP or have regressed to the posture of an "unpolitical civil servant."

town, and I became an active member from the spring of 1923 until the fall of 1925. I still like to think back on my *Wehrwolf* days when I went to many a German Day or a flag consecration beyond my neighboring area, as far as Nordhausen, Halle, and Leipzig. The spirit of comradeship was wonderful. Politically, we tended to be conservative and monarchistic. But after a brilliant rise in 1923-1924, the *Wehrwolf* movement fell apart throughout Germany and in my home area. And the fault was the lack of a deliberate political sense of direction.

At about that time, in the fall of 1925, I first became acquainted with the National Socialists. The leader of the *Wehrwolf* group in the neighboring town was a Free Corps veteran and old Hitler man. He took nearly his entire group into the Hitler movement and, by an insistent, well-aimed recruiting effort got some of my comrades to join also, following the dissolution of our group.

The respondent joined, and blamed his dismissal and the Jewish auditor for his sudden *Judenkoller*. Two cousins of his had joined even earlier, also from a *Wehrwolf* background.

How Stages One and Two Fit Together

Practically all the respondents were in stage one and stage four, the outset and the goal. But quite a few skipped either stage two or stage three or both. Let us take a closer look at these groups. First of all, how do the different groups of stage one differ from one another and which of them were most likely to become involved in stage two?

In search of plausible explanations of the transition from one stage to the next, we do well to recall the incisive effect of World War I as a kind of watershed between imperial Germany and the politicized postwar society of Weimar. Typically, a professional military man or civil servant would claim that, before the great collapse in 1918, he was quite "unpolitical," that is, unconcerned about partisan politics. He was content to "do his duty for Kaiser and Reich" which meant, of course, that he was directly involved in the exercise and manipulation of administrative and political power within the system. The defeat, the ignominious flight of the Kaiser, and the take-over of power by Socialist leaders he had previously viewed as the subversive enemy suddenly politicized what may have been a latent sense for the exercise of power all along. The "unpolitical" soldier or administrator became an eager politician or counter-revolutionary.

The "unpolitical" farmer or *petit-bourgeois* in a traditional social setting, on the other hand, experienced the war and its aftermath in a rather different way. A breakdown by spatial mobility (location experience) shows the "unpolitical traditionals" to be overrepresented among those who never moved from the place of their birth, as well as among recent migrants from the countryside. Many of them were uprooted by border struggles in the east. A breakdown by occupation of their fathers shows them up as being most often farm boys, and as socially less mobile than the other groups. Another breakdown, by geographic location, shows them to be most heavily from rural and small-town (2,000-10,000) areas. We can conjecture, then, that these unpolitical traditionals were mobilized mostly by the indirect effects of the war on the traditional social structure surrounding them. It is worth noting, also, that the traditionals exhibited a relatively strong sense of cultural shock in 1918-1919 at the "signs of moral disintegration" and dissoluteness in German life after the war, when they came back to their communities.

The agricultural crisis so well described by Rudolf Heberle with respect to Schleswig-Holstein, and other economic strictures on small-town life, combined with the unsettling social effects of the draft, rural emigration, and the cultural menace of metropolitan life, may have politicized some people long before they ever saw any red or brown shirts in their neighborhood. Nevertheless, traditionals were often the first in their area to found an NSDAP group, or at least they did so far more often than the other groups. They also tended more to blame the revolution on the machinations of international Marxism and did not become involved in counter-revolutionary activities in 1919 or 1923 at nearly the rate the military-civil servants did.

By way of contrast, the young parochials probably represent the most direct and natural route toward politics. To the extent that they were apolitical chiefly for reasons of age, they simply came to discover politics along with other functions of adult society. The passage of women's suffrage and the emancipating impact of the war on the families of enlisted fathers are probably at least as potent factors of politicization as reaching the voting age.

What were the causes or stimuli that motivated a formerly unpolitical person to fling himself into quasi-military action? It obviously makes a difference what his pre-political stage was like. There is a considerable generational difference, for example, between, on the one hand, the young parochials (including women and others parochial for personal reasons) and unpolitical youth group members and, on the other hand, the rest of the groups. The first two entered stage two when two-thirds or more of them were only 20 years old or younger. They obviously both belonged mostly to the postwar generation. Fifty to 60% of the other three groups of stage one, the traditional unpolitical social groups, the unpolitical military-civil servants, and the prewar participants, entered stage two when they were already 26 or older. A breakdown of these three groups by age shows that 85.6% of the traditional social groups, 99.1% of the military and civil service group, and the whole prewar-participant group was born in 1901 or earlier.

By the same token, the early age cohorts in the entire sample are made up of overwhelming majorities of three-fourths or more of unpolitical traditional-social and military-administrator groups until we get to the cohort born between 1895 and 1898, which has only two-thirds of unpolitical respondents. This age cohort was barely old enough to be drafted in 1914, that is to say, it was subjected to the brutal war experience at a most malleable age. The following cohort, from 1899 to 1901, the last one drafted, contains only 46.1% of the unpolitical strata. After that, the unpolitical share declines drastically to 19.3% for 1902-1905, 10.3% for 1906-1908, and 5.3% for the rest. It would seem to be justified, then, to speak of World War I as an enormously politicizing event for the whole sample and, perhaps, for German society as well.

As they entered the quasi-military stage (two), the various groups of stage one differed strikingly from one another. The military-administrator respondents were relatively the most involved (61.1%), chiefly in the Free Corps, vigilantes and irregular army units fighting foreign invaders and domestic insurgents, and among the *Stahlhelm* veterans. The traditionally "unpolitical" social groups were the least involved in stage two (32.3%), although they contributed a sizeable share of the vigilante organizations (25.8% of the latter) and also figure among *voelkisch* groups such as the *Schutz-und-Trutzbund* or the early NSDAP (23.3%). As Lohalm has shown, many *Schutz-und-Trutzbunders* rallied to the Nazis when their organization was outlawed in 1922. Persons politically involved before 1914 are strongly represented among the extreme left-wing opposition. The largest group (113 cases), the young parochials, by way of contrast, played only a modest role in the Free Corps and vigilante organizations, that is to say, in the more purely military counter-revolution. Instead, they are overrepresented among the more ideological counter-revolutionary groups, such as the *voelkisch* paramilitary shock-troops of *Oberland* and *Wehrwolf* (52.8% of these), the *Schutz-und-Trutzbund* and pre-1925 NSDAP (43.8%), *Jungdo* and even the Communist Red Front (53.1%) and, of course, the swashbuckling *Stahlhelm* (46.8%). The young parochials evidently represent in this case the harbingers of Weimar politics, the rise of political soldiers of all kinds, rather than just a counter-revolution in the sense of reaction to revolutionary attempts.

The image of the much-maligned Weimar Republic in the eyes of our sample runs the gamut of the familiar stereotypes, with predictable highlights in the perception of each of the groups. The traditionals, for example, felt a strong dislike for the "party state," i.e., the multi-party system and pluralistic pressure groups. They also objected to the predominance of capitalism and high finance and, of course, to the economic troubles, often with nostalgic glances at imperial Germany. The military-administrators were more concerned with the "prominent role" in the Weimar system of Jews and Socialists or Communists. To the young parochials, however, the Weimar Republic was "a system run by the black (Catholic) and red parties" and they longed for its replacement with the Third Reich. The youth group members, on the other hand, stressed chiefly their double-barreled criticism of both the liberal capitalism and the Marxist elements of Weimar. Jewish and alien, "un-German" influences were another preoccupation with this group's image of the Weimar Republic.

Militarization in Youth or Middle Age

What factors or circumstances brought about the militarization of half the sample? Since the respondents discuss their motives in detail, a tally was made of the reasons given for entering stage two. Their reasons for quasi-military involvement generally revolve around the war and the revolution.

FD-40: Catalyst for Stage Two

	Number	Per cent
Fronterlebnis	11	4.1
Impact of war at home	11	4.1
Shock of defeat, Versailles	15	5.5
Shock of territorial loss, border struggle	27	10.0
Shock of foreign occupation	38	14.0
Shock of revolution, fall of old order	58	21.4
Opposition to revolutionaries	56	20.6
Shock at new Weimar leaders	33	12.2
Antisemitic predisposition, Judenkoller	22	8.1
	271	100.0

The group militarized by the impact of war, defeat, and territorial losses (64 cases) has the following characteristics: Its birth-dates are concentrated in the years 1885 to 1898, with emphasis on the war generation. Nearly one-third of it came from the fought-over border areas in the east or had resided at one time abroad or in the German colonies. We could add to this the persons mobilized by the shock of foreign occupation (38 cases), who are much younger and two-thirds of whom are from the occupied German areas in the west. Nearly half of these two war-mobilized groups lived in Berlin or other metropolitan centers during the 1928-1933 period. Half of the first war-mobilized group has blue-collar workers or farmers as fathers, and a number of its members rose from a farm background. The fathers were predominantly nationalistic or belonged to moderate parties. In World War I, this group was heavily (46.6%) composed of enthusiastic soldiers, and yet it also had a particularly large element (19%) of people disillusioned with the war, often after initial enthusiasm. The comradeship of the trenches, the *Fronterlebnis* of common hardship and hatred of the enemy was a deeply moving experience in their lives, although they were prepared to accept the final defeat without bitterness. After the war, some of them (25.5%) participated in or sympathized with domestic insurgency while others (42.6%) marched or sympathized with Kapp in 1920. In 1923 they were in disproportionate numbers in the various *voelkisch* groups. The Weimar Republic was to their minds a heartless system run by Marxists and capitalists. They typically joined the NSDAP only after it had become a substantial minority in their area.

The other larger group was militarized chiefly by the shock of revolution and the desire to oppose the revolutionaries (114 cases). They were in disproportionate numbers recent rural-urban migrants or had never moved from the place of their birth, although at the time of the Nazi surge two-thirds of them were living in Berlin or other metropoles. They include disproportionate numbers of military-civil servants, women, and white-collar employees. Their fathers were often (43.1%) artisans or shopkeepers. There are more people in this group in a state of social decline (18.5%) than elsewhere, and their situation also shows up in the condescension of their solidaristic views, a solidarism mixed with fear and resentment toward the lower classes. They also include considerable numbers of enthusiastic non-combatant soldiers and youthful victory-watchers (30.1%) of World War I. Their fathers were nationalistic (47.7%), authoritarian or militaristic (16.9%), or quite unpolitical (13.8%), and the sons evidently tended to serve in the war with undaunted loyalty and enthusiasm. When the war ended in defeat and revolution, they experienced an acute sense of cultural shock which they verbalized with such complaints as the "moral and social disintegration" and absence of order in society, the "dissolute women," and "immoral Communists," and the shock of the end of monarchy. Their reaction to the revolution and to the German military defeat was to blame international Bolshevism and the Spartakist movement. Such a premise clearly pointed the way toward counter-revolutionary activities in the Hitler movement, in militant veterans' organizations such as *Stahlhelm*, or in the *voelkisch* *Wikingbund*. Their image of the Weimar Republic, in addition to the stress on both Marxism and liberal capitalism, emphasized their dislike for the multi-party state of Weimar.

As for the rest, those motivated by antisemitism are only 22 cases, but another 33 express their shock at the Weimar leaders. Such an expression, it will be recalled from our discussion of cultural shock,[6] usually goes with a good deal of prejudice. Antisemitism as a primary catalyst for entering stage two shows a remarkably even distribution over all the age cohorts, while all the other response clusters tend to be concentrated in the age cohorts of war generation and victory-watchers (1890-1905). Recent rural-urban migrants, especially in Berlin, and the spatially immobile in small-town and countryside were particularly strong in this anti-semitic group, as were the professions and managerial personnel and sons of military-civil servants. These antisemites typically either never attempted to rise in society or climbed from the level of the city proletariat rather than from the countryside. They espoused the slogan of *Volksgemeinschaft* (solidarism) mostly as argued by the middle class or to a lesser extent from below. Their political personality also comes to light in breakdowns relating to their socialization. In World War One they were particularly inclined to blame civilians, draft-dodgers, or shirkers for their problems. Their fathers were either of strong politically antisemitic or *voelkisch* views, or nationalists. Their school environment was nationalistic, *voelkisch*, or marked by conflict with Jewish teachers or fellow students. Many participated in or sympathized with the Kapp *putsch* of 1920, and a majority belonged to the NSDAP or other *voelkisch* groups in 1923. They often founded or helped to found the NSDAP local in their area, at a rate far higher than that of any other group. What attracted them to the party in many cases was the ideology. Their image of the Weimar Republic, as we would expect, is that of a system run by Jews. They constitute something of an ideological core-group of the early Nazi party.

[6] See above, pp. 180-182.

Social and Socialization Background of Stage Two Groups

Since we have spent considerable time in Part Two on the various counter-revolutionary movements mentioned in FD-38, there is no need for illustrations or examples. Let us just take a brief look at the crosstabulations with indices of social background and socialization experiences.

The *Stahlhelm* and *Jungstahlhelm* people of the sample are fairly evenly distributed over our age spectrum, with particular concentration in the last age cohorts (born 1895-1901) to be drafted (29.2%) and those (1906-1916) who missed the draft age by far but may still have been enthusiastically watching their fathers or older brothers fighting (32.7%). Spatially rather mobile, they were nevertheless predominantly in small and middle-size towns and rural areas during the 1928-1933 period. Their occupations were mostly the professional military or civil service (29.8%), farming (12.8%), and the retired military, occupations also frequently found among their fathers.

Their military service generally was longer than that of any other group, often including peacetime and full wartime service, although half the *Stahlhelmers* in the sample saw no military service at all. Needless to add, there was no disaffection with the war effort among them, but an intense solidarity of the *Fronterlebnis* against both the enemy and civilians and shirkers in their own camp. At the end of World War One, they also tended to blame the civilians and the Kaiser for having failed to stick it out to the end. Their home environment was rather unpolitical or colored by conventional political views more than by nationalistic, *voelkisch*, or militaristic views although these latter categories predominate heavily in the whole sample. The *Stahlhelmers* felt a sense of shock at the fall of the monarchy and the symbols of the old order (26%), and at the new leaders of the Weimar Republic, whom they blamed for the "shame of the country." At the time they entered stage two, 21.3% of them were under 18 and 46.8% under 25. And they were motivated to join chiefly by the impact of war and defeat (36.4%), the shock of foreign occupation (15.2%), and their antisemitic inclinations (12.1%).

The Free Corps, border defense troops, anti-occupation commandoes, and other irregular military units fighting foreign troops present a somewhat different picture. Many of them had been abroad, in the colonies, or had moved all over the country. Most of these volunteers came from among the military or civil service, the urban working-class, or the white-collar occupations. It is worth noting that this group more than the others suffered unemployment or other economic losses prior to 1928. In terms of upward mobility, moreover, this was the most static group (50% made no attempt to rise) and its social climbers were mostly people leaving the farm (26.1%). Their home environment tended to be nationalistic, militaristic-authoritarian, or unpolitical.

They were indeed enthusiastic soldiers who loved the comradeship of the trenches (46.6%), or youthful victory-watchers (25.9%). Their reaction to the defeat and revolution was a mixture of two elements, blaming the civilians and the Kaiser and blaming the Bolsheviks and Spartakists, or other foreign conspiracies such as French economic or Polish ethnic interests. They were quick to verbalize their cultural shock of 1918 with complaints about the moral disintegration of society, "the rabble taking over," or the absence of "order and discipline" in society. Unlike the *Stahlhelm* group, which played a significant role in militant veterans organizations in the crisis year of 1923, the Free Corps group was heavily engaged in activities allied to the Hitler *putsch* (26.4%) and actions against the French occupation (18.9%). They were also somewhat younger, with 43.1% under 21 and three-fourths under 26. Among the reasons given for their militarization, the most prominent was the impact of defeat, loss of territory, and the occupation (53.7%), ahead of the shock of revolution and a sense of opposition to the revolutionaries.

The *Buergerwehr* and *Wehrwolf* groups present a third pattern, although we have to bear in mind some differences that separate the substantially older and locally rooted vigilante groups from the membership of highly mobile military freebooter units such as *Oberland*, *Brigade Erhhardt*, or *Wehrwolf*, who are on the average about six years younger. Nearly two-thirds of the latter had been too young for the war and many had been a part of that lost generation of 1902 which was "shattered by the war" without having served in it. Some were, in fact, disaffected from the war effort. There were disproportionate numbers of people from the disputed eastern border areas in these groups. During the main period of the rise of the Nazis, the *Buergerwehr* group was more heavily found in larger towns and in Berlin, while the *Wehrwolf* groups resided more in small towns and rural areas.

By occupation, the *Buergerwehr* people often were military-civil servants or pensioners (48.3%), whereas the *Wehrwolf* groups tended to be white- or blue-collar workers and farmers (together 65.8%), who in disproportionate numbers lost their jobs or livelihoods during the depression of 1929-1933. Over one-third of the fathers of both groups were military men or civil servants and like numbers, especially among the *Wehrwolf* members, had artisans or small businessmen for fathers. Disproportionate numbers of their families either were in social decline (20%) or rising from the urban proletariat into the middle classes, chiefly by means of education. Their home environment was often (19.5%) characterized by a militaristic or authoritarian father, but just as often by moderate politics. *Wehrwolf* groups also had strong *voelkisch* or anti-semitic home and school experiences.

Their reaction to the great change of 1918 is curiously ambiguous. The youthful *Wehrwolf* people complain mostly about the "moral disintegration of society" and the "absence of order and discipline," evidently a fashionable line at any age, whereas the locally rooted *Buergerwehr* group is concerned about the fall of the monarchy and the traditional symbols nearly as much as about law and order. By the same token, the *Buergerwehr* blames the defeat of the country mostly on the Spartakists and Bolsheviks, while the *Wehrwolf* also points to the failure of the Kaiser and the civilians to support the men at the front. Both agree on placing the blame for the revolution on "the Marxists," but the *Wehrwolf* also blames the Jews. In the critical year 1923, as many as 25.3% of both groups belonged to the *Stahlhelm* or other militant veterans' groups. The *Buergerwehr* people were on the average 23 years old when entering stage two, as compared to a median age of 19 for the *Wehrwolf* groups. The chief catalyst for both groups, according to their own account, was their shock of the revolution and sense of opposition to the revolutionaries.

The last large, significant group of the stage of militarization are the pre-1925 *voelkisch* action groups and NSDAP. Disproportionate numbers of this group were from the disputed eastern border areas or from occupied territory (36.5%) or had but recently migrated from the countryside to the cities. Large numbers, in fact, were in Berlin or in other metropolitan areas, or at least in larger towns over 10,000, during the declining years of the republic. Disproportionate numbers were military-civil servants, white-collar, or women. Their fathers were also mostly military-civil servants or artisans. More than any other group, they suffered unemployment or economic losses during the Great Depression. Much like those of the last group discussed, their families were either in social decline or rising from the city proletariat. They consequently argued for the vaunted *Volksgemeinschaft*, either from a middle-class position or from the vantage point of the *Fronterlebnis*, though some also exhibited a pronounced class-consciousness. It is worth mentioning that these *voelkisch* groups, including the NSDAP, also were more highly educated than any of the other groups.

They were also comparatively high (54.3%) in persons who never served in the military, as well as in those who were youthful victory-watchers. Over one-half of them were inclined to blame Germany's defeat chiefly on the Spartakists and international Marxism, with some antisemitic overtones. One-fourth laid the revolution at the doorstep of the Jews, while another third blamed the Marxists or the Weimar parties. The home environment of disproportionate numbers (20.9%) of this group was *voelkisch* or antisemitic while the bulk had nationalistic fathers. The *voelkisch* groups evidently experienced more of a cultural shock in 1918 than the other groups, which is to say that they were more alienated from society. At the head of their list of complaints are the Jews, the press, and the new leadership of the Weimar Republic, followed by the absence of order and discipline, the fall of the monarchy and the traditional symbols, and the "moral disintegration of society." Along with the *Stahlhelm*, the Free Corps, and the *Wehrwolf* groups, the *voelkisch* groups were highly (39.6%) involved with the Kapp *putsch* of 1920. In 1923 one-third of the group participated in or sympathized with Hitler's beer-hall *putsch* while another third belonged to other *voelkisch* parties such as Ludendorff's *Deutsch-voelkische Freiheitsbewegung* or the *Deutsch-Soziale Partei*. Their median age of 24 on entering stage two was comparatively high, with 43.8% of them between 26 and 56 years of age. Their outstanding motivations for militarization were an antisemitic predisposition (20.4%) and the shock of foreign occupation (20.4%), though most of them (44.4%) mention the shock of the revolution as their chief catalyst as does the rest of the sample.

Stage Two and Stage Three

Considering the uneven passage of the respondents through the two middle stages, we would naturally want to know how stage two respondents passed through stage three. A good one-fourth of the sample, to begin with, never passed either through militarization or politicization, but went directly from the prepolitical phase on to the NSDAP. About one-fourth went only through politicization and less than a fourth (22.3%) only through militarization prior to joining the party. This leaves about one-fourth who went through all four phases. Let us examine each of these four groups more closely for clues to their make-up.

The group that went from militarization directly into the party has a disproportionate share of *Wehrwolf, Stahlhelm,* and pre-1925 Nazi or *voelkisch* action group members, in declining order. As many as 70.6% of all the one-time *Wehrwolf* members of the sample went this route, a sign of the kinship of the two groups, at least in the eyes of young contemporaries. One-fourth of the only-militarized[7] came from the occupied areas, where many of them, in fact, were jailed or fined and expelled by the occupation. They lived in small and medium-sized towns and their age cohorts were concentrated among the war and postwar generations. By occupation they tended to be working-class, farmers, or pensionists, and many of them became unemployed or bankrupt during the Depression. Their fathers were mostly businessmen, farmers, and artisans and the sons were somewhat upwardly mobile. They tended to have a rather limited education. What they liked best about their first youth group was demonstrations and political violence, and their greatest dislike were "un-national" or separatist views. They were disproportionately (37.4%) involved in partisan street fights while still youths and accordingly tended to be classified as politically militarized youths. Disproportionate numbers of them reported a *voelkisch*, anti-semitic, or militaristic home environment, or conflict with their fathers. They also tended to report conflict with Jewish fellow-students or teachers and a conventional or *voelkisch*-antisemitic school setting.

What about those who skipped phase two, especially the only-politicized? Nearly half of them were in moderate parties such as the DVP, Center, SPD, or DNVP. Their birth-dates tended to cluster at both ends of the scale,[8] to particularly the earlier. The spatially immobile and rural-urban migrants tended to predominate among them, which gave them a disproportionate share of rural and metropolitan (Berlin) residents. They included many women, pensionists, and business and professional people who for obvious reasons stayed out of paramilitary organizations, but also substantial numbers of blue-collar workers. Their fathers tended to be businessmen, farmers, or artisans, and the respondents mostly made no attempt to rise above the station of their fathers. They included considerable numbers of people who had joined the Socialist or Communist youth, or agricultural, religious, and conservative youth

[7] For technical reasons, the following breakdowns include also respondents who went directly from stage one to stage four and therefore have a bias on the younger cohorts.

[8] The very young cluster (1909-1916) probably again represents the respondents who skipped both phases two and three, and went directly into the party.

groups of the established parties[9] as their first youth organizations. Their likes and dislikes in youth groups were quite different from the only-militarized. What they liked best was hiking, sports, and cultural appreciation, and they disliked class distinctions, or a lack of social conscience, but also the advocacy of class struggle. Their most extreme youthful activities tended to be electioneering, proselytizing, or military training, and their youthful postures tended to be fully politicized, authoritarian, or pre-political parochial. Their home environment stressed mostly an identification with the moderate parties or with nationalism and the same was true of their school settings.

A good example of some of the motives for joining political parties is a farmer's son, born 1879 (no. 318), who became a mailman. Wounded several times, decorated and promoted during the war, he later obtained a better position in the postal service. "In 1921 I joined the SPD for a year and a half without becoming active. When I began to see through the horse-trading in the *Reichstag*, especially their designs to reduce the size of the civil service, I quit. Then I joined the DNVP for another year and a half. But this party disappointed me too and I left it, firmly resolved never to get into another party." Both of these parties had shown real solicitude for civil servants, but evidently not enough for the respondent. Years later, in 1927, he became acquainted with Hitler's *Mein Kampf*, and joined the Nazi party four years later, as an activist propagandizing from house to house.

And what about those who went through both step two and step three? Since they presumably went through militarization first, we can approach them from this side. The Free Corps and vigilante fighters against domestic and foreign enemies tended to become involved in electioneering, and nonmilitary political activity especially with the pre-1925 NSDAP and *voelkisch* parties, but less so with the DNVP or other conventional parties. A good third of these two groups and also of the *Stahlhelm* veterans, however, only hovered at the door step of partisan politics, merely shopping around or expressing distrust toward all the parties. The *Wehrwolf* and other groupings in the four-stage group are too small to permit statistical inferences, except for a handful of *Jungdo* members who became involved with the DVP and the pre-1925 NSDAP and *voelkisch* parties.

[9] A disproportionate share of respondents also joined the HJ or SA first, but these obviously belong to the group that skipped both middle phases. The same group also showed up with a stress on marching and street fighting before the age of 26.

We still need to clarify the relationship between those who were recorded as quasi-militarily involved with the pre-1925 NSDAP and *voelkisch* action groups such as the *Schutz-und-Trutzbund*, and those who became politically involved with the pre-1925 Nazis and *voelkisch* parties such as the *Deutsch-voelkische Freiheitsbewegung* or *Deutsch-soziale Partei* (DSP). These two groups overlap only by about one-third. Half of the quasi-militarily involved early *voelkisch* or Nazi activists were never politicized in stage three. The rest tended to join the DNVP. And nearly one-fourth of the politically involved early *voelkisch* or Nazi party members never went through the stage of militarization. Those that did were mostly with the vigilantes, the Free Corps, and *Jungdo*. The heterogeneity of the pre-1925 *voelkisch* movements and NSDAP permitted all kinds of political experiences and routes of development.

Activities at Stages Two and Three

Leaving the pre-1925 Nazis aside for the moment, we can ask ourselves whether it was the presence of violence-minded men in it that made the Nazi party a violent movement as it rose to power in 1933, or whether it was the presence of the Nazi party that encouraged previously non-violent people to band together for their violent push into power. It is probably impossible to give a final answer to any chicken-and-egg question, but we can at least take a closer look at what activities these later Nazi recruits actually engaged in before the NSDAP entered their lives (FD-44). What kind of people were they before they became post-1924 Nazis? We can also examine how the historical settings of the Weimar Republic relate to these activities of the middle stages, two and three. More particularly, we will want to test the hypothesis of some contemporary historians that the entire Nazi revolt grew out of the counterrevolution of Free Corps and vigilante leaders who had already been steeped in violence during what we call the middle stages.

The two violent middle-stage activity groups and also the marchers in FD-44 are worth a closer look because of their prominent role in Nazi violence and proselytizing. They appear to represent a personality type whose violent propensities form a constant in their political lives. Their violence as stormtroopers was due, we may conjecture, to their violent personalities rather than to the goals of the Hitler movement. In fact, we can go a step further and suggest that the movement gave them a good excuse for doing what they wanted to do anyway. Perhaps the early Nazi movement would have been less violent had it not been for their presence. If there is such a thing as a violent personality type, then, let us examine how it differs from the less violence-prone groups.

FD-44: Activities Reported at Stages Two and Three

	Number	Per cent
Voting only	29	7.3
Attendance at rallies, meetings	134	33.9
⌐ Electioneering	24	6.0
⌐ Held office	26	6.5
⌐ Military training	12	3.0
⌐ Marching, demonstrations	53	13.3
⌐ Organized violence	70	17.6
⌐ Individual violent encounters	25	6.3
Provocation	25	6.3
	398	100.0

A brief glance at the crosstabulations of these middle stage activities (FD-44) shows the violent activities among them to be highly related to the war generation (1895-1901) and, perhaps, to the victory-watchers (1902-1905) as well. The marchers of these stages, by contrast, are the youngest of the lot, with a good two-thirds born after the last cohort drafted in World War One. The non-violent groups tend to be older.

If we look at what they liked best about their youth organization, the activity groups are also clearly highlighted. Those attending meetings and electioneering already indicate, after sports and cultural appreciation, a preference for marching with an ideological purpose (61.3% and 62.5% respectively). The demonstrators have the same preference (62.5%) plus a little interest in violent action (5.4%) which grows with those in the group engaged in organized violence to 36.8% who already liked violence best in their youth group. In this group, indeed, 19.4% engaged in street fighting and another 56.7% in Free Corps-style violence before they were more than 25 years old. Nevertheless, with 22.9%, this violence-minded group is far behind the marchers (57.8%), and people in individual violent encounters (39.6%), in the number of "politically militarized" youths in it. The reason for this is the large number of hostile militants (40%) among the violent of stages two and three. This leaves us with the impression that the Nazi stage indeed tended to represent a climax in the political development of these respondents, as marchers turned into stormtroopers and political violence became carefully channeled.

When we inquire from what group of stage one the marchers and the violent of stages two and three came, the answer is as follows. The youthful marchers came mainly from among the prepolitical parochials and the unpolitical youth movements, in other words, from the "political youth" of Weimar. By contrast, the violent came mostly from among the formerly "unpolitical" military-civil servants of stage one. This casts an appropriate light on the violence of the middle stages. Crossing the activity groups with stage two, moreover, clearly shows 56.3% of the violent to have fought with a Free Corps or the like against a foreign enemy (including the occupation) and 16.9% against domestic insurgents. Their violence, in other words, was related to the tail end of the war rather than to the utopia to come. The rest belonged to the *Wehrwolf* or the pre-1925 NSDAP or *voelkisch* action groups. The marchers, conversely, tended to be with *Wehrwolf*-type groups, the *Jungstahlhelm*, or also the pre-1925 NSDAP or *voelkisch* organizations. They were very young when they became involved in these activities, two-thirds of the marchers being under 21 and two-thirds of the violent being under 26 at the onset of their stage two. Their motives tend to be the shock of defeat and revolution for the violent, and the French occupation, or an antisemitic predisposition for the marchers.

The link between the Free Corps activities and later Nazi membership is not always very clear even though it is tempting to link the earlier violence with that under the swastika. One of the clearer cases is a contractor's son, born 1895 (no. 467), who was caught abroad in Riga by the outbreak of the war and interned by the Russians until his escape early in 1918. He still enlisted but saw no action which may have encouraged him to volunteer for the Free Corps Epp that "liberated" Munich from the soldiers'-and-workers'-councils in 1919. He went on to participate in the suppression of the Ruhr uprising in 1920, and "after the dissolution of the Free Corps it was *a matter of course* for me to join the still young Nazi movement" (italics supplied). He participated in the beer-hall *putsch* and received a medal of commemoration for it from the Fuehrer. Nevertheless, he dropped out and rejoined the stormtroopers only in 1930 when the movement was once more going strong.

This matter of successive waves of right-wing agitation is a common phenomenon in the Abel *vitae*. It can be explained by the state of mind required for militant activity. Unless the movement can keep going a breathless atmosphere of struggle and agitation, many of the members will drop out. It can also be related to the historical circumstances of the Weimar Republic which experienced its first two right-wing waves as a result of external causes, the anti-revolutionary and anti-Versailles backlash of 1919-1920 and the French invasion of 1923. It was not until 1929 that the right-wing demonstrated with its grand campaign against the Young Plan, that a crisis atmosphere could be artificially produced and sustained by ceaseless agitation. And Hitler, of course, prepared his own wave of agitation which aroused the more people the harder he drove himself and his campaign.

The ebb and flow of right-wing agitation is well-illustrated by an East Prussian retail clerk, born 1902 (no. 495), who, like so many, joined the movement twice. The first time was around 1925, but his Nazi local did not last out the year. Then the momentum of agitation built up again in 1931 and he joined a second time, for "now the struggle really started." He served with the squads to protect Nazi rallies all over the area, proselytizing all the while to build up sufficient fighting strength against the KPD and the *Reichsbanner*, whom he accused of cowardly running away and of injuring their antagonists in particularly nasty ways. According to the respondent, the left-wing militants used to fight and demonstrate with the help of children and women who on occasion would lift their skirts to show their *derrières*, shouting "*Nazi verrecke, Hitler verrecke!*" the exact equivalent of the hoary Nazi cry "*Juda verrecke*" (Death to the Jews). The respondent also tells of a siege laid to his residence by "50 reds" who were chanting obscenities and songs like "*Wenn Naziblut von unseren Messern spritzt*" (When Nazi blood drips from our knives), another reversal of a grisly antisemitic tune. The respondent must have been a real brawler who liked to brag about the large number of foes he and his comrades allegedly fought. He continuously accused the Prussian police of harassment and of collusion with "the reds."

As for stage three, half of the marchers and the violent tended to skip it altogether. Those marchers who did not tended to vote for or participate in the pre-1925 NSDAP or *voelkisch* parties. And the violent who did not skip stage three often expressed a distrust of all parties. Whatever involvement in stage three they reported, at any rate, the marchers tended to experience before and the violent after their early twenties. Their motives for getting involved, moreover, tended to be reaching voting age or unemployment, for the marchers, and the shock of defeat and occupation or a sense of opposition to the revolutionaries, for the violent of stages two and three.

Middle-Stage Activities and Stage Four

How did the middle-stage activities prepare the respondents for stage four? The marchers did not content themselves with marching with the NSDAP, but numbered 35.4% marcher-fighters (MFs), 32.3% marcher-fighter-proselytizers (MFPs), and 21.5% marcher-proselytizers (MPs). Those engaged in middle-stage violence included 41.4% MFs, 22.9% MFPs, and 12.9% MPs. In other words, they were long on violence and short on proselytizing. Only the electioneers and those involved in individual violent encounters had high numbers of MFPs (31-32%) comparable to the violent, but far less of the other salient stage-four categories. Those who merely voted or attended meetings, and even the electioneers of the middle stages, instead tended to have many MPs and more mere members in stage four. Thus, a distinct line separates the mindless sluggers of war and counter-revolution from the ideological concerns of the rest.

The age at which the middle-stage activity groups started stage four also sets them off clearly from one another. The marchers are the youngest Nazis, one-fourth under 21, and nearly two-thirds under 25. Those engaged in individual violent encounters are next, with two-thirds under 31, still well ahead of the organized violent of the middle stages. Those who merely voted, attended rallies, canvassed or held office tended to join the party after the age of 35 which may also account for their reserve toward Nazi violence. One-fourth of those who only voted and canvassed, in fact, were over 45 when they joined.

What were their motives for joining? The mere voters were motivated by their economic troubles, including the agricultural crisis, by "government repression," and by "the rough opposition of the Communists." Those who attended rallies and the electioneers, by comparison, were also smitten with ideological fervor and with the "dynamic impression" of the Hitler movement. The marchers, and the individually and collectively violent, on the other hand, all stress friction with the occupation, the opposition of the Communists, and the spirit of comradeship most.

We can also relate the middle-stage activities to the organizational memberships of the chief periods of the Weimar Republic (Table IV-1).[10] The table ends with the year 1930, after which nearly all the respondents were in the Nazi party anyway. The totals for 1925-1928 and 1929-1930 are lower because they do not include non-members. It has to be read in two parts, the periods before and after the reconstruction of the NSDAP in 1925, because we considered pre-1925 Nazi or *voelkisch* activities as part of stage two or three and only the reconstructed NSDAP as stage four.

Regarding the first two periods, there is a deceptive continuity between the end sums in each column which hides the very substan-

[10] For a more detailed breakdown of organizational memberships for each period, see below, pp. 360-362. The quasi-military groups include veterans, Free Corps, vigilantes, and *Wehrwolf*, *Oberland*, *Brigade Ehrhardt*, etc.

Table IV-1: Middle Stage Activities and Organizational Memberships[a]

Activity	Period	None	NSDAP voelkisch	Conserv. & Jungdo	Quasi-milit. organizations	Republican & Left opposition	Totals (n)
Voting only	1919-1921	19 (73.1%)	3 (11.5%)	2 (7.7%)	5 (19.2%)	2 (7.7%)	26 (100%)
	1922-1924	11 (42.3%)		6 (23.1%)	4 (15.4%)		26 (100%)
	1925-1928	—*	10 (71.4%)	4 (28.6%)			14 (100%)
	1929-1930	—*	15 (100%)	—			15 (100%)
Attendance	1919-1921	69 (51.9%)	18 (13.5%)	11 (8.3%)	21 (15.8%)	14 (10.5%)	133 (100%)
	1922-1924	62 (47.3%)	30 (22.9%)	13 (9.9%)	19 (14.5%)	7 (5.3%)	131 (100%)
	1925-1928	—*	51 (63.0%)	18 (22.2%)	7 (8.6%)	5 (6.2%)	81 (100%)
	1929-1930	—*	84 (89.3%)	9 (9.6%)	—	1 (1.1%)	94 (100%)
Electioneering, holding office	1919-1921	20 (41.7%)	6 (12.5%)	7 (14.6%)	10 (20.8%)	5 (10.4%)	48 (100%)
	1922-1924	20 (40.8%)	16 (32.7%)	5 (10.2%)	5 (10.2%)	3 (6.1%)	49 (100%)
	1925-1928	—*	21 (55.3%)	9 (23.7%)	6 (15.8%)	2 (15.3%)	38 (100%)
	1929-1930	—*	37 (88.1%)	5 (11.9%)	—	—	42 (100%)
Demonstrations, milit. training	1919-1921	29 (46.8%)	13 (21%)	3 (4.8%)	9 (14.5%)	8 (12.9%)	62 (100%)
	1922-1924	6 (9.4%)	22 (34.4%)	9 (14.1%)	20 (31.3%)	7 (10.9%)	64 (100%)
	1925-1928	—*	32 (60.4%)	3 (5.7%)	16 (30.2%)	2 (3.8%)	53 (100%)
	1929-1930	—*	49 (89.0%)	4 (7.3%)	—	2 (3.6%)	55 (100%)
Organized political violence (incl. street-fighting)	1919-1921	10 (13.5%)	6 (8.1%)	3 (4.1%)	55 (74.3%)		74 (100%)
	1922-1924	17 (23.6%)	21 (29.2%)	5 (6.9%)	28 (38.9%)	1 (1.4%)	72 (100%)
	1925-1928	—*	30 (73.1%)	4 (9.8%)	7 (17.1%)		41 (100%)
	1929-1930	—*	47 (95.8%)	2 (4.2%)	—		49 (100%)
Individual violence, provocation	1919-1921	23 (46.9%)	5 (10.2%)	5 (10.2%)	9 (18.4%)	7 (14.3%)	49 (100%)
	1922-1924	5 (10.2%)	24 (49.0%)	5 (10.2%)	8 (16.3%)	7 (14.3%)	49 (100%)
	1925-1928	—*	28 (71.8%)	4 (10.3%)	4 (10.3%)	3 (7.7%)	39 (100%)
	1929-1930	—*	40 (93.0%)	2 (4.7%)	—	1 (2.3%)	43 (100%)

* Non-membership was not recorded for these periods—which, of course, weights all the percentages for the other entries.

tial changes at hand. All the memberships of these periods relate
to middle-stage activities, of course. But the change probably occurred not so much from one kind of membership to another as
within each group of organizations. Thus, for example, the 55
quasi-military respondents who were engaged in organized violence
in 1919-1921, the counter-revolutionary period, cannot just be
assumed to have switched to *voelkisch* or Nazi groups by 1922-
1924. Many of them, of course, just dropped out of their Free
Corps or vigilante groups altogether. Others may have de-escalated
their activities without necessarily leaving their organization or
group of organizations. The 28 quasi-military respondents who report involvement in organized violence in 1922-1924, moreover,
are not necessarily identical with the 55 violent counter-revolutionaries of 1919-1921 and may have been with different organizations, such as the anti-occupation, anti-separatist, veterans', or
Wehrwolf groups prominent in 1923.

As for the 1925-1928 and 1929-1930 periods, their growing
NSDAP share has to be seen in the light of the fact that all the respondents eventually joined the NSDAP. The post-1924 *voelkisch*
respondents who were not in the party are negligible (3) in number. Those listed as in the NSDAP in either of the two periods,
however, must have engaged in middle-stage activities before becoming Nazis or they would not appear in this crosstabulation. The
95.8% in the NSDAP column who appear as having engaged in
organized violence in 1929-1930, for example, engaged in it in the
pre-1925 NSDAP or in another middle-stage group before joining
the NSDAP, in either the same or a previous period. This may help
to explain what looks like a premature disappearance by 1930 of
the whole sample into the Nazi party when we know that a large
percentage (27.7%) joined it only after 1930. The implication appears to be that the respondents who were engaged in middle-stage
activities tended to join the party earlier and faster than those who
were not. The latter, moreover, seem to have made up a particularly
large share of those who joined it after 1930, perhaps belonging to
the wave of opportunists and the politically naive of which the literature on the Nazi landslide likes to speak.

Middle-Stage Activities and Weimar History

Aside from the organizational memberships which give political
color and name to the middle-stage activities, we can also crosstabulate the latter period by period with the historical record of
political activities of our respondents. Thus the phases of each life
can be related to the familiar periods of Weimar history. This will

bring out the behavioral continuities of these early Nazis throughout Weimar history, although it may not separate stage-four activities from those of the middle stages. Crossing biographic activities with periodized activities should help us to locate the middle-stage activities among the periods of Weimar history. Table IV-2 has been marked[11] to show the extent to which the middle-stage activities indeed coincide with appropriate activities during the first two periods. Wherever the entries coincide, they show a disproportionate bulge. The periods 1929-1930 and 1931-1932 show smaller bulges and often two or more of comparable disproportionality. Evidently most of the middle-stage activities occurred before 1929.

This table is interesting also in that it shows the manner in which the respondents whose middle-stage activity was, for example, "voting only"[12] went on from there to more intense activities, either during the same or in following periods. There is an element of confusion because of the respondents who went through both stages two and three and who are therefore entered twice in the table, once with their quasi-military and once with their political activity. But the table clearly shows that among each middle-stage activity group, for example, the involvement in violence and proselytizing grew apace from period to period, although no group was as violent in the 1931-1932 period as those who had already been violent before 1925 when the Free Corps and counter-revolutionary violence stood at its highest point. In the milder middle-stage activities, demonstrations also register a hefty increase, evidently as an outlet of the increasing radicalization of these respondents. Among those whose middle-stage activity was marching and demonstrating, conversely, the percentage of mere demonstrators goes down as they "graduated" to political violence or proselytizing. Since the periods after 1924 also register the progress of Nazi members who joined in 1925-1928 or 1929-1930, this radicalization or escalation of extremist activities also reflects how individual members intensified their involvement over the years.

The line of distinction between the middle-stage and the post-1924 Nazi activities on the table can be drawn roughly when we cross the middle-stage activities with the date of joining the NSDAP. Those respondents who report individual violent encounters in stage

[11] The marks represent the highs in each row of crosstabulated printout. The third and fourth rows tended to have two or more such highs, indicating thereby the greater dispersion of the activities.

[12] The entries under political "interest, voting, and attendance" are made up of shopping around among parties, voting only, and following public affairs closely.

Table IV-2: Middle Stage Activities and Weimar Period Activities

		Interest, voting & attendance	Electioneering only	Demonstrations, electioneering & provocation	MF, violence & electioneering	MP, Proselytizing & electioneering	Totals (n)
Voting only	1919-1924	27 (90.0%)	—	—	3 (10.0%)	—	30 (100%)
	1925-1928	23 (65.7%)	1 (2.9%)	4 (11.4%)	2 (5.7%)	5 (14.3%)	35 (100%)
	1929-1930	14 (40.0%)	1 (2.9%)	6 (17.1%)	4 (11.4%)	10 (28.6%)	35 (100%)
	1931-1932	9 (27.3%)	1 (3.0%)	5 (15.2%)	5 (15.2%)	13 (39.4%)	33 (100%)
Attendance	1919-1924	105 (78.9%)	3 (2.3%)	3 (2.3%)	10 (7.5%)	12 (9.0%)	133 (100%)
	1925-1928	97 (62.6%)	9 (5.8%)	11 (7.1%)	16 (10.3%)	22 (14.2%)	155 (100%)
	1929-1930	59 (34.7%)	13 (7.6%)	28 (16.5%)	28 (16.5%)	42 (24.7%)	170 (100%)
	1931-1932	11 (6.3%)	16 (9.1%)	43 (24.6%)	38 (21.7%)	67 (38.3%)	175 (100%)
Electioneering, holding office	1919-1924	16 (34.8%)	7 (15.2%)	3 (6.5%)	3 (6.5%)	17 (37.0%)	46 (100%)
	1925-1928	16 (30.2%)	14 (26.4%)	2 (3.8%)	9 (17.0%)	12 (22.6%)	53 (100%)
	1929-1930	4 (6.8%)	6 (10.2%)	6 (10.2%)	18 (30.5%)	25 (42.4%)	59 (100%)
	1931-1932	1 (1.6%)	3 (4.8%)	9 (14.5%)	20 (32.3%)	29 (46.8%)	62 (100%)
Demonstrations, milit. training	1919-1924	6 (9.1%)	2 (3.0%)	40 (60.6%)	6 (9.1%)	12 (18.2%)	66 (100%)
	1925-1928	12 (17.3%)	3 (4.3%)	27 (39.1%)	12 (17.4%)	15 (21.7%)	69 (100%)
	1929-1930	5 (5.9%)	2 (2.4%)	28 (32.9%)	30 (35.3%)	20 (23.5%)	85 (100%)
	1931-1932	1 (1.1%)	1 (1.1%)	25 (26.6%)	35 (37.2%)	32 (34.0%)	94 (100%)
Organized political violence (incl. street-fighting)	1919-1924	10 (12.4%)	—	5 (6.2%)	66 (81.5%)	—	81 (100%)
	1925-1928	23 (36.5%)	1 (1.6%)	11 (17.5%)	23 (36.5%)	5 (7.9%)	63 (100%)
	1929-1930	17 (22.7%)	3 (4.0%)	11 (14.7%)	26 (34.7%)	18 (24.0%)	75 (100%)
	1931-1932	—	3 (3.4%)	16 (18.0%)	42 (47.2%)	28 (31.5%)	89 (100%)
Individual violence, provocation	1919-1924	6 (10.5%)	1 (1.8%)	11 (19.3%)	17 (29.8%)	22 (38.6%)	57 (100%)
	1925-1928	6 (9.5%)	7 (11.1%)	18 (28.6%)	16 (25.4%)	16 (25.4%)	63 (100%)
	1929-1930	4 (6.0%)	4 (6.1%)	17 (25.8%)	19 (28.8%)	22 (33.3%)	66 (100%)
	1931-1932	1 (1.4%)	3 (4.2%)	18 (25.0%)	21 (29.2%)	29 (40.3%)	72 (100%)

two or three were the earliest to join, with 30.6% before 1925 and 63.2% by the middle of 1929 which in itself is noteworthy.[13] The middle-stage demonstrators, like most of the other groups, have less than a tenth in the pre-1925 party, but by mid-1929 they too had 58.2% in the party. If we apply these figures to Table IV-2 it becomes clear that the bulk of the period activities after 1928 for these two groups were not middle-stage activities, but Nazi activities. The other middle-stage groups had between 30 and 49% in the party by mid-1929, except for "voting only," which had only 29.6%. The two mildest middle-stage groups, voting and attendance, also had the largest percentages (32-37%) that joined only after May 1931, while all the others had only 10-20% such late joiners.

Ideology and Attitudes

Some of these differences, as they relate to youth groups and to the other stages, have already been explored. But there is, for example, the manner in which the respondents were introduced to the NSDAP. None of the two violent groups report having been introduced by relatives, which happens to be the most salient route of introduction of the marchers and of the voting and attendance groups. We may get the impression that the individually or collectively violent were already considered so deviant within their families that no one undertook to get them acquainted with an even wilder group, the NSDAP. Instead, they became introduced mainly by going to Nazi rallies, being taken there by friends or colleagues, seeing Nazi demonstrations or street fighting, or becoming aware of the Nazi ideology. Perhaps what they saw there appealed to their latent hankering for violence.

Qualitatively, their ideologies offer no great differences from those of the other groups. Those involved in organized violence, of course, tend to be revanchists and superpatriots, as one would expect the Free Corps and vigilante fighters to be. They also frequently have antisemitism as their dominant ideological theme. But the attendance and electioneering groups are no less often antisemitic. The individually violent tend to be Hitler and Nordic-German cultists. Again the attendance and electioneering groups equally stress the Nordic-German cult. The marchers too share this preoccupation but they more often stress the *Volksgemeinschaft*. Except for revanchism and superpatriotism, these themes do not amount to anything like an ideological predisposition for violence.

[13] The dates of joining were coded according to how they coincided with important periods of party growth and are not in conformity, therefore, with the activity periods.

As to their objects of hostility, the individually violent and the marchers tend to stress anti-Marxism, while the organized violent prefer an all-encompassing hate-list of Marxists, reactionaries, and Jews. If you are going to fight at all, you might as well ritualize your displacements. By comparison, the attendance and electioneering groups like to add only the Jews to their anti-Marxism, while the voting group tends to stress the "reactionaries, liberals, Catholics," etc. Their attitudes toward their political enemies clearly mark off the two violent groups, of whom 42-46% like to refer to the enemies as rodents, subhuman, immoral, and the like. Again the ritualization of hatred in the language of the *outré*. Half the marchers and all the other groups express some understanding of, even liking for, their political antagonists.

On the antisemitism scale, about 40% of the voting and the organized violence groups give no evidence of prejudice at all. The most prejudiced are the electioneers and those involved in individual violent encounters, with over three-fourths each, followed by the demonstrators with little less. The individually violent and the marchers, indeed, stand out with delusions of a Jewish conspiracy and anecdotes involving Jews. The electioneering group, and also the attendance group, each have about a third that suddenly caught the *Judenkoller*. Aside from antisemitism, their ethnocentricity clearly sets off the two violent groups again from the rest. They tend to vent their spleen particularly on aliens and alien influences, including ultramontanism, in Germany. The voting, attendance, and demonstration groups, by way of contrast, project their hatred instead on the allegedly inferior foreign nations and, especially the attendance group, on their hostility toward Germany.

Are the two violence groups and the marchers "authoritarians" in the conventional sense of political psychology? In all three groups, the respondents tend to express strong hostility toward the police and government authority. The electioneers and the attendance groups show more of the authoritarian syndrome, with extreme leadership cult and an obsession with authority. The voting and attendance groups also criticize the weakness of the multi-party state of Weimar.

It is not easy to classify their personality types even by raising the question of what seems most excessive about each *vita*. The two violent groups, to be sure, tend to show a high degree of group conformity—so do the electioneers—and of personal insecurity or self-pity. The marchers, along with the voting and electioneering groups, instead stand out for extremes of leadership cult. The voting and attendance groups, finally, exhibit a good deal of irrationality, even paranoia, and high cultural shock. The most disturbed are not the same as the most intensely involved. Perhaps engaging in violence and closely identifying with this fighting movement helped some to pull themselves together.

To pursue this question further, we might look at the nature of their participation in the Nazi party. The two violent groups indeed seem to have gotten a sense of personal integration out of the movement's struggle itself, while the young marchers of the middle stages were mostly gratified with its spirit of comradeship. The three milder groups got a sense of personal integration from the pursuit of an utopian goal or from the leadership cult of Hitler.

These attitudes toward the movement relate to the actual roles played in the party. The marchers and those engaged in individual violence often (one-third) held important local party offices and had the highest percentage in the SA or SS (80-84%). The organized violent of the middle stages are noticeably less often in important party offices (18.8%) and in SA or SS (74.6%), but compensate for this by holding many more important offices in the stormtroopers organization. Here again, there is the link which goes from the minor officers' ranks of the war generation through vigilantes and Free Corps to the officers of SA and SS. Among the three milder activity groups of the middle stages, party offices (except in the functional organizations) and stormtrooper membership are decidedly lower. In fact, only 25.9% of the voting, 44.6% of the attendance, and 66% of the electioneering group were stormtroopers and only a few held any offices in the SA or SS.

The two violent groups and the marchers of the middle stages, not surprisingly, were also engaged most (45-51%) in marching and fighting under the swastika, with one small difference. Those engaged in organized violence in the middle stages are noticeably underrepresented among the stormtroopers who fought "day and night" during the final struggle of 1931-1932. Such zeal, apparently, would have gone beyond the ritualized violent behavior of these men. Besides, if they were indeed of the war generation and had fought in the counter-revolution, they were probably in their early thirties by then (median date of birth 1898) and perhaps a little old for purposes of "day-and-night" fighting and campaigning. The voting, electioneering, and attendance groups instead concentrated on proselytizing and canvassing.

The attitude of these last-mentioned three groups toward the use of violence tended to be one of regret or of realistic acceptance of violence as the price of victory. Among those involved in violence, the balance between self-pitying masochists and bullying sadists varied considerably. Among the attendance, electioneering, and demonstration groups it was around three masochists to two sadists. For the individually or collectively violent, however, it was nearly three sadists for every two masochists, especially among those engaged in organized violence in the middle stages. We have already considered the factor of youth in connection with this self-pitying attitude, although the attendance group was not exactly young (median date of birth 1893). It may be related more to the socialization (and vicarious socialization) of wartime, when hatred and killing were officially sanctioned, while growing up among the taboos against violence of a peaceful society, prewar or postwar, may require special rationalizations for political violence. The individually violent were several years younger than the organized violent, younger also than the electioneering group. But then individual violent encounters probably require a propensity for sudden outbursts or seizures which may well generate a different line of rationalization than the collective efforts in a Free Corps.

TWO

Stage Three: Politicization

If there is any generalization broadly applicable to the generational differences in our sample, it would be the greater ease with which the younger cohorts approached politics. Respondents of the postwar generation often comment on the "unpolitical minds" of their parents and contrast them to their own lively interest in politics from an early age. To be sure, there were also exceptions, such as the young *Wehrwolf* man quoted earlier[1] who went directly into the NSDAP, or older respondents who had been with prewar parties. But, by and large, politics came harder to the prewar and war generations. Many of their members experienced a deeply rooted discomfort at their encounter with the electoral politics of the new and "old" parties of Weimar who now held the power in their weak but greedy grip and whom they had evidently not taken very seriously under the authoritarian empire.

There are many accounts of the confusion of the returning soldier and other unpolitical souls when they first had to prepare to vote. Some tell touching stories of how they went from party rally to party rally across the entire ideological spectrum to prepare for their civic duty. All the party speakers and platforms sounded good to these innocents. Yet their innocence quickly soured and turned into alienation when they found it impossible to make up their minds among this welter of deceptive promises and grandiloquent phrase-making.

Let us examine how the different pre-political backgrounds of stage one fit the scale of politicization experiences of stage three. At first, there is the paradox of age. The unpolitical military-civil servants were the most politicized group with nearly two-thirds involved in spite of their age, presumably because they were all along deeply involved with the exercise of power in the empire regardless of their disclaimers of political interest. The prewar-involved naturally show about the same rate of involvement. Both of these groups had one person out of five or six, respectively, in the pre-1925 NSDAP or the *voelkisch* parties, and stand out also with dis-

[1] See above, pp. 318-319.

proportionate numbers of respondents who express a strong distrust of parties. The unpolitical Youth Movement and other youth groups, by contrast, number only about one-third that has gone through the stage of politicization. The other two groups, the unpolitical traditionals and pre-political youth each had about half their numbers go through politicization with varying emphasis. We must conclude then, that the often-asserted political precocity of Weimar youth does not seem to apply to the partisan electoral politics of stage three, but rather to the politically militarized kind of stage four. Within the Abel sample, at least, the older respondents clearly engaged more in stage three than did the young hotspurs. But they also did so at a much more mature age than the average of 20 years of the two younger groups—namely, in their early thirties.

Social and Political Profiles of Stage Three Groups

The distinctions among the different politicization groups of stage three, those distrustful of parties, those shopping around, members of the DNVP, of the moderate parties (SPD, DDP, DVP, Center, etc.), and of the pre-1925 *voelkisch* and Nazi parties deserve a closer look.

There are some notable differences in the basic makeup of these five groups. To begin with, the postwar age cohorts (born 1902 or later) tended to miss the stage of politicization altogether and went directly into the Nazi party. They were the vanguard of the political youth revolt of the Weimar Republic. On the other hand, 51.7% of those distrustful of all parties were born before 1895 and so were 60.3% of the German Nationalists (DNVP), the rest being mostly in their youth affiliate, the *Bismarckjugend*. Members of the republican parties were notably younger (64.8% born 1890-1905) and so are those who were shopping around among the parties and the pre-1925 NSDAP and *voelkisch* followers. The last-mentioned group, however, had a considerable contingent (42.7%) also in the older age brackets born between 1860 and 1894, which may account for the overtones of prewar political antisemitism in the *voelkisch* groups. This pre-1925 group was hardly a group rooted in regional traditions, but was spatially highly mobile (29.4%) and in disproportionate numbers from the border areas or from sojourns abroad or in the colonies. Sixty-three and eight-tenths percent of it lived in Berlin or other metropolitan areas at the time of the Nazi surge.

The distrustful group can be further characterized as follows. Not unlike the unpolitical traditionals of stage one, they were often business and professional men or farmers as were their fathers. One-third of them lived in communes under 10,000 inhabitants and some were recent rural-urban migrants who swelled the numbers of the upwardly mobile. Their distrustfulness of parties was complemented by their stress on *Volksgemeinschaft* from an upper- or middle-class point of view or on the basis of the *Fronterlebnis*. Their fathers and school environment were for the most part nationalistic. They grew up in disproportionate numbers in poverty (36%) or as orphans or near-orphans (14%), often having had to work before the age of 14 or as unskilled laborers in their early teens, when others could learn a trade. With such a childhood, naturally, they were so lacking in self-assertion that they tended to join the NSDAP in their locality only after it had grown into at least a substantial minority (67.4%), a striking contrast to other groups such as the pre-1925 NSDAP and *voelkisch* groups.

The egalitarian *Fronterlebnis* of the war also patterned their reaction to the defeat for which they blamed the Kaiser, the civilians, and international Bolshevism. Coming home in 1918, they were deeply disturbed by the changes they saw. They were shocked by the signs of "moral disintegration," the fall of the old order and its symbols, and the absence of order and discipline. Next to the Spartakists and international Marxists, they also blamed the Jews. The distrustful did not get involved in stage two as much as the other groups did, except for some participation in Free Corps and *Wehrwolf* activities. Some sympathized with or were involved in the Hitler *putsch* of 1923 (19.6%). At the time they expressed their distrust of all parties, it is worth noting, one-third of them were already between 26 and 35 and nearly another third over 35 years of age. Their activities during stages two and three, apart from the Free Corps and *Wehrwolf*, tended to be limited to voting (24%) and attendance at political meetings and rallies (48%). Their distrust of parties was evidently touched off by a nagging concern about the things that seemed to be wrong with the country—namely, the Weimar leadership, the economic troubles, the impact of defeat and occupation, and the red revolutionaries. When they finally joined the NSDAP, many (28.3%) remained mere members or sympathizers, although equal numbers (30%) were fired up enough to demonstrate and proselytize for the cause. Relatively few (35%) engaged in organized violence, because, among other things, half of them were already over 35 and three-fourths over 30. Among their reasons for joining, police and governmental repression (15.6%) and economic crisis (8.9%) stand out, followed by friction with the occupation and ideological or antisemitic fervor.

The conservative (DNVP) group tends to fall into two categories of nationalistic experience. They were either well-rooted and spatially immobile (36.7%), or their feelings had been kindled by encounters with other nations in the border areas or in foreign or colonial experiences (22.4%). Nevertheless, no less than 61.7% of this group lived, in 1928 to 1933, in Berlin, where the DNVP had been politically powerful prior to the Nazi landslide. By occupation they were mostly military or civil officials (37.5%), or sales and secretarial staff; they included a disproportionate share of women. Their fathers were also mainly military-civil servants (44.7%), including many of high standing, or artisans. Decline in family status and upper-class prejudices in this group played a role which links the fading glories of the imperial establishment to the imperial promise of the rising Nazi movement. The solidarism of the military and civil service and of white-collar workers seems to be the DNVP approach to Hitler's *Volksgemeinschaft*. The father's politics were often colored by authoritarianism or militarism, or by conservatism or other moderate prewar philosophies. Their school environments, more than their homes, were nationalistic. Their reaction to the war was again typically establishmentarian: they showed a pronounced hostility toward civilians and shirkers (34.4%) and supported the slogan of *Durchhalten* (sticking it out). Their cultural shock at the changes of 1919 was in particular a reaction to the fall of the monarchy and the symbols of the old order (36.7%) and to the "moral disintegration of society." They blamed the defeat on international Bolshevism, and the revolution on the mutineers and Spartakists (40.5%).

Though the German Nationalists did not participate much in stage two, their inclination led those that did into the *Buergerwehr* and similar anti-insurgent groups. In 1923, they participated in the counter-revolutionary stirrings mainly through their own party. The reasons cited for joining the DNVP or its youth affiliate in the first place stressed the motives of opposition to the red revolutionaries (46.9%) and opposition to the Weimar leaders, who were probably perceived as differing only in the degree of "redness." When the Nationalists finally joined the NSDAP so many of them (59.6%) were over 35 (21.3% over 50) that their large numbers of mere members or sympathizers (35.4%) need not surprise us. Their chief reasons for joining the Nazi party were the dynamic impression of the Hitler movement (28.6%) and generalized complaints about the economy and the rough opposition of the "reds" (14.2%). The difference in age is so important that it may be well to stop here for a closer look at some of the cases of older respondents.

Examples of Older Nazi Recruits

The older the respondent, the more likely he was to be affected by the socio-economic dynamics of imperial and Weimar society. One particular case of a rather violent farmer and vintner, born 1891 (no. 444), demonstrates this in a subtle way. He had settled down with a family before the war, but his reserve status and sense of patriotic duty brought him directly into the war until grave injuries in 1915 sent him home. As he viewed the postwar development, his distorted perception becomes clear:

> After the collapse of the war we experienced sad scenes and events in our fatherland. The Marxists, and especially the then powerful Social Democrats, dissolved all the hitherto extant German traditions. Not only did they chase away the Kaiser and the kings, but they chastised all *voelkisch* ideas and replaced them with international, liberal-capitalistic ideas which they made predominant in Germany.

This simpleton belonged to the DNVP, but became disenchanted with this party's "lack of social concern for the mass of people." In 1928, the Nazi siren song of "blood and soil" began to reach the respondent just as he was on the verge of losing his farm and vineyard. Economic crisis and political radicalization went hand in hand. Two years later he was bankrupt, joined the party, and soon became a stormtrooper in "daily service whenever the occasion demanded it." And yet his prewar antecedents left him with a law-and-order streak even while the police were after him:

> In the year of the great struggle, 1932, we were often persecuted by the police measures of the government of that day which attributed to us all kinds of punishable deeds. Thus, I was punished for "resisting state authority" just because I had stopped the police from beating up a comrade of mine. On another occasion I was arrested and locked up for holding and turning over to the police a Communist who had knifed a stormtrooper.

He felt strongly that the government ought to deal with impeccable justice with those who set out to overthrow it.

> In August 1932, an arrest order and wanted posters were issued against me and other comrades. After 13 weeks of hiding I was betrayed, arrested, and locked up in jail. In court I was sentenced to five months for disturbing the peace just because I and other stormtroopers went to help some comrades who had been assaulted and beaten up by the Marxists. On another charge of causing a riot (*Aufruhr*), the

prosecutor proposed twelve years at hard labor (*Zuchthaus*) and I received three years of prison. All I did was to straighten out a gendarme who during a search of the house had been uncouth and abusive to my wife while I was in hiding. But after 3½ months in solitary confinement I got out thanks to the amnesty of Christmas 1932 and could go back to serve the cause.

Another example is a very business-minded accountant, born in 1876 (no. 454), whose rise from his modest antecedents—his father was a policeman—turned into ruin in the late 1920s. He already had contact with the *voelkisch Schutz-und-Trutzbund* in 1919. He joined the NSDAP formally in 1930, at the age of 54, held minor local offices in it, and seems to have participated in an amazing amount of violence for his age. "There were confrontations and brawls with the SPD who were gradually joined by the Communists as well. Fortified with faith and loyalty in the Fuehrer I repeatedly escaped death." In halting German with atrocious spelling he relates how he and 16 comrades held off two police detachments that wanted to arrest the entire SA Storm of 200 men in his area. He also tells of two incidents of alleged left-wing student unrest at the university in early 1932 during which he received serious injuries.[2]

Another case in point is that of a mine worker, born in 1889 (no. 447), unemployed since 1926, who suddenly discovered the Nazi party in 1929 without ever having been interested in politics before. He immediately became a stormtrooper and fought many battles "in order to reconquer a job for myself." As he describes it, "I literally hungered to be able to pay my dues while I was unemployed."

A rather different case of this sort is that of an itinerant carpenter born in 1873 (no. 420) who settled down before the war after many years of wandering. He served in the war and upon his return, for undisclosed reasons, could not find a job even though he had a wife and five children to support.

> When in 1923, for the first time, I heard the soldier Adolf Hitler, I realized after years of searching for truth and justice, that my place could only be with these men of true deeds. . . . In 1927 I turned my back on the idle and joined the active fighters of the SA. After that time I participated courageously in the demonstrations carrying the flag of the group. During the years of the struggle I tasted many a meeting-hall and street fight with the menace of the red street mobs and their screeching women.

[2] More plausibly, these were incidents of the Nazi campaign to take over the universities.

In this case, the respondent's reference to turning his back on "the idle (*Nichtstuer*)" suggests that perhaps at 45 he never quite managed to get back into a regular peacetime career after the interlude of war. Perhaps it was this middle-age crisis of aimless idleness which led him into the arms of the pied piper from Braunau.

Another respondent, born 1895 (no. 404), an elementary-school teacher and the son of a teacher, was motivated primarily by a seething class resentment against the better-educated upper classes in imperial society. He volunteered for the war and won decorations and promotions. A partial invalid in the end, he fitted his war experience into his social views; only heroic achievement counted, not class or rank. In the hospital at war's end, the respondent took the events of November 1918 very hard, with equal venom for the spineless capitulation of his upper-class garrison commander and for the "notorious dodgers" who took over. As soon as he was well enough, minus one eye, he joined the Free Corps Epp to "liberate Munich from the council dictatorship." Back in the classroom in the occupied Palatinate, furthermore, he joined the conspiratorial Organisation Consul to fight the occupation and the separatists.

He and 15 like-minded men founded the first NSDAP local in Kaiserslautern as early as October 1924. "As a stormtrooper and SA leader I have fought through the entire path of suffering and triumph of the movement in the Palatinate." The respondent's social background evidently did not permit him a candid description of what this involved, but we can guess.[3]

The Younger Stage Three Groups

How do the younger groups such as the followers of the republican parties and those shopping around among the parties differ from the older groups? Unlike the older ones, both are rather high in people who never moved away from where they were born (spatially immobile). They are also more at home in medium-sized communities rather than in Berlin. Their occupations are often blue- or white-collar jobs (49.1%), business or the professions, or even farming.

[3] This kind of candor appears to be more typical of the working-class or very young respondents. As one worker and worker's son, born 1893 (no. 369), freely relates, by comparison, "as a stormtrooper, I participated in many meeting-hall battles. . . . In Fuerstenwalde, it was very hard to hold a meeting. Only after about the tenth try did we 30 to 50 Nazis manage to hold out against the many hundreds of Marxists and Communists. . . . [In 1930] I and the two SS comrades broke up a Social Democratic meeting at the *Schuetzenhaus*. . . ."

Their fathers were often military-civil servants (36.3%), or also workers or farmers. Their level of education is considerably below that of the Nationalists. They often come from a personally deprived childhood, having lost a parent at an early age. Their reaction to the war was frequently a change from enthusiasm to disaffection. The cultural shock of the shoppers-around arises from the sense of moral disintegration and the fall of the old order. The republicans, who frequently seem to have been converted chiefly because of their antisemitism, stress the new power of the Jews and the press. They tend to blame the "rabble" and the Western powers for the revolution, and the Kaiser and the civilians for Germany's defeat.

Persons of working-class origin in those days in Germany tended to become politicized much earlier than those of middle-class origin. In our sample, they joined the republicans or began shopping around at such an early age that nearly a third of them were under 21 and 11.9% were under 18. Nevertheless, their activities at stages two and three were not notably inclined toward marching or organized fighting, except for some of the shoppers who had been in the *Stahlhelm*, Free Corps, or *Buergerwehr* in stage two (36.2%). When they finally joined the NSDAP, they were prominent in marches, violent encounters, and in proselytizing (together 69.3%), three key activities. Over one-half cite their ideological fervor as their chief reason for joining.

The pre-1925 followers of *voelkisch* parties and of the NSDAP, finally, were again a highly mobile lot with many persons of border area or foreign background. No fewer than 63.8% of them lived in Berlin or other metropolitan areas during the crucial period of 1929-1933. Many of them were business or professional people, students, pensionists, or military-civil service types. Their fathers were often artisans (31.1%). Many (19.8%) suffered economic losses already before 1928. Regarding their upward mobility, half of them made no attempt to rise, though others rose from a farm background. For a movement aiming at solidarism, this group is rather high in pronounced, class-conscious responses and barely above par in solidaristic answers. More than 40% of them had engaged in street-fighting or other organized violence, and another one-fourth in demonstrations, before they were 26 years old. Their home environment tended to be unpolitical, *voelkisch*-antisemitic, or militaristic-authoritarian, but not particularly poor or deprived.

Their attitude toward the war was positive and enthusiastic, with an edge of vindictiveness toward civilians and dodgers. Their sense of cultural shock after the war was pronounced and emphasized the absence of order and discipline (34.7%) and the theme of moral disintegration. The civilians and the Kaiser as well as international Bolshevism were blamed for the German defeat. The revolution was laid at the door of the Spartakists and mutineers (34.7%), of the Jews, and also of the new Weimar leaders, as far as the respondents cared to distinguish among these three. Consequently nearly one-third had joined *voelkisch* or Nazi groups in the years 1919-1921 and another 25.9% belonged to the various quasi-military organizations. In the following three years, including the year 1923, the number in *voelkisch* or Nazi groups rose to two-thirds, of which more than half claimed some involvement or at least sympathy with Hitler's beerhall *putsch.*

Their reasons for joining the pre-1925 Nazi or *voelkisch* parties stressed incidents of personal political friction or awakening interest in politics, and the impact of defeat and foreign occupation, but not the economic troubles cited by the followers of the republican parties. The group was heavily involved in demonstrations (22.4%) and in individual provocations or violent encounters (18.8%). When they joined or rejoined the NSDAP after 1924, in fact, they bore a lion's share of the marching, fighting, and proselytizing (77.6%) that was to be done, even though their ages averaged out around 33 years. The foremost reasons bringing them to the party were the dynamic impression of the Hitler movement (25.5%), their ideological fervor (45.9%), and the comradeship expected among the stormtroopers (10.2%), perhaps a recapturing of the *Fronterlebnis.*

Pre-1925 NSDAP and Voelkisch Members

The early NSDAP and *voelkisch* members are worth a closer look even though the accounts of that period are rarely as explicit as those of the main fighting period of 1928-1933. Whether because of the passage of time or because of the greater frankness of the youth rebellion Nazis of that second period, the pre-1925 followers are rather reticent about what they did and what their feelings about it were. Let us look at a few anyway, since they will not be discussed in depth anywhere else in this book.

An example of a member of the *voelkisch Schutz-und-Trutzbund* and a very early Nazi is an ex-colonial military-civil servant born in 1882 (no. 368). The lost war and German postwar society—he fought in South West Africa—did not make his and his wife's readjustment any easier.

I had lost all my savings of 15 years in South West Africa when I was captured by the English. Uprisings, war, and unrest there and now the revolution in Germany. . . . I could figure out the internal situation in Germany only very gradually, since my views in South West Africa had been established quite differently. Everyone just looked out for his own nation . . . and yet there was peaceful international coexistence. Not so in Germany where all eyes were on foreign countries and our own people, the country, and the *Reich* counted for nothing. An undisciplined bunch of all conceivable parties and ideologies, each only aware of the consequences of his actions and intent. Devoted only to the moment, with excesses of all sorts, a terrible disappointment for all of us who had suffered and fought for this nation.

The respondent got married in 1919, at the age of 37, to a like-minded farmer's daughter. "Thus we joined the truth-seekers of the *voelkisch Schutz-und-Trutzbund* together. And already in 1920 we both joined the NSDAP in Wuerzburg. Here we found what we hoped was going to save Germany from her deepest humiliation." The respondent felt cheated out of a decent civil service career after 18 years of military service by the "system" which gave all the better jobs to the "Novemberlings." He did receive a menial position with the railroads, though, and subsequently a number of transfers to punish him for shamelessly proselytizing on the job. Yet, wherever he was transferred, he just kept on recruiting and organizing new locals in order to "plant the seeds for Hitler's idea." His wife likewise kept organizing Nazi Women's League groups. We classified the respondent's involvement among the stage two responses because he showed no interest in electoral politics.

Another farmer's son, an electrician born in 1901 (no. 354), is an example of a *voelkisch* party member. As he relates,

In my youth I was not much interested in politics. My nationalistic parents gave me a strictly patriotic education, and I sharply rejected Marxism. . . . I soon became convinced that the mistakes of the Marxist economic system were going to bring about the complete ruin of our economy and of our role in international affairs. I was strongly interested in the Jewish question, but distrusted antisemitism at first because I was not aware of the Jewish role in politics and economy. Only after hearing several lectures given by the *Deutsch-voelkische Frei-heitspartei* (DVFP) did I realize the deleterious effect of the Jews in the political and economic area. In 1922 I became a member of the DVFP in Landsberg an der Warthe. My political interest had now awakened and I began to follow the beginnings and the growth of the NSDAP.

He became a Nazi only in 1930, evidently having sat out the decline or absorption of nearly all autonomous *voelkisch* groups in the NSDAP.[4]

A relatively old member of the pre-1925 NSDAP (born 1872, no. 336) was a war invalid who was in Munich at the time of the end of the war.

> I experienced the whole shameful collapse, the revolution, the Soldiers-and-Workers Council Republic etc. I saw how almost the whole people became politically degenerate (*verlumpt*) which deeply demoralized me and my strictly patriotic attitude. It became very clear to me that the horse-trading of the political parties would never bring about radical change.
>
> Then I heard for the first time Adolf Hitler in the first big *Hofbraeuhaus* rally and new hope came into my heart. I told myself "that is my man"; he and no one else has been called to pull the German people out of the morass. I joined in August of 1923 and received membership no. 40821. I did my share in steady quiet work to help spread the movement as well as I could. Even the unfortunate events of November 9, 1923, could not stop me. I remained true to the swastika flag.

In rare cases, the militant activism antedates involvement in the pre-1925 *voelkisch* movements. A railroad engineer, born in 1876 (no. 324), describes his postwar political activities as follows:

> My principle of action was always to break up the associations affected by the Social Democratic-Communist virus and to disturb their meetings with heckling. After the glorious days of the November Republic I joined the DNVP. After merely half a year, the Jewish question began to arise and I left for the German Nationalist Voters Association and ran on their ticket for the Charlottenburg city council.
>
> But I did not stay there either, because now the *voelkisch* idea was spreading and so I joined the DVFP, of which I became a treasurer. I did this for two years until I saw the first signs of our *Fuehrer* Adolf Hitler. Then one fine day, I and another person now in the party broke up the *voelkisch* movement in Charlottenburg to make way for the NSDAP.

Sooner or later the respondent would have done the same to the NSDAP. The violent temper is more obvious with another respond-

---

[4] See also no. 325, born 1879, who in turn belonged to the DSP, the *Schutz-und-Trutzbund*, and the *Deutsch-voelkische Freiheitspartei* (DVFP), an offshoot of the DNVP, in the early 1920's. He joined the NSDAP as soon as it was reconstituted in 1925, although he had to keep his membership hidden because he was a civil servant.

ent, born 1886 (no. 321), a military-civil servant who returned from the war limping on a cane.

> At the Potsdam station in Berlin I was stopped by a horde in uniforms with red armbands who demanded that I take off my Iron Cross, First Class, and the other insignia. I responded to this imposition with hearty whacks of my cane, but the horde knocked me down and only the intervention of some railroad officials saved me from my predicament. From that moment, a white-hot hatred burnt in me against the November criminals. Barely restored to health, I volunteered to quell the insurrection. I took part in the storming of the *Vorwaerts* building, of the Marstall, and in the other battles in Berlin.

Eventually he also joined Kunze's DSP, but not for long because the growing NSDAP attracted his attention with its lusty brawls. He became involved in a major meeting-hall melée even before joining and was arrested. But from that time on he had found the "real spirit of the front" in the Nazi party.

Motives for Politicization

What reasons do the respondents give for becoming interested in the electoral politics of the Weimar Republic? The reasons are still similar to those given for entering stage two, but there is a noticeable decline of the direct impact of the war and of the violence of revolutionaries and counter-revolutionaries. The emphasis instead shifts from the immediate happenings of the revolution and counter-revolution to opposition to the long-range significance of the change in power, even though the respondents still refer to "the revolution" and "Marxism" as if the Spartakists had succeeded in taking over the Weimar Republic. Opposing the Weimar leadership, therefore, differs from opposition to the Marxist revolution only by the degree of a sense of reality.

FD-43: Catalyst for Stage Three

	Number	Per cent
Fronterlebnis, impact of war	21	7.1
Shock of defeat	22	7.5
Shock of occupation	19	6.5
Opposition to revolution, Marxism	90	30.8
Opposition to Weimar leaders	48	16.4
Economic troubles, inflation	22	7.5
Reached suffrage age	41	14.0
Friction with political opponents	8	2.7
Other (Nazi party becomes available)	22	7.5
	293	100.0

Social Background of Stage Three Motivation Groups

How do these political motivation groups differ from one another? We combined the war, defeat, and occupation groups as well as those whose interest in politics resulted from such external causes as reaching voting age, political friction, or the availability of a Nazi local organization. The second grouping is obviously the youngest of the five groups, with over half born after 1898. The small group blaming its politicization on its economic troubles is the second youngest. The group politicized by opposition to the Weimar leaders, with over one-half born before 1890, is the oldest group, followed by those who oppose the "Marxist revolution."

By occupation, the two youngest groups and their fathers were mostly workers, while the two oldest have a disproportionate contingent of military-civil servants among them. Those opposed to the Weimar leaders also include many farmers. Their fathers, for that matter, tended to be either farmers or military-civil servants. The anti-revolutionary group includes many business, professional, and white-collar respondents. Its fathers tend to be businessmen and artisans. Those Nazis who were politicized by war and occupation have disproportionate numbers of white-collar employees and women among them, while their fathers tended to be businessmen.

There is a surprising degree of continuity of occupation and status between the generations. We get the impression, also, that the older cohorts represent mostly the once unpolitical military-civil servants, farmers, and bourgeoisie, while the younger groups may be acting more from current socio-economic causes such as working-class miseries, unemployment and the like. Those politicized by economic troubles, in particular, show a noticeable difference between their many businessman or artisan fathers (40%) and the many white-collar or blue-collar respondents among the sons (60.9% as compared to 35.0% of the fathers). They obviously include a disproportionate number of families socially stagnant or in social decline, a feature shared by the anti-revolutionary group. By comparison, the respondents politicized by war and occupation are often upwardly mobile from an urban background. The opponents of the Weimar leadership as well as the new voters and those politicized by the local availability of the NSDAP tend to be upwardly mobile from a farm background.

Does religion have anything to do with these subtle undercurrents of politicization in the Weimar Republic? Once more, it is the failure to state their affiliations which most tellingly distinguishes the groups. No one will be surprised to find the young economic-trouble group the most secular with 77.3% who fail to indicate their religious affiliations. Living mostly in secularized Berlin and other Protestant areas, they are evidently concerned more with solvency than with salvation, except in matters political, if there. The other young group, the new voters etc., are far more religious (only 50.8% failed to state their affiliations). Those politicized by war and occupation are second in secularism (74.5%) and then come, surprisingly, the anti-revolutionaries (70%), an older group whose establishmentarian faith in Kaiser, Reich, and the Wilhelminian bourgeoisie may well have taken the place of religion in their lives. They also have the highest number living in religiously mixed areas or areas dominated by the opposing religious affiliation.

Youth Groups and Politicization

Did involvement in youth groups contribute more toward militarization or toward politicization? The stage two groups naturally included a large contingent (89 cases; 39%) whose first youth organization was a Free Corps or a vigilante or military training group, as compared to the stage three respondents (51 cases; 21%). Furthermore, since the militarized were quite a bit younger than the politicized, the latter had a much larger number who belonged to the older age cohorts and, consequently, were in no youth group at all. Yet, on balance and with some qualifications, the politicized of stage three did belong more to appropriate quasi-political youth groups. They were far more often in conservative groups such as the *Bismarckjugend* (DNVP) or the DHV Youth, especially those who were politicized by war and occupation, or by opposition to the Marxist revolution. They also participated more in the Socialist or Communist youth groups than did the stage two respondents, whose "reds" were militarized mostly by war and defeat, presumably fighting on the side of the revolutionaries. The politicized reds tended to derive their interest in politics from their economic troubles or from coming of voting age. Though the figures are small, the militarized in turn tended to be in unpolitical youth organizations more often than were the politicized of stage three.

What the politicized liked best about their first youth organization is also considerably less dramatic than with the militarized. Whereas 13.8% of the latter liked violence best, only 7.5% of the politicized, and chiefly the younger, cohorts did. The militarized also stressed marching, rallies, and uniforms more (16.1%) than did the politicized (13.7%). On the other hand, the latter liked the spirit of comradeship and hiking and cultural appreciation (31.6%) more than did the militarized (25.3%). Their youthful dislikes present a similar picture. The politicized objected most to class distinctions, a lack of social conscience, socialist militancy, or to the ideological overtones or leadership of their youth group. The militarized instead criticized "un-national views" or the lack of political direction and action. The youthful disposition, it would appear, is likely to determine either militarization or politicization. And so are the external challenges of the historical situation or family traditions of militarism or civilian courage.

The differences also extend to our classification of youthful postures. The militarized, for example, have noticeably more hostile militants (20.8% as compared to 11.2%) and "politically militarized" youths (27.5% as compared to 19.5%) than the stage three respondents. The latter in turn have the edge with the "fully politicized" (11.2% as compared to 9.3%), authoritarian (8.8% as compared to 6.4%), and "pre-political parochial" youths (16.3% as compared to 12.3%). Consequently, we would expect them also to show a differential in their involvement in youthful violence. The militarized, indeed, include 21.2% in partisan street fights (cf. 17.6%), and 24.4% in Free Corps-type organized violence (cf. 17%), while the politicized have the edge in demonstrations and provocation (20% as compared to 17.6%) and in proselytizing and electioneering (18.2% as compared to 16.6%).

The political color of the home environment, which we alluded to briefly, also differs though perhaps not drastically enough to explain why some people became militarized and others politicized. The militarized had more militaristic (13.5% as compared to 11.3%) and *voelkisch*-antisemitic (14.7% as compared to 10.7%) fathers than the politicized. That a *voelkisch* home environment made more for militarization rather than, as expected, politicization, appears to be a reflection of the nature of antisemitic prejudice. We are not just dealing with a partisan political ideology, but with a sickness that drives people on to violent deeds. The politicized again had more often a conventional political (12.5% as compared to 10.3%) or even unpolitical (15.5% as compared to 13.5%) home background.

Biography and Historiography

It may be well to pause here in order to gain an overview of the whole process. There are two ways of charting the course of the respondents toward the Nazi movement. We can proceed by following the stages of their *bios*, their individual lives, or we can follow the historical periods of the Weimar era in the hope of laying bare the challenges of each period and the responses of the Nazi recruits to them. Whenever we have brought in the periodization rather than or juxtaposed to the biographic stages of political mobilization, historiography has received its due. For the sake of completeness we have also made a record of the organizational memberships and activities of the Abel respondents in the various periods in question. The reader has already encountered these statistical breakdowns in crosstabulations. Here are the complete listings by period. From them we can gather the extraordinary diversity of the political careers of our respondents as well as the rates of their eventual absorption into the NSDAP.

FD-48: Organizational Membership, 1919-1921

	Number	*Per cent*
None	318	56.8
Voelkisch groups:		
DSP-*Deutsch-soziale Partei* (*Kunze*)	8	1.4
Schutz-und-Trutzbund	14	2.5
Voelkisch-sozialer Block	2	.4
NSDAP, 1920-1921 (or fronts)	8	1.4
Other *voelkisch* groups	26	4.6
	58	10.3
Quasi-military organizations:		
Anti-occupation, -separatist, -Polish groups	11	1.9
Other veterans' groups	24	4.2
Buergerwehr, vigilantes	27	4.8
Free Corps, irregulars	54	9.5
Oberland, Ehrhardt, Consul	4	.7
Other quasi-military groups	1	.2
	121	20.3
Conservative-bourgeois opposition:		
Jungdo, bourgeois opposition	4	.7
DNVP	27	4.9
Regional, agricultural parties, borderland groups	3	.6
	34	6.2
Republican parties, left opposition:		
SPD	12	2.1
DDP	2	.4
DVP	5	.9
Center Party, BVP	2	.4
Other republican group	1	.2
USPD	7	1.2
KPD, red militants	7	1.2
	36	6.4
Grand total:	567	100.0

From the very beginning of the republican era, the later Nazi recruits overwhelmingly tended to be in right-wing groups hostile to
the republic. It will be recalled that many respondents were partial
to or involved in the Kapp *putsch* of 1920. This initial hostility to
the establishment hardly waned during the second period (FD-49)
when the great crisis of 1923 brought the republican government
to the edge of a right-wing takeover, not by the histrionics of Adolf
Hitler in Munich, but by the broader plans of the right wing all over
the country. The *voelkisch* groups of 1922-1924 in our sample have
more than doubled their number of the earlier period. Eighty and
eight-tenths percent of their earlier number are still with them. Like
numbers have joined them from among the previously unorganized

FD-49: Organizational Memberships, 1922-1924

	Number	*Per cent*
None	261	45.4
Voelkisch groups:		
DSP	10	1.8
Schutz-und-Trutzbund	7	1.2
Voelkisch-sozialer Block	5	.9
NSDAP, 1922-1923	32	5.6
Nazi fronts, 1924	18	3.2
Deutsch-voelkische Freiheitsbewegung	40	7.0
Other *voelkisch* groups	20	3.5
	132	23.2
Quasi-military organizations:		
Anti-occupation, -separatists	17	3.0
Militant veterans' groups	21	3.7
Stahlhelm, Jungstahlhelm	26	4.6
Other veterans' groups	14	2.5
Free Corps	4	.7
Zeitfreiwillige	14	2.5
	96	17.0
Conservative-bourgeois opposition:		
Jungdo, bourgeois opposition	17	3.0
DNVP	30	5.3
Other conservative groups	1	.2
	48	8.5
Republican groups, left opposition:		
SPD, Socialist union	14	2.5
DDP, DVP	5	.9
Center, BVP	4	.7
KPD, Red Hundreds, RFB	10	1.8
	33	5.9
Grand total	309	100.0

and from a combination of the other three groups. The other groups have progressively less continuity between the first and second period. Only 62.2% of the conservative-bourgeois opposition groups of the first period are still with them in the second period, even though the share of this group grew. Among the quasi-military groups only 40.7%, and among the republicans and left-wingers, only 37.1% of the members of the first period are still there in the second period.

In the third period, the *voelkisch* members are all united in the reconstructed NSDAP, which by 1927 has already increased substantially. Three-fourths of the *voelkisch* members of the first period are again with it and nearly the same percentage of the second period. A third of the reconstructed party came from previously uncommitted persons and another one-sixth from the quasi-military groups of earlier periods. More than half of the additional growth of 1928 likewise came from among the uncommitted, and another one-fifth from earlier quasi-military groups.

FD-50: Organizational Memberships, 1925-1928

	Number	*Per cent*
None	262	44.9
In NSDAP, 1925-1927	166	29.1
In NSDAP, 1928	47	8.0
Quasi-military organizations:		
Stahlhelm	33	5.6
Other veterans' groups	9	1.5
	42	7.1
Conservative Bourgeois opposition groups:		
Jungdo, bourgeois opposition	10	1.7
DNVP	20	3.4
Other conservative groups	21	3.6
	51	8.7
Republican groups, left opposition:		
SPD, Reichsbanner	2	.3
DDP, DVP	3	.5
Center Party	3	.5
Pacifistic group	1	.2
KPD	4	.7
	13	2.2
Grand total	581	100.0

In the first year of the fourth period, 1929-1930, the NSDAP again added substantial numbers from among the previously uncommitted (39.5%) and half that number from earlier quasi-military groups. In 1930, it picked up half of their increase from the uncommitted, 19.3% from pre-1925 *voelkisch* members, and another 15.8% from quasi-military groups.

FD-51: Organizational Memberships, 1929-1930

	Number	Per cent
None	153	26.4
In NSDAP, 1929	277	47.6
In NSDAP, 1930	122	21.1
Stahlhelm	7	1.2
Other veterans	3	.5
Jungdo	1	.2
Agricultural opposition	1	.2
DNVP	9	1.5
Other conservative groups	3	.5
SPD, *Reichsbanner*	2	.3
KPD	2	.3
DDP	1	.2
	581	100.0

The entire process of growth looks, at least within the confines of our sample, like a process of rapid absorption of the previously uncommitted and of a sizeable quasi-military reservoir of Nazi recruits. We have to bear in mind, though, that we can measure only the different rates at which the groups within our sample join the NSDAP, because we have no representation of groups which did not join by the early thirties nor of any early *voelkisch* group members or Nazis who dropped out.

Let us now compare the breakdowns for each period:

Table IV-3: Organizational Memberships, 1919-1933 (in %) (FD 48, 49, 50, and 51)

	1919-1921	1922-1924	1925-1928	1929-1930	1931-1933
None	56.8	45.4	44.9	26.4	—
Military organizations	20.3	17.0	7.1	1.7	—
Conservative and bourgeois opposition	6.2	8.5	8.7	2.4	—
Republican parties and Communists	6.4	5.9	2.2	0.8	—
NSDAP and *voelkisch groups*	10.3	23.2	37.1	68.7	100.0
Totals	100.0	100.0	100.0	100.0	100.0

The periods in Table IV-3 are those of the revolution and counter-revolution, the crisis of 1923, the quiet period, the onset of the depression, and the height of the struggle. As for the growth of the NSDAP, the other *voelkisch* groups played a significant political role only prior to 1925. While there were, of course, rivalries and incompatibilities, some of the pre-1925 *voelkisch* groups were direct antecedents or front organizations (e.g., DSP or *Frontbann*) and merged completely with the resurrected Nazi party of 1925. Very few respondents who eventually joined the NSDAP were in a *voelkisch* group after 1925.

The tabulation of the political activities the respondents engaged in over the Weimar years (Table IV-4) also shows the gathering

Table IV-4: Political Activities Reported, 1919-1933 (in %)
(FD 52, 53, 54, and 55)

	1919-1924	1925-1928	1929-1930	1931-1933
Voting, political interest	25.7	26.4	13.7	2.8
Interest in various parties	21.4	18.8	8.6	1.3
Electioneering only	6.1	7.1	6.4	5.0
Marching, demonstrations, and electioneering	13.4	14.6	18.6	21.9
Marching, electioneering, and proselytizing	10.0	16.9	27.0	37.8
Political violence and electioneering	23.4	16.2	24.7	31.2
Totals	100.0	100.0	100.0	100.0
	(n=471)	(n=548)	(n=686)	(n=746)

Note: Multiple entries account for totals in excess of 581.

of the storm. The number of respondents rises from period to period and the weight shifts toward the marching, fighting, and proselytizing typical of the full-fledged movement. Moreover, the responses of marching and fighting of the early period (1919-1924) generally do not include electioneering. The Weimar Republic opened on years of militarization and it was not until the depression era that the national election campaigns rose to the fever pitch of political soldiering. The year 1932, finally, was the peak of the Nazi *crescendo* as one election struggle followed the other—one presidential and two parliamentary elections—and many respondents report marching, fighting, and proselytizing "day and night" to the point of physical and mental exhaustion. It was at this point that the era of political soldiering had reached its absolute peak and would have started to decline, had not the circumstances and certain men in responsible positions looked with favor upon the man of the hour, Adolf Hitler.

THREE

The Beginning of the End

Many of the Abel respondents wrote or implied that when "the system" of Weimar had provoked them long enough and they finally took the plunge into the brown movement, their decision was the beginning of the end of "the system." They may have had rosy visions of the future which were eventually dashed by the iron fist of the Fuehrer and his henchmen. They may not have envisaged the horrors the Third Reich was going to bring. But there is no mistaking their heartfelt desire to put an end to "the system." Why they felt this way is a subject worthy of further exploration, both in the short-range sense of their immediate motives for joining the party as well as in the long-range sense of what they expected to accomplish by their membership and activity. We shall return to the long-range aspects later.

The Motives for Entering Stage Four

A word of clarification is necessary before we can take a closer look at the motives for joining the party suggested by the respondents. In a way, this entire book is devoted to an exploration of their motives and yet we have had to admit the limitations of our quest from the very beginning. At this point we shall call "motives" only the plausible explanations given or implied by the respondents themselves for joining the Hitler movement. No attempt will be made to probe into the motivations behind these "motives" except for the light shed upon them by the various crosstabulations which link them to the deeper strands of social and political motivation explored elsewhere in this book.

A good three-fourths of the responses (FD-47) refer to motives such as the ideological fervor, the dynamic impression of the movement, or the spirit of comradeship among the stormtroopers, which mostly represent the momentum of the storm gathering over a politically passive population. Of these three, a sense of dynamism in humdrum lives and of belonging among comrades is deeply rooted in all modern societies and need not surprise us. The ideo-

logical fervor and antisemitism of the respondents may perhaps
seem the most autonomous and pre-extant. But as a motive the latter also represents not a static condition but a dynamic process by
which certain predispositions were activated and channeled by the
presence of the movement. The vague elements of Nazi ideology
and the generally diffuse and unpolitical nature of antisemitism
needed the politicizing and militarizing stimulus of the dynamic

FD-47: Catalyst for Stage Four

	Number	Per cent
⌐ Sense of repression by police, government	27	3.8
⌐ Incidents of mistreatment by police, establishment suffered or observed	35	4.9
Friction with occupation	22	3.1
Rough opposition of political enemies, Communists etc. (incl. "threat of red revolution")	45	6.4
Ideological fervor, antisemitism	310	43.8
Dynamic impression of Hitler, or NSDAP	173	24.4
Spirit of comradeship in SA	58	8.2
Economic troubles	38	5.4
	708	100.0

Note: Multiple entries.

movement to draw further converts into the activist frame of mind
of the pre-1933 NSDAP. The following crosstabulations will give
depth to this characterization of the motives for entering stage four.

A Social Profile of Stage-four Motives

When we compare the distribution of the age cohorts over the different motives for stage four, several salient features stand out. The
youngest cohort (born 1909-1916) tends to cite such motives as
the comradeship among the stormtroopers, or a sense of being repressed by the police or the establishment in government and society. Those a little older (born after 1902) also stress friction with
the occupation and the "rough opposition" of the Communists or
other political enemies. In fact, comradeship and the occupation are
the only motives which have more than half of their respondents
in the postwar generation. Their economic troubles, on the other
hand, tended to motivate the war generation (born 1890-1901) in
disproportionate numbers. The "oldest" motives were the dynamic

impression of the Hitler movement and the ideological fervor which each had a good fourth of their respondents in the age cohorts born before 1890.

Despite their comparable ages, however, the last-mentioned two groups did not join the party at the same time. They constituted two successive waves of older Nazi recruits. Those attracted by the dynamism of the movement tended to join late, with some 48.2% coming after the *Reichstag* elections of 1930, and a good fourth after May of 1931. Only those complaining about being repressed joined this late, perhaps in part because of the prohibition of NSDAP membership in the civil service. Fifty-eight and seven-tenths percent of the ideologically motivated group, by comparison, joined before the 1930 elections (as against 51.8% for the dynamic group). Only the much smaller groups motivated by the comradeship of the stormtroopers or by friction with the occupation tended to join any earlier.

The dynamic impression of the movement was particularly beguiling to the women, the military-civil servants, and to white-collar respondents. The military-civil servants and the women were also motivated by a sense of general repression and by ideological fervor. The workers in the sample, by comparison, were more often motivated to join by the rough opposition of the Communists, economic troubles, two experiences close to their lives, or by their sense of being repressed. Business and professional respondents mention the stormtrooper comradeship before their economic difficulties, the occupation, or ideological fervor as their motives. White-collar respondents, in addition to the dynamic impression of the movement, were also motivated by economic troubles and ideological fervor. The farmers, finally, cite the comradeship of the stormtroopers, the occupation, economic troubles, and ideological fervor, in this order, as their motives.

Since so much speculation about these motives has filled many a book, it may be well to stop here and comment on the motives of these occupational groups. The small number of economically motivated responses in itself should cast further doubt on many of the economic interpretations of the Nazi revolt. The blue-collar fears of Communist power and the appeal of comradeship to young workers, businessmen, and farmers also are hardly surprising.

The general sense of being repressed which so many workers, women, and military-civil servants express invites comparison with the same feelings current among young radicals in the contemporary United States. Here as there, a more objective picture would have to stress the helpless floundering of a weak government unable to contain the erupting domestic turbulence. The Nazi civil servants, at least in Prussia, were probably the only ones who could lay an objective claim to repression by the establishment of the day. Nevertheless, a sense of repression is evidently natural to a violent, revolutionary movement even in the midst of a permissive, democratic society. The thrust and direction of the ideological-fervor group, which accounts for well over half the sample, and of the sizeable group lured by the dynamic impression of the movement will have to be explored further. Who are these people who were sucked in so easily by the political whirlwind of Hitler and at a comparatively late stage of the movement?

The Wide Swath of the Movement

Both groups have a surprisingly high percentage of the borderland Germans (70.2%) of the sample and three-fourths of the highly mobile respondents. More than a third of them, indeed, lived in Berlin during the era of Goebbels' conquest of the city. Among the occupations of their fathers, the ideologues had disproportionate numbers of artisans. Those attracted by the dynamism of the movement tended to have high military, professional, or businessmen as fathers, from whom they may well have learned elitist expectations. But they were less often in social decline, for example, than those motivated by comradeship or by friction with the occupation. Instead, the ideologues tended to have made no attempt to rise socially from a rural background. Those attracted by dynamism tended to be upwardly mobile from an urban background. Both tended to be Protestant and to live in Protestant areas more than most of the other groups.

In their youth group life, both tended, for reasons of their age, to have had no group affiliation (about one-third) or to have been in a conservative or nationalistic group. The ideologues, apart from this, often had been in an agricultural or religious, or a Socialist or Communist, group, and surprisingly many of them had joined the SA or Hitler Youth (HJ) directly. What the ideologues liked best about their youth group, moreover, were marching, rallies, and ideological direction. They disliked a lack of ideological guidance. Those with a hankering for dynamism tended to prefer sports and cultural appreciation, or violent action. They disliked, conversely, "un-national views" and a lack of political direction. The quest for a sense of direction and guidance is here obviously a key to their attitude toward the rising Nazi movement.

Their most extreme youthful activities varied considerably. Both groups disproportionately acquired military training, but the dynamic group was more violent in street fighting and the Free Corps type of violence. The ideologues were more often absorbed by demonstrations, provocation, and proselytizing. For this reason, they had the highest proportion of "fully politicized" youth among them, and even somewhat more than their share of the "politically militarized," though not nearly as many as those motivated by the comradeship among the stormtroopers, or by friction with the occupation. The dynamic group, in spite of its violence, stands out only with its numbers of "pre-political parochials," who evidently stem from the older cohorts antedating the wave of youth organizations of the 1920s.

Both groups tended to have a rather friendly work environment. The political color of the home among the ideologues was mostly *voelkisch* or unpolitical. Among those yearning for dynamism, it was more often militaristic or patriotic than with any other group. Their school environments similarly stressed patriotism, while that of the ideologues disproportionately was *voelkisch*-antisemitic, often with conflicts with Jewish fellow-students, or identified with the conventional parties. Thus the two groups showed their distinctive character long before being attracted by the movement.

As to their childhood settings, there is a curious difference between the sheltered and the freewheeling childhoods among the well-to-do. The sheltered tended to hanker for dynamism, perhaps to make up for their constrictive childhoods, while the freewheeling had a disproportionate share of fervent ideologues and antisemites. The latter also included more than their share of highly disciplined and orphaned childhoods. By and large, however, neither of the two groups grew up under particularly deprived circumstances as compared to the rest.

The Impact of War and Revolution

As for the impact of the war and its aftermath, the ideologues have more than their share of those whose initial enthusiasm gave way to disillusionment toward the end. They also include quite a few war invalids and ex-prisoners of war. The dynamicists, on the other hand, show more of the qualities of the legendary front generation. They tend to have served with merit, often winning decorations or promotions. Many of them stress the egalitarian *Fronterlebnis*. When they came home, consequently, many of them experienced a sense of cultural shock at the absence of order and discipline, the institutional changes, and the "moral disintegration" of Weimar society. The ideologues share the last-mentioned kind of shock, which is really an indication of their alienation, but otherwise they tend not to have experienced any cultural shock at all. Evidently one does not always need to be alienated from society in order to be a fervent Nazi ideologue. Like other members of the war generation, the dynamicists tend to blame the Kaiser and the civilians for the German defeat or to express great but diffuse emotions about it. The ideologues, by comparison, tend to take it in stride.

Typical perhaps of the relevance of the war experience to the path of the dynamicists toward the NSDAP are the following examples. They both illustrate in their political careers the shadow of the war which, according to one respondent (no. 489) had "only seemingly ended in 1918 with the shameful, dictated peace." Especially those who were too young, or otherwise unfit, to be drafted often acted like an automaton programmed for war and hence unable to settle down in peace. One respondent for example, born in 1900 and drafted in May, 1918 made up in belligerent patriotism whatever he missed in combat service in the last months of the war. "The great war did not spare the children. We boys in particular nearly outdid the older ones in love of the fatherland and enthusiasm." The respondent went to rallies of nearly all the parties during the republican era and "I always had the feeling I did not belong there." Finally, spurred on by his "search for a savior from national humiliation," a virulent *Judenkoller*, and acute xenophobia, he found what he was looking for, the NSDAP. He joined "and immediately became a stormtrooper as well . . . a fighter for the Third Reich marching to victory in the brown shirt. . . ."

Another respondent, born 1902 (no. 426), who just missed being drafted immediately joined the Free Corps to fight the Poles in Upper Silesia. "There my urge for soldiering could realize itself." The Free Corps impressed him also with its classlessness in the relations between officers and men and its personal ties to the early Nazi movement. "Here for the first time I discovered the satisfactions of being a political soldier." He joined the party and SA in 1927 and, when asked to form his own SS Storm, he crowed: "I had reached my life's goal: to become a soldier."

The attitudes of the two groups toward the revolution differ considerably. The ideologues tended to blame the Jews or the Weimar parties (SPD, DDP, and Center) for the revolution. Those yearning for dynamism simply blame the mutineers or the Spartakists, or unspecified rabble of the streets. They became heavily involved, as a consequence, with the Free Corps against the Poles, in the Kapp *putsch*, with vigilante groups, and also with veterans' organizations and their military training programs, while the ideologues tended to be hardly involved at all.

The two groups also rival each other in their hatred of the occupation, but not in their actual involvement in the struggle against it. Here the ideologues tended to get themselves expelled for participation in the passive resistance, while the dynamicists tended to be jailed and expelled for violent acts of resistance. In 1923, the latter were about as often involved in or sympathetic to the Hitler *putsch* as the ideologues—that is, more than any other group. But the fervent ideologues also had substantial numbers in *voelkisch* parties, other conventional parties, or in militant veterans' groups. They were, quite clearly, more broadly involved in Weimar politics throughout the early years, while the membership of those yearning for dynamism was limited to quasi-military and conservative groups. Nevertheless, over one-half of both groups was in the NSDAP before 1928 and another 13-20% joined that year, earlier than most other groups.

The Four Stages

Let us examine how these two groups went through the four stages. The ideologues tended to come from among members of prewar political parties (8.1%) including the political antisemites, and from unpolitical bourgeois or farming circles (31.4%). A good third of them were simply pre-political parochials at stage one. The respondents yearning for dynamism, on the other hand, are made up mostly of one-time "unpolitical" military-civil servants (21.2%) or the similarly unpolitical bourgeoisie or agricultural (36.5%).

In stage two, the dynamicists in considerable numbers were in Free Corps and vigilante groups, while the ideologues were more often in the *Wehrwolf*, in *voelkisch* action groups, or in *Jungdo*. The ideologues tended to enter stage two when they were either under 21 or over 36, whereas the dynamic group was evenly distributed over the starting ages. Their motives for entering this stage tended to be the shock of war and defeat, or of the occupation. The ideologues were propelled either by their antisemitic predisposition or by their opposition to the revolutionaries.

More than half of both groups never went through stage two, but this is barely true with regard to stage three of those enamored with the dynamism of the Nazi movement. The ideologues were far more involved in this stage of politicization. In particular, they shopped around among the parties or expressed strong distrust toward them. And a fair number of them, as of the dynamicists, voted or electioneered for the pre-1925 NSDAP or *voelkisch* parties. The rest of those devoted to dynamic action tended to be with the DNVP or the *Bismarckjugend*, two rather unlikely vehicles to still their yearning for dynamic leadership. The two groups tended to become politicized rather late in their lives, with over half of the ideologues and nearly two-thirds of the dynamic group already over 25 and 25-30% over 35 years of age. This forms a strong contrast with the early politicization of all the other groups we focus on, especially those motivated by comradeship or by friction with the occupation.

The reasons cited by the two groups for becoming politicized differ only slightly. More than any other group they tended to be motivated by their sense of opposition to the "Marxist revolution" and to the Weimar leaders. Many of them probably equated these two, the republican leadership and the alleged revolution. It is worth noting that this emphasis implied less attention to war and occupation and less motivation by economic troubles or by coming of voting age than was true among the other groups. Their activities in stages two and three tended disproportionately toward violence among those hankering for dynamic action, though no more than with several of the younger groups. The ideologues instead tended to become involved no further than attending rallies and electioneering.

When they reached stage four, however, those motivated by ideological fervor and antisemitism were notably ahead in violence (MF and MFP), while the dynamic group did more marching and proselytizing (MP) than any other group. The ideologues had actually fewer MFs than most groups, but they had more marcher-fighter-proselytizers than all but the group motivated by the comradeship among the stormtroopers. Perhaps a few examples of dynamic MPs and ideologue MFPs will illustrate the character of many members of these two motivation groups. The reader will have to bear in mind, however, that hardly any case ever seems very typical of anything. It is in the statistical averages that we find the relationships we have examined.

A Few Examples of MPs and MFPs

Most of the dynamic marcher-proselytizers seem to be of the war generation (1895-1901), although the war experience is usually not the only determinant of their proselytizing ardor. An example of a mixture of the war-invalid syndrome with the effect of political friction on the job is a railroad worker born 1897 in poverty (no. 402). With an arm disabled from a war injury, he joined the *Verband nationalgesinnter Soldaten* in 1920, which earned him a great deal of hostility on the job but also some secret supporters. "My parents gave me a nationalistic education and no one can ever drum it out of my head." He sympathized with the Kapp *putsch*, the Schlageter cult, and Hitler's defense in court after the beer-hall *putsch*. He complained bitterly about the economic burdens laid upon the Germans and about hungering his way through the inflation of 1923 so that his children could eat. "Thereby I was literally torn out of the bourgeois way of life and nothing was radical enough for me. To maintain my family and fight for a better standard of living for it, any means was good enough for me."

The respondent was very bitter about the party and government leaders "who lived like millionaires," while he was unable to spare the dues for any organization other than his trade union. When the spreading Nazi agitation reached his area, his wife went to the first rally, returned all aglow, and dragged him along to the next rally.

> Later still I learned that there had been a terrible brawl at that first rally. But my wife persuaded me to come along and I did her the favor. I stood in front of the hall until the stormtroopers arrived to protect the meeting. All of a sudden a gang of punks no older than 17, 18, 19 began to attack the people who were arriving. I raised my voice in protest against this outrageous way of treating German citizens (*Volksgenossen*) and nearly got clobbered too. I kept thinking about this for several days. Meanwhile, some older men around here decided to get together to put a stop to this by founding an SA Storm under the leadership of my brother.

His outraged remarks and the role of his brother intensified the friction at his job and eventually the reluctant recruit came around to joining the NSDAP (1930). His reluctance soon turned into zeal. He began to proselytize at work, which often brought the friction close to blows. He also spent late hours canvassing and demonstrating until his labors bore the fruit of scores of new stormtrooper units sprouting everywhere. He viewed the Third Reich primarily as a means to raise the living standards of the whole people.

Often the effectiveness of a proselytizer depended on his job or on his organizational connections. A good example of this is a very ambitious retail clerk born 1894 (no. 430), the son of an active Social Democratic mother and a nationalistic father. The respondent joined the Retail Clerks' Union (DHV) before the war. During the war, he was in an intelligence unit because of his knowledge of languages. The end of the war meant to him "as a young businessman, that now Germany was cut off; we had lost everything." He witnessed "the acts of terror and banditry of the Communist rule in Munich" and its suppression by the Free Corps, and later the occupation regime in the West. But politics did not hold his attention, apart from attending a few SPD meetings. A 1923 speech of Hitler in Munich left an impression, but in the occupied area, according to the respondent, Nazi activity and even newspapers were suppressed. Actually, he was too busy preparing to acquire by examination the secondary-school certificate, which he had missed and which he found indispensable for social and economic advancement, no mean undertaking for a person of his modest education. "As a man of grade-school background I had learned especially during the war that I was at a disadvantage as compared to the 'one-year reservists,' despite my conduct and seniority at the front. After the war, too, I often experienced my lack of a better education in the struggle for existence. I soon realized that the certificate was more and more important in the republic and that the slogan 'an open road to the achiever' was sheer deception."

Once he had passed his examination, however, he became more and more involved with the NSDAP. In 1928, he attended rally after rally and witnessed many fights.

I had become a convinced Nazi and went proselytizing from one man to the other in spite of much scorn and hostility. I realized more and more clearly how capitalists and Jews were progressively exploiting us and systematically making us cowardly and timid. It gave me great satisfaction in 1929 to put my signature on the petition against the Young Plan, as only a few like-minded people were doing. I often felt close to despair about the utter indifference of the German people.

The views of the respondent are no surprise coming from a DHV member, but now there is a new note, the lonely despair of the extremist. His connections permitted his election to the Employees' Council of the I. G. Farben concern in 1930-1931 and in turn catapulted him into a high DHV office when the movement won power. In the meantime, his anxiety drove the respondent on toward violence. "When in 1932 the struggle for the existence of the movement became harder and harder, I realized that the final battle could not be avoided. I joined the stormtroopers in October 1932. I expected an all-out armed clash with 'the system' since we just could not seem to get ahead any more in spite of all the electoral battles." The armed clash, of course, never occurred because the Reich President capitulated and appointed the chief of the invaders instead of defending the constitution as he had sworn to do.

The ideologues are noticeably more preoccupied with Nazi goals and ideas. The ideological emphasis frequently came out earlier than just with the Nazi movement. Fairly typical is another clerk with I. G. Farben, born 1900 (no. 432), who was already with the *voelkisch Schutz-und-Trutzbund* right after the war and tells about the antisemites he met in this organization. The French occupation outlawed the group, so its members joined *Wehrwolf*. The respondent read and distributed the antisemitic *Eisenhammer* and wrote occasional articles for the Nazi paper *Rheinfront*. In 1928 he was already so convinced of the righteousness of the Nazi cause that he proselytized and propagandized for it even before joining. He joined in 1930 and continued his work while being unemployed.

Nazi women, who could not do any fighting, often became proselytizers because of their beliefs. A poor Silesian weaver's child born 1897 (no. 459) who learned weaving, a locksmith's trade, and worked in many jobs including domestic service is a good example. Following the war, she shopped around among the parties, appalled at their number and in search of one that might promise real salvation.

> I searched and searched but there was none that offered salvation from all this hopeless misery. If you went with open eyes through all this chaos, you could tell that there was someone behind it all trying to pull our fatherland into the abyss. I attended SPD and DNVP meetings but they bored me to tears. Then I went to Communist rallies where Karl Liebknecht and Rosa Luxemburg spoke. Again my innermost feelings revolted. Those Communist rallies brought out the antisemite in me.

The respondent married an unpolitical man who "just lived thoughtlessly from day to day"; but she continued her search. She came in contact with the DSP of Knueppel-Kunze and voted for it once "as the lesser evil." She learned about Hitler through his widely publicized court trial following the beer-hall *putsch*.

Her marriage foundered and in 1924 she moved in with her child with her sister and brother-in-law. The latter was already a Nazi and *Frontbann* member, and brought home Nazi literature and the book *Mein Kampf*. But the party still was not very successful in Berlin until the arrival of Dr. Goebbels and his grand campaign and monster rallies. "For us women it was always a special delight to go to one of the great rallies in a red area. Most of the time it was dangerous, too, because the red mob of indoctrinated Communists always brought about a big battle." She joined the Nazi party in 1928 and began to proselytize by loaning a copy of *Mein Kampf* to prospective recruits, giving them tickets to a play by Goebbels, or trying to take them to some rallies. It was not easy.

Many of the respondents from Berlin tell the story of the Reverend Mr. Stucke, who dared speak up against Goebbels and was manhandled in a Nazi rally, with the result that the party was outlawed for a year. The respondent has a different version of the incident: "Our party was forbidden for a year just because we helped a provocateur, who was supposedly a minister, to a little fresh air." The decree outlawing the party only restrained it from public activity. It failed to stop the proselytizing and left undaunted the proselytizing spirit of the faithful, as the respondent readily testifies. She chronicles the growth of the movement in Berlin to the day of the takeover.

Ex-Communists in the NSDAP

Of particular interest also are former Communists who came around and became ardent Nazis. One such case is a teacher's son born 1895 (no. 493) who came upon hard times after the war. On being discharged from the service, he first served with the *Grenzschutz* in Poland, then in the police in Stettin. He tried his hand at running a grocery store in Berlin and failed.

> As a result of this impoverishment and crisis I became a Communist and had important functions as an organization and propaganda supervisor. I also was a leader of the Red Front [RFB]. I quit the party in 1929 because I could no longer agree with the orders from the Soviet Union. I attended every rally [of other parties] and became more and more dissatisfied with myself and the world till I went to an NSDAP rally. But I was still suspicious and not to be soon persuaded to join a party again. Yet on the election nights the old fighting spirit would seize me again and so I went back to battle my comrades of today.

The pains of withdrawal from his intoxicant were hard to resist at campaign time. When a Nazi leader offered him the leadership of an NSDAP local, in any case, he decided to accept it, even though he expected a good deal of personal hostility from his former Communist comrades. They called him names, but evidently refrained from physical attacks. He recruited other ex-Communists and, "shoulder to shoulder with our good old SA, we cleaned out the red pigsty."

Another such case was a young merchant marine man and construction worker born 1907 (no. 492) who became unemployed in 1928. "I therefore joined the KPD and now the political battle got started." In 1930, a friend persuaded him to attend a Nazi rally, and soon he was talked into joining the stormtroopers. When his fellow-workers saw him in the brown uniform, the following encounter ensued the next morning at work:

> When I showed up at my place of work the next morning, I was received with the International and cries of *"Nazi verrecke!"* But they

left me alone when I gave no answer and just laughed. After our breakfast break I had to listen to a KPD member who tried to "learn" me the goals of the party. When he noticed I was paying no heed, he started to whistle the International and I began to sing the Horst Wessel song. Suddenly there were five, six men around me telling me to shut up, and that fellow-worker held his shovel under my nose and said he'd bash in my Nazi mouth. . . . I told him that he too would see the light some day and march with the SA. . . . [A month later] he came with me to a party meeting and became a stormtrooper himself. When the others on the construction site found out, another four men joined the SA.

A third ex-Communist is the young son of a furniture factory owner, born 1905 (no. 466), who in 1922 worked in a strange central German town among members of the Red Hundreds.

I had never been interested in politics until then . . . but soon I fell for their Communist proselytizing and became a fellow-fighter of the Red Hundreds without understanding the real purpose and idea of the Communists. . . . In another town I experienced the first street battle when we Red Hundreds tried to break up a German Day celebration. To our surprise we were beaten and had to flee. That day I saw the first *voelkisch* Hundreds with a blood-red swastika banner and a picture of Hitler with pine branches around it. Their courage and flair cast a spell on me.
In those days, the NSDAP put the Jewish question in the foreground. I began to read *voelkisch* literature and particularly Theodor Fritsch's *Handbook of the Jewish Question*. Then I joined the *voelkisch* Hundreds and thus the wonderful and bitter hours began in my life which I would never have wanted to miss.

The respondent spent his 18th birthday in jail for distributing *voelkisch* literature at the time of the Hitler *putsch* of 1923. Back with the movement in 1926, he went to one inspiring rally after the other, and had an opportunity to meet Goebbels and the Fuehrer in person. He viewed the cause as a fight of the old Germanic tribes against the Jews and "inferior races." Once he also reports violence but not his own. He reports that at a monster rally in 1928 in the Berlin *Sportpalast*, the police lost control over the crowds and even shot at the stormtroopers when they tried to "defend themselves against *Reichsbanner* and Communist assailants." Twenty-nine stormtroopers were injured. The respondent likes to ornament his account with ringing phrases but says very little about his own activity except as a bodyguard of Goebbels during a speaking tour. He held a fairly high SS office, considering his age.

These cases of ex-Communists who became fervent Nazis illustrate the interchangeability of extremist movements. For the young in particular, changing from the Red Front to the brown shirt appears to have been no more unusual or consequential than a change of juvenile gang membership in a big city. The smell of battle and the fighting spirit held the same promise in either camp. Perhaps the anecdote which tells about the boasting of a group of brawny new SA recruits in a "red" village near Munich is not so farfetched after all. They boasted that they had followed the red flag even before there was a swastika in its middle.

Age at Stage Four

The ideologues and the dynamic group did not enter stage four very early. Neither group, for example, joined between 12 and 17, as those motivated by a general sense of repression or by comradeship tended to do, or between 18 and 20, as did those motivated by friction with the occupation, by comradeship, or by the rough "Communist opposition." Both the ideologues and the dynamic group stand out among those who entered stage four between 21 and 25, an age young enough to go in for street violence. Even in that age group, the occupation- and comradeship-motivated groups are more prominent.

The ideologues again stand out among those who joined between 31 and 35, but again far less than the groups motivated by economic troubles and by the rough Communist opposition, who also dominate the age group that joined between 26 and 30. From then on through the higher age groups, the two groups begin to dominate. They have, in fact, more than a fourth each who joined after the age of 40 and one-tenth after the age of 50. These groups, then, appear to be motivated largely by something other than the youth revolt of the Weimar Republic. Let us take a look at some examples of older marcher-proselytizers which illustrate the diversity of personality types and motivations.

One respondent of this description is a carpenter, born 1873, who owned his own shop (no. 383). He served in the imperial army in peacetime and again in the war, and, during the course of the latter, contracted a virulent case of *Judenkoller*. After the war he began to order antisemitic literature from the well-established hate-peddler, Theodor Fritsch, and posted it secretly on telephone poles and public benches, in waiting-rooms, cafes, and the like. He also joined the *Deutsch-voelkische Freiheitsbewegung* and, in 1926, the NSDAP which allowed him to be an *Ortsgruppenleiter* until 1929 "when my nerves had suffered too much to go on." He complains about how hard his "great struggle" was and how he encountered hostility and was accosted at times. There is an air about his *vita* as if the Nazi movement was really his own production and his comrades had joined him in his work, rather than he the movement.

Another respondent was a pastry cook and café owner in Berlin, born 1879 (no. 460), who had always abstained from political involvement and instead concentrated on the prosperity of his business. In the mid-1920s, however, Nazi customers who had a regular table in his establishment got him interested in Hitler and his movement. He prides himself on being one of the first to advertise in the party organs and on always having put his car at the disposal of party transportation needs. Above all, he was involved in some major demonstrations and in proselytizing in and around Berlin, often by car.

His café and pastry shop, naturally, suffered from his political involvement and had to be sold in 1931. But he was resourceful enough to start a stormtrooper uniform supply business, together with two comrades. "We gave credit too, especially to needy SA comrades, and thereby helped the movement," and probably themselves as well. Perhaps, it was this attitude the NSDAP often referred to as "creative Aryan capitalism" to distinguish it from "destructive Jewish capitalism."

One of the more difficult things to understand is how a truly conservative person could ever become an enthusiastic Nazi. Here is an example of a wallpaper hanger born in 1884, who spent a part of his professional training with an uncle in Switzerland (no. 381). The respondent settled down with a family in Switzerland before the war and was repeatedly asked to become a Freemason, but declined. He joined the German army in 1914 but because of his health saw little action until the last months of the war. After the war he was permitted to return to Switzerland, but under humiliating circumstances.

> The returnees gathered in Singen where we were taken over in closed formations by the Swiss and taken to five days of quarantine in Frauenfeld/Thurgau. Here began the path of suffering for us Swiss Germans. The train first took us to Winterthur where each returnee underwent a criminal investigation. The train to Frauenfeld had military guards with rifles, and at the Frauenfeld garrison there were strong teams of armed guards. We were led through the town to the scorn of the populace. On the sixth day, the day of our release, we were once more escorted with rifles to the station. All this treatment and humiliation were bearable only because our freedom was just around the corner.

Now the lies of the newspapers against us Germans, which during the war had been launched in great number by the entente, came out. We were back with our families, but our respect and honor as Germans were lost. We remained the barbarians, *les boches*, and were continually treated with scorn and contempt. My speaking out publicly and representation of Germans gave me a hard time. I would have been expelled, had I not been the secretary of the German Assistance League.

The respondent describes the boycotts and job discrimination against Swiss Germans and their children and relates how he finally "had it up to the neck" and moved his family to Germany in 1922. "I could not suppress my German thinking and feeling and finally had to take the consequences." Significantly, he devotes nearly half of his *vita* to these Swiss tales.

Living in Bavaria, he joined the veterans organization *Bayern und Reich* and conducted its military training program for two years.[1] At the same time he was evidently close to the Bavarian branch of the Center party (BVP), a curious mixture of Catholic and nationalistic conservatism. But he also felt that they were too hard on Hitler, whom he heard twice in 1923. The super-patriotism he had learned in postwar Switzerland evidently militated against his conservatism. He moved from his veterans' group to the *Stahlhelm* while becoming increasingly more enamored with National Socialism. Long before he left the *Stahlhelm* (1930) and before he joined the party (December 1932), he was already speaking out publicly for the Nazis and proselytizing for them while making his daily rounds as a paper-hanger in people's homes. His conviction and eloquence were so great, he boasts, that many Communists respected him, too.

Nazi Ideology and Motive for Joining

The Nazi party, it is often alleged, promised many different things to different people and many people joined for rather disparate reasons. How did a person's main ideological theme tie in with his immediate reason for joining? A closer examination of the views and attitudes of our two groups will show what elements lay behind their ideological fervor and dynamic attraction to the movement. The ideologues, for example, more than any other group viewed the Weimar Republic as the *Judenrepublik*, a republic run by the Jews.

[1] On this organization, see also Andreas Werner, *SA und NSDAP*, unpublished doctoral dissertation, University of Erlangen-Nuernberg, 1964, pp. 31-34, 54-56.

The dynamicists, and also those motivated to join by comradeship, criticize mostly the "multi-party state" and the "Marxist-liberal system. And the respondents motivated by the occupation or by felt repressed tended to complain about Weimar as a capitalistic system. And the respondents motivated by the occupation or by "Communist opposition" saw it as a system dominated by the red and the black (Catholic) parties.

What were the dominant ideological themes of the two mainstream groups after they were in the party? The ideologues tended to be antisemites and, to a lesser extent, devotees of the *Volksgemeinschaft*, and of superpatriotism. The respondents hankering for dynamic leadership, on the other hand, tended to be Nordic-German cultists, or revanchists, or also devotees of the *Volksgemeinschaft*. They also paid their tribute to the Hitler cult, though not as much as did respondents motivated to join by comradeship, economic woes, or friction with the occupation. The last-mentioned also were superpatriots first of all, while the economically troubled tended to be antisemitic. Those motivated to join by the "Communist opposition" showed an emphasis similar to the dynamic group: Nordic-German romanticism, revanchism, and the *Volksgemeinschaft*. Revanchism was also particularly dear to the comradeship-oriented, while the *Volksgemeinschaft* was especially important to the group that felt repressed. Thus the motives for joining by and large form natural links to the themes of ideology.

As for their hate-lists, both the mainstream groups to about two-thirds stress anti-Marxism and to another 15 percent add the Jews to this formula. Those who joined because of their economic troubles or because of feeling oppressed also tend to stress the "reactionaries" as an object of their hostility, which goes well with their anti-capitalism. Those motivated by friction with the occupation heavily tend to have all-inclusive hate-lists, and we meet them again at one extreme of the attitudes toward political enemies. They and, to a lesser degree, the respondents with economic troubles and feelings of repression tend to speak of their enemies in the *outré* terms of rodents, immoral, etc. The two mainstream groups, surprisingly, tend instead to express a certain liking or understanding for them and would like to win them over.

On the scale of antisemitic attitudes, the ideologues have the highest score (69.8%) of involvement. They tend, in particular, toward delusions of conspiracy and, less so, toward sudden *Judenkoller*. Those who were motivated by economic troubles or by friction with the occupation have that sudden prejudice more often. Respondents motivated by the rough opposition of the Communists speak of threats and counter-threats more often than do the ideologues. The dynamicists were relatively less prejudiced although they had more than their share of tellers of prejudiced anecdotes.

The two mainstream groups were also less ethnocentric toward aliens and foreign nations than were some of the other groups, especially those motivated by friction with the occupation. Their attitudes toward authority, moreover, tended to decry most of all the "messy multi-party state," especially among the ideologues. The dynamically motivated also paid homage to an extreme sort of leadership cult. A craving for law and order, or an obsession with cleanliness, was more typical of those who were motivated to join by their sense of being repressed or by the comradeship of the stormtroopers.

Their relationship to the party is particularly instructive with the two mainstream groups. In their introduction to the party, for example, the ideologues tended to be attracted by Nazi rallies and demonstrations or to be introduced by a friend or fellow-worker. The people of the dynamic group, on the other hand, were generally introduced by a relative or were attracted by their awareness of the Nazi ideology. The implication seems to be that the latter were less likely to go to the public spectacles by which the party made its presence known. Instead, they became aware of it through reading the newspapers or perhaps Nazi literature.

To a higher degree than any other group, the two mainstream groups held local offices in the party. At the same time they tended far less often to be stormtroopers. Especially the dynamic group, of which the reader will recall a high degree of Free Corps or other middle-stage violence, had less than half of its members in SA or SS, far fewer than, for example, those motivated by the occupation (92%) or comradeship (80.3%). Consequently, their activities in the party rank below all the other groups in street violence and especially in "day-and-night" campaigning in 1932. Instead, they excelled in proselytizing and participation in demonstrations and electioneering.

Their attitude toward the party, in a word, was characterized by the satisfaction of fighting for utopia. For the ideologically motivated, in particular, the striving for utopia tended to be the integral experience of their extremist career. The dynamic group also battened upon the classless comradeship of life in the party and upon the leadership cult. This utopian attitude of the large group of ideologues is also borne out by a measurement of the ideological or pragmatic character of their thinking. The ideologues tended to be on the ideological side, though on a low or medium level of political understanding. The dynamic group, by comparison, tended to be pragmatic, but mainly in the low and narrow way befitting their more or less military background.

Motivations for Stages Two, Three, and Four

We can, finally, compare the reasons for entering stage four with those for entering the middle stages. A look at the changing distribution of the reasons for moving from stage to stage (Table IV-5) is revealing in what is shown about the impact of external events and antagonists. The salient causes mobilizing the unpolitical to leave stage one, such as the war, the revolution, or the French occupation of the Rhineland all pale before the attraction of the Hitler movement in the final stage. From their own accounts, the drawing power of the Nazi movement evidently lay not merely in negations such as anti-Communism or anti-republicanism. It was a positive force of enthusiasm, whatever we may think of it today, a virulent faith inspiring large numbers of people to march and fight and proselytize for the greater glory of the cause.

Table IV-5: Catalysts for Stages Two, Three, and Four (in %)
(FD 40, 43, and 47)

	2	3	4
Impact of war, territorial losses, French occupation	37.6	21.1	3.1
Shock of revolution, opposition to revolutionaries	42.1	31.7	6.4
Economic troubles, other reasons	—	7.5	5.4
Opposition to Weimar leaders, police repression	12.2	16.4	8.7
Ideological fervor, dynamic impression of Hitler Movement	8.1	23.3	76.4*
Totals	100.0	100.0	100.0

* Note: The 76.4% motivated by ideological fervor etc. at stage four is composed of 43.8% professing great ideological or antisemitic fervor, 24.4% stressing the dynamic impression of Hitler and his movement, and 8.2% citing the spirit of comradeship among the stormtroopers.

FOUR

The Violence of the Brown Columns

The brown-shirts were not necessarily the most violent movement of the Weimar Republic or of the period between the wars in Europe. There were many other fascist movements and also violent syndicalist and Communist movements whose involvement in political violence may have been as great or greater. Unfortunately, we have no equivalent to the Abel data on any of these movements and cannot compare them to find out how they differed from our group of early Nazis. The detailed accounts of political violence of the Abel respondents, in any case, allow us to examine the behavioral dynamics of the Nazi movement, which may well have been, after all, not so different from other extremist movements then or at any time since.

Stage Four: The Post-1924 Nazi Party

Stage four was the end goal of the process we are describing, the making of extremists. Unlike our treatment of the earlier stages, in this one we divided the stage four respondents according to the character and intensity of their participation in Nazi activities (FD-45).[1] The breakdown can be read as given or in overlapping

FD-45: Stage Four: Participation in Nazi Activities

	Number	Per cent
Mere members or sympathizers	154	26.4
Marching, demonstration, rallies, electioneering (M)	37	6.3
Marching, etc., and fighting (MF)	144	24.5
Marching and proselytizing (MP)	118	20.2
Secret proselytizing	13	2.2
Marching, fighting, proselytizing (MFP)	111	19.0
Political provocation	8	1.4
	585*	100.0

* Multiple entries.

[1] Although Abel specified party membership as a condition for the essay contest, 11 respondents give no evidence of actually having joined the party.

categories. If we add up all the respondents engaged in demonstrations, for example, no fewer than 70% answer that description. Forty-three and five-tenths percent altogether were engaged in street fighting or meeting-hall brawls. However, it seems more useful instead to work out the three combinations that are most typical of movements of this sort, marching and fighting (MF), marching and proselytizing (MP), and marching, fighting, and proselytizing (MFP). These groups need to be compared with each other and with the less violently engaged.

In arriving at stage four and the particular Nazi activity a respondent engaged in, how much difference did his antecedents make? Was a Nazi from an unpolitical military-civil service past likely to be more violent than one from an unpolitical farmer of stage one? The most violent (MF and MFP) were those young respondents from a pre-political parochial (youth) or unpolitical youth group (59.3 and 52.1%, respectively) setting. The least violent were the members of the pre-war parties (19.5%), probably because of their age. The unpolitical traditionals and unpolitical military-civil servants compensated for their underinvolvement in violence by more engagement in proselytizing (25-29%).

As for stage two, the largest percentage of violent Nazis (76.5% MF and MFP) came from former members of *Wehrwolf, Oberland, Brigade Ehrhardt*, and the like, followed by former Free Corps, anti-Polish, and anti-occupation fighters (56.6%). All the other stage-two groups contributed between 40 and 49% Nazi fighters. The combination of proselytizers (MPs and MFPs) of stage four was supplied best by former *Jungdo*, pre-1925 NSDAP or *voelkisch* groups, *Stahlhelm*, and *Wehrwolf* members (47-54%). The contribution of stage-two respondents to the violence, but not to the proselytizing, appears to have been far greater than that of stage three. From the stage of politicization, the largest percentage of fighters were former members of moderate political parties (50%), followed by members of the pre-1925 NSDAP and *voelkisch* groups (45%). The rest of the stage-three groups contributed no more than between 31 and 37%. Fifty-eight and eight-tenths percent of the pre-1925 Nazis and *voelkisch* members were proselytizers, while the moderate and conservative party members and those distrustful of all parties engaged only to 40-42% in proselytizing.

The Mere Members

There are some basic divisions among these groups regarding their ages and geographical origin. As we would expect, the mere members are substantially older (only 11.9% born after 1901) than the marchers (M), marcher-fighters (MF), or the marcher-fighter-proselytizers (MFP) (54, 56.3, and 45%, respectively, born after 1901), but not much older than the marcher-proselytizers (MP) (only 26% born after 1901). It would appear that the last-mentioned group was just as zealous about its contribution to the cause but perhaps less suitable for organized violence for reasons of age. During the crucial fighting period also, it is worth noting that the two older groups lived predominantly in Berlin and, in the case of the MPs, also as farmers in rural areas. The Ms and MFs, by contrast, were more often in other metropolitan areas and, together with the MFPs, in small and medium-sized towns (up to 40%). By occupation, the two older groups are often (up to 30%) military-civil servants and include quite a few women. The younger Ms, MFs, and MFPs are mostly blue- and white-collar workers or with business and the professions.

Apart from their age, the mere membership group can be characterized as follows. They were the sons of military-civil servants (30.2%), including some of high standing, artisans and businessmen (35.3%), and farmers (21.8%). They often had come in but recently from a rural background in a Protestant area. The fathers were often of moderate political persuasion, or militarist-authoritarian, or nationalist. Unlike many of the other groups, the mere members tended to join the party only after it had become at least a substantial minority in their localities, that is to say, mostly after the middle of 1930. They were enthusiastic soldiers and the *Fronterlebnis* meant a great deal to them. Neither the defeat, the cultural shock, nor the revolution elicited much of a distinctive response from them except that they blamed the revolution particularly on the Jews. They participated little in 1923 or in any stage-two organizations except for the vigilantes. In stage three, they chiefly tended to follow the DNVP, shop around among the parties, or evince distrust of all parties. At the time they joined the post-1924 NSDAP, over 60% of them were already over 35, and 31.2% in fact over 45 years of age. Their chief reasons for joining were economic troubles, police and governmental repression, and the dynamic impression of the Hitler movement. Their objections to the Weimar Republic were the traditional criticisms of capitalism, the image of a Jewish-controlled system, and the multi-party state.

The Marcher-Proselytizers (MP)

The marcher-proselytizers (MP) had mostly farmers (28.2%), independent businessmen (16.5%), or workers (26.2%) as fathers. In fact, many of them had but recently risen from a farm background (21.2%). Parental politics were often moderate, as was the school environment. They frequently had to work before the age of 14 or perform unskilled labor instead of learning a trade. When they joined the party, often between 1928 and 1930, unusual numbers of them were the founders or co-founders (42.2%) of the local, or at least part of the first nucleus (20.6%). Their reaction to the war was one of enthusiastic service and great appreciation for the *Fronterlebnis*. Their sense of cultural shock emphasized especially the fall of the monarchy and the old symbols, and secondly the absence of order and discipline. The civilians, the Kaiser, and international Bolshevism bore the blame for Germany's defeat, and the latter was also blamed for the revolution, along with the Weimar leaders. Many of the MPs report having been in *voelkisch* parties or having at least sympathized with the beer-hall *putsch* of 1923 (31.3%). Some were in the *Stahlhelm*. Their ages upon joining the post-1924 NSDAP were comparable to those of the mere members. Their most pronounced reasons for joining were the dynamic impression of the movement (30.9%), the rough opposition of the Marxist (7.4%), and their ideological fervor (47.5%). Most of the older examples of the preceding chapter were MPs.

The Marchers and Electioneers (M)

The group that engaged only in demonstrations, electioneering, and rallies (M) resided in large numbers in the countryside (35.1%) and in large cities (24.3%) other than Berlin. By occupation, many were blue-collar workers (28.9%), business and professional people (18.4%), or farmers (10.5%). There were also many women in this group. Their fathers were often military or professional people of high standing. The social mix of high and low of the Ms also accounts for their view of *Volksgemeinschaft* from an upper or lower class, rather than the prevailing middle-class angle, as well as for their relatively high level of education. Their home environment tended to be nationalistic, their school environment more of moderate political coloration. They joined the party only when it had become a substantial minority locally, generally after August of 1929. Their reaction to the war included a good deal of disaffection after initial enthusiasm (26.9%) as well as significant numbers impressed by the *Fronterlebnis*, or marked by captivity or injury suffered (15.4%). They tended to feel that moral disintegration had occurred in German postwar society and blamed the civilians and the Kaiser for the German defeat, about which many felt sadness or rage (33.3%). The revolution they blamed on unspecified rabble, on international Bolshevism, and on the new Weimar leadership.

In the postwar years 1919 to 1921, the Ms consequently joined conservative or bourgeois opposition groups, *voelkisch* groups including the Nazis, and republican or Communist outfits. In 1923, many (19.4%) participated in or sympathized with the beer-hall *putsch* in Munich or were in other, legitimate political parties. Their participation in stage-two activities was rather limited except for some Free Corps activity. In stage three, they stood out only with shopping around among the parties or in joining the DNVP. When they entered stage four, 21.6% of them were under 21 and 40.5% under 25 years old. Their most prominent reasons for joining were the spirit of camaraderie among the stormtroopers, police and governmental repression, and the dynamic impression of the Hitler movement. Although their involvement did not go beyond marching, as far as we can tell, it would seem that the behavioral dynamics of such marching tended to point toward heavier involvements, such as MF or MFP, in their future.

Some Examples of Marchers

Here are some examples of marchers, demonstrators, and devotees of political rallies. A young *Wandervogel* enthusiast born in 1909 (no. 405) tells of his weekend wanderings from one youth hostel to the other, a knapsack on his back, flying a black-white-and-red pennant, and singing a marching song.

> We were often thrown out by the youth hostel keeper because we allegedly provoked the Socialist Workers Youth (SAJ) with their black-red-yellow[2] and red rags. One day I also heard of Adolf Hitler. I liked his battle against the government of the day and especially against the Jews; and when I read *Mein Kampf*, I became a most enthusiastic antisemite. I frequently went to meetings of the *voelkisch-sozialer Block* and joined the youth affiliate of this movement in 1926.

As the NSDAP grew apace in his area, he joined the stormtroopers at the age of 18 and participated in all the marches, rallies, and propaganda campaigns. He loved the big rallies and the grandiose annual *Reichsparteitag*, and reports with pride that he served for two years as a drum major with the SA marching band. He felt deeply honored when, although he was barely 24, he received the

[2] The substitution of yellow for gold in the description of the Weimar flag was a common antisemitic slur against the republic.

golden commemorative medal on the Day of the Old Guard in 1934.

Another respondent, a carpenter's son and young worker, born 1904 (no. 399), was repeatedly unemployed in the early half of the 1920s. He married in 1927 and had two children, but his marriage ended in divorce owing to his wife's unfaithfulness. "In my desperate situation I was thrown into the arms of the Communist party. That was in 1929, for my wife was always cheating on me. Injustices on the job and elsewhere in life and the great poverty of many of my comrades drove me into political activity." He felt that the Social Democratic leaders were hypocrites living well above the scarce means of their followers. The KPD turned out to be another disappointment for him. He accuses its leaders of empty promises and of "having like cowards gone abroad." After two years, presumably in 1931, he became acquainted with the NSDAP and was favorably impressed by its spirit of solidarity and patriotism. "My decision could only be to make up to my German brothers for having fought them in the past. My innermost feelings drove me into the SA."

Another respondent is an Austrian-born borderland German born in 1898 (no. 400) who tells of bloody brawls between Czech and German youngsters in his childhood. He bitterly reports the defection of Czech and Slovak regiments in mid-1918 and the cession of the Sudetenland to the CSR. The Sudeten German *Volkswehr* in which he had fought in 1919 was dissolved and its members sought out and persecuted. He fled to Germany just ahead of a six-year prison sentence. In Germany, he became active and held office in the trade unions, but was rather disillusioned by the empty promises of the Weimar governments. He joined the Independent Socialists (USPD) in 1922 and the KPD for half a year in 1923 until he "noticed that its leaders were non-working Jews." Then he attended meetings of the *Deutsch-voelkische Freiheitspartei* but was not particularly impressed by it. When Hitler rebuilt his party in 1925, however, the respondent joined immediately and served as a stormtrooper through thick and thin, going to jail and losing his job, among other sacrifices. His attitude was characterized by a strong cult of leadership.

Another marcher was the son of a rural-urban migrant from East Prussia, born 1910 (no. 375), who describes his childhood locale in Berlin as follows: "We lived in a street popularly called New Jerusalem because many Jews lived there. Here as elsewhere, poison was brewed and distributed and our children's souls had no idea. The war was over. The soldiers returned home, cheated of all those years and enormous sacrifices by people incapable of feeling or thinking German." The respondent describes his childish glee while observing how the medals and stripes were ripped off the soldiers' uniforms by revolutionaries—until his father, too, returned and set him straight on the matter. His parents joined the DNVP and took him to many DNVP meetings.

In 1926, the respondent joined a nationalistic gymnasts' association (*Turnerbund*) and there met a stormtrooper who must have left a deep impression on him. For there ensued arguments at school when he began to propagandize for the movement without belonging to it.

> I had a poetic vein and attached some verses on the movement—I regarded myself already as a follower—to classroom blackboards. . . . In 1927 we were beaten up badly on a trip when we were singing Nazi fighting songs and wearing swastika pins. . . . Unfortunately I was rather on the short side and my parents always succeeded in dissuading me from becoming a stormtrooper.

He joined the party only in 1929 and claims that his apprenticeship would not permit him to join the SA. Nevertheless, he participated in many demonstrations and rallies. "Now the final years of the struggle against the November system started which we had to destroy with every trick and artful chicanery, if our whole people was not to perish hopelessly in immense chaos. . . ." In 1933, he comments, the leaders of the enemy fled abroad, leaving their followers in the lurch. "We were not interested in staging another bloody revolution like the one of 1918. Our revolution was to be one of leading men back to the people and to themselves. There were still a few who openly opposed us, but they soon were taught some sense at an appropriate place." After this reference to the Nazi terror of 1933, the poet goes on to describe how the movement hoped to brainwash the rest of the people, now that it had won power.

There are many others who, like another young respondent, born 1913 (no. 397), were taken in by the sight of the stormtroopers singing and marching: "The uniforms and the flags! What stouthearted fellows!" They joined at a tender age, 16 in this case, very eager to march along with the SA.

The Marcher-Fighters (MF)

The marcher-fighters were obviously more advanced in revolutionary consciousness although they were the youngest of all the groups. MFs were often from the French-occupied areas (31.3%) and included many highly mobile people, mostly from middle-sized towns and metropoles other than Berlin. Large numbers among them were blue- (45.8%) or white-collar (19.7%) workers, or farmers (9.9%). Their fathers had been workers (25.9%), artisans (22.3%), or military-civil servants (17%). Half of their families had made no attempt to rise and an unusual number (16.5%) were in social decline. Of the few upwardly mobile, only those rising from the city proletariat stand out (24.8%). A fair number exhibit no class consciousness or solidarism (27.6%), while others are solidaristic only from nationalistic experiences (13.3%), such as the *Fronterlebnis* or the struggle against the occupation. In areas of mixed religion or dominated by a majority of another religion, the MFs are significantly more numerous than those living among their coreligionists.[3] They tended to join the NSDAP only when it had become a substantial minority in their area. In the war, they were enthusiastic soldiers with some animosity toward civilians and draft-dodgers, and, like the Ms, a disproportionate share (one-fourth) of war invalids and POWs, who may well have felt particular ire at the disparagement of military honor after the war. Like the Ms, also (but not the MFPs), the MFs report little in the way of cultural shock at the big change of 1919 although, again like the Ms, they felt great sadness or rage at the German defeat (31.9%). For the revolution, they blamed "the rabble" or the Western powers, international Bolshevism, or the Jews.

Fifty-five and four-tenths percent of them, indeed, were already either marching or engaged in organized violence in the first five years of the republic. In stage two, they were with the Free Corps and the *Buergerwehr*, and in *Wehrwolf* type organizations. In 1923, many were involved in anti-occupation activity or were members of militant veterans' or *voelkisch* groups. In stage three, many were distrustful of parties or just shopping around, or actually in republican parties. Half of them were under 25 and a fourth under 21 when they joined the NSDAP. The reasons for their joining were the stormtroopers' spirit of comradeship, unemployment, and clashes with the occupation or with the Communists. The dates of their joining cluster around two points, the period of 1925 to 1927 (27.3%) and that following the 1930 elections which brought a lot

[3] In a country with considerable religious strife and prejudices, violence is evidently related highly to minority feelings of discrimination. The entire sample divided 26.8% to 19.8% into religious majority and minority area respondents, while the MFs did so 17.6% to 23.9% and the MFPs 18.4% to 22.3%.

of old war-horses into the NSDAP. During the height of the battle in 1931-1932, indeed, the MFs were by far the most violent group (76.2%) in the NSDAP.[4] Their perception of the Weimar Republic tells much about their mental make-up. Thirty-three percent stress that Marxists were "running the republic," with overtones of longing for deliverance. Another 10.7% stand out for raising the traditional objections to Weimar capitalism.

The outstanding characteristic of the marcher-fighters, next to their awesome bent for violence, was their almost complete failure to engage in the other essential activity of an extremist movement, proselytizing. As Table IV-6 shows clearly, they did far less proselytizing than either the MPs or the MFPs. Were they the mindless sluggers of the movement? Let us take a closer look at their ideology and attitudes.

Table IV-6: Demonstrations, Violence and Proselytizing, 1919-1932
(in % of MFs, MPs, and MFPs)

		1919-1924	1925-1928	1929-1930	1931-1932
MFs	Demonstrations	16.0	16.8	15.6	13.9
	Violence	39.4	35.3	58.5	76.4
	Proselytizing	6.4	3.4	4.8	8.5
Totals		61.8	55.5	78.9	98.8
MPs	Demonstrations	12.1	9.0	19.2	20.6
	Violence	15.9	4.1	9.0	9.7
	Proselytizing	17.8	25.4	44.9	62.9
Totals		45.8	38.5	73.1	93.2
MFPs	Demonstrations	26.7	21.9	23.7	26.2
	Violence	18.8	23.9	30.6	32.1
	Proselytizing	16.8	26.3	37.6	41.2
Totals		62.3	72.1	91.9	99.5

Ideology of MFs, MPs, and MFPs

The MFs differ pronouncedly from the MPs and MFPs in their dominant ideological motifs. The latter two tend to emphasize anti-semitism, the Nordic-German cult, and the *Volksgemeinschaft*. The MFs, by way of contrast, emphasize the Hitler cult, revanchism,

[4] With 39.4% engaged in violence in 1919-1924, 35.3% in the quiet years of 1925-1928, 58.5% in 1929-1930, and 76.2% in 1931-1932, the MFs were on the average twice as violent as the MFPs.

and superpatriotism. They are evidently, in spite of their youth,[5] a kind of missing link to the violent nationalistic and counter-revolutionary strains of the immediate postwar era and 1923. Their hate-lists, as compared to those of the other two groups, tend to be either the all-embracing kind or simply anti-Communist and anti-Socialist. They also felt a lively hatred for the police and the government. The MFPs likewise stressed their anti-Marxism, while the MPs instead tended to pillory the "reactionaries" and the Jews. On the antisemitism scale, indeed, the MFs (and also the Ms) were the least prejudiced, with 38.8% giving no evidence of bias and another 19.4% engaging only in mild verbal projections. A good third of the MPs, by comparison, were suffering from *Judenkoller* and, like the MFPs, about one-eighth indulging in personal antisemitic anecdotes. The MFPs, furthermore, stand out with an unusual number (23%) of persons who speak of conspiracies and hint at threats and counterthreats. Aside from their antisemitism, the MFs (and Ms) show relatively less ethnocentricity than the other groups except for a pronounced phobia against aliens in Germany. The MPs and MFPs are more preoccupied with the hostility and alleged inferiority of foreign nations in general.

There is further evidence that the MFs were merely the foot-soldiers of the movement who, for reasons of their own, did the dirty work. Seventy and four-tenths percent of the MFs held no office in the Nazi party, in striking contrast to the MPs and MFPs, of whom two-thirds and three-fourths, respectively, were in party offices. The MFPs, in particular, held more than their share of higher offices and special functions. On the other hand, the MFs had the highest percentage of respondents who immediately joined the SA stormtroopers (69.7%) and of those who graduated to the SS (14.2%). Nearly three-fourths of the MPs were in neither the SA nor the SS. The MFPs came close to the high involvement of the MFs, but tended to join the stormtroopers a year or more after they had entered the NSDAP. The MFs consequently held a lot of offices in the SA or SS, more than the MFPs, but they tended to be the lower offices of *Truppfuehrer*, or *Rottenfuehrer*. The MFPs held just as many of the higher offices, such as *Sturmfuehrer* or *Sturmbannfuehrer*, and in addition a number of special organizing functions.

Although the MFPs held as many or more SA and SS offices, the MFs did far more of the fighting in streets and meeting-halls. Only

[5] Half of them joined the post-1924 NSDAP at the age of 25 or younger, and 70.9% joined it before they had passed the age of 30. This contrasts with 36.7% of the MPs, 59.4% of the Ms, and 65.7% of the MFPs who joined before they were past 30.

in the most intense category, campaigning and fighting "day and night" in 1932, did the MFPs clearly have the edge over the MFs. We get the impression that even in political violence there was some stratification which assigned the common or garden variety of violence in quantity to the MFs, while the MFPs are involved in a more rarefied way. To begin with, their concern with ideology and proselytizing makes them far from mindless, rather men "with malice aforethought." They also tend to join the party first and warm up to the stormtrooper role later. This makes their "day and night" fighting something of a climax of their extremist career, rather than just an increase in quantity of the same mindless slugging that seems to have attracted them to the MFs to begin with.

Their attitudes toward their political enemies add further depth to this insight. The MFs tended to see them with the eyes of the *outré*, and to calling them subhuman, rodents, etc., more often than the MFPs. The MFs also often betray their instinct for physical aggression toward them or refer to them as traitors or as an abstract conspiracy. By contrast, 45.3% of the MFPs and 63% of the MPs (cf. 29.1% of MFs) express a liking toward the enemies and a desire to win them over. Curiously, the attitude of the MFs toward violence tended to be masochistic and self-pitying as compared to the sadistic MFP bullies. Evidently, concern with ideological rationalizations and with proselytizing is an effective way of assuaging any guilt feelings that may be associated with breaking the societal taboo against violence.

In view of this record, it is hardly surprising that the MFs derived their greatest satisfaction in the movement from the struggle itself and from the Hitler cult. The MFPs instead stressed the classless comradeship and, less strongly, the struggle and the satisfactions of striving for utopia. This utopian consciousness was quite dominant among the MPs although they also appreciate the classless comradeship of the movement. In this connection, it is worth juxtaposing all these satisfactions of Nazi membership to the grosser one of expecting a job or promotion as a reward. The latter expectation, interestingly enough, was highest among the mere Nazi members (about 10%) and lowest among the Ms, MPs, and MFPs (2-5%). The MFs included 8% with this expectation who evidently believed that they were entitled to something like a pension for their pains. To them, apparently, utopia was not enough.

Personalities of MFs, MPs, and MFPs Compared

What were the formative experiences in the lives of the MFs, as compared to the other groups? They seemed to be the experience of youthful comradeship and educational or literary influences, two experiences the MFPs tended to share. Many MFs also were deeply impressed by an experience of social humiliation or unemployment and so were many MPs. Otherwise, the MPs tend to have been formed by the war and its aftermath. Many MFPs also projected alleged episodes with Jews or aliens as their formative experiences, whch may well be a reflection of their ideological preoccupation.

If we ask ourselves what is oddest about each of the cases, the MFs stand out with disproportionate numbers of very insecure, self-pitying respondents and, like the MFPs, with many who seem to have had a great desire to merge their individuality with the movement (group conformists). The MFPs also have more than their share of persons with an extreme case of leadership cult. The MPs, on the other hand, include disproportionate numbers of respondents who suffered high cultural shock or exhibited extremes of irrationality or paranoia. There are indeed many MFs who were possessed of a low ideological kind of understanding of politics or who were political dimwits or hold a romantic view of politics. The MFPs and MPs, in this order, were considerably more perceptive in their grasp of Weimar politics.

In their personal lives, too, the groups differ markedly. The MPs, for example, tend to have their families and especially their spouses in the NSDAP, too. The MFPs often have the whole family in the party, a sign of the penetration of family life and marriages by the Nazi virus. The MFs, by contrast, seem to be loners, for their family involvement lags far behind the other groups. This is also the impression we get from their patterns of political friction. The MPs stand out for friction on the job, at their business, and in their neighborhood, and the MFPs for friction at school, in the family, or at home. The MFs, by comparison, in disproportionate numbers report having been fired or boycotted (economic suicide) or having gone out of their way to seek out friction. While these locales can also be found to a lesser extent among the MFPs, their very nature suggests a lack of social integration.

Here are some more or less typical MF cases. One is an illegitimate child, born in 1903 and raised by grandparents (no. 490), who had to work as a teenage dockworker to support them. He was pressured to join the union and, when he refused, life became difficult for him on the job. So he quit and volunteered instead in 1919 for the border protection units of the *Reichswehr* which sent him to various places for action. When he returned to civilian life in 1924, again he encountered Communists and Socialists dominant in most employment situations, which greatly offended his patriotic soul.

> The decisive change in my political view of the world occurred in 1932 after several NSDAP rallies when I met my current *Obersturmfuehrer* [with the same name as respondent] at work, who had long served in the SS. This man got me so enthusiastic about the goals of the *Fuehrer* that I joined without hesitation. After an overwhelming rally in May 1932 I joined both the party and the SS in order to contribute to the realization of the ideals and goals of the *Fuehrer*.

The respondent had evidently found the father substitute he was looking for. "There ensued a time of plenty of battles and sacrifices. We dropped everything and rushed into the fray, taking the gaff and insults of the reds. They never had the guts to attack us few comrades physically. But I shall always remember the wonderful times when we broke up many an opposition rally or demonstration and chased them away."

Another young respondent, born 1907 (no. 488), witnessed at close hand the suppression of the Ruhr uprising of 1920 by the Free Corps Epp and the French occupation of 1923, which was rather painful to him and his family. He emerged with a deep-seated hatred for the French and a strong aversion to the reds and the republican parties. Expelled to Kassel by the occupation, the respondent immediately joined the *voelkisch Jungsturm*, which offered him *voelkisch* indoctrination and military training. Years later, while studying agriculture, he became an agricultural trainee under another *Jungsturm* leader and rejoined. His new youth group, however, fell under the spell of an old Free Corps fighter who indoctrinated the boys and their leader with National Socialism. The entire group joined the stormtroopers in August of 1930.

> And then we former *Jungsturm* men worked untiringly under and for the swastika banner. In rain or shine, with or without a speaker, we went into the villages every Sunday to make propaganda. From here many an SA *Trupp* and base and many an NSDAP local were started. I really hated to leave Prechtau when I changed jobs and went to Dortmund. Here I joined the SS and liked the service in it even better. It was harder, full of responsibility, and more dangerous, especially in the red industrial center where I did all kinds of things for the SS.

Another respondent, born in 1910 (no. 480), an East Prussian dentist's apprentice and the son of a long line of peasants and country teachers, fancied himself the descendant of the fighting Knights of the German Order. He relates how his father had to make the school available to political meetings which turned out to be "mostly Marxist and for preaching wild tirades of hatred to rile up the agricultural workers against the lords of their estates. If they don't yield to your demands, class-conscious workers, string them up at the nearest willow tree!" Although the respondent was only nine at the time, these experiences deeply impressed and politicized him.

His two older brothers showed an early political interest and read right-wing newspapers, periodicals, and books. They were being indoctrinated by a *voelkisch* secondary school teacher. Every Saturday night there were big discussions at home, which increasingly focused on the *voelkisch* movement and, inevitably, on Adolf Hitler. The respondent's brothers soon became active Nazis, distributed propaganda in the villages, and began to proselytize and campaign "all by themselves," for there was no NSDAP local there prior to 1928. The respondent, barely 17, attached a swastika pennant to his bicycle and soon became acquainted with a Nazi recruiter who stopped to talk to him and then insisted he join as soon as he turned 18. His brothers joined too, and so did a baker's apprentice, "a man who could meet any physical terror most forcefully, a good boxer, nimble and energetic." The respondent anticipated not only a lot of terror from the dominant Marxists in his town, but also scorn and derision from the right, presumably from the DNVP.

His first big rally, complete with the usual brawl, was staged in 1929 when there were only ten stormtroopers in the local. They had substantial reinforcements from two other places and stood up well to "superior red forces." The respondent's comments on the speaker, Erich Koch, who later became a prominent Nazi leader, are remarkable for their typically over-determined accents: "Erich Koch, by his passionate profession of faith in Adolf Hitler, gave me and my brothers the final commitment to and unconditional confidence in Hitler and his movement." One can sense behind the overstatement his desperate attempt to dedicate himself to a cause bigger than himself, whatever it might be.

The respondent participated in many demonstrations and propaganda campaigns, and considered the protection of Nazi meetings "his innermost duty." He depicts the nature of his idealistic, but obviously non-ideological commitment as follows:

A non-Nazi who has not experienced the enormous elementary power of the idea of our *Fuehrer* will never understand any of this. But let me tell these people as the deepest truth: Whenever I worked for the movement and applied myself for our Fuehrer, I always felt that there was nothing higher or nobler I could do for Adolf Hitler and thereby for Germany, our people and fatherland. . . .

When I say so little in this *vita* about *my external life*, my job, etc., this is only because *my real life*, the real content of my life is my work for and commitment to Hitler and toward a national socialist Germany. . . . Hitler is the purest embodiment of the German character, the purest embodiment of a national socialist Germany (italics supplied).

The respondent concludes with vignettes from his life as a storm-trooper. He relates how once, on the night before a rally, the news-papers were full of reports of a meeting-hall battle elsewhere in which the stormtroopers all ended up in the hospital with severe injuries, some in critical condition. The respondent slept badly and had dreams of violence. Mother cried but Father was proud to see the determination of the respondent and his brother, in spite of all forebodings, to go out and fight.

The respondent also relates his impressions when he first heard Hitler speak, and his elation at attending the *Reichsparteitag* of 1929 in Nuremberg where he also saw "the immortal hero of our movement, Horst Wessel." His father, who took in the respondent during his frequent interludes of unemployment, finally left the DNVP, which had made him a *Kreistag* deputy, and joined the NSDAP, just before dying.

Another respondent was a peasant's son, born in 1900 (no. 474), who served in the last months of the war and subsequently volun-teered for the Free Corps Epp. Between 1920, when the Free Corps was disbanded, and 1930, when he became a stormtrooper, he seems to have limited himself to his occupational life. He gives no clue as to his motivation for returning to the fighting just as he passed the symbolically significant age of 30. He tells about the difficulties of "us two young and not very articulate Nazis" in the midst of an "ex-tremely black [i.e., Catholic] community" in the rural Allgaeu where he was subjected to "every conceivable harassment."

He participated as a stormtrooper in all the demonstrations and propaganda campaigns of 1931-1932, and especially in Hitler's presidential campaign. In 1932 he joined the SS in his native village and there he was "beaten up but good a couple of times." The police, too, were repeatedly after him for "political offenses" and, therefore, he welcomed the amnesties of 1932 and 1933. He never tells us what contribution he made to these violent encounters ex-cept for a hint, on the occasion of the declining Nazi vote of November 1932. He went to an inn to listen to the election returns on the radio along with many "black" fellow-villagers. "I got a little excited because of our loss of votes and before long I got my due from the black brothers" who had already called him a super-Hitler when he came in. In a rural setting, somehow, such encounters seem not much different from the usual St. Martin's Day brawls.

Another respondent was a young carpenter, born in 1907 (no. 451), who professed great sympathy for the imprisoned Hitler of 1924. As soon as a Nazi local had been established in his area, "in spite of the repression of the French and the black-red-and-yellow men behind them," the respondent became a stormtrooper. He likes to dramatize the resistance of his "red" town to the blandishments of the Nazis.

> Only a man who fought side by side with me at the time can understand what it meant to be a stormtrooper in a Marxist strongpoint. If you were openly for Hitler, you were likely to be knocked down in the street and thrown in jail. Almost every Sunday or weekend, we went into the villages to take the flame to the people. When we old fighters undertook such a propaganda campaign, we were not sure whether we would ever see our families again. Wherever we went we encountered resistance and I took home many a smarting reminder.

With such a complete accounting of the hostility and violence shown to him, the respondent naturally saw no need to mention anything he had done.[6]

Another respondent, born in 1903, the sixth of a tailor's 12 children (no. 416), was an extreme devotee of Adolf Hitler. He lost two brothers in the war and grimly recalls months of living on a little bread and vegetables during the Allied hunger blockade. He also remembers incidents of venality of "Jewish" military supply and transport officials and working side by side with "draft-dodgers and labor agitators," which early made him an antisemite and anti-Marxist, he claims. His political education was intensified by the French "who with their black and yellow troops raped our girls and women, plundered our mines, cut down our woods, and outlawed our German convictions." The occupation jailed him at the age of 16 for undisclosed reasons.

In 1920, his superpatriotism led him to the *voelkisch Schutz-und-Trutzbund*. He first heard of Hitler in 1921, but was taken aback

---

[6] Other youthful respondents were less reluctant to communicate how they enjoyed "tanning the hides of the Moscow disciples." See no. 471, born 1915.

by the word "socialist" in NSDAP. In 1922, he and his *Schutz-und-Trutzbund* comrades, after a thorough study of the Nazi program, joined as one man. The respondent does not tell us how he fought the Marxists in 1923, but he mentions that the French kept locking him up or searching his parents' home about two to three times a week. He tangled with the separatists at one time in 1924 and emerged badly beaten up and in need of weeks of medical care.

In 1925 the respondent immediately rejoined the reconstructed NSDAP and SA and participated in many a meeting-hall battle in the following years. There are also glowing reports of the first time the respondent listened to Hitler and of an incident following this speech:

> When the *Fuehrer* left nobody knew what it was like in the streets. We were still listening to the echo of his wonderful words in ourselves when suddenly a shout went through the meeting place: Hitler is in danger! Everyone rushed out into the street. The Communists had broken through the police cordon and were attacking the car of the Fuehrer. Now we had to take action. We stormed out against the superior numbers of the Communists and they had to retreat. I had never before had the wonderful feeling of risking my life to protect my Fuehrer.

The respondent gloried in big demonstrations and rallies that showed the power of the movement; the bigger the better. "With renewed strength we went about storming the strongpoints of Marxism and enlightening the people. We were not interested in winning the votes of the people, but in recruiting fighters for Germany. The elections to me . . . were only a sign that the people are beginning to think. . . . Our comrades did not die to win elections, but to free our people of Marxism and reaction. . . ." The respondent believed that Hitler was appointed Chancellor in 1933 in order to forestall an imminent Communist uprising.

Another respondent, born 1905 (no. 415), grew up in grinding poverty and was obsessed with worry about his family's livelihood. His reading of historical books and the experience of occupation and separatism inclined the respondent to a *voelkisch* view.[7] In

---

[7] See also no. 142 (born 1903), another respondent whose conflict with the occupation led him to found his own SA under a cover name (*Bluemchen*). He also combined a long list of injuries and punishments with a love of big rallies and battles where he could "prove my faith to our people and Fuehrer Adolf Hitler . . . it was indescribable with how much joy we attacked the red beasts." A similar case is no. 411 (born

1926 he joined the party, together with two brothers. His description of his trials and tribulations abounds with masochistic verbiage. But he also tells in some detail of the great stormtrooper demonstration and following meeting-hall battle in Idar-Oberstein. The approximately 400 stormtroopers had already been attacked sporadically if bloodily during the demonstration.

> One after the other, our four speakers had their say, interrupted by furious howling and catcalls. But when, in the ensuing discussion, an interlocutor was reprimanded for saying, "We don't want the brown pest in our beautiful town," tumult broke out. There followed a battle with beer steins, chairs, and the like, and in two minutes the hall was demolished and everyone cleared out. We had to take back seven heavily injured comrades that day and there were rocks thrown at us and occasional assaults in spite of the police protection.

According to the respondent, this encounter was typical of others and there were some 400 dead and thousands of injured Nazis by 1933.[8] His capacity for feeling persecuted, however, was not exhausted with the Nazi takeover. He describes the "18 months of blessed reconstruction and rebirth of the German people" until he turned in his *vita* in August 1934 as follows:

> One would never have believed that anyone could dare to disturb the peace in Germany. We expected the struggles in our souls caused by the fight of the foreign countries against us and the boycott of German goods by a Jewish campaign . . . but the whole German people, which stood solidly behind Adolf Hitler, simply could not believe the treason of the unfaithful of June 30, 1934. It was particularly incredible that some of the oldest fighting comrades of Adolf Hitler would break the faith. With his customary and heroic activism, the Fuehrer intervened like a man and stopped the treason. Again the German people was freed from a danger so great it boggles the imagination.

There are many similar testimonials to the Roehm purge in other Abel *vitae*, all worthy of the testimonials at the Moscow purge trials of about the same time.

Our last case of a marcher-fighter is the son of a painter born in 1901 (no. 408) who was already in military auxiliaries like *Jugend-*

1902), also an occupation-motivated bully who relished beating up his opponents.

[8] See also the Severing memorandum reprinted by Gotthard Jasper in the *Vierteljahreshefte fuer Zeitgeschichte*, vol. 8 (1960), 280-289 on the political violence and the number of casualties.

wehr at the age of 7 and in 1914 tried to play soldier at the front together with a buddy until an officer spotted them after a week and sent them home. He describes the immediate postwar period movingly but quite inaccurately as "a chaos, with traitors, rabble, and scoundrels carrying on . . . and the SPD and KPD regime completely corrupting German morals." Like some of the other occupation fighters, he gleefully recalls the rout of the separatists in 1924 in Pirmasens. His flight to the other shore of the Rhine took him directly into the *voelkisch-sozialer Block* and from there to the NSDAP. Like several other Abel respondents, he belonged to the notorious Pirmasens stormtroopers "who acquired a reputation for always thoroughly cleaning up at meeting-hall battles and other brawls." They were sent all over the southwest, including to the previously mentioned rally in Idar-Oberstein where "Dr. Ley ordered us to disarm the police and gendarmerie."

The respondent's fondest recollection is of a 1930 street battle in Pirmasens, "a red strongpoint, where we really settled accounts with the Communist rabble." He also glories in other battles in 1932, including one which resulted "in a beautiful postlude in court. We were accused of murder and of disturbing the peace. The coming revolution fortunately got us off or we would not have gotten out of jail so soon."

The Marcher-Fighter-Proselytizers (MFP)

The last of the larger groups, the marcher-fighter-proselytizers (MFP), is the epitome of the Nazi storm against the established authorities. By origin heavily from highly mobile strata or rural-urban migrants, they were living mainly in medium-sized towns of 2,000 to 100,000 residents (40.5%). By occupation, business and professional people (18%), blue- and white-collar workers (48.6%), and military-civil servants (22.5%) stand out among them. Military-civil service (19.6%) and artisans (20.7%) predominate among the occupations of their fathers. There are many respondents who were upwardly mobile (41.8%), especially up from the city proletariat by means of a better education. Yet no other group was as hard hit by unemployment or bankruptcy before 1928 (22.5%) and even more during the depression (38.3%).[9] There is a parallel here for the social dynamics of revolution as many historians and social scientists from Crane Brinton to James C. Davies and Ted Gurr have explained them.

[9] The averages for the entire sample are 16.2% before and 25.6% after 1928.

This was also the sprouting dragon-seed of the last years of the war. Due to their youth, 55.6% of the MFPs, 67.6% of the Ms, and 58.9% of the MFs saw no military service at all. Dispropor-tionate numbers (17.9%) of the MFPs viewed the war with dis-affection after initial enthusiasm, but also with hostility toward the civilians and shirkers (22.4%) who would not "stick it out." They tended to blame the defeat on international Bolshevism. Many were youthful "victory watchers" (26.9%). Their fathers were often militaristic, *voelkisch*, or unpolitical, and their school environment was disproportionately reported as *voelkisch*, or nationalistic. They frequently had to go to work before they were 14 years old (11.7%) which adds deprivation and hard luck to the seeds of militarism and antisemitism. Their cultural shock of 1919 was expressed mostly in the form of objections to "moral disintegration" and the absence of order and discipline, arguments which must have had a propa-gandistic meaning to these young people different from what their elders were referring to. The MFPs, like the older zealots of the MPs, also mention the Jews and the power of the press in this con-nection. They furthermore show strong feelings about the French occupation (44.4%) and many of them (19.4%) report having been expelled from the occupied areas for their part in the passive resistance of 1923.

Nearly half of them were pre-political parochials in stage one. In stage two, the MFPs were highly involved in such groups as *Wehr-wolf* (12.7%), the bourgeois and left-wing opposition to the repub-lic (8.2%), *Stahlhelm* (11.8%), *voelkisch* action groups (15.5%), and the Free Corps (12.7%). In stage three they were in the *voel-kisch* groups, including the early NSDAP (23.4%), as well as in the DNVP (9%) and in moderate parties (11.7%). In 1923, too, they were more involved than the other young groups, the Ms and MFs, in particular in militant veterans' groups (11.9%), other legitimate parties (17.4%), and participating in or sympathizing with the beer-hall *putsch* in Munich (20.2%). It is difficult to escape the conclusion that, unlike most other groups, the MFPs were political activists throughout the fourteen years of the unhappy republic.

When they finally joined the NSDAP, they stand out among those that founded or co-founded local organizations (41.2%) or at least were a part of the first nucleus in their locality (20.6%) in proportions rivalled only by the older zealots, the MPs. In fact, by mid-1929 60.5% of the MFPs are already in the party. Forty-two and three-tenths percent of them were at the time under 25, and 65.7% under 30 years of age. They were attracted chiefly by the stormtroopers' comradeship (12.1%) and driven to join by their own ideological fervor (45.4%).

A Few Examples of Marcher-Fighter-Proselytizers

Since the MFPs embody all the essential qualities of an effective member of an extremist movement, there is a special quality about many of the *vitae*, be they long or short. We shall attempt to give a complete picture of their essentials. Further cases of MFPs appear in the next chapter on the young Nazis. A good example is a young carpenter, born in 1908, the son of a bricklayer (no. 409), who tells how during his apprenticeship he met and joined some young people who liked to go on "marching exercises into the environs every weekend singing soldiers' songs." The respondent was 17 and greatly enthusiastic about the spirit of comradeship in this group. He "really liked the wonderful romantic life in nature," especially camping overnight. During these camping trips two older comrades who were already with the SS indoctrinated the boys with national socialism. "As soon as we had more or less mastered the basic ideas, they took us to NSDAP meetings. We got to know the faults of the other parties and the great idea of our Fuehrer and thus became political soldiers of the movement." In 1926 and part of 1927 the respondent served as a stormtrooper without having joined the party. Finally he was officially enrolled and began proselytizing:

> And so we were forever trying to recruit new members for our idea, which was particularly difficult because of the French occupation of the Palatinate. But we were not to be discouraged. We fought on with redoubled effort which soon bore fruits in the growth of the SA, despite some setbacks. . . .
> We were not spared brawls with people of different conviction and there was often a court trial afterwards. As our *Sturm* grew enough to be divided, we looked for a new hangout in the reddest part of town, in fact quite close to the Communist headquarters. . . . Since the Communists were so close there were often massive clashes, and we were exposed to many a danger.[10]

This technique of seeking confrontations with the Communists was evidently copied from Goebbels' effective approach to the "conquest of Berlin." The respondent concludes with the thought that he cannot go into details about his six years of life as a stormtrooper because "there would be no end to it."

The attention of the Nazis to recruiting youths was a fairly com-

---

[10] See also no. 451 (born 1907) another MFP of a similar nature.

mon device. In fact, we have a case of such a recruiter in the same area, born perhaps 1902 (no. 413), who in 1923 ran a *voelkisch* youth group, *Sturmvogel*, for the "religious and patriotic education of youth." He became a Nazi in 1925 and took over the youth section of the party which he later turned into the Hitler Youth. He believed in the Nordic-Germanic line and in Hitler and knew how to treat youth to the Youth Movement atmosphere of hikes and "rap" sessions (*Heimabende*) while discreetly proselytizing for the cause. He also engaged in some fighting during the big push and received his share of bruises and injuries as he continued to play the role of the pied piper: "Here we went, a small handful of German youths marching through need and misery, in faithful comradeship. . . . Neither hunger nor need, nor even feelings of depression could stop us."

Another young man, the son of a Bavarian mail coachman, born 1909 (no. 481), and a gardener by trade, met a stormtrooper at work who told him all about the movement. In 1929, attending an agricultural college in another town, the respondent discovered that his roommate was a Nazi:

> We looked at each other in amazement, each saying to the other: Why didn't you tell me sooner you were a "Hitler." It was not so easy in those days. The school had forbidden it and many were a little afraid. Now we were both delighted and, at the next party meeting, I was enrolled. . . . I became a stormtrooper; there were only twelve of us. It was embarrassing for me at school to go to my daily SA service. I had to wear a coat over the uniform and put the cap in my pocket. . . .
>
> Soon we had a rally . . . with SPD and Communists filling the hall and I experienced one of the first meeting-hall battles. But everything went well. *The second battle came out a lot better.* Strasser was supposed to come . . . instead all hell broke loose. There was not one of us who did not get it with a chair or a beer stein. Our *Sturmfuehrer* got it the worst; he had a couple of stab wounds. (italics supplied)
>
> Then we had a big demonstration in Munich which was something new for me. People insulted us, even spat out in front of us. The women were the worst. They even dared to grab us by the brown shirts. In some streets there were brawls; and I got something on my foot. On the way home we were full of joy, having gotten off as well as we did. Our slogan through cities and villages was always "Germany awake!"

The respondent goes on to describe other big demonstrations, on foot and by truck, apropos of the 1929 campaign against the Young Plan. He transferred to another town and reports a lot of friction with Bavarian Center party (BVP) members on the job there. He had joined the SS meanwhile and, in spite of threats to fire him, recruited a number of his young assistants for the SA and SS.

> Then came a big meeting where a DDP representative spoke . . . we went there too, of course. We only wanted to break it up, which we succeeded in doing. Our local leader really would have liked to speak there but they would not let him. In a short while, chairs and steins, etc., began to fly and a huge battle developed in the beer garden. The police attacked us with drawn sabers and several of us were severely injured, including a Hitler Youth member. The whole town was in an uproar. They were going to storm our party hangout but we were prepared with mallets and the like . . . then we were outlawed but went right on serving the cause.

In 1932, finally, the respondent was fired for his political activity and went home, feeling sorry for himself. He refers to the Nazi takeover as "the revolution" and ends with assurances that he will always fight on to the death for his Fuehrer.

As with the MPs, particular interest is aroused by MFPs with a Communist background. We have a couple of which the wife (no. 390) reports that her husband, no. 391 (born perhaps in 1903), used to be in the KPD in his salad days before he settled down and married her. In 1927, to her alarm, he started bringing home Nazi literature, and one evening she saw him leaving with a swastika armband. As it turned out, he had already been a stormtrooper for some time. His addiction to extremist causes had caught up with him again. An agricultural laborer, he was often unemployed.

His first rally in Giessen was disbanded by the police before it could be broken up by the large number of opponents present. "After this failure we tried each in our own way to recruit new members." He also distributed the *Hessenhammer*, an antisemitic hate sheet, and went with his comrades by truck wherever their protection was needed. There was no violence in the first years "since no one took us seriously," but it was almost impossible to get the owners of meeting-halls to rent them out for NSDAP meetings. Innkeepers would not even allow teams of two or three uniformed stormtroopers to peddle their newspapers inside, and the respondent often found himself ejected.

In 1929, the respondent reports the first street fights and increasing meeting-hall protection activity in preparation of the campaign for the 1930 elections. His brother was injured on that occasion. During the campaign itself, at one rally, the respondent's erstwhile friends were "so enraged that they attacked us with rocks and bottles and other thrown objects in a narrow street. Many rocks came my way because I was carrying the pennant of the *Sturm*, but they hit instead the policemen standing by the curb." The respondent needed a police escort to get home.

Another time he and seven others dared not walk home to Giessen from a meeting because "ten times our number of Communists" were returning the same way. They feared bloodshed and spent the night in a haystack instead. "It is impossible to describe all the rallies in detail. There were hundreds of rallies and demonstrations where we did our service." The respondent was particularly pleased with the foundation of a Nazi trade union (NSBO). He describes the bitter depression days:

> Misery had grown so much among the people. Almost all of us were unemployed. I also was out of a job again. Hundreds of SA comrades had no home or shelter because they had to leave their families as a result of political friction. . . . Hence, SA Homes were established all over the Reich and also in Giessen. We needed all kinds of things to furnish the home and, having no money, we went around for days asking for gifts from the burghers of Giessen. We got what we needed. We had a bedroom-lounge and a completely equipped kitchen. I took care of the food by driving a truck from village to village collecting food.

The respondent tells how the government ordered the homes closed by a police commando. But the fight went on and became ever more intense. For the Hessian Landtag elections of 1931, monster rallies were held in which thousands crowded in so eagerly that there were injuries among them. The respondent graduated from stormtrooper work to political organizing and propaganda planning functions although he still had to endure physical dangers in chauffeuring Nazi speakers, as well as occasional police searches and one arrest.

Another renegade was a self-styled former Marxist and member of the "red" Metal Workers Union (DMV). This respondent, born 1898 (no. 440), lost his job as a result of a prolonged strike and was shocked to learn that his union would not help him with minor funds for transportation to a new job. He also accuses the Metal Workers Union of poor representation of workers' interest. He moved to the Palatinate in 1925, but his Marxist education conflicted greatly with the political opinions current in his new environment. Only prolonged exposure to Nazi rallies and literature slowly brought him around from his initial opposition to the NSDAP. "The decisive turning point for my later actions was my reading of Adolf Hitler's book *Mein Kampf*. Although the content was often and especially at the beginning hard to understand, the discussion of the labor question, which is so thorough and true, gave me the push to join the party in late fall of 1929." He became a stormtrooper leader and engaged in intensive proselytizing:

Since I was full of the idea I began to spread it. Although it was slow going, I kept thinking back on my own political development which had pointed me in a different direction. It was relatively easy to convince young people and bring them into the party. But with their [older] relations it was often necessary to point out the faults of the other parties again and again and to make clear with all my energy the will and desire of national socialism. Our untiring proselytizing for the new view of the world thus created a movement which by its steady growth was bound to come to power some day.[11]

MFPs and MPs in Weimar History

The purity and intensity of the MPs and MFPs suggest a historical comparison between their respective memberships and activities throughout the period. Table IV-7 shows the striking similarities among their membership records, although the age difference shows up in the form of a substantially faster rate of mobilization among the MFPs. Table IV-8 shows the functional differentiation between the young MFPs and the older MPs. The former did far more fighting, while the latter evidently concentrated on propaganda and proselytizing, especially after 1929.

[11] See also no. 443 (born 1902), a respondent who tangled with the occupation and fled and who worked among Communists. His description of the time of the struggle is notable for the stress it places on the recruiting function of political violence. "After every Marxist attack we got new recruits," whose sympathy was evidently mobilized by the vicarious experience of being roughed up by the reds.

Table IV-7: MFP and MP Organizational Memberships, 1919-1930 (in %)

		None	Voelkisch & NSDAP	Conservative bourgeois opposition	Quasi-military organization	Republicans and extreme left	Totals
1919-21:	MP	60.7	9.2	5.4	18.5	6.2	100.0
	MFP	48.6	10.3	8.4	24.3	8.4	100.0
1922-24:	MP	49.2	23.4	7.1	14.8	5.5	100.0
	MFP	33.0	23.9	14.7	22.9	5.5	100.0
1925-28:	MP	45.6	17.6	11.8	19.1	5.9	100.0
	MFP	49.4	17.6	16.5	11.8	4.7	100.0
1929-30	MP	32.1	64.1	3.1		0.7	100.0
	MFP	8.1	85.6	5.4		0.9	100.0

Table IV-8: MFP and MP Activities 1919-1933 (in %)

		Voting, shopping around, campaigning	Marching, electioneering & provocation	Marching, electioneering & proselytizing or propagandizing	Marching, electioneering, & fighting	Totals
1919-24:	MP	64.2	12.1	17.8	15.9	100.0
	MFP	37.7	26.7	16.8	18.8	100.0
1925-28:	MP	61.5	9.0	25.4	4.1	100.0
	MFP	28.4	21.9	26.3	23.4	100.0
1929-30:	MP	27.0	19.2	44.8	9.0	100.0
	MFP	8.1	23.7	37.6	30.6	100.0
1931-33:	MP	6.9	20.6	62.8	9.7	100.0
	MFP	0.5	26.2	41.2	32.1	100.0

Youth and Extremism

What is it that makes young people more open to radicalism or extremist violence of every sort? Is it a matter of body chemistry, or youthful physiology, the rising sap which in many European peasant societies makes young peasants engage in brawls on Saturday night? Are the middle-aged more cautious because they have lost the quickness of step and nimbleness necessary for successful violence? Is it a matter of the social obligations imposed on a person by marriage, parenthood, and job responsibilities by the time he gets a little older? Or are the minds of young people still fermenting with immaturity, high with newly discovered, intoxicating ideas on nearly an empty mind? Does their imperious radicalism stem from their inability as yet to grasp and tolerate the enormous complexities and ambiguities of industrial societies? Is it a matter of upsetting events and conditions such as foreign occupation, borderland struggles, or discrimination abroad which will unhinge a young mind more decisively than an older one?

We have no definite answers to offer to these questions except the confirmation that age indeed seems terribly important in our study of Nazi extremism. And it is not only the age at which the respondents entered stage four which tends to separate them by their degree of involvement, their preoccupation with prewar or war issues, or their engagement in violence. It is also the age at which they became militarized and politicized which seems to influence the degree and kind of their involvement in middle stage activities. And, furthermore, the time lapse between the onset of their earlier involvements and their entry in stage four is also likely to reveal significant differences in the process of becoming a Nazi activist. Let us take a closer look first at the ages at which the respondents entered the middle stages.

Ages of Politicization or Militarization

Some readers familiar with the American literature on political socialization may have raised their eyebrows when they saw in the last section that we set the upper limit of Weimar youth politics as high as 25 years. But our chief interest is in the awakening of a conscious interest and commitment, rather than in the exploration of childhood learning, for which we lack adequate information. A look at the table of ages when the Abel respondents (FD-39, 42, 46)

FD-39, 42, 46: Ages at Stages Two, Three and Four

Stage	Age 12-17	18-20	21-25	26-35	36-72	Totals (n)
Two	54 (19.8%)	58 (21.4%)	67 (24.6%)	60 (22.0%)	33 (12.2%)	272 (100%)
Three	23 (8.9%)	37 (13.6%)	65 (23.9%)	81 (29.7%)	65 (23.9%)	271 (100%)
Four	16 (3.0%)	58 (10.4%)	101 (18.1%)	180 (32.2%)	194 (36.3%)	559 (100%)

entered stages two, three, and four shows how late the majority became in this sense politicized.[1] Even if we take into account the small number of persons involved in prewar politics, such a late starting age would seem to be surprising. Militarization, which after all depends largely on the presence of a war or revolution, occurred much earlier in people's lives and with no one later than his 56th year. The one-fourth of the respondents who skipped the two middle stages and went directly in the NSDAP, are probably concentrated especially in the younger cohorts of stage four.

When we crosstabulate these starting ages for stages two and three with other dimensions, we get a clearer view of their significance in the political development of the respondents on their way to Nazi extremism. If we take the principal occupations of the respondents, for example, both the militarized and the politicized show considerable age differentials. The working-class respondents in both groups tend to have started in stage two or three below the age of 26, and often under the age of 18. The farmers and white-collar workers also began early. Military-civil servants, by comparison, started mostly after they were 25. Business and professional respondents also started late, but among them the politicized began much later than did the militarized. This tends to confirm other findings about the political socialization of social classes in pre-1933 Germany.

How does upward mobility affect the age of militarization or po-

[1] A more detailed breakdown of the ages at the beginning of stage four appears below, page 425.

liticization? Among the militarized, being in social decline appears to be particularly frequent among those mobilized before the age of 18. We can assume that the family decline may push young people into militant causes at an early age. No fewer than 54.5% of the decliners were under 21 when entering stage two. The upwardly mobile from an urban background also tended to be disproportionately militarized (73.7%) when they were only 25 or younger, a reminder of the social profile of the American race rioter of the 1960s. Among the politicized, the urban climbers also tend to enter stage three when they are still rather young, but there are very few young decliners. In both the militarized and the politicized groups, finally, the upwardly mobile from a farm background tend to enter their respective stages rather late in their lives. Perhaps the social mobilization of leaving the farm competes with and retards political mobilization.

Early Political Mobilization and Youth Settings

The ages of beginning a given stage also throw some light on the nature of the process by which the respondents arrived at youthful postures such as being "politically militarized." No fewer than half of the politically militarized of stage two entered this stage between the ages of 12 and 17, and another third before they were 21. These early-militarization groups also include three-fourths of the young victory-watchers of World War One. Evidently "political militarization" happens very early and, at least in many cases, the vicarious experiences of the war effort are a likely cause of it. Among the politicized of stage three, the politically militarized are more evenly spread over the age spectrum from 12 to 25 and so are the victory-watchers of World War One. Here, however, half of the "fully politicized" youths entered stage three between the age of 12 and 20 and another one-fourth before they were over 25. The fully politicized of stage two are concentrated between 18 and 25. In either case, becoming fully politicized also seems to be a process that is likely to be completed rather early in a person's life, as compared to the other posture groups.

What about the hostile militants? Among the stage-two respondents, over half of them became militarized before the age of 21 and another third between 21 and 25. But among the politicized of stage three, only 23.3% entered before they turned 21 and another 43.3% between 21 and 25. The authoritarian and pre-political youths, finally, entered stages two and three rather on the late side, especially stage three. An authoritarian or parochial youth posture, it would appear, is a poor vehicle for early politicization or militarization.

What kind of home environment tends to make for early militarization or politicization? It depends on where we draw the line. Among those of stage two under 18, the respondents reporting a *voelkisch* (33.3%) or conventional political home background (26.3%) stand out. Among those under 21 it is the children of militaristic fathers (54.5%). In stage three the respondents from *voelkisch* and conventional homes also stand out with 16-17% under 18 and about 40% under 21. The slowest to become politicized are those with a militaristic father. Respondents from nationalistic or unpolitical homes are not much quicker, a demonstration again of the power of the home environment. The school environments tend to confirm these relationships.

How do childhood settings influence early involvement? Among the stage two respondents those reporting an orphaned or personally deprived childhood stand out both among those under 17 (31.8%) and between 12 and 20 (68.2%). Children born in poverty were militarized mostly after 25 (55.7%). Between the sheltered and the freewheeling well-to-do, the sheltered are slightly ahead among the categories of early militarization. Among the stage-three respondents, the picture is very similar with regard to the orphaned and, conversely, the poor. But among the economically secure, it is the freewheeling who are politicized earlier than the sheltered, as indeed we would expect.

The Early-Militarized and the Stages

What pre-political state (stage one) was likely to lead to the earliest militarization? As we might have anticipated, the pre-political parochial stage (of youth etc.) has the largest share (83.3%) of those militarized under 17 and also the largest (62.1%) share of those between 18 and 20. Respondents from unpolitical or pre-political youth groups such as the Youth Movement are second in early militarization. A young Berliner born 1906 (no. 376), whose father had died early, joined the *Wandervogel* at the age of twelve and learned there "to appreciate Germany and German kind." "In the summer of 1926, for the first time I learned something from a fellow apprentice about Hitler and his idea, National Socialism . . . and recognized it as the only idea appropriate to Germany. This was the *Volksgemeinschaft* I had dreamed of for a long time. And so *it was a matter of course to become a stormtrooper*." (italics supplied) He seems to perceive nothing incongruous in this matter-of-fact decision, although in the next sentence he proceeds to show how enormous a step he had taken from the gentle way of life of *Wandervogel* hikes and youthful fellowship. "Now a new life began for me as my quiet life turned into one of battle. Meeting-hall fight followed meeting-hall fight. There were propaganda marches and campaigns in Kottbus, Pasewalk, Frankfurt an der Oder, Wiesenburg, Trebbin, etc." The respondent, a goldsmith by trade, lost his job and became a chauffeur instead. He tells the story of how he and his "comrades" survived the outlawing of the NSDAP in Berlin in 1927. "Of course we comrades did not just part company as the chief of police seemed to imagine. We had fought together too many hours and we deeply believed in the mission of Adolf Hitler. Now came the time of in-gathering and of quiet proselytizing. We stormtroopers of the Kreuzberg section formed the Sporting Club South West [as a camouflage]."

Another respondent of the same age (no. 385), but in Frankfurt am Main, joined the *Grossdeutscher Jugendbund* and began to attend Nazi rallies as early as 1923.

Early in 1924 I joined the outlawed NSDAP. During the *Reichstag* campaign of May 1924, we had a fight with a Communist poster commando which put me out of action for three weeks with a head injury. As soon as I had recovered I was back in the first line.

With the refounding of the party in 1925, I officially became a stormtrooper. . . . In repeated clashes with political enemies I often sustained injuries. In November 1927, *Reichsbanner* men stabbed me in the chin during a raid, which resulted in severe damage to my lower jaw and the destruction of three teeth. The steadily increasing terror of the Marxists in 1927 and 1928 forced my father to sell his shop in the Marxist center of the city, as we were no longer secure in life or limb and we were suffering from boycott. In mid-1928, my father opened the Inn *Zum goldenen Reichsapfel* . . . which soon became a chief base of our party comrades. But here too we suffered much under the terror.

Early in 1930, I transferred to the SS. I shall never forget one day, October 22, 1930, when Severing [Prussian Minister of the Interior–SPD] spoke to the police in Frankfurt. After the meeting the policemen literally hunted down one Nazi after the other. I was caught in one of the hunts and manhandled by three police officers who beat me unconscious in front of my father's business. Nineteen or 20 policemen then invaded our inn and the excitement brought on a nervous breakdown for my 56-year-old father. I was unable to work for six months.[2]

[2] This incident was the cause of one of the innumerable motions of Nazi deputy Kube before the Prussian diet, against various big-city chiefs

The respondent in no way indicates any active involvement in street violence such as we might expect of a stormtrooper. Everything is done to him, the innocent, patriotic victim by the beastly antagonists, be they Communists or policemen. The bulk of his account, in fact, is this list of the bruises and persecutions he received and suffered. To see the world in this light appears to be one of the ego defenses of being a political extremist. To reinforce the solidarity of the movement and to face down the patent deviancy of his actions and beliefs in the midst of a common-sense world, he has to believe he is incessantly being persecuted for his righteous struggle for utopia.

What organizations of stage two did these early-militarized respondents pick? Between 12 and 17, it was mostly groups like *Jungstahlhelm*, *Wehrwolf*, *Oberland*, *Jungdo*, or the Red Front. Among the 18- to 20-year-olds, the Free Corps, vigilantes, and again *Wehrwolf* and *Oberland* were frequent choices. What were their predominant motives for joining these militant groups? The shock of the occupation stands out as a motive both under 17 and among the 18- to 20-year-olds. An antisemitic predisposition was a strong motive among the youngest (12-17) and the oldest (35-56) to be militarized. The impact of war and revolution, by contrast, seems to have been strongest in motivating those between 21 and 35 to enter stage two.

It is a rare case for an older respondent to be involved in violence. Here is one which reads like a guide to the counter-revolution. A technician, born 1881 (no. 548), describes his upbringing as "Christian, strictly nationalistic, but even then antisemitic" and anti-Marxist. He served in 1903-1905 and again in the war and volunteered afterwards for the navy to fight "red plunderers" and then for the Iron Division (Free Corps) to fight the Bolsheviks in the Baltic area. Wounded and in the hospital for six weeks, he developed a "mortal hatred" for the Bolsheviks, whom he accuses of all kinds of atrocities and outrages. Since the Iron Division was "betrayed" by the German republican government and had to fight its way back the hard way, the respondent also felt a "white-hot hatred for our Social Democratic Ministers and their Jewish hangers-on." He also claims that the government's breach of promises of financial support to the Free Corps fighters in 1920, when the units were disbanded, was one of the reasons for the Kapp *putsch*, in which he

---

of police. Kube claimed that the Frankfurt chief had given each of the three officers involved 50 marks and a vacation. *Sammlung der Drucksachen des Preussischen Landtags*, 4. Wahlperiode, pp. 182-183.

participated, too. He barely escaped the massacre of Captain Berthold's men in Harburg at the hands of "a Marxist-led mob."

A few months later, he followed another call of the government, "with another sack of promises," to fight the Communist uprising in the Ruhr area. He was finally retired to civilian life in August 1920 and, after a two-year interval of working as a technician, learned about the Hitler movement. "Like lightning, the idea went through my soul: Here is the right man. You are his and he will lead us from humiliation back into the light." In December 1922, he was asked to join the resistance against the French, and in particular to be a liaison to Schlageter, an old Free Corps acquaintance from Kurland. Both Schlageter and the respondent were caught, but the respondent suffered only mistreatment and expulsion. Then he joined the Black *Reichswehr* and experienced with it the abortive right-wing *putsch* of Kuestrin in 1923.

Once more in civilian life and on the verge of remarriage—his first wife had died in childbirth in 1920—his past caught up with him in 1925.

> I was arrested by the Marxist judicial authorities on charges of a so-called *Fememord* (political execution), involving traitors of the people who could not be nailed legally. We Black *Reichswehr* soldiers had to do it with the silent consent of the government and the *Reichswehr*. But since Herr Ebert (the Reich President) and his comrades were involved in corruption . . . they had to distract people's attention and the Jewish press invented the campaign against the *Fememord* which cruelly ended my livelihood.

The respondent's critical remarks on Weimar justice should be compared with the consensus on the pronounced right-wing bias of the courts. In any case, the prosecution could not obtain a conviction. The respondent and his superior officer were released because of illness and eventually amnestied in 1930. He was jailed once more in the investigation of a bombing attempt on the *Reichstag* which he did not commit. While in jail he met another old Free Corps buddy, Ernst von Salomon, who had been involved in political murders. Long before that time he had already been in the *Deutsch-voelkische Freiheitspartei* and in 1929 he joined the NSDAP, at the age of 48. He helped to build up the volunteer labor service and served on a welfare commission together with his "mortal enemies who lay in waiting for me at night in the streets," his violent mind imagined.

As we follow their progress to stage three, the early-militarized continue to diverge from the later-militarized in noticeable ways. Those militarized between the ages of 12 and 17, for example, stand out among the politicized for such middle-stage activities as voting, attending various political rallies, or shopping around among the parties. Unlike the later-militarized groups, they seem to have been readily available for all kinds of political options. The groups between 18 and 35, by contrast, either tend to express strong distrust of all parties or to join conventional parties such as the DVP, SPD, or DNVP as their stage three. Membership in the pre-1925 Nazi or *voelkisch* parties is an option more popular with those who were militarized after the age of 25, or even between 35 and 56—in other words, the war and prewar generations. The chief motive for becoming politicized for the early-militarized (12-20) was simply becoming eligible to vote rather than such runners-up as opposition to the Marxist revolution or the shock of war and occupation.

Early Mobilization and Extremist Activities

The young hotspurs of stage two were highly involved in demonstrations and political violence prior to joining the Nazi party. Those militarized between the ages of 12 and 17 participated to nearly one-half in rallies and demonstrations and to more than a third in organized violence or violent encounters. Among those militarized between 18 and 20, the violent percentage grows to 50.8%, while another 21.1% is engaged in demonstrations. The violent share remains near the 50% mark also among those militarized between 21 and 25 and begins to decline only over 30.

The same young hotspurs are in the forefront of stormtrooper activism in stage four. Seventy-one and five-tenths percent of those militarized between the ages of 12 and 17 are either marching and fighting (MF) or marching, fighting, and proselytizing (MFP) in the NSDAP, while a mere 10.7% are engaged in the less violent combination of marching and proselytizing (MP). Sixty-five percent of those militarized between 18 and 20 years of age are likewise MFs or MFPs, while there are only 15% MPs. Among those militarized between 21 and 25, the proportion of MPs all of a sudden rises to 27.7% and remains in that neighborhood also for those militarized at 26 or above. The MFs and MFPs drop to 50.8% between 21 and 25, 31.1% between 26 and 35, and 26.4% above 35. Thus, early militarization in stage two can be said to be a direct cause of the violent behavior of the stormtroopers in the early 1930s.

It is tempting to look for the motives of the early-militarized in joining the NSDAP, but such an inquiry yields disappointing results.

They mention the comradeship in the SA (12- to 17-year-olds) or the dynamic impression of the Hitler Movement (18- to 20-year-olds), but we have the feeling that these age cohorts are less able to perceive or to communicate their true motives, which appear to stem from the dynamism of the youth rebellion of those days. With regard to their ideological themes as full-fledged Nazis, the earliest-militarized stress somewhat the Hitler cult and the Nordic-German cult. The 18- to 20-year-olds of stage two stress revanchism, Nordic-German culture, and superpatriotism. The younger ones also show more than a touch of virulent antisemitism. Their attitude toward being in the Nazi movement gives us the only deeper clue to their motivation. Both early-militarized groups in disproportionate numbers do experience a sense of personal integration through the struggle itself, rather than from the goals of the movement. That indeed seems to be the spirit behind the youth rebellion, great emotional tensions which could tear a person apart if he (or she) did not find his mental balance and a sense of personal integration in the hectic struggles of an extremist movement.

Here is an example of a respondent who joined *Oberland* at the age of 17 and became a stormtrooper two years later. As so often, it was the clash with the French occupation which eased the transition from bourgeois civility to political soldiering. A young Palatinian born 1906 (no. 439), he was still going to the *Gymnasium* when the occupation came in 1918: "My political awakening occurred at the time of the deepest humiliation of the German people. My homeland, the beautiful Rhine Palatinate, was occupied in November 1918 by French troops under the conditions of the armistice." It is difficult to separate the external causation from his inner compulsions which he likes to clothe in curiously dialectic formulations. He claims that the "increasingly harsh" occupation measures turned his chivalrous respect for the French into hatred, and adds that "the Jews were in cahoots with the occupation." The encouragement of an antisemitic teacher and of his own parents turned his antisemitism into a veritable teenage *Judenkoller* which determined his political course in the years to come. In 1923, the French took over the railroads and expelled his father, a railroad official, with his family for participation in the passive resistance. The son arrived in Munich just in time to witness the beer-hall *putsch* and, a few months later, barely seventeen, he joined *Bund Oberland*, which had been outlawed for participation in the *putsch*, under the cover name *Deutscher Schuetzen-und Wanderbund*. On his return to the Palatinate, in 1925, he encountered the first efforts of the reconstructed NSDAP to gain a foothold.

At the founding meeting of the Neustadt an der Haardt local of the NSDAP in June 1925, I formally became a member and have since fought indefatigably for this party. Our first public rally was broken up by Marxists of both shadings. We were still but a handful and too weak to combat this well-organized, Jewish-financed power. But things were soon going to change. The *increasing* mismanagement of the red-black [SPD-Center] governments worked for us and recruited more and more fighters for us. The *increasingly* bolder spreading out of Jewry in politics, the economy, and the arts nourished antisemitism. And yet our struggle would have been in vain had not our brilliant Fuehrer Adolf Hitler led the fight.

I helped to protect innumerable, often bloody Nazi rallies against our political enemies. I participated in many demonstrations to propagate our idea, first with the SA, and, after July 1930, with the SS. I shared joy and suffering with my comrades. Attacks by the red bandits did not intimidate us. We gave blows whenever they meant to give them to us. Thus our first great success in the *Reichstag* elections of 1930 finally arrived, a great reward and satisfaction to me after all our efforts and sacrifices. . . . (italics supplied)

Early Politicization and the Stages

Just as with the early-militarized, the early-politicized tend to come from among the pre-political parochials and the unpolitical youth movements of stage one. The youngest among them report either having been in the *Bismarckjugend* (DNVP) or just shopping around among different parties. Those between 18 and 20 also joined moderate parties such as the SPD or DVP. Many were politicized by the occupation experience. Most of the early-politicized lived in small-town or rural areas. Those politicized between 12 and 20 heavily belonged to left-wing, conservative, and bourgeois youth groups such as *Jungdo*. Unlike the rest of the stage-three respondents, the early-politicized were highly involved (about 40%) in partisan street-fights and also disproportionately in electioneering, and demonstrations (also about 40%) during their first 25 years of life, but not necessarily before joining the Nazis. Those politicized between 12 and 17, consequently, are made up of two-thirds "politically militarized" and one-eighth "fully politicized" youths. Among those politicized between 18 and 20 the politically militarized are only a good third and the fully politicized a good fourth. Evidently early politicization, particularly under 18, speeds and intensifies the escalation of extremism even more than early militarization does.

An example of an early-politicized respondent is a young construction worker born about 1910 (no. 520) who was evidently very much under Social Democratic influence during his teenage years and who, in fact, fills his whole *vita* with refutations of all the SPD arguments against the Nazis. He joined the Nazis in March 1930 and immediately began to proselytize among his fellow-workers in his own way:

> In spite of persecutions, harassment, scorn, and ridicule, I made clear to people in precisely these words what the NSDAP meant for an organized worker in his struggle for existence: These are no empty phrases and slogans like with the SPD which has used them for years to trick the people. Adolf Hitler means it square and fair with you. He is really going to provide work and bread. Trust him and vote for him.

He went into the villages, proselytizing from door to door, telling people about Hitler's program, and inviting them to rallies. "These rallies brought me a lot of arguments and beatings. The SPD and KPD were allies who often beat me black and bloody, especially in the years 1930-1933. They were forever tearing down my posters and putting theirs up. At night I would return, tear down theirs and replace them with mine." The respondent may not have been the most eloquent and persuasive speaker in the Nazi stable, but his persistence and sincerity obviously brought results.[3]

What motivated the early-politicized to become so involved? There is an interesting progression of shifting emphases over the age spectrum. Among the groups from 12 to 25, coming of voting age and political friction at school or on the job are, of course, prominent reasons. But other motives soon make themselves felt. Among the 12- to 17-year-olds the shock of defeat and occupation also stand out and, for those politicized between 18 and 20, defeat and occupation account for almost as large a proportion as does voting age. With this age group also, economic troubles such as unemployment become an important factor—which is even more true of those politicized between 21 and 25. The other motives recorded, opposition to the "Marxist revolution" and to the Weimar leaders, disproportionately motivated those who became politicized after the

---

[3] See also the very young no. 570 (born 1912) who was already passing out handbills for a *voelkisch* party in the presidential elections of 1925. In 1930, he was hit with a police truncheon while attending a Nazi rally. He promptly joined the party and became an MFP. There is also no. 577 (born 1911), who also campaigned in 1923 and 1925, but for the DNVP. In 1928 he was with the *Stahlhelm* for two years and in 1932 he joined the stormtroopers and became an ardent MF.

age of 25. The war also figures as a prominent cause for those politicized after the age of 35.

Is there a noticeable difference between the activities the early-
politicized engaged in at stages two or three and what they did at
stage four (Table IV-9) after joining the NSDAP? Yes, their middle stage activities tended to be milder though similar in kind. At
the middle stages, the early-politicized between 12 and 20 tended
to engage mostly in demonstrations and electioneering, unlike the
more violent early-militarized. For the 18- to 20-year-olds, however,
individual violent encounters or provocations began to play a prominent role. Those politicized between 21 and 25 were heavily engaged in organized political violence (18.8%), individual violent
encounters (18.8%), and demonstrations (20.3%). The group between 26 and 35 still had one-fourth involved in organized or individual violence, but the emphasis had shifted back to electioneering, attendance at rallies, or merely voting. Those politicized after
they are 35 show an even stronger shift in this direction.

Table IV-9: Age at Stages Two and Three and Stage-four Activity (in %)

Age at stage		March-ing	MF	MP	MFP	Provoc.	Other	(n)	Per cent
				Stage Four Activities					
12-17	Two	3.6	41.1	10.7	30.4	3.6	10.7	(56)	100
	Three	8.7	39.1	13.0	17.4	4.3	17.4	(23)	100
18-20	Two	8.3	31.7	15.0	33.3	3.3	8.3	(60)	100
	Three	7.9	36.8	18.4	28.9	2.6	5.3	(38)	100
21-25	Two	4.6	24.6	27.7	26.2	—	16.9	(65)	100
	Three	1.5	27.3	19.7	27.3	1.5	22.7	(66)	100
26-35	Two	6.6	9.8	26.2	21.3	1.6	34.4	(61)	100
	Three	8.5	9.8	26.8	20.7	2.4	31.7	(82)	100
36-60	Two	5.9	17.6	29.4	8.8	—	38.2	(34)	100
	Three	10.4	9.0	26.9	10.4	1.5	41.8	(67)	100
All	Two	5.8	25.4	21.4	25.4	1.8	20.3	(276)	100
All	Three	7.2	19.9	22.8	20.7	2.2	27.2	(276)	100

Early Mobilization and Nazi Activities

Do the ages at which the respondents were militarized or politicized influence the intensity of their extremist involvement with the Nazi party? Table IV-9 clearly shows that there is a connection. Early militarization and early politicization have nearly the same effect except for the smaller numbers of the early-politicized. Respondents who were mobilized early in their lives are far more likely to participate in street violence (MF and MFP) than are those who were not mobilized until they were over 25. At that point the numbers of the violent drop below 50% and in their place the marcher-proselytizers (MPs) and other, non-violent activists become prominent. This confirms the link between the youth rebellion and Nazi street violence. Respondents who were mobilized early in their lives were obviously more prone to violence than those who were militarized or politicized after the age of 25.

Table IV-10: Age at Stages Two and Three and SA Membership (in %)

Age at stage		Not a member	Joined immediately	Joined later	Graduated SA to SS	(n)	Per cent
12-17	Two	14.3	51.8	16.1	17.9	(56)	100
	Three	19.2	57.7	7.7	15.4	(26)	100
18-20	Two	8.5	55.9	20.3	15.3	(59)	100
	Three	21.1	57.9	7.9	13.2	(38)	100
21-25	Two	32.8	50.0	12.5	4.7	(64)	100
	Three	29.5	50.8	14.8	4.9	(61)	100
26-35	Two	55.6	38.9	5.6	—	(54)	100
	Three	57.5	26.0	12.3	4.1	(73)	100
36-60	Two	63.3	26.7	10.0	—	(30)	100
	Three	75.4	19.3	5.3	—	(57)	100
All	Two	31.6	46.8	13.3	8.4	(263)	100
All	Three	45.5	38.4	10.2	5.9	(255)	100

The rate at which the age groups of politicization or militarization joined the stormtroopers or failed to do so once more also sets off the early-mobilized from the later-mobilized. The early groups also tended to "graduate" to the SS, Hitler's bodyguard, in considerable numbers. There is a difference, however, in the rate at which they joined the SA immediately or later. The stage two respondents generally joined the stormtroopers more often than the stage three respondents did, especially the early-militarized. The early-politicized, on the other hand, were more likely to join the SA immediately and not a year or so after joining the party. Those politicized between 21 and 35, by comparison, tended to join later rather than immediately, possibly because their politicization motivated them to join the party first without joining its paramilitary organization. At any rate, this consideration did not seem to apply to the early-politicized or, for that matter, the early-militarized.

There is yet more to be said about age. It is worth noting, for example, that the ages at which respondents became politicized tend to cluster with only a short lapse of time with those at which the respondents joined the Nazi party. Those who entered stage three between 12 and 17, for example, tended to join the NSDAP between 18 and 20. Those who became politicized between 18 and 20 tended to be in the Nazi party by the time they were 25 and so forth. We shall come back to this point when we discuss the speed with which the respondents traversed the four stages.

Early Politicization and Nazi Ideology

What motivated the early-politicized to join the NSDAP? All the age groups under 25 prominently mention the spirit of comradeship among the stormtroopers, as we would expect. They also cite in disproportionate numbers having been stirred up by friction with the occupation regime. In addition to these factors, the very young (12-17) mention a climate of general or personal repression by the police and government, a sentiment echoed more recently by American radical college youth. Those between 18 and 20 also stress the rough opposition of the Communists and other political enemies as a reason for joining. Respondents between 21 and 25 also mention unemployment or the agricultural revolt as important reasons for entering stage four. The later-politicized, on the other hand, stress such motives as the dynamic impression of the Hitler movement or their ideological, often antisemitic, fervor as their reasons for joining. The group which became politicized between 26 and 35 years of age also cites government repression and unemployment as motives for becoming Nazis. It is remarkable, in any case, that the dynamism of the movement and ideological ardor did not make as big an impression on the early-politicized as on the older groups.[4]

Further light is thrown on the motivations of these groups by comparing their dominant ideological themes after they had entered the NSDAP. Those who were politicized between 12 and 20, tend to be most impressed by the slogan of the social *Volksgemeinschaft* and by Hitler himself, themes which evidently responded to certain personality needs of this age group. The older group among them also tends to feel an appreciation of Nordic-German culture as its dominant theme. Those politicized between 21 and 25 are mostly Nordic fanatics or Hitler cultists or superpatriots. In the older cohorts (26-56) the themes change and the preferred motifs are revanchism, superpatriotism, and antisemitism. The difference is evidently one between the postwar "political youth" and the war and prewar generations. This difference also comes out in their hate-lists, which mark off the early-politicized as more anti-Marxist and the over-25 groups as more antisemitic.[5] And it is also characterized by the sense of personal integration of the early-politicized by the struggle in the movement rather than by the utopian goals which inspired those over 25.

The Ages of Each Stage Compared

It is enlightening to set the ages at which the respondents entered the different stages side by side (FD-39, 42, 46). To begin with, their youngest and oldest diverge considerably from stage to stage. The youngest among the militarized started at the age of 12 and the oldest was 56 when he started out in stage two. Among the politicized of stage three, the youngest was 13 and the oldest was 60. Stage four, finally, had no one under 14 and its oldest was 72.

The comparison clearly shows, moreover, that militarization tends to crest early in the 21 to 25 range and to wane rapidly after this age, while politicization does not reach its peak until after 26 and declines more slowly than militarization does. The onset of stage four, finally, is still more broadly spread from the age of 18 to the early fifties, with the median at about 31.

[4] It should be noted that these are relative measures. Ideological fervor accounted for 40-43% of the early-politicized and 48-52% of the later-politicized. The dynamism of the Hitler movement was cited by 13-20% of the early and 22-27% of the late groups.

[5] On the shadings of antisemitism scale, however, the differences seem to boil down mostly to the much higher incidence of *Judenkoller* among the later-politicized. The earliest cohorts (12-17) in fact, have the highest share (22.2%) of respondents with delusions of conspiracy.

FD-39, 42, 46: Ages of Entry in Stages Two, Three, and Four

	Stage Two	Stage Three	Stage Four
	54	23	16
12-17	(9.2%)	(3.9%)	(2.9%)
	58	37	58
18-20	(10.0%)	(6.4%)	(10.0%)
	67	65	101
21-25	(11.9%)	(11.6%)	(17.4%)
	36	46	97
26-30	(6.2%)	(7.9%)	(16.9%)
	24	35	83
31-35	(4.1%)	(6.0%)	(14.2%)
	16	28	57
36-40	(2.6%)	(4.8%)	(9.7%)
	6	12	58
41-45	(1.0%)	(1.9%)	(9.9%)
	8	15	38
46-50	(1.3%)	(2.6%)	(6.5%)
	3	10	51
51-	(0.5%)	(1.5%)	(9.0%)
	309	310	22
NA, not in this stage	(53.2%)	(53.4%)	(3.5%)
Totals	581	581	581
	(100.0%)	(100.0%)	(100.0%)

This impression of the age spread is increased when we compare the dates of birth of these age groups for stage four. The Nazi movement appears to have appealed equally to all the older age cohorts, so that the birth dates of each age group are clustered within a few years. Between 70 and 80% of those who joined between 46 and 50 were born between 1878 and 1884. The same percentage of those joining between 41 and 45 were born 1885-1889; and of those 36-40 were born 1890-1894. The age groups under 30 tend to be more scattered over a wider range. This is to say that for the prewar generations, the appeal of the Nazi revolt tended to be concentrated in just a few years of the movement, perhaps when it was at the height of its campaign to conquer the country. The war and postwar generations were more likely to join at different ages in their lives even though they had less leeway between growing up and the end of the period under consideration.

This view is confirmed and made more precise when we cross-tabulate the onset of stage four in each respondent's life with the date he joined the party. A good half to three-fourths of the respondents who joined when they were 31 or older joined only after the 1930 elections, after which the movement evidently began to "age" faster. Respondents who joined before they reached 31 tended to join before mid-1930. Forty to forty-five percent of those who joined between the ages of 18 and 25, in fact, did so before 1928, and especially between 1925 and 1928. Three-fourths of the pre-1925 sample and two-thirds of the reconstructed party of 1925-1928 joined when they were under 30.

In the light of this discovery, then, we also have to recognize that these young recruits of the pre-1925 and reconstructed party tended to belong to age cohorts of the war (1895-1901) or immediate postwar (1902-1909) generation, respectively. Their formative historical periods, then, are the war experience as a participant or teenager (victory-watcher). Or, for the second group, it was the war experienced as a child between, say, 8 and 15, and the revolutionary and counter-revolutionary violence of the postwar years experienced as a participant or a witnessing young adult. The impact of all this violence undoubtedly helped to form the attitudes of these young Nazis although it may not explain the attitudes of the older and later recruits to the cause.

We have to distinguish then, between a wave of youth revolt sparked by the violence of war and revolution and, perhaps, a second, younger wave involving cohorts clearly beyond the impact of these two events of 1914-1920, though not necessarily beyond the impact of the events of 1923. We do indeed have some very young respondents, mostly born after 1908, for whom war and revolution are evidently ancient history and the only political reality at hand is the attraction of the exciting Nazi movement. The date of birth alone, however, is not as important in this respect as are the influences of the home and of the social setting.

Examples of Two Youth Revolts

A good example of the war-related youth revolt is a messenger boy born 1907 (no. 465) in Spandau, who in 1924 successively belonged to a patriotic veterans' group, the *Jungstahlhelm*, and then the *Frontbannjugend*, which eventually led him and all his comrades into the SA.

> My time with the *Frontbann* was the best time of my life. The comradeship, the whole time of struggle, in electioneering, in demonstrations, or in protecting meetings. I was there when one of our first victims in Berlin . . . was shot to death by a Jew on *Kurfuerstendamm*. But then I also got something to remember just as nearly every comrade got. After a meeting . . . we fellows from Spandau, about 20 of us, went to the railroad station pursued by perhaps 150 Communists, who caught up with us at the station. I remained behind at the door, was

pushed aside and stabbed with a knife, which cost me a rib. That happened . . . in 1926. I had to sit it out for a year because of this injury.

Having been cornered by a far superior force and the character of the injury, of course, heightened the glory of "the best time" of the respondent's life. Another respondent, born 1903 (no. 468), a scion of the upper classes with an unfulfilled yearning to have served in World War One, writes "I am glad to live in this age" because he evidently sees stormtrooper life as a reenactment of sorts of the war itself.

An example of the "now generation" of 1930 is a very young DHV member born 1911 (no. 472), with a sharp awareness of class discrimination along with an intense dislike for the SPD, who faced down his father's disapproval and economic adversity "because there was nothing more wonderful than the SA service!" He joined in 1929 and was in many a battle. He proselytized on the job, among relatives, and in the DHV, and busied himself with tasks of organization. His exclamation is echoed by another young veteran of many battles, a baker born 1909 (no. 477) who joined in 1931 and wrote: "The fighting period was hard but also wonderful," and by one born 1914 (no. 479) who, after joining the same year, comments, "My first tests under fire by no means deterred me; on the contrary, they really bound me to Hitler's idea."

There are so many distinctive types of this second youth revolt that we may hesitate to generalize beyond broad statistical categories. Here is a sampling to give the reader an idea of the extraordinary diversity at hand. There is the Nazi student with an early propensity for violence. A theology student, born 1911 (no. 494), was expelled from his *Gymnasium* because of his conflicts with the teachers. The entire upper class (*Prima*) of that school, according to the respondent, participated in SA brawls without having joined and, of course, without the knowledge of their parents. His own violence brought fines and adverse publicity and, finally, government attention. The Prussian Ministry of Education initiated an investigation against him and came very close to taking away his graduation diploma (*Abitur*), which in Weimar Germany was almost the only key to upper-middle-class status. At Breslau University he joined the traditional student fraternity Arminia, but resigned when the fraternity brothers would not stand for his stormtrooper membership. He joined the NS St.B and held office in it in 1932 while living, by his own choice, "in the reddest part of town," involved in the stormtrooper activities of marching and fighting. "This year," he comments, "made me a true National Socialist." It also got him and ten other Nazi students arrested for undisclosed reasons. To the dismay of his parents, disciplinary proceedings were initiated and the "vindictive establishment" took away his scholarship and tuition waiver. "We poor SA students," he comments in self-pity.

Another distinctive type is the youthful wanderer born 1910 (no. 485) who describes his small-town youth as the scourge of the neighborhood "through my activities as an Indian chief who enjoyed great hunts and campfires to roast chickens, cats, and geese." He was apprenticed to a Munich druggist but preferred hiring out as a farm hand after his apprenticeship, one of many short stints of employment in his wanderings all over Germany and Switzerland. "Since I was chiefly interested in seeing a lot of the world, I never stayed long in one job but moved on as soon as I had a little money in my pocket." He dug potatoes, picked fruit, and, at the age of 18, became a volunteer assistant on many estates of East Germany, the Black Forest, and Switzerland with the *Artaman* movement.[6]

He became smitten with the Nazi movement and Hitler's speeches in Munich as a 15-year-old and joined in 1928. He reports with pride his participation in several major demonstrations as a storm-trooper, including one in Weimar which ended with detainment for two days for "defacing the walls." He never makes clear what attracted him to the Nazi movement except that the great marches and the uniforms may have appealed to his romantic soul.

Even when members of the second wave of political youth recall the events of the revolution they are not as deeply involved as the first wave was. A civil servant's son born 1911 (no. 533), for example, witnessed the attempted storm of the city hall of Eisenach in 1919 and saw workers shot by the police and then buried. But to him this was just another tableau of history, like other things he later read in the paper as a teenager. There is an allegation of betrayal, reminiscent of the claims of American radicals regarding the betrayal of the American dream,[7] when he scorns the republican promises of a bright future, the "life in dignity and beauty," as a fraud. This, too, is a common theme among the Abel respondents. Then in 1930-1931, immediately before his *Abitur*, a stressful time when other German students may contemplate suicide, the respondent joined the Nazis. He saw a stormtrooper demonstration, and one man in particular marching in formation, his eyes radiant while

[6] There is a considerable number of *Artamanen* in the Abel collection.

[7] See, for example, Charles A. Reich, *The Greening of America*, Bantam Books (Random House), 1971, pp. 236ff. or Keniston, *op. cit.*, on the "end of the line."

blood was streaming down over his face. The respondent was spell-bound and sold his soul to "the holy community of the brown fight-ers" which his school had forbidden him to join. And he became a new man, or a Peter Pan in flight from his adolescent crisis: "I no longer belonged to myself, but to the movement. Bourgeois life with its pleasures, with dancing and games, no longer mattered to me."

A Social Profile of the Young Nazis

How did the respondents who joined the party before they were 21, or 26, differ from the older recruits? In their location experience, there is quite a concentration of people from the occupied areas in the groups under 31 as compared to the older Nazis. The stimulus of foreign occupation evidently loses its potency with the age of the respondent. The youngest recruits (14-17), tend to be from a spa-tially immobile setting. The experience of borderland struggles, on the other hand, seems to be relevant at all ages. The older Nazis also tend to have had foreign experiences, especially before the war, which may help to explain their eventual recruitment by the party. Finally, there is an unusually high percentage of rural-urban mi-grants among them, which suggests that perhaps the restlessness which drove them to migrate in the first place also was a factor in their extremism. Or, more likely, these respondents may well have settled down after their successful migration only to feel all the more unsettled and threatened by the forces of change in German postwar society.

Their occupations and location at the time of the most intensive Nazi campaign also separate the young from the old. The younger groups tend to be from small and medium-sized towns. The inter-mediate age groups (21-35) have up to one-fourth rural residents, while the older respondents (36 and older) are heavily metropoli-tan. As for their occupation, the young Nazis up to 30 years of age are heavily blue-collar and, less often, white-collar or farmers. Among those who joined at the age of 31 or later, business and pro-fessional people and, increasingly, military-civil servants stand out. These differences may also reflect shifts in the composition of the movement from the earlier "younger" phase to the recruitment of older cohorts after 1930.

How were these age groups affected or perhaps even motivated by the socio-economic dynamics of the period in question? The younger groups tended to have workers or artisans as fathers, the older ones businessmen, farmers, or military-civil servants. The younger ones tended to be upwardly mobile from an urban working-class background. Among the older groups, the trend was either upward mobility from rural antecedents or stagnation. There were also quite a few in social decline concentrated at interesting points in the life cycle of the individual, namely at 18-20, 26-30, and 36-40. We could speculate that social decline is most easily turned into political extremism among the very young and among those in the crisis of approaching 40. But what might have been the panic of approaching 30 except perhaps a fear of soon being "over 30," which in German social life, too, is something of a watershed dividing the carefree young from responsible middle age.

The social dynamics are mirrored better in the different ways the age groups conceive of *Volksgemeinschaft*. Those who joined when they were over 30 tend to view it mostly from a middle-class perspective or as national solidarity toward the outside which neatly gathers their social background and contact with borderland and foreign settings under one heading. Those who joined earlier, by comparison, tend to crave the solidaristic *Volksgemeinschaft* more from the vantage points of either the social underdog or the declining upper classes who seek acceptance. There are other elements of unrelieved contrast, such as the substantial number of 21- to 25-year-olds with strong class consciousness and those under 18, who tend to be blissfully unaware of the class patterns of German society.

This youngest group also turns out not to have suffered in any way from the Depression or other economic troubles, while those between 18 and 30 include as many as a third or more economic casualties of the Great Depression. The motivation of the very young is evidently purely psychological rather than socio-economic, and the same tends to be true of those who joined the party after the age of 40. There is, however, a middle section between the ages of 25 and 40 which had more than its share of economic troubles in the years before the depression. Still, there is little sustenance here for an economic interpretation of National Socialism.

Youth Activities and the Young Nazis

The overlapping of our study of youth activities in the preceding section with this inquiry into the young Nazis has created some ambiguity. We need to know how the age structure of these Nazis fits into the larger picture of Weimar youth activities. To begin with, it is worth noting how the number of respondents in each age group who belonged to no youth group at all rises rapidly from less than 7% of those under 26 to half of the respondents aged 36-40 and around three-fourths of those over 40. From this, we can estimate the beginning of mass youth culture in Germany to be around the turn of the century. Among those over 50, 82.9% were never in a youth group setting. A disproportionate number of the groups over 35 who did belong, moreover, was in unpolitical organizations.

What organizations, then, were dominant among the political youth? Among the 26- to 35-year-old joiners, the tendency was to belong to a military training group, a Socialist or Communist youth group, or the religious or agricultural youth. The 14- to 25-year-olds, by comparison, tended to have joined the NSDAP or Hitler Youth directly or else to have been in the *Jungdo* or other liberal or bourgeois groups first. There is the impression, as we get down to the earlier joiners that there is an increasing tendency to shortcut the preliminaries on the way to Nazi membership. Those who joined the party between the ages of 21 and 25 have the most diverse youth memberships, including also conservative groups such as the *Bismarckjugend* (DNVP).

When we examine the record of military service of the age groups of stage four, one good reason for the sharp separation between those who joined before and those who joined after the age of 30 becomes abundantly clear. Eighty to ninety percent of those over 30 served in the German army, including, among those over 35, 40-50% peacetime enlistees or professional soldiers. The age groups from 30 to 50 saw the heaviest service in World War One. Respondents over 50 were less involved in the war than in peacetime soldiering. Of those who joined the Nazis at 26-30 years of age, only two-fifths served; the younger groups saw practically no military service. The victory-watchers are concentrated among the groups between 21 and 30. Having grown up in war and violence, the younger respondents may well have felt a great urge to march and fight in private armies of all sorts, including the stormtroopers.

Are there differences in childhood settings among the age groups? The groups under 26 tend to come from a *voelkisch*-antisemitic home. Those who joined after they were 40 tend to have had militaristic fathers or at least nationalistic parents. The age groups in between often come from an unpolitical home or from parents with loyalties to the conventional parties. Their school and peer environments follow similar patterns. Among most of the groups over 25, the childhood settings were disproportionately marred by a disciplinarian upbringing. The younger groups, under 30, on the other hand, often tend to have grown up without fathers or without both parents. But, except for the poorer middle groups from 26 to 35, affluence and poverty seem to be balanced in the childhoods of most groups. The middle groups are the same that often became unemployed or bankrupt before 1928.

The Young Nazis and the Four Stages

Following the younger and older recruits of the NSDAP through the four stages will shed some light on their political career patterns. We begin with their pre-political phase (stage one), which again clearly separates those over and under 30. The younger groups tend heavily to come from a personal-parochial stage, mostly being still too young to participate, or from relatively unpolitical youth movements, while the older groups come almost exclusively from unpolitical bourgeois or farmer circles, similarly unpolitical military-civil service positions (30-50% each), or prewar political involvements.

Their involvement in stage two is less clearly outlined. The youngest (14-20) and oldest (36 and over) tend to have skipped this stage entirely. Of the younger groups that did not, the *Wehrwolf*, *Jungdo*, and *Stahlhelm* tend to claim the lion's share. Free Corps or vigilante activity is more typical of the 26- to 40-year-olds, since the era of the Free Corps was in 1919-1920. Action with the pre-1925 NSDAP or *voelkisch* action groups literally spans the age groups from 21 to 50.

Their motives for becoming militarized do not distinguish the age groups very clearly from one another. To be sure, the shock of the occupation was a prominent militarizer among the younger Nazi recruits, and disproportionate numbers of those under 26 were militarized by their antisemitism. But this prejudice also drove many of the recruits over 40 into stage two. Other causes, such as the shock of war and defeat, are well-distributed over most age groups.

With stage three the division between the age groups is clearer, although between one-half and three-fourths of those under 31 never went through stage three at all. Those who did, among the groups under 21, tended to shop around among the parties, since they could not even vote. Respondents between 25 and 30 often belonged to the moderate parties, the DNVP, or the pre-1925 NSDAP or *voelkisch* parties. Among those who joined the party between 26 and 30 there was an increasing reluctance to make a commitment. Over 30, the pattern was dominated by the preferences of an older generation in German politics. There was a great tendency to express a strong distrust of all parties, or to be in the DNVP, or in the pre-1925 NSDAP or *voelkisch* parties.

The motives cited for entering stage three, however, fail to separate the age groups at the same point. Predictably, disproportionate numbers of the youngest recruits were politicized simply by reaching voting age, becoming involved in political arguments, or economic troubles. But this set of motives also predominated among the groups up to the age of 36. The shock of the occupation is also an important politicizing motive for those who joined the party before they were 26. The "oldest" of the motives prominent among Nazi recruits over 40 was a sense of opposition to the Weimar leaders.

The most extreme activities at stages two or three can be expected to separate those under and over 30. The older Nazi recruits tended to limit themselves to voting, attending rallies, electioneering, or holding office, while the younger ones stand out with demonstrations, provocations, and individual violent encounters. The young groups also had the lion's share of organized political violence (57%), although the groups between 30 and 40 (29.2%) were pretty violent, too. The most violent groups, the Nazi recruits between 21 and 40, and especially between 30 and 40, included many who coincide with the participants in Free Corps and vigilante activities in 1919-1922.

The distinction between the younger and the older groups is repeated in stage four itself, though with an important difference. Again the older groups tend to limit themselves to mere membership in the party, but this time they also have almost a monopoly on marching and proselytizing (MP). The younger groups, by way of contrast, are heavily involved in demonstrating (M), marching and fighting (MF), and marching, fighting, and proselytizing (MFP). Fifty-nine and four-tenths percent of the Ms, 70.9% of the MFs, and 65.7% of the MFPs, as compared to only 36.7% of the MPs and 18.4% of the mere members, joined the party before they were 31. Herein among other things lay the advantage of youthfulness of the NSDAP, which was considerably younger in its membership than any other Weimar party save the Communists. How could the gerontocracy of the Weimar Republic ever hope to meet the threat of these marching, fighting, and proselytizing columns of young Nazis?

Intervals from Stage Two to Four

Let us imagine for a moment that becoming a Nazi extremist is a process comparable to a fever or a mental breakdown, which both have to run their course before the respondent can become well again. If these analogies applied, it would be very important to know how long each respondent took to get from the onset of stage two or three (or the end of stage one) to stage four. We could conceive of all kinds of significant differences which might be discovered between those who progress fast and those who move slowly from phase to phase. We constructed for this purpose a scale from 0 to 9 and more years that a respondent might take from stage two to stage four, and then crosstabulated the intervals with various other variables and attributes.

The average interval from stage two to stage four is nearly eight years, we were surprised to learn. That the length or shortness of the intervals is strongly related to the motivation of the respondent can be demonstrated by crosstabulating the interval with whether the respondent was one of the first in his area to join the party. Almost half of those who were founders or cofounders of the party local went from stage two to stage four in less than five years, as compared to only a good fourth of those who were among the first half-dozen or so to join, or even less among those who joined only when the movement was already a substantial minority or well on its way to power. On the other hand, of course, there also were external circumstances, such as the lapse of time between militarizing events, the revolution or occupation, and the appearance of the Nazi party in the respondent's area.

With regard to age, there is a drastic difference between the generation born before 1899, which has 45-65% respondents who took nine years and longer, and the last war cohorts and first postwar cohorts (born 1899-1905), who include only about 28% such sluggards. Respondents younger than that may not have had the time between their pre-political youth and joining the Nazi party to take nine years or more for anything. Among those born 1909-1916, the second wave of youth revolt, more than half accomplished the transition from stage two to stage four in under four years, and among those born 1906-1908 in barely five years. For the next cohort, that born 1902-1905, the victory-watchers, the halfway mark was not reached until seven and a half years had elapsed. This indicates some limitation on the vicarious socialization by the war effort even though the lapse of time between 1918 and the reconstruction of the party alone is about seven years. This is something of a measurement of the two waves of political youth rebellion in the Weimar Republic, for they appear to have intensified their political involvement much faster than any of the preceding age cohorts, and faster than the time lapse would explain.

Are some location settings more conducive to rapid extremist escalation from stage two than others? In the occupied areas, and quite likely as a result of foreign occupation, one-fourth of the respondents reached stage four in two years or less and 40% reached it in four years or less. Perhaps, there was some kind of "occupation choler," a virulent outbreak of extremism, under the impact of the occupation. None of the other groups can come close to this rate in the occupied areas, not even the borderland cases. The slowest are the rural-urban migrants, of whom over half took nine years or more and less than one-eighth under five years. The rate is just as slow among rural residents, while towns and cities between 2,000 and 100,000 seem to have been the best setting for rapid extremist escalation.

We have already discussed many of the occupation-motivated, and the reader may recall that, in most of them, conflict and expulsion indeed led in short order to involvement with *voelkisch* action groups or the Nazi party. We can contrast this to the effect of the experiences of borderland struggles or of the internal colonial in the example of the son, born 1904 (no. 436), of a Social Democrat who in 1908 had followed the invitation to homestead in the Province of Poznan. The son experienced the Polish uprisings and the well-armed border vigilantes of *Grenzschutz Posen-West* of the immediate postwar era until "in January 1920 the German government of the day disarmed and withdrew the *Grenzschutz* troops behind the line determined by the Versailles Treaty and left the whole area to the Poles without a fight." The miseries of expropriation and expulsion intensified the respondent's hatred for the Weimar parties. He was so intent on winning back his "homeland" by force that he joined the German army just for the military training it afforded him. In 1926 he came in contact with the Nazis and, after learning about the goals of the NSDAP, joined it the same year, aged 22. Peddling his Nazi literature, in particular the *Eisenhammer*, he soon became known as a Nazi in a "red" town. He lost his job and, unable to pay the dues, his party membership as well.

> In 1930, when the movement began to gain ground more rapidly, I joined again as an active stormtrooper and . . . [because of his military training] was soon made a *Scharfuehrer* and then a *Truppfuehrer*. . . . After the street battle of November 1930 in Edigheim between the *Reichsbanner* and the SA and SS, more active elements came to the fore. The years 1931 and 1932 passed with constant fighting and proselytizing. After many a successful meeting-hall and electoral battle we thought that now our Fuehrer would come to power . . . but not yet. . . .
> We SA men here in Oppau were almost all unemployed. With a

wife and child, I got ten marks on the dole. We lived on that a whole week, paid my dues of RM 1.30, the party paper, and the dues of the NSBO [Nazi union]. I went out every night to protect our propaganda and election rallies. We were laughed at, ridiculed, and punished, but never lost our faith in Adolf Hitler and his mission. Even after his appointment as Chancellor by Field Marshal von Hindenburg we lay in waiting many a night in case the Communists would rise up, which they would have done if our Fuehrer had not gone after them with an iron fist.

Regarding the respondents' occupations, the differences were not great, but the slowest were the military-civil servants and the "fastest" the blue-collar workers, a difference probably due to age more than to occupation. The father's occupation seems more relevant here. The children of businessmen and of military-civil servants were nearly twice as fast as workers' children, although the latter may well have become interested in politics at an earlier age.

The different childhood settings offer only minor differences. The respondents' upward mobility or lack of it appear to bear a strong relation to his rate of extremist escalation. Respondents in social decline, in particular, were quick to go on from stage two to four, one out of five in two years or less, and nearly half in less than five years. As will be remembered, social decline is sometimes alleged to be one of the dynamic causes of fascism and prejudice. We can add to this the many cases in which economic troubles and decline clearly coincided with increasing involvement. The second-fastest group are those upwardly mobile from an urban background, just like the American race rioters of the 1960s.

Were respondents who belonged to a youth group quicker to move from stage two to stage four than those who did not? The answer is affirmative. Except for those in unpolitical youth groups and those who immediately joined the Hitler Youth, members of conservative or bourgeois (*Jungdo*) youth groups were twice as likely to have crossed the interval in only three or four years as were those older respondents who had never been in a youth group. The fastest, of course, were those who joined the HJ or SA right away, or after another youth group, but while they were still no older than 25.

Did the war experience speed up the course of the extremist fever? On the contrary, the respondents without any military service were nearly twice as fast as those with it, which may of course have been due to the youth of the former. But there is also a perceptible difference between those who had already served in peacetime or were professional military men and the wartime volunteers and draftees who were the slowest of the lot. Even the young victory-watchers were not much faster than the average and only half as fast as the other, younger respondents who never served.

Other indicators of the effect of the war and its aftermath suggest that being a prisoner of war or war invalid, feeling great hostility toward draft-dodgers and civilians in general, experiencing cultural shock at the new elites of Weimar society or at its "moral disintegration," participation in Free Corps activity and the Kapp *putsch*, or at least sympathy with the latter, and of course any kind of anti-occupation activity were all highly related to rapid extremist escalation.

Did the father's politics or the school and peer environment tend to speed the progress from stage two to four? It did indeed, provided the home or school influence was *voelkisch*-antisemitic or at least related to the conventional parties. The childhood settings give little differential except for showing up those from poor childhoods as slower in this respect than the economically secure. This is confirmed by the record of those who had to work before they were 14, although respondents who had to work as unskilled teenage laborers tend to be just as fast as the middle-class children who did not have to work until the age of 17 or later.

Experiencing friction within the family or at school and seeking out personal confrontations also mark fast progress toward stage four both from two and three—though not much faster than being fired or boycotted for political reasons. As pointed out earlier, however, the reason might be just as much in the provocative behavior of the respondent as in a hostile environment. Such provocative behavior, in fact, would fit very well our assumption that there is a deviant personality in the fast respondents which will out regardless of the consequences.

Entering the NSDAP

How did the speed of moving from stage two to stage four relate to the different motives for entering stage four, the party? By far the fastest are those who cite friction with the occupation. More than half of them take less than three years to make the transition. They are followed by those who were attracted by the spirit of comradeship among the stormtroopers, of whom one-fourth made it in less than three years. All the other groups are rather close together, with a small head-start for those who mention the "rough opposition of the Communists" or their economic troubles as motives, both again rather "young motives." The slowest, with more than half taking nine years or more, are those who point to the dynamic impression of the Hitler movement. Evidently, this group admired in the NSDAP what it did not possess in itself, dynamism.

The respondents who joined the party in the years after the 1930 elections are generally the slowest, evidently having sat out the years since their quasi-military involvement right after the war. By contrast, the quickest and probably most highly motivated are the pre-1925 Nazis and *voelkisch* members and also those who joined between 1925 and 1928 for the first time. One-fourth or more of both of these groups let no more than two years elapse between entering their stage two and joining the reconstructed NSDAP, and about half join in four years or less. The manner of their introduction to the party, moreover, places the greatest stress on being introduced by a friend or fellow-worker as a much faster route than awareness of the ideology, introduction by a relative, or going to Nazi rallies and demonstrations.

Their involvement with the movement further bears out these differences. Respondents who graduated from the SA to the SS, or who at least were SA men, were about twice as fast as those who never became stormtroopers. In fact, a fourth to a third of the stormtroopers made the transition within three years. It is small wonder, then, that respondents who engaged in campaigning, marching, and fighting, especially "day and night," were also much faster than those who only marched and proselytized, although the latter were also a little older. In their attitude toward the movement, moreover, the fastest seem to have been motivated mostly by the Hitler cult and the spirit of comradeship as compared to the much slower group that derived a sense of personal integration from the struggle itself. Some of these differences, of course, also reflect differences in age which we have already explored. It goes without saying that the younger groups nearly always tended to be faster than their elders.

Their ideological themes as Nazis, finally, seem to involve higher or lower rates of extremist escalation, too. The fastest were the Nordic-German romantics and, much less so, the Hitler cultists. Revanchism and antisemitism were among the slowest, in part because they are "older" themes and in part because quasi-military involvement in either one probably started early in the Weimar Republic. The NSDAP, after all, was not immediately a logical choice for revanchists or even for political antisemites, but only one among many better-established groups.

On the antisemitism scale, there are no great differences in the speed of escalation to report, not even as compared to those who give no evidence of prejudice. Their attitudes toward violence, on the other hand, show up the masochists and those who regret violence as more than twice as fast as, for example, the sadist bullies who of course tend to have been in the war. The same is true of respondents who refer to their political enemies as subhuman, rodents, etc. They are more than twice as fast as those who see them as traitors or as an abstract conspiracy, which makes the language of the *outré* another deviant symptom at least among stage two respondents. On a comparison between the more pragmatic and the more ideological casts of mind, finally, the ideologically-minded respondents are by far the faster in their extremist escalation. Pragmatism appears to have been an inhibiting factor on the way to the Nazi party.

From all this, we can compose an archetype of the fast stage-two-to-four Nazi, a person "overdetermined in an overdetermined way," who has the following characteristics: He was born after 1908, the son of a businessman in decline, who fought the French occupation and had political friction at school, in a medium-sized town, and who joined the party or Hitler Youth directly or right after belonging to *Jungdo*, at any rate at an early age. Alternatively, he might have been in the war, but emerged from it a POW or an invalid, full of venom toward civilians and draft-dodgers, shocked at the new leaders of Weimar society or at the moral disintegration of German postwar society, a Free Corps fighter, Kapp *putsch*ist, or pre-1925 Nazi or *voelkisch* partisan. He may also have joined the NSDAP for the first time between 1925 and 1928, attracted by the spirit of comradeship of the stormtroopers and introduced by a friend or fellow-worker. He immediately became a stormtrooper, marching and fighting "day and night," believing passionately in Hitler, and graduating soon to the SS. He was a romantic about Nordic and German culture, doctrinaire about matters of ideology, and regretful or masochistic about violence in spite of his heavy involvement in it and his reference to his political enemies as subhuman.

We must not forget the one-fourth of the sample which is beyond this measurement because they went through neither of the middle stages. Here is an appropriate example[8] of very rapid escalation in this group, a very young respondent born 1910 (no. 382). At the age of 15, he attended a commercial school at Koblenz, where he went to his first Nazi speech—by Gottfried Feder, a *Reichstag* deputy and the author of the official National Socialist program:

[8] See also no. 507, another account mentioning only the injuries received and persecutions suffered by a young man (born 1907) who started out tangling with the occupation in Baden.

The streets around the meeting place were filled with nervous people. I entered half an hour early and found in the vestibule a beautiful brawl going on. Before I knew it, someone had torn the black-white-red ribbon [the respondent's father was a nationalist] from my lapel and I was involuntarily drawn into the fight. The handful of National Socialists defending the hall against an enemy a hundred times stronger could hold out only because the Marxists had to fight their way up a staircase. . . . There were injuries on both sides till the police cleared everyone out. But the Nazis who had been the victims of the attack were treated as if it had been their fault. These happenings made me instinctively a National Socialist, a process reinforced later by my intellectual grasp of the goals of the NSDAP as they were presented in the inspired speeches of party comrade Feder and *Gauleiter* Grohe.

Quite typically, the respondent asserts, his commitment antedated and was far deeper than his "intellectual grasp" of the ideology.

Barely 16, I joined the party and fought and propagandized eagerly for the new view of the world. . . . The enemy proceeded from ridicule to terror as our numbers began to grow. Meetings were broken up and comrades returning alone were assaulted and beaten bloody. The rabble often received me at night with a hail of stones. The political terror was augmented with economic terror. We were boycotted and terrorized by the authorities and by the public.

My parents had a nursery which rapidly suffered dwindling returns. So they forbade me any public activity. For a while I used to leave the house in civvies and change to my stormtrooper uniform at the house of a comrade. My parents finally had to give up the store because of the boycott and even our garden produce had to be sold out of town, because all the hotel owners here were either Freemasons or loyal to the government.

The young monomaniac ignores the obvious interpretation that it was his activity which threatened to ruin his parents' livelihood. Instead he says:

The enemy used any conceivable means to force us to capitulate, but the greater the terror, the more fanatically we fought on. Prior to the elections we did not get to see our beds for two weeks.[9] Every night we put up posters and guarded them and tore off those of the enemies; we painted slogans on streets, fences, and rock walls, painted over those of the enemies, or "corrected" them with appropriate additions. Since there were not enough activists to do this, we could never afford to rest. When the days were not long enough to pass out leaflets, they

[9] See also no. 392, another "day-and-nighter."

had to be shoved under the doors at night. Sometimes we spent whole nights making up flyers or painting posters because there was rarely enough money to have them made. Like criminals we used to sneak through the streets at night so as not to arouse the attention of the police and of the enemies. We were not motivated by hopes for a position, or for the gratitude of posterity, but only by blind obedience to the Fuehrer. . . .

The Interval Between Stages Three and Four

In comparing the rates of escalation from stage two to four with those from stage three to four, we have to remember that militarization generally occurred during the early years of the Weimar Republic. Politicization, therefore, tended to occur much closer to the period of the most broadly-based struggle for power of the Nazi party and the transition from stage three to four was consequently shorter. This is particularly obvious in the age distribution, where those born after 1902, the postwar generation, also steeply accelerate their rate of escalation to the point where two-thirds and more have made the transition in four years or less.

In their location experience, the intervals for the politicized likewise make those from the occupied areas and also highly mobile respondents stand out as fast. As with the militarized, residents of towns and cities are faster than rural respondents, but so are the residents of metropolitan areas other than Berlin, which is rather slow because of its many older respondents. By occupation, the workers, women, and business and professional people are faster than, say, the military-civil servants. Unlike the militarized, workers', artisans', and businessmen's children are much faster than those of military-civil servants. And the upwardly mobile, especially from a rural background, also are faster than those in decline.

Youth group membership, as with the militarized, often accelerated escalation, and so did never having served in the military. But the peacetime or professional soldiers moved from stage three to four no faster than the wartime draftees and volunteers. The effects of the war and its aftermath were also weaker, except for the impact of anti-occupation experiences. But involvement in 1923, especially in Hitler's *putsch* or in the *Ruhrkampf* was an important factor for both the militarized and the politicized.

Their fastest home environment, oddly enough, was an unpolitical one, or a *voelkisch* home environment, at least after an interval of only one year or less. School settings offered little difference, but with the childhood settings there was a considerable head-start among the orphans and personally deprived, in addition to the faster progress of respondents with economically secure childhoods such as we already observed with the militarized.

What were the motives which brought the stage-three respondents into the party fastest? Friction with the occupation, the stormtroopers' comradeship, and their ideological fervor, including antisemitism, were the fastest, far ahead of such reasons as complaints about the repressiveness of police and government or the opposition of "the Communists." As with the militarized, the respondents who joined the NSDAP before 1928 were by far the quickest to join, with three-fourths making the transition in four years or less. Those who joined between 1928 and 1930 were progressively slower, and after the 1930 elections half the new members had taken eight years or more from their politicization as defined here. Perhaps this made them more mature and experienced, but it also denotes weakness of motivation.

As for their introduction to the party, in contrast to the stage-two respondents introduction by a relative was the fastest approach, followed by introduction by a friend or colleague, but again far ahead of becoming aware of the Nazi ideology. Evidently partisanship was more compatible with family members as go-betweens than was quasi-military activity.

SA or especially SS membership goes with more rapid progress toward the NSDAP and those marching and fighting "day and night" are somewhat faster than the rest, but not by as much as among the militarized. In their attitude toward the movement, only the spirit of comradeship stands out as a chief satisfaction of the faster cases. Their attitudes toward violence hardly permit a distinction between the masochists and the sadists, the two fastest groups, but make out those who regret violence to be a slow group of old fogies. But by the same political reasoning by which the more highly motivated evidently approve of violence, they also tend to express a liking or understanding for their enemies and would like to win them over. The language of the *outré*, which was so typical of the faster militarized cases, is rather a mark of the slow among the politicized. They are evidently too intelligent for such lapses of self-control.

The most frequent ideological theme of the faster cases, finally, is the Nordic-German cult above all, but not the Hitler cult. They too were more often ideological than pragmatic. For this reason they frequently introduce themselves by way of an anecdotal encounter with Jews or aliens which thus forms their "formative experience" or symbol of self-representation. A great many of the faster cases also present the experience of youthful comradeship as their symbol, an obvious youth symbol. What seems the most unusual about the faster cases of the politicized? High cultural shock is their most frequent feature, while among the fastest of the militarized, it tends to be a high degree of group conformity such as we may indeed find in a well-adjusted soldier. High cultural shock, however, the reader will recall, denotes a deep alienation from Weimar society, which evidently characterizes those who most quickly found their way from stage three to stage four.

If we were to compose an archetype of the fast stage-three-to-four Nazi, he would also be very young, from a medium-sized town or a metropole, a worker and worker's son or upwardly mobile from a rural background. He would have been in a youth group and, in 1923, involved in either the beer-hall *putsch* or the anti-occupation struggle. He would be an orphan or from an unpolitical or *voelkisch* home environment. He would have joined the party before 1928 and while rather young, introduced by a relative and attracted by his own ideological fervor or the stormtroopers' comradeship. He would have been a stormtrooper, marching, fighting, and proselytizing, perhaps even "day and night," and have gotten much satisfaction from the spirit of solidarity in the movement. He, too, would be a Nordic-German romantic, rather antisemitic, and alienated from German society, but inclined to express some understanding toward his political enemies.

The Best Time of My Life

"The time of the great struggle," wrote one respondent, born 1903 (no. 433), "was the best time of my life." This phrase mirrors well the sense of meaning their participation shed on many young Nazi lives. Being a part of what they viewed as a great historical effort seemed to give meaning to even the most undistinguished existence. It even shines through matter-of-fact accounts in quasi-military report style such as the following account of a Pirmasens shoemaker's son born 1906 (no. 434), whose job career is typical of the times. He was unable to find a job as a cook, for which he had been trained, worked for a while in his father's shoe shop until the shop could no longer support him, and then joined the Voluntary Labor Service as an agricultural assistant. In 1930 he found a job as a public baths attendant and then again in a shoe factory before entering the unemployment rolls. The Nazis in 1933 gave him a job as caretaker of a sports field and, finally, as supervisor of the municipal street-sweepers. His political career, by way of contrast, was glamorous:

> In 1923 I joined the National Socialist movement as an active member and stormtrooper. A year later I was in a bloody meeting-hall battle at Waldfischbach where an SA comrade . . . lost his life. . . . In the following years until the takeover of power by our movement, I participated in all the rallies, demonstrations, etc., we had in Pirmasens or elsewhere in the Palatinate. From this participation, I frequently suffered injuries. A particularly bad one I incurred 1929-1930 in Worms when we broke up a theater performance. I was stabbed in the head and in the back. Because of my political activity I was frequently in conflict with the German police and court authorities and received many jail sentences and fines. The French military court in Kaiserslautern also sentenced me. . . . In 1929 I was appointed a *Sturmfuehrer* in Pirmasens. After a Christmas celebration in 1932, I got into a brawl with Communists which led to my arrest on charges of disturbing the peace. But I was never tried because our movement took over the power in the country.

Reading between the lines, it is obvious that his fighting years and his career in the movement supplied the high points of his life.

The same interpretation seems to apply to a worker's son born 1906 (no. 464), who grew up among Berlin Social Democrats and Communists and belonged to a Socialist sports club and to the Communist Youth (KJ). The latter group, in fact, sent him to infiltrate the *Bismarckjugend* and other right-wing groups in order to wean away their working-class members. The plot misfired in that the respondent left the KJ for a right-wing group in 1921 and henceforth had to endure physical assaults by his erstwhile buddies. His new group, called *Stellung* (front-line position) eventually merged with the Nazi front *Frontbann*, and he campaigned for Ludendorff for President in 1925.

> I still recall . . . that election Sunday when we reported at 6 a.m. and were ordered to pass out flyers. . . . From the opening of the polling stations I stood without any relief holding up my election poster at Schloss-Strasse. At first the [red] comrades would not even let me stand there until a policeman assured me of my place. It was a stormy Sunday for me and I had to run away at least once every hour.
>
> Afterwards, four of us ran into the entire Red Front (RFB) of Charlottenburg at Schiller-Strasse. If we had not each carried with us that famous walking cane and one of us a gas pistol we might not have survived.
>
> My SA period was with *Sturm* 33 which was led by real men . . .

guiding us in those days. Our *Sturm* hangout in the Hebbelstrasse was our home. The Communists ran into granite here. The hours I experienced here were too wonderful and perhaps also too hard to write down. Our *Sturm* 33 was called the Killer *Sturm* (*Moerdersturm*) and there was not one stormtrooper in it who had not been worked over at least once by the reds on his way to the hangout. . . .

The worst period of struggle was the years 1931-1932 when the Communists gradually began to peter out. The last decent workers turned their backs on the KPD and we were fighting only the underworld, wrestling clubs, etc.

He did mention that unlike some of his comrades he never lost his job. But, the real life of this young man was something quite similar to the world of juvenile gangs. The only point of orientation left was evidently the KPD as the antagonistic rival gang. Whether he belonged to the one or the other was not a matter of ideology, but of group loyalty and gang fights.

It is easy to lose one's way in the trackless world of special personal motives and circumstances which we will explore further in the chapters ahead. One good way of conceptualizing the process of becoming an extremist, however, is still the assumption of a powerful missionary urge, for whatever personal reasons, to reform the world in the image of the ideology. Manifestations of the intensity of this urge speed up the process, and a long list of retarding factors, beginning with the life cycle of the respondent, can slow it down or stifle it altogether. The role of violence in this process can be quite ambiguous, because violence may be a purpose in itself in some cases, as with the "mindless sluggers," and a manifestation of the missionary urge in others. The young extremists are a prime example of fast mobilization chiefly because they lives exhibit few retarding factors. It is also conceivable that there are special psychological aspects of growing up and of political deviancy that may tend to intensify the ideological urge itself. Let us take a closer look at the beliefs and attitudes of the Abel respondents.

PART V

Nazi Ideology and Attitudes

There is by now an international literature totalling many hundreds of volumes and thousands of articles in scholarly journals or parts of learned books that deal with Nazi ideology. They range from enlightened anti-Fascist manifestoes and polemics and serious philosophical treatises to the literature on "German thought from Luther to Hitler" which was admired in the Anglo-American intellectual community but a generation ago. Rarely has so much intelligence been wasted on so unpromising a subject. To be sure, there were some minor Nazi leaders such as Alfred Rosenberg or Walther Darré who attempted to fashion snatches of personal belief into an ideology for the movement. Their efforts were not widely adopted in the NSDAP. Hardly any of the Abel respondents mention any of them, except for Hitler's *Mein Kampf* and the official party newspapers and periodicals. There were also a few popular writers, rarely mentioned in the Abel *vitae*, such as Paul de Lagarde, Julius Langbehn, Moeller van den Bruck, and other "conservative revolutionaries" whose respectable cultural pessimism and political fantasies performed a valuable service for the not so respectable NSDAP.[1] Although they were neither in the Nazi movement nor its beneficiaries, they fashioned the intellectual bridges over which many conservatives and bourgeois intellectuals could find their way to the brown masses. However, this does not make their thought *the* Nazi ideology either.

More prominently mentioned by many Abel respondents are the prewar groups and publications of political antisemitism, especially

[1] See, especially Fritz Stern, *The Politics of Cultural Despair*, Berkeley: University of California Press, 1961, Klemens von Klemperer, *Germany's New Conservatism*, Princeton University Press, 1957, and George L. Mosse, *The Crisis of German Ideology*, New York: Grosset & Dunlap, 1964, and the sources cited there. Many of the *voelkisch* groups and the conservative revolutionaries shared a strong aversion to the Nazi movement which they regarded as too "democratic" and too "political," i.e., too much involved in fashioning an effective mass movement.

one Theodor Fritsch (1844-1933), whose *Handbook on the Jewish Question* went through an awesome forty editions between 1888 and 1936. Other publications of his *Hammerverlag* were also read and distributed further by some of the political antisemites in the sample. Another name that comes up frequently is that of Richard Kunze (*Knueppelkunze*), an antisemitic propagandist of the prewar Conservative party who later continued to attract followers in a separate movement. This prewar antisemitic element and its ramifications in the Weimar setting[2] come closest to supplying a kind of ideological core, especially if we throw in scattered *voelkisch* ideas that crop up here and there in the autobiographies of the Abel collection. However, even this *voelkisch*-antisemitic core is too limited in its acceptance and salience among the bulk of the Abel respondents to serve as a basis for studying the movement as an ideological movement. There may be layers of ideological attitudes that distinguish the rather activistic group before us from the broad range of middle-class voters and sympathizers whose support was perhaps more highly related to *voelkisch* and patriotic appeals. But there is no escaping the conclusion that we cannot truly understand the minds of these rank-and-file Nazi activists by intellectualizing their motivations into an ideological system of ideas. Instead, we need to examine the mixture of ideas, phobias, and prejudices on their minds which form a coherent political subculture that is more amenable to psychological than to intellectual analysis.

For this purpose, we propose to abandon the search for logical consistency and first principles and to concentrate instead on understanding the relationships among certain beliefs, attitudes, and actions. First of all, we shall catalogue and relate the main themes of Nazi ideology to other indicators and attributes. Even though there may be little relation among the themes, the cosmogonies of various subgroups of the sample and their long-range expectations obviously deserve attention. Then, we shall shift to an examination of the feelings and subjective attitudes of the respondents toward the system in which they lived and fought, the Weimar Republic, the public authorities, and their political antagonists. From their subjective orientation toward the system we move to the murky

[2] See especially the discussion of the Youth Movement and of Weimar in Mosse, *The Crisis of German Ideology*, pp. 171-279, and Pulzer, *The Rise of Political Anti-Semitism in Germany and Austria*. On the *voelkisch* ideology, see also Rolf Geisler, *Dekadenz und Heroismus*, Schriftenreihe der Vierteljahreshefte fuer Zeitgeschichte, no. 9, Deutsche Verlagsanstalt, 1964, and Martin Broszat, "Die voelkische Ideologie und der Nationalsozialismus," *Deutsche Rundschau*, vol. 84 (1958), pp. 53-68.

depths of their hatreds and prejudices, especially antisemitism and ethnocentricity, the harbingers of the great crimes of the Third Reich. Antisemitism is no more an idea or an ideology than a common obscenity is. It is a state of mind that comes in different shadings and degrees of intensity which are likely to be highly related to other attitudes and to behavior. Finally, we turn to the respondents' attitudes toward themselves, their own roles, and what we can glimpse of their personalities. This combination of various perspectives, we hope, will add up to a fairly complete picture of the political subculture of the early Nazi movement despite the inadequacy of the sample and of the information it supplies.

There is also some question about what depth of belief is required to constitute an element of ideology. Like those in other young extremist movements, the early Nazis had an inspirational style all their own. It is difficult to describe this spirit of "idealism" outside the rhetoric of some of the speakers, and it is not at all a matter of ideological content. A few of the younger respondents have caught the melodramatic style and present their *vitae* as a series of inspiring moments. A furniture manufacturer's son and gardener's apprentice born 1905 (no. 466), for example, describes the mood of the faithful at the time of the collapse of the beer-hall *putsch*, his first personal encounter with Adolf Hitler, and other momentous occasions including the following one:

October 9-10, 1926: The first National Socialist Freedom Day of the Mark Brandenburg in Potsdam. Six hundred brown shirts under the command of SA leader Kurt Daluege, we are marching along the old army route once followed by General Luetzow into Potsdam. A field prayer service was held before the sacred house in which the remains of the great Soldier King Frederick William I and of his great son, the *Alter Fritz* [Frederick II], are resting. We would rather have gone to the old garrison church and would have bowed our heads at the sight of the old flags of the Brandenburg regiments, praying for their blessing for our struggle. But the edict of the established church authority barred us from entry.

That night in the festival hall of the airship port, Dr. Goebbels, the drummer of the Ruhr area, spoke to us. His speech made the meeting into a church service. The hall is no longer on the sands of Brandenburg, but a cathedral in the plains of Flanders. Young war volunteers now are the parishioners who are crowding closer and closer to the altar. . . . Dr. Goebbels no longer speaks as a party man, but as a Fuehrer who has returned from the fire of the first front lines to inspire new reserves and lead them into battle.

And so on from one heroic occasion to the next one. The English language hardly suffices to translate his sacral symbolisms and exalted style. In spite of all his references to church service, the respondent is anything but a man of Christian devotion. And neither Goebbels nor the respondent ever served in the war. His real ideology is mentioned only in a brief aside about his familiarity with *voelkisch* literature and Fritsch's *Handbook of the Jewish Question.* All this inspirational imagery would have been readily understood, however, by other young Nazis, especially if they too were of the victory-watcher generation. For still younger recruits, other Goebbels speeches could be just as moving. The same respondent, for example, describes in his breathless style another speech at the Berlin *Sportpalast*:

> *September 29-30, 1928:* . . . Dr. Goebbels speaks of the problem of the prewar period: the unknown worker, the worker of hand and brain. And the backbone of the war effort, the unknown soldier. . . . Both grew into the symbol of our time, the unknown stormtrooper, who fights and bleeds according to his inner law, without being forced to. These are the legions of the freedom fighters, the future of our nation. Their antagonist is the symbol of the state of today, the policy of Gustav Stresemann. . . . The coming revolution will smash one of the two. In our camp is Germany. Let us march forward over the graves.

One can imagine how these young men must have viewed themselves and their historical role, drunk with their own words or with those of a brilliant demagogue. This rhetoric and the shared sentiments, furthermore, must have helped to create a sense of group solidarity capable of summoning forth extreme exertions and sacrifices from many a young stormtrooper. As Hitler had once pointed out so aptly, one did not win a truly dedicated following by making all kinds of promises but rather by demanding the last in effort and sacrifices. Many of his followers did not even require any ideological food for thought. The inspirational tenor of the rhetoric was quite enough for them.

Main Themes of Nazi Ideology

Before we try to look at the *Weltanschauung* of the individual respondent, there is the question of the level and nature of his (or her) understanding of the political world around him, as some of the Abel respondents are noticeably less perceptive or more ideological than others. Then we recorded the main ideological themes stressed by each respondent after he had become a Nazi. Since many respondents describe their progress toward the party as a development which often led them through other organizations and sets of ideas, we could hardly assume that the respondents always had the same ideas. Finally, we also recorded the expectations of the respondents in 1934 when the Abel *vitae* were collected. This information is the last attitudinal hint of coming orientations as they passed the boundary between an extremist fringe group and the awesome potentiality of being in power.

The Level of Political Knowledge

The Abel respondents vary widely in their political acumen. Some knowledgeable observers have been tempted at times to deny them the possession of any intelligence or judgment whatever. We tried to avoid any bias by using as the criterion the ability of the respondent to understand all, a major part, or only little of the complex political scene of Weimar. "High, pragmatic," for example, bears the parenthetical legend in the codebook "understands the major groups of Weimar politics and society and their respective roles." "High, ideological" was interpreted as "sees the whole picture but through ideological lenses." "Medium" was "understands system but with major flaw, e.g., no understanding for labor." "Low, ideological" is "cannot see the whole picture because of obsessive concern of some sort." The rest are self-explanatory. For purposes of cross-tabulation, these categories were collapsed in two different ways. One separated them into high, medium, and three low groups, ideological, pragmatic-narrow, and romantic-dimwit. The other juxtaposed all ideological to all pragmatic (including the medium) groups, and left the rest in a third group.

FD-73: Level and Nature of Political Knowledge

	Number	Per cent
High, pragmatic	24	4.7
High, ideological	27	5.3
Medium	82	16.0
Low, ideological	198	38.3
Low, pragmatic	23	4.5
Low, narrow (military or civil service blinders)	74	14.4
Low, dimwit, incoherent	67	13.1
Low, romantic hero to self	19	3.7
	514	100.0

A Social Profile of Knowledge Levels

The most obvious way of confirming the relevance of our measurement is to test it against the level of formal education. The highly knowledgeable respondents, indeed, turn out to have the largest number of people with at least an *Abitur* (34.9%), and with *mittlere Reife* (23.3%), together 58.2%. They are followed by the medium-level group with only 44.2% and the low level groups with only 10-25% of the same educational attainments. The least-educated group are the dimwits and romantics, of whom one-third had no more than the customary eight years of primary school and another one-half primary plus vocational training. When we compare the ideologically minded with the pragmatists, moreover, the latter are, with 18.8% with *Abitur* (cf. 13.2% of ideologists) and 24.8% with *mittlere Reife* (cf. 14.2%), noticeably better-educated.

As to their ages, the low-ideological and dimwit-romantic groups predominate among the postwar generation (1902-1916), followed by the high groups. The low-pragmatic-narrow respondents, on the other hand, stand out among the prewar and, together with the medium group, the war generations. These two main elements, the narrow military-civil servant mentality from before and during the war, and the masses of uncomprehending young followers after the war, fit the picture that we have gained from other indicators. The juxtaposition of ideological and pragmatic inclinations adds a further dimension. As we would expect, the ideologically motivated predominate among the postwar generation, while the war generation is relatively pragmatic.

Would we expect political intelligence among the early Nazis to be concentrated in Berlin or in other metropolitan areas? The dimwit-romantics and the medium-intelligent groups are over-represented in small towns and rural areas, to be sure. But the highly intelligent are outnumbered in the metropolitan areas by the low-pragmatic-narrow group, which probably includes many former military or civil servants. The low-ideologists are most at home in rural areas and in metropoles other than Berlin, which seem to be the best places for ideological brooding at any level. Regarding their location experience, furthermore, it is remarkable that no other experience seems as likely to kindle ideological-mindedness—especially low-ideological-mindedness—as being from the occupied areas.

The various occupational groups of the sample differ sharply in the level of their political understanding. The white-collar group and the military-civil servants have the largest share of high- and medium-level respondents. The women and blue-collar respondents have the most low-ideological and romantic-dimwit responses, and are generally more ideological than the rest. Similar statements can be made about the occupations of the fathers of the respondents. The high and medium responses are most frequent among the sons and daughters of military-civil servants, including some of high rank. Low-ideological responses tend to be typical of the children of workers, businessmen, and farmers. And the dimwit-romantic responses are especially frequent among the descendants of artisans and farmers.

Is social mobility related to a propensity for ideological thinking? The most ideological, it turns out, were respondents upwardly mobile from an urban background or in social decline. Both groups also include a disproportionate share of the highly knowledgeable. The upwardly mobile from a rural background, by comparison, have an abundance of the low-pragmatic-narrow political understanding typical of many military-civil servants. A socially static environment, finally, seems to be the ideal breeding grounds for unusual numbers of dimwit-romantics and low ideological types. There can be no doubt that social mobility and an urban environment enhance political intelligence.

Finally, there is a strong relationship between ideological thinking and religion which requires closer examination. The more ideological respondents, both high and low in level, tend to be Catholics and to live in a Catholic area, or, alternatively, they could be Protestants or Catholics but living in an evenly mixed area or in one dominated by the opposite religious majority. The Protestants and Protestant areas, by comparison, tended to be pragmatic or dimwit-romantics and narrow. Catholicism seems to breed ideology even in its apostates.

Main Ideological Themes

Our record of the main ideological themes held by the respondent after he joined the Nazi party is, by definition, not an inventory of his ideas on various subjects. It only brings out his emphasis, thereby opposing, for example, the revanchists to the antisemites even though the Nazi revanchists may well have been somewhat antisemitic and the antisemites frequently rather revanchist. We can supplement the one-dimensionality of this index by crosstabulation with other measurements. It also does not measure the intensity of belief except as belief in one issue may be contrasted with belief in another issue by the same respondent. To compare intensity of belief among several respondents, we have to use separate indicators such as the ethnocentricity scale. Since antisemitism was one of the central concerns, however, our breakdown tries to separate the full-blown ideology of political antisemitism from the cases in which we can hardly speak of an ideology, even though the verbal stereotypes indicate the prejudice.

In our nomenclature, a Nordic nut emphasizes the virtues of a Nordic or Aryan race, while a German romantic is beholden to the cultural and historical traditions of old Germany *as he inter-*

FD-60: Main Ideological Theme (while in NSDAP)

	Number	Per cent
No ideology worth noting	19	2.6
⌐Strong ideological antisemite	63	8.5
└Incidental antisemite (e.g., use of verbal stereotypes only)	38	5.1
⌐Nordic cultist	11	1.5
├German romantic	21	2.8
└Blood and soil	11	1.5
Revanchist, law-and-order	42	5.7
Superpatriot, nationalist	166	22.5
Social *Volksgemeinschaft* (solidarism)	234	31.7
Hitler cult	134	18.1
	739*	100.0

* Multiple responses.

prets them, and often in the vein of cultural pessimism. These two and the blood-and-soil category were combined to form a general group of *voelkisch* beliefs.[3] A revanchist is a person who would

[3] *Voelkisch* ideology, as described by Fritz Stern in *The Politics of Cultural Despair* or by George Mosse in *The Crisis of German Ideology*, of course, also tends to include antisemitism, superpatriotism, and soli-

have liked to resurrect the glories of the German army and, frequently, to fight the war over or at least to eliminate the reparations, rescind all cessions of territory, and abolish all other limitations imposed upon Germany by the Treaty of Versailles. The super-patriot borders on these sentiments but with emphasis on popular feelings of outrage at the foreign occupation, contempt and suspicion toward foreigners, and loyalty toward Germany and the Germans. The other categories are self-explanatory.

A Few Examples of Ideological Themes

Examples of the *voelkisch* Nordic-German-agrarian romantics are frequent, but not always very quotable. A retired major, born in the 1880s (no. 43), for example, spends pages to create an allegoric landscape with his Fuehrer striding through gloom and clouds toward a sun-drenched mountain peak. He goes on to describe in similar abstractions the "undermining of the great sacrifices of the front by alien Jews and paid and deluded traitors of the people who sowed fraternal hatred and civil war." He sets up ideals of German kind, German womanhood, German honor, and German manhood, and claims that they were stripped of all good qualities, "while Jewish *literati* and the Jewish press raged and pulled everything into the mud." Especially the "essentially decent and honest worker was poisoned to the quick." An early member of the *Deutschvoelkische Freiheitspartei*, the respondent soon encountered the NSDAP, where he claimed to find "the front-line spirit and the proper emphasis on the fatherland, the German people, German kind, and social concern." Like many *voelkisch* ideologues, and like many of the antisemites, the respondent was oddly preoccupied with political illusions or "fata morgana" and the hidden "wire-pullers" who try to deceive the people. He was also an avid proselytizer and, with his entire family in the NSDAP, frequently engaged in door-to-door propaganda.

Another example is a woman born about 1895 (no. 44), who "due to my inherited, sound feelings" used to volunteer to sing *Deutschland, Deutschland ueber Alles* despite the teasing of her classmates. "It was not a matter of vanity with me, but from the desire of my heart." Canvassing for the People's Party (DVP) after the war, she wanted to "struggle for the German soul" and "peel off the alien layers from the German soul," until she became disillusioned with the DVP and got married. After the failure of her mar-

---

darism, but the separate investigations of these topics in this book suggested that it would be better not to lump everything together.

riage, she was vehemently attracted to the Nazi movement because of its stress on "the *race question!!!!*" (punctuation and italics of the respondent): "*With this an ideological leader could not make any money. For this he needed idealism, faith in ultimate verities for which we have been ardently longing for all these years, knowingly or not. Yes, our people needed idealism, the awareness of the meaning of the words: to be a member of a certain people!!!!*" (italics and punctuation of the respondent).

Thus, she joined the "rows of the fighters for the genuine, pure racial soul." She also mentions some philologists and archeologists of the "Nordic Ring" who gave her the solace that the race in its substance of heroism was not yet beyond repair. A few poets and thinkers are also thrown in, although the "people's healthy instinct" is given more credence than the corruptions of intellect in producing "the high point of creative and fighting existence: the religious expression of the life of the whole German people." National Socialism bears nothing materialistic but "the God-willed law of the racial soul." Therefore, the party "can lead the people back to the well-springs of life and to the native soil of the beliefs proper to the race (*arteigen*). Someday, therefore, it will enable Germany to be the liberator of all Nordically determined peoples and show them the way to a proud and free nationhood, untouched by any corrosive alien spirit."

Another respondent (born about 1898, no. 45) traces his ancestry through generations of soldiers. He also traces the history of "the Germanic peoples" to freedom-loving, nomadic herdsmen and hunters. Since this "race" produced many famous men, he argues, "we, the blood representatives and descendants of this race, demand to participate in the fortunes of this world on the most justified an incontrovertible authority." Germany's current fate is the result of "hate-filled neighbors who are continuing the war through the peace," and of "dishonorable, miserable weaklings and traitors," namely the "Marxist do-gooders" who are "seeking salvation in international brotherhood" and thus blindly contributing to the destruction of Germany. The phantoms chased by the Marxists, however, were not their own invention but "imported by Jews as thoughts alien to the race." He adds that "Germany is the strongest fortress against the Jewish plans for world domination. If this fortress falls, all of Europe goes." The respondent evidently propagandized for the *voelkisch* cause for half a decade and knew several Nazis in Berlin before joining up in 1930. What caused him to turn from the anti-political *voelkisch* associations to the NSDAP, according to his own account, was witnessing a police charge against

Nazi demonstrators. Seeing them brutalized and hearing their cries of pain kept him awake all night and he joined the next day.

Another respondent is an Austrian born 1906 (no. 69), who proudly relates his father's involvement with Schoenerer and the prewar *voelkisch* groups in Austria. The son likewise joined a *voelkisch* youth group, *Adler und Falken*, and read up on the pseudo-scientific literature on race and the agricultural calling of the true German. He mentions specifically H.F.K. Guenther, Hahne, Darré, and Himmler in connection with joining the *voelkisch Artamanen* movement, agrarian volunteers on the great estates:

> In 1924 Professor Willibald Hentschel called up the German agricultural college movement, *voelkisch* youth, and the whole paramilitary movement to volunteer service in German agriculture to keep out the alien migration from the east, and to prepare the best of German youth for settlement there rather than flight from the countryside. He came up with the concept rooted in National Socialism: A people that thinks it is too good to work its own soil has no right to it and will, in the course of nature, be wiped out by those to whom it delegates this task.

A good example of a superpatriot is a bricklayer born 1891 (no. 428), who, though serving in the army and in the police, until 1926 always abstained from politics. He discovered his divergent opinions only when he began to work among Social Democrats and Centrists at I. G. Farben. With a feeling of shock, the respondent quotes an SPD colleague to the effect that "There is no fatherland named Germany for me. Wherever I fare well and make a lot of money, that is my fatherland." While the other fellow-workers nodded agreement, "Red anger rose into my face and I wanted to give him a vehement answer. But when he asked what camp I was in, I had no reply. Home (*Heimat*) and fatherland were everything to me, a piece of myself. And that man was denying the fatherland for which we had fought and bled for four years." The respondent made a serious effort to learn more about Marxism, but in the end he rejected its international and militant features in favor of a "German socialism."

Another superpatriot was a young metalworker, born 1907 (no. 1) who, as an ardent victory-watcher with two brothers in the war, used to ring the church bells with every new German victory. He was deeply moved by the death of a brother and two cousins in the war and greatly depressed by the German defeat and the revolution. As a metalworker of ardent patriotic convictions he had a very hard time among the "reds." He hardly improved his popularity by his activism in nationalist youth groups, displaying the black-white-and-red flag, and presenting patriotic plays in Prussian uniforms. He had joined the NSDAP by the time he was 18.

A great many of the superpatriots were people from the occupied areas who often combined a strong identification with the war effort with hostile involvement with the French occupation, sometimes as a result of participation in the passive resistance, sometimes as a natural consequence of direct conflict.

Social Background of Ideological Groups

If we compare the main ideological themes by date of respondents' birth, the ideological profiles of the postwar, war, and prewar generations emerge. The postwar generation, for example, has the largest share of those without any ideology (68.4%), of Nordic-German-agrarian romantics (39.1%) and of Hitler cultists (38.9%). These three themes are particularly heavy among the cohorts born 1906 or later. The war generation, narrowly defined (1895-1901), has its emphasis on Nordic-German culture, the *Volksgemeinschaft* (it includes many who suffered economic disaster before 1929), and, especially if we include the 1890-1894 cohort with its many peacetime and professional soldiers, revanchism. The prewar generation (born 1860-1894) has more than half of the antisemites and revanchists (including those born 1890-1894) and almost as many of the superpatriots. In the light of the literature on Nazi ideology, it is worth stressing in particular that the *voelkisch*, Nordic-German-agrarian cult, which some writers regard as a sinister nineteenth-century crypto-Nazi tradition, is far more typical of our postwar and war generations. Antisemitism again, which the literature tends to attribute to the 1920s to the extent that it acknowledges it at all, appears to be more heavily represented among the older respondents. It is this motif which seems to be the poisonous legacy from the nineteenth century, the fatal flaw of all Nazi idealism.

Revanchism and superpatriotism, on the other hand, are understandable, defensive attitudes of a stiff-backed older generation faced with the destruction of much it held dear. It comes as no surprise to find the prewar and professional military motivated by revanchism. The reader may also recall the switch in the home and school environments of many Nazis from nationalism or patriotism to *voelkisch*-antisemitic influences. Here the antisemitism of the prewar generation evidently began to poison the wellsprings of the generations to come under the cover of *voelkisch* ideas.

Does the size of the community of residence during the years 1928-1933 have anything to do with the varying ideological emphases of our Nazi respondents? There are some notable differences. The Hitler-worshippers, for example, are heavily concentrated in small towns and rural areas, while the antisemites and revanchists tend to be metropolitan, especially from Berlin. The Nordic-German romantics tend to live mainly in medium-sized cities (10,000-100,000) while superpatriots and devotees of the *Volksgemeinschaft* (solidarism) mostly live either in metropoles or in rural and small-town areas. The location experience groups also have distinctive ideological profiles. Respondents with foreign or colonial experience tend to be chiefly revanchists or antisemites. The borderland Germans are mostly Nordic-German romantics or Hitler-worshippers who probably considered the Austrian corporal one of their own. Respondents from the occupied areas tend to be superpatriots or also worshippers of Hitler, who promised them a national rebirth. By way of contrast, rural-urban migrants are mostly antisemites, superpatriots, or solidarists, all evidently influenced by issues related to the migration and melting-pot experience. The spatially immobile tend to be revanchists and solidarists. Those highly mobile are mostly without any ideology, or Nordic-German romantics, or also antisemites. Two of the last-mentioned groups, the readers may recall, were among the more violent of the sample.

Did occupational groups or social classes have an ideological cast of their own within the Nazi panoply of issues? Military-civil servants tended to be revanchists or superpatriots, naturally, but the sons and daughters of this profession were more often Nordic-German romantics, antisemites, or solidarists. Workers and workers' children both tended to be solidarists. But workers also opted heavily for the Hitler and Nordic-German cults, and many of them had no ideology worth noting. The children of workers, on the other hand, also included many superpatriots and revanchists, since the military was a road to social advancement in the empire. White-collar Nazis tended to be antisemites or revanchists. Business and professional respondents were mostly antisemites or superpatriots, while the children of businessmen were more often Nordic-German romantics or revanchists. The women respondents tended to be Nordic-German romantics or dedicated to the Hitler cult as their dominant theme. Farm families, finally, were the most warlike background. The children of farmers tended to be revanchists, superpatriots, or solidarists. And farmers were most frequently revanchists or solidarists.

The advance or decline in status between father and son consti-

tutes the basis of our measurement of social mobi
in social decline tended to stress the Nordic-Ger
cults or revanchism—one perhaps to feel precious
salvation, and the third to get even with the world. T₁
no attempt to rise above the station of their parents
be revanchists or else they were solidarists. The gre₁
seems to be between the upwardly mobile of town and ι
latter were mostly revanchists and superpatriots. The ſ ₋ιre
more likely to be Nordic-German romantics, solidarists, or antisemites.

Nazi Ideology and Religion

There are many accounts among the Abel *vitae* of the conflicts respondents experienced with the Catholic religion (rarely with Protestantism). Their own scruples were often reinforced by the stubborn resistance and open hostility of the church and of the Catholic
community. We have already quoted some instances of this earlier.[4]
An example of the Catholic resistance is in the political *vita* of a
worker and farmer's son born 1891 (no. 473), who served his
country from 1912 until 1918, one of seven sons in the war. Two
died and one lost an arm. "After my discharge I had a hard time
settling down to the still and peaceful life. I kept thinking of re-
enlisting with some outfit but my mother did not approve of it." In
1924, at the age of 33, he married a girl against the will of his
parents and had to leave home. His political interest was engaged
in 1923 by the treason trial of Hitler which he "followed avidly" in
the Nazi newspaper *Voelkischer Beobachter*. When the NSDAP
came to his area, he joined immediately, and so did twelve of his
fellow-workers. At this point the local resistance started, beginning
with liberal hecklers at the first rally, a teacher "who still has not
grapsed this ideology today (1934)," and the local *Bauernbund*
leader, "to whom we and a few courageous farmers gave the right
answer." The ensuing Nazi electoral advances and a propaganda
campaign of selling Nazi newspapers and forcing leaflets even on
the unwilling mobilized the Catholics.

In particular the church itself and the Catholic associations preached
hatred and intrigues against us. They even passed out leaflets in the
cemetery. Once, when I was putting up Hitler posters in public places
for the coming elections, one of this most Christian gang said, "You
can't even go to church anymore without getting angry with all these
Hitler heads."

[4] See above, page 87 ff.

The chairman of the BVP [Bavarian Center Party] here handed out his leaflets to his flock and so I gave him some of ours. He said sarcastically, "That is the right man indeed who will help you, that foreign scalawag.[5] You could not find a better one. . . ." The local priest said in his Sunday sermon on election day that this time there ought not to be 200 or even 20 Hitler votes . . . there were 220. . . .

But we could do no better here than elsewhere; we were marked and working with our faithful followers did not do us much good. As soon as we had conquered a few souls of the people, the black [Catholic] brotherhood intervened with hatred and intrigues on such a nasty level that our converts often fell back into their old beliefs.

The Catholic solidarity held admirably tight, at least until the capitulation of the Vatican in July, 1933.

When my seven-year-old in 1932 had a swastika on his school pack, the teacher reprimanded him and the clergy mentioned me in the Christmas Sunday sermon. Three weeks later they invited my wife to come to Christian indoctrination because she had been delivering the [Nazi] *Nationalzeitung*. . . .

We were not able to raise our number of members during the fighting years, unfortunately, despite our many propaganda rallies. On the contrary, by August 1932 there were only five of us who held out and we had to merge our local with that of a neighboring community.

The respondent finally took over the local leadership himself after vainly offering it to several local "job-hunters and big shots who did not have the guts to stand up openly for national socialism but would rather stay in good stead with the clergy, the BVP, and the *Bauernbund* [a liberal, regional peasant party]."

But there are also other dimensions of the religious question which are better explored with statistical means. The Abel respondents include 24.1% Protestants, 9.4% Catholics, and 66.5% who failed to state their affiliation. Disproportionate numbers of Catholics were antisemites, superpatriots, or solidarists. The Nordic-German romantics, by comparison, tended to be Protestants. The revanchists and Hitler cultists, and most of those without any ideology tended not to state their denomination—which in the Weimar setting may have denoted secularism. As to their religious area, however, the revanchists mostly lived in a Protestant area, the Nordic-

---

[5] The word was *Schlawak*, a Bavarian epithet vaguely referring to Slovaks. The respondent points out, by the way, that this BVP leader also happened to be Austrian-born and that he reminded him of that fact.

German romantics and solidarists in Catholic areas, and the superpatriots in evenly mixed areas. When we control for whether a respondent lived in an area dominated by his coreligionists or in a mixed area or in one dominated by the other major religion, superpatriots and devotees of the Hitler cult disproportionately turn out to live mostly in a religiously heterogeneous setting. By contrast, antisemitism and the Nordic-German-agrarian cult are most at home in a religiously homogeneous setting. This kind of integral nationalism seems to flourish in the absence of cultural conflict.

So much of Nazi ideology is at a mental level which, in a relatively well-educated population, never fails to astound foreign observers. Are there differences in the mental level of the various issues emphasized by the respondents? As far as formal education is concerned, the Nordic-German romantics with 48.6% of at least a six-year secondary education (including 27% with *Abitur*) are the best-educated, followed by the revanchists (35.7%) and the antisemites (32%). Education is evidently no sure remedy for prejudice but, as we have seen, can actually intensify it. Those without any ideology and the superpatriots have the most limited education. As for their level of political understanding, the best-informed ones are the solidarists and the Nordic-German romantics. The least-informed are those without any ideology, who include many of low intelligence who to themselves are romantic heroes, and the revanchists, who are very often low-pragmatic or narrow. The antisemites and the Hitler cultists include many low-ideological or dim-wit-romantic respondents. The same two groups also stand out as notably more ideological in their thinking than the rest.

The "System" and the Other Actors

How did these ideological groups view "the system" of the Weimar Republic? Two-thirds of the antisemites, naturally, viewed Weimar as the *Judenrepublik*, a system run by Jews. One-third of the Nordic-German romantics gave the same verdict, while the others tended to call it a "Marxist-liberal system." Revanchists and superpatriots differ substantially on this issue. The revanchists, who were older, tended to stress their objections to the "multi-party state" and to raise the traditional anti-capitalist arguments. The superpatriots, on the other hand, liked to call it a Marxist or Marxist-liberal system, or to clothe their yearning for a fascist utopia in laments about the "black [Catholic] and red parties." The *Volksgemeinschaft* solidarists also stressed Marxism or Marxism-liberalism and also the multi-party state as the divisive influences they hated in the republic. The Hitler-worshippers, finally, emphasized the red and black parties, multi-partyism, and capitalism as the chief obstacles to salvation. The convergence of their various images of the republic and their chief themes of ideology hardly requires pointing out.

Whom did they identify as their chief enemies? The most common reply among all the respondents was the Marxists, or Communists and Socialists (62%), but only the devotees of the Hitler cult and the Nordic-German romantics placed disproportionate stress (75.7% and 68.6%, respectively) on anti-Marxism. Not surprisingly, the antisemites added the Jews to the anti-Marxist package. The revanchists and solidarists, on the other hand, tended to rail against reactionaries, liberals, Catholics, and the like, a distinctly anti-establishmentarian response. The superpatriots and, to a lesser degree, the antisemites, finally, liked to lump together all the objects of their hatred into one comprehensive list, a sign of the ritualization of displacement.

Their attitudes toward their political enemies, to the extent to which they expressed them in their *vitae*, often (47.7%) expressed some understanding for the enemy and a desire to convert him. This attitude characterizes well over half of the solidarists and the Nordic-German romantics. The antisemites and, to a lesser degree, also the Nordic-German cultists, tend to refer to the enemy as traitors or as an abstract, faceless conspiracy. The revanchists, superpatriots, and Hitler worshippers, on the other hand, stoop to the language of the *outré*. Worse yet, nearly one-third of those who have no ideology whatever speak of their political enemies in a way that mirrors their physical aggressiveness.

Motives for the Stages of Mobilization

It is difficult to imagine that these "dominant ideological themes" evolved suddenly, after the respondent joined the NSDAP, and without any relationship to his political motivations earlier in his development. Let us take a look at how they relate to the sets of motives which brought each respondent successively into the stages of mobilization.

The antisemites, for example, tended to be militarized (stage two) mostly by their antisemitic predisposition or a sudden outbreak of *Judenkoller*. They were politicized (stage three) by the shock of defeat and occupation and their sense of opposition to the new Weimar leaders. They finally joined the post-1924 NSDAP, mostly driven by their ideological fervor. Many of them had already been in the pre-1925 Nazi party or other *voelkisch* groups. The Nordic-German romantics tended to be militarized by their sense of opposition to the revolution and politicized by the shock of defeat and occupation, or by economic troubles. They entered stage four mainly because of the "rough opposition of the Communists" and the dynamic impression of the Hitler movement. The antisemites evidently were motivated by their politicized prejudice from the very beginning, while the Nordic-German cult seems to have been more like a private ideology whose adherents are stirred up by historical or personal crises or other external stimuli.

The revanchists were militarized mostly by the shock of defeat and territorial losses and by their opposition to the revolution. They were politicized mainly by the demands of the suffrage and by the shock of defeat and occupation. They tended to be attracted to the party by the soldier-like spirit of comradeship, by the dynamic impression of the movement, and by the "rough" Communist opposition. The superpatriots, on the other hand, were militarized mainly by the shock of foreign occupation and less by the shock of defeat and territorial losses. They were politicized mostly by the suffrage and by their sense of opposition to the "Marxist revolution." They tended to be motivated to join the party mainly by friction with the occupation. The differences between the two groups clearly outweigh their similarities.

The solidarists were mobilized mostly by their opposition to the new Weimar leaders (for both middle stages), which shows the anti-Marxist tenor of their solidarism. They were militarized also by the impact of defeat and politicized by economic troubles, since many of them belonged to the working class. They tended to be attracted to the party by their sense of being repressed and by the dynamic impression of the movement or, less frequently, by their ideological fervor. The Hitler worshippers were militarized mostly by their opposition to the revolution and to the Weimar leaders. They were politicized by the shock of defeat and foreign occupation, by their economic difficulties, and by their sense of opposition to the "Marxist revolution." The stormtroopers' comradeship, economic troubles, and friction with the occupation were their chief inducements to join the party. Both these groups seem distinctly more politically purposive than the last two we discussed, and rather like the antisemites. On the whole, the profiles of the ideological groups have by this excursion become more differentiated rather than more cohesive or unified. Except for the monomanic consistency of the antisemites, the dominant ideological motives each seems to have evolved in complex and different ways through the various stages, reflecting the special challenges and irritants of each historical situation.

Ideology and Prejudice

Generally speaking, the Nazi respondents distinguished clearly between their flesh-and-blood political enemies—the Communists, Socialists, or other antagonists—and the distant, alleged conspiracy of the Jews. Even the anecdotal encounters some of them present are mostly meant to make a point about the story-teller rather than to provide factual accounts. Our antisemitism scale attempts to measure prejudice along a continuum ranging from "no evidence" over "mild verbal projections" and sudden *Judenkoller*, to such prejudiced anecdotes and, finally, to the paranoid stage which mixes delusions of threatening conspiracies with thinly veiled counter-threats.

Let us examine to what extent this prejudice applied to all the different ideological groups. The lowest in prejudice are those without ideology and the revanchists, who have 39.3% with no evidence and another 21.4% with only mild verbal projections. The Hitler-worshippers, the superpatriots, and the solidarists are next-lowest with around half in the no-evidence or mild-projections categories. Of over a hundred antisemites, on the other hand, about half had *Judenkoller*, one-fifth told personal anecdotes, and over a fourth had the combination of paranoia and aggressiveness. The Nordic-German romantics were the second most prejudiced with one-fourth with the *Judenkoller*, a twelfth with anecdotes, and one-fifth paranoids. The milder groups had between 20-35% with *Judenkoller*, 4-12% story-tellers, and 7-14% paranoids.

In their ethnocentric feelings aside from this prejudice, a further dimension emerges. The antisemites, far more than any other Nazi group hated aliens and "alien forces" such as the Catholic church or international organizations of any sort in Germany. Their xenophobia is shared to a more modest degree by the superpatriots and the Nordic-German romantics. By way of contrast, the revanchists and, to a lesser degree, the superpatriots concentrate their ethnocentric aversion on the foreign nations outside and on their "encirclement" of Germany. The solidarists show the least ethnocentricity, while the Nordic-German romantics and the Hitler-worshippers like to stress how "inferior" alien nations are.

There are also the attitudes toward authority which according to the theory of the "authoritarian personality" are supposed to underlie other fascist attitudes. Our measurement found little support for this theory from our admittedly limited evidence. The antisemites tend to be mostly critical of the manifestations of the multi-party state, and so are the solidarists. The revanchists and superpatriots are closer to the stereotype, showing a concern with law and order, authority, and, positively or negatively, with police functions. The Hitler-worshippers and, to a lesser degree, the Nordic-German romantics are preoccupied with the leadership cult. Authoritarianism does not seem strongly related to antisemitism or xenophobia.

In the Nazi Party

As we have argued earlier, holding a party office and political violence are different styles of extremist behavior. Let us take a closer look at the relevant differences among the ideological groups. With half holding no party office and one-fourth holding very minor posts, the revanchists are the least often in party offices, followed at some distance by the superpatriots and the Hitler-worshippers. The Nordic-German romantics, on the other hand, most often hold special organizing functions or are local chairmen. Higher offices can be found mostly among the antisemites, the solidarists, and the Hitler cultists.

By way of contrast, the revanchists have the highest proportion of stormtroopers (71.8%). Only the small group without any ideology has more (77.3%) and they hold even fewer offices. The smallest number of stormtroopers (50% or less) is found among the antisemites and Nordic-German romantics, whose physical courage evidently did not match their rhetoric. The antisemites, furthermore, have the largest percentage of respondents who became stormtroopers only a year or more after joining the NSDAP, with evident reluctance. The superpatriots, solidarists, and Hitler-worshippers all have nearly as many who immediately joined the SA as the revanchists, but far fewer who joined later or who eventually "graduated" to the SS. Nevertheless, these three groups had nearly as many SA or SS *Sturmfuehrer* or *Sturmbannfuehrer* as did the revanchists, even though the latter had more low-level stormtrooper offices.

The record of activities in the Nazi party confirms the impression that those without ideology and the revanchists do most of the fighting, followed by the Hitler cultists and the superpatriots. The antisemites and, with a handful of highly involved exceptions, the Nordic-German romantics, content themselves with demonstrations, electioneering, and proselytizing. As pointed out in an earlier chapter, this amounts to a system of stratification between those who do the dirty work and the party organizers and ideologues. Their attitudes toward violence round out the picture. The revanchists and those who have no ideology at all, and also the antisemites, stand out for their bully-like sadism. The Hitler-worshippers and the superpatriots, by comparison, tend to be self-pitying masochists.

These skewed distributions of ideology, prejudice, office-holding, and violence, among other things also make for an inverse relation between intense antisemitic prejudice and involvement in street violence (Table V-1). We can line up all the ideological groups ac-

Table V-1: Prejudice and Violence in Ideological Groupings (in %)

Antisemitic prejudice		Street-fighting	
(in % paranoid, anecdotic, and choleric)		*(in % fighting in the NSDAP)*	
Antisemites	(93.3)	Antisemites	(30.5)
Nordic-Germans	(54.3)	Nordic-Germans	(34.7)
Solidarists	(50.3)	Solidarists	(36.4)
Superpatriots	(50.0)	Superpatriots	(36.5)
Hitler cult	(46.7)	Hitler cult	(36.4)
Revanchists	(39.3)	Revanchists	(42.9)
No ideology	(7.1)	No ideology	(52.6)

cording to their prejudice and engagement in street-fighting while in the Nazi party and obtain clearly opposite trends. The most likely reason for this inverse relationship is an equivalence in function between violent acting out and the more introverted, symbolic acting out that is violent prejudice. If we assume approximately the same inner tensions in all the early Nazis, some evidently discharge them with their fists or other bizarre behavior; the prejudiced persons discharge them by mental contortions. In either case, the acting-out behavior is likely, and perhaps even intended, to shock society and to bring about retribution of sorts as long as society conforms to common-sense social prerequisites. Once a society is taken over by people given to this kind of autistic behavior, however, there is a wholesale change in the psychological situation. Not only is the society henceforth mad, but the acting-out behavior loses its point of reference and, thereby, one of its special gratifications—namely, a reaction of shock and authoritative punishment. This was one of the reasons why the early Nazis so often felt jolted and disillusioned by their own takeover in 1933.

Personality and Ideology

We cannot hope to give more than an inkling of what might be the relationship between personality types and these ideological patterns. Let us begin with the presumably formative influence in the life of each kind of respondent. For the antisemites, it tended to be either alleged episodes with Jews or aliens or an educational or literary experience. The Nordic-German romantics mostly spoke of the experience of youthful comradeship or of the defeat and revolution in this vein. The revanchists and the superpatriots both stressed the *Fronterlebnis*, the former adding youthful comradeship and defeat and revolution as the Nordic-Germans had, while the superpatriots tended to stress alleged episodes and educational experiences as the antisemites did. The differences between revanchists and superpatriots indeed resemble those between the Nordic-Germans and the antisemites. The solidarists, naturally, liked to cite social snubs or economic hardships, as well as youthful comradeship. And the Hitler cultists again cited educational influences or economic and social snubs.

Our second question is the pathological one, what feature of each case is the most unusual. Here nearly one-half of the antisemites fall under the rubric of "irrational, paranoid, or grossly unbalanced account." The Nordic-German romantics, by comparison, tend to have suffered particularly severe cultural shock or alienation from German postwar society, and to exhibit a good deal of personal insecurity. This group indeed exhibits a certain preciousness and emotional dependency on the social environment which may have made it particularly vulnerable to cultural shock. The revanchists mostly exhibit high cultural shock, too, as well as a desire to merge completely with the movement such as some of the examples in the last section have expressed.[6] The superpatriots share these two traits and, furthermore, show a high degree of personal insecurity. By contrast, the solidarists and the Hitler-worshippers mainly have an extreme kind of leadership cult. The former also tend to exhibit high cultural shock while the latter show a great deal of personal insecurity.

Their personalities also play a role in their relationship to the party. The chief satisfaction of the antisemites, for example, tended to be the expectation of a job or a promotion, while the revanchists and those without ideology derived their satisfaction from a sense of personal integration from the struggle itself. The division into beneficiaries and fighters is a familiar one by now. The superpatriots, the solidarists, and the antisemites also partook of a strong utopian consciousness looking toward a still distant goal. The Nordic-German romantics, on the other hand, were satisfied mostly with the Fuehrer cult and the classless comradeship of the movement. The

[6] See above, pp. 395-397 and 426-429.

Hitler-worshippers, of course, derive their satisfaction from this cult of leadership.

One reason why the antisemites were so conscious of job opportunities can be found in their record of friction endured. Close to one-third of them lost their job or livelihood for allegedly political reasons. The reader will recall, however, from our discussion of personal friction[7] that there is a fine line between this kind of economic suicide in the midst of a depression and mere friction on the job because of being found out or political disagreement with fellow-workers or employers, such as was more characteristic of the Nordic-German romantics, the revanchists, and the superpatriots, all of whom in general report less friction. The political ostentation of the antisemites, which ruined their livelihood, is part of the self-revelation, the "coming out" of the extremist identity crisis which may be increased by the shocked reaction of the social environment and, in extreme cases, may bring on mental disintegration.

It is worth noting, however, that the locale of friction chosen by the antisemites was quite different from the neighborhood settings popular with the Nordic-German romantics, those without ideology, the Hitler-worshippers, and the solidarists. It was different also from the family and school settings typical of the last two groups. Except for a few cases in a school setting, political antisemitism seems to lend itself better to the rather public scene of the open market or place of employment, where it is also easier to feel victimized by public boycotts or conspiracies. In spite of the pseudo-biological basis of the ideology itself, the family[8] and neighborhood settings are perhaps too much dominated by personal relationships to lend themselves well to this kind of self-display.

Expectations in 1934

The Abel collection was completed in 1934, at a time when each respondent was still full of some of the earlier crusading fervor and yet also reassured by the triumph of the movement and by the over-generous recognition that the Hitler regime began to receive from various sources abroad. Most of the Abel respondents end their *vitae* with a general statement of hope or expectations for the future. Some of these, at first glance, looked like hackneyed slogans,

[7] See above, part III, pp. 257 ff.

[8] The antisemites frequently had their spouses in the party, too, as compared to the much larger percentages of revanchists, superpatriots, and solidarists who had no Nazi family members. But their marital relationship is never depicted as providing an audience for their self-revelation, but rather as a kind of togetherness in delusion.

but on closer examination they are worth some exploration. To be sure, the sentiments and hopes of rank-and-file members of the party are by no means a sure guide to what the leadership may have had in mind, especially not in such an authoritarian movement as the NSDAP. Nevertheless, the rank-and-file expectations in 1934 do reveal the extent to which the hundreds of thousands of members indeed wanted what the Third Reich was to bring. There is no better way of seeing through many of the *post facto* rationalizations of early Nazi idealism than to let the early Nazis of this collection speak for themselves.

FD-74: Expectations in 1934

	Number	Per cent
⌈ National resurgence, foreign expansion	35	6.4
⌊ Europe to be freed of Jews, Marxism	26	4.7
National renaissance within	278	50.7
⌈ Economic recovery	28	5.1
⌊ Social restitution, reordering, restored status, prestige	26	4.7
Individual pay-off (hoped for or received)	48	8.7
⌈ 1000-year *Reich*, ideological brainwash of all people	47	8.6
⊢ Internal purge, revenge	13	2.4
⌊ May Hitler live long	48	8.7
	549	100.0

Some of the respondents express their hopes and expectations at great length. Others again have just a single line, such as "We shall go on working and helping with the construction of the national socialist state, until every German understands the Nazi ideology, true to our oath: We shall fight to the death for our *Fuehrer* and his idea." This totalitarian response came from a young metalworker (born 1907, no. 1).

A Catholic son of a farmer, born 1872 (no. 49), describes how the ascent to power "went into our black city like a thunderstorm. We purged and we cleaned up. There was to be only one leader and that was Adolf Hitler." Another respondent (no. 99), who joined only in February 1933, was attracted by "the thought of Hitler to purge Germany of people alien to our country and race who had sneaked into the highest positions and, together with other criminals, brought my German fatherland close to ruin." Another totalitarian, born 1896 (no. 6), writes: "We needed a total reordering of all areas of public life. January 30, 1933, finally brought us the triumph over parliamentarism and thereby the beginning of a national renaissance." Another respondent, born 1900 (no. 21), wrote with unintended ambiguity, "We National Socialists don't want to engage in petty revenge; we are used to thinking big and to action on a grand scale."

A more concrete involvement in the future is related by a milk-man's son born 1893 (no. 527), who early in 1933 tried to infiltrate the Communist party as an SS dissident in order to learn more about its local organization and membership:

> At the time of the national revolution, little happened except for a few well-known ringleaders being arrested by the police. . . . I knew that the KPD would stick together and that there was literature, even weapons, with some of their functionaries. We told the police (mean-while we had become the auxiliary police) but nothing happened. So we went and collected the literature and weapons ourselves after duly intimidating the persons in question. . . .
>
> I had to remove old election posters from the walls with a team of KPD inmates, which gave me an opportunity with favors and gifts to win over some of weak character . . . to work for us. We tracked down some distributors of SAP (a leftwing Socialist group) newspapers. They were all rounded up by us and have meanwhile been sentenced. In June 1933 some of my spies told me about some new Communist cells which we took out and interned. A group distributing the red B.Z. newspaper was also arrested and taken to Oranienburg [a concentra-tion camp].

The respondent, who had been unemployed, soon joined the crimi-nal police, as a result of his successful sleuthing. He also reports careful surveillance of some "unregenerate former *Stahlhelm* mem-bers" in his city government who had joined the NSDAP but still engaged in occasional acts of sabotage and chicanery against the party. In this case, the expectations of the unemployed respondent had obviously become merged with the repressive purposes of the Third Reich.

Other respondents, especially those who were already Hitler-wor-shippers, end on a note of eulogy for the great and glorious leader. A bricklayer born 1893 (no. 18), who suffered under the class bar-riers of the old society, has this to say:

> The leader of this movement, Adolf Hitler, was its symbol, the in-exhaustible source that gave all his co-workers never-ending energy, prudence, and steady courage whenever these threatened to wane. All I could feel but not express in my mind I found in the movement. That is why I joined and why I shall remain with it together with many hun-

dreds of thousands until my death. We want to thank divine providence for giving us such a man, Adolf Hitler, and pray that he will be preserved for the nation and the whole world for a long time, as long as his blessed mission is not yet completed.

An example of the hope for social and economic restitution is a retail clerk born 1893 (no. 24), who believed in the *Volksgemeinschaft* and in the *Fronterlebnis* of World War One, when he had become an officer. In 1934, his hopes are that "youth may learn from our struggle to avoid the sad mistakes of disunity, discord, envy, and hatred. Class arrogance on the one hand and class resentment on the other must and will be forgotten concepts. Long live the national socialist *Volksgemeinschaft*, long live peace and reconstruction, and the proud Third *Reich*. God grant us further that youth will never forget the dead of World War One and of the brown movement. . . ." There is no need to document here the many cases in which respondents expected or actually received individual rewards for their loyalty in the form of a position or promotion.

The attitude of the borderland German is well-portrayed by the eloquent account of a former Socialist from the poorest part of the Sudetenland, born 1901 (no. 466). After describing the tragedy of the fall of Hapsburg and of the confusion of a young man without a country and miseducated by the war, he relates how he fell between the millstones of ethnocentricity and ideology. Drafted by the Czechs, he turned pacifist and was turned in by Social Democratic Czech officers for spreading pacifist internationalism and carrying German Social Democratic newspapers. The Czech army made him a German superpatriot, the wishy-washy German SPD a Red Front sympathizer. And the moderation of the Sudeten German Ethnic Association (*Heimatbund*), which expelled him for stirring up their young members, made him receptive to the Nazis. Soon he became so deeply involved with the stormtroopers that "I no longer asked myself if I was doing the right thing. All we could do was to defend ourselves. There was no time to think." The respondent expresses his expectations in 1934 in simple words:

> From childhood on, I have been longing to be accepted in the *Volksgemeinschaft* of all. Again and again I was rejected and regarded as not belonging there, either because my father was a Social Democrat, or because we were poor—they always found a reason. . . . These fateful hours brought me to the path toward becoming as good a National Socialist as I can . . . Germany has found a *Fuehrer* and so have I, a poor, rejected comrade of the people (*Volksgenosse*). Germany must

win respect again and the millions of Germans who are still outside under the knout of foreign peoples must be brought back into a *great German fatherland vast in space.* (italics supplied) I trust in the ability of the *Fuehrer* to accomplish this and will be glad to help him as ever.

Another respondent, a worker born 1894 (no. 452), in 1918 "swore to myself with gnashing teeth to pay back the traitors who had allowed the enemy to win and thus brought intolerable shame on the German name." In 1934 "my most ardent wish is that Hitler may succeed soon in freeing Germany from unemployment and regain her well-deserved equal rights among all the nations." Another, younger man, born 1908 (no. 65), a product of the ethnic problems of the borderland, became a desperado of the stormtrooper movement, thrown out of the University of Koenigsberg and frequently in flight from the police. When the movement triumphed and saved him from further prosecution he wrote: "I could not go back to my career, having lost all financial support [his father disowned him]. Fate was knocking me around, but as I have faith and hope for Germany's future, I also believe in my own."

Some respondents also give revealing glimpses of the great onrush of bandwagon jumpers onto the movement in 1933. One young pastrycook's apprentice, born 1909 (no. 72), fled after an extraordinarily violent stormtrooper career from a warrant for arrest for throwing a tear-gas bomb into a large SPD meeting. After many scraps with the police, he relates: "When I was made an auxiliary policeman after the seizure of power, the very same policeman who had tried to arrest me in 1932-1933 for wearing a stiff black hat and red tie [during the ban on SA uniforms] greeted me most cordially. I just could not help laughing." Another respondent, a locksmith and farmer's son, born 1897 (no. 58), relates:

> After the seizure of power, things changed dramatically. People who had hitherto scorned me were now overflowing with praises. In my family and among all the relatives I was now considered number one, after years of bitter feuding. My *Sturmbann* grew by leaps and bounds from month to month so that (from 250 in January) by October 1, 1933, I had 2200 members—which led to my promotion to *Obersturmbann-fuehrer* at Christmas time. The more the philistines lauded me, however, the more I came to suspect that these scoundrels thought they had me in the bag. . . . After the incorporation of the *Stahlhelm*, when things came to a stop, I turned on the reactionary clique which was sneakily trying to make me look ridiculous before my superiors. There were all kinds of denunciations against me at the higher SA offices and with the public authorities. . . . Finally, I succeeded in being appointed

local mayor . . . so that I could break the necks of all the prominent philistines and the reactionary leftovers of the old times.

Undoubtedly, many an old stormtrooper fell victim at this stage to the intrigues of the established forces of German society who were as eager to trip up a vulgar, local Nazi upstart as they were to be coopted by the Nazi regime.

Social Background of Nazi Expectations

For purposes of crosstabulation, we combined the first two responses as imperialism; likewise economic recovery and social restitution as one category; and finally the last three as totalitarian utopia. Let us begin by relating the expectation groups to the dominant ideological themes. The antisemites turn out to be hoping for imperial resurgence, socio-economic restitution, and, as before, individual payoffs for themselves. The Nordic-German romantics dream of imperial expansion and, even more, of the totalitarian utopia of the 1000-year Reich with overtones of total indoctrination and purges of heretics. The revanchists also have visions of renewed empire, and they share with the superpatriots and the solidarists the hope for a national renaissance within, presumably a rebirth of patriotic sentiment and dedication to national greatness. The solidarists combine with this a material concern with social and economic restitution and, in particular, payoffs for themselves. The Hitler-worshippers and those without any ideology, finally, dream of the totalitarian utopia in which the internal enemies are purged and all Germans worship an immortal Fuehrer.

From this initial measurement we can take our cues. Socio-economic restitution and the hopes for a payoff are probably the most understandable and harmless expectations which could be held by any victorious political party. National rebirth within is more enigmatic, although its traditional overtones render it similarly understandable for any right-wing movement. More sinister are the imperialistic appetite and the hope for a totalitarian utopia. Let us take a look at the social background of these groups.

How were these expectations distributed over the generations? The postwar generation tends to hope for a national renaissance and an individual payoff, especially the younger cohorts. The victory-watcher cohort (1902-1905) is more intent on the totalitarian utopia of the 1000-year Reich. The war generation (1895-1901) tends to dream of a Nazi empire and, because of its economic troubles between 1919 and 1928, of social and economic restitution. The prewar generation is the most payoff-minded and the least hopeful of a totalitarian utopia, which seems more typical of those born after 1890. The "oldest" expectations (of people born before 1890) are imperialism, national renaissance, and a payoff for themselves.

Do these expectations vary by the size of the community? The hope for social restitution and economic recovery, for example, tends to be held mostly in rural and small-town areas (under 10,000), where the economic troubles may well have left a more lasting impact. The expectation of individual rewards is more heavily held in metropolitan areas. Nazi imperialism likewise is mostly a metropolitan phenomenon, while the totalitarian utopia is more typical of towns and country. Their location experiences tie in with these variations. The rural-urban migrants are the most imperialistic while highly (spatially) mobile respondents are more hopeful of the totalitarian utopia. The immobile seem interested neither in imperialism nor in totalitarianism. Respondents with foreign or colonial experiences tend to be imperialists, while the borderland Germans would settle for a national renaissance which in their case may denote a kind of imperialism, too. The respondents from the occupied areas, finally, tend toward both imperialism and totalitarianism, a telling demonstration of the contribution of the occupation toward the Nazi movement.

But these expectations do not readily fit into the patterns of social mobility. Respondents in social decline, for example, express little enthusiasm for social restitution or economic recovery, although they more often expect rewards than the others do. Instead, they stress imperialism and totalitarianism. It is the upwardly mobile, interestingly enough, who are most intent on socio-economic restitution in order, perhaps, to salvage the symbols of their social rise. They also hope for a national renaissance, probably for the same purpose. The socially static hope for social restitution and for the 1000-year Reich.

Did different occupational groups have different expectations? The military-civil servants, naturally, hope for imperial and national renaissance. But their imperialism is topped by that of the white-collar employees and the farmers, both of whom, along with the women and blue-collar workers, also tend to dream of the totalitarian utopia. The business and professional respondents, by comparison, are satisfied with hopes for economic and social restitution. They and, to a lesser degree, the farmers evidently constitute the reactionary strain of the movement in the Marxist sense, rural or small-town, and socially static, while the groups which advocate both totalitarianism and imperialism, or totalitarianism alone, are the socially mobilized phalanx of the Nazi revolution.

Religion, too, seems to have a subtle effect upon the distribution of the expectations. Catholics are less often imperialists or totalitarians than are Protestants. At the same time, imperialism flourishes more in Protestant areas, while totalitarianism tends to be more frequent in Catholic areas. Perhaps we have to remember also the traditions of Protestant Prussia and the Catholic nature of much of the French-occupied territory. At any rate, respondents in religiously mixed or religious-minority areas (where the respondent is in the minority) are considerably more imperialistic or totalitarian than respondents in religiously homogeneous settings. Not unlike spatial and social mobility, the underlying factor of religious dissension seems to enhance the limitless, nihilistic striving for empire and totalitarianism.

Expectations and Ideological Attitudes

The formative experiences of each expectation group provide a good way to approach their attitudinal dimensions. The totalitarian expectations tend to be typical of respondents whose attitudes were fashioned by educational or literary experiences, although it would be an exaggeration to refer to them as intellectuals.[9] The experiences of 1918 or of social snubs and unemployment also played a role with this group. The imperialists tend to present anecdotes of alleged encounters with Jews or aliens as their "formative experience." They were also especially influenced by defeat and revolution and by educational experiences. Those hoping for a national rebirth, on the other hand, tend to have been formed by the *Fronterlebnis* or by the experience of comradeship in a youth group. The groups hoping for social and economic restitution and for an individual payoff, finally, heavily tend to be influenced by social snubs and unemployment. This comes as a surprise, at least with those hoping for social restitution, since we have assumed that respondents complaining about social humiliations were an element in favor of basic social reform, even revolution. Were they so elated by the spurious symbolic triumphs of the Nazi victory that they were now ready to settle for social restitution, a restoration of other people's status and prestige, economic recovery, or an individual payoff? Evidently, consistency is too much to ask of the Nazi social revolutionaries.

[9] The totalitarians are less well-educated than the imperialists, those thirsting for economic and social recovery, or the advocates of national rebirth. Only those expecting a payoff have still less formal education.

How do the hatreds characteristic of an extremist movement relate to their expectations? The anti-Marxists or anti-Communists turn out to be the dominant element among those hoping for a totalitarian utopia. The imperialists tend to favor either adding the Jews to their anti-Marxism or an all-inclusive hate-list. Those who hate "reactionaries," liberals, and Catholics tend to hope for a national renaissance or for social and economic restitution. The latter preference, which is also shared by those with an all-inclusive hate-list (i.e., one including reactionaries, etc.) again demonstrates the dubious character of the social-revolutionary pretensions of the Nazi movement.

How did the expectations in 1934 relate to the attitudes expressed toward the political enemies before the Nazi victory? The imperialists who, it will be remembered, were dreaming of freeing Europe of Jews and Marxists, tended to speak of their political enemies mostly as traitors or as an abstract conspiracy. The totalitarians, on the other hand, who were dreaming of internal purges and brainwashing until all Germans would agree with them, tended to refer to them, in addition to "traitors" and "a conspiracy," as "subhuman, rodents, immoral" and the like, a chilling forecast of the political terror to come—and already in progress against political opponents in many instances.

The fate which the Third Reich had in store for the Jews, on the other hand, is not clearly indicated by our data at this point. If we relate the expectations to the antisemitism scale, for example, the least prejudiced group turns out to be those hoping for national rebirth, with 53.2% giving no evidence of bias. They are followed by those hoping for a totalitarian utopia (25.9% no evidence). The most intense prejudice, in the form of 32.7% speaking of threat and counter-threat, is among the imperialists, followed by those hoping for an individual payoff (27.5%) and for social and economic recovery (23.3%). It is difficult to explain this distribution except by somewhat farfetched theories: 1) that the persecution and genocide was not part of the old fighters' expectations in 1934 and that it was in fact closely linked to the imperialistic drive toward the east,[10] and 2) that the economic scapegoat mechanisms indeed link socio-economic crisis, individual or collective, to antisemitic prejudice. We tend to discount the economic-scapegoat theory too easily because

[10] See also Karl Schleunes, *The Twisted Road to Auschwitz*, Urbana: University of Illinois Press, 1969, who describes the gradual escalation of Nazi transgressions against the Jews through the stages of sporadic boycotts, legislation, expropriation and emigration, and finally, genocide.

of its transparent falsehood and rationalizations or because of the tautology of a dyed-in-the-wool antisemite going to economic ruin under vociferous antisemitic charges and recriminations. In either case, the explanation is not exactly one of rational purpose, but then no one really expected it to be. Our crosstabulation, in any case, does not pretend to indicate the rationality or the origins of the prejudice but only to relate its intensity to certain other obsessions.

To pursue this line of inquiry a little further, let us also take a look at the ethnocentricity (other than antisemitism) of the respondents. The least ethnocentric, according to our measurement, are those hoping for an individual payoff and, next, those dreaming of national rebirth. By comparison, the totalitarians display pronounced hostility to aliens and "alien forces" (including the Catholic church) in Germany. The imperialists also hate aliens and consider foreign nations definitely inferior. Only those intent on a national renaissance tend to express hostility and fear toward the foreign powers "encircling Germany." One gains the impression that Nazi imperialism was more concerned with integral nationalism and alleged racial superiority than it was with the very real hostility and oppression by the victorious Western powers. To the extent that the drive for a racist empire was supposed to be a revenge for World War One, then, it seems to have been curiously deflected in the Nazi mind along the lines of least resistance, toward the inside and toward the east, from where there was little threat or even hostility for Germany.

TWO

Disaffection from "The System"

The broader dimensions of Nazi ideology which have often received a flattering amount of attention may bear the character of a cosmogony or quasi-theology. The murky depths of some of the most abstruse ideas of the lesser-known Nazi ideologues indeed hint at such implications.[1] But to the ordinary Nazi, and certainly to the Abel respondents, this dimension of their vaunted *Weltanschauung* seems to have been practically nonexistent. The vast majority was probably totally ignorant of it and the few who may have heard of it preferred not to comment on it in any way. This is sufficient justification for us to proceed instead along the lines familiar from other studies of political culture.[2] In this section, we shall explore in particular the respondents' attitudes toward the Weimar Republic, toward authority, and toward their political antagonists, the "enemies" and the police.

The Weimar Republic or, for short, "the system," was the object of vitriolic scorn from many sources of the anti-republican right and, not infrequently, from the extreme left as well. To many right-wingers and especially to the *voelkisch* and Nazi parties, it was at best a *Zwischenreich* (inter-regnum) between the rather unsatisfactory Bismarckian (Second) Empire and the utopia that was yet to come, the Third Reich.[3] The conservative right wing, as far as it could be distinguished from the radical right, frequently regarded "the system" as the forces of chaos, corruption, and subversion which had betrayed and undermined the old order.[4] The dividing line, among other things, involves their assessment of the causes of the German defeat and the revolution. Let us take a look at how the Abel respondents viewed the republic.

[1] See, for example, Wilfried Daim, *Der Mann der Hitler die Ideen gab*, Institut fuer Politische Psychologie Wien, Munich: Isar, 1958.

[2] See, especially, Gabriel A. Almond and Sidney Verba, *The Civic Culture*, Princeton: Princeton University Press, 1963, chap. 1.

[3] See also Fritz Stern, *The Politics of Cultural Despair*, chap. 14.

[4] See especially Annelise Thimme, *Flucht in den Mythos*, Goettingen: Vandenhoeck, 1969, pp. 65-103 on the DNVP attitudes toward "the system" and its presumable origins.

FD-56: Perception of the Weimar Republic

	Number	Per cent
Marxist-(KPD, SPD) run system	45	9.4
"Liberalistic-Marxist" system	111	23.1
⌐Liberal system, capitalism, high finance,		
monopolies	14	2.9
⌐Traditional objections (empire was better),		
economic disorder	25	5.2
⌐Republic run by "blacks and reds"	27	5.6
⌐Utopian objections (looking forward		
to Third Reich)	22	4.6
Jewish-run republic, alien or un-German		
culture	144	30.1
Respondent dislikes multi-party system	89	18.5
Respondent likes Weimar (more or less)	3	0.6
	480	100.0

Their different perceptions, at first glance, are confusing because of the way they overlap. But, actually, these are all highly fictitious labels to begin with, including even the seemingly clear label of "the Marxist-run system" because it hardly represents the political realities of Weimar. The "liberalistic-Marxist" label was a very common way of attacking capitalism *and* Marxist internationalism at the time of the drive against the Young Plan of reparations (1929). Liberalism by itself and the traditional objections to the republic, on the other hand, remind us of the fact that, to the man in the street, prewar economic prosperity was not the result of free enterprise but rather of the political order of the empire. The objections to the "republic of the blacks (Catholics) and reds" generally tended to depict these parties as the forces of the *Zwischenreich* and to look forward to its future replacement. The objection to the *Parteienstaat*, the multi-party state of Weimar, is spurious too, in the sense that the empire also had six to eight parties even though their representatives were less powerful than those under the republic. Only if it is compared to the rising Nazi autocracy does this objection take on concrete meaning. It is worth emphasizing, finally, that hardly any of our respondents express even a little liking for the Weimar Republic. The system affect among them, to speak with the political culturists, was overwhelmingly negative.

Social Background of Perceptions of Weimar

How do the generations differ in their perception of the republic? The postwar generation, and especially the cohorts born after 1905, tend toward the utopian line, including the dislike for the multi-party system. The war generation, and often a good portion of the victory-watcher cohort (1902-1905) as well, tend to perceive Weimar as a Marxist-run or a "liberalistic-Marxist" system. The prewar generation (born before 1895) mostly inclines toward the traditional, anti-capitalistic objections or to seeing Weimar as the *Judenrepublik*.[5]

By location of residence during the fighting years of 1928-1933, the antisemitic response comes mostly from Berlin, while the traditional, anti-capitalistic one is so strong in rural areas as to suggest that it is frequently based on the long-standing agricultural crisis. Many of the critics of the *Parteienstaat* also come from the countryside, where political or ideological diversity may well have been rare. The utopian and antisemitic responses are as much as two-thirds metropolitan. The anti-Marxist perceptions, by contrast, come heavily from small and medium-sized towns.

There are some notable differences in perception among the occupational groups. Military-civil servants, business, and the professions tend to see the republic as Jewish-run. Blue-collar and white-collar workers mostly compare its "red and black parties" to the utopian Third Reich. The farmers perceive the republic most often as Marxist-run or engage in the traditional anti-capitalistic criticism. Women tend to be either anti-Marxist or antisemitic in their perception. If we consider the occupation of the father, the accents shift, but not much. The antisemitic response is still most typical of the children of military-civil servants and businessmen. Artisans' children turn out to be the most traditional and anti-capitalistic. Respondents who take the utopian approach tend to be military-civil servants' or businessmen's sons or daughters. The critics of the multi-party state, finally, are mostly farmers' sons.

Do the respondents' attitudes reflect their socio-economic circumstances? Like the farmers, the respondents who are upwardly mobile from the farm are mostly critical of multi-partyism and alleged Marxist control of the republic. Those moving up from an urban background most often see it as a liberalistic-Marxist system or take the utopian tack. Evidently as a rationalization of their circumstances, those in social decline tend to raise the traditional, anti-capitalistic objections. Respondents who never attempted to rise above the station of their parents also raise the traditional criticisms and, moreover, perceive Weimar as the *Judenrepublik*. Their economic fortunes during the bad years of the Weimar Republic follow a generational pattern but not quite as we would expect. Those who

[5] See also the remarks of Schleunes, *The Twisted Road to Auschwitz*, pp. 47-48 on the pernicious slogan of the "Jewish Republic."

raise utopian objections and criticize the *Parteienstaat*, the youngest of the lot, tend already to have failed financially before 1928. The antisemitic and traditional anti-capitalistic responses, which come mostly from the prewar generation, tend to be typical of those who became casualties of the Depression. Those raising the criticisms of Marxist control or of the "liberalistic-Marxist" system tend to have had normal economic careers without sudden crises, and yet they were mostly of the war generation. The attitude groupings toward the Weimar Republic evidently shift very considerably the generational incidence of economic crisis.[6]

War, Defeat, and Revolution

We would expect the attitudes of the respondents toward the Weimar Republic to be closely related to their experiences and attitudes during and after World War One. Those who see the republic as Jewish-run, indeed, also tend to show particular hostility toward draft-dodgers and civilians during the war; the two kinds of extrapunitive prejudice evidently are highly related. Those with a utopian bent, who also tend to be the youngest, often turned from enthusiasm to disaffection from the war effort. The same is true of respondents with traditional anti-capitalistic objections to Weimar. By contrast, those who are dissatisfied with the liberalistic-Marxist system and the multi-party state tended to be enthusiastic soldiers from the beginning to the end.

In their attitude toward the German defeat, the utopians and traditional anti-capitalists tended to display great emotion: fury, sadness, or resignation. Blaming the Kaiser or the civilians for the defeat, on the other hand, was more typical of those objecting to "liberal-Marxism" or to multi-partyism. The antisemites and anti-Marxists tended simply to take the defeat in stride. Nevertheless, the two last-mentioned groups report having been shocked by the "moral disintegration" of German postwar society. The cultural shock of the enthusiastic soldiers who object to the liberalistic-Marxist system was mostly caused by the fall of the symbols and institutions of the old order and the new Weimar elites. The critics of the *Parteienstaat*, finally, tend to verbalize their cultural shock over the absence of order and discipline in postwar society. There is an authoritarian note in both complaints.

As for the "revolution," those who see in the Weimar Republic the *Judenrepublik* heavily blame the Jews also for the revolution. The opponents of the party state and of "liberal-Marxism" tend to

[6] Cf. above, part I, pp. 42-43.

blame the Weimar parties or the navy mutineers of 1918. The utopians and the traditional anti-capitalists tend to blame the West, international Bolshevism, or unspecified "rabble" for the upheaval. Given their attitudes toward the revolutionaries, the antisemites were disproportionately involved with the Free Corps and vigilantes against the Poles and domestic insurgents and also with the Kapp *putsch*. The utopians also played a considerable role in that *putsch*, while the traditional anti-capitalists played a comparable one in Free Corps and vigilante organizations against domestic insurgents. The critics of the "liberalistic-Marxist system" tended to belong to quasi-military groups, but saw little action. Those objecting to the multi-party state, finally, and the antisemites as well, mostly express a strong hatred toward the insurgents.

An example of the intertwining of motives is an "internal colonial" born in Metz in 1905 (no. 427) who was expelled by the French first from there and then from the occupied Rhineland because his father, a railroad official, participated in the passive resistance. Bitter and "already an antisemite" from his home environment, this victory-watcher was immediately attracted by the Hitler movement in Munich in 1923, although he first joined the quasi-military *Vaterlaendische Verbaende* (VVM) there. He participated in the Hitler *putsch* and repeatedly lost jobs "because of my political convictions" and activities. About the Weimar Republic he says:

> Ever since I was small, my education at home and the life of a large garrison town inspired me to consider my love and loyalty for the fatherland the highest good. How could I join an outfit which publicly engages in high treason, calls loyalty to the fatherland insane, and betrays and enslaves the whole German working people with its criminal policy. Having been expelled twice I have experienced that international "solidarity" on my own body.

The respondent clearly identifies the Republic with the left-wing parties and seems hardly aware of the subversive or revolutionary nature of his own conduct against the existing order.

Another respondent, a farmer's son born 1891 (no. 444) and wounded in the war, scored in particular "the chaotic and corrupt party system [*Parteienwirtschaft*]" and "liberal-capitalistic thinking" paired with Socialist internationalism. He also accused the "Marxist and Jesuit tendencies," in other words the red and black parties, of spreading hatred toward the NSDAP and keeping it from putting an end to the "steep decline of the German people."

In 1923, when the Weimar Republic was nearly overcome by its right-wing enemies, the perception groups behaved as follows. Disproportionate numbers of those who viewed Weimar as the *Judenrepublik* participated in or sympathized with the beer-hall *putsch* or belonged to *voelkisch* action groups or parties. Those opposed to multi-partyism tended to be in militant veterans' groups, while many utopians were embroiled with anti-occupation activities. The anti-Marxists, finally, tended to be in other political parties.

Perceptions of Weimar and Ideology

If we relate the respondent's perception of the system to religion, some interesting connections come to light. Respondents objecting to the multi-party state or to the liberalistic-Marxist system, for example, tend to be Catholics and to live in a Catholic area. The German Catholic subculture, apparently, was less tolerant of ideological diversity and of the free marketplace than were the Protestants. The utopians and those calling Weimar Marxist-run either tend not to indicate their religious affiliation and, by a considerable margin, to live in evenly mixed areas, or to live in areas dominated by the other religion. Respondents who object to the alleged Jewish control or the capitalism of the Weimar system tend to be Protestants and to live in an evenly mixed area.

The perceptions of the Weimar Republic are clearly aligned with the dominant ideological motives of the respondents. Those complaining about the "liberalistic-Marxist system" naturally tend to favor the *Volksgemeinschaft* or, to a lesser degree, superpatriotism, and the Nordic-German cult. The anti-Marxists tend to be superpatriots. Those who call Weimar the *Judenrepublik*, of course, are above all antisemites. The traditional anti-capitalists tend to be revanchists or devotees of the Hitler cult. The utopians likewise are mostly Hitler worshippers and also superpatriots. And the critics of multi-partyism are, in this order, revanchists, Hitler cultists, and solidarists.

How do the perception groups differ in their level of political understanding and in the ideological or pragmatic character of their thinking? Those complaining about the "liberalistic-Marxist system" are the most intelligent, while the respondents who view the republic as Marxist- or Jewish-controlled are lowest in their political grasp. The last-mentioned group, along with the utopians and the critics of the *Parteienstaat*, have around 40% of low, ideological types.[7] The anti-Marxists and traditional anti-capitalists, by

---

[7] The utopians tend to be the best-educated of the perception groups with nearly half with at least a secondary education and 18.8% with

comparison, abound in dimwits, low-romantic types, and the kind of pragmatic narrowness typical of military-civil servants of the lower ranks.

Given their images of the Weimar Republic, what do these respondents hope for in 1934? The antisemites, typically, tend to dream of empire or to expect an individual payoff. The utopians, the anti-capitalists, and the anti-Marxists, in this order, mostly hope for the totalitarian 1000-year Reich. The foes of "liberal-Marxism," furthermore, are thinking of social restitution and economic recovery, which appear to be persistent concerns with this group. The last-mentioned group and the critics of the multi-party state are also dreaming of a national renaissance. Sometimes their anticipations are laced with an awareness of the wave of opportunists crowding into the NSDAP after January 1933. As a young respondent, born 1915 (no. 7), yearning for delivery from "the black and red functionaries" and the "black and red system," put it, he knew "that many had now joined the party who did not belong in it, but who had sized up the situation and joined anyway, thinking you have to turn with the wind." The correspondence of most of the criticisms of Weimar to the respondents' expectations in 1934 seems striking indeed.

The System and the Nazi Party

The perception groups vary a good deal in their dates of joining the NSDAP. Those who call the republic Jewish-run and the utopians already made up the bulk of the pre-1925 party. The utopians and those who speak of a Marxist republic also figure prominently in the years of reconstruction of the party, 1925 to mid-1929. More than half of the critics of multi-partyism and of the traditional anti-capitalists, by contrast, joined only after the 1930 elections. These last two groups also are the more rural groups in the sample and may well have been drawn in only as the movement expanded into the hinterland of the cities to which political competition at first tended to limit itself.

This progression is confirmed by the patterns of stormtrooper membership and activity. The utopians and those who speak of a Marxist republic have the highest membership in SA and SS (77.6 and 63%, respectively). They also have the highest number of people who became stormtroopers directly upon joining the party, and also the largest numbers of "graduates" to the SS. By contrast, those

---

Abitur. The respondents who object to multi-partyism are the next best-educated.

criticizing alleged Jewish control, the "liberalistic-Marxist system," and the traditional anti-capitalists not only joined the SA and SS less often, but frequently only a year or more after joining the party. The anti-Marxists and utopians, consequently, are the most heavily involved in the street-fighting and in meeting-hall brawls. The critics of the "liberalistic-Marxist system" and of alleged Jewish control are the most involved in proselytizing, while the traditional anti-capitalists and the critics of the multi-party state tend to limit themselves to electioneering.

The satisfactions drawn from membership in the NSDAP present yet another dimension of life in the party. To the traditional anti-capitalists, and the utopians, there was great satisfaction in the struggle itself. These two and the critics of the *Parteienstaat* also were attracted to the movement by their cult of Hitler. Those opposed to the "liberalistic-Marxist system" and to the "Marxist-run republic" praise in particular the classless comradeship of the party in addition to, for the anti-liberal-Marxists only, a sense of striving for utopia. This utopian satisfaction is also shared by those who call Weimar the *Judenrepublik*.

Images of Weimar and the Other Actors

How are the images of "the system" intertwined with the respondents' perception of other actors in the system? Those who see the republic as Marxist-run naturally see Marxists as their chief enemy. The critics of the liberalistic-Marxist system and of multi-partyism tend to combine anti-Marxism with a hatred of "reactionaries," liberals, and Catholic politicians, an anti-establishmentarian sentiment also shared by the traditional anti-capitalists. Respondents who consider the Weimar Republic Jewish-run naturally tend to concentrate their hostility on "Jewish Marxists." On the antisemitism scale, in fact, they show far and away the heaviest prejudice of any perception group. Forty-three and one half percent of them developed a case of virulent *Judenkoller* at some time in their lives. Another 14.3% tell prejudiced anecdotes, often with a sexual angle, and as many as 27.9% (as compared to 3-13% for the other groups) speak of conspiracies that have to be countered with threats or counterconspiracies.

As for their attitudes toward their immediate political enemies, finally, more than half of the critics of liberal-Marxism and multi-partyism express some understanding for the enemies and would like to win them over to the cause. Those who speak of a Marxist or Jewish republic tend to refer to their political opponents in the language of the *outré*. The utopians and respondents raising traditional anti-capitalistic objections tend to speak of them as traitors or members of an abstract conspiracy.

Perception of Political Enemies

Fighting political opponents with violence or other extreme means is an essential aspect of the life of a political extremist. Hence his perception of the nature of the enemy and his attitude toward him are an important facet of his relationship toward his political environment. The Abel respondents expressed their attitudes toward their political opponents along a range which begins with liking or at least understanding some of them and ends with expressions of a physical aggressiveness which is clearly beyond the pale of normal human attitudes. Between these two, there are, for example, the ritual assertion of the proselytizer that he would like to win the enemies over, or at least their rank and file. There are also the shadings between the abstract, flesh-and-bloodless images of the enemies as the established power, a conspiracy, or simply as traitors on the one hand, and the all-too-colorful language of the *outré* on the other. The significance of these categories will become clearer from the crosstabulations with other variables.

Some respondents sound more than one note on this subject. One phrase-maker, born about 1890 (no. 8), calls the enemies "traitors, seducers of the people . . . who enslaved and sold the German people, delivering it to people of an alien race." Then he turns on "the red flood . . . Moscow's mercenaries . . . the red mob intending to disrupt the meeting, carrying instruments of murder . . . hordes of red murderers lurking in the dark, not daring to attack us." And yet he also proclaims "death to the seducers, but a brotherly hand for the seduced followers" and boasts about having returned "the stray sheep to the people." The respondent's several themes obviously required multiple coding.

A more typical *outré* was a schoolteacher born 1898 (no. 31) who at 17 volunteered for the war. He relates how he and others who had interrupted their secondary schooling were going back to school in 1918, ostentatiously wearing their field-grey uniforms in the face of the "hatred of the red coolies in Braunschweig" and with a deep loathing for "the unsoldierly, sloppy conduct of the guards of the red ruler of Braunschweig, who was a mere tailor master." "People of that ilk want to lead sixty million Germans toward a better future, a people of the most industrious workers, the bravest soldiers, and great scholars and artists." He took a teaching job in the hope of influencing young people and was involved in violence with a vigilante group. He refers to the "red murder mob . . . the screaming, screeching hordes . . . hate-filled, furious faces worthy

FD-70: Perception of Political Enemies

	Number	Per cent
Respondent likes them (some of them)	32	8.2
Respondent would like to win them over	148	37.8
Enemies are all-powerful, the established power	33	8.4
They are an abstract conspiracy	14	3.5
Traitors	35	8.9
They are sub-human, rodents, murderers, etc. (outré)	83	21.2
They are immoral, venal, unclean, etc. (outré)	32	8.2
Physically aggressive (including concentration camp guards, 1933-1934)	15	3.8
	392	100.0

of study by a criminologist" after he became a stormtrooper, and his account leaves no doubt about what he did to them.

Another typical *outré* was a Lower Saxonian retail clerk, born 1894, who was a prisoner of war in France for most of the war (no. 32). He encountered violent revolution and counter-revolution in 1918 and at the time of the Kapp *putsch*, when he witnessed how "the red rulers of Harburg and Hamburg armed the rabble of the Polish quarters and . . . animal-like women and criminals went at Captain Berthold's [Kapp *putsch*] troop with kicks and knives . . . killing them like dogs." He played a prominent role in the DHV and joined the counter-revolutionary *Orgesch* group "to gather freedom fighters against the Bolshevist murder gangs of Max Hoelz and others . . . [such as] the Polish murderers and arsonists in Upper Silesia." He describes the "red" reaction to the first rally after the NSDAP came to Harburg and the respondent joined: "The Reds were foaming with rage. The Jewish newspapers were spitting poison and gall." This is the authentic language of the *outré*.

A Social Profile of Attitudes Toward Enemies

The different generations vary noticeably in how they refer to the political enemy. The few physically aggressive respondents heavily belong to the postwar generation. The *outrés* are slightly ahead of the others both in the postwar and the war generations. By way of contrast, the respondents referring to an abstract conspiracy tend to be more often from the prewar generation and are often rural-urban migrants. The respondents expressing a liking for their enemies tend to be from small town and rural areas. The *outrés* are the most metropolitan group and tend to be highly mobile or never to have moved from the place of their birth.

The different occupational groups vary greatly in their attitudes toward their enemies. Military-civil servants and farmers tend to express a liking for them. Business and professional people and white-collar workers, as well as women, tend to refer to the opponents in the language of the *outré*, which perhaps came easy to the German bourgeoisie in the face of the rising Marxist parties. Blue-collar workers instead stress the image of an abstract conspiracy, either of traitors or of a hostile establishment. "We were hunted" or "persecuted." The children of blue-collar workers, by contrast, and those of military-civil servants and businessmen as well, tend to use the expressions of the *outré*, especially in urban settings. The children of farmers and artisans, on the other hand, speak of abstract conspiracies. And the sons and daughters of high professional or military persons, as well as of most farmers, would like to win the enemy over to their cause, though undoubtedly from reasons as different as the pretensions of leadership of the upper classes and the primordial unity of the rural community.

Objects of Enmity

Even though our tabulation aims chiefly at attitudes toward political enemies, it would be rather unlikely if one kind of hostility were completely separable from other kinds in an individual's mind. When it comes to the respondent's hate-list, for example, it turns out that those who show hostility chiefly to the Communists and Socialists are most likely to use the language of the *outré*, or to betray their physical aggressiveness. This language is also the preference of those with an all-inclusive hate-list. Those who rail at the establishment of "reactionaries," liberals, and Catholic power tend to express some liking for the enemy, possibly thinking chiefly of the "misled workers and union members." Respondents who like to add the Jews to their anti-Marxism tend to refer to the enemy as an abstract or traitorous conspiracy.

An example of such anti-Marxist attitudes is a clerk and part-time musician born 1893 (no. 527), whose socialization in this respect began during repeated boycotts of his father's milk store by "the Marxists." His father was a religious man who refused to join the SPD in his "red" neighborhood. *Voelkisch*-antisemitic indoctrination by university students who had volunteered for his artillery unit, and a feeling of shame about a momentary flirtation with the revolution in 1918 did the rest. Soon he referred to the red flag as "a blob of blood," to the soldiers' councillors as "arrogant, brash, and dishonest," and to the revolutionaries as "Spartakist criminals" or "the rabble of Spartakist procurers."

On the antisemitism scale, those who reveal their physical aggressiveness show the least prejudice, possibly because they are already acting out all their hostility with no holds barred. Those who express a liking for the enemy also are less biased than the rest, although they are given to telling prejudicial anecdotes. The *outrés*, who act out their inner tensions with their outrageous language, have an unusually high proportion of cases of sudden *Judenkoller* when the sickness within them must have violently broken through the surface of civility. The most prejudiced are those who see their enemies as an abstract conspiracy. Nearly one-third of them are aggressive paranoids.

Their ethnocentricity, aside from antisemitism, has a somewhat different twist. Here the *outrés* turn out to be the strong alien-haters, although the counter-conspirators are not far behind. But the first degree of emphasis among those believing in an abstract or traitorous conspiracy is on hating and distrusting foreign nations. Those who express a liking for their enemies show the least ethnocentricity although they also tend to believe that alien nations are inferior.

The attitudes toward the political enemies also relate strongly to the respondents' attitudes toward authority. The *outrés* and also the physically aggressive tend to exhibit a fundamental hostility and disrespect toward all police and government authority. Far from being authoritarians in the accepted sense of the word, they are really rather disorderly people. The counter-conspirators, by comparison, more often display an extreme Hitler cult or the authoritarian syndrome composed of an obsession with order and cleanliness to the point of respectfully criticizing the police for not maintaining order. Those who express a liking for the enemy and would like to win him over, on the other hand, heavily criticize the pluralistic order of Weimar and its multi-party and parliamentary system. Theirs is an institutional sort of authoritarianism.[8]

Attitudes Toward Authority

Many of the socio-psychological examinations of National Socialism and other pseudo-conservative movements put a person's attitudes toward authority in the family, in school, or in police and government in the center of their concept of the *authoritarian personality*. The Abel *vitae* did not allow a complete test of the familiar

---

[8] They are also the best-educated of these attitude groups, with nearly a third of respondents with at least a secondary education (*Mittlere Reife*).

theory of the genesis of authoritarianism either in an authoritarian childhood or in a disturbed relationship of the child toward his father, the repository of primary authority in imperial and Weimar society.[9] But we can try to examine the limited childhood record that we do possess against the patterns of authority attitudes at hand.

FD-72: Attitudes Toward Authority

	Number	Per cent
(1) Respondent complains about "multi-party state," parliamentarism, group struggles	48	10.5
(2) Same, but respondent blames "devisive Marxists" or "Jews"	145	31.5
(3) Same, but respondent is a leadership cultist	33	7.2
(4) Extreme Hitler or leadership cult	43	9.4
(5) Preoccupied with leadership and police authority	15	3.3
(6) Obsessed with order, cleanliness	25	5.4
(7) Respondent criticizes police for not maintaining order	74	16.1
(8) Hostile and disrespectful toward police, government authority	76	16.6
	459	100.0

The attitudes in FD-72 were combined in two separate patterns for purposes of crosstabulation. In one pattern we collapsed all the leadership cultists (3,4,5) into one and all those preoccupied with order and police authority into another category (6,7,8). In the other pattern we combined instead all who complained about pluralism (monists—1,2,3) and the authoritarians (5,6,7). The last-mentioned category is particularly noteworthy since the respondents in it show strong respect for police authority in spite of their criticism of it for not maintaining order.

Social Background of Authority Groups

The youngest of the authority groups is the one that shows hostility toward all police and government authority, with nearly half in the postwar generation. The monists or anti-pluralists, by way of contrast, are the oldest authority group, with nearly a third in the prewar generation alone. These two groups represent rebellious youth

[9] See esp. Theodore W. Adorno, Else Frenkel-Brunswick, D. J. Levinson, and R. Nevitt Sanford, *The Authoritarian Personality*, New York: Science Editions, 1964 (first published by Harper, 1950).

and the unity of the old empire, so to speak. The leadership cultists (4,5,6) are the next oldest. The anti-authoritarians (8) also have the lowest proportion of metropolitan residents and nearly one-fifth of them live in rural areas. Many are in social decline or upwardly mobile from an urban background.

The authoritarians (5,6,7) tend to be military-civil servants and business and professional people, or the sons and daughters of businessmen and of workers. Many of them were rural-urban migrants. These evidently were the people obsessed with order and cleanliness according to the German pseudoconservative stereotype of the "good German."[10] The hostile anti-authoritarians, by comparison, were workers and farmers, in other words, from the lower classes and often from the occupied areas. White-collar workers, women, and the children of farmers play a prominent role among the anti-pluralists.

Religious affiliation also sets off the authority groups from one another. As we would expect, the anti-pluralists and authoritarians both tend to be Catholics rather than Protestants. The anti-authoritarians are mostly Protestants or fail to indicate their affiliation. And they often lived in religiously mixed areas or areas dominated by a faith other than their own. Again it would seem that there is a connection between religious dissensus and this strong hostility to all authority. The anti-authoritarians also happen to be the best-educated with a slight edge over the anti-pluralists and a considerable one over the authoritarians and the leadership cultists. The levels of formal education, of course, tend to be lower for the older cohorts and higher for those born in the twentieth century.

There is a tendency in the literature to discount or ignore the role of religious feelings in the formation of political beliefs. To give an example of the feelings between Weimar Protestants and Catholics, in addition to the welter of other hostilities, we can cite a construction engineer, born 1896 (no. 6), who remarked on his feelings as a soldier at war's end:

> The population of the area where we were stationed was devoutly Catholic and voted for the Center party. Only a small part of the industrial workers voted SPD. The attitude of the population, under the influence of the Catholic clergy, was not exactly friendly toward us soldiers, who had only wanted the best for Germany. Since I was from a purely Protestant region, I just could not understand it at all and kept thinking about it. Such a contrary attitude toward soldiers I had encountered only from Marxists and not from people with property, from the bourgeoisie.

[10] See also Thimme, *Die Flucht in den Mythos*, pp. 114-115.

The respondent could well have added that Catholics were viewed with at least as much hostility where he came from. Or he might have remembered the decades of tension between the Catholic Rhineland and the Prussian monarchy and military.

Childhood and Authoritarianism

Short of clinical investigations and with respondents who were living in an age prior to the popularization of psychology, there is not much we can expect of the Abel data, however fascinating a more systematic look into Nazi childhoods might have been. Let us examine what little there is. Our record of childhood settings, it will be recalled, distinguishes among poor, personally deprived (orphaned), and highly disciplined childhoods, and divides the economically secure settings into sheltered and freewheeling childhoods.

The respondents with strict, disciplinarian, or authoritarian upbringing tend to be extreme leadership cultists or hostile anti-authoritarians. The orphans are most often authoritarians or also anti-authoritarians, a pattern which fits the theories of "ambiguity toward authority." Poor childhoods apparently lead to extreme leadership cult, or an identification with powerful men. A sheltered childhood often produces anti-pluralism, while a freewheeling one leads to hostile anti-authoritarianism and, also, to anti-pluralism. It would appear, then, that the leadership cult is highly related to a disciplined or poor childhood, perhaps by way of compensation or by identification with the "enemy." Authoritarianism occurs most frequently from personal deprivation (orphans) and especially from growing up without a father. Anti-pluralism seems to develop mostly from economically secure childhoods whether sheltered or freewheeling. And the hostility to all police and government authority comes most often from disciplinarian, orphaned, or freewheeling childhoods, in this order. These statistical relationships make any simple cause-and-effect relation seem unlikely, with the sole exception of authoritarianism and being without a father. There is a triumph of free will in the fact that disciplinarian childhoods often produced anti-authoritarian hostility,—as the child rebelled against mistreatment—but so did a freewheeling upbringing or growing up fatherless.

Respondents with an authoritarian or disciplinarian childhood are worth a closer look. One of the oldest respondents, born 1868 (no. 132), was the son of a Prussian division commander who retired after the Franco-Prussian war. He describes his mind as the product of the old Prussian ideas of King Frederick William I, imbued with a sense of duty, truthfulness, integrity, and thrift. "Authority in the state and in the family were considered the pillars of the social order. Birth and property imposed obligations of . . . service." He enrolled in a cadet corps in 1880 and seven years later became a lieutenant. After three decades of officer service abroad and in German colonies, he witnessed the "meanness, cowardice, and miserable character" of the revolution at home. He was "so overwhelmed by the daily impression of degradation and lowness that [he] had no hope for a resurgence of the German people." In the late twenties, finally, the dynamism of the Nazi movement and especially his observations of its effect on people attracted him to it:

> After the little speakers I heard also the important figures of the movement. But what really engaged me was to observe the effect on the audience and to feel the posture and expression of the SA. Never in my life have I seen such a sense of trust, so much dedication, so much unity of feeling among accidentally gathered crowds as the large mass rallies in Danzig where Goebbels and Frick spoke. Here was once more a German people one could join joyfully, a fatherland, and a home.

The lonely old nobleman and imperial officer, whose alienation was probably compounded by his decades of residence abroad, had found a sense of belonging.

Another respondent, born in 1889 (no. 190), lost his father at the age of 7 and was thenceforth raised by a very strict uncle who forced him to take up a postal service career he loathed. His real love was for the stage, and he endured all kinds of privations in order to follow his inclination. Most of his account is a long description of his feuds with his uncle and his mother over what he was to be and of the misery he had to go through because his uncle threw him out of his house when he found out that the young man had secretly pursued his interest in acting. His mother liked his brother better, he believed, even after the latter fell in the war, "because he was a lieutenant." The respondent shows no particular ethnocentricity and communicates no particularly strong feelings that could have motivated him to join the NSDAP, except for a seething resentment of all titles, privileges, and class snobbery. His only authoritarian feature was his immediate rallying to Hitler after listening to a single Hitler speech, and maybe even this was a tribute more to Hitler's histrionics, than to his leadership qualities.

A third respondent is the son of an army sergeant who later became a policeman. The respondent is a school principal born 1896 (no. 196). He tells of his childhood as a Protestant among Catholics, and of his father's "inflexible character which got him into trouble with his superiors." The father received a transfer to an area where it took his military bravado to prevail against the forces of crime and popular disrespect. The respondent had a rather free-wheeling adolescence, in any case, although his father forced him to become an engineer's apprentice rather than a teacher. The war changed his situation and enabled him, afterwards, to pursue his true inclination. In 1918, he identified with the SPD but increasingly developed a virulent *Judenkoller* against certain party leaders. By 1923 he had joined an unnamed *voelkisch* anti-occupation organization plotting a popular uprising against the French. From there he graduated to the NSDAP in 1930 and soon served as an *Ortsgruppenleiter* of the party.

An example of an authoritarian upbringing is a locksmith, born 1889 (no. 263), who grew up not just in poverty but with an acute sense of deprivation:

> I had a childhood different from others whose parents had good positions and whose every wish was fulfilled. I grew up in the bitterest poverty and soon I was possessed of a deep seriousness. . . . At the age of eight I was already earning my living with hard work on a farm. In school I was ambitious and sought to excel with industry. The hard work did not stop me from dreaming about the illusory goals that were going to be the content of my later life. I wanted to become a doctor, and my teacher tried everything to get me a scholarship, but the poverty of my parents prevented me from reaching that goal. Thus I had no childhood full of boundless joy and letting oneself go in play like all my classmates. . . .
>
> My upbringing was strictly supervised and every influence that could have been bad was kept away from me. My parents lived strictly according to bourgeois values and thus they also laid the foundation for my later attitudes.

The boy went to work in a factory to support the parents and he "never had any recreation except for gymnastics." Then he became a locksmith's apprentice and, as soon as he had completed his apprenticeship, he "felt an urge to travel. The native soil was too confining, my thoughts too fantastic. And even though I was only 18, my way of looking at the future was different and my ideas quite alien from those customary in my hometown. Good books were my best friends and they nourished my dreaming and longing."

In his wanderings he always preferred the countryside to big cities. In the war he had a hard time adjusting to the military discipline until the comradeship and the purpose of serving the fatherland took hold of him. Pacifistic and unpatriotic propaganda, in particular, seemed like a personal threat to his integrity. All along it seems that the respondent's authoritarian upbringing was not so much an original cause of his peculiarities, although it may have accentuated them.

The great patriotic effort of World War One and the "betrayal of the iron front" quickly brought his maladjustments to the point of crisis. The thought of all that dying at the front for nothing deeply alienated him from the new Weimar government. He ended up an invalid and, although he had gotten married, a solitary figure trying to find a new niche in life. At this point he had a violent outbreak of *Judenkoller* and convinced himself from literature about the Jews and Freemasons that the whole war was the result of a gigantic conspiracy. He spent most of the republican era unemployed and watching the Nazi movement, oddly fascinated with its martyrs and casualties and their hostile treatment by the daily press. The casualties of the year 1932 finally induced him to join. His morbid fascination with death even led him to look forward to his own demise in the last sentence of his *vita*.

It is quite clear that the authoritarian nature of these childhoods is circumstantial rather than attitudinal and that they have no obvious adult consequences. In fact, we simply cannot be certain from the respondents' accounts alone of how authoritarian their upbringing may have been. It is not unlikely that a respondent of intensely authoritarian upbringing would have depicted his childhood in a more misleading light than someone in a normal setting.

The authoritarians mostly report a school and peer environment colored by identification with the moderate parties and frequent troubles at school, especially as a result of having been moved from one school to another. Both the hostile anti-authoritarians and the extreme leadership cultists tend to report a *voelkisch*-antisemitic school environment and more than their share of conflicts with Jewish teachers or fellow-students. As the reader will recall, the responses to this question generally suggest that a highly prejudiced person will tend to select teachers and provoke incidents that match his prejudices. The anti-pluralists mostly report an educational and peer environment of nationalistic or moderate political color, which once more goes to show the relative normality of their Nazi attitudes and perceptions.

The parental politics or political home environments are aligned in similar ways. The authoritarians mostly report an identification with moderate political parties and more than their share of father-son conflicts. Of militaristic fathers they have no more than an average share. The hostile anti-authoritarians tend to have *voelkisch*-antisemitic fathers and also more than their share of father-son conflicts. In this case, the antisemitic home environment very likely was a cause of prejudice, since a child cannot pick his parents although he may in time rebel against them. The anti-pluralists tend to be from a patriotic or unpolitical home environment, while the leadership cultists do not show any very pronounced central tendency.

Authoritarianism and the System

How did the authority groups relate to Weimar politics and to other actors on the Weimar scene? The authoritarians strongly tended to view the republic as a "liberalistic-Marxist system." The hostile anti-authoritarians mostly saw in it the system of the "black and red parties" that deserved to be replaced soon by the Third Reich. They also tended to raise the traditional anti-capitalist objections or to view it as the "Marxist-run" republic. The respondents with extreme leadership cult stressed exactly the same features as did the anti-authoritarians. The largest group, the anti-pluralists, naturally objected to the multi-party character of Weimar most, but tended to see it also as controlled by the Jews.

According to their dominant ideological motif, the hostile anti-authoritarians tended to be superpatriots or, to a lesser extent, Hitler cultists. The authoritarians were mostly revanchists, and the leadership cultists, naturally, worshippers of Adolf Hitler. The anti-pluralists tended to be antisemites, solidarists, or Nordic-German romantics. These attitudes were reinforced by the other patterns of hostility. The authoritarians, for example, heavily tended to concentrate their hatred on the Communists and Socialists—which, together with their revanchism, marks them as counter-revolutionaries rather than as the utopian kind of Nazi. The leadership cultists were more inclined to add the Jews to their anti-Marxist pattern. The anti-pluralists railed mostly against the "reactionaries," liberals, and Catholics, but also against the "Jewish Marxists." The hostile anti-authoritarians, finally, tended to prefer the all-inclusive hate-list, the hallmark of ritualized hostility.

How do the authority attitudes relate to various kinds of prejudice? On the antisemitism scale, the anti-pluralists turn out to be the most prejudiced, with far more than their share of cases of *Judenkoller* or delusions of conspiracy. The extreme leadership cultists are next, with a disproportionate propensity to tell anti-semitic anecdotes about themselves. The hostile anti-authoritarians surprise us by being the least prejudiced, and the authoritarians also are relatively less prejudiced even though they have nearly as many anecdote-tellers and paranoids as do the anti-pluralists. It would appear, then, that authoritarianism and even hostile anti-authoritarianism are not at all as highly related to political antisemitism as we would have expected or as the literature would lead us to believe.

It seems more plausible to argue that the anti-authoritarians, authoritarians, and leadership cultists were already acting out their inner tensions in extreme behavior in lieu of an acute display of prejudice. The anti-pluralists, on the other hand, had seemed so relatively moderate on most other issues that we have to assume that extreme prejudice simply was their style of acting out what other extremists may have acted out in other shocking or deviant ways.[11]

Aside from antisemitism, the ethnocentricity of the authority groups follows a different pattern. The hostile anti-authoritarians rank very highly in hatred for aliens or "alien forces" in Germany, including the "ultramontane" Catholic church and other "international forces." The authoritarians not surprisingly focus on hostile foreign nations, as we would expect them to do. The leadership cultists exhibit hardly any ethnocentricity except for a little xenophobia. And the anti-pluralists are mostly preoccupied with the alleged inferiority and hostility of the foreign nations around the fatherland. Authoritarianism here seems somewhat more highly related to hostility toward the outside world and, with the hostile anti-authoritarians, to xenophobia. In any case, ethnocentricity and antisemitism appear here to follow rather different paths.

[11] Gordon Allport also stresses the fixation of prejudiced persons upon an institutional focus such as the nation-state or a particularly unified kind of nation-state. *The Nature of Prejudice*, Garden City, N.Y.: Doubleday (Anchor), 1958, pp. 380-381.

THREE

Dimensions of Nazi Prejudice

National socialism is in itself an *outré* subject and, after Auschwitz and Nazi aggression in World War Two, few aspects of it could be more *outré* than its cultivation of hatred toward the Jews, toward other nations, and toward any other objects of Nazi hostility. These hatreds, moreover, were not just personal quirks or the incidental byproducts of the Nazi struggle for power. They were a rather well-understood functional prerequisite of the revolutionary Nazi movement and of the totalitarian regime that followed. Our examination of Nazi ideology, more than any other part of this study, has shown how little the Nazi movement was motivated by shared, constructive goals of any kind. Instead, the movement owed its solidarity and dynamic drive to the skillful manipulation of fears and hatreds which were rather common in Weimar society and, for that matter, elsewhere in the Western world and in Eastern Europe. Antisemitism, in particular, was Adolf Hitler's Big Lie which attracted hundreds of thousands to his cause. The hatreds of the lost war and the social malaise of a disintegrating class society added to the store of hostilities the Nazis could manipulate.

Once the movement had propelled its leaders into absolute power, the built-in hatreds and the collection of haters they had attracted began to have the potential power of one of the major industrial nations of the world. The hatreds took on a life of their own, as autistic fantasies of hatred began to turn into actual policies of an increasingly well-armed government. German rearmament made it possible for the Nazi leadership to prepare for its war of aggression, the collective acting-out of the fantasies of revenge for long-forgotten humiliations. Totalitarian control made it possible to act out the anti-Communist and anti-Socialist hatreds in Germany. And the combination of the initially successful imperialistic drive to the east with totalitarian control made possible the slaughter of millions of European Jews.

As Hannah Arendt has persuasively pointed out, none of these acted-out hatreds fulfilled any rational purpose or followed any vital necessity except for the warped logic of hate-filled minds.[1] The empirical material of the Abel collection, of course, gives us few clues to the function of prejudice for the movement and the regime. Instead it allows us to document the presence of extraordinary amounts of prejudice and hatred in the respondents, a feature which still has to be fully acknowledged in much of the literature.[2] It further permits us to ascertain different degrees of prejudice and to relate them to the background, socialization, and other attitudes and behavior of the respondents.

Our scale begins with the respondents whose *vitae* contain no evidence of their prejudice. There is no telling how many of them deliberately omitted this theme, either because they anticipated a negative reaction from an American readership or because in their social circles there was a sense of shame attached to talking about such phobias. In a manner of speaking, all the other cases can be considered those without a sense of shame about their prejudice. A truly prejudiced person, according to Gordon Allport, implicitly tends to assume that everybody shares his prejudice. Many Nazis are known to have regarded the United States of the early thirties as a country with plenty of antisemitic prejudice. We can safely assume that a considerable number of those who give no evidence of prejudice were indeed not "truly prejudiced" in this sense and had other motives for joining the NSDAP. This may have been true especially with some of the younger, more naive respondents. It is

FD-62: Shadings of Antisemitism

	Number	Per cent
No evidence	146	33.3
Mild verbal projections, or party clichés	63	14.3
⌐ Sudden *Judenkoller* from cultural shock, 1918	84	19.1
⌊ Sudden *Judenkoller* from economic, personal crisis	38	8.6
⌐ Relates alleged episodes with Jews	43	9.8
⌊ Relates episodes with sexual angle	9	2.0
Preoccupied with "the Jewish conspiracy" (implying counter-threats)	57	12.9
	440	100.0

[1] *The Origins of Totalitarianism*, new. ed., New York: Harcourt, Brace and World, 1966, pp. 423-429, 452.

[2] Books which clearly tackle the pivotal role of the hatreds and phobias in Nazi policy, such as Schleunes, *The Twisted Road to Auschwitz*, are still rather in the minority.

hard to imagine a reasonably perceptive, mature person who would join the NSDAP without being fully aware of its chief issue.

The next entry on the scale is that of mild verbal projections and clichés such as we would expect among Nazi social gatherings. We can assume that persons of weak prejudice would use the language of prejudice in a perfunctory way to establish rapport with their fellows.[3] From this weak motivation there is a huge step to the severity of *Judenkoller*. A good one-fourth of the respondents report rather clearly how under the impact of a personal crisis or the cultural shock of 1918 they suddenly became virulent antisemites. As the word *Judenkoller* indicates, these choleric explosions signify considerable intensity and a kind of rupture in the continuity of the respondent's mental life. Great inner tensions, but not necessarily a pronounced prejudice, may have been present for years prior to the sudden outbreak. "Coming out" as a raving antisemite would release the tensions and focus them on the object of the displacement. Afterward, the restored balance is rationalized with a reinterpretation of the respondent's life which may take the form of a personal anecdote with which he explains his prejudice to himself and to others. The content of these alleged episodes usually involves primary elements such as good faith, personal honesty, decency, sexual probity, or parent-child relations, rather than the broader stereotypes of conspiracy or grand economic manipulations.

The anecdote-teller is a confirmed, self-rationalizing antisemite, but he is still a person relatively at a static balance between his displacement and his rational self. He can leave his scapegoat alone except for symbolic vilifications. At the last point in our scale, however, there is no longer even a sense of balance between the person and his sickness, but the dynamic disequilibrium of paranoia. Cornered by his surging fears of "the conspiracy" and of personal persecutions, the paranoid is a dangerous man. He has become a "political antisemite" who feels compelled to take political action against the object of his displacement. He will lash out at his imagined tormentors, plot counter-conspiracies against their alleged conspiracy, and go around propagandizing to warn people about the fancied menace. There are many stories about the distribution of handbills and attaching of posters and stickers on walls, park benches, and places of public convenience. The sight of these dirty

---

[3] See especially the interpretation of the use of prejudiced language in popular agitation to establish rapport between the demagogue and his audience by Leo Lowenthal and Norbert Guterman, *Prophets of Deceit*, New York: Harper, 1949.

old men (and women) peddling their social pornography would be rather ridiculous, if the consequences had not been so chilling.

Social Background of Prejudice Groups

There are considerable age differences among the prejudice groups. By far the youngest group, with nearly half of its members born after 1901, are those who indulge only in mild verbal projections. The next-youngest group are those whose *vitae* give no evidence of prejudice. The relative youth of these two groups tends to confirm our speculation that naive young respondents may indeed have stumbled into the Nazi movement without strong antisemitic motivation. By far the oldest groups are the *Judenkoller* groups, with more than half born in the prewar generation (before 1895) and a good three-fourths before 1902. This suggests that the choleric outbreak tended to occur at a mature age—about 30 or even later. We have already mentioned the significance of passing the age of 30 in German society. The cholerics may well tend to be men who had failed to pass from young adulthood to middle age in a creditable way. The other two groups are more evenly distributed by age.

As for the size of the community of residence, the no-evidence and mild verbal groups tend to be more rural, while the three most prejudiced groups are heavily metropolitan, especially from Berlin, which housed nearly half of the paranoids. Rural-urban migrants figure prominently but not unexpectedly among both the choleric and the paranoids, while most of the anecdotes are told by respondents who never moved from where they were born.

By occupation, the choleric tended to be military-civil servants or business and professional people—in other words, respondents particularly vulnerable to the defeat and red scare of 1918. Military-civil servants were also prominent among the story-tellers, while business and professional respondents had more than their share of the paranoids. The farmers and the workers were the least antisemitic. White-collar workers and women tended to limit themselves to the milder verbiage, but they also tell anecdotes and, in the case of the white-collar workers, included a disproportionate number of paranoids.

Does prejudice relate to downward social mobility, as some American research has suggested?[4] Respondents in social decline indeed stand out among the choleric and the paranoid. However,

---

[4] Bruno Bettelheim and Morris Janowitz, *Dynamics of Prejudice*, New York: Harper, 1950, pp. 59 and 150, and Allport, *The Nature of Prejudice*, pp. 209, 216-219.

the upwardly mobile from a farm background more than match their *Judenkoller* and those moving up from a city background are every bit as paranoid, and tell many anecdotes to boot. We have already encountered the choleric rural-urban migrants, who probably overlap with the farm climbers, two paragraphs earlier. There may well be enough of a rupture of conscience, or of maladjustment, in rural-urban migration to create the inner tensions for the choleric outbreak and the displacement. The city climbers, the reader will recall from part one, tended to be in the forefront of all Nazi activities. They show the most evidence of prejudice, while the least evidence is found among those who never tried to rise above the station of their fathers.

Some of these motives also come out in the varying interpretations of the vaunted *Volksgemeinschaft* (solidarism) by the prejudice groups. The most choleric were the solidarists from below, followed, naturally, by those claiming national solidarity against the outside world. The choler of the former may well have been related to the wrath of the social underdog against his "betters." The most likely to tell anecdotes, however, were respondents who had either no class consciousness at all or very strong and unsolidaristic class feelings. Their fathers tended to be workers or high military and professional people. The most paranoid were the solidarists from above, who may well have felt particularly threatened by the Socialist and trade-union movements and by the erosion of their own status. The paranoids, indeed, tended to have military-civil servants or high military and other professional persons as fathers. Economic crisis, as such, seems to have little bearing on the intensity of prejudice. The largest incidence of *Judenkoller* and of anecdote-telling was among respondents who suffered no unusual economic strictures. Those who became unemployed or whose businesses failed before 1929 tended to show no great evidence of prejudice. The casualties of the depression of 1929-1932, to be sure, had more than their share of mild verbal projections and slightly more paranoids than the average for the whole sample. But even here the relationship between the self-initiated friction and true external, economic causation of prejudice remains obscure.

Is antisemitic prejudice a function of the decay of a particular faith, or of secularization? The Protestants of the sample are noticeably more prejudiced than either the Catholics or those who state no religious affiliation. But they stand out chiefly for mild verbal projections and for their paranoia. The Catholics more often have *Judenkoller* and, particularly often, indulge in prejudicial anecdotes. The latter tendency probably is related to the well-established

German Catholic tradition of telling nasty anecdotes about the priesthood. If anecdote-telling thrives in Catholic areas, paranoia seems to be most common in evenly mixed areas.

Is formal education an antidote to prejudice? Not exactly. Those with no evidence of prejudice turn out to be the least educated, while the paranoids and those using only mild verbiage have the highest number with *Abitur* or even university study. The choleric tend to have attained a secondary school education (*mittlere Reife*). When we pit ideology against pragmatism in their political understanding, however, there is a clear progression from the slighter to the more extreme forms of prejudice. The more intense the prejudice, the more ideological the cast of mind, particularly of the "low, ideological" sort, although there are surprising numbers of highly intelligent people among the paranoid.

Antisemitism in the Nazi Party

It is interesting to find out how the intensity of prejudice in our sample relates to the holding of party offices and to the partisan activities the respondents engaged in. Was intense prejudice an advantage or a hindrance in a party career? We can imagine that the heaviest antisemites might have been an embarrassment to the party. The evidence is somewhat ambiguous. The groups with the fewest party offices (53-54%) were the anecdote-tellers, the choleric, and those with no evidence of prejudice. Respondents who engaged in mild verbal projections, by contrast, held many offices at the local level, a fact that ties in with their perfunctory use of the party clichés of antisemitism. By far the most office-holding group (70.2%), however, were the paranoids, of whom 38.6% held offices such as special organizers of functions, speakers at rallies, *Ortsgruppenleiter*, higher-level offices, or legislative mandates. The prominence of the political antisemites in this area in spite of their patent mania clearly heralded the course of the Third Reich.

The relationship of prejudice to stormtrooper membership, on the other hand, is somewhat at variance with the pattern of office-holding in the party. To be sure, the mild-verbal and the paranoid group held the highest percentage of members here, too, while more than half of the choleric and the anecdote-tellers never became stormtroopers. But this time those who gave no evidence of prejudice are also highly involved, and rival even the paranoids in their percentage of men who graduated from the SA to the SS. We have to remember that the original function of the stormtroopers was to act not against the Jews but rather against the paramilitary formations and raiding parties of the extreme left. It was only at a rather late stage and mostly after Hitler came to power that stormtrooper violence began to turn on Jewish fellow-citizens.

The patterns of office-holding in the SA and SS further confirm this impression. Here most ranks up to the *Sturmfuehrer* and *Sturmbannfuehrer* levels turn out to be held by respondents who give no evidence of prejudice. Even the mild-verbal group has no more stormtrooper ranks than the choleric (32%). Only the paranoids are once again heavily represented in the higher level offices.

The partisan activities tell a similar story. The paranoids were the most heavily involved in street fighting and meeting-hall brawls, often "day and night." The next heaviest fighters were the mild-verbal and the no-evidence groups. The cholerics and anecdote-tellers were noticeably less involved, especially in "day-and-night" fighting at the peak time, 1931-1932. Instead they stood out for proselytizing and electioneering. The story-tellers were still a good step ahead of the cholerics in fighting and behind them in proselytizing. Here, it would appear, they reveal themselves as having gone a step beyond *Judenkoller* toward the fighting stance of the paranoid political antisemites.

The anecdote-tellers also have a slight edge over the cholerics in getting a sense of personal integration out of the struggle itself. To be sure, neither group comes close to the disproportionate numbers of no-evidence and paranoid respondents for whom this sense of integration from the struggle is the chief satisfaction in the party. The cholerics and the story-tellers instead tend to feel uplifted by the thought of striving for utopia and, among the cholerics only, by the Hitler cult. The mild-verbal group tends to be gratified by the classless comradeship in the movement and not much more by the struggle itself than the cholerics and story-tellers.

The upshot of this and the preceding comparisons is, then, that there is a rather important difference here in the degree of political mobilization of the various prejudice groups. If it is chiefly those with no evidence of prejudice and the paranoid, and perhaps to a limited extent the mild-verbal group, who are driven by a deep inner need for the political struggle, then the strong prejudice of the choleric and the anecdote-tellers may indeed be an inhibiting factor on political activity other than proselytizing. As *Judenkoller* and facetiousness turn into paranoia, however, prejudice evidently drives people into violent and aggressive political actions—which explains the consistently leading role of the paranoids in office-holding and in stormtrooper violence. The no-evidence group participated without inhibition in stormtrooper activities but evidently held few offices in the NSDAP precisely because of its lack of prejudice. The party was dominated by the political antisemites and even the mild-verbal group seems readily to have followed their maniacal leadership.

Childhood and Prejudice

The genesis of strong prejudice is a fascinating topic which deserves detailed exploration with clinical methods. The Abel *vitae*, unfortunately, allow only broad categories of childhood settings to be compared and, for obvious reasons, they tell more about adolescence than about childhood. Respondents who grew up in poverty show the least prejudice. Those with a disciplinarian upbringing and the orphans, on the other hand, have the highest number of paranoids and fewer respondents who exhibit no prejudice. Here the theories of the "authoritarian mind" of a disturbed father-son relationship seem obviously to apply.[5] Of the economically well-off childhoods, the freewheeling are high in prejudice, especially in *Judenkoller*, while the sheltered are among the least prejudiced of all the groups. Considering the importance attached to freewheeling childhoods in some cultures, including our own, this is a startling discovery. The break-down-like *Judenkoller*, moreover, is about the last consequence we would expect of a freewheeling childhood unless, of course, we view this freewheeling permissiveness, from a conservative point of view, as self-destructive.

The influences of the parents, especially the father, follow predictable lines. The least prejudiced by far are the children from an unpolitical home environment, followed by those from a nationalistic or patriotic environment. The most prejudiced, as we would expect, are the children of *voelkisch* or antisemitic parents, who also supply the largest percentages of aggressive paranoids and of the mildly verbal, as well as more than their share of tellers of prejudiced anecdotes. Most of the choleric, however, come from nationalistic or militaristic homes where they may well have learned to identify closely with the glories of the empire that disintegrated in 1918.

Their reported school environments follow similar lines. Those who report an influential *voelkisch*, antisemitic, or Nazi teacher, or conflict with Jewish fellow-students, are the most prejudiced and include the largest numbers of paranoids and story-tellers. Students in a nationalist school environment are more likely to engage in mild verbal projections or to have *Judenkoller*.

[5] It has become customary to speak of "an ambivalence toward the parents" rather than of authoritarian childhood influences. See for example, Allport, *The Nature of Prejudice*, p. 374.

We have no record in most cases of when or at what ages the prejudice began, but we can look into the ages at which strongly prejudiced persons became politicized or militarized, or joined the NSDAP. Stage two (militarization) respondents who were under 18 or over 35 tend to be the most antisemitic, with emphasis on *Judenkoller* and anecdotes. The paranoids are most frequent among those who were militarized between 26 and 35. Regarding stage three (politicization), those who entered it under 26 tend to be paranoids and to tell anecdotes, while those over 25 are more often victims of *Judenkoller*. With respect to the age of joining the party, finally, those under 21 and between 40 and 50 have the most paranoids. The cohorts who joined after the age of 35 tend to have suffered more than their share of *Judenkoller*. The general impression is one of the very young and the middle-aged joining forces in prejudice.

To account for the very young, we need only crosstabulate antisemitism with the youthful postures to find that the paranoids heavily tend to be classified as "hostile militants" in the first 25 years of their lives. To account for the older semesters, and their *Judenkoller*, we can look back in Weimar history to 1918-1919. The choleric, it turns out, experienced the cultural shock of 1918-1919 far more often (82.5%) than any other prejudice group, and mostly in the form of shock at the "moral disintegration" of German postwar society or of shock at the new Weimar elites in society and government. For many respondents, perhaps as many as one-seventh of the sample, their *Judenkoller* outbreak and the cultural shock of 1918-1919 are the same. The consequences of this choler on the political development of respondents also show up in our statistics, in the age intervals of the transition from the middle stages to stage four, the NSDAP. The choleric were faster than any other group in moving along the ladder of extremist escalation. There must have been a massive *Judenkoller* wave throughout Germany in 1918-1919.

It stands to reason that a person of strong antisemitic prejudice may also express other hostile feelings. However, we could just as easily argue that one kind of displacement obviates the need for other displacements. Let us examine the relevant crosstabulations. When we look at the list of objects of hostility, the large group of anti-Communists and anti-Socialists are the lowest in prejudice, with 37.4% showing no evidence of it, even though they are not far below the average in the number of paranoids. The highest and most severe prejudice prevails among those who habitually link the

Jews to their anti-Marxism and who also have the largest shares of paranoids, cholerics, and anecdote-tellers. Respondents who vent their spleen on "reactionaries," Catholics, and liberals generally make only mild verbal projections, but they also tell anecdotes. The Nazis with the all-embracing hate-list are the second most prejudiced group and stand out in particular for their *Judenkoller* and their story-telling. Except for anti-Marxism, then, there is little evidence that one displacement makes others unnecessary.

The relationship between the respondents' prejudice and their attitude toward their political enemies, presumably the Communists and other antagonists of their fights, gives an added dimension to this. The cholerics are prone to calling their political enemies subhuman, rodents, and the like, in a clear demonstration of parallel displacements. The paranoids, logically enough, prefer to call them traitors or an abstract conspiracy, another parallelism. The storytellers and, less often those giving no evidence of prejudice, finally, tend to express a liking for their political enemies and a desire to win them over which obviously could not be parallel to any antisemitic feelings they had.

Regarding their other ethnocentric feelings, nearly a fourth of the sample gives no evidence of either prejudice. The paranoid antisemites exhibit a very strong hatred of aliens and "alien forces" in Germany (xenophobia). All of the other, more prejudiced groups show more than their share of this phobia. The story-tellers, paranoids, and cholerics also tend to stress the inferiority of other nations, while the mildly verbal group more often stresses the hostile foreign nations outside (chauvinism). Again the displacements appear to be clearly parallel except for the not unrealistic perception of Germany's wartime enemies as hostile. The primary objects of ethnocentric displacement are aliens in Germany and the obverse of a flattering national self-image, "inferior foreign breeds."

The Prejudiced Personality

In spite of the tempting topic, we have to content ourselves with rather limited indications of the prejudiced personality, because of the limitations of the data. Let us take a look at the whole configuration of each case and at a few attitudes and aspects revelatory of personality. First of all, there is the formative influence or experience distinguishing each case. The mildly verbal group stresses the experience of youthful comradeship and of social or economic humiliations. The cholerics, as we would expect, tend to be influenced by *Fronterlebnis*, educational or literary influences, or alleged encounters with Jews or aliens. The anecdote-tellers, of course, report encounters with Jews or aliens, as well as educational experiences, even more often than the cholerics but they also tell stories of social or economic humiliation. The paranoids, finally, relate alleged encounters, the defeat and revolution of 1918-1919, and the experience of youthful comradeship as their formative experiences.

The social settings of party membership also tell something about the personality of the respondent. The fully mobilized paranoid, it turns out, was less likely than members of the other prejudiced groups to have any family members save rather distant ones in the party. He was a loner. The spouses of cholerics, by way of contrast, were often members too, and the mildly verbal group tended to have practically their whole family in the NSDAP. The tellers of prejudiced anecdotes are a link to the paranoids, many with distant relatives and more than their share of whole families in the party. The general impression is that the paranoids were loners whose pseudopolitical obsessions were their whole lives. Interestingly, respondents who give no evidence of prejudice and who, as will readily be recalled, were quite involved in the fighting and far less in party offices also tend to be loners. After all, a person who joins an antisemitic movement just for the sake of fighting and without showing any antisemitic prejudice is psychologically rather marginal, too. By contrast, the choleric married to a party member and the mildly verbal conformist whose whole family were Nazis seem socially well-integrated. The lack of social integration of the anecdote-tellers is also documented by their extraordinarily high rates of political friction reported in family or school (25%), and of political boycotts or firings (36.4%).[6]

How did these people view themselves? Their dominant ideological motives tended to be antisemitism with all the groups of heavier prejudice, beginning with the cholerics. Small proportions of the paranoids also were Nordic-German romantics or revanchists, the two themes which were also dominant among the mildly verbal group. In their attitudes toward political violence, those who were physically involved were rather low in prejudice (56-61%) and differed strikingly depending on whether they were sadists or

---

[6] Oddly enough, the paranoids report not nearly as much political friction in any of these settings in spite of their fears of persecution. Their political mobilization evidently made them less likely to cause friction with their environment since they had a good outlet for their self-representation, their political roles.

masochists. The sadistic bullies who were biased heavily tended to be paranoid antisemites, while the prejudiced masochists more often inclined toward verbalisms, *Judenkoller*, or anecdotes. Sadism obviously inclines the violent to all-out mobilization and paranoid aggression, while masochism holds them back. Perhaps the impact of the war, which removed the inhibitions against violence, also accounts for the mobilization of prejudice. Most cholerics incline toward the realistic acceptance of violence as the price of victory. Respondents who express a dislike for or regrets about the violence are even more restrained in their prejudice than the masochists who, as the reader may recall, are characterized by their self-pity and guilt feelings in connection with heavy participation in fighting.

Our final measure is of the pathology of each case in terms of its most abnormal feature. Respondents showing an extreme degree of leadership cult, group conformity, and masochism or insecurity are among the least prejudiced. The cholerics and anecdote-tellers, and most of all the paranoids, by way of contrast, show a high degree of irrationality and a lack of balance in their accounts. Nearly one-sixth of the sample falls into this combination of strong prejudice and irrationality. Some of the cholerics and the mildly verbal also show a high degree of cultural shock.

Examples of Antisemites

It is difficult to select among the wide variety of antisemitic respondents some that could be called typical. The real genesis of their prejudice tends to remain obscure in any case, even though the presentation may include an attempt to make it plausible. Quite frequently, a respondent's account invites all kinds of speculation about what really happened or how much he (or she) ever understood his own development.

A "typical" case of social decline is an aristocratic country judge's son, born 1893, who had an upper-class education and held an officer's patent until he literally fell off a horse, ruining his officer's career (no. 139). His accident did not stop him from fighting with the Free Corps and the vigilantes in Berlin. After the war he became in turn an agricultural trainee, commercial trainee, insurance representative, accountant, public employee, and, after many intervals of unemployment, a taxi driver in the years 1928 to 1932. His inherited money was lost in the inflation as a consequence of a bad investment with a company by which he was employed. Even the taxi business did not yield enough to support his wife and two children, and he supplemented his income as a doorman and care-

taker for a public agency. His political involvement, he claims, grew
from the idle conversations of taxi chauffeurs waiting for customers.

> The idle sitting-around at taxi stands, caused by the bad economic
> situation, led to constant political discussions among the chauffeurs
> [and other idlers there]. Since there was many an old soldier of like
> mind in the company I worked for, we soon went about systematically
> influencing our Marxist colleagues. The conduct of the Jews in the
> west of Berlin and the fact that 80-90% of the customers were Jews
> was a great support for our undertaking.

The respondent joined the party only years later when renting
two rooms of his flat to a party local. Thus far, this account creates
a superficial impression of a kind of "taxicab theory of antisemitism"
in which the envied, well-to-do customers are equated with the Jews
by the down-and-out hack drivers. Even at that, we can surmise that
the antisemitic angle was one of the few effective lines to use in the
conversion of "the Marxist colleagues." As it happens, this respondent wrote two *vitae*, one accounting for his military and economic
career, the other about his political development. In the latter, he
wrote, among other things, how he viewed the role of prejudice in
his political life: "I felt a strong aversion toward anything Jewish
since I had been in school. It was reinforced by my father's views
and *pushed me gradually* and under deteriorating economic circumstances into political activity, though not immediately with a political party. In particular a political feud in the [company] where
I worked in 1923 stirred up my interest in politics." (italics
supplied)

There is no reason to doubt the respondent's assertion that it was
his prejudice that drove him into politics, although we might accord
his father a more prominent role. In any case, it is worth noting that
it took a great deal of economic strictures and, in the end, something of a *quid pro quo* in the rental of his rooms to the NSDAP to
make this warped soul crawl out from under his rock and join a
party. Quite probably, there were many more such antisemites who
remained, as he should have, aloof from politics.

Another respondent of the same age, born 1893 (no. 24), was
a commercial employee who volunteered for the war. He served
with enthusiasm, and soon as an officer, until he was wounded in
1918. Convalescing from his wounds and "a stomach ruined by the
diet of the trenches" in a South German spa during the darkest days
of the war, he suddenly experienced *Judenkoller*: "Without any
influence from any other source, an insight came into my life which
was decisive for my later development as a Nazi. I became an anti-

semite because of what I was witnessing daily." And he describes the promenade area of the spa, Bad Kissingen, with two rows of benches, one for the military convalescents, the other for the guests of the spa.

[In the one row,] miserable, undernourished, shot-up soldiers in their old deloused uniforms. Many of them were so weak from their wounds and privations that they barely existed . . . on the miserable hospital food. In the other row, the guests were chattering, constantly eating fruit or cakes, the ladies in elegant robes, high modern boots . . . , diamonds on their hands and around their fat necks, with arrogant, un-German conduct which bore no relation to the hard times, laughing and joking indecently. The gentlemen of this exquisite society were well-nourished . . . and very busy. Stock quotations were flying through the air. . . . The guests were at least . . . 85% Jews.

The respondent stresses that he had never been an antisemite before "although I had always had a barely conscious racial aversion to Jews." The collapse and revolution further politicized his "barely conscious racial aversion" and turned it against all the economic and political abuses he could pin on the Jews. While he does not identify the politics of his parents or other early influences, it is a safe guess that here, too, a modicum of prejudice antedated his experiences in Bad Kissingen. He shows no awareness of the logical gap between the individual examples alleged by him and the global sweep of political antisemitism.

A case of *Judenkoller* without antecedents or earlier prejudice, but with an authoritarian upbringing in poverty, is that of a locksmith born in 1889 (no. 263), who felt a great urge to roam through the German countryside and a hatred for the city. A soldier in peacetime and in the war as well, he took the German defeat and the "revolution" very hard:

The partisan squabbles took an even greater hold of the people. The Jews had laid such a foundation and they had managed to prepare all this inner corruption behind the façades. Wherever you looked, wherever you went to talk to people, you found Jews in the leading positions.

And so I was seized by such a tremendous hatred that once, in 1922 at a war invalids' meeting, I launched into the open struggle against the Jews without realizing in my innermost mind the consequences to which their regime was to take us. I began to search. I bought books that threw some light on the Jewish way of life and its goals. I studied Freemasonry and discovered that, according to the documents handed down, this terrible war had long been prepared and planned. Although they tried to tell us that the war was our fault, I suddenly realized that it was all a game of intrigues, a net of lies without equal in world history.

The *Judenkoller* here had turned into paranoid delusions of global conspiracy. The respondent was unemployed for years and very lonely until, in 1932, he joined the brown movement, where he developed a peculiar fixation on the martyrs and casualties of the struggle.

Another respondent born about 1891 (no. 192) tells about being spanked repeatedly by his father, a loyal domestic servant with Jewish families for nearly half a century, for showing hostility toward his father's employers. The son's complaints soon were transmuted from the hostility of Jean Genêt's play *The Maids* to the corrosive envy of an employee of a Jewish textile businessman in Frankfurt. By 1924, his hostilities had become focused so specifically on "the Jewish question, capitalism, Freemasonry, and Jesuitism" that "these questions became the content of my life." He began to propagandize for his new beliefs and soon lost his job because of the conflict between the "dirty thinking and actions of my boss and my blood-related feelings." His wife shared his prejudice and, with plenty of time on their unemployed hands, they soon discovered the Nazi party together.

His wife, born 1896 (no. 193), also wrote a *vita* in which she disclosed that her innkeeper parents, like her husband's father, were rural-urban migrants. One of eight children, she was also very strictly raised but, as she relates, also with kindness and justice. In spite of the resistance of her father to her early and lively interest in politics, she became very well-informed and aware of the significance of the war, "regretting that I was not a boy who could go out and defend the fatherland." She was very upset about "the collapse of a skilfully undermined system which already carried the seeds of its own subversion. . . . The German people was led by a horde of criminals who in turn were led by the wire-pullers of the International, the Jews." Her two brothers joined the SA in 1923-1924, and the girls in the family were strongly attracted by Hitler's *Mein Kampf* and other Nazi literature. The respondent participated in demonstrations and shouting slogans in the streets "until we were hoarse." In 1929 she attended the big party rally in Nuremberg, where she first encountered her great and glorious leader of the years to come.

Some antisemitic respondents are physically so aggressive that we need not be in the least surprised about the direction taken by the Third Reich. A high Prussian civil servant, born 1885 (no. 28), was so outraged by defeat and revolution that he went from one rally of the left to the next to heckle and harass prominent Socialists, republicans, and revolutionaries. In close cooperation with the Kapp *putsch*, he proposed to suppress the general strike with armed force. In November 1918, he attempted to call a mass meeting against the revolution and, subsequently, he founded innumerable nationalistic organizations for civil servants, officers, and Catholics, mostly as fringe groups of the DNVP. His aggressive hatreds included not only Marxists, "the *Reichstag*, the red headquarters," the "treasonous and godless Social Democrats," but also the Center party and the Catholic church, that "imperialist world power," and the Democrats (DDP), "all Jews." His antisemitism he describes as "an instinctive aversion for the Jewish race" which in 1919 turned into a mania. He relates: "Whenever a Jew was carrying on impertinently on the elevated or on the train and would not accept my scolding without further impertinence, I threatened to throw him off the moving train . . . if he did not shut up immediately." This sociopath of a civil servant also threatened Marxist workers with a gun and with his boot during the Kapp *putsch*, according to his own account. His egomania evidently drove him to create ever-new fringe groups in which he could play the cock of the walk. As soon as he was no longer in the center of things, he would stage major provocations, get into trouble with the law, or simply lose interest in the group. "I always took it to be a weakness of my political enemies in the civil service that they let me get off so easily every time," he wrote with the innocence of the sociopath who is asking to be restrained. Apart from a court trial for disturbing the peace, two disciplinary proceedings, and denials of promotion, he seems to have met his match only once: he was beaten up by Communists, he claims, in a fracas that cost him a few teeth and his gold watch. He joined a *Nationalsozialistische Freiheitsbewegung* briefly in 1924 and was a *Kreisleiter* until he lost interest and resigned. In 1930, he once more worked for the NSDAP as a secret mole burrowing in the bureaucratic warren, and joined officially in 1932. On coming to power, the party promoted him to the rank of *Oberregierungsrat* and gave him a position in the Prussian Ministry of Commerce.

Another respondent illustrates the curious ambivalence of some antisemites who like Adolf Eichmann[7] not only had friendly social

[7] See for example, Hannah Arendt, *Eichmann in Jerusalem*, Viking Press, 1963, pp. 28-33, 38-42, 56-65. Eichmann was born in 1906 and

contacts with Jews but at times even showed some interest in or identification with Jewish groups and symbols. A banker's apprentice, born 1897 in an occupied area (no. 438), he began his political activities in 1920 by heckling at SPD, DDP, and Center party rallies "whenever nationalistic principles were denigrated under the eyes of the French." He attributes such denigration in particular to Jewish speakers. After his expulsion from the occupied area in 1923, he remained aloof from politics until the presidential election campaign of 1925. He propagandized in a Catholic association for Hindenburg until that group threw him out "in a tumultuous session on election day, after I had announced my vote." He lost his bank job for undisclosed reasons and returned deeply disgruntled to his home town:

> My hatred for the Jewish bankers and stockbrokers was all that remained. I tried to penetrate deeper into the Jewish character. Getting together with the Jews, Kahn and Mohr, who had gone to school with me, I learned that some so-called Hitler boys were carrying on in Germersheim and bothering the chosen people. One night in the summer of 1926, Mohr lifted my disguise with a rash remark in front of my younger brother. I decided to take up the fight against these two Jews. . . . I joined the young leaders of the NSDAP local in Germersheim and right after a lecture . . . about the "world vampire of Judaism," I signed up with enthusiasm. I'll make no secret of the fact that I was regarded upon entry at first as a spy for Kahn. But I soon convinced my new comrades otherwise by intensively distributing copies of the *Eisenhammer*. . . .

This stalwart "fighter against Jews, Freemasons, and the Black [Catholic] International" evidently employed the familiar mechanism of trying violently to dissociate himself from what might seem to the public, including his own brother, a friendly association. As in so many cases of prejudice, there is a curious mingling of private and public motives.

There is a certain plausibility about outbreaks of *Judenkoller* among military-civil servants under the impact of defeat and revolution or of small businessmen when economic crisis strikes. Few people are mentally so stable that we cannot picture them going through a breakdown in which "my hatred against the Jews grew by leaps and bounds, and I became certain that the Jews are Germany's misfortune" (no. 523, born 1886). What requires explana-

---

had been in the *Wandervogel* and in a quasi-military youth organization before joining the NSDAP and SS in mid-1932.

tion is not the private breakdown and use of scapegoats, but their translation into public political action. Let us examine some of the paranoids who turned their private manias into activist careers.

A good many of the paranoids are simply *voelkisch* partisans from the earliest times. A typical case is a druggist, born 1888 (no. 11), who was already in the antisemitic Retail Clerks Union (DHV)[8] before the war upon the advice of his boss. Following the war, in 1922, he joined the *Deutschvoelkische Freiheitsbewegung*, held a local office in it, and soon switched to the NSDAP and the SA. He says very little about his beliefs but rather describes how his drugstore was boycotted by Communists, and Socialists and denied deliveries by "a certain industrial enterprise in town." He also fails to indicate whether, as a stormtrooper, he engaged in any demonstrations or fighting. "Our National Socialism was purely a matter of sentiment (*Gefuehlssache*)," he states after indicating a good deal of proselytizing and of "ruthless action" for the cause in earlier years.

Another such activist was an executive of a shipping firm, born 1898 (no. 12), who joined the *Schutz-und-Trutzbund*[9] in response to the "betrayal of the German front by the new rulers" and Jewish war profiteers. He spent much of the republican era abroad, away from "the alien racial elements now abroad in Germany," but in contact with like-minded people in Holland, where he also read *Mein Kampf*. In 1929, the campaigning against the Young Plan not only brought him back to sign the petition, but also enlisted him in the NSDAP. He became a stormtrooper and Nazi speaker "although my firm had nearly 60% foreign and especially Jewish customers." He undertook to proselytize and organize party cells among the "red sailors" of the Rhine shipping traffic and claims to have been in an *SA Sturm* where executives, public prosecutors, businessmen, workers, and the unemployed were cooperating in perfect harmony. At the time he wrote his *vita*, the respondent was the political director of his local.

Another old antisemite, born 1886 (no. 271), was a civil servant who tells of his father's allegiance to such nineteenth-century political antisemites as Ahlwardt, Stoecker, Henrici, and the *Deutscher Antisemitenbund*. The respondent and his brother had been militant

[8] On the *voelkisch* character of the DHV, see also Iris Hamel, *Voelkischer Verband und nationale Gerwerkschaft*, Frankfurt: Europaeische Verlagsanstalt, 1967.

[9] On the rise of the postwar antisemitic movement including the counterrevolutionary *Schutz-und-Trutzbund*, see especially Lohalm, *Voelkischer Radikalismus*, especially chapters 2, 4, and 5.

members of the DHV since 1912 and he was also in the *voelkisch Deutschsoziale Partei* of Hamburg and the *Deutscher Turnerbund*. The writings of Fritsch, Duehring, Claass, and Dahn, he asserts, convinced him of the pernicious role of Jews in recent German history from Stahl and Marx to the contemporary German press. The respondent seems to have suffered a *Judenkoller* in 1912 and then to have gone on to severe paranoia, which caused him to see Jews everywhere in the government and to agonize over the question of whether Jesus was a Jew. His account of his war and postwar experiences is an unbelievable jumble of such mutterings. The Freemasons and the Catholic Center party also receive their share. The respondent spent most of his Weimar years with the DNVP, feeling "inhibitions" about joining the NSDAP. Finally, in 1932, after three years of withdrawal from politics, he attended a Nazi rally and arrived at the sudden realization that "this was what I had been looking for since 1912." It is cases like these which dispel this writer's concern about the possibility that the Nazi party, in helping to collect the *vitae*, may have removed the more embarrassing cases.

Our last example is another civil servant, born in 1879 (no. 291), who grew up in an orphanage because of the early death of his mother and served in the military before and during the war. In his thirties he read H. S. Chamberlain's *Foundations of the Nineteenth Century* and "through a friend in the police, got to know the slums and criminal quarters of the big city, the breeding places of the corruption of the people (*voelkische Zersetzung*)." He was "highly aware, despite the outlawing of political activity among the soldiers, of the progress of Marxism and the corruption of the people. The call of Chamberlain in the great world struggle and the bugle call of Dietrich Eckart [a Nazi writer] after the war took me among the freedom fighters of Adolf Hitler."

In 1922, the respondent founded and led the Wuerzburg local of the NSDAP. "I was *Ortsgruppenleiter*, stormtrooper, and a soldier, but this time a political soldier." He participated in the beer-hall *putsch* and, during the outlawing of the party, was a candidate for the *Reichstag* on behalf of the *Nationalsozialistische Freiheitspartei*. After Hitler's release from prison, he helped to reconstruct the party and the SA in Lower Franconia.

He met Hitler many times and, in addition to Chamberlain, read *Mein Kampf* and the writings of Gottfried Feder. His deepest wartime impressions culminated in "the appearance of Negro divisions against our heroically fighting nation" and "the Germanic tragedy of the sons of our blood brothers, who emigrated to the United States, coming back to turn the fortunes of war against us." He ends his rantings with a flourish:

A true follower of Hitler had to be determined to eliminate the consequences of the shameful Treaty of Versailles and thus to push open once more the door to life, which has been slammed on our people and its children; to vanquish the culture-destroying, godless, Jewish Marxism and Bolshevism again, and thus to banish the great menace in Europe—nay, in the world at large. This was a struggle not just for the existence of the German people, but of the white race in general.

This old fighter and early Nazi leader undoubtedly thought he knew what he was talking about and fighting for, even if his rantings made little sense then and now. There is a difference between the unserious talk of an American right-wing demagogue, such as Loewenthal and Guterman have analyzed in their book[10] and very similar rantings by the leaders of a popular mass movement about to come to power in a modern nation-state. The difference can be deadly indeed, even though the rantings are just as illusionary as those of the demagogue, who may be content to fleece his audience of gifts and contributions.

Ethnocentricity Aside From Antisemitism

Another and parallel prejudice is that against aliens or foreign nations. Our tabulation shows the distribution of xenophobic themes in the Abel sample. To begin with, there is a slight, if somewhat debatable, difference between respondents who show no prejudice and those who seem unaware of the outside world. Then there are

FD-71: Ethnocentricity Other than Antisemitism

	Number	Per cent
No ethnocentricity	220	46.0
Unconcerned about outside world, parochial	54	11.3
⌐ Foreign nations dangerous, hostile (encirclement)	47	9.8
⊢ Projective, likes others' nationalism, attributes economic envy, hostility to them	11	2.3
∟ Scores foreign press criticism of Nazis	9	1.9
⌐ Venom against aliens in Germany	65	13.6
⊢ Anti-Catholic hatred (beyond political friction)	7	1.5
∟ Vague reference to alien "international" forces, or conspiracy	25	5.2
Alien nations are inferior	40	8.4
	478	100.0

[10] Especially in *Prophets of Deceit.* See also the antisemitic rhetoric of no. 274 (born about 1892), a military-civil servant who undertakes to defend the assassination of Rathenau and other political (*Feme*) murders by rightwing zealots.

three categories of hostile perception of foreign nations, all of which we shall call chauvinistic. There are another three themes of xenophobia. There are some Protestant regions, especially in the north, where anti-Catholic prejudice was so strong as to be quite comparable in intensity to the hatred of aliens or Jews. Anti-Catholicism also was an important ideological motive among certain racist or *voelkisch* ideologues in Austria or other Catholic areas.[11] The theme of alien inferiority is simply the obverse of delusions of national or ethnic superiority. We will not go into as much detail on ethnocentricity as on antisemitism, because the former issue is more on the surface and requires little explanation. Nevertheless, it may be worth relating this prejudice to wartime experiences and attitudes.

The three generations differ slightly in their commitment to the different ethnocentric themes. The "youngest" attitude, represented by half its respondents in the postwar generation, is unconcern about the outside world. The next youngest exhibit no prejudice. The "oldest," by comparison tend to display the ideas of inferiority and superiority among nations. This group, as well as the chauvinists and xenophobes, has particular strength among the members of the war generation (born 1895-1901). The non-ethnocentric and the parochials are also noticeably more from rural and small-town areas. The highly mobile among cities tend toward xenophobia.

Which occupational groups were the xenophobes and which the chauvinists? To begin with, workers, farmers, and women are relatively free of ethnocentricity. The most chauvinistic are the military-civil servants and, less so, the white-collar employees, who are more often xenophobic. Delusions of ethnic superiority are particularly popular with women and, less often, with military-civil servants and business and professional men. If it is a matter of the father's occupation, however, the children of military-civil servants tend to be far more often convinced of German superiority and more xenophobic than they are chauvinistic. It is as if there were a generational progression from chauvinism to xenophobia. The sons and daughters of high military or professional people or of artisans tend to be more chauvinist, but those of businessmen are balanced between the two, and those of farmers are more xenophobic.

Social mobility also has a bearing on the choice between the two or three alternatives. Respondents moving up from the farm and social decliners are not particularly ethnocentric. Those who never

[11] See George Mosse, *The Crisis of German Ideology*, pp. 159, 231, 257.

attempted to rise, by comparison, tend to be chauvinists. The upwardly mobile in the city, again, are xenophobes or obsessed with German superiority. This is somewhat surprising if we are inclined to
think in terms of the ethnic tensions of the melting-pot of rural-
urban migration. But integral nationalism evidently is more at home
with the next generation that grows up in the urban environment.
It is their burning social ambition which turns upon the alien or
exalts their own national identity.

The different interpretations given to the vaunted *Volksgemeinschaft* also tell the story. Ethnocentricity is highest (71%) among
those who call for national solidarity against the outside world and
who, naturally, tend toward chauvinism and feelings of national
superiority, often as a result of their *Fronterlebnis*. But it is also
rather high (53.1%) among respondents of strong class-consciousness and the solidarists of the middle (48%), who take out their
social frustrations on the aliens and on the inferiority of "lesser
breeds." Ethnocentricity, by comparison, is much lower among the
solidarists from below (22.8%) or above (43.2%), or among
those innocent of class feelings (41.5%), who tend slightly toward
chauvinism. The strongly class-conscious may hate the alien more
because he cannot readily be fitted into their social scale of values,
but the solidarists of the middle (mostly military-civil servants and
white-collar workers) hate him simply because he is an alien.

Religion and education also add some significant differences.
Protestant Nazis tend to be far less ethnocentric, but more chauvinistic than Catholics or those who failed to indicate their religion.
Catholics are more convinced of the inferiority of other nations.
The most xenophobic are those who state no religious affiliation.
German education gives a doubtful demonstration of its humanistic
character when we learn that the best-educated of the sample incline toward the belief in the inferiority of other nations. Thirty-
seven and one-tenth percent of the respondents holding this belief completed their secondary education (*mittlere Reife*) and 17.1% have
the *Abitur*.

War and Revolution

If we look for the dominant ideological motive of the ethnocentricity group, we learn that the antisemites and the Nordic-German
romantics were also by far the most ethnocentric (56.8% and
55.8%). The antisemites were heavily xenophobic, and the romantics inclined toward visions of national superiority and toward
chauvinism. The superpatriots shared this approximate balance be-

tween xenophobia and chauvinism, while the revanchists were heavily chauvinistic. These relationships are not unexpected, but they suggest that we should take a closer look at all the experiences that might contribute to the ethnocentricity of the respondents.

It is particularly interesting to observe whether certain contacts with foreign nationalities seem to have predisposed a respondent more toward chauvinism or toward xenophobia. Foreign birth or sojourn seems to produce chauvinism; borderland or occupation experiences more heavily relate to xenophobia. Both of the last-mentioned seem to result in a rather high degree of ethnocentrism, especially the experiences with the French occupation (71%) which we have found to be so potent a stimulus to Nazi involvement.

The ethnocentric groups also differ somewhat in their military service patterns. Those who never served, mostly the postwar generation, are noticeably less ethnocentric (38.6%) than the war and prewar generations. Those who served in peacetime, in particular, are the most ethnocentric (50%) and both rather chauvinistic and xenophobic. As for their war experiences, the most ethnocentric (76.6%) and especially chauvinistic group are the bitter-enders, with their hostility toward draft-dodgers and civilians in general. They are quite convinced of the inferiority of other nations but not nearly as xenophobic as, for example, those whose initial enthusiasm turned to disaffection with the war. Those who stress the egalitarian *Fronterlebnis* also tend to be chauvinists. The youthful victory-watchers, also tend to be more heavily chauvinistic than xenophobic.

In their reaction to the German defeat, the most ethnocentric (86.3%) are those who blame the *Kaiser* and the civilians. They are mostly chauvinistic or believe in the inferiority of other nations. Even respondents who blame Marxists and Spartakists for the German defeat more often are chauvinists rather than xenophobes. Only among those who reacted with diffuse emotion and who were also rather young are the xenophobes the prominent element. As for the revolution, however, the xenophobes clearly tend to blame international Bolshevism or the Jews. The territorial changes in the east, of course, may well have tended to blur the national status of some revolutionary leaders—Hitler himself did not acquire German citizenship until the early 1930s. The chauvinists tend to blame the Weimar parties, the Jews, or the Spartakists and mutineers for the revolution.

The direct impact of the occupation, by way of contrast, mostly made xenophobes out of those who were punished, jailed, or expelled by the French. Respondents who only express hatred or distaste for the occupation, on the other hand, were more often chauvinists. The question of whether the displacement went toward the aliens inside or toward the obvious enemy outside evidently was greatly influenced by actual conflicts and friction.

We are still unable to explain completely why some ethnocentrics insist on hating aliens rather than foreign nations, which would have followed more logically from the experience of international conflicts. One prevalent reason so far has been the parallel nature of antisemitism in various contexts to xenophobia. In their perception of the Weimar "system," too, those who view Weimar as the *Judenrepublik* rank high in xenophobia as well as in the belief in other nations' inferiority. But there are also other factors present. Respondents who raise the traditional anti-capitalistic objections to Weimar are just as xenophobic, and those who look beyond the regime of the "red and black" parties toward utopia are far more so. We must be dealing with an intense integral-nationalistic impulse here which probably interacts with other attitudes as well. Let us examine what other attitudes bear the highest interrelationship with xenophobia.

With regard to the objects of hostility, the strongest xenophobic impulse is found among respondents with the all-embracing hate-lists; 42.9% are xenophobes. The next most xenophobic group are respondents who vent their spleen on "reactionaries," Catholics, and liberals (24.6%), well ahead of the anti-Marxists (13.4%) and the antisemitic anti-Marxists (12.7%). If the all-embracing hate-list reflects the intensity of free-floating hostility or a high propensity for displacements, this would seem to be a typical feature of Nazi xenophobia. On the antisemitism scale, it will be recalled, the xenophobes most heavily tend to be paranoids, cholerics, or tellers of prejudicial anecdotes. In their attitude toward political enemies, the xenophobes are mostly physically aggressive or *outrés* who probably considered aliens also as "subhuman," rodents, immoral, etc. In their attitude toward authority, too, the xenophobes heavily tend toward hostility vis-à-vis the police and government authority.

In their level of political understanding, the xenophobes are mostly of the low-ideological type or of medium intelligence, which makes them considerably more ideological than any other group. Their formative experiences tend to be alleged encounters with Jews or aliens or an educational or literary experience. By comparison, those who believe in German superiority and the chauvinists also cite such alleged encounters but they are also strongly influenced by the war and by their *Fronterlebnis*. The attitudes toward violence of the xenophobes heavily emphasize attitudes of physical involvement, and more often masochism than sadism.

The pathology of xenophobia yields disproportionate numbers of irrational paranoids and of the insecure or masochistic. By comparison, the chauvinists and those who believe in German superiority tend to have much more often a severe case of cultural shock from the events of 1918-1919. In 1934, finally, the expectations of the xenophobes more than those of anyone else were set on empire and on totalitarianism within it. Here we obviously have a very important element of the Nazi attitude, a kind of core group even though its ideological profile is far from clear.

Dimensions of Hostility

At first glance, there may seem to be some duplication in the effort to measure Nazi hostility apart from antisemitism and ethnocentricity, not to mention the other ideological and attitudinal indicators. However, the importance of sorting out the various overlapping dimensions of the political culture of the Nazi movement suggests a strategy of overlapping measurements in the hope of winnowing out each motive by itself and its relation to the others. This measurement (FD-61) began as an attempt to inventory the hostilities of the respondents by their chief objects. Since crosstabulation requires a certain amount of consolidation, however, the emerging categories are less clear: Antisemites, anti-Marxists, anti-establishmentarians, and the all-embracing or intense leftover of hatred shall be the labels. The last-mentioned also includes motives of a more private sort, such as a hatred of particular individuals which has somehow become politicized.

By far the largest of our groups are the anti-Marxists, whose prominence raises the question whether and to what extent the Nazi

FD-61: Chief Objects of Hostility

	Number	Per cent
Jews, the "conspiracy"	53	12.5
Jewish Marxists, Communists	9	2.1
Socialists, Free trade union leaders	34	8.0
Communists	45	10.6
Marxists in general	190	44.7
Catholics, Church, Center party	19	4.5
Liberals, capitalists	33	7.8
Reactionaries	7	1.7
All of above	10	2.4
Others (personal hostilities)	24	5.7
	424	100.0

movement was an anti-Marxist movement. Historically there was an intense feeling of rivalry with Socialism among the more labor-oriented elements of the Nazi movement and a strong sense of opposition to Communism and Socialism among the bourgeois Nazis. But the *vitae* rarely show a case in which a passionate anti-Marxism could be cited the principal motif. There is frequently an eloquent expression of regret about how the Social Democrats alienated the German workingman from his fatherland and, on occasion, an expression of the desire to win him back from the "reds." There are also plentiful descriptions of fighting against Communists and *Reichsbanner* in the streets and meeting-halls, along with deprecatory remarks about these opponents. But no Abel respondent, with the possible exception of a Russian emigré or two, exhibits anything like the anti-Communist crusading spirit familiar from certain contemporary American groups and campaigns. Perhaps a real flesh-and-blood enemy does not lend itself as well to the manipulation of paranoid fantasies as does one that is either distant or a mere figment of the popular imagination. In any case, anti-Marxism as a crusade does not appear to have moved the respondents as deeply as did some of the other attitudes we discussed earlier in this section.

Social Background of Hate Groupings

How do the anti-Marxists and the other groups relate to the different Nazi generations? The anti-Marxists, of whom 39.9% belong to the postwar generation, are among the youngest. More than half of them were born after the turn of the century. Only the small group of the intense haters is that young. The oldest group are the antisemites. The youthfulness of the anti-Marxists suggests that their anti-Marxism had little to do with the prewar Socialist movement, but rather constituted a hostile reaction to the well-entrenched and powerful SPD and KPD of the Weimar years. Thus it contains strong elements of anti-establishmentarianism just as the older anti-reactionary attitude did. Many respondents, indeed, in spite of the occasional involvement of their own parents, considered the Socialist and labor movement an outdated legacy of the past or an obnoxious monopoly over union-controlled jobs or welfare benefits limited to holders of "red" party-member cards.

The anti-Marxists tended to live either in Berlin or in rural areas, as compared to the anti-reactionaries and intense haters who more often lived in large towns or other metropolitan areas. The anti-Marxists, furthermore, mostly lived in the place of their birth, or they might be highly mobile among cities, but they were not as often rural-urban migrants as were the antisemites and the anti-reactionaries. The borderland respondents also tended to be strong anti-Marxists because they considered the SPD an obstacle to ethnic unity and also because they felt betrayed by a Socialist government in Berlin. They were also anti-reactionary, a trait they shared with respondents from the occupied areas where the impact of foreign occupation seems to have loosed an avalanche of displacements on all kinds of targets other than the occupiers.

By occupation, the anti-Marxists tended to be workers, as we would expect them to be, but also women, and military-civil servants. Business and professional persons were more frequent among the antisemites or among the anti-reactionaries, who also had a greater share of white-collar workers and as large a proportion of military-civil servants. The disaffection and sense of rivalry with the Marxist labor movement was evidently their predominant motive. We can tentatively extend the inquiry into the preceding generation by looking at the occupations of the fathers. The anti-Marxists had mostly military-civil servants and workers as fathers, while the fathers of anti-reactionaries tended to be farmers or workers. There may well have been a working-class Tory tradition present here.

Many working-class Tories are upwardly mobile people who spurn the existing trade union movement because they feel that they can do better by themselves. Others again feel so well integrated into a hierarchic society that their shock at Socialist pushiness outweighs their interest in their own advancement. Our anti-Marxists tended not to attempt to rise above the station of their fathers and may have felt envious of the success of the Socialists and unionists as individuals in the Weimar Republic. Many were in social decline and may have resented successful Socialists all the more. The anti-reactionaries, by comparison, were upwardly mobile and evidently more preoccupied with the capitalists, Catholics, and other established circles who may have been reluctant to accept them. The anti-reactionaries tended to be Catholics, which may explain their hostility toward the Catholic establishment. The anti-Marxists, by comparison, were mostly Protestants or respondents who failed to indicate their religion. Historically, winning the loyalty of the German worker in Protestant areas involved fighting the SPD, while in Catholic areas the *Sozialverein* and Catholic labor associations were often better-established than the SPD and the Free Trade Unions. Our data clearly bear this out.

The Reaction to Defeat and Revolution

The great shock of the year 1918 hit the various hate groupings quite differently. The cultural shock of the antisemites chiefly took the form of complaints about social and moral disintegration and shock at the press and the new Weimar elites. The anti-Marxists instead were shocked about the fall of the old order and the disparagement of the glories and military symbols of the empire, as well as about the new Weimar elites. To see this in the appropriate light, we have to remember how young they were at the time. Very few of them actually mourned the passing of a social order they had experienced only as children. The anti-reactionaries instead tended to complain about the absence of order and discipline.

Their reaction to the German defeat gives us a first clue to their motivation. Unlike the antisemites and anti-reactionaries, who tend to blame the defeat on the *Kaiser* and the civilians, the anti-Marxists heavily blame it on the Marxists and Spartakists. More than half of them, of course, had never served in the military and, of those who had been in the war, many became disaffected, but evidently they quickly changed their minds at the "Marxist excesses." There were many victory-watchers among them, too. Their reaction to the "revolution," moreover, was mostly to blame the Spartakists or mutineers, or unspecified rabble, or the Western powers. The anti-reactionaries instead tended to blame the Weimar parties, and the antisemites the Jews for the revolution. The motive of the anti-Marxists for becoming militarized (stage two) tended to be the shock of defeat and their sense of opposition to the red revolutionaries, certainly a plausible reaction.

Our second clue has to come from the youth-group background of the anti-Marxists, since so many of them were rather young at the time of defeat and revolution. The fathers of the anti-Marxist respondents tended to be militarists or *voelkisch*-antisemitic, while the anti-reactionaries, for example, more often had fathers of moderate political color or an unpolitical home environment. The anti-Marxists also report a *voelkisch*-antisemitic school and peer group environment and more than their share of orphans and childhood poverty.

As for their first youth group association, one in ten of the anti-Marxists turns out to have been in a Socialist or Communist youth group. A good many also joined *Jungdo*, or bourgeois groups, or were in a Free Corps or military training group before they turned 26. What they liked best about this first youthful association was its spirit of comradeship, marching and ideological direction, or just demonstrations. And what they liked the least were "un-national views" or the ideology and leadership of their group. It looks as if their dislikes and very likely their antisemitism led them to defect from their Socialist or Communist youth groups and to drift into the

NSDAP. Quite a few, in fact, joined the Hitler Youth or the storm-troopers to begin with. As their motives for joining the NSDAP (stage four), indeed, many cite the "rough opposition" of the Communists, or the dynamic impression of the Hitler movement. Anti-Marxism seems to have been a convenient umbrella to cover a wide range of bourgeois or ex-Socialist youthful attitudes.

Ideological Attitudes and the NSDAP

Among the dominant ideological themes of the Abel group, anti-Marxism plays no role at all. When we cross it with these themes, in fact, most of those "without any ideology" turn out to be anti-Marxists. Hitler-worshippers, Nordic-German romantics, and solidarists, in this order, make up the bulk of the anti-Marxists. Relatively low on the antisemitism scale,[12] they are also the lowest in other forms of ethnocentricity. Only in their attitude toward authority do they exhibit an extraordinary amount of authoritarianism and of extreme leadership cult.

Their level of political understanding tends to be rather low and of the dimwit-romantic or low-pragmatic sort, as compared to the highly intelligent anti-reactionaries, or the low-ideological anti-semites. This corresponds to the differentials in their formal education, of which the anti-reactionaries have the most and the anti-Marxists the least. The antisemites have quite a few members with a lot and quite a few with very little education. The expectations of the anti-Marxists in 1934 tended to be the dream of the totalitarian 1000-year Reich, with hints of purges and brainwashing. Their pathology indeed suggests special movement qualities for this direction: A high degree of leadership cult and of group conformity.

These qualities also highlight their role in the Nazi party. The chief satisfactions of the anti-Marxists in the party, for example, tended to be the Hitler cult and the spirit of comradeship of the stormtroopers, as compared to the utopian consciousness exhibited by the antisemites and the anti-reactionaries. In contrast to these other groups, also, the anti-Marxists held only rather minor local offices in the party. They were far more heavily involved with the stormtroopers than were the antisemites and anti-reactionaries, and yet the latter two held the more important offices there at the *Sturm-fuehrer* and *Sturmbannfuehrer* levels. The anti-Marxists did most of the fighting, while the antisemites concentrated more on proselyt-

[12] This is low only in relative terms. In absolute numbers the very large group of anti-Marxists still supplies more than half of the paranoids on that scale.

izing, and the anti-reactionaries on electioneering. This did not pre-
vent the anti-Marxists from a masochistic attitude toward violence
and yet a distinctly *outré* manner of referring to their political
opponents. It is not unfair to say that the anti-Marxists were mostly
the foot soldiers of the movement. Eugen Kogon in his *Theory and
Practice of Hell* describes the typical SS guard in his concentration
camp as a simple man with a few fixed ideas in his head. Such a
fixed idea without much ideological underpinning was probably the
stereotypical anti-Marxism we are examining here.

FOUR

Extremism and the Self

How does an extremist, in particular a Nazi, see himself? We have repeatedly received the impression that the Abel respondents never saw themselves as the ridiculous figures or monsters that they seemed to the world or their victims. Some considered themselves romantic heroes or idealistic knights in shining armor on a crusade to save the fatherland. Others were obsessed by their phobias to the point of paranoia. Some even allowed their obsessive fantasies to take complete charge of their lives and to drive them on into a pseudopolitical life of hectic action. Others again reveal a cold-blooded cynicism which ignores the idealism of some of their fellow-fighters and instead concentrates on thrills and pay-offs. By and large, the Abel respondents seem to be driven people. They often blame their personal background or the broader historical circumstances for the direction their lives had taken.

Interpreting Their Own Lives

To determine how the Abel respondents viewed their own lives is not an easy task. But we can try to explore the subject from various angles. There is, first of all, the question of how they present the course of their own lives. Theodore Abel had asked for an account of their political development but this was not always what he received. About one-eighth each of the respondents instead describe their lives either as the product of the great upheaval of their times, of the war, the "revolution," or the economic and cultural crisis, or as the product of personal problems of various kinds. In a sense, those blaming history are merely less self-assertive than are those who are describing their political development as if to say: It turned out this way because we wanted it. Respondents who blame their personal problems, on the other hand, are not just casualties of their society and frequently of their mixed-up family relations, but tend to have a sociopathic streak. What else are we to think of a case such as the young worker quoted earlier who claimed that his wife's unfaithfulness had driven him into the Communist party? Or of the woman clerk who insisted that the interest of some Jewish males in her "delicate blondeness" had caused her to be an antisemite? The emotional forces at work here are no doubt powerful and persuasive, but common sense balks at accepting these explanations at face value.

FD-78: Interpretative Emphasis

Chief emphasis on:	Number	Per cent
International forces, war	3	0.5
Domestic Politics	48	8.0
General economic crisis, disorder	8	1.3
Cultural pessimism, disorder	14	2.3
Personal economic problems	20	3.3
Personal, family problems	46	7.7
Social class problems	15	2.5
Own political development	444	74.4
	598	100.0

Social Background of Interpretation Groups

The age distribution among the historical, personal, and political interpretation groups, shows up important generational differences. The political development group is far younger than the others, with 39.2% in the postwar generation. Here the greater politicization of German youth since the turn of the century is making itself felt. The oldest group is the one troubled with all kinds of personal problems, with nearly one-half born before 1895. The historically determined group has the highest number of members of the war generation, which pinpoints the date of their overwhlelming historical events at World War One and its aftermath.

The respondents preoccupied with their personal problems tended to be either rural-urban migrants living in Berlin or still in small-town or rural surroundings. Some of them, according to their own account, wrestled all their lives with siblings, parents, or wives. Women in particular tended to blame their personal or historical circumstances, which throws a significant light on the status of women in those days. Farmers and white-collar respondents mostly blamed history, while workers, military-civil servants, and business or professional people mostly spoke of their personal political development.

The interpretative emphasis also relates to the dimensions of prejudice. Regarding objects of hostility, for example, the respondents with personal hangups tend to be antisemitic or anti-reactionary. It is the respondents who describe only their own political development who are the anti-Marxists. On the antisemitism scale, the historical cases tend toward *Judenkoller* or paranoia, while the personal complainers mostly tell prejudiced anecdotes. The most ethnocentric respondents, again, are the historical cases, which stress in particular xenophobia and chauvinism. The personally wronged respondents, by comparison, tend to believe in the inferiority of other nations and, to a lesser extent, to be chauvinists.

The Excess and the Defect

As mentioned earlier on many occasions, we also catalogued the pathology or psychological marginality of each case according to excessive traits of one sort or another. Respondents showing extreme degrees of leadership cult, cultural shock, paranoia, or group

FD-77: Psychological Marginality

	Number	Per cent
High cultural shock	63	19.3
High leadership cult	70	21.4
High personal insecurity	13	4.0
High masochism, self-pity	29	8.9
High group conformity	108	33.0
High paranoia	33	10.1
Irrationality, incoherence, gross imbalance	11	3.3
	327	100.0

conformity, for instance, were considered psychologically marginal and were categorized as in FD-77. Group conformity was defined as a propensity to want to merge the self with the movement. What constituted excess, of course, was a matter of judgment and common sense, although in most cases excess spoke for itself too clearly to leave any doubt about its abnormality.

A Social Profile of Psychological Marginality

The age differences among these psychological groupings are great. The two youngest are the conformists and leadership cultists with 48.1% and 41.4%, respectively, in the postwar generation and about three-fourths born after 1894. These two groups evidently represent the youthful wave of the Nazi movement. The oldest group is the one that suffered great cultural shock, with 60.4% born before 1895. Nearly that old were the paranoids, with 55.7% born before 1895. These two groups appear to be the prewar- and war-generation converts to the cause. The masochists are evenly distributed over the age cohorts.

The rural-urban differences are just as clear. The young leadership and conformity groups, it turns out, are concentrated in the rural and town areas, while all the others are highly metropolitan. They are evidently a part of the Weimar youth revolt. Nevertheless, the two young groups also tend to be rather mobile among towns as compared to the spatially immobile or rural-urban migrants among all the other groups. There is the distinct impression that we are really recording generational patterns of spatial mobility rather than psychological patterns. Respondents from borderland or occupied areas also show up heavily in the two young groups, while those with foreign experiences mostly complain about a high cultural shock.

By occupation, the leadership cultists tended to be white-collar or, as with the conformists, workers or farmers. The wave of Nazi youth hardly came from privileged homes. The fathers of the leadership cultists were mostly military-civil servants and the fathers of the conformists were either the same or workers or artisans. The masochists and insecure were mostly women or workers. The cultural-shock and paranoid groups heavily tended to be military-civil servants. The culturally shocked also were often women or white-collar respondents, while the paranoids heavily tended also to be business or professional people.

This social profile is further clarified by relating the psychological groupings to the patterns of social mobility. Respondents suffering from severe cultural shock tend to be upwardly mobile from a farm background. Or to put it a different way, their painful rise from rural antecedents evidently made them more vulnerable to the shattering experiences of defeat and revolution. The paranoid also tend to be upwardly mobile, but from the urban proletariat. For both of these groups, especially to the extent they chose the military-civil service as their avenue of advancement, the additional strains of the year 1918 were evidently too much to bear and they became extremists. The masochists and insecure tend to be in social decline— another kind of social drama that may well produce despair, especially if it is politicized by the dramatic circumstances of history. The situation is somewhat different with the two younger groups because of their youth. The group conformists tend to be in the same status as their parents, which says nothing about their social motivation. The leadership cultists, on the other hand, are mostly upwardly mobile from the urban proletariat, which should remind us of our earlier findings about the activism and violent behavior of this mobility group. We have repeatedly compared it to the profile of a race rioter in the United States of the 1960s.

As the Leaders So the Men

These personal characteristics are not so far from what the court psychiatrist Gilbert noticed in interviewing 21 of the high Nazi figures in the dock at the Nuremberg trials.[1] He found them to be generally sociopathic, aggressive, paranoid, schizoid, highly suggestible, authoritarian, emotionally unstable, and egotistical. Such a catalog also describes much of Hitler's personality. We can assume, of course, that the leadership would embody these qualities to a far higher degree than would the rank and file. Nevertheless, we have already encountered a number of extreme paranoid examples in the preceding section. Here is another example, a small businessman, born about 1896, who ran a poultry, fish, and venison shop in Berlin (no. 255). The respondent describes his return from the war and adds: "The mob was in control of the streets. It was quite impossible at the time to found a national movement; anyone showing nationalistic conviction was immediately knocked to the ground." The respondent tells about one of his train trips to buy merchandise and how he saw some leaflets of the *Schutz-und-Trutzbund* lying around in one of the train compartments. The leaflets contained an invitation to come to a meeting of the group, and triggered in him a mixture of paranoid fear and adventure. "Secretly and furtively I took a leaflet. If any of the other passengers had seen me take it, they would have recognized me as a nationalist and thrown me through a window of the moving train. You would not believe how these beasts were putting pressure on people dissenting from them." He went to the meeting, which turned out to be composed of only a handful of people. They talked him into organizing a local of the *Schutz-und-Trutzbund*, which he succeeded in doing at great expense of money and effort. At a mass rally of the organization in Berlin's Circus Busch in 1922, the respondent experienced his first major meeting-hall fight with Communists, and later a Communist raid on his headquarters. The respondent also fought with the Protestant Parents' Association against the secularization "of our Christian schools" plotted by "the Communists and Social Democrats and many, many ministers."

> One Sunday, the Serious Students of the Bible (*Bibelforscher*) held bible meetings all over, and the city of Berlin made all conceivable rooms available for this purpose. But the real purpose of these bible

[1] See G. M. Gilbert, *Nuremberg Diary*, New York: Farrar, Straus, 1947, and especially his *Psychology of Dictatorship*, New York: Ronald Press, 1950.

meetings was to prepare the people for the time when "god" was supposedly going to crown the Jew, Rathenau, king. So we went and
broke up many of these meetings. A short time later Rathenau was
murdered (?) and, of course, they were looking for the "assassin" in
our midst.

The assassination of Rathenau, regardless of the respondent's
doubt, was very real and led to the outlawing of the *Schutz-und-
Trutzbund*[2] and of a police auxiliary to which the respondent and
many of his co-conspirators belonged. The conspirators trans-
formed themselves into a reading club [*Lesezirkel*] and went on
proselytizing until the *Deutschvoelkische Freiheitspartei* was
founded by a dissident DNVP faction (Wulle, Graefe, Goldebee).
The respondent participated in this foundation and was commis-
sioned to develop protective squads for the meetings of the new
party. These stormtroopers were used almost daily in 1923 and saw
many bloody battles. They were also involved in the abortive coup
of the Black *Reichswehr* the same year. The respondent also describes the setting in which he lived.

> As I mentioned . . . I lived in the second story [*Hochparterre*] in the
> middle of the Communist cauldron. They would long since have hanged
> me and my family if we had not had party comrades walking in and
> out from morning till night. There were always, moreover, ten to fifteen
> men present [preparing handbills]. Police captain S. from the precinct
> here was a like-minded friend and protected my place against attacks
> as best he could.

Having described how secure his residence was, he promptly tells
how he went out of his way to bring about a major siege. "In 1925,
at the time of the presidential elections, I for the first time hoisted
my six-foot swastika flag out the window. It was probably the first
swastika flag in all of east Berlin. The Communists tried to pull it
down, but they found out that there were armed party comrades behind the curtains guarding the flag. So they let it be." Later the respondent, in order to make sure that unemployed Nazis would get
their due, became a welfare volunteer. He tells how he made his
rounds checking out applicants: "With a gun in my pocket I took
care of my job without regard to partisanship. Because of my self-
confident and energetic demeanor no one dared assault me." He
claims that his Socialist and Communist clients were "amazed how
a Nazi could have so much understanding of poverty" and that he

---

[2] See Lohalm, *Voelkischer Radikalismus*, chap. 15, for an account of
the court prosecutions and trials following the assassination.

soon won their confidence. The respondent manages to tell his story of the fighting years in Berlin without once mentioning Josef Goebbels. It is remarkable that a person with such strong paranoid fears was capable of sustained organizing activity in the party and in the Nazi welfare apparatus (NSVW) of which he eventually became a *Kreisleiter* in Berlin. Perhaps it was the constant fear of attack and persecution that spurred him on to counter-attack and to organizing a counter-movement.

In other cases, paranoia is less directly related to personal fears and linked instead to *voelkisch* antisemitism and anti-Freemasonry. A well-educated son of a businessman born 1896 (no. 229) relates that his father was with the *Deutscher Antisemitenbund* and that his grandfather knew Stoecker well. Their example and the anti-semitic *Staatsbuergerzeitung* in the house "early impressed me with the Jewish question." The teenage son also helped in getting out the vote for the prewar Conservative Party and belonged to the *Wandervogel* in Steglitz. His agricultural apprenticeship in East Prussia was interrupted by the war. The respondent volunteered and ended up a lieutenant and a prisoner of war. "During my captivity I did not want to see or hear anything about the goings-on in Germany. I was horrified to read the names of the new German cabinet ministers, nothing but Jews. . . . I could not bear to listen to the translated press reports from Germany once or twice a week."

Upon his return to his agricultural apprenticeship, he began to read *voelkisch* newspapers again, especially Kunze's *Deutsches Wochenblatt*, and also books. He ordered "the well-known stickers with the quotations of great Germans about the Jews. . . . I began to carry on the war [against the Jews] all by myself. I could not find any comrades of like mind, but there were some helpers among the workers and artisans on the estate who took the stickers to the right people." Back in Berlin, the respondent joined the *Deutsch-sozialer Bund* and read reams of further material, including the *Protocols of the Elders of Zion*. The organization disbanded and he went on to join the *Deutschvoelkische Freiheitspartei* (DVFP). But in the meantime, he had read of new disclosures "about Freemasonry, [its role in causing] the World War, and about the workings of the secret powers." And since the DVFP concerned itself little with the "secret conspiracy of the Freemasons, which had become my main interest," the respondent dropped out of this party. Eventually, and from reading Nazi newspapers such as *Der Angriff*, he drifted into the Nazi party, though hardly as an activist—which might have interfered with his illusionary world. Yet he shares the feelings of uneasiness of many a *voelkisch* convert to the NSDAP:

I had the hope and belief that I had finally found a movement which wanted to be more than just an antisemitic club. And yet I asked myself often in the early days whether our movement would make it. In my innermost feelings, sometimes, I feared for it. But slowly we advanced and the more I got to know National Socialism the more I became part of it. Much of what had moved me as a schoolboy and as a young adult, often only subconsciously, was reawakened by our *Fuehrer*. I had learned to appreciate comradeship at the front and now I rediscovered it in the movement. The war in enemy territory and during my captivity had taught me that we Germans need to become a different people, with different mind and different soul. So I became a Nazi because I am a German, which to me is *one* and the same thing.

If this respondent had not been not living in a world of delusions, we might puzzle over his reference to his reawakened youthful feelings, presumably in the *Wandervogel* and under the influence of his *voelkisch* home environment. Or about his insistence that the German people would have to change rather than to return to its old identity. In any case, these phrases are an expression of alienation.

Ideology and Attitudes

It stands to reason that at least some of the kinds of psychological marginality we have described must be highly related to other attitudes and beliefs. Religion, for example, differentiates quite noticeably between the conformists who tend to be Protestants and the leadership cultists who are more often Catholics or do not indicate their denomination. The culturally-shocked, who have the highest number of respondents (75%) who fail to state their religion, tend in this secular direction. The paranoids have a far larger number who indicate their religion; they incline toward Catholicism. Now what could it be about Catholicism that might produce a tendency toward leadership cult, paranoia, and masochism? It goes without saying that these Catholics are mostly defectors or, at best, rather nominal Catholics, although they stand out among a group of believers of high solidarity. And quite a few of them parade their wounded conventionalism when they report with indignation how the church "persecuted" them for their Nazi beliefs and activities, or how it denied their brownshirt buddies a Christian burial. Perhaps leadership cult and the other personal quirks mirror certain religious attitudes in transition to secular indifference.

How did these groups see the Weimar Republic? The conformists mostly saw it as the Marxist republic. The leadership cultists, and also the masochists, raised the traditional anticapitalistic objections to the republic, or looked forward to its replacement by the Third

Reich. The paranoids saw it as the *Judenrepublik*. The culturally-shocked criticized only the "liberalistic-Marxist system" and multipartyism. Here the connections between the forms of psychological excess and the underlying defects of prejudice begin to appear.

By dominant theme of ideology, the paranoids indeed tend heavily to be antisemites. The masochists are mostly Hitler-worshippers, or superpatriots. The leadership cultists, of course, tend heavily toward Hitler-worship. The conformists tend to be revanchists or superpatriots. They also include a disproportionate number of respondents with no ideology worth noting. Inasmuch as an ideological preoccupation constitutes a good motive for loyalty to the movement, a high degree of group conformity may well remove the necessity for an ideological motive. The culturally shocked group is made up mostly of Nordic-German romantics, revanchists, and solidarists, a reflection of its desire to preserve and defend what it views as having been destroyed by the crisis of 1918.

The chief objects of hostility of the culturally-shocked were the reactionaries, liberals, and Catholics, oddly enough. The reason may have been that these forces evidently did not share the chaotic vision of Weimar society of the Nazis, who promptly accused them of hypocrisy, just as the Weimar Communists regarded the Social Democrats as the worst hypocrites. Contemporary American liberals have become accustomed to similar abuse from radicals for not sharing their deep alienation from society. The leadership cultists and conformists tended to be anti-Marxists. And the paranoids and, to a lesser extent, the masochists mostly vented their spleen on the Jews and on "Jewish Marxism."

On the antisemitism scale, the irrational-paranoids are by far the most heavily prejudiced, followed at some distance by the masochists. The group conformists and the cultural shock group are at the other end of the scale. Again, the desire to merge one's self with the group appears to remove the necessity for antisemitism as a motive for loyalty to the NSDAP. The conformists also rate very low in ethnocentricity, and the leadership cultists are nearly as low. The paranoids are the most ethnocentric and excel especially in the belief in German superiority and in hatred of aliens. The masochists show a weak tendency toward xenophobia. The culturally shocked are the second most ethnocentric group, with heavy emphasis on chauvinism and on the belief in German superiority.

In their attitude toward their political enemies, on the other hand, the conformists turn out to be particularly aggressive and to make heavy use of the language of the *outré*. The more they rely on the support of the group, it seems, the more they engage in verbal displacements. Only the paranoids and the masochists have comparable numbers of *outrés* and, furthermore, many who refer to the enemy as traitors or an abstract conspiracy—as we would expect, especially of the paranoids. Respondents with high cultural shock and those with extreme leadership cult tend to express a liking for the enemy and a desire to win him over. The leadership cultists also tend to regard their enemies as traitors of a conspiracy.

Finally, the psychological groupings show rather different degrees and kinds of attitude toward authority. The conformists and the masochists show the greatest hostility toward police and government authority. The paranoids are preoccupied mostly with the multi-party state of Weimar, a concern shared by the cultural shock group, which also includes some genuine authoritarians. The leadership cultists, finally, exhibit not only extreme Hitler cult, but also some of the authoritarian preoccupation with order and cleanliness.

The Leadership Cult

This is a good time to pause and look more closely at the phenomenon of the leadership cult which played such a crucial role in attracting and maintaining the loyalty of many new converts to the cause. Adolf Hitler had an extraordinary talent as an orator and also as the manager of the growth of his own public image. According to the estimate of his own press chief, he had addressed more than thirty-five million Germans before coming to power.[3] Once he had found his style of speaking after a first year of impassioned outbursts,[4] of "hurling the burning brand among the masses," his appearances became more and more carefully staged events for which the crowd, the timing, the music, and even the weather had to be just right. A myth grew up about "Hitler weather" and about his carefully calculated manner of appearance at these occasions which forms a striking contrast to what we know otherwise about his social awkwardness and slovenly, Bohemian manner of dressing. Hitler's audiences, by stage management as well as by autosuggestion, built up their expectations to the point of hysteria even before there was that famous stirring in the crowd which indicated his always late but well-timed arrival. In many cases, among the Abel *vitae* and in general, hearing Hitler was all it took to motivate a person to join

[3] Otto Dietrich, *Hitler*, Chicago: Regnery, 1955, p. 17. This figure, however, probably includes overlapping attendance figures of many of his devoted listeners at the major rallies.

[4] See especially the description of this first year in Fest, *The Face of the Third Reich*, pp. 17-19.

the party. Of the other Nazi speakers, only Goebbels was even re-
motely as successful an orator.

Albert Speer, who joined the party when he was a university assistant in 1931, has given a description of his first Hitler speech,
along with the rationalizations born of his years in power and in
prison. The speech, meant exclusively for Berlin university students,
was held in a run-down beer-hall ordinarily used by the working
class: "The room was overcrowded. It seemed as if nearly all the
students in Berlin wanted to see and hear this man whom his adherents so much admired and his opponents so much detested. A large
number of professors sat in favored places in the middle of a bare
platform. Their presence gave the meeting an importance and a
social acceptability that it would not otherwise have had."[5] Thus
the setting was carefully prepared for the upper middle-class students' flinging themselves into an atmosphere of proletarian politics.
"Hitler entered and was tempestuously hailed by his numerous followers among the students. This enthusiasm in itself made a great
impression on me." Speer goes on to describe his surprise at the
"respectable-looking" business suit, the "reasonable modesty," and
"sober tone" of the demagogue whom the press had always pictured
as shrieking, in a brown uniform, and with a swastika armband. Hitler typically began "in a low voice, hesitantly and somewhat shyly,"
but with growing self-confidence. Soon

> his pitch rose. He spoke urgently and with hypnotic persuasiveness.
> The mood he cast was much deeper than the speech itself, most of
> which I did not remember for long. . . . I was carried on the wave of
> the enthusiasm which, one could almost feel this physically, bore the
> speaker along from sentence to sentence. It swept away any skepticism,
> any reservations. . . . Hitler no longer seemed to be speaking to con-
> vince; rather, he seemed to feel that he was expressing what the audi-
> ence, by now transformed into a single mass, expected of him.

We have already encountered the reactions of some of the Abel
respondents to the *Fuehrer*.[6] Let us take another look at how some
of them viewed Hitler on the occasion of their first encounters or
in general. Even after years of membership and activity in other
right-wing groups, they often felt his impact profoundly. A young
public employee, born 1908 (no. 38), reports having been active
in the *Jungsturm* since 1924 and having heard quite a few prominent speakers such as Ludendorff and Hugenberg. He became well

[5] *Inside the Third Reich*, New York: Macmillan, 1970, pp. 15-16.
[6] See above, pp. 105-106.

acquainted with national socialism before joining and claims to have been involved in many arguments at work and in the streets defending "the cause of the Fuehrer."

> On April 20, 1932, in Kassel, for the first time I heard the *Fuehrer* Adolf Hitler speak in person. After this, there was only one thing for me, either to win with Adolf Hitler or to die for him. The personality of the *Fuehrer* had me totally in its spell. He who gets to know Adolf Hitler with a pure and true heart will love him with all his heart. He will love him not for the sake of materialism, but for Germany.

George Orwell's minions in *Nineteen Eighty-four* could not have loved Big Brother more.

Another respondent, a German-Russian aristocrat, born in 1892 (no. 90), who had alternately fought the Bolsheviks and tried to get a commission in the Red Army "for there was no bread outside it," made his living as an emigré by lecturing on Soviet Russia. He relates how he walked out in boredom from his first Hitler speech in 1923 and how he viewed Nazi audiences with distaste. But his loneliness and the threat of deportation eventually drove him to join the NSDAP in 1930. The SA was reluctant to take him because of his foreigner's status, but in time he got into the SS. In 1932, a German Communist asked him to address a group of Communists at a private home and there was a spirited exchange, during which the respondent feared he might be roughed up. "I did not let them provoke me, however, because I had a good and true mission to carry out. Very calmly I told these deluded people that Russia meant nothing to them as Germans. I said, 'even if you are still Communists today, Hitler loves you.'" As a result, the next day, the respondent claims, fourteen Communists applied for membership in the NSDAP, and he goes on:

> Yes, it is love that Hitler brings to save his people from disastrous Marxism, but also from other enemies. His love for the people comes from his heart. . . . Love for his people is the essence of his power to wake up the slumbering and to inspire them. . . . The German people today stands overwhelmingly behind Hitler, the unselfish, the lover. Soon the whole world will recognize that Hitler is a man of love . . . who would like nothing better than to see all the nations of the world extend a brotherly hand to each other.

The respondent even cites St. Paul on the power of love in this context.

The power to evoke such quasi-religious ecstasy often gets lost in the respondents' phrases. With some, the penchant for phrase-making is so strong that it is difficult to separate words and meanings. A metalworker's apprentice, born 1903 (no. 416), who was an antisemite from his boyhood days and deeply involved with the fight against the separatists and the occupation, went the usual route from the *Schutz-und-Trutzbund* (from 1920) to the early NSDAP (in 1922). Five years later he experienced his first Hitler speech. "In 1927 I and my comrades had a chance to look into the eyes of our Fuehrer and to hear from his mouth how Germany could be saved. I shall never forget this, for I think that our Fuehrer radiates a power which makes us all strong." Another phrase-maker, born 1907 (no. 326), glories in "what comrades we had who would forsake wife and family, father and mother, and risk their lives and livelihood, simply everything, in order to follow the flag with the sacred emblem, the swastika!" Then he says: "In Nuremberg in 1929, for the first time I saw the *Fuehrer*. How his blue eyes [sic] sparkled when his stormtroopers marched past him in the light of the torches, an endless sea of flames rippling through the streets of the ancient Reich capital." Another example is an antisemitic, anti-Marxist respondent, born 1905 (no. 427), who became involved with the Nazi movement after having been expelled from the occupied Rhineland. As he explains:

> I did not come to Hitler by accident. I was searching for him. My ideal was a movement which would forge national unity from all working people of the great German fatherland, united by bonds of blood and of language, one which would honor labor, fight for social justice, and bring the son long lost from years of subversion, the worker, back to his father's house, the German fatherland.

The respondent adds an expression of his exaggerated Hitler cult in his curious mixture of biblical and Socialist rhetoric: "The realization of my ideal could happen through only one man, Adolf Hitler. The rebirth of Germany can be done only by a man born not in palaces but in a cottage."

The women respondents, finally, show a particularly high degree of Hitler cult, though their motives are no clearer than those of the men. "Only Hitler's idea could be the one salvation of Germany," sighed a nurse (no. 457) who, born in 1906, early lost her mother. An impoverished estate owner's antisemitic daughter, born 1871 (no. 456), who also became a nurse and a welfare worker, writes about the advent of Hitler to power: "It was as if the sun was shining more friendly and people were breathing easier." A working-class woman of nearly the same age, born 1873 (no. 347), whose political background mixed the influence of antisemites like Ahlwardt with active participation in the SPD, writes: "In 1926, I finally found the *man* who had the moxy (there's only *one such man* once in a while) to grab the tiller and save his people from foundering and doom." There can be no question but that an extreme of this devotion is a pathological feature indeed. It is unlikely that these intense images of leader-worship were widely shared outside the party and its auxiliaries.

Psychological Groups and Personality

Of the different psychological groups, the leadership cultists, followed by the cultural-shock group and the conformists, have the most formal education.[7] The paranoids and, next, the masochists are the least well-educated. The culturally-shocked also show the highest degree of political understanding, although they have a disproportionate number of pragmatic-narrow types such as might be found among military-civil servants. The paranoids are the lowest in political intelligence and number, in particular, a great many low-ideological and dimwit-romantic types. The masochists answer the same description. And so do the group conformists except for an additional feature, a disproportionate share of pragmatic-narrow respondents.

The psychological groupings also differ in how they set the accents on their own lives. The paranoids in disproportionate numbers develop their story from their personal difficulties or from the historical circumstances, anything but their self-willed political development.[8] The masochists and, less so, the culturally-shocked also blame their personal problems for their development, while the leadership cultists more often present themselves as the products of historical circumstances. The group conformists are the only ones who tend to relate chiefly their political development, as they were instructed to do by Professor Abel.

Their expectations in 1934, finally, tend to relate the excessive features of their respective groupings to appropriate remedies of what appear to be their underlying defects of personality. The paranoids more than any other group tend towards German imperialism: Conquer Europe or the world and no more threatening

---

[7] Thirty-five and three-tenths percent of the leadership cultists had completed at least a secondary education (*mittlere Reife*).

[8] This trait fits in well with Allport's feature of "externalization," which characterizes the prejudiced personality. *The Nature of Prejudice*, p. 379.

conspiracies will be possible. Their second-best remedy is an individual payoff of some sort. The masochists also hope to salve their wounds with such a reward. Those suffering from extreme leadership cult tend to yearn for the 1000-year Reich, with overtones of totalitarian brainwashing and purges. Similarly totalitarian, but also hoping for a national renaissance, are group conformists. As the reader will recall, these two totalitarian groups are the youngest. The culture-shock group, finally, dreams of national rebirth within.

Attitudes Toward Violence

In what sense can attitudes toward political violence be said to contribute something to our understanding of the selves of the Abel respondents? Attitudes toward violence, especially when related to their actual behavior, reveal an important part of the self-image. They are reflections by the respondents, however distorted, on his own acting-out. We carefully tried to record whether or not the respondent actually was involved in political violence. And, if so, we ascertained whether he felt constrained to make up excuses for his violent acting-out and described his encounters mostly in the terms of what was done to him (masochist) or, to the contrary, whether he just waded into battle self-confidently, taking pleasure in his and his fellow stormtroopers' physical prowess (sadist). These two attitudes emerged distinctly, though they were often blurred by reference to the respondent's group rather than himself. However, in a violent movement of this sort the group naturally takes over much of the acting-out function and an individual may well identify more purely (and with greater impunity) with the blows struck or received by his fellows. There was also a large number who seemed to take the violence in stride as the price of victory without indulging in unusual postures. Some gave the impression of acting out their

FD-68: Attitudes Toward Political Violence

	Number	Per cent
Regret of violence, war	36	9.1
Verbal abuse only	14	3.6
Realistic or romantic acceptance of violence		
(with or without involvement)	155	39.6
Physically involved:		
High masochism	23	5.9
Medium masochism	31	7.9
Group masochism	51	13.0
Bully, sadism	77	19.6
Group sadism	5	1.3
	392	100.0

violent urges by verbal abuse only. Others actually expressed regret about the violence, usually implying that it was too bad that the brown revolution could not succeed any other way.

Let us first clarify the relationship between these attitudinal groups and their actual involvement in various extremist activities in the NSDAP, including political violence. First of all, a few of our physically involved were so before they joined the party—for instance in the Free Corps—and may have been merely nominal members or engaged only in electioneering or marching in the NSDAP. The bulk of the physically involved were marcher-fighters (MF) or marcher-fighter-proselytizers (MFP), two groups of whom no member expressed any regrets about the violence or gave the impression of merely verbal abuse of the enemy. The combined masochists were made up of 41.9% MFs, 26.7% MFPs, and 17.2% marcher-proselytizers (MP) and provocateurs. The sadists included 24.1% MFs, 39.1% MFPs, and 20.6% MPs and provocateurs. The considerably higher percentage of MFPs and MPs of the sadists evidently means that proselytizing fervor supplies rationalizations and removes the inhibitions against acting out in violence. The masochists, by the same token, have to make up excuses or to make out their involvement as something imposed on them because they have not yet convinced themselves of the purpose of the crusade. Those who realistically accept violence also include more modest numbers of MFs (21.8%), MFPs (25%), and MPs and provocateurs (20.5%).

Examples of Masochism and Sadism

An example of a sadist is a teacher, born in 1898 (no. 31), who volunteered for the war and, in 1920, fought in a vigilante shock troop against red insurgents. In 1929, he became involved with the Nazis, and he relates how his *Sturmbannfuehrer* "called us up to fight against the red murder mob, who had killed many a brave stormtrooper. The struggle was going to be harder and harder, and would forge us into a unity just as the past World War had done with us soldiers." The respondent tells of nocturnal election poster operations.

We especially liked to go into the areas where the enemies were living. We took down their posters and put up our own instead. Climbing in the dark was not hard to learn. Undesirable encounters were occasions for the exercise of comradeship as well as opportunities for a manhunt. There were muffled cries, sometimes also brief screams, dull blows, and by the crack of dawn the spook was over.

He also describes major clashes in this vein, such as the quick mobilization of his *Sturm* one evening to help protect a Nazi rally in a neighboring town against red raiders.

> We all gathered at the entrance of the town and put on white scarves, and then you could hear the thundering marching of our column of about 250 men. Without weapons but with clenched fists, we marched in strict order and iron discipline into the catcalls and screaming of the crowds before the meeting-hall. They had sticks and fence boards in their hands. It was 10 o'clock at night. With a few maneuvers in the middle of the street we pushed the crowd against the walls in order to open up a path in the middle. Just at that moment, a carpenter drove through with a small truck and a black coffin in it. As he went by, one of us said "Well, let's see whom we can put in there." The screams, catcalls and whistling grew ever more intense.
>
> The two rows of our column stood still, charged up with energy. A signal, and we go marching into the hall where a few hundred loudmouths are trying to shut up our speaker. We came just in time, marching in step along the walls until we had closed the ring around them, leaving an opening only at the entrance. A whistle sounds. We tighten the ring. Ten minutes later we trumpeted our Horst-Wessel song after the guys we put out in the fresh air. The meeting goes on while outside all hell breaks loose. We then escorted the speaker back out cutting once more through the swirling mob in closed formation.

The respondent, who soon became a *Sturmfuehrer*, also wrote a fighting song for "his boys" which said, among other things, "Whenever we are forced to fight by the enemies of the German people, we swing our fists as long as we deem necessary." On another occasion during a major clash, the respondent tells of a comrade stabbed in the groin and of others who were shot at while trying to help him. "Now we dropped all inhibitions. If we had so far used only our fists and belts, we now tore the boards off a nearby fence and did a complete job. Unfortunately, the police stopped us from finishing it. The murderer was taken in injured and got jail for his bloody deed." The appointment of Hitler as chancellor once more unleashed the respondent's aggressiveness as he anticipated a red uprising upon the signal of the *Reichstag* fire.[9]

[9] See also the chilling account before the Prussian diet in 1932 of the wave of assaults, murders, and raids on the SPD and other left-wing groups on the occasion of the rescision of the order suppressing the SA by Chancellor von Papen. *Sammlung der Drucksachen des Preussischen Landtags*, 4. Wahlperiode, 1930-1932, pp. 320-325.

We were prepared; we knew the plans of our enemies. I had put together a shock troop [*Rollkommando*] of my *Sturm* from the most daring of the daring. We lay in wait night after night. Who was going to strike the first blow? And then it came. The signal in Berlin and similar signals all over the country. And finally the order releasing our tension: Hit them [*packt zu*]! *And we did hit them.* It was not just a matter of . . . you or us, but of getting the Bolshevik murder face to wipe off its wanton grin, and of saving Germany from the bloody terror of undisciplined hordes." (respondent's italics)

It is worth noting that this respondent was seemingly free of anti-semitic prejudice or social resentments, but literally embodied the brutality and anti-Marxism of the war generation. As he describes the "national revolution," it was "the spirit of the frontline comradeship, risen from the smoke of the sacrificial vessels of the war, and finding its way into the hearts of the awakened German people."[10]

Social Background of Violence Attitude Groups

How are these attitudinal groups distributed over the generations? By far the youngest group are the masochists, with well over one-half in the postwar generation. This may well imply that having missed serving in the war, this group also missed the brutalization of war and warlikeness which is as likely as anything to remove any inhibitions about violence. The sadists, by comparison, have the largest share not only of the war generation itself, but also of the adjoining cohorts, those born 1890-1894 (a cohort including many professional soldiers) and the victory-watchers. There can be no question about the effect of the war on their violent attitudes and behavior. This is less true of those who realistically accept violence. They tend to be older, as are those who regret violence and, most of all, those content with verbal abuse. The last-mentioned two groups, with 41.2% and 64.3%, respectively, in the prewar generation (born 1860-1894), are a demonstration of how successful prewar society had been in banking the fires of violence even among future converts of the Nazi movement. Although their age, of course, contributes to their non-involvement in street-fighting, they evidently have non-violent attitudes as well.

As for their occupations, the masochists tend to be workers or business and professional people. They are mostly the sons of work-

[10] There are many other examples of sadists, such as no. 501 and 537. They are not all as purely the product of the war as was our example.

ers, artisans, or farmers. The sadists tend to be farmers or workers. Their fathers are mostly businessmen or workers. Respondents who accept the violence as the price of victory tend to be military-civil servants, white-collar workers, or business and professional persons. Their fathers also tend to be military-civil servants. The workers are evidently the most involved in violence, masochistic or sadistic. The tradition of German labor militancy, along with the depressed condition of labor, may also have helped to reduce inhibitions toward violence. The farmers in many parts of the country have never been particularly squeamish about violence, though of the Saturday-night variety rather than political violence. For the bourgeois respondents, the need to rationalize was more likely to be strong because of bourgeois notions of dignity and civilized behavior. Yet there may also have been a strain of tough-fisted fascism in the German bourgeoisie. Respondents from the occupied areas and from the borderlands were also masochistic more often than sadistic in spite of the stimulus of violent encounters.

Violence Attitudes and Ideology

Whether the attitudes on violence bear any relation to other beliefs or attitudes still needs to be demonstrated. For example, it is not surprising that the masochists tend not to state their religion, nor that those who express regret at violence do. What is surprising is that the sadists tend to indicate their Protestantism, and that those who simply accept violence more often than not state their religious affiliation. Were these the stormtroopers with God on their side? The masochists also tend to live in areas of evenly mixed religion, a feature we commented on earlier.

In their levels of education, these attitudinal groups vary quite considerably. By far the best educated, with 37.5% with at least a complete secondary education, are the respondents who take political violence in stride. They are followed by those who express regret about violence. The least-educated are the sadists, followed closely by the masochists. Considering that the younger cohorts are generally better-educated than the older ones, this difference appears to relate to the attitudes themselves. It may well be that to the sadists and masochists, engaging in political violence not only answers deep inner needs but also offers them illusions of status and prestige which the educational system never permitted them. In their level of political understanding, consequently, the same groups tend to be high or low, but there are notable differences. Over one-half of the masochists and also of those who regret the use of violence are of the low, ideological type that we have found to be most typical of the minions of a totalitarian movement. Both the masochists and the sadists, furthermore, have more than their share of dimwit-romantic types, while the pragmatic-narrow kind abounds among the sadists and those who regret the violence. This distribution indicates the presence of different elements, such as the sadism of the military-civil servants or the low-ideological and romantic elements of the Weimar youth revolt.

Similar elements come out in substantive issues. In their perception of Weimar, for example, the masochists tend to look forward to the replacement of the "red and black parties" with the Third Reich or, like the sadists, they call Weimar the Marxist-run republic. The sadists see it as the "liberalistic-Marxist system" or as the *Judenrepublik*. Those older respondents who accept violence as the price of victory also consider the republic Jewish-run, or criticize its multi-party character or its capitalistic ways. The dominant ideological themes of the masochists are the Hitler cult or superpatriotism. The sadists tend to be revanchists, antisemites, or to have no ideology worth noting. Those who take the violence in stride are mostly Nordic-German romantics, solidarists or, to a lesser degree, antisemites. There is a curious note of ambiguity in how antisemitism comes out in competition with some, and differently with other, obsessions. If we pair antisemitism with anti-Marxism, in fact, both the masochists and the sadists turn out to be mostly anti-Marxists, give or take a little "anti-reactionary" phobia among the sadists. By contrast, it is those older respondents who realistically accept violence who show a greater tendency toward antisemitism and even more toward hatred for reactionaries, Catholics, and liberals.

The mystery is cleared up by applying the antisemitism scale. Both the sadists and the masochists, with 43.5% and 38.6% showing no evidence of prejudice, are among the lowest in prejudice and certainly lower than those who accept violence in this category (27%). However, the sadists also have the highest number of respondents who speak of conspiracies and counter-threats (24.2%) of any group. And while those who take violence in stride stand out with their *Judenkoller*, their anecdote-telling, and their milder verbal projections, the masochists are not far behind them. In other words, to the extent the sadist are prejudiced they tend to be fully mobilized into aggressive, extrapunitive paranoids, while the other two physically involved groups are more apt to resort to autistic forms of venting their spleen. Even so, those who accept the violence have slightly more than their share of aggressive paranoids.

The interrelationships between the attitudes receive further depth with the consideration of the respondents' attitudes toward their political enemies. More than two-thirds of those who regret violence and those who take it in stride express a liking for at least some of their opponents.[11] The masochists tend to refer to their enemies as traitors or an abstract conspiracy. Both the sadists and masochists heavily use the language of the *outré* on their opponents, topped only by those given to verbal abuse. The sadists, moreover, supply four out of five of those respondents whose physical aggressiveness shines through their description of the enemy. They also supply most of the respondents who went out of their way to seek out political friction. Both the sadists and the masochists, moreover, are high in ethnocentricy, and in xenophobia more than in chauvinism. The sadists, moreover, tend to emphasize the alleged inferiority of other nations.

In their attitudes toward authority, also, the sadists and masochists rank high in hostility against the police and government authority and in their obsession with order and cleanliness. The masochists are particularly high in the last-mentioned authoritarian features and indulge also in extreme leadership cult. The three other groups, by comparison, are far more preoccupied with the pluralistic multi-party state of Weimar.[12] Their expectations in 1934, finally, round out the picture. Those who accept the violence mostly hope for a national renaissance and for an individual pay-off for their efforts. The sadists tend to be either imperialists or to dream of the totalitarian utopia of the 1000-year Reich replete with internal purges and universal brainwashing. The masochists have the same tendencies, though to a lesser extent, and hope also for individual rewards. In their own sick way, these two groups were closer to the emerging rationale of the Third Reich than were those who took the violence in stride. Their intense emotional involvement with the violent acting out of the pre-1933 movement pointed beyond the thin façade of national rebirth to the collective violence of terror and aggression that lay ahead.

Self-Representation and Formative Experience

Is it really possible, in self-representation or biography, to present the origins or meaning of an entire life through a Goethean symbol or simile?[13] Some of the respondents present their stories self-consciously by relating personal experiences which *in nuce* are to ex-

[11] Only 24.7% of the masochists and 28% of the sadists express such a liking.

[12] This preoccupation accounts for 64-73% of these three groups, as compared to only 26.5% of the masochists and 36.8% of the sadists.

[13] Goethe uses the word *Gleichnis*, but his meaning is far broader and more philosophical than ours in this context.

plain their lives as a product of social humiliations, family troubles, the *Fronterlebnis* in World War One, clashes witnessed between revolutionaries and counter-revolutionaries, the reading of a book, the experience of comradeship in a youth group, alleged encounters with Jews or aliens, or with the French occupation and the like. Others make no such effort at self-representation, but tell stories in which such formative experiences play an obvious role in the un- folding biographies. We have taken both at face value and lumped them together in full awareness of the risks involved. We have no way of knowing whether the symbolic happenings volunteered by the respondents or the seemingly crucial experiences related by them were indeed the chief or the only formative influences on their lives. But they are undoubtedly important themes on their minds which deserve our attention.

FD-76: Formative Experience or Influence

	Number	Per cent
Fronterlebnis, World War One	101	13.8
1918 defeat, revolution, occupation, etc.	175	23.8
Comradeship in youth group (25 or younger)	75	10.2
Educational or literary influence	131	17.8
⌐Social snub, humiliation	29	4.0
└Not finding a job or other personal economic crisis	43	5.9
⌐Alleged episode with Jews	37	5.0
└Alleged episode with aliens	55	7.5
Other	88	12.0
	734*	100.0

* Multiple entries.

The formative influence groups are rather clearly distinguishable by generations. If we take military service as a distinguishing device, for example, 79.7% of those who were formed by the experience of youthful comradeship were in the postwar generation and never served in the military. The same is true of 60.3% of those claiming a great educational or literary influence in their lives, and of 57.3% of those relating symbolic or formative encounters with Jews or aliens. These three then, tend to be typical experiences forming the minds of the postwar generation. The war generation figures prom- inently among those influenced by the *Fronterlebnis* (58.2%), or by unemployment or social humiliation (42.9%).[14] The peacetime

[14] The average in the non-service postwar generation is 51.4%, in the war generation (wartime service only) 34.4%, and in the prewar gen- eration (peacetime or professional service) 14.2%.

and professional soldiers, mostly of the prewar generation, were formed heavily by the *Fronterlebnis* (27.5%) and by the defeat and its consequences (21.2%).

It is in the light of these generational overtones that we should view also the other social indicators. Thus it comes as no surprise that rural-urban migrants tend to be formed by the *Fronterlebnis* and by the defeat, for rural-urban migration took place largely among the prewar generation. The spatially immobile, by comparison, include both this element and those formed by youthful comradeship, who are also present in unusual numbers among the highly mobile. The highly mobile among cities also have more than their share of another postwar group, those influenced by educational and literary experiences. The war generation, with its *Fronterlebnis* and socio-economic difficulties, finally, is evenly divided between the spatially immobile and the highly mobile.

Respondents from the occupied areas, by comparison, tend to be formed mostly by alleged encounters with aliens and Jews, especially the former, and by educational or literary influences. Borderland Germans often cite the experience of youthful comradeship as crucial. Respondents with foreign or colonial experiences, finally, tend to relate influential educational or literary encounters or the trauma of the defeat.

Occupation gives the formative influence groups a different dimension. The *Fronterlebnis* and defeat groups tend to be military-civil servants, farmers, or, among the *Fronterlebnis*-formed only, business and professional people. Those with job or social traumas tend to be farmers, women, or business or the professions. Youthful comradeship and educational experiences particularly characterize workers and white-collar Nazis. Alleged experiences with aliens or Jews are most frequent among white-collar respondents and military-civil servants. Respondents in social decline tend to be motivated by youthful comradeship or by educational experiences. The upwardly mobile from the urban proletariat are formed mostly by the experience of comradeship in youth groups and by encounters with aliens or Jews. Those who never attempted to rise above the station of their fathers tend to have been influenced by economic or social humiliations, by youthful comradeship, and by the trauma of the defeat. The farm climbers, finally, combine stress on the "older" experiences of *Fronterlebnis* and defeat with the "young" experiences of encounters with aliens or Jews and educational-literary influences.

The concept of educational or literary influences deserves a brief example from the *vita* of a housepainter, born 1898 (no. 140). He was very concerned about the deteriorating situation of the trades and the politicization, if not subversion, of labor which clashed with his patriotic and religious (Catholic) upbringing:

> After the war I became very much interested in politics and eagerly studied newspapers of all political shadings. In 1920, for the first time, I read in a right-wing paper an advertisement for an antisemitic periodical and became a subscriber of the *Hammer* of Theodor Fritsch. With the help of this periodical I got to know the devastating influence of the Jews on people, state, and economy. I still must admit today that this periodical was for me really the bridge to the great movement of Adolf Hitler.

After voting for a few years for the *Deutschvoelkische Freiheitsbewegung*, which "was antisemitic but lacked the right heads," the respondent began to attend Nazi rallies and joined up in 1926. "I put several books of Th. Fritsch and Henry Ford at the disposal of my local group." Many respondents also point to an educational experience with an influential nationalistic, *voelkisch*, or even left-wing teacher or influential adult.[15]

Formative Experiences and Prejudice

Do certain kinds of formative influences predispose a person to have particular ideas or to vent his (or her) spleen on given targets? In their dominant ideological motif, for example, those who cite encounters with Jews and aliens naturally tend to be antisemites or superpatriots, which is also true of those influenced by education or literature, along with a goodly share of Hitler worshippers. Those who were formed by economic or social humiliation naturally tend to advocate the *Volksgemeinschaft*. The *Fronterlebnis* predisposed people to be revanchists or superpatriots, while the effect of the defeat and its consequences seems to have been to produce Nordic-German romantics, revanchists, and solidarists. The comradeship experience, finally, created Nordic-German romantics, solidarists, and revanchists. The linkage is not always obvious.

Which formative influences seem to encourage anti-Marxism rather than antisemitism? The experience of youthful comradeship tends to produce anti-Communists and anti-Socialists, probably be-

---

[15] See, for example, a bookkeeper's son who was given writings of Luxemburg, Liebknecht, and Toller by an older colleague, "a Communist of truly noble character." But in the end, the respondent relapsed into a patriotism with racist overtones and became an SS *Sturmfuehrer* (no. 526).

cause of the political color of the youth groups involved. The *Fronterlebnis* and social humiliation groups on the other hand, tend to be more hostile to reactionaries, liberals, and Catholics. Those who claim crucial encounters with aliens or Jews tend to be anti-semites or to have an all-inclusive hate-list. The latter is also the tendency of respondents with an educational or literary formative experience. And those who were formed by the impact of defeat and revolution are mostly antisemitic and anti-Marxist. It would appear that there are few direct relationships, but rather general tendencies toward prejudice which are encouraged more by some than by other formative influences.

On the antisemitism scale, for example, the most prejudiced are the respondents who tell of encounters with aliens or Jews. Yet their number of fully mobilized paranoids is almost matched by those who were formed by the trauma of defeat or by youthful comradeship. Their anecdote-telling is nearly matched by the products of socio-economic humiliation and of educational experiences. Their *Judenkoller* is, in fact, exceeded by that of the *Fronterlebnis* and educational experience groups. Depending on where we draw the line, prejudice is rather evenly distributed throughout these groups.

The picture is somewhat clearer with ethnocentricity, where those with alleged encounters with aliens or Jews have far and away the highest degree of the phobia. They stand out particularly with their belief in the inferiority of other nations and almost as heavily with their xenophobia and their chauvinism. The *Fronterlebnis* group is the next most ethnocentric, but at some distance. The least ethnocentric are those who were formed by social or economic humiliation or by the experience of youthful comradeship. Those who relate a crucial educational or literary experience were relatively high in antisemitism and they also show a good deal of xenophobia.

PART VI

Life in the Party

Most of this inquiry has been preoccupied with the motives and reasons which may have impelled a person to join the pre-1933 Nazi party. We have left few stones unturned in our search for the circumstances and obsessions which impelled the Abel respondents toward this end. Once they did contemplate joining, however, a new life began, with new friends and antagonists, new activities, and a new life style. There are several distinct areas of interest here that we should examine with care. One is the timing, manner, and setting in which the actual joining took place. Another area is the complex of stormtrooper membership, activity, and orientation which characterizes so much of the life of the party prior to Hitler's appointment as Reich Chancellor on January 30, 1933. The stormtrooper organizations, SA and SS, completely changed their original roles after this date and after the Roehm purge of mid-1934. The third area of interest encompasses the careers on which the Abel respondents embarked in the NSDAP and in affiliated organizations both before and after 1933.

The Brownshirts Come to Town

When a respondent joined the NSDAP, he completed the process of traversing the four stages of political mobilization we discussed earlier. As we have already seen, however, the final commitment was a complex process of many factors which we have to consider with some caution. On the one hand, the life stories of many of the respondents literally seem to strain toward this end in ways going far beyond the understandable license of self-interpretation with the benefit of hindsight. In the autobiographies there is plenty of evidence that the Nazi movement was indeed tailor-made to fit the needs and yearnings of most of the Abel respondents.

On the other hand, we must not overlook the signal importance of the timing, the setting, and the opportunity, when the brownshirts came to each town and neighborhood. There are many stories of would-be Nazis waiting for years for a likely leader and movement to come along. While they waited they were sometimes absorbed in more harmless movements or kept their political mania hidden from anyone but their intimates—a private eccentricity rather than a public threat. There are also stories of people seemingly unaware of their potential inclination in this direction and certainly not searching for anything like the Hitler movement. Once the brownshirts ostentatiously came to town and began their propaganda work, their person-to-person proselytizing, and their deliberate policy of demonstrations and violent confrontations, however, even the less-motivated became curious and many of them stumbled into the movement.

We have recorded the chronological order (the date when the respondents joined) as well as the situational sequence, i.e., how soon after the first local appearance of the Nazis they joined the brown mass movement. We also kept track of the circumstances of joining as reported by the respondent: whether he was introduced to the party by a relative or a fellow-worker, or whether he was really attracted by an awareness of its ideology, however he may have perceived it. These several aspects and their relation to other factors should throw sufficient light on the process by which the NSDAP carried on its recruitment before 1933.

The Date of Joining

We divided the dates of joining, as far as they could be ascertained,[1] according to the phases of national party growth and between land-mark elections. As can be seen, the sample has only a small number of pre-beer-hall-*putsch* members if we discount those who joined Nazi fronts in the interim between Hitler's arrest and the refounda-

FD-57: Date of Joining the NSDAP

	Number	Per cent
Before November 1923	20	3.5
November 1923 or 1924	25	4.4
1925	43	7.5
1926	35	6.1
1927-May 1928	49	8.6
June 1928-mid-1929	65	11.4
Mid-1929-Dec. 1929	42	7.4
January 1930-Aug. 1930	42	7.4
Sept. 1930-mid-1931	114	20.0
Mid-1931-March 1932	75	13.2
April 1932-January 1933	60	10.5
	570	100.0

tion of the NSDAP early in 1925. Nearly a fourth of the sample, by comparison, joined during the reconstruction period between 1925 and the *Reichstag* elections of 1928 when the NSDAP won a mere twelve seats.[2] The winning of a majority in the municipal elections of Coburg in June 1929 and, in December of the same year, 11.3% of the vote in the state elections of Thuringia were the way-stations to the next landmark, the *Reichstag* elections of September 1930. In these elections, to the great shock of many observers, the brown flood had suddenly grown to 6.4 million voters (18.3%), which brought 107 Nazi deputies into the *Reichstag*.

Let us compare the Abel sample with the actual composition of the party (Tables VI-1 and VI-2). This pre-1928 one-fourth obvi-ously exceeds the share of the 1933 NSDAP which joined before 1928. Another good one-fourth joined between the elections of 1928 and September 1930, bringing their combined numbers to

[1] Some respondents suggest that the party was not always prompt in registering their admission, sometimes causing them to join twice at considerable intervals. In some cases, also, respondents were rather vague as to the time they joined and we had to make an estimate.

[2] Its popular vote was 809,000 or 2.6% of the total. These electoral results tended somewhat to underrepresent the state of the growing move-ment. See Orlow, *The History of the Nazi Party, 1919-1933*, pp. 128-133.

well over one-half (56.3%) of the sample rather than a mere 15%. Our sample has about one pre-1930 respondent for every 400 in real life. This bias of the Abel sample is important to note inasmuch as there was considerable suspicion in party circles of the allegedly

Table VI-1: NSDAP Membership Before and After 1930 Elections

Joined	Parteistatistik, I, 16	Abel Sample
Before 1930 elections	129,563	321
	(15.3%)	(56.3%)
Sept. 1930-Jan. 1933	719,446	249
	(84.7%)	(43.7%)
Total in Jan. 1933	849,009	570
	(100.0%)	(100.0%)

opportunistic or careerist Septemberlinge[3] who presumably jumped onto the bandwagon only after it was well under way. Thus we have far more of the authentic old fighters than the party actually had at the time of Hitler's appointment as chancellor, not to mention the vast influx of opportunists after that date.

Table VI-2: Ratio of Respondents to Party Members

By date:	a) Membership	b) Abel	c) b in % of a
Nov. 1923	55,000	20	.036
Dec. 1925	27,000	88	.33
Dec. 1926	50,000	123	.25
Dec. 1927	73,000	157	.21
Dec. 1928	109,000	204	.19
Dec. 1929	116,000	279	.24
Dec. 1930	170,000	387	.23
Dec. 1931	390,000	464	.12
Dec. 1932	900,000	557	.062
Jan. 1933	849,000	570	.066

We can pursue this subject further by comparing the ratios between the official membership figures from year to year with those of our sample. As Table VI-2[4] indicates, the ratios hold up pretty

[3] See also Orlow, The History of the Nazi Party, 1919-1933, p. 209 and the many slurs scattered throughout both volumes of the official Parteistatistik.

[4] These cumulative, rounded figures are taken from Abel, The Nazi Movement, p. 311, with the exception of the years 1929 through 1933. For the year 1932, official sources such as the Brockhaus encyclopedia list greatly inflated figures in excess of a million. The missing figures have been interpolated by a curve from the known points in September 1930 and January 1933. According to Fest, The Face of the Third Reich,

well until 1931 and decline still further in 1932. A plausible explanation for this declining rate may consist of three factors: One, the late-comers to the movement had less pride in their own political development and hence less to tell and less motivation to participate in the contest. Two, the essay contest was understood to be meant primarily for the really "old fighters." And three, the older fighters saw in the essay contest a special opportunity to remind the party of their efforts and pains on its behalf. This last point is supported also by the general feeling among the old fighters in 1933-1934 that they had been forgotten by the party.[5]

To be sure, the charge of opportunism against those who joined after September 1930 was not always appropriate. In spite of its electoral triumph of that year, the NSDAP was still only the second-largest party, after the SPD, in the *Reichstag*. There were still many anti-Nazi battles and police measures ahead before the final triumph. In May 1931, the party won a plurality in the state of Oldenburg. In April 1932, running for *Reich* President against the aged von Hindenburg, Hitler won an awesome thirteen and a half million votes, a figure the NSDAP barely topped in the *Reichstag* elections of July, 1932. It had not been enough to beat von Hindenburg in the run-off, but it constituted an ample plurality in the *Reichstag*. In November of the same year, in another *Reichstag* election, the Nazis lost two of these thirteen millions, and there was probably a noticeable drop in morale and in the numbers of new recruits to the cause. But then, two months later, Hitler was appointed anyway and the ensuing new wave, encouraged by the harassment and suppression of Communists and other opponents, set a high-water mark of seventeen million votes (44%) for the NSDAP.

Age and Location Experiences

For the purpose of crosstabulation, we collapsed the different periods of joining into seven groups of comparable size—the early Nazis (pre-1925), three before, and three after the middle of 1930. The early Nazis typically have a full two-thirds in the war genera-

---

p. 32, "in 1926 the party still had no more than 17,000 members, a year later only about 40,000, and . . . in 1928 . . . 60,000." If these figures are current, then our pre-1929 Abel respondents represent one and a half times as much of the real strength of the party at that time, which amounts to an even greater bias on the early years of the party. Hans Volz, *Daten der Geschichte der NSDAP*, 10th ed., Berlin, 1939, p. 21, agrees with Abel's early figures and may well have been their source.

[5] See also the remarks in *Parteistatistik*, II, p. 282.

tion (1890-1901) and among the victory-watchers (1902-1905). Those who joined between 1925 and the 1930 elections tended to be on the young side with 36-46% born in the postwar generation. Respondents who joined after mid-1930 are again quite a bit older, with nearly two-thirds from the prewar generation (born before 1895). Except for a small element of the very young (1909-1916), the *Septemberlinge* were not exactly a part of the youth revolt of Weimar society.[6]

A substantial part (up to one-third) of those who joined the party prior to mid-1929, including the early Nazis, came from the occupied areas. The borderland Germans, on the other hand, tended to join only after that date, years after they had encountered struggles at the ethnic border. As for their location, it is interesting to note that, prior to 1928, the Nazi recruits tended to come from the larger towns and cities. Between 1928 and the 1930 elections, evidently in reflection of the expansion of recruitment into the rural hinterland, the bulk of the recruits tended to be in rural or small-town locations under 10,000 inhabitants. After 1930, finally, the emphasis shifts to Berlin where Josef Goebbels had already been at work for four years "conquering the city." A good third of those joining between mid-1930 and mid-1931 and nearly half of those who joined after mid-1931 were in Berlin at the time.

How does the chronological order in which the respondents joined relate to the local progress of the party? As we would expect,

FD-28: Local NSDAP Progress at Time of Joining

	Number	Per cent
Among the first five to join	45	11.0
Cofounder of local	71	17.4
The first at the job, school	10	2.4
Organizer of functional group	15	3.7
In nuclear group (6-20)	58	14.2
Among nucleus at work	11	2.7
Among substantial minority	171	41.8
Among majority	21	5.1
Bandwagon jumper	7	1.7
	409	100.0

[6] To put it a different way, those who joined after the 1932 elections include no less than 22.4% over 50 and over one-half over the age of 40. Half of those who joined between mid-1931 and mid-1932 were over 35. A good half of those who joined between the 1930 elections and mid-1931 were over 30. If the Nazi party had not come to power in 1933, it seems, the growing influx of older members might well have wiped out its advantage of youthfulness over the "old" SPD and other republican parties.

respondents who were the first to join in their area or were founders and cofounders of their NSDAP local organizations tend to have joined before 1925 or in the period between 1925 and 1927. There is also a concentration of such local founders right after the 1930 election, 27 cases out of a total of 142 post-1930 joiners; they probably represent a core of the more highly motivated among the *Septemberlinge*. Respondents who report having been part of the first local nucleus of, say, half a dozen members tend to have joined between the elections of 1928 and 1930. Those who joined when the movement was already a substantial minority locally—in other words, when it could defend itself better but also attracted more massive hostility—are scattered all over the joining periods of the reconstructed NSDAP up to the 1932 elections. Those who jumped onto the bandwagon only when it seemed headed for victory, finally, tend heavily to have joined only after these elections.

As for the ages and locations of these groups, there are striking correlations. The local founders tend to be from rural or small-town areas and to have been born after the turn of the century. The nuclear group is mostly in large towns (10,000-100,000) and of the war generation (1890-1901). Those who joined when the movement constituted a substantial local minority are more evenly distributed, though with a distinct prewar (1885-1894) and a postwar bulge (1902-1908). The bandwagon-jumpers tend to have been born before 1890. Both of the last two groups tend to live in metropolitan areas at the time of the chief struggle, 1928-1933. It would appear, then, that the movement spread from the postwar generation and from rural and small-town origins into further layers of the population.[7]

Table VI-3: Location and Local NSDAP Progress (in %)

	Metro-politan (100,000 +)	Large town (10,000-100,000)	Small town (2,000-10,000)	Rural (Up to 2,000)	Total
Local Founders	28.7	17.1	24.7	29.5	100.0
In first nucleus	37.7	31.9	13.0	17.4	100.0
Among large minority	56.7	18.7	11.1	13.5	100.0
Bandwagon	71.6	7.1	14.3	7.1	100.0

[7] Local founders also stand out among respondents from the borderland and occupied areas and among those who never moved from where they were born. The ethnic border, friction with the occupation, and spatial immobility were apparently factors making for strong and early motivation to join the NSDAP.

Table VI-4: Age and Local NSDAP Progress (in %)

	Born 1860-1889	Born 1890-1901	Born 1902-1916	Total
Local Founders	19.1	35.1	45.8	100.0
In first nucleus	18.8	48.0	33.2	100.0
Among large minority	21.0	34.5	44.5	100.0
Bandwagon	42.9	39.3	17.8	100.0

Occupation and Social Mobility

When we crosstabulate the chronological group with occupation, some of the shifts occurring in the party itself emerge. The pre-1925 party had more than its share of white-collar workers and military-civil servants.[8] The reconstructed party from 1925 to the 1930 elections, by comparison, had substantially more blue-collar workers and farmers, and business and professional people, than did their predecessors. After the 1930 elections and especially after mid-1931, the Abel sample tends to consist once more of military-civil servants, white-collar workers, and women.[9] As Table VI-5 demonstrates, our sample has a rather inflated share of military-civil servants, especially after 1930, and its workers and white-collar respondents before and after 1930 rather show the opposite trend from that documented in the party statistics.[10]

Table VI-5: Members' Occupations Before and After 1930 (in %)

	Members before 1930	Members 1930-1933	Abel before 1930	Abel 1930-1933
Workers	26.3	32.5	32.6	20.2
White collar	24.0	20.6	17.0	20.6
Business & professions (including students)	19.9	18.5	14.1	13.2
Civil servants	7.7	6.5	16.1	25.2
Farmers	13.2	12.5	7.5	9.2
Others & pensionists	5.3	5.3	6.2	5.6
Housewives	3.6	4.1	6.5	6.0
	100.0	100.0	100.0	100.0

[8] The strong artisan and professional element described, for example, by Georg Franz-Willing, *Die Hitlerbewegung: Der Ursprung 1919-1922*, Hamburg and Berlin: Schenck, 1962, pp. 126-135 is less conspicuous in our sample.

[9] According to *Parteistatistik*, I, p. 70, the *Septemberlinge* included a larger share of women than the pre-1930 party had.

[10] The figures for the membership in Table VI-5 are taken from *Parteistatistik*, I, pp. 69-70. The cut-off point in 1930 is September 18,

As to the local progress of the NSDAP at the time the respondent joined, the most highly motivated local founders tend to be farmers, the retired, or business and professional people. There is also a substantial (25.8% and 15.9% respectively) but not disproportionate share of blue- and white-collar founders. The military-civil servants mostly show up only in the first local nucleus (6-20 persons), while typical latecomers appear to be white- and blue-collar workers or women.

There is also the question whether it was the Great Depression that led the ranks of the Nazi party to swell so dramatically after mid-1930. The Abel data, in any case, give no support to this theory. On the contrary, it is those who joined the NSDAP before the 1930 elections and especially before 1925 who tended to be the victims of the Depression. Most of those who joined after the 1930 elections either suffered no particular economic crises or they had difficulties prior to 1929. The respondents who joined prior to 1928 also tended to have suffered unemployment or bankruptcy prior to the Depression. Relating this factor to the local progress of the party at the time of joining, we also find the Depression victims mostly among those who joined when the movement was already substantial. The local founders tended to have had a normal economic career.

The relationship between upward mobility and the chronology of joining the NSDAP is not particularly revealing. The early (pre-1925) Nazi party, to be sure, tended to be predominantly in social decline or upwardly mobile from an urban background. Those who joined between 1925 and 1930 tended to have made no attempt to rise socially. After 1930, the party tended to attract more often the upwardly mobile from a farm background, men and women of an older generation. The late joiners also had a disproportionate share of respondents who embraced *Volksgemeinschaft* from an upper-class point of view, evidently ready to forego their class privileges in exchange for social acceptance in a changing age. If we relate social mobility to the local progress of the party, more than half of the local founders turn out to be people that failed to rise above the station of their fathers, who had often been farmers and military-civil servants. Social decline plays a negligible role in motivating respondents to join early. The upwardly mobile from the city proletariat stand out only among the bandwagon jumpers.

It is also worth noting that the local founders in a dispropor-

___

the date of the elections. The Abel figures for women include some gainfully employed.

tionate number of cases are Catholics or live in predominantly Catholic areas. We might think this was due to the headstart of the movement in the Catholic south, but Catholics do not appear to stand out in the chronology of joining until after the 1930 elections.[11] The local founders also tend to have less formal education than those who joined when the movement was already a substantial minority or even larger.[12] Perhaps it took such rural simplicity of mind to take up the cause of the brown salvation movement or to believe in its brand of national revivalism. The local founders also report a surprisingly large number of mental or physical breakdowns.

Youth Organizations and the Chronology of Joining

The Weimar youth culture, with its constantly changing organizations and the youth migration from the more harmless to politically militant groups, presents a confusing picture to the historian. At what stage, he would like to know, did the NSDAP attract recruits from which group of youth organizations? The pre-1925 party, according to our sample, tended to draw recruits from the Socialist or Communist youth, from conservative or DHV groups, including nationalistic athletic leagues, and from bourgeois youth groups such as *Jungdo* or the Hindenburg Youth (DVP). The reconstructed NSDAP of 1925-1927 drew from the same sources, and heavily also from the Free Corps[13] and other military training or veterans' groups.

In the years until the Coburg elections of mid-1929, the influx from the paramilitary and conservative groups slowed down and a new phenomenon appeared, the evident result of the second wave of the Weimar youth revolt. Beginning in 1928, and up to the 1932 elections, disproportionate numbers of youths and young adults were recruited directly into the Hitler Youth or stormtroopers without first going through other youthful associations. After the 1930 elections, also, there were substantial numbers, presumably of the prewar generation, who never belonged to any youth group. This election also signals a wave of recruitment of respondents previously in conservative or leftwing youth movements as the Nazi drive

[11] Respondents in Catholic areas do stand out among those who joined before 1930.

[12] The pre-1925 members, however, have the largest number of respondents with at least a completed secondary education.

[13] As the reader may recall, youth-group membership was defined as any voluntary association other than labor unions or professional groups to which a respondent belonged during the first 25 years of his life.

gathered momentum and attracted the more activist, young following of these "old" parties of the republic.[14]

We can carry this game of finding out what other groups the Nazi
recruits came from a good deal further by relating this chronology
to the periodized prior organizational memberships. Thus nearly
a third of the pre-1925 Nazis were in 1919-1921 in a *voelkisch*
group, such as the *Schutz-und-Trutzbund*, and about another fourth
were in the Free Corps or other paramilitary or vigilante organizations. The reconstructed party of 1925-1927 drew its recruits largely from paramilitary and left-wing extremist groups and, of course,
from people who had never belonged to any other group before. In
1928-1929, the party began to attract former *Jungdo* and other
bourgeois or conservative members, and again many of the previously uncommitted. After that period, there set in intensive recruitment from the *Stahlhelm* and the DNVP, as well as from former
left-wing and *Jungdo* members.

What did the respondents like best and what did they like the
least about their first youthful association? Those who joined prior
to 1930 certainly liked violence, marching, strikes, and military
training better than did the *Septemberlinge*, whose greatest likes in
their youth group tended to be the sense of comradeship, sports,
hiking, or cultural appreciation. By the same token the pre-1930
Nazis tended to dislike most a lack of ideological leadership or of
political direction and action; those who joined later express more
scattered dislikes, especially of labor militancy. The bent for violence seems most pronounced among those who joined before 1925
or in the first years of reconstruction, 1925 to 1927. The pre-1925
Nazis, in fact, included no fewer than 61.9% who engaged in partisan street fights or organized violence before they reached the age
of 26. Their immediate successors of the reconstructed NSDAP
nearly match this figure, with 54.3% similarly engaged. Those who
joined after 1927, as young men, tended to demonstrate, proselytize,
electioneer, and went in for voluntary military training. Fewer than
40% engaged in youthful violence. Evidently, the pre-1928 Nazi
party was popularly viewed as a tough, swashbuckling outfit for
congenital brawlers, while after that date its image became a more
seriously political one.

The influence of the politics of the respondent's parents among
the early or late joiners is more difficult to assess. Typically, the

[14] The Nazis made much of the fact that the DNVP, the SPD, and
other republican parties were so dominated by the older generation that
ambitious young men had no chance of attaining positions of leadership.

local founders' parents tended to be *voelkisch*-antisemitic or loyal to the conventional parties, or there was conflict between father and son. This combination occurs again among those who joined before 1928, and especially before 1925. In their school settings, too, the local founders tend to pick out *voelkisch*-antisemitic or conventionally political teachers as important, and the same is true of those who joined before 1928.

Enter the Nazi Party

It would stand to reason that those who joined the NSDAP at different stages might have done so in different ways and for different reasons. The most frequent ways in which people in our sample were introduced to the party were through witnessing demonstrations or violence in the street or at rallies, reading about the party's ideology, or through a friend or colleague. Those who joined the party prior to 1928 tended heavily to be introduced by a friend or fellow-worker. This is also true of the local founders, who obviously needed some help to find their party. It is remarkable, though, that it was not due to their reading about the party's ideology. This ideological route is more typical of those who joined in 1928-1929 or as part of the first local nucleus, and again of the bandwagon-jumpers and of those who joined after mid-1931. The force of the demonstrations and rallies was most potent in attracting the respondents between the 1928 and the 1932 elections, probably because of the rapid spreading of the brown movement. This was also the manner in which those respondents were attracted who joined only when the NSDAP constituted a substantial minority or even the local majority. During this end-phase, and especially in 1932, many respondents tended to be introduced to the party by relatives.

In other words, as the movement grew from a lunatic fringe to something approaching the mainstream of German politics, there was a visible progression through various modes of introduction. It began with the friend or colleague as a mediary who took the respondent to Hitler just as he might have taken him to see an exotic freak show or prize wrestling match. Then, the increased movement began to intrude upon the respondent in the form of demonstrations, street violence, or public rallies that were too frequent to be freak shows any more.[15] Finally, the movement had enough legiti-

[15] Fest gives an example of the hectic pace of Nazi activities when he relates that in the summer of 1931, 4,135 mass meetings were held by the numerous Weimar parties in the province of Hessen-Nassau, including almost half by the NSDAP alone, as compared to only 450 by the SPD and 50 by the Center party. *The Face of the Third Reich*, p. 35.

macy to be introduced within the family[16] and to make its ideology respectable. This last-mentioned feature again speaks clearly against the theory that Nazi ideology was a prime mover or that it was some kind of German orthodoxy in the public mind from the beginning.

We can also go back to the motives for entering stage four, the party, and relate this to the chronology or the local progress of the party at the time of joining. The leading motives for joining of the pre-1928 party, and in fact up until mid-1929 were friction with the occupation, ideological or antisemitic fervor, and the comradeship of the stormtroopers. With the local founders, likewise, it was ideological fervor and friction with the occupation, but also the dynamic impression of the Hitler movement which attracted them. Ideological fervor is evidently quite different from being attracted by a "reading of its ideology." We are reminded of the curiously apolitical and public-shy attitude of many of the antisemites in our sample as contrasted to the politically mobilized paranoids. The latter are evidently the ideologically fervid early joiners, while the former may be the passive, older recruits of the end-phase who tended to join because they "read about" the Nazi ideology. During the middle period of 1928 to mid-1930, the motives tended toward the comradeship of the SA, the economic and agricultural crisis, a sense of government repression, and the "rough Communist opposition" that were said to have brought the respondents into the party. The two last-mentioned motives and the dynamic impression of Hitler also characterize the last phase after mid-1931—evidently a rather different climate of public opinion.[17] Again these shifts correspond more or less to the changing motives of those who joined only when the movement had grown locally to greater size.

A look at the antisemitism scale confirms our hypothesis regarding the difference between the "ideologically fervid" and those who "read about" the Nazi ideology in the papers and in propaganda materials. Those who joined in the years of reconstruction, 1925 to 1927, indeed have the highest percentage of paranoids and tellers of prejudiced anecdotes. Those who joined after May 1931, by comparison, stand out with their *Judenkoller* and with mild verbal

[16] In our tabulation of whether the respondent had any members of his family in the party, those who joined after 1930 show a tendency to have their whole family in the NSDAP.

[17] See also the telling description of this atmosphere in 1932-1933 in William S. Allen, *The Nazi Seizure of Power, The Experience of a Single German Town, 1930-1935*, University of Chicago Press, 1965, chap. 1.

projections. Only the pre-1925 Nazis have a higher percentage of *Judenkoller*. During the interval, especially between mid-1929 and mid-1931, there is a relative decrease in prejudice, especially of the virulent kind. Incidentally, those who joined in 1925-1927 also have by far the highest percentage of xenophobia. In their expectations in 1934, they tend to be imperialists.

The dominant ideological motives of the respondents also show significant variations according to when they entered the party. Among the earliest (pre-1925) Nazis, the dominant motive was Nordic-German romanticism, followed at some distance by revanchism, superpatriotism, and the Hitler cult. After 1924, anti-semitism became the dominant motive. In 1928, the ideological motives reverted to revanchism, superpatriotism, and the Hitler cult, until the onset of the Depression brought a stress on the *Volksgemeinschaft* and, once more, on antisemitism. These were evidently the changing ideological motives that the newly joining members saw in their party.

We can gain a similar impression also from the formative or influential experiences of the respondents. Among both the pre-1925 and the 1925-1927 Nazis, alleged encounters with aliens or Jews were the most frequent influence, augmented, in the case of 1925-1927, with educational or literary influences and the experience of youthful comradeship, two typically "young" experiences, as the reader may recall. Beginning with 1928, experiences of unemployment or social humiliation became more prominent, for obvious reasons. The *Septemberlinge*, on the other hand, had somewhat different patterns beginning with those who joined between mid-1930 and mid-1931. They once again stress educational-literary influences and alleged episodes with aliens or Jews. And the last groups of Nazi recruits, after mid-1931, present their *Fronterlebnis* or the experience of defeat in 1918 as their formative experience. This surprising choice, more than a decade after the war, has to be seen in the context of the revived myth of the "front generation" which was nurtured so carefully by the *Stahlhelm*, the right wing, and even by the Bruening government at that time.[18]

The shifting ideological motives according to the local progress of the NSDAP show up the local founders as predominantly anti-semites, superpatriots, and solidarists. Those who joined only when the movement already had a local nucleus more often tended to be revanchists or Nordic-German romanticists. Some had no ideologi-

---

[18] See the description of Bruening by Koppel Pinson, *Modern Germany*, p. 469.

cal motive at all. This shift illustrates well the significance of the distinction between a highly-motivated local founder and the group-oriented joiners of a nuclear group. Those who joined only when the movement was a substantial local minority, furthermore, tended to be Hitler worshippers, as the group they were joining was no longer an intimate, small group. The motives of the bandwagon-jumpers were scattered over the spectrum with a few high points, such as revanchism, Nordic-German romanticism, antisemitism, or no ideology at all.

Offices or Violence

Once a respondent was in the party, he had an opportunity to express his life-style either by acting out his hostility in violent action or by attaching himself to a career within the pre-1933 movement. The patterns of office-holding vary quite substantially according to when the respondents joined the party. Typically, those who garnered higher-level offices, such as speaking or organizing functions, or the offices of *Ortsgruppenleiter* or *Reichstag* deputy, had joined prior to the Coburg elections of 1929. Those who joined between the elections of 1928 and 1932 tended to hold minor local offices and, from about mid-1931, many held offices in the new functional organizations such as the NSBO (labor), NS St.Bd. (university students) or NSBB (civil service). Since our information ends in 1933-1934, it is not surprising to find that over half (57.9%) of those who joined after the 1932 elections held no office at all. But to find the same thing true of those who joined in 1925-1927 requires an explanation.

A partial answer may be found in the patterns of membership in the stormtroopers. Those who joined the party for the first time in 1925-1927 have a higher percentage in the stormtroopers (75.7%), and especially in the SS, than any other group. The pre-1925 Nazis are still the closest with 73.8%, perhaps a fitting demonstration of their tendency to prefer violence to legality. In the years from 1928 to mid-1931, the SA and SS membership drops to between 60 and 70% and, with the arrival of older recruits after May 1931, to less than 40%. There is no surprise in the heavy involvement in the SA of the early, *putsch*ist movement, but there is in the same feature of the 1925-1927 era, during which the role of the SA was rather in limbo.[19] The pre-1925 Nazis also hold more ranks in SA and SS

[19] See esp. Orlow, *History of the Nazi Party, 1919-1933*, pp. 89-90. Although he refused to accord the SA the prominent place it had had before 1926, Hitler did not resolve the question of whether the party was to succeed through elections or coup d'état until November of 1927.

(57.1%) than anyone else, while the 1925-1927 recruits (49.4%) are only slightly ahead of those of 1928-1930 and hold more higher level ranks.

The other half of the answer lies in their relative youth and actual participation in Nazi violence. With 46.9% engaged in political violence, the 1925-1927 Nazis were far and away the most violent of the chronological groups. The other pre-1930 groups tended to have 39-42%, and those after 1930, 19-37% engaged in political violence. The 1925-1927 Nazis may well have included many a "mindless slugger" or other people whom the NSDAP found it necessary to ease out of the party after 1933. As the *Parteistatistik* of 1935 stated so eloquently when discussing the problem of the disgruntled old fighters:[20] "There are still many old party members who in the SA in the fighting years endured great privations. Fate made them into mercenary types [*Landsknechtstypen*]. Hence they have various faults which fail to justify their further role in the party." A considerable number of the 1925-1927 Nazis came directly from the paramilitary activities of the Free Corps, vigilantes, and anti-occupation underground. As many as half of those engaged in Nazi violence in this group appear to have such a violent background. Rather than holding party offices, therefore, they seem to have derived their satisfactions from violence pure and simple.

Personal Introduction to the Party

We have already had a glimpse of the significance of the various ways people became introduced to the NSDAP. These modes of introduction are worth a closer look. A breakdown (FD-59) illustrates the prevailing methods of recruitment, either by evangelistic rallies and demonstrations or by publicity and propaganda.[21] The prominence of rallies and demonstrations is hardly surprsing considering the great efforts of the pre-1933 NSDAP to attract and maintain good, charismatic speakers, and its insistence on making itself heard and seen. The years when Hitler was not allowed to speak in some states, the temporary suspension of the party in Berlin, and the measures to forbid the stormtroopers to march and to

[20] Vol. II, p. 282. The comment went on to express a desire, on the one hand, to do something for the old warhorses and, on the other hand, to expel altogether from the party those whose conduct was acutely embarrassing.

[21] Abel gives a breakdown without further comment of "first contacts with National Socialist Party" for his original sample of 600: 18% not given, 16% friend, 5% co-worker, 33% meetings, 30% family influence, and 25% printed material. *The Nazi Movement*, p. 314.

wear uniforms were obviously significant weapons against the spread of the brown movement, however much some of the Abel respondents would like to deny this,[22] especially when the NSDAP was still a fringe movement. The other prominent recruitment devices, propaganda and publicity, also represented a large investment of time, effort, and funds on the part of the party members and the leadership. As long as the fledgling party could be ignored by the media of communications, its burden of making itself heard required immense and largely futile efforts against a curtain of silence in the press. Only a skilful strategist, such as Josef Goebbels in Berlin, knew how to turn the well-deserved loathing of the established political forces by constant provocation to the Nazi advantage.

It is important to note how few of the respondents were swayed by a *proselytizing stranger*. This is not to say, however, that the role played by proselytizing was small. First of all, much of the most effective proselytizing effort was directed not at total strangers but

FD-59: Personal Introduction to the Party

	Number	Per cent
⌈Through a close relative or spouse	23	4.6
└Through a distant relative	7	1.4
⌈Through a friend or colleague	86	17.3
└Belonged to a group which joined in toto	25	5.0
⌈Attended rally, heard speakers, saw marching	174	35.2
└Witnessed street violence, incidents, provocations	11	2.2
Read Nazi literature, newspapers, aware of ideology	162	32.7
Approached by proselytizing stranger	8	1.6
	496	100.0

at relatives, friends, and especially at colleagues. For this kind of missionary effort to succeed on a person-to-person basis, outside the evangelistic rallies, the target evidently has to know the proselytizer. Hence, proselytizing tended to employ existing social ties and structures and may well have accounted for the lion's share of all the introductions by relatives, friends, or fellow-workers. Furthermore, the line between propagandizing and proselytizing is quite fluid and difficult to draw. Proselytizers generally used propaganda material in

[22] Cf. also the comment of Orlow on the effect of the dissolution of the SA, SS, and HJ in 1932. *History of the Nazi Party, 1919-1933*, p. 252. By 1932, of course, the growth of the party was no longer so dependent on public display as it had been earlier.

persuading new recruits. They often scattered leaflets, say, in their employees' lounge, waiting to see who would pick one up and read it. Then they involved their "mark" into a conversation and, if he seemed interested, tried to take him to rallies or discussions (*Sprechabende*) of their party local.

A Few Examples of Introduction to the Party

Let us look at a few examples of the different kinds of personal introduction to the NSDAP. A typical rally-goer was a young clerk, born 1910 (no. 4), whose political interest was stirred up by the occupation of the Rhineland. He considered joining the *Stahlhelm* or *Jungdo* in his town but found neither of them to his liking. The *Stahlhelm* was not "revolutionary enough" and *Jungdo* "lacking in the comradeship I considered necessary for a successful revolutionary struggle." Barely 18, he went from one party's rally to the next.

> One evening before the *Landtag* elections of 1929 I attended first a DNVP, then a Centrist, and finally an NSDAP rally. The speakers of the first two meetings came up with the usual fine words and comments about their programs, but I heard no tangible proposal on how we as a people could get out of our misery and return to honor. The speaker of the new movement, however, was quite different. I was swept along not only by his passionate speech, but also by his sincere commitment to the German people as a whole, whose greatest misfortune was being divided into so many parties and classes. Finally a practical proposal for the renewal of the people! Destroy the parties! Do away with classes! True *Volksgemeinschaft*! These were goals to which I could commit myself without reservation. The same night it became clear to me where I belonged: To the new movement. It alone gave hope of saving the German fatherland. Thus I entered the Hitler Youth and found what I had sought: real comradeship. . . . Soon I was appointed local leader (*Ortsgruppenfuehrer*) of the NS *Schuelerbund* (high-school students' federation) and experienced and led the fight in the front lines.

More of a mixed case of introduction by a fellow-worker and rally-going was a gardener's son and apprentice, born 1908 (no. 5), whose father was a superpatriot and bitter anti-Marxist and anti-revolutionary. The son joined the DNVP youth and canvassed actively for the DNVP in the face of all kinds of friction at work. He also had a growing suspicion that his DNVP buddies, the "sons of better families" were leaving all the dirty work to him. His apprenticeship completed, the respondent began to work in his parents' gardening business where an older employee, a pre-1924 Nazi, began to fill him in on the NSDAP. His DNVP friends always referred to the Nazis as "brainless fantasy-spinners." He still voted for the DNVP in 1929 even though its phrase-making seemed emptier and its "youth leaders" more aged every year. In the fall of 1929, he finally quit in disgust and swore never to join another party. But the excitement of the September elections of 1930 did not permit the respondent to remain aloof for long:

> Like most people I often went to election rallies, and also to a Nazi rally. The speaker of the evening, a well-known National Socialist of the Ruhr area, tore off the masks of all the parties from left to right with a ruthlessness that had no equal. This was too much for the police officer present, a Socialist of course, and he dissolved the meeting without a good reason. I was so incensed about this repression of opinion that I quickly decided to join at the end of the meeting.

A clearer example of introduction by a friend is a construction engineer born 1896 (no. 6), who was instrumental in Free Corps recruiting at the end of the war even though he claims "I never paid any attention to politics." He was quite aware, in any case, of the political events following the end of the war, such as the abortive Kapp *putsch*, which he welcomed. After the French occupation of the Ruhr, he "often discussed Hitler and his goals with a friend who was an adherent of the *Deutschvoelkische Freiheitsbewegung*." He became a fellow-traveler and, for example, accompanied the local NSDAP group to Hitler's first speech in Essen after his release from prison. "The clear examples cited by Hitler and his sincerity inspired me to admiration, and so did the *élan* of the whole meeting. I heard so many fundamentally new things that it took time for me to digest it all. From this moment on I went to nearly all the Nazi rallies and made their thinking my own." He did not join formally until late in 1928, however, citing especially the poor attitudes of the DNVP, the opposition of the Communists, and the repressive actions of the Prussian police as his immediate reasons.

An example of a respondent attracted by "reading about" the Nazis or by perusal of Nazi propaganda is a professional naval officer, born 1890 (no. 14), who was full of pride in the *Fronterlebnis* of the German soldier. He believed the German navy was betrayed by the new provisional Weimar government, especially by Matthias Erzberger. He was involved in local actions to suppress the workers'- and-soldiers' councils in Wilhelmshaven. About a year after the end of the war he obtained a transfer to a municipal administrative position in the Rhineland though with evident reluctance:

As professional soldiers we had no opportunity to become involved in the politics of the country. Only when I entered civilian life did I realize into what chaos Germany had sunk through the revolt of 1918. As a person who for many years [13½] had known nothing but discipline and order, I could not find my way any more in the Germany of that time. In 1921 I joined the *voelkisch Schutz-und-Trutzbund*.

With this organization he fought the separatists in 1922 and nearly lost his freedom as a result of a bloody clash. During a vacation in Bavaria in 1922-1923 he first heard of the Nazis and of Hitler. "I acquainted myself with the program of the movement and committed myself to it body and soul." He also heard Goebbels speak a couple of times in 1924, but joined only in 1929 after a Hitler speech and in defiance of the edict against Nazi membership for civil servants. In this case, the disorientation of cultural shock and the military background had already mobilized the respondent in the *Schutz-und-Trutzbund*. But his age and evident lack of activist motivation delayed his joining up despite his awareness of the Nazi ideology which obviously corresponded to his own prejudices.

An example of a person introduced by a close relative is an industrial clerk, born in 1901 (no. 15), who on occasion switched to blue-collar jobs because the pay was better. He had been raised by his devout, patriotic mother after losing his father at the age of three. Disillusioned with the war and the miserable food supply, he became interested in Socialist and Communist literature and joined a Communistic trade union. The "excesses" during the workers' 1920 uprising in the Ruhr soured him on the Communists, but he still remained a pacifist and socialist for a number of years. In 1926 he first happened to hear about the NSDAP and to read a copy of the Nazis' *Voelkischer Beobachter*:

The contents were of great interest to me. They put into words what I felt inside. But the description of the SPD I found objectionable. I got so enraged, I put down the paper because it kept referring to the black-red-golden flag as black-red-and-*yellow* which I regarded as very insulting and nasty. . . . When I saw the first SA men in uniform, I was just as unsympathetic as the rest of the populace. Much of this was due to the brown uniform, which reminded me of the Belgian occupation troops and the cap which looked like the Austrian army, an outfit not exactly known as great soldiers. People used to call these first Hitler men scornfully Comrade Laceboot (*Schnuerschuh*).

However, the respondent's attitude changed slowly but surely because his younger brother (he had four older siblings) began to bring home Nazi propaganda material.

My younger brother, who had been with the *Marinejugend*, became associated with this little [Nazi] circle and joined it after a short while. Every now and then he would bring me the *Voelkischer Beobachter* [VB] and invite me also to discussion evenings although I did not want to go. We often had vehement arguments about the contents of the VB. He also brought home various other pieces of Nazi literature which I read with great interest. Most of all, I was fascinated by the Jewish question, to which I devoted my attention. I acquired all kinds of tracts and counter-tracts to clarify the question in my mind, looked up passages in the Old Testament, translations from the Talmud, and the *Protocols of the Elders of Zion* by Alfred Rosenberg [sic]. I compared past and present and finally broke with Marxism, Communism, and democracy.

His *Judenkoller* reached its climax after a turbulent left-wing rally at which the featured anti-Nazi speaker was a former SPD deputy allegedly convicted eleven times for morals offenses and accorded the status of *non compos mentis* by a court. Since the SPD still tolerated this man as a leader, the respondent turned away from it and attended his first NSDAP discussion evening.

A party comrade . . . spoke about Marxism and national socialism in such a vivid way that I realized that this was precisely the way I felt inside. When he declared that nationalism and socialism were not opposites but in reality one and the same, I was ripe for national socialism and joined the party. . . . I began to save money to buy the uniform I had once derided, and subscribed to the weekly *Der Nationalsozialist*. I had the best comradely relations with the other party members. We eagerly discussed the Nazi ideology and became more and more firmly committed.

While the role of the respondent's younger brother was pivotal, this case has many of the other elements as well, the influence of Nazi propaganda literature, attending a Nazi meeting, and also the background split between patriotic and socialist loyalties. Like other Socialists and Communists in the Abel collection, the respondent was alienated from the left by an outbreak of *Judenkoller*. There is also an air of the revival meeting in his description of the discussion evenings (*Sprechabende*) at which the members sought to strengthen each other's faith.

Social Background of Introduction Groups

How do these different modes of introduction relate to the three generations of early Nazis? By far the youngest, with about half in the postwar generation, is the group introduced by a friend or colleague. Only about one-third of the groups which became acquainted with the NSDAP through a rally or through a relative are in the postwar generation. The group which was attracted by the propaganda and publicity has the largest number of members of the war generation (1895-1901) and, along with those introduced by a relative, nearly half in the prewar generation (born before 1895). As the reader will recall, both of these groups tended to join the NSDAP rather late, which may mark off these modes of introduction as less appropriate to the activists.

Being roped in by rallies or demonstrations, on the other hand, is particularly frequent among inhabitants of rural areas, a fact that obviously reflects the impact of Nazi campaigning there. Those introduced by friends or fellow-workers, by comparison, tend to live in small and larger towns (2,000-100,000). By occupation, both the rally-goers and those introduced by friends and colleagues are most often workers or pensioners. Those persuaded by the ideological propaganda are often military-civil servants, farmers, business or professional people, or white-collar workers. There are evidently social-class-related differences between going to an extremist political rally and being attracted by an awareness of the ideology of the party. The former is more proletarian and the latter more typically bourgeois. Those introduced by relatives include disproportionate numbers of women (36.7%), whose social contacts and freedom to attend rallies were probably rather limited.

In their patterns of social mobility, the typical rally-goer turns out to have been in social decline or socially static—which may well have been the best condition to favor these occasions. Those who had been introduced by friends or colleagues were upwardly mobile from urban backgrounds or also in decline. Respondents attracted by the propaganda tended to be upwardly mobile from either a farm or a city background. The handful of people signed up by a proselytizing stranger, as on other crosstabulations such as with age or number of military-civil servants, strongly resembled the last-mentioned group. Their views of the Nazi slogan of the *Volksgemeinschaft* bring out further features of the social dynamics. The rally-goers were composed mostly of persons with either strong class-consciousness, no awareness of class at all, or solidarists from below. This extreme social heterogeneity appears not to have hampered their intense experience of the emotional solidarity these rallies aimed to achieve. Those who were successfully propagandized were, as expected, mostly solidarists of the middle or from without, that is from the *Fronterlebnis* or other encounters with the outside world. The respondents introduced by a friend or colleague tended to be solidarists from below or from above[23] who are seeking acceptance at the warm bosom of the *Volksgemeinschaft*.

Personal Introduction and Youth Settings

We can look at the process of personal introduction also as part and parcel of the broader patterns of political participation. Attending rallies, reading propaganda leaflets, or the act of joining a militant movement are all varieties of participational behavior. There are some striking relationships, for example, between patterns of youthful participation and the modes of personal introduction to the party. Thus, the respondents who were introduced by friends or colleagues are by far the most active before the age of 26, having participated in partisan street-fighting, electioneering, proselytizing, and in the Free Corps type of violence. In our classification of youthful postures they include many who are either politically militarized or hostile militants. Those who were roped in through rallies and those introduced by relatives are much more of the spectator type, with only moderate participation in demonstrations or individual provocation. Those susceptible to Nazi propaganda, again, show a different if not unexpected paramilitary pattern: they tend to be involved in Free Corps or vigilante activities or in voluntary military training groups.

The close link between work and activist politics, which comes out in the many cases where respondents were introduced to the party by fellow-workers or in the pattern of proselytizing on the job, is a good reason to look closely at the youthful work setting as well. The two groups whose members most often lost their livelihoods during the Depression, the rally-goers and those introduced by friends or colleagues, also report the most friction on the job, often with disastrous consequences. Those who were susceptible to propaganda, by comparison, tended to experience a friendly work environment. Since they were older, their economic troubles usually took place before 1929 or not at all.

One would hardly expect the ideological attitudes of the various introduction groups to differ substantially but they do. Respondents introduced to the party by friends or colleagues, for example, tend to have antisemitism or superpatriotism as their main ideological

[23] The reader may recall that many of the solidarists from above turned out to be skilled workmen or foremen rather than members of the middle or upper classes.

motives. The rally-goers, by way of contrast, are mostly revanchists, Nordic-German romantics, and, incidentally, anti-Marxists. Those introduced by relatives are frequently Hitler worshippers. Those attracted by the propaganda, finally, tend to be solidarists, revanchists, or superpatriots. They furthermore tend to be particularly hostile to "reactionaries"—which also fits into their military-civil servant background.

What do these unexpected differences signify? Evidently the activists introduced by friends or fellow-workers were attracted to the party largely by their own virulent antisemitism. On the antisemitism scale, indeed, they turn out to have the largest percentage of paranoids who speak of conspiracies and threats. The rally-goers are a good deal more conventional, with their vintage revanchism, anti-Marxism, and *voelkisch* romanticism. These three elements evidently constituted what the NSDAP meant to them.

The rally-goers, those introduced by relatives, and the group attracted by Nazi propaganda, nevertheless, have a rather high number (about one-third) of respondents with *Jundenkoller* and not a few who tell prejudiced anecdotes. It would appear that the antisemitism of these latter groups was the autistic type described in *The Prophets of Deceit* by Leo Lowenthal and Norbert Guterman, and was satisfied by projective verbalisms rather than the activism of the first-mentioned group. And the few respondents introduced by relatives represent something of a classical combination of autistic prejudice with the leadership cult, as the Adorno study of the "authoritarian personality" describes it.[24] This group also tends to show an obsession with law, order, and cleanliness.

From this description, it is hardly surprising to find that those who were introduced to the party by friends or fellow-workers have the largest percentages among the stormtroopers and engaged in political violence. Those attracted by the ideological propaganda, by way of contrast, have the largest share of party offices including many at the level of *Ortsgruppenleiter*. Being socially middle-class or at least white-collar, they were far ahead in this respect of the more proletarian rally-goers.

Family Members in the Party

Being introduced to the party by a relative, especially a close relative or one's spouse, raises the question of the role of the family in

[24] For a persuasive, psychoanalytic argument linking Nazi prejudice and leadership cult with Oedipal fantasies, see also Daim, *Der Mann der Hitler die Ideen gab.*

membership. Of 27 respondents so introduced, the entire families of 22 (81.5%) were in the party. Another three had only their spouses and two distant relatives in the party. Such total envelopment by the family of what to other respondents is obviously more an individual adventure gives joining and belonging to the NSDAP a rather different character. The reader may recall also that such family membership tended to occur more often toward the end of the fighting years when electoral successes had given the party a good deal of legitimacy. The only other group which tends to have the whole family in the party is that of the rally-goers, with about half in this position. Family membership seems compatible enough with their spectator style. By way of contrast, those introduced by friends or colleagues tend to be in the party by themselves (38.1%), or at the most to have their spouses in it (26.2%). Respondents who fell for the Nazi propaganda closely resemble them except that with them having their spouses in the party is the dominant tendency. That political extremism should be for loners is hardly news. That it also seems appropriate for couples we have already encountered in our examination of prejudice. Prejudice can be shared to provide cement for a brittle marriage.

A breakdown of family membership before 1933 shows the surprising extent to which the NSDAP itself must have had more than one member from each family involved. It is not unlikely that other parties such as the SPD, KPD, and Center party, and to a lesser degree the DNVP, DVP, and DDP had similar amounts of family memberships. While a good fourth of the Abel respondents were loners, another one-fourth had their spouses in the party, too. Almost half of the respondents had several close relatives or practically the whole family in the party. Since we have insufficient information on the marital status and family life of the respondents, this is worth a closer look.[25]

Social Background of Family Membership

There are some interesting features about the ages and occupations of these groups. The loners are the youngest group, with 39.6% of the postwar generation and another 33.3% of the war generation (born 1895-1901). Those with more or less the whole family in the

---

[25] The group reporting their spouse in the party and those reporting children or the whole family in the party were very likely married at the time, while the other half and especially the loners were less likely to be married. Abel notes that 48% of his original sample were married while the rest did not give any information on this point. *The Nazi Movement*, p. 313.

FD-75: Family Members in NSDAP

	Number	Per cent
No other member of respondent's family in party	48	25.1
Spouse in party	47	24.6
⌐ Parents in party	15	7.9
⊢ Children in party	31	16.2
⊢ Siblings in party	24	12.6
⌊ Whole family	17	8.9
Distant relative in party	9	4.7
	191	100.0

party are on the average six years older even though they include a disproportionate number of the youngest cohort (born 1909-1916). The oldest group is the one with only the spouse in the party, with no less than two-thirds born before 1895 and a median age, in 1933, of 43.

According to their location experience, the typical whole-family respondent was from the occupied areas or he never moved from where he was born. He often lived in a fairly large town. Disproportionate numbers of respondents with foreign or borderland experiences, surprisingly, turn out to have been loners, which would seem to cast some doubt on the nazifying effect of their experiences which were likely to be shared by their families. The loners often lived in rural or small-town areas. The couple members tended to be rural-urban migrants and often lived in Berlin. They were mostly military-civil servants, while the loners tended to be farmers or blue- and white-collar workers. One-fifth of the whole-family types were women, which illustrates the Nazi slogan: "If we enroll a man we get only him. But if we recruit a woman member we may get her entire family." Nearly two-thirds of the women respondents who supplied information on family membership were in the whole-family category.

The socio-economic dimensions are also worth a closer look. As it turns out, an unusual number of the loners lost their fathers before they were 18 years old. They also tended to have lost their livelihoods prior to the Depression. The whole-family members, on the other hand, have the largest number of parental hardships such as bankruptcy, death, or both parents working, and yet they did not become economic casualties under the republic as often as the other groups. The couples, despite their relatively secure childhoods, most often fell victims to the Great Depression.

The home environment, or rather its political color, lends further depth to our understanding of the relationships involved. As it turns out, a disproportionate number of the whole-family types came from a *voelkisch* home, which, of course, supplies a rather obvious reason why the whole family tended to join the NSDAP. Seventy-one and two-fifths percent of the respondents reporting a *voelkisch* or antisemitic father fall into this category. The couples type, by comparison, tended to be from a patriotic or a militaristic home. Their war experiences, too, mark them off as enthusiastic soldiers or hostile bitter-enders. The loners had unpolitical or moderate fathers or report conflict between father and son.

Family Membership and Violence

Before they passed the age of 25, the loners tended to be in Free Corps or militant veterans' groups and to express a special liking for marching with an ideological purpose, and political violence. Those who had their whole family in the party, by comparison, were more interested in youthful comradeship and marching together. From this and the foregoing we would expect the loners (who were also the youngest) to be by far the most violent Nazis. As it turns out, however, the family types were not far behind the loners who had 30% marcher-fighter-proselytizers (MFPs) and 20% MFs. The whole-family members had 27.4% MFPs and 14.3% MFs. The members with a spouse in the party instead concentrated on marching-and-proselytizing (27.1%) in which they were ahead of the family types (22.6%) and the loners (14%). On balance it appears that the whole-family members are really the most dangerous of the species, socially well-integrated and with equal fortitude in fighting and in proselytizing.[26] Political violence and ideological extremism are evidently not just a product of loneliness and alienation, but they thrive just as luxuriantly in a context of family and motherhood.

[26] Their youthful and adult motives join hands poignantly when we tabulate the immediate reasons of the family types to join the party. Their predominant reasons are the comradeship among the stormtroopers and their ideological fervor. The loners were more often motivated by a sense of general repression and the Communist opposition; the couples stress economic troubles and the dynamic impression of the Hitler movement.

TWO

The Sacred Freedom Fighters

"The SA man," wrote the SA leader Franz Pfeffer von Salomon in an SA decree delineating the functions of the stormtroopers as against those of the party organization (PO), "is the sacred freedom fighter. The party comrade is the instructor and skilled agitator. Political propaganda seeks to enlighten the adversary, to dispute with him, to understand his viewpoint, to go into his ideas, up to a certain point to agree with him—but when the SA appears on the scene, this stops. They are out for all or nothing. They know only the motto . . . : Strike [them] dead! You or me."[1]

The large private army of the stormtroopers indeed gave the pre-1933 NSDAP a distinctively fascist character. Before 1925, and especially after the beer-hall *putsch*, the SA under Captain Roehm was to all effects and purposes the core of the Nazi movement. During the years of reconstruction, Hitler managed to get rid of Roehm for a while, but the sizeable SA formations remained and attracted thousands of Free Corps men and other militants and brawlers at a time when the party organization was languishing. Joachim Fest estimates the SA at a strength of 70,000 by the time of the 1930 elections when Roehm came back from Bolivia, where he had served as a military instructor. The Depression then brought another 100,000 flocking to the SA soup kitchens and SA homes by mid-1931. At the same time, the criminal elements in the SA[2] and their terrorist activities in the "fight for control of the street" against the Communists came more and more to the fore. According to the

[1] Quoted by Fest, *The Face of the Third Reich*, pp. 142-143.

[2] *The Face of the Third Reich*, pp. 143-145. If this figure is correct it would amount to about 54% of the pre-1930 membership, whereas the share of the stormtroopers among the Abel respondents until the 1930 elections amounts to about 69.5%. Werner, in *SA und NSDAP*, pp. 544-552, indicates the total membership as 77,000 in January 1931, 91,000 by March, 119,000 by April, not counting 4,500 SS members, but inclusive of 5,000 in Austria. By November 1931, it was 221,000, in January 1932, 291,000, in August, 445,000, and by January 1933, an estimated 700,000, or 83.5%.

police reports of Berlin and other big cities, the brown and the red brawlers soon developed a style of bloody confrontations as predictable as the rush-hour traffic. The police made great efforts to separate and sidetrack their mutual raids and confrontative demonstrations, but in the end they always managed to find each other for another free-for-all.[3]

FD-65: Membership in SA, SS

	Number	Per cent
Not a member	213	38.7
Joined SA when entering movement	232	42.2
Joined SA a year later	33	6.0
Joined SA two or more years later	33	6.0
Graduated from SA to SS	39	7.1
	550	100.0

Our breakdown of the SA and SS membership of the Abel sample shows the heavy preponderance of those who joined the stormtroopers directly upon becoming Nazis. We can surmise that these respondents were attracted by the stormtrooper role, the quasi-military uniform, and the quasi-legitimation of violence more than by the Nazi ideology. Those who joined the SA a year or more later were evidently undergoing a process of extremist escalation from milder, though perhaps more ideologically motivated, party membership to greater militancy. For them the step toward violence constituted an intensification of their involvement. The SS was in those days still a bodyguard for Hitler and other Nazi leaders, although some of its elitist features were clearly emerging. Let us examine the differences between these groups more closely.

A Few Examples

There probably is no such thing as a typical non-stormtrooper, since the group is so large and heterogeneous. Nevertheless, a not too untypical example is a Thuringian weaver's son born 1889 (no. 16), who before the war learned the brewer's trade and joined the *Deutscher Brauerbund*. Like the millers, the brewers were a very traditional trade with strong *voelkisch*-antisemitic overtones. This

[3] See Werner's description of the struggle in Berlin, *SA und NSDAP*, pp. 580-583, and his discussion of the role of the SA *Sturmlokal* (hangout) and of the martyrs who even in death and injury were made to serve the cause. The wounded had to head demonstrations in order to document the "red terror" and the pictures and stories of the dead and their families were a favorite propaganda material of the Nazi press.

respondent volunteered for a crack regiment of the peacetime army and loved the army life. He comments on imperial Germany:

> Politically speaking, things were orderly and clean in our fatherland, with the exception of the Social Democrats, who claimed to be the sole representatives of the working-man. But it was my innermost conviction that there was many a face among the leaders that had no German features, and names that were not customary German names. Luxemburg, Liebknecht—what was hidden in these names? Mueller, Scheidemann, they may have been Germans, but their innermost soul was lost to the fatherland.

He enlisted again in 1914 and was wounded so severely that he would never again lift a barrel from the cart. Sent home in 1916, he claims to have witnessed how "the Jews and Freemasons," including Rathenau, betrayed the country for money. He joined the *Kyffhaeuserbund*, a veterans' organization, and, in 1931, the NSDAP after having attended a number of meetings and witnessed violence. He held a minor party office (*Amtswalter* and precinct captain) and participated every Sunday in demonstrations in the Communist parts of Duisburg to provoke "terrorist attacks." Three of his sons were in the Hitler Youth after 1931, and his wife was also active in the party. His strong *voelkisch* convictions, his age, and the late date of joining are typical features of the non-storm-trooper.

An example of a respondent joining the SA directly as he became a Nazi is a locksmith, born 1905 (no. 20), in the Rhineland who was something of a victory-watcher with a touch of truancy during the war:

> The mighty war broke out and nudged my childish mind with a gentle but powerful moment of enthusiasm that made me mature beyond my years. I had only one desire at the time, to grow up as fast as possible in order to participate in the great happenings of the war. Our field-grey men won victory after victory and soon I was so convinced of the imminence of the final triumph I stayed away from school and failed to do my chores at home. The result was flunking a grade and daily beatings at home.

His personal problems were magnified by the experience of the defeat. But his patriotic feelings did not keep him from joining the SPD and the Socialist trade union (FDGB), which made him a shop steward over 200 fellow-apprentices. At the time of the Rathenau assassination, the respondent became disillusioned with the SPD, having read a *voelkisch* brochure about Rathenau, and he joined the *Bismarckjugend* (DNVP). But this group evidently did not satisfy him either. It was too much lacking in social conscience and "too superficial in its German and national consciousness." With the withdrawal of the French occupation from the Ruhr, the NSDAP began to appear in his area and, "in October 1925 I became an SA man and a National Socialist." It is no coincidence that the respondent lists his stormtrooper role first.

He was involved in a good deal of violence although he mentions only how he "was persecuted by the authorities, hassled and fired by employers, and attacked and assaulted by the red murder pest on the principle 'death to the hateful fascists.' " In spite of his seemingly ideological objections to both the SPD and the *Bismarckjugend*, this respondent gives the impression of rather shallow ideological commitment. Once in the party, he typically treasured the comradeship of the stormtroopers and made a cult of his undying loyalty to Hitler and the movement. But as for his ideological baggage, he was evidently travelling light or he could hardly have stood years of membership among both Socialists and conservatives.

An example of a respondent who joined only a year after becoming a Nazi is a Pomeranian miller born 1904 (no. 19). He learned his *voelkisch* convictions from the millers' periodical, *Deutscher Mueller*, which was edited by none other than Theodor Fritsch. The respondent is full of seething social resentments because he had to leave his father's mill to an older brother and join the journeymen proletariat. He claims to have been involved in posting handbills for the NSDAP already in 1924, but did not join formally until 1928. After a year of friction, sabotage, and physical attacks at work, he also became a stormtrooper, but only a year later. Beginning in 1930, furthermore, he worked to organize the new Nazi union (NSBO) in industry in the face of what must have been considerable physical danger. In 1931, he reports, he received severe head injuries with the leg of a chair in a Communist rally he must have entered for purposes of disruption or provocation. A year later he had a nervous breakdown right after the July elections, during which he had campaigned for a seat in the *Reichstag*. In his case, the presence of strong ideological convictions evidently slowed down his becoming a stormtrooper and also assured him of a political role as a legislative candidate.[4]

---

[4] His name was seventh on the party list in his district, which was evidently not enough to sweep him into office with the landslide of 1932. Thus he was obviously not the first choice of his party.

Age and Social Background

How did these three groups of stormtroopers compare in age with those who never joined? The latter were considerably older, with nearly two-thirds born in the prewar generation (1860-1894). By comparison, the SS graduates had almost two-thirds in the postwar generation (born after 1901). Fifty-four and three-tenths percent of those who directly became stormtroopers were also born after 1901.[5] Respondents who became stormtroopers after some delay are more evenly distributed over the age spectrum of the Abel sample. These generational cohorts imply that the SS men and the immediate stormtroopers typically joined between the ages of 18 and 30, the delayed stormtroopers somewhat later, and that the non-storm-troopers tended to join the NSDAP only when they were over 30, and especially after the age of 35.

As for their location experiences, the "instant" stormtroopers and SS graduates strongly tended to be from the occupied areas. They also tended to be highly mobile among cities. The borderland respondent, by contrast, often did not become a stormtrooper. Respondents who had resided abroad or had been colonials tended to join the SA only later or not at all. The influence of these location experiences evidently varies rather considerably. The SS men and immediate stormtroopers, furthermore, tended to live in rural areas or small and medium-sized towns, while the non-members and de-layed members of the SA were mostly metropolitan.

What occupations and social class origins distinguish these stormtrooper groups? The SS men and instant stormtroopers heav-ily tended to be blue-collar workers or farmers. The fathers of the SS men were mostly artisans or businessmen, while the immediate stormtroopers tend to have workers or military-civil servants as fa-thers. Except for the fathers of the SS men, then, there was very little petit-bourgeois background. Those who joined the SA only later were mostly white-collar employees and the sons of military-civil servants or farmers, which may well have made for more ideological awareness. The non-members, finally, were mostly military-civil servants and women, a telling demonstration that the military-civil servant strain in the Nazi movement made its contribution on ideological grounds rather than because they were "specialists in violence" or particularly violence-prone.

[5] Another 26.3% of the instant stormtroopers and 33.3% of the SS men were of the war generation (born 1895-1901). The former also have a disproportionate number in the 1885-1889 cohort which may well represent a group of peacetime and professional soldiers.

One out of five SS men and instant stormtroopers had lost his father before he reached adulthood, more than in any other group. Forty-two and two-fifths percent of the SS men, 32.3% of the delayed, and 29.5% of the instant stormtroopers had also lost their livelihood during the Depression, and 10-19% before the Depression. The non-members, by way of contrast, tended to have economically secure childhoods and normal economic careers, with only a fifth falling victim to the Depression. The difference can be accounted for not only by their age but also by the probable consequences of stormtrooper activism on the economic situation of a respondent.

The instant stormtroopers also tended to be in social decline or not to have made the attempt to rise, while the SS men were heavily in social decline, a situation that seems to increase the propensity for extremist violence. The delayed stormtroopers, by comparison, tended to be upwardly mobile, especially from an urban background. We can suppose that they had more to lose by their turn to violence than did the social decliners. The non-members too, were often moving up from the farm.

About three-fourths of the instant stormtroopers had only an elementary education, which makes them the least educated group of the Abel sample. The delayed stormtroopers and the non-members had the highest proportion of people with the *Abitur* and some university study. In spite of the attraction of the SA and SS to university students, it appears, the typical jackbooted stormtrooper was a man of rather limited education along with proletarian status or origin.

The Stormtroopers and Youth Settings

How did the stormtroopers fit into the diverse youth settings of the Weimar Republic? What prior youth group memberships were most conducive to becoming a stormtrooper? How did the home and school environment of SA or SS men differ from that of non-members? As for the prior youth group memberships, nearly half of the SS members and nearly one-third of the instant stormtroopers were with the Free Corps, vigilantes, or militant veterans' groups during their first 25 years of life. They also came in disproportionate numbers from left-wing youth groups such as the Socialist or Communist Youth or the Red Front (RFB). Revolution and counter-revolution obviously made their contribution here to the Nazi violence. The instant stormtroopers also tended to come from bourgeois or conservative youth groups such as *Jungdo* or the *Bismarckjugend*, or to have joined the SA or Hitler Youth directly. The delayed stormtroopers significantly include many conservative, bourgeois, or unpolitical youth group members as well as many respondents who first went from another youth group to a *voelkisch* group rather than to the NSDAP. Since these other *voelkisch* groups generally had no equivalent to the brownshirted brawlers, these respondents were evidently interested in something more than uniforms and violence. They also had more than their share of people whose first youthful association was with the party itself or the Hitler Youth, and who may well have required a warm-up period before they were ready for the stormtroopers.

Table VI-6: First Youthful Association of Stormtroopers

	Not a member	Joined SA immediately	Joined SA later	Grad. from SA to SS	Totals (n)
Free Corps, Militant veterans	25 (21.6%)	62 (53.4%)	12 (10.3%)	17 (14.7%)	116 (100.0%)
DNVP, DHV, Nat. Athletic Association	10 (27%)	17 (45.9%)	7 (18.9%)	3 (8.1%)	37 (100.0%)
No Youth Association	86 (60.6%)	34 (23.9%)	17 (12%)	5 (3.5%)	142 (100.0%)
Agricultural Catholic Youth Group	2 (20%)	6 (60%)	1 (10%)	1 (10%)	10 (100.0%)
Jungdo, DVP, DDP, etc.	16 (28.6%)	28 (50%)	9 (16.1%)	3 (5.4%)	56 (100.0%)
SAJ, Red Front, SPD	8 (21.6%)	24 (64.9%)	1 (2.7%)	4 (10.8%)	37 (100.0%)
HJ, Other NS Young Org. 1st	12 (18.2%)	37 (56.1%)	11 (16.7%)	6 (9.1%)	66 (100.0%)
Unpolitical Organizations	11 (55%)	5 (25%)	4 (20%)	—	20 (100.0%)
Sums	170 (35.1%)	213 (44%)	62 (12.8%)	39 (8.1%)	484 (100.0%)

Typically, the instant stormtroopers and SS graduates liked violence and marching with an ideological purpose best about their first youthful association. The delayed stormtroopers, by comparison, liked comradeship and marching better. The non-stormtroopers doted most on sports, hiking, or cultural appreciation, or also on comradeship. The future street fighters evidently distinguished themselves at an early point in their careers with their likes and dislikes. Our classification of youth postures brings out these qualities in sharp profile. Half the SS men were *politically militarized* youths, and so were 41.1% of the instant stormtroopers. Hostile militants and the fully politicized make up another prominent part of the latter. The delayed stormtroopers are more evenly distributed over all the youthful posture groups. The non-stormtroopers, finally, stand out for a large share of pre-political parochials or authoritarian youths.[6] The SS and the instant stormtroopers clearly constituted the cutting edge of the Weimar youth revolt as far as it was in the Nazi movement.

The school and home environments of the stormtroopers hold some surprises. The fathers of the instant stormtroopers tend to be *voelkisch* or in conflict with their sons. The school environment of the latter, too, is mostly *voelkisch* or marred by conflict or frequent changes of school. The presence of conflict is hardly surprising in this context of violent men. The SS men tend to emphasize *voelkisch* teachers but their fathers are more often just patriotic. The delayed stormtroopers also tend to have *voelkisch* teachers and unpolitical or patriotic fathers. Somehow, we expected the parental environment of the SS men and delayed stormtroopers to be more often *voelkisch* than that of the instant stormtroopers. Evidently the early SS was not noticeably more ideological than the instant stormtroopers. The delayed stormtroopers, with their background of unpolitical youth groups, may well have received a similarly retarding influence from their unpolitical or patriotic fathers. The non-members' fathers were mostly militaristic, loyal to conventional parties, or unpolitical.

The childhood settings shed further light on the home environment of the stormtroopers. The instant stormtroopers tended to grow up as orphans (17.5%) or had disciplinarian childhoods (10%). The SS men were also distinguished by many orphans, or grew up in poverty or, if in economically secure circumstances, in a freewheeling kind of childhood. Except for this last-mentioned hint of SS elitism, an economically secure or bourgeois background seems to have been a definitely retarding influence on becoming a stormtrooper. Delayed stormtroopers particularly tended to come from a sheltered, economically secure home.

The Influence of War and Counter-revolution

What influence did the war and its aftermath have on the stormtroopers of the Abel collection? Was the SA really a movement of

[6] The non-stormtroopers account for only 8.3% of the politically militarized and 25% of the hostile militants even though they were 37.5% of the sample in this crosstabulation.

front soldiers who simply wanted to keep on fighting the lost war? To begin with, 61-68% of the SA and SS men in our sample never saw any military service in their lives.[7] The victory-watchers make up one in five of the SA and SS men. A small but disproportionate element of the SS men and instant stormtroopers, moreover, are respondents who disliked their military service or became disaffected during the war. Whether these men constitute a core of persons hostile to any authority and whether there was a carry-over of the urge to march and fight is difficult to tell. Some readers may recall the anti-war demonstrations of Vietnam veterans of 1971 and the curious urge to march in uniformed formation displayed by many who had become deeply disaffected from that war effort. It is the delayed stormtroopers and non-stormtroopers, in any case, who tend to be the typical enthusiastic World War One soldiers or bitter-enders with pronounced hostility against the enemy, civilians, or draft-dodgers. The evidence, in other words, is against assuming the presence of a link between a positive war experience and the political soldiering of the SA or SS.

What about the effect of revolution and counter-revolution aside from youthful associations? The instant stormtroopers and the SS men tended to blame the revolution on the old order, on unspecified rabble, or on international Marxism. The delayed stormtroopers blamed mostly the Weimar parties or international Marxism. It was typically the non-stormtroopers who tended to blame, after the Weimar parties, the Jews. The instant stormtroopers, and to a lesser extent the SS, consequently tended to have a disproportionate share (10-13%) of former Free Corps or vigilante fighters.[8] More than half of the quasi-military members of that time, indeed, were among these two groups. The non-stormtroopers, by comparison, betray their loyalties to another age with their strong but passive hatred of the insurgents and their participation in the Kapp *putsch*. Some of them even were among the insurgents at the time or in other republican or left-wing groups, while others tended to be in *voelkisch* or conservative groups. Even in 1923, the non-members were more often involved in the Hitler *putsch* or the early Nazi party than

[7] This should be compared with the non-stormtroopers of whom only 42% missed the military service and 22.1% were peacetime or professional soldiers.

[8] The share is not very large because three-fifths of the entire sample were not at all involved in any counter-revolutionary activities in 1919-1921. The motivation of these three-fifths appears to lie in the youth revolt.

were the instant stormtroopers, who tended to come from other legitimate parties, from the anti-occupation underground, and from militant veterans groups. Thus it appears that some of the most highly motivated stormtroopers came out of the counter-revolutionary movement without reflecting much of the influence of the war experience.

Entering the Party

Both the instant stormtroopers and the SS men, the reader may recall, tended to join the Nazi movement before mid-1929 and especially in the era of reconstruction between 1925 and 1927. By the beginning of the year 1931, the SA is said to have numbered some 77,000 men[9] of which 273 (0.35%) were in our sample, considerably more than the percentage we have of party members who joined prior to the 1930 elections. The stormtrooper element of the pre-1930 party thus is rather over-represented in the Abel sample, possibly for the same reasons as those for the over-representation of pre-1930 NSDAP members. Even before the 1934 purge, the old stormtroopers must have had the feeling that they had been used by the party organization to do the dirty work. From 1933 especially, the party was enjoying the fruit of the stormtroopers' labors with no thought of sharing the spoils of office with them. The SS men and immediate stormtroopers were introduced to the party mostly by friends or fellow-workers or, in the case of the instant SA men, also by witnessing rallies or demonstrations. The delayed or non-stormtroopers, by comparison, were more often attracted by the ideological propaganda of the Nazis. The attitudes of the instant stormtroopers and SS men toward the party were characterized chiefly by a sense of personal integration gained from the struggle itself. The non-members, by way of contrast, tended to gain their sense of integration from the pursuit of utopia, or from the expectation of a material reward such as a job.

Rather typically, office-holding and political violence remained separated. The instant stormtroopers rarely held any office in the party itself. The SS men did a little better, holding a few higher-level offices and even *Reichstag* mandates. By comparison, the delayed stormtroopers frequently held party offices, both minor and at the *Ortsgruppenleiter* level. The non-members held many minor and functional offices. The three types of stormtroopers, on the other hand, did hold SA or SS ranks except for about a third of the SA men and only one out of ten of the SS men. There are no particular

[9] See above, p. 581 fn. and Table VI-2, p. 557.

differences in the patterns of holding SA ranks between the instant and the delayed stormtroopers.

In their activities as full-fledged Nazis, on the other hand, the instant stormtroopers and SS men were noticeably more violent than the delayed stormtroopers, who made up for this by more often fighting "day-and-night" or by proselytizing. Although 55-59% of the three kinds of stormtroopers were engaged in political violence, this was true of only 7% of the non-stormtroopers. On the other hand, nearly two-thirds of the latter (cf. 23-29% of the stormtroopers) engaged in proselytizing, electioneering, and propaganda. Joining the SA or SS obviously meant a great likelihood of becoming involved in violence, and this pattern was particularly clear with those who immediately joined the SA or who "graduated" from the SA to the SS before 1933. Not joining the SA, by contradistinction, held a greater likelihood of involvement in proselytizing, propaganda, and in party offices.

Stormtrooper Beliefs and Attitudes

In their attitudes toward violence, the three kinds of stormtroopers and even the non-members are all split between masochism and sadism in about the same proportion—about three masochists for every bully. The instant stormtroopers and SS men also more often report having been fired, friction at school or in the family, or deliberate confrontations with political enemies; they also include the lion's share of respondents whose physical aggressiveness speaks through their *vitae*. The instant and the delayed stormtroopers, furthermore, like to use the language of the *outré* about their antagonists. With about one-third *outrés*, these two SA groups turn out to be rather characteristic hate-groups. One-fourth each of the SS men and the delayed stormtroopers prefer to refer to the enemy as a conspiracy or as traitors. The non-members are more disposed (55.8%) to express a liking for the enemy or a desire to win him over.

In their ideological motifs, the three stormtrooper groups differ from the non-members chiefly by having more revanchists and more respondents without any ideological notions to speak of. They differ little from each other except for the SS, which has more Hitler-worshippers and Nordic-German romantics, and the delayed stormtroopers, who have more antisemites than the rest. The three stormtrooper groups also are considerably more anti-Marxist than the non-stormtroopers. If we compare the groups with regard to the nature and level of their political understanding, the stormtrooper groups turn out to be a good deal more ideological in their thinking than are the non-members. The instant stormtroopers and SS men, in particular, tend to be romantics, dimwits, or of the low, ideological type, and the delayed stormtroopers are noticeably more aware of the political complexities of Weimar. All this confirms our earlier impressions of the different stormtrooper groups. Ideology and political knowledge were not a matter of great concern to the typical stormtrooper.

What about the prejudices typical of the Nazi party? On the anti-semitism scale, over one-half of the three stormtrooper groups gives no evidence of prejudice or voices only the milder sort of verbal projections. The non-stormtroopers, as expected, show a much higher incidence of *Judenkoller* and, together with the delayed stormtroopers, of telling prejudicial episodes. But when it comes to the fully mobilized paranoids and their mutterings of the great conspiracy, the stormtrooper groups and especially the SS are again ahead of the non-members. They are also considerably more xenophobic than the non-stormtroopers. While there are many stormtroopers who seem to have been in the SA chiefly for the marching and the violence (50-53%), in other words, there is a core group (14-19%) of political antisemites among them for whom an advanced degree of prejudice may well have been the chief motive of their violent ways.

We can end this examination of the stormtroopers by taking a look at their personal features. Forty-three to 50% of the three stormtrooper groups (as compared to 18% of the non-members) had no other members of their families or only distant relatives in the party. This tendency toward being a lone wolf is strongest among the delayed stormtroopers and SS men. The instant stormtroopers and SS men also stand out with extremes of leadership cult and a strong desire to merge completely with the movement. The delayed stormtroopers and non-members, by comparison, suffered from high cultural shock, and the non-members also showed a high degree of irrationality.

Their formative experiences, finally, set the appropriate accents on their lives: The SS men and delayed stormtroopers tended to be formed by educational or literary influences, while the instant stormtroopers more often seem to have been influenced by the experiences of youthful comradeship or unemployment. These experiences clearly set off Weimar youth from its elders, the non-stormtroopers, whose formative experiences were the *Fronterlebnis* and the cataclysms of 1918-1919. In 1934, the expectations of the instant stormtroopers and SS men tended toward building the totalitarian 1000-year *Reich* with overtones of purges and of brainwashing everybody. The SS men and delayed stormtroopers, in other words the more deliberate of the lot, also stressed German imperialism or the resurgence of German power in Europe. It is quite typical, furthermore, that the non-stormtroopers tended to hope for social and economic recovery instead. They also tended to tell their life-stories as if their political development were the result of world historical circumstances. The three stormtrooper groups, being part of the Weimar youth revolt, instead concentrated on their political development or blamed personal circumstances for it.

Ranks Held in SA and SS

More than half of the SA and SS members in our sample held ranks in the stormtrooper organizations. This appears to be an unusually high percentage of chiefs as compared to Indians until we recall the strong pre-1930 bias of our sample. Since the actual movement grew to more than five times its pre-1930 strength by 1933, it stands to reason that most early stormtroopers would have been given leadership roles by the time of Abel's essay contest. In fact, we must wonder why some did not attain rank. Perhaps some of the crosstabulations will shed light on this question. Many of the non-ranking stormtroopers may have either joined only toward the end or delayed their SA or SS membership until the last fighting years.[10]

FD-66: SA and SS Ranks Held[a]

	Number	Per cent
Rottenfuehrer, Scharfuehrer, Oberscharfuehrer	57	31.5
Truppfuehrer, Obertruppfuehrer	50	27.6
Sturmfuehrer, Obersturmfuehrer	47	26.0
Sturmbannfuehrer, Obersturmbannfuehrer	15	8.3
Special organizing functions	12	6.6
	181	100.0

[a] These stormtrooper ranks compare with German and American army ranks as follows: The *Rottenfuehrer* (*Obergefreiter*) is a Corporal: The various *Scharfuehrer* (*Feldwebel*) ranks correspond to U.S. ranks from Sergeant to Sergeant Major; *Truppfuehrer* is not a rank but a function of leading a team or detail and usually combined with one of the ranks mentioned already. All these categories were combined as "lower leaders" for crosstabulation. The "middle echelon" leaders include several *Sturmfuehrer* (Lieutenant) and *Sturmbannfuehrer* (Major to Colonel) ranks. Special acknowledgment for this information is due Professor Karl H. Kahrs of California State University at Fullerton, who was a research assistant on the project. See also Werner, *op.cit.*, p. 536, on the reorganization of 1931.

[10] One hundred eighty-one SA and SS men held SA or SS ranks. Of the SA and SS men who did not, 61 were instant stormtroopers, 20 delayed stormtroopers, and only 4 had graduated to the SS which may have involved foregoing an SA rank.

We divided the stormtrooper ranks into lower ranks and a middle echelon of leadership.[11] These two levels differ from each other clearly, for example, in the date they joined the NSDAP. Sixty and two-fifths percent of the middle echelons had already joined before mid-1929, as compared to only 44% of the lower leads. The bulk of the latter (83.2%) joined before May 1931, a date after which the broad flood of the *Septemberlinge* filled up the cadres of the early fighters.

The middle-echelon leaders also tended to be noticeably older than the lower leaders, who were in turn no older than the storm-troopers at large. While 64.1% of the SS men and 54.3% of the in-stant stormtroopers were of the postwar generation, this was true only of 56.1% of the lower leaders and 42.2% of the middle eche-lon. On the other hand, even the middle echelon was younger than the non-stormtroopers, who had only 15.9% in the postwar generation.

Disproportionate numbers of middle-echelon and lower SA or SS leaders came from the occupied areas or, in the case of the mid-dle level, also from the border areas in the East where the SA, for several years, had been part of a voluntary border-protection army against the threat of Polish invasion. The lower leaders, moreover, tended to live in rural or small-town areas or, like the middle echelons, in larger towns (10,000-100,000) rather than in the metropolitan areas typical of many non-stormtroopers. Perhaps the anti-metro-politan affect of the Nazis was strongest among the stormtrooper leadership and a good deal less sincere among the older, non-storm-trooper party members.

A comparison of the occupational composition of the SA and SS leaders with the total SA and SS membership as well as the non-members (Table VI-7) illuminates the internecine struggle in the Nazi party over the role of the "socialist component" in national

[11] These stormtrooper ranks compare with German and American army ranks as follows: The *Rottenfuehrer* (*Obergefreiter*) is a corporal; the various *Scharfuehrer* (*Feldwebel*) ranks correspond to U.S. ranks from sergeant to sergeant major; *Truppfuehrer* is not a rank but a function of leading a team or detail and usually combined with one of the ranks mentioned already. All these categories were combined as "lower leaders" for crosstabulation. The "middle echelon" leaders include several *Sturm-fuehrer* (lieutenant) and *Sturmbannfuehrer* (major to colonel) ranks. Special acknowledgement for this information is due Professor Karl H. Kahrs of California State University at Fullerton, who was a research as-sistant on the project. See also Werner, *SA und NSDAP*, p. 536, on the reorganization of 1931.

socialism. As can be readily seen, the stormtroopers are far more heavily blue-collar and white-collar workers and farmers than the non-stormtroopers, who tend more often to be military-civil servants, business or professional people, or of course women. The blue- and white-collar element and the frequently dependent or bankrupt farmers among the stormtroopers naturally insisted on the "socialist" emphasis while Hitler and the party organization in general were less than enthusiastic about yielding to their demands.[12]

Table VI-7: Occupations of SA and SS Leaders and Members (in %)

	Middle echelon	Lower leaders	SA and SS members (incl. leaders)	Non-members	Abel sample
Military-civil servants	17.5	11.4	12.7	32.3	20.7
Business and professional men	11.1	13.3	11.9	14.3	13.1
White-collar employees	25.4	11.4	24.0	14.3	18.5
Blue-collar workers	39.7	47.7	42.0	16.6	33.1
Farmers	6.3	16.2	9.1	5.5	7.8
Women	—	—	.3	17.1	6.9
Totals	100.0	100.0	100.0	100.0	100.0

Between the stormtrooper leaders and followers, the differences seem to have been rather minor except for the unusual number of military-civil servants in the middle echelons, probably a small token of carry-over from military or Free Corps ranks into the stormtrooper leadership. At the highest levels of party and SA, as is well known, Free Corps and military officers of the highest rank were more frequent. But among the rank and file, the military-civil servant element clearly tended to be outside the stormtrooper organization. Lower and middle-echelon leaders also differ from each other in various ways: The lower leaders numbered more workers and farmers and the middle echelon favored military-civil servants and white-collar employees, true to the iron law of oligarchy.

The occupations of the respondents' fathers show that the last-mentioned differences are no coincidence. The *Sturmfuehrer* and *Sturmbannfuehrer* heavily tend to have military-civil servants or even high military officers as fathers while the *Scharfuehrer* and the like tend just as heavily to be the sons of workers or, to a lesser de-

[12] See especially Orlow, *History of the Nazi Party, 1919-1933*, chapter five.

gree, of artisans and farmers. Both leadership groups have a disproportionate number (22-23%) of respondents who had lost their
fathers before they reached maturity. Both groups also tend to be in
social decline, especially the middle echelons, while the lower leaders often made no attempt to rise above the station of their parents.
The non-stormtroopers were generally more upwardly mobile, especially from the countryside. Some middle-echelon leaders, just like
the stormtroopers at large, tended to be upwardly mobile from the
city proletariat, evidently a part of that second generation of
urbanites which we have observed throughout this book as particularly active and rebellious. The educational level attained, finally,
marks off the lower leaders as far below the average for the Abel
sample. Even the middle echelon barely holds its own. It appears
that it did not take much brains to lead the mindless sluggers of the
Nazi movement and that such leadership was often a compensation
for social decline or frustration.

Prior Group Memberships

In a movement dedicated to ideological reliability, did the stormtrooper leadership have to come from purer sources than the Nazi
membership at large? What about the small but conspicuous number of converts from the extreme left? Could they only become
street-fighters, but not the leaders of street-fighters? And what about
the SA recruits from among the quasi-military and Free Corps organizations? How dominant an element do they constitute at the different level of SA or SS leadership?

Disproportionate numbers of both leadership groups came from
quasi-military youth groups or youthful (25 or younger) membership in the Free Corps (25-29%) and from left-wing youth (7-10%).
The lower leaders also received more than their share (18.1%) of
recruits who after their first youth group joined a *voelkisch* organization prior to becoming Nazis. It could be true, however, that this
detour in their progress toward the NSDAP tended to set them back
in years so that they did not attain any higher rank before 1933. It
could also be true that their greater concern with ideology was a
hindrance among the cynical freebooters of the SA and SS. What
the two leadership groups liked best about their first youth group
was political violence, especially among the middle echelons, and
demonstrations among the lower leaders.

Over one-third of the middle-level stormtrooper leaders, as compared to one-fifth or fewer of the lower leaders and the stormtroopers at large, were in the Free Corps, vigilante, or other militant veterans' groups in 1919-1921. One-fourth of them was involved in

quasi-military or anti-occupation groups in 1922-1924. Interestingly, the middle echelon was less often in the pre-1925 *voelkisch* or Nazi movement than were the lower leaders, the stormtroopers in general, or even the non-stormtroopers. The overlapping periods and the role of the early NSDAP among the counter-revolutionary groups confused the picture somewhat. To clarify, 60.4% of the middle echelon, altogether, were involved in the Free Corps, vigilante, and other quasi-military organizations (*Wehrverbaende*) before 1923 as compared to only 19.7% of the lower leaders, 22.8% of all the stormtroopers, and 13% of the non-stormtroopers. There can be little doubt that the *Sturmfuehrer* and *Sturmbannfuehrer* of the sample tended to recruit themselves from the Free Corps and other counter-revolutionary, quasi-military groups and not from the pre-1925 *voelkisch* and Nazi movement. The middle echelons thus constitute the chief link between counter-revolution and the post-1924 NSDAP.

Table VI-8: Military Service of SA and SS Leaders and Members (in %)

	Middle echelon	Lower leaders	Immed. SA	Delayed SA	Grad. SS	Non-storm-troopers
Peacetime and war service	12.5	9.2	10.6	5.6	10.8	22.1
Wartime service only	39.3	26.5	28.4	29.6	21.6	35.9
No military service	48.2	64.3	61.0	64.8	67.6	42.0
Totals	100.0	100.0	100.0	100.0	100.0	100.0

This separate quasi-military strain also had more roots in war and prewar military experience than can be found among the lower leaders or the stormtroopers at large. Where the latter have nearly two-thirds who saw no military service at all, the middle echelon have less than half. Nevertheless, they are less representative of the vaunted "front generation" than are the non-stormtroopers who, of course, are also older than the middle-level leaders of the SA and SS.[13]

Beliefs and Attitudes of Stormtrooper Leaders

The stormtrooper leaders more often came from a home characterized by conflict between father and son, by *voelkisch*-antisemitic

[13] In the tabulation of "formative experiences," too, the middle echelon does not stand out for the war or counter-revolutionary experiences, as the non-stormtroopers do, but for alleged encounters with aliens or Jews and educational-literary influences.

views, or by conventional political loyalties than did the storm-troopers at large or the non-stormtroopers. In their school environment, too, they stressed the *voelkisch* element, especially among the lower leaders who frequently also report conflict with different school environments. Significant numbers of the middle echelons, however, also stressed the patriotic nature of their school environment as one would expect of former quasi-military fighters.

The stormtrooper leaders of both levels were naturally highly involved in violence. Two-thirds of them report such involvement, including one-fourth of the middle echelons, who during the end-phase of the republic were out campaigning and fighting "night-and-day." The lower leaders, like the stormtroopers in general, were somewhat more inclined to view violence as something done to them (masochistically). The middle echelon, as befits Free Corps officers, were noticeably more aggressive, sadistic bullies who had no great compunctions about a "merry civil war."

This violence-mindedness and belligerent attitude also makes itself felt in the reports of political friction. Disproportionate numbers of both leadership levels report having sought out friction and caused confrontations. The propensity for conflict and violence seems to form a syndrome that often goes back to conflict with the parents or with the school environments. In their attitudes towards their political enemies, also, the two leadership groups have unusually high proportions of those who use the language of the *outré* or whose sheer physical aggressiveness comes through in their *vitae.*

The eventual elitist ascendancy of the SS over the SA surfaced early in the distinction between the SS as special bodyguard corps as compared to the meeting-hall protection squads which were the primary function of the SA. When we cross the leadership categories with the different stormtrooper groups, both the instant and the delayed stormtroopers tend to be lower leaders. Only the SS men clearly tend to be of the middle echelon of *Sturmfuehrer* and *Sturmbannfuehrer.* Very few SS men in the sample, in fact, are without a rank (10.5%); nearly a third of the SA men are. This raises the question, among other things, of whether ideology had anything to do with these bifurcations in recruitment.

Unlike the stormtroopers at large, whose dominant ideological motives we have discussed above,[14] the middle echelons tend to believe mostly in the Hitler cult and the *Volksgemeinschaft.* The lower leaders are closer to the averages for the stormtroopers at large. They stress revanchism and superpatriotism or have no ideology

[14] See above, pp. 591 ff.

worth noting. Being more often of blue-collar or working-class origin, they also vent their spleen on the Marxists, while the middle echelon pick the "reactionaries" in their own social class as a target. The *Sturmfuehrer* and *Sturmbannfuehrer* are also more future-oriented. This is borne out by their expectations in 1934, when 41.5% of the middle echelons, as compared to 32.9% of the lower leaders, hope for German imperial expansion and for the totalitarian utopia within. The middle-echelons are evidently a power-hungry mob.

On the antisemitism scale, it will be recalled, the stormtroopers at large are relatively less prejudiced than the non-stormtroopers except for fully mobilized paranoids. The same is true with the stormtrooper leaders. The middle echelon, in particular, exceeds the averages at both extremes and is also heavily inclined toward xenophobia toward aliens in Germany. The lower leaders exhibit this prejudice in a less pronounced fashion and are otherwise relatively low in ethnocentricity. It remains for the non-stormtroopers to show, in addition to antisemitism, a great deal of chauvinism toward foreign nations, as one would expect of the war and prewar generations. Thus the stormtrooper movement appears not to be particularly nationalistic in the traditional sense, but rather xenophobic and integralistic.

Are the stormtrooper leaders authoritarians? No, they most heavily tend toward expressing hostility toward police and government, especially at the middle level. The lower level, which inclines more toward ideological thinking of a low caliber, identifies to a very high degree with the movement. The middle echelons are not quite that ready to merge their egocentric selves with the group, although many of them indulge in an extreme leadership cult. At this level, perhaps, Nazi leaders had developed the Goering syndrome of feeling that they were a law unto themselves.

THREE

The *Goetterdaemmerung* of the Weimar Republic

In the last years of the Weimar Republic, it was not only the economic despair of the Depression that reached a climax. Relatively unrelated to and hardly "caused" by the economic troubles, a mood of political despair and adventurism spread through the political parties from the right to the center. Weimar democracy and parliamentary government were written off in favor of authoritarian solutions by politicians, professors, and journalists who had until then given lip service in support of the republic. The hour of the Hugenbergs and von Papens had arrived and, irresponsibility was mistaken for charismatic leadership.

At that moment, the Nazi party, too, felt the uplifting winds of this change in the popular mood. After all, it had preached irresponsible adventure and dictatorship long before anyone else. As new recruits began pouring in at the grassroots level, however, there was an important difference as compared to the Weimar leaders of the right and center. The new Nazi recruits were much closer to the cutting edge of the Depression: Young workers who lost their jobs or had never found any, farmers hit by the agricultural crisis, shopkeepers unable to weather the storm, and many more living in constant fear of losing their livelihood. The party immediately strove to take advantage of the widespread malaise and, in particular, offered voluntary welfare services to stricken members, and bed and board in its *SA-Heime* to young toughs willing to fight its battles "night and day." The rapid succession of electoral battles in 1932, moreover, involved even activists who still had their job in "day-and-night fighting" in the sense of constant proselytizing and propaganda on the job, marching and fighting during every waking hour, and getting very little sleep during the peak periods of the struggle. True to the old German soldier song "*Was schert mich Weib, was schert mich Kind, sollen sie betteln gehen, wenn sie hungrig sind . . .*,"[1] the day-and-nighters neglected family and job in their

---

[1] "Who cares about his wife; who cares about his child. Let them go begging if they are hungry . . ." This line was quoted or paraphrased by several respondents.

abandon to the all-out Nazi struggle for the stakes of power. They were carried away by the *Goetterdaemmerung* of the Weimar Republic, fighting against what they took to be the evil gods of Weimar, the ruin of Germany, and unaware of what they themselves were bringing upon the country.

Reported Activities in the Nazi Party

Let us take a closer look at the phenomenon of the day-and-night fighters and how they differ from other Nazis. To be sure, we have already categorized and discussed Nazi activities within the framework of the four stages of extremist escalation. This present measurement of reported Nazi activities (FD-67) has a somewhat different focus from the categories of stage four. With the latter, we attempted to winnow out three plausible combinations (MF, MP, and MFP) of the three "quintessential extremist activities," marching, fighting, and proselytizing. This time we are more interested in obtaining a scale of increasing involvement from mere electioneering to campaigning "day and night" in 1931-1932. The day-and-nighters naturally constitute a kind of spearhead among the various kinds of street fighters (both MFs and MFPs) who have dropped everything else in their lives, friendships, social, family, and job obligations, in order to be completely a part of the Nazi struggle for power.

FD-67: Reported Activities in the Nazi Party

	Number	*Per cent*
1) Electioneering only	95	13.5
2) Marches, rallies only	46	6.6
3) Individual provocation, speech-making only	27	3.8
4) Proselytizing	229	32.6
5) Streetfights, *Saalschlacht*	37	5.3
6) Combination 1, 2, 5	162	23.1
7) Same combination "day and night"	22	3.1
8) Combination 1-5 "day and night"	40	5.7
9) Combination 1, 2, 4	44	6.3
Totals	702*	100.0

* Multiple responses.

The MF-MP-MFP categories of stage four and our new categories overlap to a degree. Seventy-one and two-fifths percent of the MFs and 56.7% of the MFPs are among our new electioneering-demonstrations-street-fighting groups (5), (6) (7) and (8). But the MFPs have more day-and-nighters (19.4%) than the MFs (11.5%), and they also include a substantial number (33.1%) of provocateurs-proselytizers (3) and (4). By the same token, nearly half of the MPs are in that last-mentioned category of provocation and proselytizing, while the mere marchers (M) are concentrated among the electioneers-demonstrators (1), (2), and (9). Our chief interests will be to contrast the day-and-nighters to the less involved groups.

A typical day-and-nighter was the "son of a genuine Prussian civil servant," namely of a Catholic teacher, born 1900 (no. 22), studying to be a teacher himself. Resentful of the "revolution" and the republic, the respondent joined the anti-republican DNVP in 1920 and, in 1921, the *Schutz-und-Trutzbund* "because it was anti-semitic and I regarded the Jews as the cause of the revolt of 1918." Like many other graduates of teachers' colleges in those days, he could not find an opening for many years and in the meantime became a blue-collar worker in a lock factory. Thus he experienced the life and political views of the "red" working-classes and found himself regarded with suspicion both by his fellow-workers and by the bourgeois Nationalists (DNVP) and his *voelkisch* friends. In 1922, he attended a Nazi rally at which he became enthralled with the oratorical talents of Hermann Esser and joined, even though there was no NSDAP organization anywhere in his area. He had lost his factory job "as a consequence of leaving the DNVP" and became a railroad worker. In 1923, he had to leave town because of a collision with the occupation. Later the occupation jailed him for three months and then expelled him for involvement with the resistance. He took odd jobs and, as soon as the NSDAP was re-established in 1925, reported to the nearest *Gauleitung*. After his first major and very turbulent rally in 1926, "three years of the most tiring struggle set in which demanded financial as well as psychological sacrifices of every comrade. Night after night, leaflets for which we ourselves had to pay had to be distributed. Every month there was a rally . . . which always gave our little local of 5-10 men 60 marks of debts since no innkeeper would rent us a hall without advance payment."

> In those days it was a matter of course that every new party comrade had to be a fighter and therefore had to join the SA right away. And these party comrades and SA men had to be used at all the rallies in Oldenburg and Bremen as well. At one rally in Bremen . . . we had 35 men from Bremen, 12 from here, and 18 from Oldenburg . . . the entire SA of the Oldenburg province, and we had to face a superior foe of 400-500 Marxists. It was 45 kilometres from the city of Oldenburg, 15 kilometres from here, and all this by bicycle. . . .

The respondent describes how the party gradually established bases and locals around his own red-dominated town toward the day of the final assault. At first, only manual workers and farmers joined the movement, he explains, until the Young Plan campaign of 1929 drew in *Stahlhelm* members and increasingly bourgeois circles. In 1929, after seven years of waiting, he was finally offered a teaching position and devoted himself faithfully to this career for over a year. "But the longing to be an active fighter again became stronger and in 1931, when day after day our brave SA men were being truncheoned, I simply could not resist any longer and went back to active service." Since as a teacher he was not allowed to belong to this subversive organization, he became a roving Nazi speaker under a false name. After less than a year he was recognized and threatened not only with the loss of his job but with excommunication by the Catholic Church. However, he persisted in his speeches against the Center party and the threats appear not to have been carried out. He even founded a chapter of the Nazi Teachers' Federation (NSLB) in his area.

Another example of "day-and-night" fighting is a young farm worker, born 1909 (no. 126), from Lower Saxony with a great urge to join the cavalry. The cavalry would not take him "because of a weak eye (left)." He observed the political scene with a jaundiced eye, resentful of the republican government and wishing that there be "only one party which gets rid of all the other parties and represents all the occupations." In 1930 he became aware of the expanding activities of the NSDAP and went to several of its rallies. He induced his father to subscribe to a Nazi newspaper and, during a prolonged bout of illness, read much of the literature of the party. "It left a lasting impression on me, even though I had at first viewed the party with suspicion."

"Here and there in the fatherland," he knew, "SA men were murdered, stabbed, assaulted, and knocked down." Nevertheless he announced to his parents upon recovery

that my place was in the SA to help save my terribly threatened fatherland from its internal enemies. . . . The existing NSDAP groups multiplied and grew, rallies and other meetings became more and more frequent, and the terror against us more potent all the time. Often there were meeting-hall battles which were mostly started by the SPD and KPD members in order to suppress Nazi rallies and to render the NSDAP harmless. The SA of the protection squads, *always in the minority*, bitterly resisted their efforts. The discipline of the SA, *its external behavior and appearance* caused me and several comrades to join both the party and the SA. . . . (italics supplied)

Now the fight began even in our peaceful village. The SPD men started to taunt us, tease us, call us the most shameful names. We did not let it bother us. I became a political leader and did my duty as an SA man. I was on the road nearly every night, in part to serve as a stormtrooper, in part to go to political meetings and rallies outside of town or to propagandize in the village. We had to win over the misled people to our idea, our ideology. Sometimes the police (which was always present) disbanded our rallies or outlawed them. But the greater the terror, the more our fighting spirit grew. The [Nazi] press, periodicals, speeches all planted national socialism deeper in me. Just before the frequent elections, our hardest work set in. We propaganized the misled people, pointed out their "fine labor leaders," showered leaflets and newspapers on all houses in the village, glued up posters and strung banners across the streets.

Having once more insisted that "all the brawls were always started by the opponents," the respondent signed himself a *Rottenfuehrer* of the SA.

An unusual case is a miller's second son, born 1904 (no. 19), who was full of social resentments because he had to make his way as a laborer among Marxist workers and condescending bourgeois employers. He reports conflicts with Communists even before he joined the party in 1928.

I received membership no. 128425 and immediately became active. I thought of one thing only: Either we win and gain the rights of labor or Bolshevism wins out and chaos comes. They soiled my place at work, sabotaged me, raised suspicions against me, denounced me with the boss, and attacked me with chairs and benches in the common room. . . . These terrorizing acts and the weeks before the major elections formed the high points.

We can read his unstable state of mind between the lines.

Our victory depended on whether or not we got the workers. Hence we had to organize the struggle in the factories even if the red mob might kill us. In March 1930 I and [another man] were the first to build up the NSBO in the Ruhr area. Even the oldest fighters who had never shied away from confrontation with the red rabble did not want to join the fight in the factories. Very, very slowly we gained a foothold. The national NBSO office was established only in January of 1931. We in the Ruhr industrial area were just a few dozen among millions. We would run off leaflets by night and distribute them the next morning. In part we had to rely on unemployed comrades since we had to work.

The respondent once received a head injury in a Communist rally which he had probably invaded as a provocateur.

> Then came the fighting year, 1932. Elections after elections rained upon us. We had no money, while our opponents were loaded. We ran off handbills and banners and held many small meetings. I was put up as a candidate . . . for the *Reichstag* in 1932. I had to work the night shift the week before the elections. Working at night, organizing propaganda during the day, I slept about twelve hours during the entire week. The political criminal police [sic] paid me two visits. They searched the apartment but found nothing.

In August of 1932, the respondent had a nervous breakdown but remained active.[2]

There are many other cases in which a respondent tells how "day and night we went through the industrial area from rally to rally [as protective squads]" (no. 12, born 1898).

A final example is a day-and-nighter who gives a telling picture of the atmosphere among the stormtroopers (no. 5, born 1908). He tells of his patriotic education and of his years with the DNVP until, in 1930, he joined the NSDAP out of a sudden impulse of indignation about a police order closing down a Nazi rally. "The difference between the DNVP and the NSDAP . . . became clear to me right away. There was a very different air. When I reported for my first SA service and addressed my *Sturmfuehrer* with 'Sir,' he gave me an answer I cannot repeat here. But I liked it so much that I became convinced I was in the right outfit." The respondent tells how his opponents tried to prevail upon his fiancée to leave him or to make him leave the movement, and how he was denounced as "a Nazi, a murderer of workers," and harassed economically.

> The terror in the streets increased. They had found out that they could not silence us by ignoring us. . . . Very rarely did they manage to get one or the other stormtrooper to want to quit . . . those were usually people who had joined us for some reason other than fanatical enthusiasm for our idea. I liked it better every day. Now I really got to know the spirit of comradeship. Many people I once had rejected as inferior I now found serving in the ranks, and I learned to appreciate them. I learned in practice the truth that birth and estate mean nothing and merit everything.

[2] About 12 of the respondents report having suffered similar lapses as a result of the struggle and 22 report hospitalization. Another eight suffered nervous breakdowns in the war and 32 report poor health as a result of the war. There is no way of estimating the number of unreported nervous crises.

I soon became accustomed to the many propaganda rallies where we had to serve as protective squads, the marches and demonstrations which led us through the streets of our hometown or neighboring towns, and the howling of the enemies and the quiet enthusiasm of our adherents. I could not imagine a life without them. I became so used to it in fact that I more and more lost contact with my old friends. They had become strangers to me and no longer understood me either. They thought that I would in time come back to spending convivial evenings with them as I once used to do every night and considered it odd that I had no time for these pleasures any more. . . .

Thus I had soon lost all contacts of my earlier years and knew only one thing, the NSDAP and its goals. My wife—it was 1931 and I had gotten married meanwhile—often anxiously tried to persuade me to quit at least the SA. It was in vain. I had gotten so deeply into it that I simply could not break away. I took part in the great SA rally of October 1931 in Braunschweig[3] and came back more fanatical than ever. *I had seen the size of the movement, its coiled power, and nothing could wean me away.* I never missed an SA service and could not have forgiven myself if I had ever neglected my duty once I knew it. (italics supplied)

Like a man possessed, the respondent's enthusiasm carried him to poetic heights. But there can be little doubt that he sincerely felt this way.

Meanwhile, the year 1932 arrived and one election chased the other. Presidential, *Reichstag, Landtag* elections, God knows what, . . . We gained with every election. Ever more comrades joined us. The pressure of the enemy increased but so did our strength. I had become the drum major and felt so richly rewarded that I would not have wanted to exchange places with anyone. Often, when something special was going on, the *Sturm* was waiting in my apartment. I had become the Nazi-Wilmskoetter [respondent's name]. Bruening outlawed the uniforms and disbanded the SA. Our apartments were searched and we were watched every step of the way. I was supposed to give up my flag—they never got it. The Communists were lying in waiting when I came home late at night and I had to resort to detours. My wife cried whenever I left, begging me to think of our child. I did think of him. I wanted to give him a better fatherland than my father had been able to leave me.

[3] For six hours, over 100,000 SA and SS men paraded past Hitler. It had taken 40 special trains and 5,000 trucks to take them there. See Ernst-August Roloff, *Buergertum und Nationalsozialismus 1930-1933, Braunschweigs Weg ins Dritte Reich*, Hannover: Verlag fuer Literatur und Zeitgeschehen, 1961.

Carried away by this consuming passion of his life, the respondent seems to be a good example of the drawing power of the Nazi movement. He ended up a propaganda director of his *Ortsgruppe*, a function for which he seemed indeed to possess the skill. He was one of the rare old fighters who did not express bitter resentment against the flood of new members who sought to jump on the bandwagon in 1933. We are left to wonder, though, whether he did not also suffer withdrawal symptoms once the romantic struggle for power ended and he had to settle for a more pedestrian life.

There are some similarities between this extremist passion and certain aspects of drug addiction, both in their social aspects and in their individual motivations and rewards.[4] It is the combination of "comradeship" and the sense of personal integration derived from the struggle or from the pursuit of utopia which "turned on" these Nazi activists. Given the availability of more intense activities, many showed a craving for heavier and heavier doses of the stimulant. There may have been some "bad trips," that is, negative experiences with the Nazis or encounters with the police or the Communists. And there were also overdose crises such as mental or physical breakdowns as a consequence of ever-increasing involvement. The coming to power of the NSDAP put an unexpected end to the struggle activities, leaving many an old fighter high and dry. The sudden withdrawal may well have figured in the personal problems and embarrassing conduct of many an activist in 1933-1934. It may also have played a role among their motives for writing a *vita* for Professor Abel.

A Social Profile of Nazi Activity Groups

Which generations are most heavily represented among the various activity groups? More than half of the street-fighting groups (5), (6), (7) and (8) belong to the postwar generation. The day-and-nighters among them differ from the other street-fighters in having fewer victory-watchers (born 1902-1905) and more from the sec-

[4] See also the study of the Jesus Movement, "Mainlining Jesus: The New Trip," *Transaction*, Spring 1972, pp. 50-56, by Robert Lynn Adams and Robert Jon Fox, who found that 62% of their respondents over 18 and 44% under 18 had used narcotics and three-fourths had also been in the peace movement prior to becoming "Jesus people." To these "drug-and-peace" respondents, the authors argue, their new religious and politically conservative involvement is the functional equivalent of their earlier involvement with drugs and radical politics which they could henceforth do without.

ond youth revolt (1906-1916), fewer prewar and more members of the war generation (35.5%) among them. The groups that engaged only in electioneering and the provocateurs-proselytizers are distinctly older, with about one-half each in the prewar generation.

In their location experiences, the day-and-nighters tend to be living in small or medium-sized towns and not to have moved from the place of their birth. Quite a few of them also come from the occupied areas (as do the other street-fighters) or from the border areas in the east. The groups involved only in electioneering and demonstrations, by way of contrast, have a high proportion of highly mobile respondents. As compared to the immobility of the day-and-nighters and the many rural-urban migrants among the other street-fighters, high mobility appears to go with less involvement in violence.

As to occupation, the day-and-nighters tend to be blue-collar workers or in business or the professions. The other street-fighters are even more heavily blue-collar or else white-collar employees. Military-civil servants, by comparison, are far more likely to be provocateurs, proselytizers, or simply engaged in electioneering. Their contribution to Nazi street violence is minor. The day-and-nighters tend to be either static or upwardly mobile from the urban proletariat. They do not seem to share the conspicuous concentration of respondents in social decline among the other street-fighters and among the electioneers and demonstrators. Neither is there among the day-and-nighters the heavy component of upwardly mobile respondents from a farm background typical of the older groups. In other words, they bear some resemblance to the "portrait of a race rioter" in the United States in the 60s.

The economic fortunes of the respondents during the Weimar Republic reveal one of the conditions essential to day-and-nighting as compared to other forms of violent behavior. Two-thirds of the day-and-nighters were either unemployed or bankrupt during the Depression (41.8%) or even before 1929 (23.9%). The other street-fighters had only 44% (including 28% due to the Depression) such economic casualties, a figure not very different from that of the demonstrators-and-electioneers. With the older groups, the electioneers and provocateurs-proselytizers, the economic casualty rate drops to 30.1% and 36.3%, respectively. We have to remind ourselves, however, that there is no simple cause-and-effect relation between political extremism and economic misfortune. Whether a very active respondent loses his job because of his hyperactivity or whether he steps up his activity after the loss of his job for lack of something better to do remains beyond the reach of our method of analysis. The respondents certainly cannot reliably tell us.[5]

Youth Settings and Day-and-Night Fighting

What sort of youth organizational background and attitudes might be responsible for the high pitch of political exaltation that seems to lie behind day-and-night fighting? How does it compare with the rest of the violent Nazis? The day-and-night fighters tend heavily to come from paramilitary (including Free Corps) youthful associations. Many of them also came from *Jungdo* or other bourgeois youth groups, or changed to another *voelkisch* group before becoming Nazi, an indication of ideological commitment. Paramilitary youth backgrounds and converts from left-wing youth are prominent among the other street-fighters.

In their attitudes toward their first youth organization, the day-and-nighters heavily stress the spirit of comradeship and sports or cultural appreciation as the things they liked best. Demonstrations run a poor third among the day-and-nighters and second among the other street-fighters, whose first choice was violence. The impression, then, emerges that it is the other street-fighters, with their early liking for violence and their violent revolutionary and counter-revolutionary antecedents, who are more specifically oriented toward physical violence as a purpose in itself. The day-and-nighters rather seem oriented toward the struggle of the movement for victory, and their violence is a function of that struggle rather than a purpose in itself. Consequently, they tend heavily to be politically militarized youths, while among the other street-fighters there is an equal tendency to be hostile militants.[6]

This ideological-mainstream quality of the day-and-night groups is confirmed further by other indicators. Unlike such violent groups as the instant stormtroopers, for example, the day-and-nighters have far less than their share of respondents whose fathers died before they were 18 years old. Their fathers tend to be *voelkisch*, unpolitical, or in conflict with the respondent. The other street-

[5] Disproportionate numbers of day-and-nighters, indeed, are on record for having gone out of their way in seeking out political friction, far more in proportion than report friction in the family, at school, or having been fired or boycotted for political reasons.

[6] Both groups were equally involved in youthful street-fighting, but the other street-fighters far more often participated in organized (Free Corps) violence, while the day-and-nighter tended to engage only in demonstrations and electioneering in their younger years.

fighters, by comparison, often have militaristic or also *voelkisch* fathers.

The childhood settings of both the day-and-nighters and the other street-fighters, finally, tend to be disciplinarian (10-13%) or, in the case of the day-and-nighters only, economically secure and sheltered (27.7%). What could possibly drive a young man from a sheltered bourgeois home into the thick of day-and-night fighting is a question only an observer of contemporary youth revolt movements may be able to answer. In the case of the Nazi day-and-nighters, the current theories of bourgeois guilt feelings hardly provide an adequate explanation.

Unlike the other street-fighters and the most involved stormtrooper groups, the day-and-nighters tended to join the NSDAP either before 1925 or in the two-year period from mid-1929 to mid-1931. Thus they are not part of the conspicuous bulk of the other street-fighters, who joined mostly between 1925 and mid-1929. The day-and-nighters also tend to have been introduced to the party by friends or fellow-workers rather than through attendance at rallies like the other street-fighters. At the time they joined, finally, both the day-and-nighters and the other violent group were far younger than any of the other groups. One in five of the violent groups joined before he was 21 and nearly half before the age of 26. Only 13.4% of the day-and-nighters were older than 35 when they joined the NSDAP. The provocateurs-proselytizers, by way of contrast, had only one-fourth who had joined before the age of 26 and almost half over the age of 35.

Only negligible portions of the day-and-nighters and the other street-fighters were not in the SA or SS (6-7%), a description fitting one-third to two-thirds of the other groups. It should be noted, however, that the other street-fighters were more often instant stormtroopers or SS men than the day-and-nighters, who tended to be delayed stormtroopers. The reason appears once more to have been an element of deliberateness and ideological commitment among the day-and-night fighters. They also tended to hold more of the higher stormtrooper ranks than did the other street-fighters, of whom a larger percentage held a rank in the SA or SS. In their attitude toward the Nazi movement, both violent groups differ sharply from the rest in their stress on a sense of personal integration through the struggle and on the satisfactions of classless comradeship in the movement. As we said earlier, these are the hallmarks of the Nazi addiction. The day-and-night fighters emphasize these angles even more than do the other street-fighters and, moreover, tend to expect material rewards or jobs for their pains. This expectation may have been due more to their high rate of unemployment or bankruptcy than to their mercenary character. The other street-fighters, by way of contrast, may have felt that their engagement in violence was its own reward.

Beliefs and Attitudes

In what way do the beliefs and attitudes of the day-and-nighters differ from the other street-fighters, not to mention the other groups? In their main ideological themes, the day-and-nighters tend to be Nordic-German romantics or superpatriots, again typical mainstream themes. The other street-fighters are mostly revanchists, Hitler cultists, or have no ideology worth noting, except perhaps a stereotypical anti-Marxism. On the antisemitism scale, both violent groups are relatively low in prejudice when we compare them to the electioneers or the provocateurs-proselytizers. Nevertheless, nearly one-fourth of the day-and-nighters are paranoid antisemites, far more than in any other group. Their day-and-night fighting, in other words, may well have been the acting-out of severely disturbed minds.

Are these differences also reflected in other attitudinal measurements? In their attitudes toward political violence, both violent groups stand out with expressions of deep emotional involvement with violence. But the day-and-nighters are proportionately more often sadistic bullies, while the other street-fighters tend toward feeling sorry for themselves and making excuses. Ideology and prejudice, in other words, supply enough rationalization for the violent behavior of the day-and-nighters so that they need not feel guilty. In their attitudes toward their political enemies, on the other hand, it is the other street-fighters who tend to call them "subhuman," rodents, etc., or whose physical aggressiveness even shines through their descriptions of their antagonists. Describing the enemy in the language of the *outré*, of course, is also a rationalization of violence toward him. The day-and-nighters typically prefer to call them traitors or a conspiracy. We are evidently dealing here with two rather different attitudes toward violent involvement with an enemy: (1) the rationalizations of masochism and dehumanization of the enemy, and (2) ideology and prejudice together with aggressiveness released from all restraints by delusions of conspiracy.

What kind of people were these day-and-nighters and the other street-fighters? The day-and-nighters have far and away the largest proportion of respondents (60% as compared to 15-23%) who had no other family member in the NSDAP. Day-and-night fighting was evidently an outlet for loners. The other street-fighters were the very opposite in this respect. Over half of them, more than any other group, had more or less their whole family in the movement. Violence to them was a family affair.

One out of five in both groups was a "dimwit" or romantic rather out of touch with the political realities of Weimar. But the day-and-nighters also had more than their share of politically very well-informed comrades, while a low, ideological type of political intelligence predominated among the other street-fighters. Both groups tended to exhibit great hostility toward police and government authority and yet also a preoccupation with law and order. Their most salient formative experience was that of youthful comradeship, and they found a sense of security in close identification with the movement to the point of self-negation.

Dominant Local Political Force

Political opinion in a context of modern popular government largely develops in dialectical interplay with the dominant political forces of a given locality. Many of the Abel respondents report whether their town or part of town was dominated by the "reds," the "blacks" (Center party), the "reactionaries" (especially DNVP or *Stahlhelm*), or a particular mixture of these Weimar groups. Since their own ideology was not exactly a potent, cohesive faith, the nature of their revolt tended to be strongly colored according to whether they were revolting against the Socialist or Communist control over the workers, the Center party's alleged misuse of Catholic solidarity, or the conservative hold on bourgeoisie and Protestant peasantry. This is a simplified picture of the complexity of Weimar politics, but the question is worth closer examination with respect to our data.

Our breakdown (FD-27) shows that more than half of the respondents who give this information were living in an environment dominated by Socialists or Communists. Other substantial numbers

FD-27: Dominant Local Political Force

	Number	Per cent
KPD, USPD	18	6.5
SPD, KPD	138	49.8
⌐ SPD alone (or with DDP, DVP)	7	2.5
├ SPD with Center (or Center with KPD)	52	18.8
└ Center (or BVP)	23	8.3
⌐ DNVP (or agricultural party), *Stahlhelm*	37	13.4
└ Other	2	0.7
	277	100.0

were in a Centrist environment, probably in a Catholic area[7] such as the Rhineland, or in a conservative, Protestant area of the rural north or northeast. Many of those in a Centrist area were in the French-occupied territory and often in rural areas. Borderland respondents and rural-urban migrants were most likely to report an SPD-KPD-dominated environment, chiefly of a metropolitan nature.

There is also an age and occupational dimension to this breakdown in that some of these revolts were more youth-related or occupation-related than others. The most youthful were those who revolted against a KPD-USPD environment, and next, against Centrist and other moderate persuasions. The former have a strong war generation and victory-watcher component, which suggests the nature of the sentiments behind their anti-revolutionary attitude. The anti-Centrists and anti-moderates were probably motivated more by the presence of the occupation than by Youth Movement sentiments. The anti-conservatives and those complaining about an SPD-KPD environment are the oldest of the lot. As for occupation, the typical anti-Socialist or anti-Communist Nazi was a blue-collar worker and not well-educated. However, some respondents reporting a heavily Communist or Socialist environment also came in significant numbers from well-off bourgeois homes. The anti-Centrists were often from well-off bourgeois homes. Anti-conservatives tended to be farmers, women, or military-civil servants. The anti-Centrists were often from a poverty-stricken, orphaned, or disciplinarian background. Nevertheless, they tended to be among the first to join (local founders), while the anti-conservatives mostly waited until the bandwagon was well under way.

The Four Stages and Local Politics

It is instructive to see how the four local political settings differ in their patterns of individual political mobilization. The small group that claimed to be surrounded by the extreme left tended to be in prewar parties or in left-wing youth itself at stage one. At stage two (militarization) the typical anti-Communist was in the *Wehrwolf* or a *voelkisch* action group including the early NSDAP. He tended to enter stage two either before the age of 21 or after 35, and for such reasons as his antisemitic predisposition or his opposition to the revolutionaries. At stage three he tended to be in a moderate party or to vote for the early *voelkisch* parties. He entered this stage between the ages of 18 and 25 and owed his politicization to coming

---

[7] As many as half of these respondents in fact indicate that they are Catholics; only one in ten says he is a Protestant.

of voting age or to economic misfortune. In either stage he was the most likely to engage in individual or organized political violence and demonstrations of any group. Half of this group became marcher-fighters (MFs) at stage four, which half of them entered between the ages of 18 and 30. Their immediate motives for becoming Nazis tended to be the comradeship of the stormtroopers and, of course, the "rough opposition" of the Communists.

The much larger group in SPD-KPD dominated areas tended to be "unpolitical" military-civil servants or traditionals at stage one. At stage two, they were in large numbers in *voelkisch* action groups, the *Wehrwolf*, or in the Free Corps. They became militarized mostly between the ages of 25 and 35, motivated by the impact of the lost war and their own antisemitic tendencies. At stage three, like the first-mentioned group, they tended to be in *voelkisch* or moderate parties, but on the average at a more advanced age, their motives being again the lost war and the occupation, or economic troubles. Their middle-stage activities were more likely to be limited to electioneering and demonstrations. At stage four, despite their being generally over 30 and frequently over 40, they numbered many MF's and quite a few provocateurs. Their most prevalent reason for joining was also the physical opposition of the KPD.

The respondents who report that the Center party and other moderate parties such as the SPD, DDP, or DVP dominated the local scene present a rather different picture. Unpolitical traditionals or members of the Youth Movement at stage one, they tended to be in the *Stahlhelm* or Free Corps at a very early age, if indeed they ever went through stage two (60.5% did not). Their motives for militarization were the shock of the occupation or of the alleged revolution. At stage three, this group again played a very limited role except for expressing strong distrust of political parties of which they became aware early, motivated by coming of age and by their opposition to the Marxist "revolution." In spite of its limited participation in the middle stages, this group was quite involved in violence and demonstrations. But once they became Nazis, again they were more likely to be marchers (M) or marcher-proselytizers (MP). They tended to be either under 25 or over 35, and were motivated largely by friction with the occupation or by economic or agricultural troubles. It should be obvious by now that this group coincides rather well with a well-known state of mind among certain parts of the Weimar bourgeoisie and peasantry.

The last group, the respondents facing an environment dominated by the DNVP or the *Stahlhelm*, tended to be unpolitical military-civil servants or prepolitical parochials at stage one. At stage two, beginning somewhere between the ages of 18 and 35, they might have been with the *Stahlhelm* or *Jungdo*, mobilized by the shock of the defeat or the revolution. At stage three they tended to be in the DNVP or still shopping around, a stage started generally after the age of 25 and for reasons such as economic trouble or opposition to the Weimar leaders. In this group then, the Nazi revolt against the DNVP and the *Stahlhelm* starts within these organizations, not from the outside. Except for some individual violent encounters, their middle-stage activities are limited to attending meetings, electioneering, and holding minor offices. When the defectors join the NSDAP, nevertheless, they supply a considerable number of MFPs (29.3%) and MPs (26.8%) although almost one-third of them were no more active than merely holding membership. Their ages of joining, with more than half over 30, indeed make them the oldest group. Their prevalent motives are the economic or agricultural troubles, the "dynamic impression" of the Nazi movement, and their ideological fervor. They too constitute an easily recognized group from the *Stahlhelm* and the DNVP.

These four groups also differ in when they tended to join the party. The group in a Communist-Independent-Socialist environment tended to join the pre-1925 NSDAP, when the extreme left was still something of a menace, or between 1925 and the 1930 elections. The anti-Centrist and anti-conservative groups, by comparison, tended to join only after mid-1929, or even after mid-1931, as the bandwagon was merrily rolling along. The respondents in an SPD-KPD environment were more evenly distributed over the time spectrum. The differences also show up in how they were introduced to the party. The anti-Communists were typically introduced by friends or fellow-workers, the respondents in an SPD-KPD area by relatives. The anti-Centrists were taken in when they went to a Nazi rally or saw a demonstration. The DNVP or *Stahlhelm* defectors, finally, became aware first of the Nazi ideology and propaganda. The last-mentioned group thus was the most motivated by ideology, or so it seems.

Ideology and Attitudes

If the groups motivated by such different antagonists really went by such differing routes to the brown movement, we would expect them also to exhibit the corresponding differences in ideology and attitudes. The DVNP and *Stahlhelm* defectors, indeed, tend to be Nordic-German romantics, Hitler-worshippers, and superpatriots. Of these, only the cult of Hitler would have taken them out of the conservative fold. The anti-Centrists stress the *Volksgemeinschaft* and superpatriotism, an emphasis that can easily be related to their poverty background and the occupation experience. The respondents from SPD-KPD-dominated areas tend to be revanchists or Hitler-worshippers, and of course anti-Marxist just like the anti-Centrists hate Catholics, liberals, and reactionaries. The anti-Communists are also mostly revanchists, but also antisemites and Nordic-German romantics in their main themes of ideology. The latter group is also the most ethnocentric and the most antisemitic, with over one-third paranoid. The large group from SPD-KPD areas is next in antisemitism.

The degree to which these groups joined the stormtroopers as well as the NSDAP declines sharply from the anti-Communists (82.4%) and anti-Socialists (66.9%) to the anti-Centrists (51.9%) and anti-conservatives (41.7%). In their attitude toward violence, however, the fewer members of a group are involved, the more they tend to be sadistic bullies. The highly involved anti-Communists are more often masochistic in their self-pity and insistence that violence is something imposed on them. They also tend more toward using the language of the *outré* in referring to their enemies.

The level of political knowledge is highest among the defectors from the DNVP and *Stahlhelm*-dominated areas. The anti-Centrists are next, although their thinking tends to be rather highly colored by an ideological cast. The two anti-Marxists groups abound in "dimwits" and witless romantics. The anti-conservatives and anti-Centrists tend to suffer from high cultural shock and alienation. The two anti-Marxist groups, finally, far outrank them in paranoia and irrationality, and in the desire to merge completely with the movement.

In their expectations in 1934, it is the anti-conservatives and anti-Centrists who show the most longing for the 1000-year *Reich* and its totalitarian leader cult and purges. The anti-Communists hope more for social and economic recovery, and the respondents from SPD-KPD territory for individual pay-offs. The two anti-Marxist groups and the anti-conservatives also set their hopes in the resurgence of German imperialism in Europe.

Attitudes Toward the Movement

The reader will recall many accounts which mirror the kinds of personal satisfactions the Abel respondents got out of belonging to the movement. A sense of personal integration, a sense of followership or of comradeship, or a job are the general categories we could pinpoint (FD-63). The respondents from a KPD-USPD-dominated area, for example, tended to derive a sense of personal integration from the struggle itself, or to get their satisfaction from the classless comradeship of the movement, or from the expectation of an individual reward, a promotion or a job. The anti-Centrists and anti-conservatives, by way of contrast, derived their sense of personal integration from the utopian vision. These categories help us to order the somewhat contradictory categories suggested by the other measurements in this section.

FD-63: Attitude toward Nazi Movement

	Number	*Per cent*
Hitler or other leadership cult	162	19.6
Classless comradeship	180	21.8
Integration per struggle	92	11.2
Integration per utopia	338	40.8
Expects, received job	54	6.6
	826*	100.0

* Multiple responses.

There are glaring generational differences among these attitude groups. The job-hunters are by far the oldest, with 48.1% born before 1895. The utopians are next-oldest, with 42% of the same vintage. Those integrated by the struggle, the fighters, are the youngest, with over one half born after 1901 and over three-fourths in 1895 or later. Those satisfied with the classless comradeship of the movement are nearly that young. And those who like to follow a leader, the born followers, are in between. The action in the Nazi movement was obviously with youth, and the accent in descending order on fighting, comradeship, and following the leader, rather than on utopia. The two older groups also tend to be concentrated in Berlin, while the fighters are more at home in medium-sized cities, and the good comrades and followers are often rural.

By occupation, the fighters tend to be blue-collar workers. Comradeship is the chief satisfaction of farmers, workers, and white-collar workers. Women and the children of military men stand out among the born followers. Military-civil servants tend to be utopians, and business and professional people are the most pay-off-minded, although the military-civil servants and farmers are not far behind in this either.

The social-mobility patterns of these groups are also instructive. The fighters tend to be socially static—which hardly fits into any theory of fascism. The upwardly mobile from a farm background are mostly utopians. The upwardly mobile from the urban proletariat typically expect a pay-off or they are good followers. Respondents in social decline tend to prize the classless comradeship of the movement most, perhaps out of a great longing for acceptance.

The struggle-oriented respondents delineate a politically violent personality quite different from others we have examined in this chapter. Let us take a look at their youthful background and special personal features, in contrast to the good comrades and the followers. As their first youthful association, the struggling fighters typically were in a Free Corps, vigilante, or militant veterans' group, which underlines their youthful liking for violence. They were indeed far more involved in partisan street fighting (40.2%) and organized violence (20.7%) before the age of 25 than any of the other groups, although they had the smallest number of veterans among them. The comradeship-oriented, by comparison, were more likely with *Jungdo* or *Stahlhelm*, or had joined the Hitler Youth (HJ) or SA directly. They preferred youthful "togetherness," hiking, and demonstrations, and engaged in far less street violence, although they included large numbers of wartime veterans and victory-watchers. The *Fronterlebnis*, in fact, was one of their salient formative experiences and many of their number suffered a severe cultural shock in 1918. The leadership-oriented, in turn, were with a left-wing or a conservative youth group (DNVP or DHV) or directly joined HJ or SA. They liked marching with a purpose and comradeship best, and engaged mostly in demonstrations, electioneering, and proselytizing in their young days. They frequently belonged to the pre-1925 NSDAP or *voelkisch* groups. All three of these groups included many politically militarized youths. The fighters had the largest number as well as a disproportionate share of hostile militants, while the other two tended to include more fully politicized youths.

Their childhoods differ less, except with regard to the politics of their parents. All three groups tend to come from economically secure, but sheltered, home backgrounds. The fighters also include a number of respondents who grew up in poverty, while the other two have a contingent of orphans (15%). Poverty and violence apparently go together, and so do the dependency needs of the fatherless with comradeship and leadership. The freewheeling childhoods are more typical of the pay-off-minded or the utopians. As for their parents' politics, the fighters tended to have militaristic, *voelkisch*, or politically moderate fathers, or to have been in conflict with their fathers. The front-generation comrades had unpolitical or moderate parents. The leadership-oriented, who were obviously the most political of the three, had *voelkisch* or nationalistic parents, or were also in conflict with them.

In the Nazi Movement

The fighters, it is no surprise to learn, have by far the highest stormtrooper membership (91.4%), as compared to around 70% for the good comrades and followers and 56-62% for the rest. Of the stormtrooper ranks, again, the fighters seem to have the lion's share, but, on closer examination, the utopians make up at least their share of the middle-echelon ranks. Both these groups, in any case, have more middle-echelon stormtrooper leaders in relation to their number of SA and SS men than all the other groups. When we look at their offices in the party, the picture changes. The fighters have the fewest party offices, while the utopians, the good comrades, and the job-hunters hold the most *Ortsgruppenleiter* positions.

The fighters' attitude toward violence tends heavily toward sadism, as does that of the much older utopians, who include many military-civil servants. Though their reasons may differ, they make no excuses for their violence. The good followers and the job-hunters, by comparison, tend toward masochism. In fact, the followers often express regrets about the violence. But they tend to refer to the political enemy in the language of the *outré* nearly as often as the fighters, who were more involved in violence. They are also highly xenophobic, as are the fighters and the job-hunters. The utopians tend to express some liking for the enemy and a desire to win him over. Their ethnocentricity expresses itself more with chauvinism and feelings of national superiority. It goes well with their background of World War One camaraderie that the comradeship-oriented should tend to express a liking for their enemies just as they are significantly less masochistic and more sadistic than the leadership-oriented respondents. The good comrades also are the only ones among the three groups that could be called authoritarian in the sense of order-and-cleanliness-minded. The fighters instead are anti-authoritarian—that is, hostile to the police—and also rather low and romantic in their understanding of politics. The leadership-oriented, by comparison, rate low, ideological. The fighters also are loners in the party, while the two other groups tend to have their whole families in it.

Once they entered the party, the fighters and the good comrades tended to show a great desire to merge their individuality with the movement (conformity) in contrast to those stressing an extreme leadership cult, which of course is also a kind of total, self-denying identification. The ideology of the struggle-oriented was either none at all or revanchism. The other two had more standard preoccupations such as Nordic-German romanticism, anti-Marxism, and, with the good comrades, solidarism and revanchism. The fighters were relatively low in antisemitism but included a number of paranoids. The good comrades were higher but mostly with mild verbal projections, while the leadership-oriented had a heavy share of cholerics.

Being oriented toward the struggle is evidently another peak manifestation of a style of being politically violent in response to strong personality needs. As with the respondents for whom the time of struggle was "the best time of my life," being involved in the physical struggle regardless of the nature of its object or of its antagonists seems to hold together and integrate rather disjointed or unstable personalities. If we compare struggle-orientation to the other ways we have attempted to classify politically violent people in this chapter, there appears to be no uniform dimension scaling the more violent and the less violent. Instead, there are different personal styles of political violence, each represented in archetypal form in a recognizable part of our sample: The pure, mindless activism of the instant stormtroopers and SS men, the Goering-type of middle-echelon stormtrooper leader, the more deliberate, ideologically motivated violence of the delayed stormtrooper or day-and-nighter, and the struggle-oriented sadist. Their individual styles and personality needs relate somewhat differently to Nazi ideology and to such features as comradeship satisfactions, group conformity, and to the leadership cult.

FOUR

A Career in the Pre-1933 Nazi Party

"The goal of the NSDAP," proclaimed the *Parteistatistik* of 1935, "is to be a *Fuehrerorden* of the German people."[1] The members, and particularly the leadership, of the party were indeed from the very beginning meant to be a self-selected counter-elite to the social and political elites of the Weimar Republic. The early office-holders in the Nazi party, not the SA or SS, were the spearhead of this new counter-elite. Let us take a look at the character of this elite in the Abel sample.

FD-64: Office Held in the Nazi Party

	Number	Per cent
No office held	243	41.5
Minor local office	117	20.0
Functional office	66	11.3
┌ Organizing/founding activity	63	10.8
├ *Ortsgruppenleiter*	53	9.1
└ Speaker	26	4.4
Reichstag deputy, high level office	17	2.9
	585*	100.0

* Multiple entries.

How do these elite groups stand out among the entire sample of early Nazis? To begin with, the local office-holders of various kinds, and especially the functional leadership, were noticeably older than those who held no party office. The minor local leaders and the functional leadership also tend to be metropolitan while the organizers, speakers, and *Ortsgruppenleiter* are more often from towns and rural areas. The latter, indeed, often include farmers and the business and professional *Mittelstand*, while the former tend to be military-civil servants, white-collar workers, and women.[2]

[1] NSDAP, *Parteistatistik*, I, p. 218.

[2] In these respects, the averages for the party leadership reported in the *Parteistatistik* are quite comparable to the Abel sample: The leaders tended to be of the war generation, especially if they joined before Sep-

Early Membership of Office-Holders

According to the *Parteistatistik* of 1935, most of the higher offices were held by persons who had joined the party before September 1930. All the *Reichsleiter* and *Gauleiter* and 70% of the *Kreisleiter* had joined before that date and, except for two of the *Kreisleiter*, all before January 30, 1933, the day Hitler was appointed Chancellor. These figures not only highlight the core of "old fighters" in the post-1933 leadership, but are remarkable in the light of the wholesale changes of the years 1933 and 1934. According to the *Parteistatistik*, 53% of the *Kreisleiter* and 44% of the *Ortsgruppen-* and *Stuetzpunktleiter* were newly appointed during these years after the incumbents either resigned or were dismissed as "unfit for the requirements of office."[3] Evidently, the new *Kreisleiter* also tended to be old fighters.

Table VI-9 shows the decreasing percentage of pre-1930 members among the lower offices of the party.[4] The leadership component of the Abel sample tapers off similarly in its percentage of

Table VI-9: Early Membership and Office-holding (1935) (in %)

	Joined before 1930	Joined 1930-1933	Joined after 1933	Totals
Reichsleiter, Gauleiter	100.0	—	—	100.0
Kreisleiter	70.0	29.0	1.0	100.0
Ortsgruppenleiter	30.0	56.0	14.0	100.0
Stützpunkt- and *Zellenleiter*	10.0	50.0	40.0	100.0
Blockleiter	3.3	25.5	71.2	100.0
Total Leaders	6.0	32.0	62.0	100.0

early members. As many as one-fourth of the higher level offices and *Reichstag* deputies of the sample were pre-1925 members, as compared to only one-eighth of the *Ortsgruppenleiter* and speakers or organizers, and 5-9% of the minor leadership. In excess of 70% of all the higher categories including *Ortsgruppenleiter* had joined

tember 1930, while the membership at large is concentrated among the age cohorts of the immediate post-war generation. Regarding their occupations, the leadership was far more often white-collar workers, civil servants, or, because of the rural expansion of the party, farmers, than was true of the members at large. See *Parteistatistik*, II, pp. 154, 213, 220.

[3] See *Parteistatistik*, II, pp. 278-279.

[4] *Parteistatistik*, II, pp. 10-11, 14.

by the 1930 elections, as compared to less than half of the minor local office-holders.[5] The functional leadership, finally, tended to have joined the party only after mid-1931, which suggests not only the relatively late development of functional NSDAP auxiliaries but also the manner in which they were established. Rather than relying on the old fighters to establish groups such as the NS Druggists' Association, the party simply coopted influential druggists regardless of how long they had been with the party.

Party Office and Youth Settings

Did membership in youth organizations have any predictive significance for a later party career? There does not appear to be one particular kind of youthful association which favors a later party career. Even the attitudes displayed toward the first youth group of the respondent tell us little, except that the office-holders were not particularly violence-prone as youth group members. They did exhibit a great tendency to hold youth organization offices beyond small-group leadership. Once an office-holder, always an office-holder. The fathers of the minor office-holders tended to be *voelkisch*. The fathers of the *Ortsgruppenleiter* or higher officers were generally conventionally political, unpolitical, or in conflict with their sons.

To the extent that they were in the war, moreover, the *Ortsgruppenleiter* tended to be bitter-enders, or even POWs or invalids. The minor officials instead gloried in the egalitarian *Fronterlebnis*. Their reaction to the "revolution" is distinctive in its emphasis on the responsibility of the Weimar parties. Nevertheless, the office-holders tended particularly not to engage in counter-revolutionary activities, with the sole exception of the minor officials, who had more than their share of Free Corps and vigilante veterans. The heritage of war and civil war thus played only a minor role among the Nazi leadership. Their attitudes toward war and revolution are underscored by expressions of ethnocentricity aside from antisemitism. The *Ortsgruppenleiter* and higher leaders were particularly high in xenophobia and chauvinism.

It is no less revealing that the office-holders in general, unlike the

[5] In the Abel sample, party office-holders were overrepresented by as much as 100% as compared to the non-office holders. Between 50 and 70% of the Abel respondents held a party office; according to the *Parteistatistik*, only about one-fourth of the members did. The least office-holding groups of the Abel sample are those who joined between 1925 and 1927 or after April 1932. The former period, it will be recalled, was one of heavy stormtrooper influx into the sample.

stormtroopers, were not likely to have their whole family in the party, but tended to be loners. Evidently, holding a party office was considered something of a lonely masculine mission, while street-fighting was not. Nevertheless, many *Ortsgruppenleiter* were characterized by a great desire to merge their selves completely with the movement, which thereby may well have become a substitute family or wife. They were married to the Nazi movement, so to speak.

Getting Involved with the Party

How did a person become involved in the organizational and propagandistic work of the extreme right of the Weimar Republic? A paranoid shopkeeper of the Abel collection, born 1882 (no. 255), gives chapter and verse on the practical and financial aspects. He initially responded to a leaflet of the *Schutz-und-Trutzbund*, a direct forerunner of the party, which invited him to a rally.

> I went there and found in a hall big enough for 300 people no more than five persons. The man issuing the invitations and the speaker asked us to a table in the corner of the hall and filled us in on the importance and the goals of the *Schutz-und-Trutzbund*. After this informative session, I and another man were asked to found a local group in the east of Berlin. Since we could no longer stand the prevalent street terror, we thought it necessary to take over the leadership of the local. When we wanted to leave following the discussion of this matter, we were obliged first to pay the rental of 20 marks for the hall. This was our first sacrifice.

The respondent and his associate immediately rented a room for the first meeting. The shopkeeper bought a mimeograph machine and ran off a number of invitations which his children, aged 8-11, had to deliver to about 50 or 60 people of his acquaintance. Of these, nine showed up; the respondent considered this a great success.

> Everybody agreed to help actively in the building up of our local. We collected from our new comrades lots of addresses which we then literally showered with leaflets and invitations. Every week now we had another public rally. I cannot tell you how much work and money had to be sunk into this enterprise until we reached a membership figure of 50. At this point we could enlarge our board and afford a good speaker now and then.

In the meantime, also, a police auxiliary composed of war veterans was formed which ostensibly was to assist the police with the suppression of crime. The respondent joined this auxiliary and twice a week had to accompany a police patrol. But he also used the auxiliary to recruit "many a comrade for the *Schutz-und-Trutzbund* so that our local became larger and larger. Other locals were similarly successful and were appearing in public." By 1922, the *Schutz-und-Trutzbund* in Berlin was presenting mass rallies in the Circus Busch.

In the years from 1920 to 1922, indeed, the *voelkisch* forerunners of the NSDAP grew by leaps and bounds. As recently as at the end of 1919, about half of the 30,000 *Schutz-und-Trutzbund* members were still derived from older antisemitic groups and parties. Within a year their number had nearly quadrupled. In 1921 they added another 40% despite state action forbidding members of police and *Reichswehr* to belong to this subversive group. The increasing inflation, a rise in the dues, and the refusal to keep any but paid-up members on the rolls also did their share to keep the numbers down. By the time the *Schutz-und-Trutzbund* was outlawed in mid-1922, following the murder of Rathenau, it had between 160,000 and 180,000 members. Thus there was a large pool of antisemitic, *voelkisch* activists, including those from the *Reichshammerbund* (Fritsch), the *Deutschsoziale Partei* (Kunze), and others which had merged with the *Schutz-und-Trutzbund*, available for the sudden surge of power of the NSDAP and the *Deutschvoelkische Freiheitspartei* in 1923.[6]

For our respondent, the increasing size of the movement and its rallies gave birth to a new problem:

> We had to be particularly careful about the big mass rallies because the Marxist and his Jewry had only now noticed that we might be dangerous to him. Now Marxism tried with all its might to disrupt the rally. We anticipated the Communist method of packing the hall beforehand by seating our people early in double rows throughout the Circus and letting in only whoever had a regular admission ticket.

Nevertheless, they had battles inside and outside the hall and ended up with a considerable number of severely injured comrades. The outlawing of the *Schutz-und-Trutzbund* and police searches did not keep the respondent and his friends down for very long. They first formed a reading club for a cover and then participated in the foundation of the *Deutschvoelkische Freiheitspartei* (DVFP), which gave them "a certain protection and allowed them to work

[6] The NSDAP had 55,000 members in November of 1923, at the time of the beer-hall *putsch*, according to Orlov, *History of the Nazi Party, 1919-1933*, p. 45. The information about the *Schutz-und-Trutzbund* stems from Lohalm, *Voelkischer Radikalismus*, pp. 89-91.

more freely." The respondent had been on the board of the reading club and, after making the merger official, promptly arranged for another large rally, and many more. He took care to engage popular speakers, especially a certain lieutenant colonel "whose gripping speeches, one could rightly say, really stirred up the populace in east Berlin." The respondent also began to recruit from among the membership a protective squad of stormtroopers for his rallies. Another stormtrooper unit had already been organized in north Berlin by another future Nazi leader, Daluege, and "now the Communist could not so easily disrupt our meetings any more." The stormtroopers were needed almost every night and brought back "many a bruise or black eye" from the frequent meeting-hall brawls.

The same respondent also permits us a glimpse of the propaganda activity[7] of his group, presumably the DVFP.

> Since we had little money in those days,[8] we had to mimeograph all the invitations and handbills ourselves. The handbills were run off in my apartment by 10 to 15 unemployed comrades. I soon did not recognize my place any more, for we worked without reserve. Now we also started again to put up [antisemitic] stickers during the night. This was quite dangerous because the Communists undertook systematically to intercept members by themselves in order to render them harmless.

Such nocturnal activity also landed the propaganda team once in a while in the police station. After a brief fling at an attempted coup d'état with the Black *Reichswehr* late in 1923, the respondent was back at his work. He had been asked to organize a new local in the southeast of town. He turned over his own local to his second chairman and proceeded exactly as he had earlier, with invitations to a rally in a large hall. The only difference was that now he could ask his old local for various kinds of support.

> By eight o'clock, the hall which was meant for 300 people was already overcrowded. The news of this overcrowding spread fast in the

---

[7] From the point of view of this man, there appears to be little difference between his life in the *Schutz-und-Trutzbund*, in the DVFP, and in the NSDAP. They succeed each other in the most natural way and the respondent hardly bothers to indicate when he switched from the DVFP to the Nazis.

[8] The *Schutz-und-Trutzbund*, according to Lohalm, started out with a substantial sum from the Pan-German League at the time of its foundation and received further funds from prominent Pan-German industrialists, businessmen, and from some deposed princes. Much of its operating funds, however, had to come from dues and gifts solicited from members. *Voelkischer Radikalismus*, pp. 100-107.

south-east and it was our best advertisement. . . . We got 52 new members and soon we surpassed the size of the old local. We also founded a stormtrooper squad with stouthearted men. Unfortunately, unemployment now became more and more frequent and no sooner did a company find out that this man or that one was a DVFP member than he lost his job.

The respondent became concerned about all these unemployed comrades and decided to look into the allegedly insufficient availability of unemployment support for his members. He became a welfare volunteer and later a local welfare official who could make sure

that nationalistic poor people got their rights, too. I was careful not to change my welfare personnel because the city councillors were all Socialists and Communists. I saw to it that young stormtroopers of the Horst Wessel *Sturm* who had been persecuted and denied assistance because of that were taken care of in my bailiwick.

At that time I also worked at [a big company] and propagandized our idea among the Communist workers there with the active support of the director and executive manager. It was here that I got our unemployed comrades jobs so that at the time of the presidential election of Hindenburg in 1925 we actually marched out of the company gate in closed formation and with a flag into the street.

After he became unemployed in connection with charges against several Nazi employees of having set a bomb in the *Reichstag*, the respondent also for a while became a *Gefangenenwart* of the party, who had to look after jailed and hospitalized comrades. "One can hardly imagine what was going on. Every day arrests of party comrades and stormtroopers were reported to me." And the propaganda activity went on: "Our propaganda work became harder and harder since even the police fought us on occasion. Every Sunday morning at six we went from house to house. My grown sons also participated in this. . . . There were always clashes with Communists on these occasions." The respondent also enumerates the other great meeting-hall battles in which he was involved and tells about the large soup kitchen the party ran for the unemployed stormtroopers. The respondent's wife, who had been involved all along, did the cooking. Finally, the respondent helped to organize the Nazi welfare organization (NSV) in Berlin. He collected used clothing, set up tailor shops to make it reusable, established local welfare commissions, and conducted courses for welfare helpers. Oddly enough, his party file gives no information about his activities or offices after 1933.

Entering the Party

How do the office-holders differ from the rest in their attitudes and behavior within the party? Regarding their personal introduction to the NSDAP, office-holders of all levels tended heavily to be attracted by the ideology and by ideological propaganda rather than being introduced by friends or fellow-workers as was typical of the stormtroopers. Those holding only minor local offices also tended to be roped in after attending rallies or witnessing Nazi demonstrations. It seems clear that the more ambitious office-holders, unlike the stormtroopers, had a strong ideological motivation. It remains to be seen what kind of ideology was most attractive to them.

There is a noticeable division between the minor and the major office-holders in this respect. The *Ortsgruppenleiter* and higher functionaries tended to be Nordic-German romantics or superpatriots. They also had a larger share of paranoids on the antisemitism scale. The minor local leaders were more often solidarists or revanchists, as we would expect from their war and Free Corps background. The stormtroopers, it will be recalled, also tended to be revanchists or solidarists, or to have no ideology worth noting. Nordic-German romanticism, superpatriotism, and antisemitism were evidently the ideological wellsprings of the pre-1933 Nazi leadership, and revanchism or solidarism only good enough for the foot soldiers of the Nazi movement.

In their attitude toward the NSDAP, also, the office-holders stand out with a sense of personal integration derived from the classless comradeship of the party and the pursuit of utopia, rather than from the struggle itself like the stormtroopers. For the most part, indeed, they left street-fighting and meeting-hall brawls, and even demonstrations, to those who held no office. The office-holders instead were heavily engaged in proselytizing and acts of individual provocation. Only a single group of office-holders, the *Ortsgruppenleiter* and local founders, seem to have been involved in political violence, and at a high degree of intensity which was perhaps a functional prerequisite of local leadership. They were fighting "day-and-night" at the height of the fighting years.

The minor office-holders and the functional leadership are the least likely to belong to the stormtroopers. The *Ortsgruppenleiter* and local founders, on the other hand, have a fair share among those who joined the SA a year or more after joining the party, or who graduated to the SS. This higher-level group also numbers quite a few middle-echelon stormtrooper leaders. Evidently it is not accurate simply to assume a bifurcation between holding party office and stormtrooper activity. There were some strong links among the holders of both party and stormtrooper offices, especially in certain areas. But these links were chiefly a feature of the years of struggle before 1933. In the 1935 statistics, a coincidence of party offices with membership in the SA or SS is the exception rather than the rule. There were less than 10% of the party leaders (only 2.7% of the *Kreisleiter* and 6.1% of the *Ortsgruppenleiter*) among the stormtroopers "because their party offices keep them too busy."[9]

Nevertheless, even at that point there were still extreme regional differences stemming evidently from the uneven historical development of the NSDAP. As many as 41.9% of the party leadership in Muenchen-Oberbayern, 36.6% in the Palatinate, 31.8% in Franconia, 31% in East Bavaria, and 24.6% in Swabia were stormtroopers. At the other extreme, in Hamburg, East Prussia, Saxony, Berlin, and Schleswig-Holstein the percentage was around 1%. The older, southeastern *Gaue* obviously had a more traditional composition which mirrored the pre-1925, fascist character of the NSDAP.

Functional Membership

In these statistical breakdowns, membership or leadership in the functional organizations of the Nazi party always played a rather atypical role. Most of the functional Nazi groups, the women's, gymnasium and university students' groups, the NSBO (labor), the Nazi civil service association, and others generally made their appearance only during the height of the fighting years when it seemed to be to the advantage of the NSDAP to attempt to penetrate the vast network of organized interest of Weimar society. Other parties, such as the SPD and DNVP, had long since blazed a trail in this direction.

FD-29: Membership in Functional Organizations

	Number	Per cent
None	299	66.3
NS women (*Frauenschaft*)	14	3.1
NS High-school students (*Schuelerbund*)	13	2.9
NS university students (*NS St. Bd.*)	8	1.8
Farmers	6	1.3
Other NS professionals	9	2.0
NS workers' cells (NSBO)	43	9.5
NS civil service	59	13.1
	451	100.0

[9] *Parteistatistik*, II, pp. 262-265.

The functional groups of the NSDAP generally started with revolutionary overtones but, by about 1928, changed their character to conform more closely to the traditional lines dear to each group. The university students (NS St. Bd.), for example, had until that date espoused a sharp opposition to the class snobbery and exclusiveness of the traditional German student corporation. In 1928, however, Baldur von Schirach became the new NS St. Bd. leader and promptly switched over to a more conventional policy of nationalistic intransigence and antisemitism which was rather typical of the student corporations in any case.

At about the same time, members of other professions, such as lawyers, druggists, doctors, and teachers, were organized also, although the general policy vacillated as to what purpose these associations were to serve.[10] In the case of the farmers and small businessmen, takeovers from within were attempted, with varying success. The largest number of functional members in our sample were civil servants who had plenty of grievances, including the government edicts against civil service membership in the NSDAP or the KPD. The Nazi civil servants formed clandestine groups to bore from within, and to proselytize and propagandize throughout the public service, including among police officers, where the NSDAP found many sympathizers. Nevertheless, the competition of the well-established Socialist and other legitimate civil service organizations put the Nazi civil servants at a distinct disadvantage, at least until Hitler's appointment in 1933.

Another and larger group of Abel respondents was in the NSBO, the Nazi workers' cell movement of the early 1930s. The Nazi workers also were not particularly effective in overcoming the defensive measures of the well-entrenched Socialist trade unions, although they undoubtedly helped to carry the brown dogma into the hitherto solid rows of labor, and to make voting for Hitler respectable among workers.[11] The NSBO was not viewed with enthusiasm by Hitler and most of the Nazi leadership, and received very little organizational or financial support from the parent organization.

A Social Profile of Functional Membership

We had already noticed in the previous statistical breakdowns that the members of functional associations of the NSDAP were relatively older than the average Abel respondent. This was particularly

[10] See also Orlow, *History of the Nazi Party, 1919-1933*, pp. 149 and 193-198.

[11] See also Hans-Gerd Schumann, *Nationalsozialismus und Gewerkschaftsbewegung*, Hannover: Norddeutsche Verlagsanstalt, 1958.

true of the typical Nazi civil servant whose age in 1933 was around 41, which puts him squarely in the prewar generation. More than half the women and student members, on the other hand, belonged to the postwar generation, with an average age of 29. The NSBO members tended to be from a metropolitan area, as did the civil servants and the other professions, the women, and the students. But there were also small-town civil servants and, of course, Nazi farmers of rural origin. On the whole, however, the functional members were far more urban than the Abel sample at large.

By occupation, organized Nazi civil servants, students, farmers, and women belonged to the corresponding categories on our list of occupations. Our NSBO members, however, tended to be mostly white-collar workers or military-civil servants rather than blue-collar workers. The lion's share (90%) of the more than one hundred blue-collar Nazis in the sample was not in the NSBO, a sign of its insignificance and marginality even in the ranks of Nazi labor. The functional members, moreover, were generally upwardly mobile and not particularly affected by the economic hardships of the Great Depression or of the pre-depression period. They were not, as a rule, driven by social or economic despair to form or join Nazi auxiliaries.

Political Motives of the Auxiliaries

What other motives could there be? About one-half of the functional members already held an office or function in a youth organization. They were quite active in their youthful years; in fact, the Nazi civil servants in military training groups and Free Corps or vigilante violence, the NSBO in street-fighting and demonstrations, and all the rest in electioneering, proselytizing, and demonstrations. As compared to the non-organized, the functional members indeed stand out as fully politicized youths and, among the civil servants only, as hostile militants. The non-organized, by comparison, were more often politically militarized youths or youthful authoritarians.

The early politicization of the functional members is evidently due in part to the *voelkisch* politics of their fathers or to conflict between father and son. Quite a few of the Nazi women, students, and others, nevertheless, are from unpolitical homes. The civil servants tend heavily to have nationalistic fathers. Considering their ages, moreover, the stimuli of war and revolution alone may well have helped their early politicization.

Half of the functional members were politically active before joining the NSDAP, including quite a few members (one-fifth) of other parties and some members (one-seventh) of pre-1925 *voelk-*

isch parties including the early Nazi party. As indicated earlier, the functional members tended to join only after the 1925-1927 period when many of the stormtroopers joined. Half of the civil servants and more than half of the NSBO, in fact, were *Septemberlinge*. Before that time, we might have expected many NSBO members to have belonged to left-wing or republican organizations, but this was just as true of the civil servants and the other groups. On the other hand, quite a number of NSBO members and civil servants belonged to quasi-military groups and, later on, to the *Stahlhelm*.

The year 1923 already saw nearly one-fourth of the functional members in the NSDAP or other *voelkisch* parties. In the years from 1925 to 1930, also, a good many Nazi farmers, women, and others were in the DNVP or in agricultural opposition groups. During the fighting years (1929-1933), finally, the NSBO members were the most involved in street violence, although even they were far behind the violent percentage of those who belonged to no functional group. In many respects, then, the functional members were a more politically minded and rather less violent lot. With the exception of those in the NSBO, they also far less often belonged to the SA or SS. They seem to embody many characteristic features of party office-holders to a remarkagle degree.

Once they had joined the reconstructed NSDAP, NSBO members and the organized civil servants tended to be quite active as marcher-proselytizers (MPs) or marcher-fighter-proselytizers (MFPs). Many of the civil servants, however, were merely sympathizers. The Nazi women, students, and others engaged chiefly in marching (M). Their immediate reason for joining the party was the dynamic impression of the Hitler movement for all the functional members, and particularly for the civil servants, who tended to be attracted by the rallies or by an awareness of the ideology. With the NSBO, a general sense of repression by and friction with the occupation also played a role. The other groups were particularly attracted by the spirit of comradeship among the stormtroopers. They tended to be introduced to the party by friends or co-workers.

If the functional members were that political, we may ask, what kind of ideological or attitudinal motives were most important to them? Typically, the Nazi civil servants were revanchists; the NSBO members were imbued with solidarism and antisemitism, which were precisely the issues that kept them away from the SPD and KPD. The Nazi women, students, and others tended to be Nordic-German romantics, devotees of the Hitler cult, or stereotyped anti-Marxists who referred to their enemies in the language of the *outré*. NSBO and civil service members also exhibited their animus against "reactionaries," Catholics, and liberals. Their expectations in 1934, apart from individual pay-offs, tended to be for the totalitarian utopia or for a national renaissance. The three functional membership groups ranked fairly high in political intelligence as compared to the non-organized. At the same time, the political understanding of nearly half of the NSBO members and of the women and other auxiliaries was of the low, ideological type. A similar share of the Nazi civil servants was of the low, narrow sort we have come to expect of the military-civil servants of the sample.

The sharp differentiation of the Nazi civil servants from the other functional members even extends to their private lives. The typical Nazi civil servant had only his spouse with him in the party while the others tended to have their whole families. We can easily visualize the difference in personality type, the shared monomania of the civil service couples as compared to the social integration of NSBO members and others. On the pathology scale, these civil servants tended to be paranoid or irrational. The NSBO members suffered from high cultural shock or an excess of masochism and personal insecurity. The women, students, and others, by comparison, yearned to merge their selves with the movement, and showed an abject devotion to its great and glorious leader.

The functional members in the Abel sample, we can conclude, are a rather select group of the party organization (PO) elite. Many of them, in fact, held other party offices as well, and particularly offices of a higher level. As we look beyond the cut-off date of the Abel *vitae*, 1933-1934, the extent to which the office-holding and functional pre-1933 elites made their mark in the Third *Reich* will become clearer.

FIVE

Third Reich Careers

The reader is likely to wonder what became of these early Nazis after the Abel *vitae* break off. Many of the Abel respondents sound so sincere and harmless that it is difficult to associate them with the monstrous misdeeds of the Third *Reich*. Since an attempt to locate and reinterview surviving Abel respondents after nearly forty years was unlikely to be worth the effort and expense, we decided instead to look up as many as were identifiable in the NSDAP membership files in the Berlin Document Center.[1] It was our hope that the information on the Third *Reich* careers of a sufficient number of the Abel respondents might shed some light on the question what kinds of early Nazis tended to make what kind of career in the totalitarian state.

The membership files thus were the chief external source consulted for confirmation of the information contained in the Abel *vitae*. As was to be expected, the information in the membership catalog had a good many limitations due to poor record-keeping and an obvious lack of interest on the part of the party in certain kinds of information. There was no record, for example, of any private wealth acquired by an old fighter as a result of his party record and, perhaps, from the expropriation of Jews and political opponents. The party evidently was not interested in recording information about a member's property or even his career in private industry. But on the whole, the other information available on each case was quite adequate, as we shall see below.

For simple party membership, the membership file provides a card which lists name, date and place of birth, date of entry into the party, occupation at that time, and the party *Gau*. These cards are available for nearly all Abel respondents. They frequently show changes of employment or advances in the same line of work, with dates. Honorary or paid party functionaries (*Walter* and higher)

[1] Acknowledgment for this work is due to Horst W. Schmollinger of the Institute of Political Science at the Free University of Berlin, whose remarks on the nature of the information are summarized here.

have an additional party statistical form (*Parteierhebungsbogen*) which, in addition to the same information, also lists occupational groups such as "worker," memberships in functional groups, the exact names and locations of the offices held (with promotions and dates), and finally, items of NSDAP uniforms in their possession.

Each SA or SS member has a further card which, in addition to the last job held, also lists the wife's name, sex and age of children, special medals or honors (with dates), military rank in the war and in paramilitary groups, entry into the SA or SS, ranks (with dates) and units there, including the *Gestapo* and concentration camp guards, and any Nazi leadership courses completed. An SA member also submitted a handwritten *vita* with information about his parents' occupation, his own education and occupation, and membership in functional organizations. SS members furthermore had to document their marriages, with *vitae*, genealogies, and medical records of both partners. Unfortunately, these detailed records are in disorder and tend to extend no further than 1942 or 1943. In many cases, the SA or SS career by that date had turned into a military career leading from the equivalent stormtrooper rank to higher officer rank.

The membership files also contain a record of expulsions, fines, and warnings by party agencies and especially by the Supreme Party Court (OPG). These cases usually include complete court transcripts. The offenses were not likely to be heroics of moral opposition, but mostly financial (embezzlement), moral, or violent in character. The NSDAP was very strict with morals offenses such as extramarital relations or exhibitionism, but very lenient with violent deeds as long as they were committed outside of the normal SA or SS service hours. Drunken involvement in brawls, shootings, even assaults resulting in death thus drew only warnings from the party. If they were committed while in service, on the other hand, they might be punished with demotion or exclusion from office. Some of the pre-1933 proceedings also include charges of collaboration with the French occupation or of insufficient fighting zeal in confrontations with the enemy.

Typical entries of this sort read "excluded from the SA by SA court (September 2, 1941), for embezzlement and theft from a comrade" (no. 564, born 1909); "expelled from the NSDAP by party district court (May 1, 1941)," with no reason given (no. 143, born 1898); or "President of NSDAP district court (July 9, 1935), dismissed from this office because of dubious conduct during the *Ruhrkampf* (August 6, 1937)" (no. 264, born 1869). Not infrequently, persons in high SA, SS, or party office were also thus demoted, suspended, or expelled altogether from their organizations, along with the average members (for example nos. 226, 239, 271, 373, 396, 400, and 407). Or a municipal functionary who was merely a party member is recorded as having resigned of his own free will and become a salesman after a party court initiated proceedings against him for maintaining intimate relations with an employee subordinate to him (no. 285, born 1893), a serious offense under German law. There are also some who voluntarily left the party, say, in 1941 (no. 164, born 1889). The party also had a nasty way of transferring the less deserving party functionaries to the Russian front (nos. 22, 80, 211) during the war.

Changes in employment or promotions were not easy to spot, at least for the period up to 1935. Members of the Nazi teachers' (*NS Lehrerbund*) or civil service associations tend to have more complete records, which may have contributed to the impression that they had particularly capitalized on their records as old fighters.[2] The few higher civil servants, independents, and professional persons among the early Nazis may have done even better for themselves. Generally speaking and without benefit of statistical demonstration, the evidence suggests that early Nazi membership alone was not enough for a spectacular advancement but that holding a party office might well have led to a Third *Reich* career. A record of pre-1933 fighting for the cause could be a boon provided the old fighter had the necessary skills of self-advertisement and that he did not constitute one of the many cases of crude, disorderly sluggers who were an embarrassment to the victorious party. A great many early members merely switched from a very modest position they had lost in private industry to an equally modest one in public employment. Stormtroopers with a working-class background often received civil service positions, especially in law enforcement. Older pre-1933 members often garnered party offices such as *Ortsgruppenleiter* after 1939, which kept them safe from the draft.

For purposes of statistical evaluation, we arrived at the following categories of a Third Reich career for the Abel respondents. The records for nearly half the sample either could not be positively identified, were not found in the NSDAP catalog,[3] had been

[2] This and the following impressions were those of the research assistant, Horst W. Schmollinger. Our approach will of necessity be broader both because of the availability of background data on each case and because statistical manipulation requires fairly large groupings.

[3] Sixty-two of the names could not be found in the membership file. The identification rested on 1) the legibility of the signature and 2) the date and place of birth. The research assistant was under the impression

checked out to judicial agencies, or contained no entry or clear evidence of a person's career during the Third Reich. Nearly one-third of the rest of the sample seems to have gotten no unusual advancement out of their early membership. Such a judgment, of course, hinges on what could be considered normal advancement during the time in question. For the crosstabulations, we lumped these cases with those who died in the period without any evidence of a career and with those who dropped out or were expelled or punished by the party. Another group, amounting to nearly one-third among the ascertainable cases, made a career of holding party office. About one-seventh were careerists in the public service and the few ascertainable careerists in private industry—who obviously under-represent the extent to which old fighters enriched themselves by hook or crook. As for the administrative careers, it was not always very clear whether a certain career with the regular police might not bring a respondent into our last and most interesting group, the bloodhounds of the terror system of the Third Reich. But we wanted to be sure to keep this last category free of the more innocuous careers.[4]

FD-79: Third Reich Career

	Number	Per cent
NA, or no clear evidence	265	45.7
Died 1933-1945 (no career)	36	6.2
No unusual advancement	86	14.8
Left party (incl. expulsion, severe punishment by party courts)	17	2.9
Party career (incl. SA and functional offices)	92	15.8
High administrative career (incl. police)	30	5.2
Minor administrative career (incl. police)	9	1.5
Business career	4	0.7
Gestapo, SS (pre-1939), SD, RSHA, concentration camp guards, occupation police	42	7.2
	581	100.0

that the personnel of the Berlin Document Center was rather inclined to withhold files where even minor discrepancies made identification doubtful.

[4] The abbreviations denote: *Gestapo* is *Geheime Staatspolizei*; SD, *Sicherheitsdienst*; and RSHA, *Reichssicherheitshauptamt*. "Occupation police" refers to the police function in the occupied areas in the East which was deeply involved with the rounding up of Jews and political enemies.

Social Origins of Old Nazi Careers

How do these groups compare with regard to age, occupation, and social mobility? The three most interesting groups, the party and administrative careerists and the enforcers of the terror, are noticeably younger than the not-ascertained or the motley group of those who died, made no noticeable gains, or were expelled. The youngest by far, with well over one-half in the postwar generation, were the terror enforcers. Their average age was about 29 in 1933, in or about the victory-watcher cohort, and hardly any of them were over 40. The administrative careerists, by comparison, had only one-third in the postwar generation and an average age of about 36 in 1933. The party careerists had an average age of about 35, and 38.7% in the postwar generation. Many of the enforcers tended to be from the occupied areas, another indication of the relevance of the occupation experience to Nazi motivations.

The administrative careerists tended to live in Berlin, while the party careerists and the enforcers more often lived in small and medium cities (2,000-100,000). As to their occupations, both careerist groups tended to be military-civil servants or white-collar workers, as would seem to be appropriate for careers in various kinds of bureaucratic organizations. The terror enforcers, however, are mostly blue-collar workers or farmers—a fact that, perhaps, made them more ready for the dirty work. Both kinds of careerists, as we would expect, were upwardly mobile, especially from the urban proletariat. The terrorists, on the other hand, heavily tended to be in social decline or had never attempted to rise. There appears to be a strong causal link between social decline or stagnation in the midst of an upwardly mobile society and their kind of sociopathic destructiveness.

There are several other such Cain's marks on the enforcers. More than any other group, they tend heavily to have lost their fathers before reaching the age of 18 (32.3%). They also show a heavy tendency to have lost their jobs or livelihoods during the Great Depression (38.6%), which might explain their readiness for any career available. They exhibit the greatest propensity (72.1%) not to indicate any religious affiliation, although not much more than the party careerists (70%). Neither one of these groups, it seems, was in the vanguard of the defense of Christianity against Communism. Those enforcers and the administrative careerists who indicate a religion tend to live in a religously mixed area or to belong to the minority in an area dominated by the other religion. In their educational level, finally, the enforcers are mostly of very modest attainments. While 45.4% of the administrative careerists and 34.6% of the party careerists completed *mittlere Reife*, this is true of only 18.1% of the enforcers.

From this preliminary evidence it becomes painfully clear what kind of person tended to go into the enforcement activities of the totalitarian state. Callow youths with minimal education, who grew up without a father and without religious commitment, workers or farmers, with families in social decline or foundering in the depression, they had no higher ambition than to subject some of their less fortunate contemporaries to the regime of terror. With the rise of the dregs of society to the top, the Nazi revolution had taken on its most characteristic meaning.

Political Socialization and Nazi Careers

Did the Nazi careerists undergo different political socialization experiences than the rest of the sample? The people who made a career of party office tended heavily to come from the *Bismarck-jugend* (DNVP), the *voelkisch* DHV, *Jungdo*, or liberal (DVP, DDP) youth groups, including those of the Youth Movement. Many of them belonged to *voelkisch* youth groups long before they became Nazis. The ideological, mainly *voelkisch* emphasis was pronounced from the very beginning. The administrative careerists came from a wider range of youth organizations, including paramilitary groups, the DNVP and DHV youth, and religious or unpolitical associations. The bloodhounds of the Third Reich, finally, largely came from paramilitary (including the Free Corps) and left-wing youth, such as the Red Front, or SAJ, or they had joined the SA or Hitler Youth (HJ) directly.

What were the attitudes of these respondents toward their youth groups? The enforcers predictably liked political violence and marching best, and "un-national views" or a lack of a social conscience the least. The left-wing converts account for the concern for social conscience. The administrative careerists liked violence best, but they also liked hiking, cultural appreciation, and a spirit of comradeship. They expressed a dislike for class-struggle slogans and for a lack of political direction and violent action. There appears to have been a distinctive military attitude about this group. The party careerists, finally, preferred hiking and cultural appreciation in the true *voelkisch* style, as well as marching with a sense of ideological direction. Their dislikes centered on a lack of social conscience and on the ideology of particular youth leaders.

An Education in Brutality

The propensity for violence of the enforcers expressed itself early in their lives. Thirty-seven percent of them were involved in partisan street-fights or meeting-hall brawls (vs. 27.3% of the party and 20% of the administrative careerists) and another 22.2% in the Free Corps type of violence (vs. 16.7% and 12.5%, respectively) before they were 26. The party careerists typically engaged more often in proselytizing and electioneering at that age, while the administrative careerists mostly were in military training groups as their most extreme youthful activity. In their youthful political postures, therefore, the enforcers tended to be classified as politically militarized (42.2%) while the party careerists were most often prepolitical *romantics*, probably of the *voelkisch* type, or fully politicized youths. All three groups had more than their share of hostile militants, especially among the enforcers (15.6%). Political militarization thus seems to have been the process leading to a career as enforcer, while early politicization or political daydreaming more likely led to a party career. The office-holding style of the party man also differentiated itself early from the violent, militarized style of politics. As many as half of the party careerists had already held an office in their youth organization, but only 36.3% of the administrative careerists and 31.5% of the enforcers had done so.

Let us take a closer look at some of the *vitae* of enforcers who were especially groomed by the Third Reich for careers in terrorist enforcement. One of the purposes of concentration camp brutality, from the very beginnings under SS *Obersturmbannfuehrer* (Lieutenant Colonel) Theodor Eicke at Dachau, was to toughen the SS guards. Eicke regarded Dachau as "his school" and, indeed, one of his early pupils there was Rudolf Hoess, the later commandant at Auschwitz. His notions of the education of an SS man in impersonal systematized brutality were shared by Himmler and Heydrich, who frequently expressed their conviction that this experience was a most desirable one.[5] There are a number of concentration camp guards and the like in the Abel collection who are worth a closer look.

One example is the son of a peasant, born in 1891, who served in the army two years before, and again during, the war (no. 444). Although he had to leave his family and his parents' vineyards behind, he felt a great patriotic enthusiasm in 1914. Gravely wounded in 1915, he spent the next four years in hospitals and emerged partly invalid. He had no comment on the German defeat, but viewed

[5] See, for example, Roger Manvell and Heinrich Fraenkel, *The Incomparable Crime*, New York: G. P. Putnam, 1967, chap. III and the chapters on Himmler, Heydrich, and Hoess in Fest, *The Face of the Third Reich*.

the "revolution" as a Marxist plot to expunge *voelkisch* traditions and to replace them with liberal capitalism and economic and political chaos. He was with the DNVP until that party, too, became too "liberal-capitalistic" for him. Much of his venom is reserved for the "Marxist and Jesuitic press" and its calumnies regarding the NSDAP, which he eventually discovered as just right for him "as a peasant at the southwest border of Germany . . . related to the people and the soil by my blood."

In 1928, he began to fall under the spell of the Nazis and their appeal to "our arch-German, undistorted peasant sense." He joined in 1930, after two years of progressive bankruptcy and fellow-travelling with the movement. A year later he helped to found an SS *Sturm* and from then on his energies were completely absorbed in fighting and propagandizing. He gives a long list of alleged harassments and false accusations by the police, beginning with a charge of resisting a police officer "because I had stopped the police from working over a comrade." It was always the police or the Communists who were at fault. In 1932 he and others were wanted by the police and, after 13 weeks, "betrayed, caught, and jailed." A court sentenced him to 5 months for breach of the peace "because I and some SS men went to help other comrades who were threatened by the Marxists." On another charge of rioting, the prosecutor wanted to put him in prison for 12 years of hard labor but the court decided on three years of jail, "because I had straightened out a police officer who had searched my house, while I was in hiding, for insulting my wife and being disorderly." He was saved by the amnesty of December 1932.

After the 1933 elections, he writes: "Today there are only a few people, either of alien blood or dedicated to nothing but money who still oppose us and our idea. It will be our task in the future, in loyal and unquestioning obedience, and with pure national socialist will, to stand by the side of the *Fuehrer, ready to strike* so that these people cannot do as they please. . . ." (italics supplied) In 1934, the respondent was a *Haupttruppfuehrer* of the SS. As the membership file discloses, ten years later he was an *Obersturmfuehrer* (First Lieutenant), no spectacular advancement. But his skills of violence had brought him to the SS Death's Head unit in Dachau.

Another peasant's son, born 1893 (no. 342), grew up with poverty and hard work and worked in various unskilled jobs before joining the prewar army. He fought in the war with dedication and was decorated for bravery, but by its end he was "tired of the war and touched by the Marxist promises of a life in dignity and freedom." He became a worker again and soon became disillusioned with "the Marxists," especially when he considered making himself economically independent. He went back to farming since his older brother had died in the war, but what remained after dividing the small farm among five brothers and sisters required extraordinary efforts and sacrifices. Under conditions of decline in German agriculture, it was a losing battle. He became radicalized but no longer in the Marxist direction. He wanted "a future in which everybody has the same right to live!"

The interest-bound political parties held little attraction for the respondent in 1928-1929. Instead, he began to read more and more about the Nazis and Adolf Hitler. At first, the objections of the Catholic clergy and of his own family held him back. But the economic deterioration in agriculture pushed aside the last doubts. In 1932, he became a member and was immediately subjected to the sanctions of the church and to friction at the school his sons attended. They were beaten up "whenever they used the Hitler greeting." His communal office was also a locale of friction. "There began for me a miserable time. I cannot describe the family conflicts [with his devout wife]. I became tougher and ignored it all, thinking only of Germany and of our Fuehrer. I accepted all sacrifices and envied the fighters in the city who could openly fight with the SPD and KPD." In 1932 he became an *Ortsgruppenleiter* and held a county office of the party. He ends his *vita* by promising "to accompany the movement faithfully, conscientiously, and aware of my duty to the end of my life, as my Fuehrer Adolf Hitler would want me to." According to his file, he followed it all the way to the Ukraine, where he was an area commissar in 1942, and to Cracow, where he was a functionary of the occupation police in 1944.

A third case is that of a worker and worker's son (no. 369, born 1893) who also served with dedication in the war. He gives no details about his life before 1926 when a Nazi rally persuaded him to join. Subsequently,

> as an SA man I participated in many battles. It was particularly hard to hold a meeting in Fuerstenwalde. Only at about the tenth try did we 30 to 50 Nazis manage to survive the onslaught of hundreds of Marxists and Communists. The Marxists did not seem to understand that we were fighting not only for a better Germany, but also for a freer lot for the worker.

The respondent casually mentions the time when he and a couple of SS comrades broke up an SPD rally. His record lists him as a *Rot-*

tenfuehrer (Corporal) in 1939 and, from 1943, as a member of the SS Guard Battalion of Sachsenhausen.[6]

While these cases were of an older vintage than most of the enforcers, there are plenty of younger ones to compare. There is, for example, the son of a village blacksmith born 1904 (no. 306), who completed the *Abitur* but could not go to a university because inflation wiped out the family's savings. The Ruhr invasion of 1923 politicized him and he belonged to the *Wehrwolf* from 1923 until 1925. He fondly remembered his days with this group, which took him to flag consecrations and German Days all over the region. "The comradeship was great. Politically, we were nationalistic and monarchistic. But the *Wehrwolf* movement, after a brilliant rise in 1923-1924, began to decline in the whole Reich and in my area. The fault was the lack of political direction."

In 1925, a *Wehrwolf* leader and former Free Corps officer from a neighboring town took his group and the respondent into the NSDAP. Two cousins of his had already travelled the same route. The respondent, a bank clerk, had just been dismissed in consequence of an audit by "a Jewish auditor" in the central office in Berlin, which awakened his mind to "the Jewish problem." He began to read Nazi literature and to set his faith in "the unconditional, goal-conscious policies of Hitler." He tells very little of his early fighting years except that it was "very hard" to increase the membership until the 1930 elections. In that year, the respondent also moved to Berlin, where he had found a new bank job, and immediately joined the SA. The electoral campaigns of 1932 were accompanied by many meeting-hall battles and SA service nearly every night. The respondent describes one major battle, taking care to stress that "the Communists provoked us in the first place." He also relates how during the suppression of the SA, his unit became the Brandenburg Sports Club and merrily went on with their drill. He concludes with a word about how "the movement began its storm after the seeming set-back of the elections of November 1932 in January . . . and pushed open the gates to power on that historical January 30, 1933." He went on to make a career with the SS, which took him to the position of a *Hauptsturmfuehrer* (Captain) in Auschwitz in 1940 and to a high rank with the SS Economic Administration looting Hungary in 1944.

[6] See also no. 478, another enforcer of the Death's Head *Sturmbann* Sachsenhausen who in 1940 was a SD *Hauptsturmfuehrer* and in 1944 held the same rank with the SS in the *Volksdeutsche Mittelstelle* of Cracow.

Of similar age was the son of a locomotive engineer, born 1904 (no. 422), who well represents the mindless hostility typical of many young Nazis in the collection. He writes with supreme unconcern about any connection between the French occupiers, the separatists, and the socialists: "Since my home was in the occupied area, as a boy already, I experienced the blessings of the International. The conduct of the separatists during the passive resistance awakened me and I was in the underground like so many patriotic Germans." He met and admired members of the *Bund Oberland* and also heard about the Hitler movement which, to his mind, embodied "German manhood (*Manneszucht*) and comradeship, unlike the republican outfits." The failure of the beer-hall *putsch* put an end to all associated groups and to his efforts to join the Nazis. But as soon as party and SA were once more available, in 1925, the respondent joined both. He gives no details about his activities with the SA or, after 1930, with the SS except to say that he always fought "in the foremost line." In 1933 he was a *Sturmfuehrer* (lieutenant). After 1941 he became a leader of the SS Guard Battalion South East.

A third young respondent, born 1903 (no. 469), was a victory-watcher who comments on his mother's strictness while her husband was away in the war. He learned farming from his father and later had to go to help him periodically because of the old man's war injuries. He also learned to drive heavy equipment, an ability that stood him in good stead until 1930 when he lost his job on an estate in Mecklenburg. As he reports, in 1929 he "had to belong to the *Reichsbanner*" for six months to keep his job. In 1932, he joined the SS, but he does not say a word about his activities there. Being unemployed left him free for stormtrooper service and he received no other job until, in April 1933, the Nazis gave him a factory job. They also put him through an SS leadership training program of six weeks, after which he was made an SS *Oberscharfuehrer* (Sergeant first class). In 1936 he joined the SS Guard Commando in the SS Camp Koenigstaedt.

A number of the original *vitae* (e.g., nos. 214, 226, 557, and 559) mention how SA and SS members were made auxiliary police the moment the Nazis took over. Their function involved especially the rounding up of political opponents of the pre-1933 struggles, mostly Communists and Socialists, into the new political jails and concentration camps. A clerk, born 1893 (no. 426), who had an extremely violent record before 1933 tells revealing details about their activities in this connection. He had already collected all kinds of inside information on the local KPD by pretending he was going to defect.[7] When the SS there became part of the auxiliary police, the respondent and his stormtrooper gang carried out unauthorized searches and seizures with such abandon that the local police was cowed into cooperation. The arrested KPD leaders were at first compelled to carry out such assignments as removing old election posters in public places. The respondent relates:

> This gave me an opportunity, by means of small favors and gifts, to win some of those who were of weak character. I got one released from protective custody who then did good work for us. Even before that we had already tracked down SAP people distributing the paper *Spartakus*.[8] . . . These people were all arrested and have since been sentenced.
>
> In June 1933 my informer led me to newly organized Communist cells which were totally captured and interned. We also found a group distributing the red *Berliner Zeitung* and they were also taken to [the concentration camp] Oranienburg.

The respondent's talents in this detective work—in his words, "my successes during the revolution"—were rewarded with a criminal police job. The violent stormtrooper bully became a police officer. His membership file lists him as an SS *Obersturmbannfuehrer* (Lieutenant Colonel) in 1944 without further indication of where and how he served the SS state.

Another testimonial of 1933 is from a teacher and war invalid, born 1897 (no. 199), who delights in gory hints about "the bloody year of 1932." His account is all too typical of the self-serving reasoning underlying the violence of the takeover:

> It is my firm conviction that we old fighters would have paid with our lives, had the Communists won power instead of us. . . . Now that it was our revolution that had come we could easily have paid the political enemy back [sic] in the same coin. But nothing of the kind happened in our suburb. We did not touch a single Communist, which surprised them more than anybody. . . . They associated streets aflame and rolling heads with a revolution. . . . But many of them interpreted this treatment as weakness and their propaganda began to show up again here. We had to hit them harder. One morning in November 1933, when everybody was going to work, the police had blocked off

[7] See also no. 162, who hints at some undercover work among the Communists for the SS.

[8] The SAP (*Sozialistische Arbeiterpartei*) was a radical SPD offshoot of which Willy Brandt is rumored to have been a member before fleeing to Scandinavia.

the roads and sixty former Social Democrats and Communists, including all their former leaders, had to go to the Police Presidium. Some returned after a few days; others had to go for several weeks to the concentration camp.

It is refreshing to hear at least some early Nazis acknowledging the SA terror which in 1933 alone led to the detention of at least 60,000-75,000 political enemies.[9] The respondent claims to have helped to take care of some of the families of inmates and asserts that they were all back in a month or two. There also were some SS men who acknowledge having been employed, often after prolonged unemployment, as auxiliary policemen in the concentration camps of Dachau or Oranienburg (e.g., no. 474, born 1900). Such early concentration camp duty does not appear in the membership files. The membership file also fails to disclose his SS membership and rank of another case (no. 162, born 1886) who tells how he participated in the executions of June 30, 1934.

School and Childhood Settings

There are, of course, also a number of other factors of political socialization, the influence of the home, the school, the work environment, and the military service which we need to consider. As for their childhood settings, the enforcers have an unusually high percentage of orphans[10] 27.3% or of children growing up away from their parents, a feature frequently connected with a high propensity for violence. The party and administrative careerists, on the other hand, have nearly half of their respondents (vs. 21.2% of the enforcers) growing up in economically secure, and especially freewheeling settings which we earlier associated with prejudice. At the same time, all three groups, and especially the enforcers, tend to come from a disciplinarian upbringing far more heavily (15-21%) than the rest of the sample. Thus we are once more faced with the question of authoritarianism or, possibly, of the "battered child" becoming a Nazi enforcer. On our scale of authoritarian motives, however, the authoritarian elements make for a rather differentiated picture. The enforcers, for example, heavily reflect hostility toward the Wei-

---

[9] See Bracher, *The German Dictatorship*, p. 358, and the description of the early mass arrest, terror, and concentration camp phase in Hans Buchheim et al., *Anatomy of the SS-State*, New York: Walker, 1968, pp. 400-420.

[10] 27.3%. The two other groups have only 6-7.5% in this category. All three have about one-third who grew up in poverty but few who actually had to work before they were 14 or while others were learning a trade.

mar police and government (28.6%) and an extreme kind of leadership cult (16.7%). The identification with the authority figure is evidently needed to legitimize the violent activity of totalitarian enforcement. The party careerists, by comparison, show a great deal of leadership cult of various shadings as well as an obsession with order and cleanliness. They show much less hostility for police and government than do the administrative careerists—perhaps a concomitant of the office-holding style.

The political color of the respondent's home and other social environments of his youth shows up a good deal of similarity between the party careerists and the enforcers. Both, for example, tend to have fathers who were militarists or identified with moderate parties. In school, both tended to pick out *voelkisch* or antisemitic teachers or peers. The administrative careerists, by way of contrast, have *voelkisch* or unpolitical fathers, but nationalistic school and peer-group experiences. Behind this seeming reversal, there are differences of generation and of social behavior. The choice of *voelkisch* school and peer influences was "in" after the time the administrators went to school, although antisemitism was already a typical "in-group-out-group" dynamic among immature minds. During their early years of work, an astounding three-fourths of the enforcers (vs. only 38.8% of the administrators and 41.2% of the party careerists) were fired or experienced political friction.

Effects of War and Revolution

In the military service, telltale patterns of conformity emerge. Nearly two-thirds of the enforcers, as compared to less than half of the other two groups, never served in the military at all. Disproportionate numbers of the two careerist groups volunteered for the war, which fits into their pattern of striving for achievement. They were eager soldiers and, apart from having more than their share of war invalids and prisoners of war, they also developed a great hostility for civilians and draft-dodgers, who seemed to be mocking their best efforts. The enforcers, too, were enthusiastic soldiers, though they had the same portion (13-18%) of people eventually disaffected with the war as did the other two groups. In the reaction of all three groups to the defeat of Germany, the most salient fact is how all three tended to blame the Kaiser and the civilians. Only the party careerists also stress the role of Marxists or Spartakists, as we would expect of politically-minded right-wing extremists. They also include a sizeable number of victory-watchers. The hostility toward the old regime, of course, marks off the NSDAP from other Weimar right-wing groups such as the DNVP. The resentment toward the civilians also expresses itself in a sense of shock at the disparagement of the symbols and insignia of the army.

Their reaction toward the alleged revolution of 1919-1920 and service in Free Corps and vigilante groups brings out commonalities between the enforcers and the administrative careerists. Both attribute the "revolution" to the machinations of the victorious West and to unspecified street rabble and, along with the party careerists, to international Bolshevism. The two careerist groups also tend to lay it at the door of the Weimar coalition parties. About one-third of the enforcers and administrative careerists (vs. only 20.0% of the party careerists), consequently were in the Free Corps or vigilante groups. The administrators also tended to participate in the Kapp *putsch* of 1920. The party careerists, by way of contrast, more often merely sympathized with the counter-revolutionary work of these groups, but did not participate in it. Nearly two-thirds of the party and administrative careerists affected by the occupation, moreover, were expelled by the French occupation, often after participating in the anti-occupation underground. Similar numbers were well aware of the Hitler *putsch* in Munich (Table VI-10).

Table VI-10: Third Reich Career and Counter-revolutionary Background (in %)

	Military service	% in counter-rev. 1919-1922		Expelled by occu- pation (in % of those involved)	% in counter-rev. 1923 Voelkisch, NSDAP, veterans' assoc.	In other parties
		Free C., vigil.	Kapp			
Party career	50	20.0	5.8	63.3	41.6	15.7
Admin. career	52.5	31.2	7.8	65.0	33.9	6.1
Enforcers	39.6	35.1	3.4	31.5	22.1	18.6
All respond- dents (average)	48.3	20.6	5.5	49.4	33.6	10.1

Administrative or Party Careers of Old Fighters

This may be a good place to stop and take a closer look at the kind of administrative careers some of the respondents made under the Third Reich. One notorious case involved the son of one of the princely families of Germany (no. 260, born 1906) who started out as a law student and aide-de-camp of Joseph Goebbels. Mixing a party career in the staff of a *Gauleiter* and as an SA *Standarten-fuehrer* (Colonel) with an administrative career, he quickly rose to the higher civil service rank of *Regierungsrat* and, in 1944, *Ministerialrat* in Goebbels' Propaganda Ministry. There are many others who from far more modest beginnings before 1933 rose to the same rank in the Economics Ministry (see no. 28, born 1885), or who started out as a flunky (*Buerohilfsarbeiter*) in an office and rose rapidly in the police to the rank of a *Polizeisekretaer* (no. 60, born 1896). Some also switched over from a lowly position in a private bank to public service, like one, born 1907 (no. 171), who became a presiding judge of a county court by 1935 and, following that, an appointive mayor of a town. A lowly sales clerk, born 1902 (no. 534), in 1940 became a member of Goering's staff in the Prussian Ministry of State.

Quite a few of the administrative careerists show their greatest advancement immediately upon the Nazi takeover. A former bricklayer, born 1897 (no. 258), and technical employee of 1933, for example, was a *Regierungsbauinspektor* in 1934. A former teacher, born 1895 (no. 404), vaulted into the state school administration as a *Kreisschulrat* in 1934 and then, by a circuitous route of party offices such as *Kreisleiter*, became the appointive Lord Mayor of a large city. Another bank employee, born 1893 (no. 272), became a civil servant (*Regierungsinspektor*) in the Ministry of Economics and during the war, in 1942-1943, got himself transferred to the Office Rosenberg in Rome. As we shall see, such immediate advancement was rare among the party careerists and for good reason. While the administrative careerists could immediately move into the offices whose incumbents were purged in 1933 for political or "racial" reasons, the party careerists found themselves crowded by droves of competitors from the outside who had suddenly "discovered" the Nazi movement.

Therefore, we are more likely to find patterns of slow or late advancement among the party men. A member holding no office in 1933, for example, might make *Ortsgruppenleiter* only by 1942 (see no. 56, born 1897) when some of his more able-bodied rivals were already in the war. By comparison, those who had acquired such offices prior to 1933 received them much sooner after their entry into the party. This is even true of women, such as a longtime stalwart of the People's Party (DVP) born 1894 (no. 44), who joined the NSDAP in mid-1930, became *Ortsgruppenleiter* in a metropolitan area still within the same year, and held this office until 1937. Such early office-holders often increased their further chances of advancement by a judiciously timed entry into the SS. One *Ortsgruppenleiter* of 1928-1930, born 1908 (no. 389), for instance, joined the SS in March 1933, rose to the rank of sergeant by 1935, and thus moved on to director of the *Kreisleitung* and the appointive position of a city councilman of a large town. Occasionally, also, an aristocrat could travel faster than anybody. A young nobleman born in 1912 (no. 379) who was still in school and at the university at the time of the take-over was evidently spared most of the discomforts of the fighting years through the special protection and immunities extended to him by his school principal and by the police. His record lists him as an SA *Truppfuehrer* in 1939, but three years later he had a fairly important job (*Hauptstellenleiter*) in the Chancellery of the *Fuehrer* of the NSDAP. Some of the auxiliary organizations also permitted more rapid advancement. A member born in 1892 (no. 500), who held no office in 1933 could be a *Kreisleiter* of the German Labor Front (DAF) in 1934.

The careers within the SS, if we consider only rank, often evolved faster than in the party organization because of the rapid growth of the SS after 1933. Of course, it was never again as fast a road from SS man to *Sturmfuehrer* (Lieutenant) as it had been during the fighting years when a man under favorable circumstances could build up his own *Sturm* within a period of one to two years. An old fighter joining the SS in 1938 might make it by 1941 (no. 450, born 1906). To get from the lowest rank to that of *Sturmbannfuehrer* (Major) might take as long as a decade (see no. 421, born 1898, no. 475, born 1900 and no. 527, born 1893). A pre-1933 *Sturmfuehrer* could be a *Gruppenfuehrer* (General) by 1938 (no. 443, born 1902; or by 1939, no. 385, born 1906) or by 1942, a time of rapidly widening opportunities in the top ranks of the Armed SS (no. 462, born 1896). To rise to such heights from the lowest rank after 1933 was evidently helped greatly by membership in the Security Service (SD), the secret police watching SS and party members (no. 440, born 1898).[11]

The SS and Gestapo (Secret State Police) were among the organizations specifically proscribed in the war crime and denazification proceedings after the war. They and later services such as the SD, the SS Special Commandos, the new Office of the Chief of the German Police (Himmler), and the RSHA (Reich Security Office) indeed were the hub of the Nazi police state, of the coercive system

[11] This respondent, a lathe worker, was an SS *Truppfuehrer* in 1933 and became an SS General in the SD Main Office as early as 1939. See below p. 663.

at the heart of the Third *Reich*.[12] There was some objection at the time of the denazification trials that a person should not be considered guilty for merely having belonged to the SS, but only for specific acts of wrong-doing. Considering the solidarity and mobility among the SS members, the deaths of victims, and the confusion of the times, such acts were rarely proven or even known beyond a small circle. Among the enforcers of the Abel collection, the membership file in the Berlin Document Center often listed very incriminating assignments which we shall examine more closely below. But there were also SS men with no such entries or with entries suggesting a different order of wrong-doing, if any.

A case of this latter sort was a young travelling salesman, born 1900 (no. 526), who complained about having had a mean stepmother since the age of ten and about losing his bookkeeper father in the war seven years later. He was drafted at the same time as many unwilling Socialist recruits but never saw any action. After the war, the respondent served some time with the *Buergerwehr* and as a *Zeitfreiwilliger*. Through a "noble Communist" friend he was also exposed to the writings of Rosa Luxemburg, Karl Liebknecht, and Ernst Toller. At every election until 1929, the respondent relates, "in his confusion" he voted for a different party. In 1929, while he was unemployed, he went to a big Nazi rally and was immediately captivated by a Goebbels speech:

> It was as if I had heard the gospel. Politically completely neutral, I immediately awakened to the significance of the idea and found what I had always been looking for: Justice and progress. Justice in the socialist demands of the program, toward the workers whose bitterness I had gotten to understand. . . . Progress in awakening the natural forces of personality and race. . . .
> It was fighting time! I had a goal and, being unemployed, I could devote myself completely to party work.

He became an SA man and propaganda assistant and served nearly every night at one rally or the other. He comments on this service: "We SA men of that period were, of course, no saints, but we never resorted to one thing: We never broke the discipline to tolerate in our midst elements who were in it only for the adventure. For we were no mercenaries (*Landsknechte*) but political soldiers fighting for a new view of the world which was to unite our whole people and lead them into a better future."

In October of 1930, the respondent graduated to the SS, which

---

[12] See esp. Bracher, *The German Dictatorship*, pp. 350-362, and Buchheim et al., *Anatomy of the SS-State*, pp. 172ff.

he describes as "on the average the best-selected material of men available in Germany in a special organization for certain tasks and with rigorous discipline." When he completed his *vita* for Abel, he was an SS *Sturmfuehrer*. By 1941, according to the Berlin files, he had become an *Obersturmbannfuehrer* (Lieutenant Colonel) in the staff of the SS Main Office. The last entry identifies him as a film director and producer with the Ufa, Tobis, and Terra companies and a functionary of the *Reichsfilmkammer*. Thus the menace of his black SS uniform with the "gold pheasant" officer's insignia was probably confined to the starlets of the motion picture sets.

But there are many others whose SS or other enforcer career ends with more ominous entries. There is, for example, a druggist from Silesia, born 1905 (no. 522), who found all parties, right and left, distasteful until the Nazi landslide of 1930 swept him up as well. He began to read the *Voelkischer Beobachter*, *Mein Kampf*, and other Nazi propaganda, and soon joined the NSDAP. He claims having witnessed "the fury and meanness of the Marxist rabble and its helpers" during an alleged assault by the "Moscow disciples" on an SA man. He also accuses the police of having deprived the injured man of available medical assistance. Then he tells of an attack of "the *Reichsbanner* hordes" on his SA home which received such "a hearty reception" that it was not repeated. According to the respondent, it was always the others, the "hordes" that attacked.

He began to proselytize among friends and fellow-workers and claims to have recruited the majority of the 18 employees of his company before his superiors, allegedly a Freemason and a left-winger, followed up on "Jewish accusations" and fired him. He went to live with his parents and, after his father's death, joined the SS. His record in the party files indicates that he joined the Gestapo late in 1933 and eventually became a *Kriminalsekretaer* with this organization in occupied Poland. In 1944, he also served with the Reich Security Office (RSHA) as an *Untersturmfuehrer* of the SS. He was obviously not just a harmless "gold pheasant."

Another case is the one of a gardener, born 1905 (no. 466), the son of a furniture manufacturer and at 17 a member of the Red Hundreds. After a clash between his Red Hundreds and the *Voelkisch* Hundreds, the respondent was irresistibly attracted by the latter and their swastika banner. He began to study *voelkisch* propaganda, including Fritsch's *Handbook of the Jewish Question*, and joined the *voelkisch* squads. His account of his years as a stormtrooper is a series of descriptions of inspiring moments presented in the special inspirational style typical of some Nazi propagandists.

He also speaks of a "common front against the Jews and the lower races" and the "final victory of the Germanic tribes." His account of violent encounters depicts the *Reichsbanner*, the Communists, and the police as the aggressors, even "animal-like murderers" but with fewer undertones of hidden brutality than the previous case. His wife was also an "old fighter" of the movement. In 1934, he was already an SS *Sturmhauptfuehrer* (Captain). Ten years later he was a *Sturmbannfuehrer* (Major) of the Armed SS on a special section on police affairs with one of the regional Higher SS and Police Chiefs. His inspirational preaching evidently masked a terrorist mind.

A third case of the same generation was a plumber, born 1904 (no. 59), who at the age of 9 had lost his father. His Catholic mother raised him to religious devotion and he joined a Catholic young men's association. Under the influence of a meeting of the *voelkisch-sozialer Block* and his own antisemitic disposition, however, he soon found himself isolated among his Catholic fellows and left the group. His experiences in the militant Metal Workers Union during a wildcat strike also were a great disappointment, in spite of enthusiastic beginnings. He quit the union and claims always to have done well in negotiating with employers by himself. In 1923, the respondent and a friend fell under the spell of a young Nazi who had been expelled from the occupied area and supplied them with information about the movement in Bavaria. Another Nazi swore them to secrecy and asked them to be ready for the call of November 9 that never came. The next day, the newspapers told about the abortive beerhall *putsch*.

The respondent was far more ideologically committed and politically active from an earlier date than most enforcers. After 1923, he helped to form a Nazi front, *Treubund*, and got into violent encounters with the local "rabble." After a short stint with the *Reichswehr*, he went back to work among Socialists and Centrists and attempted to propagandize the cause at work. Since the *Treubund* had been outlawed, too, he and his friends founded a *Stahlhelm* chapter in 1927, but after about a year the respondent moved away. In 1931, he lost his job just as the Nazis were coming to his town. A rally which ended in a wild melée with Communists, Socialists, and the police battling an SS team finally induced the respondent to join the party and the SS.

> Now the fight started in [this city]. We found some more men and women to form a local. When we were planning another meeting at the end of October, we were prepared to give the Reds something to

think about in case they wanted to disrupt our meeting. . . . I was living with my brother who wanted to throw me out so he would not have to put up with the danger of being accosted by the Reds. . . . My relatives were particularly mad at me, since they all belonged to the Center party, except for my brothers. My uncle once refused to eat for three days because I had sullied the family name by marching at the head of an SA demonstration. At the unemployment office it was like running the gauntlet, being the only SS man who needed unemployment benefits. Rocks were frequently flung at me from behind and from dark corners.

By the beginning of 1932, the respondent was already heading his *Sturm*. He tells of the comradeship and togetherness in the movement. But he also tells of "the terror of police and government against us":

> In January 1933, a comrade from the edge of town asked me to see him home because he was threatened by about 20 communists. I went with him until he was safe. Now the toughs cornered me as I re-entered the town. I defended myself and knocked one down with a heavy wrench. The police appeared and took me down to the station, where the wrench was called a weapon. I was sentenced to four days in jail. But I need not have worried for . . . our Fuehrer Adolf Hitler became Reich Chancellor a few days later. . . . Our erstwhile enemies went into hiding for fear of our revenge. . . .

This respondent joined the police in 1934 and soon began to work for Himmler's Reich Commissariat for Strengthening German Folkdom (RKF), which was entrusted with shuffling about the various ethnic minorities in the east. He became an RKF Commissar in Poland and an SS *Obersturmfuehrer* of the Armed SS in 1943. His advancement appears to have been slower than that of the other bloodhounds.

All three of these cases show certain common features, such as the early involvement in extremist violence. Evidently, the most violent pre-1933 stormtroopers simply went on to enforcer roles in which they could further indulge in brutality. They all seem to have tended to see their violent encounters in masochistic terms, that is, with the antagonists always the aggressors. Frequently, their fathers died prematurely, were absent, or were at odds with their sons. And, especially with the last two cases, there is usually a long record of previous involvement in extremist politics which prepared the respondent, stage by stage as it were, for the hostility and militant attitude he showed as a violent stormtrooper and later as an enforcer of the terror of the Third Reich. Let us take a look at the patterns of political mobilization of these groups of respondents.

Third Reich Careers and the Four Stages

How did the processes of political mobilization undergone by these three career groups differ? Were there specifically military-civil service routes for the administrative careerists, specifically ideological-political ones for the party men, and political-violence-oriented careers for the enforcers? At the pre-political stage (stage one), prior to any Weimar involvement, the administrative and party careerists often came from an unpolitical Youth Movement background. One out of ten party careerists also was actively involved in prewar political parties such as the SPD, the Conservatives, or the Antisemites. The bloodhounds of the movement, by contrast, tended to enter stages two, three, or four so early in life that before this mobilization they were too young for political interest.

At stage two (militarization) the three groups exhibit characteristic patterns. The administrative careerists tended to join the Free Corps, *Wehrwolf*, or *Stahlhelm* after they passed the age of 25, many of them probably in logical continuation of military-civil or wartime service.[13] The party careerists either tended to become militarized just as late or before they were even 18. But they did so in an ideological and political manner. They mostly joined *Jungdo*, left-wing groups, or pre-1925 *voelkisch* groups such as the *Schutz-und-Trutzbund* or the early NSDAP. One out of five in this group belonged to the pre-1925 party. The enforcers shared some of the features of both careerist groups by tending to join the Free Corps or the *Wehrwolf*, but they did so heavily before the age of 21. In fact, 70% of them became militarized before that age, as compared to only 40% of the administrative and 46.3% of the party careerists who went through stage two. Their motives for militarization round out the picture. The administrative careerists were militarized mainly by the impact of the defeat and their shock at the new lead-

---

[13] Party and administrative careerists, to begin with, more often went through militarization than did the enforcers and the rest of the sample. It is remarkable that half of the enforcers in fact did become militarized at all, considering that 57.4% of them were born in 1902 or later and hence could have been no older than 21 in 1923. This may also help to explain their early militarization, aside from organizations such as *Wehrwolf* or *Stahlhelm* that were available after 1923. But it does not detract from the youthful militarization which seems to be a hallmark of the bloodhound group.

ership of Weimar. The party careerists, by way of contrast, were militarized mostly by their own antisemitic predisposition or by their opposition to the revolutionaries. The accent is clearly on ideological motivation. The enforcers, finally, tended to be mobilized by the shock of the occupation or also by their opposition to the revolutionaries, presumably a gut reaction rather than the result of intellectual deliberation.

The third stage, politicization, was experienced by relatively few of the enforcers (44.4%), except for some who belonged to moderate parties before joining the NSDAP. Again the enforcers were remarkably young when they entered this stage. The Nazi administrators also tended to be in moderate parties or to shop around at this stage. The party careerists, by contrast, heavily belonged to pre-1925 *voelkisch* parties including the early NSDAP, or to the DNVP and its affiliates. Their age at becoming politicized tended to be over 25, in contrast to the administrators, not to mention the terror-enforcers. Among the motives for politicization, opposition to the leaders of the Weimar Republic and coming of voting age figured prominently among the party and administrative careerists. The enforcers who were mostly of working-class or farm backgrounds were more often motivated by opposition to Marxism and revolution or by economic difficulties. At both, stage two and three, nearly half of the enforcers already engaged in organized and individual violent encounters. The party and administrative careerists rather tended only toward individual violence. The enforcers also tended to demonstrate; the party men typically were engaged in electioneering or in holding office.

At stage four, in the post-1924 NSDAP, the enforcers tend to be either marcher-fighters (MF) or marcher-fighter-proselytizers (MFP). The party careerists, by comparison, tend to be MFPs or marcher-proselytizers (MP), or simply marchers (M). The accent is on fighting among the enforcers and on proselytizing among the party men. The administrators have no unusual concentrations in any one category.

Table VI-11: Third Reich Careers and Stage Four (in %)

	Ms	MFs	MPs	MFPs	Totals
Party careerists	8.6	16.1	24.7	23.6	71.0
Administrators	4.4	22.1	22.1	19.1	67.7
Enforcers	3.4	52.5	10.2	28.8	94.9

The large percentage of MFs, the "mindless sluggers," among the enforcers is particularly notable. They also join at a much younger age—45.7% under 21 and three-fourths no older than 30. The comparable figures for the administrators are 32.2% and 44.2% and for the party men 33% and 48.9%, respectively. The motives of the two careerist groups for joining the NSDAP are especially the dynamic impression of the Hitler movement and, for the administrators, also friction with the occupation. The enforcers, by way of contrast, are attracted mostly by their economic troubles or by the spirit of comradeship among the stormtroopers.

An unusual case with a "day-and-night" record of violence was a relatively old salesman, born 1884 (no. 75). He had served two years in peacetime and as a sergeant in the war. Allegedly too busy each night to follow his inclination, he finally managed through a change of business to attend a Nazi rally in 1928 and promptly signed up for the party and the SA.

> With fanatical dedication I now fought for the party and the great idea of Adolf Hitler. Although my business declined because of my entry into the party, I fought openly and recruited various new members by my example. Soon I was the most hated man with the SPD and KPD, and I never missed a rally or a meeting-hall assignment of the SA. . . . My wife had to endure the worst insults [for being the local party treasurer] and I often went after the Communists or Socialists on account of this. In spite of all the brawls which repeatedly gave me head injuries, my wife and I were not to be deterred from fighting on and doing our duty.

This account suggests a closer relation to his "red" antagonists than he admits. In 1930, when he became unemployed, he again devoted body and soul to the movement. He became a cell leader (*Block- und Zellenwart*), went to rally after rally and, as an SA *Truppfuehrer*, got involved in plenty of brawls and demonstrations. The respondent seems to have made Goebbels' theory of confronting the reds in their own lair the rationale of his fighting years. He lived right next to the local Communist hangout evidently on purpose, and apparently was the object of a good deal of hostile attention from there. His description casts a curious light on the relations between the enemies of the day:

> I was often persecuted and accosted, until I really told them off. Then—I learned this through my contacts—the local KPD held court over me and decided to "finish" me, my *Sturmfuehrer*, and another four comrades. When I heard this, I decided to confront them with this story. Two nights after that KPD meeting I passed three KPD men on the way to the SA service and they jeered aloud: "There is that Nazi

bandit." I turned on my heels and went right up to the biggest of the three and to the functionary who had presided over that meeting. If even one of us was assaulted, I told him, ten of their men were going to lie dead on the ground soon. I quietly walked away and none of our men in this area ever got his hair mussed again.

The author of this piece of *West Side Story* dialogue later seems to have done well for himself in a business career under the Nazis. More important, although he never went beyond the declining SA, in 1943 he was their Commissar of Counterintelligence (*Abwehr*) in one of the regional SA commands.

In the Party

When and how did these career groups become introduced to the party? The party careerists were the earliest to join; one-fifth was in the pre-1925 party and another fifth joined in the immediate reconstruction period. They also tended to be the first to join in their locality and often were founders of the Nazi local. The enforcers heavily joined in the years of reconstruction 1925-1927, and again right after the landslide elections of 1930. In fact, they tended to join the party only after it had become a substantial minority in their area. We would not go wrong in seeing in them the young Free Corps and stormtrooper types who crowded into the party at these times, attracted by the opportunities for violent action and little else. The administrative careerists have the highest number of *Septemberlinge*, far in excess of the entire sample. They also tended to join not immediately after the 1930 election, as did the enforcers but, with the caution befitting bureaucrats, only after mid-1931 when the further growth of the movement and its final triumph seemed likely. Here, in other words, we have the opportunists for whom the word *Septemberlinge* was really coined.

In their manner of introduction, the party careerists and enforcers conform to the model typical of the most active stormtroopers. They were introduced by friends or fellow-workers who presumably took them to a Nazi meeting, knowing that they would like it, given their previous attitudes or behavior. The administrative careerists, on the other hand, were mostly attracted by an awareness of the Nazi ideology, as were many of those who joined after mid-1931 and at middle age. Once they were in it, moreover, the attitude of both party and administrative careerists toward the NSDAP was strongly colored by the expectation of a job or other material reward, and much less by a sense of personal integration derived from the pursuit of utopia. The enforcers, by way of contrast, tended heavily to identify with the struggle itself and also with the Hitler cult that lent legitimacy to the mayhem. This combination is evidently a strong indication of the enforcer career to come.

And then comes a clear division into the styles of office-holding and of violence. Ninety-five percent of the enforcers (vs. 59.7% of the administrators and 54.8% of the party careerists) belonged to the stormtroopers, including one-third in the pre-1933 SS. These figures by far exceed those of any other grouping we have made of the sample. The difference in holding stormtrooper ranks is not quite as extreme; 45.6% of the enforcers held minor ranks (vs. 12-15% of the careerist groups) and 31.6% were *Sturmfuehrer* or *Sturmbannfuehrer* (vs. 16-26% of the careerists). The administrators, some of whom came from the Free Corps, are not far behind at the higher ranks.

On the other hand, only 38.6% of the enforcers held party offices prior to 1933, as compared to 77.9% of the party careerists and 71.8% of the administrators. The latter were almost on a par with the party men, especially at the higher levels. About one-third of both groups were *Ortsgruppenleiter* and another seventh or eighth held office in a functional organization. Clearly, the paths lead from stormtrooper to totalitarian enforcer and from party office holder to party or administrative careerist.

And it is not just a matter of organizational membership in the SA or SS. Nearly two-thirds of the enforcers report engagement in political violence in the streets or in the meeting-halls, as compared to only about a third of the two careerist groups.[14] The latter, on the other hand, made up the difference by heavy involvement in proselytizing and, at least among the party men, electioneering. In their attitude toward violence, the enforcers stand out with heavy emphasis on masochism: It is always the others who are doing things to them. This sociopathic reversal of violent roles probably continues into their enforcer roles in the Gestapo and in concentration camps. It may be a necessary prerequisite to an enforcer role, in fact, to be a sociopath who blames the victims for what he is doing to them.

Ideology and Attitudes of Careerists

Since there was a major shift in personnel in 1933, it is a matter of considerable interest to compare the pre-1933 ideology and atti-

---

[14] There is, moreover, a noticeable tendency among the most involved enforcers to be rather close-mouthed in their *vitae* about their involvement in street violence. It is hard to tell whether they are secretive because they are getting illicit pleasure out of the violence or whether they fail to talk about it because it seems unimportant to their account.

tudes of these three "successful" groups with those of the sample at large. Ideologically, the party men emphasized Nordic-German romanticism (heavily), antisemitism, and the Hitler cult, in this order. The administrators preferred instead to stress *Volksgemein-schaft* (solidarism) and revanchism. The enforcers, finally, put the stress on revanchism (heavily) and on the Hitler cult. They also include more than their share of people with no ideology of note. Curiously missing among these themes is superpatriotism, which was very important to a good fifth of the entire sample, while the Nordic-German cult had no more allegiance than about 6%. The combination of themes of the party men, *voelkisch* romanticism, antisemitism, and Hitler cult, augmented with revanchism and solidarism, indeed, pretty well describes the concerns of the Third Reich.

The attitudes toward the Weimar Republic also tell a good deal about the mentality of the different kinds of careerists. The party men tend to call it the Jewish-run republic or to yearn for the day when a Nazi utopia would replace the "red and black parties." The administrators heavily lean toward the old slogan of Weimar's "liberal-Marxist system," which is also popular among the enforcers. The latter also voice traditional anticapitalistic objections and express their dislike for the multi-party system, all rather inconsequential criticisms to motivate revolutionary violence.

What about the level of prejudice of the "successful" old fighters? As we would expect, the party careerists are highest in antisemitic prejudice, with 74% responding positively, including 27.4% with the *Judenkoller*, 13.7% telling prejudiced anecdotes, and 15.1% virulent paranoids. The administrators even exceed their share on the last two categories, but have far fewer cholerics. The enforcers, like the other groupings of violent men we have examined, are not particularly prejudiced, although they have a larger number of respondents with a sudden outbreak of *Judenkoller* than any other group. It is hard to interpret this finding except by interpreting this choler as a sign of deteriorating mental balance. That the party careerists should be the most prejudiced is hardly surprising, though the extent of virulent prejudice among the administrative careerists is. It must signify a high degree of penetration of the civil service with Nazi ideas that such men could make a career in it.

A glimpse of the personalities of these groups of men[15] emerges from their patterns of family membership in the party. Rather less

[15] Of the 36 Nazi women in our sample, only 4 appeared in any of our career groups, including 3 in a party career.

than the entire sample, they tend to have their whole families in the party. The good fellowship of the fighting years alone was evidently not enough to make a career. Instead, both the party men and the enforcers show a tendency to be loners, which is quite at variance with our earlier finding about the violent stormtroopers. Evidently the enforcers were somewhat odd even among the bulk of the stormtroopers. The administrators heavily tend to have spouses in the party. They also indicate their "formative experiences" in many cases either as the *Fronterlebnis* of World War One or as alleged episodes with aliens or Jews. The party men more often stress the experience of defeat and occupation. The enforcers claim to reflect particularly the "educational" experiences of a book, a teacher, or being unemployed. They also exhibit an extreme degree of leadership cult along with a desire to want to merge completely with the movement. These features, too, seem to be characteristic of an enforcer career later on.

In all this, it goes without saying that the enforcers were not particularly intelligent. Their level of political understanding tended to be either of the low, ideological or the dimwit-romantic type. The administrators, by comparison, were far more often very knowledgeable about Weimar politics and even the party men and women tended to come in at a medium level. In a sense, the three career groups embody more or less recognizable strains we have dealt with earlier: *voelkisch* ideologues and perpetual office-holders, the military-civil servants of an earlier regime, and the mindless sluggers of the fighting days of the movement.

Serving the SS State

The enigma of the motivations of the enforcers remains in spite of our search and the speculations about a man like Rudolf Hoess, the "face in the crowd," who ran the Auschwitz camp. Were they really just dimwitted brutes who did not mind doing the dirty jobs of the totalitarian SS state? We have already looked at one or two who rose to higher authority in Himmler's empire of terror.[16] Obviously, they do not tell us all there may be to know about their persons and conduct even before 1933. Occasionally, though, there are glimpses of the truth, at least with the benefit of hindsight. Let us take another look at some of the most deeply involved.

The birth dates of our first three cases of enforcers placed them

[16] Before the FBI confiscated about 100 cases in 1951—very likely cases involving ongoing denazification trials or investigations—there were probably a good many more such respondents.

in the victory-watchers' generation, but there are also enforcers of the second wave of youth revolt. One was a young worker born in 1914 (no. 136), who was recruited by a fellow-worker in the midst of "the Communist terror." He bore a deep resentment against the wealthy, "corrupt politicians in all parties," particularly the DNVP, against the Jews, and against capitalism. He was enthusiastic about the 25 points of the nearly meaningless Nazi program. He joined the Hitler Youth in 1930, and the SA early in 1932, when he was only 17. By an oversight no one noticed that he had not joined the party itself until after the Nazi take-over in 1933. He is rather close-mouthed about his experiences as a stormtrooper.

In May 1934, he was called to serve in the staff of the SA leadership, just in time for the blood purge of that year. But this did not hold back his advance for long. A year later he was in the Race and Settlement Office (RUSHA), where he was to remain until 1945 with the rank of SS *Obersturmfuehrer* in spite of some disciplinary measures against him at one point. RUSHA was one of the innermost cogs in Himmler's infernal machine, administering certain internal affairs and certifying the racial purity of SS members back to the year 1750. It also played a role in developing Nazi policy against Czechs, Poles, and Jews.[17] The respondent's file also lists him as an employee of the Gestapo.

Older enforcers are not absent from our collection, but they tend to have somewhat different motives. A bank clerk, born in 1896 (no. 462), who volunteered for the Guards Regiment in 1914, at the age of 17, is a good example. He was wounded in 1915 and after a prolonged stay in the hospital was sent home with 50% disability pay. He describes his feelings as a suddenly aged young adult whose active life seems to have passed its apogee: "For me as an old soldier the times after the end of the war were utterly depressing (*trostlos*). Politically, I had no idea what to do with myself. If I voted for the left-wing parties, I was voting for an improvement of my economic situation. If I went for the nationalistic circles of the day, I knew I was serving the fatherland but worsening my own situation." Supported by his evident faith in the efficacy of the ballot, this strange logic led him to the Nazis: "Thus the movement founded by Adolf Hitler provided a perfect fit for my needs. Here I found what I as an old frontline fighter had hoped for." He voted for the Nazis "from their first appearance on" and read the *Voelk-*

---

[17] See Bracher, *The German Dictatorship*, pp. 414-416, 426. See also Paul Kluke, "Nationalsozialistische Europapolitik," *Vierteljahreshefte fuer Zeitgeschichte*, vol. 3 (1955), pp. 257ff.

ischer Beobachter and all the Nazi books and periodicals "from their first issue" but joined only in mid-1930. This part of his story is one of the more implausible tales of the collection and was probably inspired by a desire to impress the local NSDAP with his early sympathy and loyalty.

The respondent almost immediately joined the SA and then the SS, all in 1930. "I participated in everything the SS did, propaganda, demonstrations, training recruits, and meeting-hall battles." He gives no detailed account, however, and concludes his brief *vita* by asserting his determination "to fight right on for Adolf Hitler until even the last German has absorbed the idea of National Socialism." His dedication to "everything the SS did" led to his rapid advancement which by 1941 resulted in an assignment in the *Haupttreuhandstelle Ost*, where the SS empire handled the loot stolen from the occupied territories in the east.[18] A year later he is listed as an SS *Gruppenfuehrer* (General) in the SD Main Office. The SD (Security Service) was Heydrich's secret police control organization for the NSDAP and was then under the Reich Security Main Office (RSHA), the hub of the SS state. By that time it had been vitally involved in ferreting out all real and potential political enemies in conquered Austria and Czechoslovakia.

Somewhat similar to the third case in his venom against the Metal Workers Union was a self-styled former Marxist lathe worker, born in 1898 (no. 440), who allegedly lost his livelihood in consequence of a prolonged wildcat strike "provoked by Marxist hate-mongers." He turned his back on the union and on the SPD. His account suggests that he may have acted with excessive militancy, though without deep conviction, on the union side during the strike and ended up blacklisted by his employer and without support from union or party. At least this would explain his fury toward union and party leaders and tell something about him as well.

In 1925, after two years of "abstention from politics" he moved to another town and began to attend NSDAP meetings and to try and understand Nazi thinking. Late in 1929 he became a member and almost immediately a minor SA chief. He tried very hard to spread the propaganda by word of mouth although he was not the most articulate or intelligent of men. His forte seemed to lie more in his unquestioning loyalty and in his penchant for violence, qualities which stood him in good stead with the Nazi regime. His file

[18] On the farflung economic empire of the SS, see also Enno Georg, *Die wirtschaftlichen Unternehmungen der SS*, Stuttgart: Deutsche Verlagsanstalt, 1963.

lists him as an SS *Truppfuehrer* in 1933. Three years later he already held an important post in the Security Service (SD); in 1939 he was an SS general (*Gruppenfuehrer*) in the SD Main Office for the South West, and in 1943 he was with the Reich Security Main Office (RSHA). Nowhere but in the SS state could a man of such limited intelligence have risen with such awesome rapidity.

Another SD man, born 1895 (no. 323), has an interesting story to tell about his school background, which somewhat resembles accounts of the failures of several prominent Nazi leaders, including Hitler himself. The son of a distiller on a feudal estate, he was sent away for his education from the age of 7, first to an uncle who was an elementary-school teacher, and then to various intermediate and secondary schools. In one class, at about the age of 11, the respondent had a monster of a teacher whose canings and arbitrary punishments reportedly sent him from near the top of the class to the bottom. He had to stay home repeatedly with "fever from beatings" and failed to be advanced at the end of the term. Eventually transferred to the *Gymnasium*, he also had his ups and downs there, and finally had to capitulate before the challenge of learning languages, especially Latin. He finally changed to a teachers' college, which turned out to be very dull and oppressive, as his penchant for sports became the object of disciplinary measures against him. He dropped out and switched to a bricklayer's career until the war broke out.

He enlisted right away and was an enthusiastic soldier who received both decorations and injuries. When the war ended, nevertheless, he was glad: "I hoped that the Social Democrats would bring about understanding and fraternization with the whole world, thus securing a just peace. My hopes were disappointed. The unrest, strikes, murders, and excesses, the humiliating peace treaty of Versailles, and the occupation of the Rhineland soon allowed me to see my mistake."

The respondent was now working for the railroads and comments with dark hints of conspiracy on a railroad men's strike in which he participated. In 1925, he became involved in Kunze's *Deutsch-Soziale Partei* but was critical of Kunze's social bias which, in his opinion, was unlikely to lead to a broad popular movement. The *Stahlhelm* with its massive demonstrations impressed him although he deplored its lack of political direction and ties to the DNVP. The SA and NSDAP, finally, which under Goebbels was just beginning to make headway in Berlin in 1927-1928, captivated the respondent with "its bravery in battling the Communists and the police," and with the big rallies and speeches in the Sports Palace. He joined the party right after such a rally and for a few months was kept from joining the SA only by the strenuous objections of his wife.

It is not clear from his account what caused his rising interest in political participation and especially in stormtrooper activity. He says that at the outset, his political interest was caused by discussions with a colleague about the ravages of the inflation of 1923, which ruined his parents' savings and "initiated the gradual decline of the whole economy." His joining of the SA was against the strong opposition of his wife who "feared to be left alone since our marriage was happy but not blessed with children and the SA was going to claim all my free time." The respondent, then aged 33, may well have become footloose because of marital disappointments or the crisis of aging.

The respondent became very involved in the organization of a viable SA *Sturm* in his town, Koepenick, and tells in glowing terms of attending a big Nazi convention in Nuremberg. He also describes meeting-hall battles in Berlin, fighting alongside the stormtroopers of Horst Wessel, and being beaten up by Communists and police. The others are always the attackers. In 1931 the respondent transferred to the SS because he could not get along with his new *Sturmfuehrer*, a man who was apparently executed in the Roehm purge of 1934, as he gleefully reports. To transfer, he had to belong all by himself to the SS of another town for there were no other SS men in Koepenick. There are shades here of his difficulties with various teachers and schools. He liked the SS and soon was asked to form his own troop, an undertaking that entailed a rank of SS *Scharfuehrer* for him.

After the ascent to power, the respondent expresses an unusual amount of bitterness about the rush of opportunists into the party and to the positions and jobs now available. Eventually, the party remembered him too and gave him a thankless civil service assignment which no one else wanted. They also assigned him a task of "political surveillance" in this job. He slowly caught on and became a functionary of the SA Main Office while working as an executive of the "political railroad police." His case is more notable for the revealing frankness with which he talks about himself than for his enforcer career, except for his final assignment as an SS Economic Administrator with the "Clothes Processing Agency," Dachau, in Oranienburg.

The last example of an SD man was a young workman, born 1905 (no. 48), who fits the pattern of the young nationalist amid Socialist workers who eventually "forced" him to join the Metal

Workers Union. As soon as he became permanently unemployed and moved in with his parents again, in 1930, he became interested in the Nazis. He read some of their literature and, early in 1931, joined the SA. He tells of SA demonstrations and of being knifed and hospitalized for six weeks. Later in the same year, he was "ordered," along with seven other SA men, to transfer to the SS.

In the SS, then, he "had to work even harder at propaganda and proselytizing, on the road every day until late at night with newspapers and brochures, or protecting rallies in towns and villages." There were compensations, such as the exhilarating experience of attending the huge SA rally of October 1931 in *Braunschweig*, at which he saw the Fuehrer, both "experiences the like of which I never had again." And there was a career waiting which began with full-time work for the SS in 1933. In 1935 he was drafted into the SD. And by 1944 he held the rank of SS *Hauptsturmfuehrer* (Captain) and Inspector of the Security Police and the SD. While he has not told us much about himself, it is striking how many of these heavies joined only after the 1930 elections and while being unemployed.

This brings us back to the question, what manner of men were these enforcers who did the dirty work in the SS-state? What can we learn from these cases? How did the enforcers differ from the other two groups of careerists and from the many other violent extremists of the Nazi Movement we have discussed above? The three groups in many ways look like groupings we have encountered earlier. The party careerists resemble the *voelkisch* ideologues and office-holders of the pre-1925 party. The administrative careerists are a mixture of the prewar military-civil servant strain, the front generation, and the more passive antisemites who jumped on the bandwagon only after 1930. The enforcers, however, have to be placed more specifically among the styles of violence we discussed earlier. In addition to their large share of the instant stormtroopers, for example, the enforcers comprise half of the pre-1933 SS members and have a surprisingly large share (19.4%) of the delayed stormtroopers. Only about one-sixth of the struggle-oriented are enforcers. Nearly one-third of the enforcers hold middle-echelon ranks and almost half of them lower ranks in the SA or SS, which makes them representative of nearly one-fourth of all the stormtrooper leaders of the sample. There are very few day-and-nighters among them, far fewer than among the party men and administrative careerists.

Apart from their high involvement with pre-1933 political violence in the SA and their heavy overlap with the pre-1933 SS and the stormtrooper leadership, we have to fall back on their personal background for an explanation of their grisly role in the Third Reich: Their social frustrations, lower-class and poverty backgrounds, lack of paternal or religious guidance, fatherlessness or disciplinarian childhoods, low education, and poor school environment seem to have turned these youths toward very early militarization, violent youth activities, and eventually Nazi extremism. They seem to have joined the NSDAP for lack of something better to do and because it promised them more violence under the cover of a legitimizing ideology and supported by a charismatic leader and a comradely organization. Hence the intense leadership cult and the stress on the comradeship of the stormtroopers and on merging individuality with the movement.

As the movement took over power in the country, the romanticism of the violent brotherhood of outlaws waned, but the new regime was just as anxious to continue to exploit their bent for violence. And it appears to have been precisely their overwhelmingly masochistic attitude toward violence[19] which made it possible for them to work as concentration camp guards and other minions of the SS-state. The masochistic attitude, which had manifested itself in the curious habit of relating all violence as if it was always initiated by the antagonists and imposed on the respondent, is an extrapunitive, sociopathic attitude that is extremely well-suited to the enforcement role. These men and many others like them probably blamed even their victims in the concentration camps for the violence they visited upon them.

[19] The enforcers had two masochists for every sadist, the administrators the exact reverse, and the party men were about equally masochists and sadists.

Summary and Conclusions

The time has come to look back and briefly to retrace the steps we have taken to shed more light on the motives of the early Nazis. We began with a description of the Abel biographies and of the likely kinds of bias they might contain. In particular, we noted how the Abel sample differs in age, occupation, geographic distribution and, most of all, in the time of joining from these same parameters in the official party statistics of 1935. It is a sample with a heavy pre-1930 bias, a time when the movement was still small and an extremist fringe group. These flaws in the sample make the frequency distributions unrepresentative, but as long as we concentrate on the multivariate relationships, they will not invalidate our findings.

The Social Dynamics of the Movement

Then we turned the spotlight on the social dynamics of the early Nazi movement in the light of various current theories. The evidence appeared to cast considerable doubt on theories explaining the socio-economic motivation of all the respondents with such simple schemes as the "lower middle-class revolt," or the fascism of social decline. There were obviously highly differentiated motive forces at work which had few common denominators except for frustrated upward mobility and an in-between or misfit status between the two powerful camps of the liberal bourgeoisie and the organized working class. The class resentments of the imperial sergeant who could never become an officer, the primary-school teacher who was held in contempt by the academically trained professions, or the half-proletarian by birth are examples as typical as were the upwardly mobile from the farm or from the urban working-class whose future was jeopardized by the economic consequences of a lost war. The patterns of social and spatial mobility, furthermore, clearly relate the age groups of the sample to German social and economic history: The older but upwardly mobile rural-urban migrants, the younger socially and spatially immobile residents of small towns and countryside, and the young, highly mobile drifters who were in social decline or stagnant. The relation of the three generations (prewar, war, and postwar) to the economic crises of the Weimar Republic also shows the highly mobile to have been far more often victimized by the Depression than were any of the other groups, and the war generation beset with economic troubles mostly in the decade 1918-1928. Nevertheless, it was not the highly mobile "outside agitators" but rather the spatially immobile who were the most involved in the political violence of the NSDAP.

Particular attention was focused on certain strata of imperial society which clearly fitted neither into the bourgeois nor the proletarian camps, such as the military-civil servants and the farmers. The former, in particular, were found to represent an "unpolitical" devotion to their duty to state or army of the empire that quickly became politicized with the fall of the old regime. However, their chief contribution to right-wing violence seems to have taken place before they joined the Nazi party, in the Free Corps and vigilante organizations of the early years of the republic. The conservative military-civil servants notably differed in their views from the anticapitalistic farmers, though both exhibit an intense and aggressive nationalism. On the other hand, the farmers show far less interest in the myth of blood and soil than the military-civil servants display in a renaissance of German power and military glory. To be sure, some of the young farm-owning respondents were indeed motivated by the agricultural crisis and by the farm revolt of 1929-1930. Others, however, stress their economically dependent status and derive from it a kind of agrarian socialism. The highly stratified nature of agricultural society suggests careful analysis of the respective exposures of early Nazis to the conservative (DNVP or *Stahlhelm*) right or the Socialist-Communist left. The evident resistance of Catholic rural society to the brown virus, side by side with the fatal weakness of rural Protestantism, also tends to emphasize the importance of faith and tradition among the rural settings.

We also took note of the considerable number of respondents whose fathers died before they reached maturity or who grew up in grinding poverty or otherwise deprived circumstances quite different from the privileged background of many other early Nazis. These different routes to National Socialism supplement the picture of the different occupational groups, the upwardly mobile military-civil servants, often coming from the countryside, the rising and the static old middle class, the static farmers, and the socially declining women. The white-collar cases in the sample were either upwardly or downwardly mobile, the blue-collar Nazis stagnant or declining. Each group had indeed a recognizable set of socio-economic motives, but the motives were not the same. It was for this reason, also, that the vaunted *Volksgemeinschaft* meant very different things to different groups. The upwardly mobile solidarists of the middle, in particular, meant by it a social prescription quite different from those who looked at the class antagonism from below or from above. It is also the solidarists of the middle who show the most antisemitic and ethnocentric prejudice.

Still another, and very potent, meaning of *Volksgemeinschaft* points at a sense of national solidarity against painful collisions with a foreign environment. Significant numbers of Abel respondents interpreted it as a rationalization of their intense nationalistic reaction to the *Fronterlebnis*, to a prolonged sojourn abroad, in the German colonies, or as internal colonials in Alsace or Poznan, to border-area experiences with alien ethnic elements, or to clashes with the French occupation in the west. We also analyzed the changing motivations of several generations of Nazi women in German society from the nineteenth century to the 1920s. Social decline, racial fantasies, and the impact of the war on their restricted status appeared to be the major determinants of Nazi allegiance.

War, Revolution, and Counter-revolution

To the extent that they were not motivated by the social dynamics of a disintegrating class society, many of the respondents appear to have been deeply influenced by the traumas of war and defeat, the culture shock of 1918, or the "revolution" and counter-revolution. The impact of each of these events and circumstances varies according to the generational differences among the prewar, war, and postwar generations. Thus the socialization of Nazis of the war and prewar generations tends to have been militaristic-authoritarian, ethnocentric and antisemitic, anti-pluralistic and law-and-order-minded. As Nazis, consequently, they were mostly revanchists and superpatriots. The war generation, and particularly the draftees and volunteers of World War One, moreover, were heavily involved in counter-revolutionary violence with Free Corps or vigilante units and came to join the NSDAP mostly before 1924 or at a rather late stage, after 1930.

The postwar generation, by comparison, tended to come from *voelkisch*-antisemitic homes and schools and to have been mobilized only vicariously, if at all, by the war and the revolutionary events. Conflict with the Franco-Belgian occupation was a major factor of political mobilization among them. As they joined the Hitler movement, particularly in the years between 1925 and 1930, they tended to be Hitler cultists, Nordic-German romantics, and distinctly struggle-oriented. The impact of the war on the postwar generation of Nazis, in other words, was rather indirect if noticeable at all.

Nevertheless, a potent combination of aggressive attitudes related to the war can be observed cutting across these generational lines. The bitter-enders and respondents reporting the deep impression left by their *Fronterlebnis*, for example, show the same syndrome of political attitudes as do the victory-watchers who never served in the war. They show a disproportionate amount of hostility toward Marxists and Spartakists, and toward the old regime and the civilian failure to "stick it out." Soldiers who sustained their enthusiasm throughout the war, and the victory-watchers, also exhibit a similar sense of cultural shock and complain particularly about the "lack of order and discipline" in postwar society and about the fall of the symbols and institutions of old.

This attitudinal solidarity, however, is not a reflection of behavioral continuity. The victory-watchers, for example, express strong support for the Free Corps and vigilante groups but rarely participated in counter-revolutionary action. Even in the middle years of the republic (1925-1928), they were generally content to participate in demonstrations rather than in political violence; the enthusiastic soldiers of World War One were still among the most violent of the early Nazis. By this time, furthermore, the rising political youth revolt of the Weimar period was beginning to take over the roles of Nazi violence, although its cohorts were born too late for the war to leave much of an impression on them. As a clue to violent behavior, the war activities were becoming increasingly irrelevant after 1925.

The reaction of the Abel respondents to the German defeat is more strongly linked to the social dynamics than is generally understood. Rural residents and the sons of farmers, for example, tended to accept the defeat without much ado even though they were generally rather nationalistic and ethnocentric. The sons of military-civil servants instead mirror the great rage or sadness which their fathers must have felt, in their displays of diffuse emotion. The children of businessmen and of workers, on the other hand, react in a violent, extrapunitive way that evidently grew out of their embattled position in either camp of the class struggle. With a vengeance, they blame the Marxists and Spartakists for the defeat, thus giving the legend of the "stab in the back" a specifically anti-Socialist note. These anti-Marxists also tend to be far more involved in counter-revolutionary violence than do the other early Nazis.

In the first years of the republic, we can sense a differential of hatred and counter-revolutionary aggressiveness grown from the defeat. It ranges from the intense and practically ubiquitous hatreds of the military strain and the anti-Marxist counter-revolutionaries to the placidity of the rural element and of the still dormant political awareness of Weimar youth. The rural element and the Weimar youth tended to accept both the defeat and the revolution. At the extremes of hatred and also at the cutting edge of antisemitic prejudice, there was also a strong sense of cultural shock at the seemingly profound changes that the lost war had brought upon German society. We conceptualized this sense of shock as the subjective experience by the returning soldiers of the various alleged changes, such as "social and moral disintegration," "lack of order and discipline," "shock at the new leaders in government and society," or anguish about the gratuitous disparagement of traditional symbols and institutions. But it would be more correct to consider this cultural shock a measure of alienation from Weimar society which was not limited to returning soldiers and rather independent of specific external events. This alienation is the most profound, we conjectured, when respondents complain about social disintegration, immorality, loose women, "strange clothes" and the like. It is less profound but more action-oriented in the "order-and-discipline" (authoritarian) version, and mildest in the tradition-mourning form.

The social-disintegration people, we found, tend to be older, in social decline or stagnant, poorly educated and frequently from authoritarian or poverty backgrounds, strongly *voelkisch* or antisemitic, but not particularly engaged in political violence. Toward their political enemies, nevertheless, they exhibit the attitudes of the *outré*. Respondents who are shocked at the new Weimar leaders often are similar in age and antisemitic prejudice to the social disintegration respondents. Those concerned about a lack of order and discipline, by comparison, tend to be of the war generation and younger. Frequently the sons of military-civil servants, they already like marching, violence, uniforms, and military training in their youth groups. In the years 1919-1923, they are heavily involved in Free Corps, vigilantes', and militant veterans' organizations. From 1923 on, they flock into the NSDAP and continue to fight there. They are the revanchist and authoritarian "military desperadoes" of the movement, especially during the middle years of the republic. From about 1925 on, the young respondents who report no cultural shock and those preoccupied with the disparagement of traditional symbols move into the forefront of Nazi action and contribute their greatest share to the SA and SS. The authoritarians, being men of military experience, on the other hand, supply more SA and SS officers.

The nature of the alienation felt by the different groups is tellingly illustrated by the curious similarities among the authoritarians and the social-disintegration people. In spite of their differences, they both tend to be sadists in their attitude toward violence, while the others incline toward self-pity and masochism. Both are revanchists and particularly devoted to the Hitler cult. Both groups also get a sense of personality integration out of the struggle itself, a feature they share with the young respondents who report no shock. But in the last analysis, this measurement of alienation cannot but separate the generations according to their differing life experiences and the emotional vulnerabilities pertaining to different phases of the life cycle. Thus we return once more to our points of departure: the insufficient primary socialization of the social disintegration respondents who later become antisemites, paranoids, and so patently irrational that only the extremist struggle can keep their personality together; and the similarly incomplete socialization of the order-and-discipline-conscious who were so warped by the war experience that they could only go on hating and fighting for the decade following 1918, fit for no human company other than the comradeship of fighting men.

Our attention also turned to the numerous Abel respondents who came to the NSDAP from the experience of friction with the French or Belgian occupation. Generally younger than the rest, they were evidently politicized and turned into superpatriotic extremists by their experiences with the occupation, whether it was the occupation or the respondent who initiated the hostilities. The anti-occupation respondents, in fact, were twice as violent as the rest and carried this propensity especially into *voelkisch* action groups such as *Oberland* or *Wehrwolf*, and into the NSDAP of the years 1925-1927. The occupation of the Rhineland in 1923 was truly a school of violence for many a Nazi recruit.

Our concern with the impact of the war and its consequences finally turned to the "counter-revolutionaries" of various sorts among the Abel respondents. They naturally fell into the three generations: The Kapp *putsch*ists were the oldest, the true reactionaries of the imperial establishment; the Free Corps and vigilante members were of the war generation; those who received paramilitary training but saw no action, and many Free Corps sympathizers, were part of the postwar generation. The Kapp *putsch*ists and the paramilitary trainees tended to have military-civil servants as fathers. All the counter-revolutionaries of 1919-1922 were considerably more class-conscious and more often from a religiously mixed area than the rest of the sample. Three-fourths of them were indeed in the war, mostly as enthusiastic soldiers, and the rest were victory-watchers.

Subtle differences in attitude characterized the various counter-revolutionary groups at a youthful stage. The Free Corps and vigilante fighters tended to be hostile militants or authoritarian youths, including many a respondent anxious to put a new leader in place of the discredited Kaiser. They were less often antisemitic than the rest, but when they were, their prejudice was full of threats. The Kapp *putsch*ists and the young Free Corps sympathizers typically were fully politicized youths and often belonged to *voelkisch*-antisemitic groups or the NSDAP at an early age. The young paramilitaries who saw no action, finally, were politically militarized youths and often quite prejudiced. All of the counter-revolutionaries tended to be more involved with youth organizations than the rest, and to have liked violent action and youthful comradeship above anything else. They frequently report conflict with their classmates, their schools, and their parents.

The second counter-revolutionary wave in 1923 was a far more political undertaking for the Abel respondents than that of the immediate postwar years of 1919-1922. The fateful year of 1923 found as many as half of the Kapp *putsch*ists and paramilitaries without action in the NSDAP or other *voelkisch* groups, who together make up the largest share of the second wave. The Free Corps and vigilante fighters, being less political, are far less often (one-quarter) in these groups and also rather unlikely to have been among the local founders of the NSDAP. With the sole exception of *Stahlhelm* members, the counter-revolutionaries of 1923 are also quite beholden to the slogan of *Volksgemeinschaft*, which goes well with their urban background and frequent economic troubles. Their involvement in political violence, finally, shows in both duration and character—partisan street-fighting rather than Free Corps type of organized action—a much higher degree of continuity with the Nazi violence to follow than that of the first wave of counter-revolutionaries. If any groups can be said to be the vanguard of the brown movement of 1925-1933, it was these right-wing revolutionaries of 1923.

In this differentiated fashion, then, the impact of war and revolution imprinted itself upon the emerging Nazi movement. There were several links to the social dynamics of prewar society, especially to the military-civil service strain, but also to the class struggle in the form of the Abel respondents' reactions to "revolution" and defeat. There were more direct links between the war experience and the counter-revolutionary activities of 1919-1922. And there was the striking politicization of the counter-revolution and war experience in the second wave of 1923 and the impact of the Franco-Belgian occupation on the Abel respondents.

The Weimar Youth Revolt

A third major factor contributing to the virulence of the Nazi movement, in addition to the social dynamics and war and revolution, was the role of the Weimar youth revolt. We attempted to relate the youthful strain in the Abel sample to the broader phenomenon of Weimar youth culture. At the outset, we noted the encompassing breadth of organized youth, which enrolled no less than 70% of the Abel respondents. Only the oldest respondents had never been in a youth group, a fact that helps to pinpoint the rise of the German youth culture in history and to link it with other social phenomena of the immediate prewar period and with the war. The war generation and the victory-watchers tended to be in quasi-military, conservative, and Youth Movement-related organizations. The latter also enrolled a goodly number of the postwar generation. The youngest cohorts of the Abel collection, a second wave of political youth (after the victory-watchers), directly entered the stormtroopers of Hitler Youth (HJ) without first going through another youth group. The defectors who joined the Nazi youth from Socialist or Communist youth antecedents were generally motivated by anti-semitism.

Those joining the SA and HJ directly and the converts from the left sustained the movement with their violence where the quasi-military youth left off, for the second half of the Weimar Republic. The likes and dislikes of the different groups mirrors their changes in orientation. The war generation, and especially the members of quasi-military groups, like comradeship, marching, and violence best—a simile of the *Fronterlebnis*. They dislike the advocacy of class struggle and "un-national views." The postwar generation prefers hiking, folk culture, marching, and ideology and disliked a lack of leadership and political direction. Among them, the Youth Movement groups tend to give the edge to hiking and cultural appreciation, while the young stormtroopers and those in other *voelkisch* youth groups prefer proselytizing. But they join in their desire for violent action or "struggle." There are also striking differences in location experiences: The great "urge to march" on which even Hitler comments derisively in *Mein Kampf* ("*die ewigen Marschierer*") seems to have come more naturally to young respondents from the occupied areas, the borderland, rural-urban migrants, the urban upwardly mobile, and families in social decline. The spatially immobile, who play such a central role, instead love group comradeship and glory in the cultural traditions.

The use of violence among the young Abel respondents exhibits several striking features worth closer examination. The most violent, both in partisan street-fighting and in the organized violence of Free Corps and vigilantes, are those who already express a liking for violent action at a tender age. They are also the least educated and frequently from a poverty or orphaned background, all of which tends to underscore their inadequate socialization. There is also a fairly clear division between those active in organized violence, who tend to be hostile militants of little political understanding, and those in partisan street-fighting and "marching with a purpose," who are more often politically-militarized or fully-politicized youths. Marching with a purpose is evidently a stage preliminary to engaging in political violence, just as the immersion of the "prepolitical, parochial youths" in group life is preliminary to marching and violence. All the youthful political postures we have sketched strain toward marching with a purpose and violence even though the life cycles of some permit them to get there earlier and with greater vehemence than the rest.

Violent acting-out of the tense minds of these youthful extremists also seems to be in inverse proportion to their antisemitic prejudice. With the sole exception of converts from the extreme left, who are both violent and prejudiced, violent minds show distinctly less bias, while the milder forms of involvement, such as the cultural appreciation of the pre-political parochials or the dedication to rallies and marching, are accompanied by increasing forms of antisemitic mania. Though their violent acting out may reduce their prejudice, however, the violent-minded still engage disproportionately in other expressions of ethnocentricity and refer to their enemies in the gutter language of the *outré*.

We took our data on political friction at work to develop a theory of extremist behavior modeled on the example of social deviancy—that is, a process of external labeling and increasing self-identification with the extremist label. The young extremists of the Abel sample, especially those who directly joined the SA or HJ, tended rather deliberately to stir up political friction by exhibitionistic acts such as wearing a stormtrooper uniform to work. Friction often intensified their extremist sense of identity and, if they were fired for their behavior, they would complain about political persecution. Seeking to separate the external causes from the actions of the respondents, we noted in particular that most of the "economic suicides" got themselves fired long before the Great Depression, and that the war and prewar generations, including many respondents in quasi-military youth groups, rarely complained about a politically "unfriendly" work environment. We are evidently dealing with manifestations of the youth revolt of Weimar, including an explosive generation gap.

Friction in the neighborhood, in the family, or at school appears to have a somewhat different character than does friction at work, which seems to be a favorite locale for extremist self-representation. In the neighborhood, family, or at school, the external causes are often more pressing. We also commented on the sense of personal isolation of the young extremists and their urge to merge their identity with the movement, as well as other parallels with Kenneth Keniston's *Young Radicals*.

Coming back to the various types of youthful posture among the Abel respondents, we constructed social profiles for each. The politically militarized turned out to be the youngest, spatially immobile ("inside agitators"), and socially stagnant or urban climbers— much like the American ghetto rioters of the 1960s. One out of four lost his father early in life, though most of them had no particular reaction to the war and never served in the military. They were rather low in their level of education, but extremely high in their involvement in political violence. They tended to be struggle-oriented and to show little ideological principle apart from superpatriotism and the Hitler cult. The hostile militants resembled them except that they were older and obviously formed by the inner fears and outer violence of war and revolution. They were also highly mobile and frequently in social decline. Their ideological motives tended to be a mixture of revanchism and antisemitism. The fully-politicized, by comparison, were younger, upwardly mobile, better-educated, and frequently from a *voelkisch* home and school background. Often infected with *Judenkoller*, they were attracted by comradeship, proselytizing, and by the figure of Hitler to the movement and tended to be Nordic-German romantics or solidarists. These were the three main groups among the young activists. The prepolitical parochials were less distinctive as a type, but resembled the fully-politicized except for belonging to the war or prewar generations.

We also juxtaposed the holding of youth group offices and violent action as mutually exclusive styles of youthful extremist conduct. Indeed, the most violent rarely held office and *vice versa*. Nevertheless, there are also other distinctions, such as between the "office-happy" generation of those who directly joined the SA and HJ, including many local founders, and the office-shy war generation of the members of conservative and quasi-military associations, who also tended to join the NSDAP only after the bandwagon was well under way. The partisan street-fighters and Free Corps fighters also differ according to their generation. Three-fifths of those engaged in organized violence (Free Corps, etc.) were of the war generation, while two-thirds of the street-fighters and three-fourths of the demonstrators and electioneers were of the postwar generation.

Finally, we took a close look at the childhoods and schools of the young Abel respondents. There appear to be two rather distinctive groupings. Those from a poverty background, orphans, and respondents with a disciplinarian childhood were less eager to get involved and yet a good deal more violent than the rest. The orphaned and disciplinarian cases were particularly antisemitic; the orphans, Hitler cultists; and the poor, solidarists. The economically secure were more eager to get involved and showed a curious division into those of "freewheeling" and those from a sheltered childhood. The freewheeling, interestingly, were far more inclined toward antisemitism, while the sheltered were often revanchists and inclined toward violence.

As for the political preferences of the parents of the Abel respondents, there appears to be a significant progression from the militaristic homes of the oldest via nationalistic, conventionally political, or unpolitical homes to the *voelkisch* homes of the younger respondents whose indoctrination took place from about the turn of the century onwards. It was this *voelkisch* generation that liked ideological direction, marching, and cultural appreciation best in their youth groups and that brought forth most of the hostile militants, politically militarized and fully politicized youths. Their *voelkisch* background, furthermore, induced it to like antisemitism, Nordic-German romanticism, and the Hitler cult after they had joined the NSDAP. Numerically, and in the degree of active service, they were undoubtedly the dominant element within the party during the "fighting years."

The Escalation of Political Violence

Once we had explored the three major "causes" of the rise of the Nazi movement, we could direct our attention to the movement itself. In particular, we could examine the building up of violent and extremist propensities among the members, their beliefs and attitudes, and the formal roles they were playing in the movement. To approach the first of these three topics, we constructed the biographic four stages of political mobilization: 1) an unpolitical or pre-political stage (at least prior to Weimar politics); 2) a stage of militarization, or quasi-military involvement; 3) a stage of politicization, or involvement with electoral politics; and 4) the stage of active NSDAP membership, subdivided according to the kind and intensity of extremist activity. To become an intensely involved activist for the cause, we suggested, a respondent had to be both "militarized" and politicized. Mere militarization would have landed him only with one of the countless uniformed veterans' organizations or irregular, counter-revolutionary combat groups. Mere politicization would have led him no further than to one of the political parties of the Weimar Republic.

We ascertained to what extent, for what reasons, and at what age the respondents had actually gone through stages two (militarization) and three (politicization) although this process of becoming "a political soldier of Adolf Hitler" need not have been all that external. About one-fourth each of the sample, it turned out, went directly from stage one to four, or through all four stages, or skipped either two or three, and all along the social history of Weimar and the empire made itself felt. A sharp division, for example, separated the older respondents who tended to have been "unpolitical" military-civil servants or immobile farmers and small-town bourgeoisie at stage one from the pre-political young and the Youth Movement members. Of the older generation of Abel respondents, only the military-civil servants were very much involved in stage two and mostly with the Free Corps and vigilante groups, having been militarized by the impact of war and defeat. The young more often belonged to groups such as *Wehrwolf, Oberland, Stahlhelm, Jungdo*, or to the early NSDAP at stage two. They are more likely to have been militarized by friction with the occupation.

Grouping the respondents by their motives for entering this stage also discloses other meaningful relationships. The "revolution," or the revolutionaries, was a catalyst for militarizing especially the victory-watchers, people in social decline, rural-urban migrants, and the spatially immobile. All these people saw it as a painful challenge to what they had acquired or held dear in life. Another stage-two catalyst, an antisemitic predisposition, reveals an important wellspring of the brown flood. Often coming from *voelkisch*-antisemitic home or school backgrounds, these respondents tended to be already in the early NSDAP or involved in the Kapp *putsch*, and frequently became local founders of the post-1924 movement.

The various stage-two groups of the Abel sample can be characterized as follows. The *Stahlhelmers* were a curious mixture of long-time soldiers and youngsters who had never served, but were evidently attracted by the militaristic exhibitionism of the group. The Free Corps, border fighters, and anti-occupation fighters were often military-civil servants, ex-colonials, people of foreign sojourn, socially immobile or up from the farm, and frequently of blue- or white-collar occupations, which were distinctly less exciting than combat. The vigilantes of *Buergerwehr*, etc., tended to be older men well-rooted in larger towns or military-civil servants. The *voelkisch* free-booters of *Wehrwolf*, *Oberland*, etc., were more often young, highly mobile though from small towns and rural areas, and also often white- or blue-collar workers who later fell victim to the Great Depression. The pre-1925 Nazis and *voelkisch* action group members were often from the occupied or border areas, or from urban areas. They tended to be military-civil servants or white-collar workers, frequently in social decline or rising from the city proletariat, and despite an average age of 24 seem never to have served in the war.

To come back to the succession of stages, the younger generation tended to skip stage three and go directly from their *Wehrwolf* or *Stahlhelm* into the post-1925 NSDAP. Many older respondents, and especially business and professional people, went only through stage three, usually other political parties, before entering stage four. Those who tended to go through all four stages were mostly Free Corps and vigilante men who would pass through a phase of electioneering, shopping around among, or expressing distrust for, all the parties on their way to the NSDAP.

We were particularly intrigued with the range of political activities the respondents engaged in at the middle stages, two and three. Were there a number of violent men who later, on joining the Nazi party, made it a violent movement? Or was it the party which made non-violent men violent? There is some merit in both explanations of Nazi violence. Those who were already involved in violence at the middle stages tended to be of the war generation, victory-watchers, or part of the rising wave of violent youth rebellion. To the extent that they participated in organized violence, Free Corps style, during the middle stages, they played a declining role in the party after 1930. They never held many party offices, although they often supplied officers for the SA. To the extent that they report individual violent encounters, moreover, we are dealing with a more virulent type of extremism. The individually violent often were politically militarized youths to start with. They were the earliest to join the NSDAP and tended to join the SA directly, as well. Their ideological emphasis is on the Hitler cult, on Nordic-German romanticism, and on antisemitism, while the organized violent were more often revanchists and superpatriots. Both of these violent types undoubtedly contributed their violence to the resurgent Nazi party and made it a more violent movement than it would have been without them.

On the other hand, there were also two further activity groups of the middle stages, the marchers and the electioneers, who were non-violent before entering stage four and who became violent while in the party. These two groups easily rival the organized and individually violent in the number of marcher-fighters (MF) and marcher-fighter-proselytizers (MFP) in the party. They also held fast to Nordic-German romanticism, the Hitler cult, and antisemitism as their ideological convictions. They were a part of the political youth rebellion of Weimar in contrast to the last two middle-stage activity groups, those older respondents who merely engaged in voting or in attending political meetings.

Stage three (politicization) tends to be a stage occupied mostly by the older respondents, even though the postwar generation has claimed to be far more politically minded than their elders. Their kind of politics, it turned out, is the politically militarized kind of a totalitarian movement, not the electoral or partisan politics of a liberal democracy. The early Nazis and *voelkisch* party members of stage three are a mixture of the prewar and postwar generations. Many other stage-three respondents merely hover at the door of electoral politics, expressing distrust of all the parties. This is particularly true of many older respondents from the border areas or foreign sojourn, from Berlin, and among small businessmen and farmers.

How did the youth settings of the only militarized (two) differ from those of the only politicized (three)? The former included many more violent and politically militarized youths and generally came from militaristic or *voelkisch* homes. The latter more often were fully politicized youths, frequently involved in demonstrations and generally from unpolitical homes or with fathers who identified with one of the conventional parties. The two middle stages generally came at different periods of the republic, two at the beginning (1919-1921 or 1923) and three during the quieter years (1925-1928), and we can correlate the period activities with the biographic record of each case to pinpoint the rates at which violence escalated in the individual lives as well as in Weimar history. The individual respondent also experienced successive waves of political mobilization and often sat out as much as a decade from one wave to the next.

The list of motives for joining the post-1924 NSDAP tends to be dominated by two things, the "dynamic impression of the Hitler movement" and the "ideological fervor and antisemitism of the respondent." The two groups motivated by these categories differ sharply from one another. The dynamicists started out as unpolitical military-civil servants, bourgeoisie, or farmers (one), often were with Free Corps and vigilantes (two), but hardly in stage three, and were content to march and proselytize (MP) at stage four. The ideologues instead came from the prewar parties or from among the prepolitical parochials (one). They were in *Wehrwolf*, *Jungdo*, or *voelkisch* action groups (two), and were mobilized by the "revolution" and by their antisemitism. Highly involved in stage three, they shopped around among the parties, expressing distrust of them, or were involved in the electoral activities of the early NSDAP or *voelkisch* parties. At stage four, the ideologues stand out as marcher-fighters (MF) or marcher-fighter-proselytizers (MFP), a far more aggressive stance than that of the dynamicists.

The division between these two cuts across some of the distinctions we drew earlier. The dynamicists were city climbers and as youths already fond of violent action, although they were mostly from sheltered, economically secure homes. They were Nordic-German romanticists, revanchists, and solidarists by ideology, while the ideologues preferred the themes of antisemitism, superpatriotism, and also solidarism. The ideologues tended to be from a freewheeling childhood and from *voelkisch* homes and fully politicized as youths. They also joined the NSDAP earlier, generally before 1930, whereas the dynamicists were attracted by the dynamicism of the movement only after the bandwagon was well under way.

There were also smaller and younger motivation groups than the dynamicists and ideologues. Some of the youngest respondents were attracted by the spirit of comradeship among the stormtroopers. This was particularly true of politically militarized youths, but also of many who had been enthusiastic soldiers in World War One, or products of the *Fronterlebnis* or of the cultural shock of returning after the war. Others, both very young and older, complained about a sense of repression by the established powers in police, society, and government, and blamed this for their entry into the party.

Once the respondents had entered the post-1924 NSDAP (four), we classified them according to the quintessential extremist activities of marching (M), fighting (F), and proselytizing (P). The Ms, similar to the marchers of the middle stages, appear to be extremists who have not yet unfolded their potential, but are obviously headed for deeper involvement. The MPs are older zealots evidently kept from violence by their age but dedicated proselytizers and missionaries for the cause. Their ideology appears to favor antisemitism,

Nordic-German romanticism, and solidarism. The MFs are the "mindless sluggers" of the movement, previously involved in the "counter-revolution," but mostly of the postwar generation. They are revanchists and superpatriots, xenophobes, and *outrés* in their attitudes toward their antagonists. The movement used them to do its dirty work without according them much of a leadership role. Violence and struggle to them is a purpose in itself even though their attitude toward violence tends to be masochistic, perhaps to make up for their guilt feelings about their violence. They include many political "dimwits" and romantics and tend to be loners in the movement, unlike the MPs or MFPs.

If the MFs and MPs are, each in their own way, defective extremists who either fail to proselytize or to fight, the MFPs are the pinnacle of extremist perfection. They are nearly as young as the MFs and are as often among the local founders and office-holders of the movement as the MPs. Business and the professions, blue- and white-collar men, and the military-civil service predominate among them. They are often upwardly mobile, especially in an urban context, and yet more affected by economic adversity than any other group. Many were victory-watchers or had militaristic or *voelkisch* fathers or a *voelkisch*-antisemitic school environment. They often come from a poverty background and had to go to work before they were 14 years old. This apparently is the explosive combination required to produce the full-fledged Nazi activist: A childhood of poverty, frustrated upward mobility in the city, militarism, and antisemitism. Unlike the MFs, their political intelligence was relatively high, and the MFPs were not lacking in social integration either. In fact, they tended to bring their whole families into the party. They tended to have joined by mid-1929, often coming from the pre-1925 NSDAP or *voelkisch* groups, the DNVP, or from more moderate parties with whom they parted company because of the attraction of the comradeship of the stormtroopers or their own ideological fervor. Unlike the MFs with their *outré* verbiage and masochism, finally, the MFPs (and also the MPs) tend to be self-righteously sadistic or to express liking for their enemies and a desire to win them over. The presence of an ideological faith evidently obviates the need for guilt feelings and for the verbal violence of the *outré*.

We furthermore investigated the significance of age and timing for the escalation of political extremism. As we had expected, the ages for entering stages two, three, and four differ considerably, and there are notable social and psychological differentials as well. Workers, for example, started the middle stages much earlier in

their lives than did military-civil servants or businessmen. Respondents in social decline or upwardly mobile in the city, those who lost
their fathers early, children of *voelkisch* or conventionally political
fathers, and those who report friction with the occupation all started
early. Children from poverty backgrounds started later. Politically
militarized youths, including many victory-watchers, tended to start
stage two before the age of 21, and the hostile militants started soon
after. Fully politicized youths began stage three before they were
26.

The earlier political mobilization sets in, the more activist the
temper and the greater the involvement in partisan violence. Unless
the middle stages were entered by the age of 25, in fact, the respondents were unlikely to become MFs or MFPs, or even stormtroopers, at stage four. To be sure, there were also differences between the early militarized and the early politicized other than that
of age. The former tended to have militaristic fathers, whereas politicization was likely to be retarded by such parentage. The preference of the early militarized also were organizations like *Wehrwolf*,
Oberland, *Jungdo*, Red Front, or *Jungstahlhelm* rather than the
Free Corps or vigilantes. The early militarized were more open to
politicization than *vice versa* and more likely to become MFs or
MFPs. They even exhibited an ideological differential above and
below the age of 18. The younger ones tended to be Hitler cultists,
antisemites, or Nordic-German romantics, while those militarized
between 18 and 20 were revanchists or superpatriots, the war-related syndrome. Early politicization was no less prone to violent development, although there the younger respondents tended to be
anti-Marxist and the older ones antisemites in addition to their common solidarism, Hitler cult, Nordic-German mania, and superpatriotism. They were motivated to join the party by the attraction
of comradeship and their sense of general repression.

What about the youngest respondents to join the post-1925
NSDAP? They tended to be the Ms, MFs, and MFPs most of whom
joined before the age of 30. Only the Free Corps types were likely
to continue being violent in their 30s. The young Nazis were mostly
from medium-sized towns, blue- or white-collar, or farmers, spatially
immobile, but often rising from the urban working class. They generally had *voelkisch*-antisemitic fathers or none at all during their
formative years. They were nearly all in youth groups, the youngest
(under 21) having gone directly into the SA or HJ. At the middle
stages, they tended to be quite active and frequently violent. Those
who joined the party after the age of 30, the break-off point for wartime military service, by comparison, were mostly from metropoli-

tan areas, upwardly mobile rural-urban migrants, and military-civil servants or businessmen and professionals. They often report disciplinarian childhoods. At stage one, they tended to be the unpolitical military-civil servants or bourgeoisie, and at stage three they often evinced distrust of all parties. These were the main generational differences in the pre-1933 NSDAP.

There was also a generational difference separating the first Weimar youth revolt of the 1902-1905 cohorts from the following wave of rebellion. The first youth generation still stood under the shadow of war, defeat, and of the "revolution" and first counter-revolutionary wave (1919-1921). The second youth revolt was influenced by the French invasion and the second counter-revolutionary wave of 1923, but essentially fed upon itself as a revolution in youthful life-styles independent of external events. This periodization has to be kept in mind as we examine the intervals between the stages of political mobilization in the respondents' lives. There is a noticeable shortening of the two-four intervals from the slow front generation (and the not much faster victory-watchers) to the fast cohorts born 1906-1908, and the even faster cohorts born after 1908.

What kind of factors would speed up this process of political mobilization from stage two? The French occupation was a powerful catalyst, especially with respondents under 18. People in social decline, especially when approaching 20, 30, or 40, and those in economic trouble, also made the transition in less time. Those recruited by friends or fellow-workers and those joining before 1925 or 1925-1928 were also fast. Blue-collar workers, urban social climbers, former youth group members and, of course, the young were among the faster groups. The front generation, as we have already pointed out, was the slowest, even slower than the pre-war generation. Some kinds of war experience, such as bitterness against civilians and draft-dodgers, being a prisoner of war, or returning an invalid seem to have speeded up the process. Other retarding influences were a poverty background, revanchism, antisemitism, sadism, and a struggle-orientation while in the movement. Those who joined after 1930, and were attracted by the ideological propaganda or by the "dynamic impression" of the Hitler movement, were rather slow. "Fast" ideological views, by comparison, were the Nordic-German and Hitler cults, masochism, an *outré* attitude, and group conformity, mostly rather "young" ideas in the Weimar context.

The escalation from stage three to stage four generally happened much faster than from two to four, since much of stage two took place before 1924. Among the fastest were respondents from unpolitical or *voelkisch* homes. Here the occupation, the attraction of comradeship, and the respondent's ideological or antisemitic fervor were accelerating factors and so was Nordic-German romanticism and group conformity. *Outré* attitudes toward the political enemy, on the other hand, were retarding influences. From both middle stages, the fastest seemed to be people with strong ideological convictions who turned out to be the founders or co-founders of their Nazi local organizations. Military-civil servants, by way of contrast, were among the slowest to become Nazis.

On balance, the best way of conceptualizing the process of becoming an extremist is still to assume a powerful missionary urge, for whatever personal reasons, to reform the world in the image of the ideology. Manifestations of the intensity of this urge speed up the process and a long list of retarding factors, beginning with the life cycle of the respondent, can slow it down or stifle it altogether. The role of violence in this process is ambiguous, because it may be a purpose in itself, as with the "mindless sluggers," and a manifestation of the missionary urge in others. The young extremists are an example of fast mobilization chiefly because there are few retarding factors in their lives. There may also be special psychological aspects of growing up that tend to intensify the ideological urge itself.

Nazi Weltanschauung and Attitudes

There are many dimensions to the subject of Nazi ideology that are worth exploring. Of these, the least promising are the ones that have received the most attention in the literature, namely national socialism as a logically consistent system of ideas, or as the outgrowth of German intellectual traditions. We proposed instead to examine the random occurrence of beliefs and attitudes—in other words, the political culture of the Abel respondents, beginning with the levels of their understanding of the complex Weimar political system. We found the postwar generation characterized by ideological preconceptions of a low order and by an abundance of political and often romantic "dimwits," especially in rural and small-town areas and under the French occupation. Military-civil servants and white-collar workers were among the more intelligent; social mobility and an urban environment evidently make for more political intelligence. The most intense ideological obsessions could be found among respondents in social decline, Catholics, and those upwardly mobile from the urban proletariat.

The main ideological themes among the Abel respondents divide the sample along generational lines: The prewar generation, contrary to popular impression, tended to be made up of antisemites

and of revanchists and superpatriots, especially military-civil servants and respondents of foreign sojourn or colonial background living in Berlin. The war generation shared this revanchism, but was
more beholden to the *Volksgemeinschaft* and especially to the
theme dearest to the postwar generation, Nordic-German romanticism, a *voelkisch* tenet of faith popular in towns and cities. Hitler-
worshippers and respondents with no ideological theme round out
the picture among the postwar generation, especially in small-town
and rural areas. Respondents from the border areas, women, and
persons in social decline combined the Nordic-German line with the
Hitler cult. Those from the occupied areas were superpatriots and
Hitler cultists. The Hitler cult seems to be the ideal stopgap for
empty extremist minds.

We also noted the generational progression from revanchist military-civil servant fathers to Nordic-German children and such
group propensities as that of white-collar men for antisemitism and
revanchism, of laborers for the Nordic-German and Hitler cults,
and of the farmers for revanchism and solidarism. Protestants
tended to be Nordic-German romantics, Catholics to be antisemites,
superpatriots, and solidarists. Areas of religious homogeneity were
particularly high in antisemitism or in the Nordic-German cult. The
confusing variety of habitats and propensities makes more sense in
each particular sphere than when it is added up into a national
trend. There is some consistency in it, though, when we learn that
two-thirds of the antisemites considered the Weimar Republic a
Judenrepublik and that many Nordic-German romantics shared this
prejudgment. Or that the solidarists were opposed to its "liberal-
Marxist" system and to the multi-party regime. Less obvious,
though contributing something to our understanding of our own
terms of reference, is the knowledge that the revanchists also hated
the capitalism and pluralism of Weimar, while the superpatriots
more specifically opposed "Marxist rule" or the red and black parties allegedly running the republic. The subtle difference between
the two images of Weimar speaks volumes about the difference between the revanchists and the more politically minded superpatriots.

We can throw the differences between the ideological groups into
stark relief also by taking each group through the stages of mobilization and relating the motives for entering each stage to the ideological theme of each group. The Nordic-German romantics, for
example, were militarized (two) by a sense of opposition to the
"revolution"; politicized (three) by the defeat, the occupation, and
by economic troubles; and attracted to the post-1924 NSDAP by
the dynamic impression of the movement or the "rough opposition"

of the Communists. The Hitler-worshippers, a similarly young group, had almost exactly the same set of motives, except that they entered stage four because they were attracted by the comradeship among the stormtroopers and spurred on by economic troubles and the occupation experience. The revanchists, though considerably older, also have roughly the same set of motives, while the younger superpatriots tend to be more often motivated by friction with the occupation (two and three). The antisemites, by way of contrast, were militarized by their antisemitic predisposition or *Judenkoller*, politicized by defeat, by the occupation, or by their opposition to the new Weimar leaders, and led into the post-1924 party (many were already in the pre-1924 party) by their ideological or antisemitic fervor. Their mania made their course all too predictable.

Let us consider the relation between these two elements, the monomaniacal antisemites and the other ideological concerns. First, to what extent are the other ideological groups free of prejudice? The antisemites, of course, exhibit the deepest bias: Half of them have the *Judenkoller*, one-fourth are aggressive paranoids, and another fifth tell prejudiced anecdotes. The Nordic-German romantics follow at some distance. The least prejudiced are those without an ideology and the swashbuckling revanchists, followed at some distance by the Hitler-worshippers, the superpatriots, and the solidarists, who have about half in the "no evidence" and "mild" categories. The bias against aliens, xenophobia, is distributed analogously to antisemitism, except that the superpatriots have it more severely and that all the other groups focus their ethnocentricity more on the foreign nations outside (chauvinism) and their "inferiority." The attitudes toward authority, despite the well-known theories, fail to follow this pattern of distribution.

Those without ideology and the revanchists, conversely, do most of the fighting in the SA and SS, followed by the Hitler cultists and the superpatriots. The antisemites and Nordic-Germans with few exceptions tend to stick to demonstrations, electioneering, and proselytizing. They have only half of their numbers in the stormtroopers, and joined them with obvious reluctance. Yet they frequently hold party offices and special organizing functions in the party while those most involved in fighting do not. This division of labor amounts to a system of stratification between those who do the dirty work and the party organizers and ideologues. It also implies a functional equivalence between the violent acting-out of street-fighting and strong prejudice in acting out the inner tensions of the early Nazis. If they discharged their tensions by fighting or other bizarre behavior they were less in need of the mental contortions of prejudice, and *vice versa*.

How do personalities and formative influences differ among the ideological groups? Antisemites and Nordic-Germans seem so close together, and yet the former include many irrational or paranoid respondents and they often present their lives as under the influence of encounters with aliens or Jews, or of an educational or literary experience. The Nordic-Germans, by way of contrast, tend to have suffered severe culture shock and to have been influenced either by the experience of youthful comradeship or by the defeat and "revolution" of 1918-1919. The revanchists resemble them in this respect, while the superpatriots cite the same formative influences as the antisemites. Both revanchists and superpatriots otherwise are products of their *Fronterlebnis*. The solidarists and Hitler worshippers share a sense of social humiliation and economic hardship, and are both quite dedicated to the leadership cult. The antisemites also include a disproportionate share of economic suicides, people who lost their jobs or livelihood because they would not desist from their prejudicial exhibitionism.

What were the expectations of the respondents in 1934, after Hitler had come to power? A significant bloc composed of antisemites, Nordic-Germans, but also revanchists, coming especially from the war generation, and from Protestant metropolitan areas, affected by friction with the occupation, and numbering many military-civil servants, white-collar employees, and farmers, hoped for the establishment of a German racial empire. The postwar generation, and especially the superpatriots and solidarists, borderland Germans, and some military-civil servants with chauvinistic memories of their *Fronterlebnis* wanted to see a national renaissance within. Social and economic restitution was desired by the solidarists, rural and small-town respondents of the war generation, by many who had been upwardly mobile, or business and professional people. More crassly, the prewar generation of Abel respondents and many antisemites and persons from metropolitan areas simply hoped for an individual pay-off for themselves. By comparison, the totalitarian utopia of the 1000-year Reich had its clientele mostly among Nordic-German, Hitler worshippers, those without any ideology, the victory-watchers, those involved with the occupation or in social decline, white- and blue-collar workers, xenophobes, and Catholics. These totalitarians included many strong anti-Marxists and liked to refer to their enemies in the gutter language of the *outré*, a chilling forecast of the regime descending upon the country. The dreams of racial empire, by comparison, seem more like a revanchism deflected against internal enemies and against the weaker East.

We also devoted some attention to the respondents' attitude toward "the system," toward other political actors in it, and toward authority in general. The various perceptions of the Weimar Republic represent, of course, rather fictitious images reflecting the different generations. Thus, the prewar generation of the Abel respondents tended to see it as the *Judenrepublik* or to raise traditional or anti-capitalistic objections to it. The war generation, including the victory-watchers, perceived it as a Marxist or "liberalistic-Marxist" system (anti-pluralists) by the Third Reich.

That image of the Jewish-run republic was held, in particular, in Berlin and other metropoles, by military-civil servants or business and professional people and their children, by women, and by the socially immobile. Such an antisemitic reaction typically came from soldiers who during the war had expressed their hatred of draft-dodgers and civilians, who accepted the defeat even though they tended to feel a sense of shock at the "moral and social disintegration" in Germany, and who blamed the Jews for the alleged revolution. They often joined a Free Corps, participated in the Kapp *putsch*, and joined the pre-1925 NSDAP or other *voelkisch* groups.

The anti-capitalists were more often farmers, in social decline, and Depression victims. They tended to become disaffected from the war effort and to react to the defeat with emotion, but nevertheless became also involved in Free Corps action and with Kapp. Their ideology was mostly revanchism or the Hitler cult. They joined the party only after 1930, even though they soon became struggle-oriented stormtroopers. The anti-pluralists tended to resemble the anticapitalists in many ways and so did the super-patriotic utopians who hoped that the red and black parties would go away. However, while the anti-pluralistic foes of Weimar tended to be rural, the utopians were typically metropolitan and more involved in the counter-revolution and the pre-1925 NSDAP.

The last important group of critics of Weimar were those objecting to its "liberalistic-Marxist" system. Far better educated than, for example, the antisemites, they were often urban climbers and believed in solidarism, superpatriotism, and the Nordic-German line. As solidarists, of course, their rejection of both bourgeois liberalism and Marxist socialism makes some sense. They were in fact strong anti-Marxists, but also anti-reactionary, and tended to go in heavily for proselytizing for the party.

The attitudes of the Abel respondents toward their political enemies also deserve special attention because of the extreme differences between the verbal incontinence of the *outrés* and those who who would like to win them over. Typically, the *outrés* belonged to the war and postwar generations, were from metropolitan areas, and they included many business and professional people, women, white-collar workers, and the children of workers, military-civil servants, and businessmen. They were also pronounced anti-Marxists, hostile to police and government, and obvious sufferers from *Judenkoller* and of xenophobia. These last-mentioned foibles fit well the image of a verbally violent person.

Those who looked upon their enemies as traitors or as a faceless conspiracy, by comparison, were more often born before 1895, rural-urban migrants, blue-collar workers, Hitler cultists, authoritarians, and extreme antisemites. The respondents who express a liking for some of their enemies and a desire to win them over tended to be from small-town and rural areas, farmers or military-civil servants, anti-reactionary, anti-pluralistic, and relatively free of prejudice and ethnocentricity.

The respondents' attitudes toward authority round out the picture of their system-related orientations. Those who were hostile to police and government, in particular, tended to be among the youngest and best-educated, from small-town and rural areas, city climbers or in social decline, workers, farmers, and often from the occupied areas. The hostile and also those characterized by leadership cult tended to have disciplinarian childhoods, *voelkisch* fathers or teachers, and friction with fellow-students, teachers, and with their own parents. Many of them grew up as orphans, which increases the impression of a disturbed relationship to paternal authority. The leadership cultists were relatively old, poorly educated, and often from a poverty background. Their ideology was the Hitler cult and they delighted in antisemitic anecdotes and in expressions of chauvinism; the hostile are more often superpatriots and xenophobes.

The real authoritarians, obsessed with order and cleanliness, tend to be military-civil servants, businessmen, professionals, rural-urban migrants, Catholics, and poorly educated. Many of them also grew up as orphans or report friction with their parents. By ideology they are revanchists, anti-Marxists, and chauvinists. The last group, the anti-pluralists, dissatisfied with the multiparty system, is the oldest and most antisemitic, and includes many white-collar employees, women, children of farmers, and Catholics. Many anti-pluralists had an economically secure, sheltered childhood. The freewheeling childhoods seem to lead more often to open hostility toward police and government. The parents and schools of the anti-pluralists are nationalistic, moderate, or unpolitical, and their ideology, next to antisemitism, is solidarism, and Nordic-German romanticism. Again the most intense prejudice appears to lie less with the authoritarians than with those who are less involved in other forms of "acting out."

We have hit upon the role of antisemitic prejudice among the Abel respondents so often that it appears to be high time to focus on it more specifically and to explore its internal dynamics. Of all the hazy ideological elements in these Nazi minds, this prejudice seems the most tangible precisely because its object is in the minds of the prejudiced persons themselves, at least at this stage. We distinguished four categories aside from *vitae* with no evidence of bias: mild verbal projections, *Judenkoller*, anecdote-telling, and aggressive paranoia, or speaking of threats and counter-threats. The underlying theory pictures the mild verbal projections as a form of social conformism; the choler as an outbreak of scapegoating in which the projective mind is still relatively at balance with its own displacement; the anecdote-telling phase as a transition to aggressive paranoia; and the latter as a dynamic disequilibrium which drives the disturbed minds on to hectic political action.

How do these prejudice groups of the Abel sample differ from one another? The no-evidence and mild groups were the youngest and tended to be farmers, workers, salaried employees, and women. The more prejudiced groups were much older, often metropolitan, rural-urban migrants, or upwardly mobile within the city. The cholerics were generally over 30 at the time of the outbreak of their choler and, along with the paranoids, frequently in social decline. The anecdote-tellers tended to be upwardly mobile military-civil servants, the paranoids business and professional people, upwardly mobile white collar workers, and the children of military-civil servants.

Their childhood experiences shed some light on the origins of their prejudice. Poverty and a sheltered childhood appear to produce the least bias, disciplinarian and orphan childhoods the most intense prejudice, particularly of the paranoid kind. Theodore W. Adorno's theory of the disturbed relationship to the father thus holds up well. A freewheeling childhood, as compared to a sheltered one, turned out to be very high in prejudice of the choleric type, in contradiction to what many American psychologists have suggested about the genesis of a democratic personality. It would be more accurate to say, however, that this finding only drew a distinction among different kinds of Nazi minds. It is entirely possible that a normal mind would benefit from rather than break under the strain of a freewheeling childhood, even though our respondents tended to become choleric.

As for the home and school environments, an unpolitical setting made for the least bias while a *voelkisch* home and school was related to intense prejudice. The cholerics tended to come from nationalistic or militaristic homes. As youths (under 26), the paranoids typically were hostile militants. The onset of paramilitary or political activity in their lives tended to be either among the very young or at middle age. The stage of militarization (two) was typically entered by the paranoids under the age of 18, and by the cholerics or anecdote-tellers after the age of 35. Though imprecise as to the exact onset of the prejudicial phase, this finding makes it doubtful that any of the cholerics or anecdote-tellers would ever develop into paranoids. The stage of politicization similarly divides paranoids and cholerics at the age of 25. At stage four, paranoids tended to enter either under 21 or in their forties. The cholerics tended to join after the age of 35 and to be rather "fast" in their transition from stage two or three to four.

We can now refine also our earlier statement on prejudice and violence or offices. The prejudiced are not uniformly low in violence, but this is true only of the cholerics and the anecdote-tellers. The paranoids and the mild and no-bias groups are highly involved in stormtrooper violence. The paranoids and the mild group also hold most of the party offices. The cholerics and anecdote-tellers probably were ruled out because they "ran off at the mouth." And those of no bias were used only for the dirty work of street violence precisely because they showed no bias. The important party offices were in the hands of the aggressive paranoids, the embodiment of our theory of dynamic disequilibrium. The mildly verbal were allowed to hold local offices precisely *because* they conformed to the Nazi rhetoric.

The paranoids and the no-bias group are struggle-oriented and do the most fighting and "day-and-night" campaigning. The mild group gets more satisfaction from the comradeship of the stormtroopers but are not far behind in fighting. The anecdote-tellers fight less and are looking forward to the coming of the racist utopia. The cholerics, instead of fighting, concentrate on electioneering and proselytizing and receive their satisfaction from the Hitler cult. Quite typically, many of the cholerics experienced a severe cultural shock (social disintegration and the new leadership) in 1918-1919 which may well have been identical with the genesis of their *Judenkoller*. As much as one-seventh of the Abel sample seems to have experienced such a crisis at that time suggesting something like a mass outbreak of political antisemitism under the impact of defeat and "revolution" in Germany.

Pursuing this question a little further, we note the prominent role of the *Fronterlebnis* and of defeat and revolution among the formative experiences of both the cholerics and the paranoids, and the intense cultural shock among the cholerics. All the more highly prejudiced groups are characterized by an extreme degree of irrationality. However, there are obviously other factors involved as well as the crisis of 1918-1919. Very typically, the paranoids are also xenophobes, and they refer to their enemies as traitors or a conspiracy. The cholerics are *outrés* in their attitude toward the enemy, while the anecdote-tellers tend to express a liking for their political enemies. The paranoids also tend to be loners, as are those without bias, neither of them having any family members in the party. The cholerics often have their spouses in the party and the mild and anecdote cases often the whole family. Finally, the paranoids happen to be sadists in their attitude toward violence while all the others tend toward masochism. Perhaps it is a matter of personality, or else the war helped to unchain their prejudice and mobilized it to the point of paranoid aggression.

How were the other forms of ethnocentricity distributed over the sample? Generally speaking, the prewar generation was the most ethnocentric and the postwar generation the least. The "oldest" ethnocentric motif was that all the other nations were "inferior." This was held especially by women, military-civil servants, businessmen and professionals. Chauvinism toward foreign nations and xenophobia were more typical of the war generation. The chauvinists, in particular, tended to be military-civil servants, white-collar workers, foreign contact people, and the socially static, Protestants, Nordic-German romantics and revanchists, bitter-enders, and victory-watchers. The xenophobes, by way of contrast, were highly mobile, white-collar workers, children of military-civil servants and farmers, and upwardly mobile in the city. They tended to be antisemites or superpatriots, from border or occupied areas, and to stand out with their all-inclusive hate-lists, their *outré* language, their hostility toward authority, and their irrational and insecure personalities.

As well as hating Jews and aliens, the early Nazis also were anti-Marxists, although their anti-Marxism appears to have been neither particularly ideological nor very intense. To be sure, the anti-Marxists were a very large group and they were also among the youngest Abel respondents. But the feeling seems to have been mostly a reaction to the would-be revolutionaries of the left, as well as to the "outdated legacy" and the monopoly on certain jobs of Weimar's well-entrenched SPD and KPD. Anti-Marxists were particularly from Berlin or from rural or border areas, workers of little education and probably resentful to the Socialist labor movement, women, military-civil servants, and the sons of workers and military men. They tended to be socially static or in decline, which may explain their envy of some of the SPD careerists of Weimar. They included many victory-watchers and men of strong cultural shock at the fall of the old symbols. They blamed the defeat on Marxists and Spartakists and were often brought into counter-revolutionary organizations by the shock of defeat and revolutions.

Their parental influences were generally *voelkisch* or militaristic, although one out of ten came from a left-wing youth group. Their ideology tended to be non-existent, or the Hitler cult, or the Nordic-German line. They were mostly authoritarians and, of course, leadership cultists. The NSDAP gave them few party offices of any importance and few stormtrooper ranks, even though they were heavily (and masochistically) involved in stormtrooper violence. Evidently, with the stop-gap ideology of anti-Marxism rather than antisemitism, they were only the foot-soldiers of the movement, in spite of their gutter language about their political enemies.

The last topic of our investigation of Nazi ideology was the extremist's perception of himself. We tried to get at this topic from several different angles. First of all, we distinguished among *vitae* written to present only the political development of the respondent; lives seem as products of such historical circumstances as the war, the economic crisis, or social disorder; and stories presenting the respondent's life as the outcome of personal, social, or family problems. The vast majority of the respondents, and especially the younger ones, business and professional men, workers, and military-civil servants just tell a straightforward account of their political development. Many members of the war generation, also women, farmers, white-collar workers, and not a few ethnocentrics, cholerics, and paranoids blame their lives on the great historical upheaval of their age. Those who blame personal problems tend to be the oldest, including many from Berlin, rural-urban migrants, women, and small-town and rural residents. They include many tellers of antisemitic anecdotes, antireactionaries, and chauvinists.

Another way to get at the extremist self was the pathological question of what was the most excessive feature of each case. The groupings obtained by this process were sharply distinguished by age and other social indices. The youngest were the conformists, who had shown an extraordinary desire to merge their selves with the movement and the extreme leadership cultists. The conformists tended to be workers or farmers, socially static and from rural, small-town, border, and occupied areas. The leadership cultists were from the same locations, but more often white-collar and upwardly mobile in an urban context. These young Turks tended to be anti-Marxist and low in antisemitism and ethnocentricity. Group conformism, in particular, seemed to be a substitute for ideology and prejudice, and an extreme leadership cult is also not exactly an ideological notion.

The two oldest groups were the irrational-paranoids and those who had suffered severe cultural shock. Of these, particularly the irrational were heavily antisemitic and xenophobic. The culturally-shocked, by comparison, condemned the Weimar Republic as a "liberalistic-Marxist" system or for its multi-partyism. They were also Nordic-Germans, revanchists, and solidarists, authoritarians concerned with order and cleanliness, and in 1934 they were still hoping for a national renaissance in Germany. The irrational-paranoids, for their part, wanted to see a German racial empire established in Europe.

Another approach to the extremist self-perception goes through the attitudes of the physically-involved toward violence. Here we were struck not only by the differences between sadists and masochists, but by the relation between ideology and these attitudes. The masochists are, generally speaking, younger and hence grew up without the inhibition-removing war experience. The sadists are composed of the war generation, professional soldiers, and the victory-watchers. Workers and farmers predominate in both physically involved groups, the workers perhaps acting from generations of labor's militancy, the farmers from centuries of violent habits. Bourgeois respondents, but also those of little education, and people from the border and from occupied areas heavily tended toward masochism.

The masochists, interestingly, include many of the "mindless sluggers" (MFs), while the sadists more often are MFPs or MPs. The presence of ideology and proselytizing fervor seems to supply enough rationalization for violence so the respondent need no longer be apologetic about it. The sadists' ideological concerns, however, are not overwhelming: revanchism, antisemitism (especially paranoids), anti-Marxism, and little else. Many sadists are "dimwits," romantics, or pragmatically narrow, yet they have the urge to proselytize. The masochists are Hitler cultists and superpatriots by ideology, and look forward to the Third *Reich* (utopians). They include many cholerics and anecdote-tellers but seem so gratified with their engagement in violence that they fail to proselytize. Perhaps the difference boils down to a difference in ego strength or self-assertiveness.

The last item relating to the extremist self was the formative experience or influence characterizing each case, including apocryphal stories told by the respondents to present themselves. Again, there are typical generational differences. The prewar and war generations tend to be formed by *Fronterlebnis*, defeat, or revolution, or by social or economic humiliation. They include many farmers, military-civil servants, businessmen and professionals, rural-urban migrants and the socially static. The postwar generation more often has formative experiences such as youthful comradeship, an educational or literary experience, or encounters with aliens or Jews. It includes workers, white-collar employees, the upwardly mobile in the city, and people from the eastern border, of foreign background, and from the occupied areas.

Typically, respondents influenced by the *Fronterlebnis* are revanchists and superpatriots, anti-reactionary, choleric, and highly ethnocentric. Those formed by defeat, revolution, and by youthful comradeship are Nordic-Germans, solidarists, revanchists, and include many antisemitic paranoids. Respondents whose formative experiences were educational or literary, and who tell of encounters with aliens or Jews, were antisemitic, superpatriotic, Hitler-worshippers, and highly xenophobic.

We began our investigation of Nazi *Weltanschauung* by assigning a rather low order of importance to the logical or rational elements in it. There are ideological themes and beliefs in it, to be sure, but there does not seem to have been a coherent faith spanning the different generations of early Nazis. Generational differences, in fact, appear to be the main matrix of the belief systems in the sample. Over-arching the ideological meaning, moreover, there are such obsessive concerns as antisemitism, xenophobia, and anti-Marxism. Of these, antisemitic prejudice is particularly intimately tied up with the violent or proselytizing behavior of the respondents and with the roles of violence or office-holding assigned to them in the movement. Ideology and behavior are thus inextricably interwoven, a fact that goes to support our point about not interpreting the Nazi movement as a movement solely or even chiefly motivated by ideas. Instead, it appears to have been motivated by two almost autonomous urges, virulent prejudice and a desire for fighting. Of the two, the prejudiced are obviously in control of the party itself while the mindless sluggers are being used to do the dirty work. The merely violent, moreover, receive their satisfactions from the comradely spirit of the movement and are all too willing to merge their extremist selves with it and its great and glorious leader. The question of extremist personality types has received some light here, but in the last analysis we have not completely penetrated its mysteries.

Life in the Party

The third major area of our concern was the individuals' lives in the Nazi party. More specifically, we tried to distinguish the respondents by the times and circumstances of their joining the party, examined the large contingent of stormtroopers in our sample, and focused on the phenomenon of the "day-and-night" fighter of 1931-1932, a particularly virulent variety of the extremist species. Then we turned to the office-holders in the pre-1933 party and, finally, to those who had made a party, administrative, or enforcer career in the Third Reich on the strength of their early membership in the NSDAP.

As for the first-mentioned topic, the times and circumstances of joining, we found two dimensions particularly relevant to our understanding of the movement—the date of joining, and whether a respondent joined when the NSDAP was just being founded locally or when it was already well on its way. To begin with, the dates of joining revealed once more the heavy pre-1930 bias of our sample, a time at which the NSDAP was still very much a fringe group and, in a sense, a purer extremist phenomenon than after the 1930 elections. Certain phases of development of the party clearly stand out according to the changing character of the recruitment: The preponderance of the war generation and victory-watchers in the pre-1925 party, including many military-civil servants, socially declining respondents, and recent converts from other *voelkisch* groups such as the *Schutz-und-Trutzbund*, "red" or bourgeois, conservative groups, the DHV, or Free Corps and vigilante groups. The 1925-1927 period of the reconstructed party more heavily attracted Free Corps and veteran elements, urban blue- and white-collar workers, respondents from the occupied areas, an increasing proportion of the postwar generation, and some of the most violent elements of the whole sample. The recruits of these early years of the movement must have given the NSDAP the character of a movement for congenital brawlers.

From 1928 on, the movement seems to have become more rural and small-townish as it spread into the countryside. It also began to receive the benefit of the second youth revolt (cohorts 1906-1916) and of further bourgeois, conservative, and *Stahlhelm* defectors. The local founders had already joined prior to 1928, and new recruits could only join existing nuclei or substantial Nazi minorities. Even the method of introduction changed from the earlier mediation of a friend or colleague of the respondent to awareness of the ideological propaganda of the Nazis or attendance at rallies and Nazi demonstrations. If before 1928 the chief motive had been friction with the occupation, ideological fervor, and the comradeship of the stormtroopers, it now became comradeship, the agricultural and economic crisis, or a sense of general repression and "rough Communist opposition" to the brown bandwagon.

After the 1930 elections again, the movement changed drastically, in particular by attracting progressively older respondents each year. Had that trend continued beyond January 1933, the NSDAP would have become just as "old" a party as its chief competitors of prewar vintage. It also appears to have become far more metropolitan and to have acquired many more military-civil servants and business and professional respondents who had never belonged to any youth group. The typical *Septemberling* was attracted to the bandwagon by the ideological propaganda of the party or may even have been introduced to it by a member of his own family, a sign of the growing legitimacy of the movement. The Great Depression was not the reason precipitating the wave of post-1930 recruits to join the Nazi party except for a few of the youngest. The typical depression victim had joined long before 1929, often as a local founder, and may, in fact, have lost his livelihood because of his extremist activities. The typical *Septemberling*, by way of contrast, suffered no economic difficulties at all or had suffered them before 1929.

How then did the ideological motives and beliefs vary among the recruits of these several phases? The pre-1925 recruits typically included many Nordic-German romantics, revanchists, superpatriots, and Hitler-worshippers, as well as many with a *Judenkoller*. The violent stormtroopers who joined in 1925-1927 tended to be antisemites and included the highest number of paranoids, anecdote-tellers, and xenophobes of any phase. They were as high in their violent involvement with SA and SS as they were low in holding party offices, even in comparison to later recruits of the period up until 1932. After 1927, once more, the ideological emphasis shifted to revanchism, superpatriotism, and the Hitler cult, while the *Septemberlinge* were motivated by solidarism and a middle-aged, non-violent antisemitism of prewar vintage.

The different ways of introduction to the movement also turned out to be related to age and social class. Introduction by a friend or fellow-worker was typical of the young workers in small and medium-sized towns, of youthful street-fighters, politically militarized youths, and hostile militants. Rallies and demonstrations were the mode of introduction for the next younger set, especially among rural and blue-collar circles who were socially static or in decline. Unlike the first group, many of whom were alone in the party, the rally-goers tended to be with their whole families in the party, and often in the SA as well. Those who were attracted by the ideological propaganda frequently were old Free Corps men or military-civil servants of the war or prewar generation as well as upwardly mobile white-collar workers or businessmen and professionals. They tended to hold the most party offices. Those who were introduced by relatives, finally, tended to be women or of the prewar generation, evidently the less actively motivated.

As for our second topic, the stormtroopers, we began by separating them into immediate stormtroopers, delayed stormtroopers, SS men, and non-members. The last-mentioned generally had joined the party only after the age of 35 and included many military-civil servants, women, and economically well-off metropolitan residents. Here, too, the military-civil servants seem to have made their contribution to the Nazi movement in matters of ideology, and not as "specialists in violence." The instant stormtroopers and SS men tended to be the youngest. They frequently grew up without a father and had a high percentage of depression casualties. Often coming from the occupied territory, rural or small-town areas, they tended to be blue-collar workers, farmers, and mostly in social decline (especially the SS) or socially static. Theirs seems to have been a case of stagnant mobility as well as of the cutting edge of the Weimar youth revolt. Those who joined the stormtroopers a year or more later than the NSDAP tended to be metropolitan white-collar sons of military-civil servants, and often from a sheltered childhood. By way of contrast, the immediate SA men often had disciplinarian, conflictual, or fatherless childhoods, and the SS men freewheeling, poverty, or also fatherless childhoods.

Typically, the delayed stormtrooper has more ideological preoccupations, including antisemitism, and is frequently engaged in "day-and-night" fighting and proselytizing for the cause at the height of the struggle. The instant SA men and SS guards, by comparison, show little ideological ballast other than revanchism and a stereotyped anti-Marxism underscored by their low political understanding and their high involvement in violence. They include about 50% "mindless sluggers" (MFs) and an unusually high (15%) number of antisemitic paranoids, although otherwise significantly fewer prejudiced persons than the other groups. The really salient qualities of these pure activists appear to be an extreme leadership cult, masochism, and an urge to merge one's self with the move-ment (conformity).

By comparison, the delayed stormtroopers are the most preju-diced, and the non-stormtroopers include many more cholerics than these two. But the latter are the products of *Fronterlebnis* and of the experience of defeat and revolution, while the delayed storm-troopers share certain formative experiences with the SS men: They both attribute their thinking, such as it is, to educational or literary experiences. And they both tend also to be loners in the party, per-haps introverts in contrast to the more happy-go-lucky SA men, whose formative experiences tend to be youthful comradeship and unemployment.

We also examined the considerable number of Abel respondents who held various ranks in the SA and SS. The middle echelon (*Sturmfuehrer*, or lieutenant, and higher) of stormtrooper leaders was distinctly older and more urban, though not metropolitan, than the rural and small-town lower leaders who in many ways resem-bled the average stormtrooper. The middle echelons also tended to join before 1929 and had a preponderance of military-civil serv-ants, though obviously of a younger generation than the many mili-tary-civil servants among the non-stormtroopers. The middle eche-lon in this respect represents a large carryover from the Free Corps and wartime officer element, the "military desperadoes." They also had an inordinate share of white-collar employees and of sons of high military officers of the empire, while the lower leaders and ordi-nary stormtroopers were predominantly blue-collar, farming, and business and professional people, a caste distinction of sorts.

What could have been their personal motives for becoming stormtrooper officers? Unlike the old non-stormtroopers who tended to be upwardly mobile, the typical middle-echelon leader was in social decline and of only average education. The typical lower leader was socially static and of very limited education in an era of expanding educational opportunities—of which Jews, foreign-ers, and women had availed themselves. He tended to have a *voelk-isch* home environment rather than the militaristic one of the middle echelons. Both leadership strata were evidently motivated by a de-sire to compensate for their social decline and stagnation by becom-ing the spearhead of a violent new elite.

Both were indeed very violent, especially the lower leaders, who included many "day-and-night" fighters and exhibited a characteris-tically masochistic attitude toward violence. The middle echelons, including many SS leaders, by comparison, were sadistic bullies who seem to have welcomed a little "merry civil war" to keep monotony

away. Both types of leaders also show a high incidence of fatherlessness or of conflict with their fathers, with teachers, and at work, and
a pronounced hatred for the police—all of which may explain both
their propensity for violence and their anti-authoritarian cast of
mind. In their references to their political enemies, moreover, both
like to use the gutter language of the *outré* and to let their physical
aggressiveness show through their words. Yet while the lower leaders conform to the stereotype of the revanchist, superpatriot, anti-
Marxist, or simply non-ideological stormtrooper who would like to
merge his identity with the movement, the middle echelons appear
to be more of an egocentric, power-hungry mob. Far from being
conformists, they indulge in an extreme kind of leadership cult
coupled with the rejection of "reactionaries" and other bourgeois
elites. Their fondest hopes in 1934 were for the establishment of the
totalitarian state within and for a German racial empire in Europe.
Their prototype could well have been the egomaniacal Goering
himself.

The "day-and-night" fighter of the peak years of the struggle,
1931-1932, appears to have been a special variety of the more ideologically motivated Nazi activist (MFP). Typically of the second
youth revolt (cohorts 1906-1916) or the war generation, he tended
to be unemployed but upwardly mobile in the city, not unlike the
American race rioter of the 1960s. In his youth background he differed markedly from other stormtrooper types. He tended to have
had a disciplinarian or sheltered childhood and to be better-educated than the typical instant stormtrooper or lower stormtrooper
leader. While the latter was often a "hostile militant" and had engaged heavily in Free Corps and other quasi-military violence before the age of 25, the day-and-nighter was more likely a politically
militarized youth who liked hiking and cultural appreciation and
contented himself with partisan demonstrations and street violence.
He tended to join the party before 1925 or after 1929 rather than
in the 1925-1927 period like the "mindless sluggers." He was usually introduced to the party by a friend or colleague rather than by
attendance at rallies like the rest of the stormtroopers. Once in it,
he became a stormtrooper only after some delay but often rose to
a middle echelon rank in the SA or SS.

His ideology and style of aggression set him off most distinctly
from the other stormtroopers. Where they were revanchists, Hitler-
worshippers, anti-Marxists, or simply without ideology, he was a
Nordic-German romantic or superpatriot. Though relatively low in
prejudice, moreover, no fewer than a fourth of the day-and-nighters
were antisemitic paranoids, which may well have been the motive

force behind their hectic acting-out. Where the others were masochistic in their attitudes toward violence and *outré* in their attitude toward the enemy, finally, the day-and-nighter was a sadist without remorse who thought of his enemies as a traitorous conspiracy. Oriented toward the struggle and the comradeship of the movement, the day-and-nighters were loners with malice aforethought and embodied a style of aggression rather different from that of the other violent Nazis, who usually had their whole families in the party.

Another interesting dimension of the process of becoming an early Nazi, which we explored only in passing, was the color of the local political environment in which the oppositional spirit first took its characteristic shape. Well over one-half of the sample reported a Socialist-Communist setting. They included many traditionally oriented military-civil servants and bourgeois respondents who found their way through *voelkisch* groups and Free Corps to the marcher-fighters (MF) of the NSDAP. Others, being mostly blue-collar and of little education, probably represent working-class elements disaffected from the SPD and the Free Trade Unions. The smaller number reporting a "deep red" (KPD/USPD) environment, by comparison, consists mostly of war generation respondents and victory-watchers whose Nazi extremism was very likely kindled by the revolutionary attempts and intentions of the far left. They include both members of prewar political parties and very young converts from left-wing youth groups who traveled through the pre-1925 Nazi or *voelkisch* groups, or *Wehrwolf*, on their way to the marcher-fighters (MF) of the movement. The left-wing converts were motivated particularly by their virulent antisemitism.

A moderate republican environment of combinations of SPD, Center party, DDP, or DVP, at least in our sample, tended to produce variations of bourgeois disaffection, especially under the impact of the occupation. These respondents typically came from traditional or Youth Movement backgrounds, went through the Free Corps and *Stahlhelm*, distrusted political parties, and eventually became marchers (M) or marcher-proselytizers (MP) of the brown cause. They include a surprising number of local founders of the movement though not nearly the proportion of stormtroopers of the anti-red and anti-deep-red groups.

Finally, there are the respondents from a conservative (DNVP) or *Stahlhelm* environment, mostly in the Protestant north or northeast, who include many farmers, military-civil servants, and women. They typically went through *Jungdo* or *Stahlhelm* and, of course, the DNVP before becoming proselytizers (MPs and MFPs) for the cause. With all these groups, their ideology tends to supply the motive for their rebellion against the dominant local political forces. The conservative converts were Nordic-German romantics, Hitler-worshippers, and superpatriots; the anti-moderates were solidarists and, on account of the occupation, superpatriots. The anti-Socialist majority was revanchist and anti-Marxist, and those rebelling against the extreme left were either revanchists and Nordic-German or extremely antisemitic and xenophobic.

We concluded this examination of the Nazi street-fighters by comparing the different satisfactions they seemed to get out of their membership in the movement. Those getting a sense of personal integration by the struggle tended to be by far the youngest and the most violent, largely coming from among urban workers of no social mobility. Their need for struggle was so great that they tend to be sadists. Next came the groups whose satisfaction consisted either in the comradeship or in the leadership cult of the movement. They were either in social decline, especially the white- and blue-collar elements, or upwardly mobile city-dwellers. They were somewhat older and distinctly masochistic in their attitude toward violence, and *outré* in their references to the enemy. These two groups found a social, or collective way of discharging their aggressions and therefore stress togetherness and leader-follower relations. The older Abel respondents instead derived their satisfactions more from the utopian vision or, more prosaically, from hopes for an individual pay-off. These groups include many military-civil servants from Berlin, business and professional people, and farmers or persons moving up from the farm. The utopians, in particular, include many middle-echelon stormtrooper leaders.

Being oriented to the struggle is evidently another peak manifestation of a style of being politically violent in response to strong personality needs. As with the respondents for whom the time of struggle was "the best time of my life," being involved in the struggle regardless of the nature of its object or its antagonists, and often to the point of physical breakdown, seems to hold together and to integrate rather disjointed or unstable personalities. If we compare struggle-orientation to the other ways we have attempted to classify politically violent people, we find that there appears to be no uniform dimension scaling the more violent and the less violent. Rather, there are different personal styles of political violence, each of which is represented in archetypal form in a recognizable part of the most violent men of our sample: The pure, rather mindless activism of the instant stormtroopers and SS men; the Goering type of middle-echelon stormtrooper leader; the more deliberate, ideologically-motivated violence of the delayed stormtrooper or day-and-nighter; and the struggle-oriented sadist. Their individual styles and personality needs each relate somewhat differently to Nazi ideology and to such relationships as comradeship satisfactions, group conformity, and the leadership cult.

To check on the degree to which the different styles of violence do or do not overlap, we can look at some crosstabulations between them. Over three-fourths of the struggle-oriented, for example, are instant stormtroopers or SS men, but only about one-sixth of these latter groups happen to be struggle-oriented. The day-and-nighters in turn are only in small part (17.9%) struggle-oriented. Many of them (30.4%) prefer comradeship or are Hitler-worshippers (13.4%). Thus it would seem fair to call the struggle-oriented a particularly violent or militant (one out of five is engaged only in electioneering or proselytizing) part of the large number of instant stormtroopers and SS men. The day-and-nighters for their part overlap very little with either group since most of them are delayed stormtroopers, including many middle-echelon leaders.

It is worth mentioning also that the struggle-oriented joined the party either before 1925 or in the years 1928-1930—in other words, not even during the peak period of 1925-1927 when so many of the mindless sluggers joined. As Table VII-1 indicates, moreover, the struggle-oriented, while having the largest number of marcher-fighters (MF) and marcher-fighter-proselytizers (MFP), are not as exclusively devoted to fighting nor as unconcerned with ideology and proselytizing (38.9%) as it may have appeared at first. They are not really all mindless sluggers, but are singled out by their need for personality integration by involvement in all-out struggle. The comradeship-oriented, by comparison, are the most

Table VII-1: Struggle Orientation and Nazi Activity (in %)

	Leader-oriented	Com-radeship-oriented	Struggle-oriented	Utopia-oriented	Average of Sample
M	9.9	6.6	4.2	5.3	6.4
MF	31.7	26.2	43.2	16.4	25.5
MP	18.0	24.0	10.5	28.7	22.3
MFP	18.0	27.3	28.4	22.6	23.0
Mere membership	18.0	12.6	6.3	24.6	18.9
Other	4.3	3.2	7.4	2.4	3.9
Totals	100.0	100.0	100.0	100.0	100.0

involved with ideology and proselytizing of the three—in fact, as much as the much older utopians who share with them the experience of war and military service, and may well reflect it in their ideological and proselytizing emphasis. The leadership-oriented, finally, have more than their share of marchers (M) and marcher-fighters (MF) which apparently does not preclude them from having been politically more involved all along, especially in the pre-1925 NSDAP and *voelkisch* groups, as we have noted. Again, political violence does not fit itself into a simple relationship to the other variables and styles of political extremism.

The last part of our investigation was devoted to the patterns of office-holding and later careers in the Nazi party. We began with a closer look at the pre-1933 office-holders, who turned out to be considerably over-represented in the Abel collection. They were the spearhead of the new counter-elite that challenged and eventually conquered the Weimar Republic. Among them, the minor local leaders are still rather similar to the rank and file of the storm-troopers, with whom they even share a stereotypical revanchism and solidarism. They include many older military-civil servants and tend to be metropolitan. The local chiefs (*Ortsgruppenleiter*) and similar functionaries tend to be business and professional men, white-collar workers, and farmers, rarely blue-collar men, and often from rural or small-town areas. The preponderance of white-collar employees and civil servants among the party bureaucracy is striking.

In their youth, the office-holders were not particularly violence-prone, but frequently held youth group offices. Except for the minor officials, they played little role in counter-revolutionary violence. Many joined the NSDAP or *voelkisch* groups before 1925, but hardly any in the 1925-1927 era or after the presidential elections of 1932. Most of them were loners in the party, which contrasts with the family membership of some of the more violent elements. The local chiefs exhibited a pronounced xenophobia and chauvinism and a strong sense of identification with the movement (conformity). Their ideology was Nordic-German romanticism and superpatriotism, and they included many paranoid antisemites. Their introduction to the party was chiefly through their awareness of the ideology of the NSDAP. They tended to be comradeship-oriented or utopians and participated far less in violence and demonstrations than in proselytizing and in acts of provocation.

A considerable number of local chiefs, on the other hand, were day-and-nighters, delayed stormtroopers, SS men, or middle-echelon leaders of the SA or SS. In the early phases of the movement, and especially in the Bavarian *Gaue*, there were some strong personal links between the party offices and stormtrooper ranks which were only gradually superseded by the bifurcation between the two that was typical of the north and east, and the ruie after 1933.

The officers of functional Nazi organizations were among the oldest functionaries, especially of the civil service association. They tended to be metropolitan, upwardly mobile, and not particularly driven by economic crises. They joined rather late and, with the exception of the Labor Cells (NSBO), were hardly involved in violence. Most workers of the Abel sample were not even in the NSBO, which instead included mostly white-collar employees and military-civil servants. The functional officers were of relatively high political intelligence and thus constitute an elite among the party office-holders. The student and women leaders among them tended to be Nordic-German romantics, Hitler-worshippers, anti-Marxists, and *outrés* to boot. The civil service leaders more often were revanch-ists. The NSBO functionaries, finally, were solidarists and anti-semites. Antisemitism always seems to play a role among the de-fectors and antagonists of the Socialist, or Communist, German labor movement.

Moving on to the Nazi careers made after 1933 by many Abel respondents, we deal with a substantially different situation. Now the party is in control of the state and there are many opportunities for rapid administrative careers. And although the original func-tions of the stormtroopers have disappeared and the SA has been drastically purged, there are new functions of enforcing the totali-tarian terror which offer careers to the unscrupulous. Last, but not least, the victorious party organization could offer careers to those old fighters who could pass the great cleaning-out of 1933 when thousands of office-holders and SA-ranks were phased out as "un-suitable" and embarrassing to the party in power. This survey, of course, also tells us what kind of pre-1933 background tended to lead to an administrative or party career, or to that of a blood-hound of the SS state. And in so doing, it links the banality, human interest, and seeming quixotic harmlessness of the pre-1933 Nazi movement with the evils perpetrated under the Third *Reich*. Let us take a closer look at the three career types and how they differed from each other.

The party and administrative careerists were mostly military-civil servants and white-collar workers, relatively well-educated and up-wardly mobile in an urban context. We might say that their career-ism in the Third *Reich* answered their hunger for social climbing in a way appropriate to their quasi-bureaucratic backgrounds. Their childhoods tended to be economically secure and mostly freewheeling. The party men, in particular, were very conscious of order and cleanliness, while the administrators were more likely to be hostile to police and government. They both typically volunteered for the war and expressed strong hostility for draft-dodgers and civilians. The enforcers, by comparison, were much younger, including more than half in the postwar generation, and consisted mostly of workers or farmers who were in social decline or static. Substantial numbers of them had experienced friction with the occupation and many lost their livelihood during the Depression. No fewer than one-third of the enforcers grew up without a father, and another third in poverty. They also had very little education and evidently little religious identification; the few enforcers who indicated their religion came from a religiously heterogeneous setting.[1] They tended to show strong hostility to the police and also an extreme leadership cult, which evidently helped to rationalize their behavior. All three career groups also had disproportionate numbers (15-21%) of disciplinarian childhoods behind them, which adds in particular to the disturbed father-son relationships of the enforcers.

The background of the enforcers marks them off as having been in Free Corps and left-wing groups or having joined the SA or Hitler Youth directly with the second youth revolt. They became militarized so early—one-third before the age of 18, three-fourths before 21, and 97% before 26—that this feature alone helps to characterize them. They particularly liked marching and violence and, in fact, participated heavily in street-fighting (37%) and Free Corps violence (22%) before the age of 26. We classified most of them as politically militarized or hostile militant youths. No fewer than three-fourths of them report friction on the job or having been fired for political reasons. The administrative careerists somewhat resemble the enforcers' Free Corps background and liking for violence, although they participated far less in street-fighting and Free Corps violence. They also belonged to *Stahlhelm* and *Wehrwolf*, though usually at a more mature age than the enforcers, who were generally militarized before the age of 21. We mostly classified the administrators as hostile militants in their youth.

The party men tended to be in bourgeois or conservative (*Jungdo*, DHV) youth groups or in *voelkisch* organizations, includ-

---

[1] The party men also rarely indicate their religion, and the administrators who do also tend to be from heterogeneous areas—that is, areas which were mixed or where they belonged to the minority.

ing the pre-1925 NSDAP (one-fifth). They liked hiking, cultural appreciation, and marching with a purpose best, but actually were somewhat more involved in youthful violence than were the administrators. We classified their youthful postures as fully politicized or prepolitical parochial. Like the enforcers, they tended to have militaristic fathers or parents identifying with the moderate parties, but then to single out *voelkisch*-antisemitic teachers as influential in their lives. The administrators, by way of contrast, report *voelkisch* or unpolitical fathers and patriotic school influences, a sign of their less over-determined bent of mind.

At the end of the war, all three groups blamed the defeat on the Kaiser and the civilians, probably a major point of distinction between the Nazis and the conservative DNVP to which some party careerists belonged. The party men also added the Marxists and Spartakists, as we would expect of such a politicized group. They participated significantly less in counter-revolutionary activities even though they expressed sympathy with the Free Corps and Kapp *putsch* activities. Their reasons for militarization typically were an antisemitic predisposition and opposition to the "revolution," while the administrators were spurred on by the defeat and the shock at the new Weimar leadership, and the enforcers by the occupation and their anti-revolutionary sentiment. The party men belonged to political parties including the pre-1925 NSDAP far more heavily than the other two groups.

The enforcers tended to join the post-1924 party chiefly in the years 1925-1927 or right after the 1930 elections, evidently following the attraction of street violence. The enforcers typically joined only when the local party already constituted a substantial minority; the party men tended to be local founders. The enforcers were usually introduced by friends or fellow-workers, as were the party men, who tended to join much earlier. One-half of the enforcers joined before they were 21, three-fourths before the age of 31. The chief motives of the enforcers were their economic troubles or the comradeship of the stormtroopers. Ninety-five percent of them indeed joined the SA or the SS. They include many SA and SS officers, and two-thirds of the enforcers report involvement in violence. Since some of the worst cases of enforcer careers are rather close-mouthed about their pre-1933 violence, as our examples demonstrate, it is likely that their involvement is much greater than two-thirds. A good three-fourths of them were classified as MFs (52.5%) or MFPs (28.8%), while the party men more likely were marcher-proselytizers (MPs), and the administrators did not concentrate on any particular combination of activities. In fact, the administrators are the true *Septemberlinge*, having joined mostly after mid-1931 in tribute to the "dynamic impression" of the Hitler movement.

It would be a simplification, however, to consider the administrators as pure opportunists. They were generally introduced to the party by their awareness of its ideology. Their own ideology tended to be solidarism and revanchism, but they also included a large number of antisemitic paranoids and anecdote-tellers. The party men were only a little higher in antisemitism and included mostly cholerics. They also tended to be Nordic-German romantics and Hitler-worshippers. The enforcers were the lowest in antisemitism, although they also had more than their share of cholerics, which may well indicate lapses of balance among their taut minds. They were, moreover, revanchists and Hitler-worshippers and included many without any recognizable ideology. Where the others expected and received a pay-off, the enforcers typically were satisfied with the struggle alone and with their leadership cult, two of the chief orientations of their lives. A third was their hankering for comradeship and desire to merge their identities with the movement. Needless to say, they were loners in the party, as were the party men, and held only half as many party offices (38.6%) as did the two types of careerists. The latter, in turn, had only a little more than half in SA or SS, engaged half as much in violence, and held twice as many party offices as did the enforcers. The administrators even rival the enforcers in the number of middle-echelon stormtrooper leaders.

Concluding Remarks

A few years ago, the eminent historian Wolfgang Sauer raised some basic questions about the directions which research on National Socialism should take or had failed to take.[2] He called, in particular, for a socio-economic theory of fascism which might supply an understanding of the social dynamics of the movement that turned out to have such a devastating impact on German and European history. Were the Nazis perhaps motivated by having been the "losers of the industrial revolution," in contrast to the liberal bourgeoisie and the Socialist labor movement? Did the Nazi movement have a true "revolutionary potential?" Was it primarily an anti-modernist, conservative movement, as Ernst Nolte has suggested?[3] We have examined the social dynamics of rank-and-file members for clues to this complex of questions and found some that point to a social-revolutionary potential of sorts. However, these socio-eco-

[2] Wolfgang Sauer, "National Socialism: Totalitarianism or Fascism?" *American Historical Review*, vol. 72 (Jl. 1967), pp. 404-424.

[3] See his *Three Faces of Fascism*, New York: Holt, Rinehart and Winston, 1965.

nomic motives could at best explain only the socio-political dynamics of a part of the sample—namely, some farmers and many of the members of the older generation of Nazis. Rather than being "losers of the industrial revolution," moreover, many Abel respondents appear to have been the losers only of the defeat-induced recession and stagnation of the postwar economy, a fate they shared with countless non-Nazis and even non-Germans in the victor nations. The social dynamics of the Nazi movement, in other words, is unable to supply a comprehensive explanation of its origins and political course, although it can shed some light on many details of social history.

A more potent source of explanation appears to be the great fall of the German national pride that came about with the defeat of 1918 and its consequences. Whether in the form of the over-reaction of respondents of foreign contacts, border Germans, former colonials, or people in conflict with the foreign occupation, or in the trauma of *Fronterlebnis*, defeat, and "revolution," here is a set of motives which explains the attitudes and overdetermined reaction of a majority of the Abel respondents. If there had been no World War One or if it had not been lost, these men and women would never have rushed into counter-revolutionary and extremist movements such as the NSDAP. This is particularly true of the military-civil servants and other militarized elements whose study Sauer also recommended. Their wounded pride turned "unpolitical" soldiers, civil servants, and even underage youths into the seething "counter-revolutionary" mobs that eventually got the better of the unhappy republic.

Although the war affected the prewar and war generations and even the victory-watchers, it cannot account for the extremism of those cohorts who followed. Even the politicized second counter-revolutionary wave of 1923 fails to provide a strong enough connecting link between the war experience and the Weimar youth revolt. It was this political youth revolt, of which especially the second wave seems to have gone directly into the SA and HJ, which gave the war-motivated movement the staying power to triumph in 1933. We undertook to follow the process of politicization in the early years of the younger respondents and to classify youthful political postures and activities. We also proposed a theory of extremist deviancy and identity which helps to resolve some of the paradoxes in the self-perception of a young extremist, and his clash with the world around him. The politically militarized youth, with some assistance from the hostile militants and the fully politicized, is the key to our understanding of the political youth revolt of Weimar. No account of the early Nazi movement would be complete without an explanation of the role of youth and of its *voelkisch* education for the brown hordes.

This book has been a study of political violence and of its relations to extremist ideologies, attitudes, personality, and the life of an extremist organization as exemplified in the pre-1933 NSDAP. What came first, the violence of the men of the counter-revolution or the violence engendered by the Nazi struggle for power, violent men or a violent movement, chicken or egg? Was the "stage of militarization" the cause of Nazi violence, or was violence caused by the super-politicization of indignant minds? As we have found, the politicized youth of Weimar was particularly interested not in electoral politics, but only in the totalitarian politics of "marching with a purpose" and in political violence almost as a purpose in itself. In fact, this is the reason why the politically militarized youth is a harbinger of this development. On the other hand, many young Nazis did not become politically militarized at an early age, but grew into the role of the "political soldier" by more gradual steps, from marching and electioneering at the middle stages to high involvement in street violence at stage four.

There is also the other chicken-and-egg question about ideological fervor or extremist political involvement. Our division into the two motives for joining, the "dynamic impression of the Hitler movement" and "ideological or antisemitic fervor," tended to separate the more traditional elements mobilized by war- and counter-revolution from the *voelkisch*-political ideologues who sustained the Nazi movement from its early beginnings into the winning stretch. The dynamicists, as the reader will recall were a passive element, even though quite violent in the earlier phases. Attracted by the dynamic impression of the movement, they were swept along by the revolutionary drive of the ideologues. Because of their deep convictions, these ideologues also carried the lion's share of the proselytizing (MP and MFP) necessary to make the movement swell into a vast quasi-religious crusade. The fighting needed for the control of the streets and the protection of speakers and propaganda efforts was left to less ideologically inclined stormtroopers, to whom the struggle supplied its own satisfactions and who played no particular role in the party organization.

Of the three combinations of the quintessential totalitarian activities, the older zealots (MP), the perfect combination (MFP), and the marcher-fighters (MF), the last deserve particular attention because they constitute something of a fascist archetype, men of action unencumbered by ideas or pity. On closer examination, they turn out to be rather pitiful figures themselves: Verbally incontinent *outrés*, or the walking wounded of a deficient childhood socialization, often fatherless, in conflict with their parents, or the battered children of disciplinarian fathers, they seem to bruise others not because they are fascist supermen. They are violent more in the manner of a person having an epileptic seizure in a crowd of accidental bystanders. Their masochism and self-pity document more truly than could any express rationalizations their attitude toward their own behavior. Nevertheless, they are driven on by their uncontrollable hankering for physical and verbal violence, and the party supplies them with appropriate ideological rationalizations, a comradeship of fighters, and the charismatic leader's blessing on carrying on what they like to do anyway. After the need for street-fighting has passed, the NSDAP even supplies them with victims in the concentration camps and in other enforcement functions, putting their sickness to grisly use for its own purposes. By that time, the ideological and prejudicial rationalizations even have the sanction of the government and the recognition of many foreign governments and international authorities behind them.

The role of violent men in politics raises further questions. As this was being written, for example, the Irish Republican Army, militant Northern Irish Protestants, and the British government in rare agreement vowed to track down "gangs of psychopathic killers," who possibly on both sides and under cover of the ongoing political tensions were said to have tortured and killed scores of victims "for thrills." Whether in Northern Ireland or in any other situation of political violence, how can we expect to draw a clear and authoritative line between a politically motivated gunman or terrorist and a thrill-killer hiding under political motives? Is it not likely, given the nature of human personality and rationalization, that a person will hide his criminal propensities from himself and others by clinging to political rationalizations? In the days of the bomb-throwing anarchists, every petty thief liked to think of himself as a righteous anarchist expropriating the expropriators, and there was no lack of similar rationalizations for maimings and killings.[4] Why should not a psychopath with a yearning for mayhem seek out a role in a violent extremist movement which will salve his guilt feelings with ideological righteousness? We now know for a fact that ideology can relieve the guilt feelings associated with political violence.

The role of violent men also has to be seen from the point of view

[4] Probably in reaction to these inevitable diversionary maneuvers, German criminologists in the 1920s used to posit "criminal types" and "propensities" which were said to be biologically anchored and associated with certain facial features. It is not known whether they ever took a good look at the stormtrooper movement.

of the party leaders and ideologues who encourage and use them. Every extremist movement has the problem of what to do with them, especially since political extremism can practically be defined by the criterion of readiness to use violence to accomplish the ends of the movement. Party leaders and ideologues of extremist movements of the right and left often openly flirt with violence in, thereby even suggesting a vicarious pleasure in what their minions may do to enemies and innocent bystanders alike. But there is a difference between encouraging the bona fide members of the movement not to shy away from acts of physical courage and encouraging "teen-age crazies" and other psychopaths to "do their thing." The insiders often can tell the difference between the two and they clearly bear the responsibility for the consequences.

Our earlier references to the role of ideology naturally raise questions about the content and intensity of Nazi beliefs. There are some intriguing passages in the Abel biographies in which respondents describe some of the criticisms made of their movement, and their own reactions to them. A Catholic worker in a nail factory, born 1879 (no. 334), relates:

> They threw at me that the Hitler movement was going to destroy both Christian churches, that it would get rid of all the crippled and unfit people, simply do away with them, and that it threatened the rights of workers and would take away their social security. They also claimed that the Nazis would like to start another war, and other lies and calumnies of which I tried to disabuse the people.

He also made a point of always going to church in order to "disprove these false charges." Another man, born 1886, a municipal clerk (no. 162), tells: "My colleagues did not trust me [in discussions] and whenever I had nailed them down, they evaded the issue with some facile trick like 'all this you say is very nice except for your damned war. If the brownshirts take over, war will come for sure.'" To the respondent, this too was a nasty lie. We may wonder what these simpletons really knew about their own movement and which of the vague and disconnected Nazi beliefs were really important to them.

According to our examination, there was precious little genuine anti-modernism among the Nazi rank and file, whatever Ernst Nolte may have found in the *voelkisch* literature.[5] Such *voelkisch* belief

---

[5] See Nolte, *Three Faces of Fascism*, and Rolf Geissler, *Dekadenz und Heroismus*, pp. 18-28 and 77-94, where especially the new faith of decadence and heroism is admirably documented, a faith that can only in minor aspects be called anti-modernistic.

elements as the Nordic-German-agrarian romanticism which was popular among some of the elite groups of our sample lacked the specificity and political punch to be a fighting faith. Obviously underlying most of this loosely formulated *voelkisch* integralism, moreover, was always the hideous face of antisemitic prejudice. Our investigation confirmed what history has already taught us about the Nazi movement: The chimneys of Auschwitz will always overshadow any of the colossal monuments by which the Third Reich sought to express a new life-style. The only other complex of beliefs really important to our respondents seems to have been that of superpatriotism, xenophobia, and revanchism, a war-related package which was hardly unique to the NSDAP. As will be recalled, the revanchist elements were relegated to a footsoldier role in the party, at least after 1927, whereas superpatriotism and xenophobia were fairly central to the beliefs of the more active elements until the takeover of power.

While we cannot claim to have developed a new body of theoretical knowledge of the dynamics of prejudice, our findings tend to put some of the theories developed by the late Theodor Adorno in a new light, especially by confirming the role of childhood and yet casting doubt on the "authoritarian" model. To begin with, what could be a more appropriate sample for studying prejudice than a collection of early Nazis speaking candidly about the things on their minds? This is also a perfect setting in which to relate "political antisemitism" to other forms of the prejudice. The nature of the data did not allow us to be more clinical, but our empirical evidence is rather clear. When prejudice turns into paranoia, often at a very young age, and with the same disciplinarian or orphaned background we have observed among several of the most violent groups, it becomes a spur to political action. The cholerics and anecdote-tellers seem harmless old fools compared to the paranoid activist. Many Nazi leaders and probably Adolf Hitler himself would have rated the paranoid classification. The paranoids of the Abel collection were among the most violent respondents and held many important party offices. We need not be surprised to find them prominent among the careerists of the Third *Reich*, even though the party men and the enforcers more often tended to be cholerics, a large category whose *Judenkoller* often coincided with the cultural shock of the defeat and "revolution" of 1918.

The personal background and character of the enforcers of the Third Reich in our study, finally, permits a revealing look into a subject about which little is known. Who were these bloodhounds of the SS state and what motivated them to take on these shocking roles? They were simply more of those men of violence and of the walking wounded we discussed earlier, sociopaths put into the service of the totalitarian regime. Though our data base on them is admittedly small, we now know something which will probably be augmented by further investigations of broader samples of Nazi and other enforcers. Perhaps someone will one day check the large numbers of SA and SS records in the NSDAP membership catalog to see whether they all have this background of fatherlessness, and whatever other information the documents can yield. In the meantime we can reflect on the violent men in other, contemporary extremist movements and wonder how many of them would become bloodhounds or enforcers if their movements ever came to power in their country. *Principiis obsta.*

In the Weimar Republic of 1922, vilification of government leaders, extremist calls for violence, assassinations of public figures, and partisan violence had grown to such proportions that the government passed the Law for the Protection of the Republic (*Republikschutzgesetz*). For seven years this law succeeded in suppressing the unrestrained verbal and physical violence to which people like the Abel respondents were inclined. In 1929 it was allowed to lapse, and once more the furies of hatred were loose on the streets of German cities. Reich Minister of the Interior Severing, in a memorandum of December 1929, documented the flood of *outré* vilifications of the republic, the Weimar constitution, the black-red-gold flag, and republican politicians which promptly issued from Nazi, Communist (KPD), and DNVP or *Stahlhelm* mouths. He also supplied an endless list of the bloody clashes and assaults which ensued among Nazi and Communist toughs every few days and often involved other victims as well. Unrestrained physical aggression by some evidently followed immediately upon the unrestrained verbal aggressions of others. Severing concluded imploringly, "The jungle-like state of politics we have sketched can no longer be tolerated in the interest of state authority, of German prestige in the world, of the security of the individual citizen, and the re-establishment of a healthy foundation of public and social life. . . . The acute illness calls for means that will instantly stop it from spreading further."[6] But the illness of violence that had German society in its grip found no effective remedies. The rest is history.

[6] See Gotthard Jasper, "Zur innerpolitischen Lage in Deutschland im Herbst 1929," *Vierteljahreshefte fuer Zeitgeschichte*, July 1960, pp. 280-289.

Appendix A: Index of Coded Items and Crosstabulations
(Frequency Distributions and other tables in italics)

Appendix B: Additional FD Tables

FD-3: Chief Location 1928-1933

	Number	Per cent
Berlin Area	189	32.6
Other metropolitan area (100,000+)	117	20.2
Large town (10,000-99,999)	92	15.9
Small town (2,000-9,999)	78	13.5
Rural-industrial, edge of town	39	6.7
Rural, small or medium farm	56	9.7
Rural, on estate	7	1.2
Other	1	0.2
	579	100.0

F-10: Religious Setting

	Number	Per cent
Protestants in Protestant area	113	20.1
Protestants in mixed area	16	2.8
Protestants in Catholic area	8	1.4
Catholics in Catholic area	38	6.7
Catholics in mixed area	4	0.7
Catholics in Protestant area	10	1.8
NA in Protestant area	260	46.2
NA in mixed area	73	13.0
NA in Catholic area	41	7.3
	563	100.0

FD-11: Level of Education

	Number	Per cent
Primary Rural	10	1.8
Primary (8 years only)	115	21.1
Primary plus vocational (apprenticeship)	230	42.2
Primary and some secondary	44	8.0
Secondary (*Mittlere Reife*)	79	14.5
Abitur only	28	5.1
University attendance (no degree)	21	3.8
University degree	19	3.5
	546	100.0

Selected Bibliography

Abel, Theodore. *The Nazi Movement*. New York: Atherton, 1965.

Adams, Robert Lynn and Fox, Robert Jon. "Mainlining Jesus: The New Trip," *Transaction*, Spring, 1972.

Adorno, Theodor W., Frenkel-Brunswiek, Else, Levinson, D. J. and Sanford, R. Nevitt. *The Authoritarian Personality*. New York: Harper, 1950, reissued by New York: Science Editon, 1964.

Allen, William S. *The Nazi Seizure of Power*. Chicago: University of Chicago Press, 1965.

Allport, Gordon. *The Nature of Prejudice*. New York: Doubleday-Anchor, 1958.

Almond, Gabriel A. and Verba, Sidney. *The Civic Culture*. Princeton: Princeton University Press, 1963.

Anthony, Katherine. *Feminism in Germany and Scandinavia*. New York: Holt, 1915.

Arendt, Hannah, *The Origins of Totalitarianism*. New York: Harcourt, Brace, 1966.

Arendt, Hannah. *Eichmann in Jerusalem*. New York: Viking Press, 1963.

Arlt, Wolfgang, ed. *Deutschlands Junge Garde*. Berlin: Neues Leben, 1959.

Bade, Wilfrid. *SA erobert Berlin*. Munich: Knorr & Hirth, 1941.

Beck, Friedrich A. *Kampf und Sieg, Geschichte der NSDAP in Gau Westfalen-Süd*. Dortmund: Westfalenverlag, 1938.

Berthold, Lothar. *Das Programm der KPD zur nationalen und sozialen Befreiung des deutschen Volkes vom August 1930*. Berlin: Dietz, 1956.

Bettelheim, Bruno and Janowitz, Morris. *Dynamics of Prejudice*. New York: Harper, 1950.

Bracher, Karl D. *Die Auflösung der Weimarer Republik*, 4th ed. Villingen: Ring Verlag, 1959.

Bracher, Karl D. *The German Dictatorship*. New York: Praeger, 1970.

Brady, Robert A. *The Spirit and Structure of German Fascism*. London: Gollancz, 1937.

Bremme, Gabriele, *Die politische Rolle der Frau in Deutschland*. Goettingen: Vandenhoeck & Rupprecht, 1956.

Broszat, Martin. *National Socialism, 1918-1933*. Santa Barbara: Clio Press, 1967.

Broszat, Martin. "Die voelkische Ideologie und der Nationalsozialismus," *Deutsche Rundschau*, vol. 84, 1958.

Buchheim, Hans et al. *Anatomy of the SS-State*. New York: Walker, 1968.

Comfort, Richard A. *Revolutionary Hamburg*. Stanford: Stanford University Press, 1966.

Conze, Werner. *Die Zeit Wilhelms II und die Weimarer Republik*. Tuebingen: Wunderlich, 1964.

Daim, Wilfried. *Der Mann der Hitler die Ideen gab*. Institute fuer Politische Psychologie Wien, Munich: Isar, 1958.

Darré, Walter. *Das Bauerntum als Lebensquell der nordischen Rasse* and *Neuadel aus Blut und Boden*. Muenchen: J. F. Lehmann, 1929 and 1930.

Deutsch, Karl W. "Social Mobilization and Political Development," LV *American Political Science Review*. June, 1961.

Dietrich, Otto. *Hitler*. Chicago: Regnery, 1955.

Dix, Arthur. *Die Deutschen Reichstagswahlen 1871-1930 und die Wandlungen der Volksgliederung*. Tuebingen: Mohr, 1930.

Duenow, Hermann. *Der Rote Frontkaempferbund*. East Berlin: MNV, no date.

Erger, Johannes. *Der Kapp-Luettwitz Putsch*. Duesseldorf: Droste, 1967.

Favez, Jean-Claude. *Le Reich dévant l'occupation francobelge de la Ruhr en 1923*. Geneva: Droz, 1969.

Fest, Joachim C. *The Face of the Third Reich*. New York: Pantheon, 1970.

Franz-Willing, Georg. *Die Hitlerbewegung: Der Ursprung 1919-1922*. Hamburg: Schenck, 1962.

Geiger, Theodor. *Die Soziale Schichtung des deutschen Volkes*. Stuttgart: Enke, 1932.

Geissler, Rolf. *Dekadenz und Heroismus*. Stuttgart: Deutsche Verlagsanstalt, 1964.

Georg, Enno. *Die writschaftlichen Unternehmungen der SS*. Stuttgart: Deutsche Verlagsanstalt, 1963.

Gilbert, G. M. *Nuremberg Diary*. New York: Farrar Straus, 1947.

Gilbert, G. M. *The Psychology of Dictatorship*. New York: Ronald Press, 1950.

Gimbel, A. *So Kaempften wir*. Frankfurt: Verlagsgessellschaft, 1941.

Glaeser, Ernst. *Jahrgang 1902*. Berlin: Kiepenheuer, 1929.

Grohe, Josef. *Der politische Kampf im Rheinland nach dem ersten Weltkrieg*. Bonn: Universitaetsdruckerei, 1941.

Guerin, Daniel. *Fascisme et Grand Captal*. Paris: Gallimard, 1936.

Gurr, Ted. *Why Men Rebel*. Princeton: Princeton University Press, 1970.

Hamel, Iris. *Voelkischer Verhand und nationale Gewerkschaft*. Frankfurt: Europaeische Verlagsanstalt, 1967.

Heberle, Rudolph. *From Democracy to Nazism*. Baton Rouge: Louisiana State University Press, 1945.

Heiden, Konrad. *Der Fuehrer.* Boston: Houghton Mifflin, 1944.

Heiss, Friedrich. *Das Schlesienbuch.* Berlin: Volk and Reich, 1938.

Heller, Karl. *Der Bund der Landwirte (Landbund) und seine Politik.* Unpublished doctoral dissertation: Wuerzburg University, 1936.

Hermanns, Will. *Stadt in Ketten, Geschichte der Besatzungs- und Separatistenzeit.* Aachen: J. A. Mayer, 1933.

Heyen, Franz J. *Nationalsozialismus im Alltag.* Boppard: Boldt Verlag, 1967.

Hitler, Adolf. *Mein Kampf.* Boston: Houghton Mifflin, 1943.

Hochmuth, R., ed. *Nationalsozialismus in der Praxis.* Berlin: Press, 1932.

Hoefler, Karl. *Oberschlesien in der Aufstandszeit 1918-1921.* Berlin: Mittler and Sons, 1938.

Horkheimer, Max. *Autoritaet und Familie.* Paris: no publisher, 1936.

Hotzel, Curt, ed. *Deutscher Aufstand: die Revolution des Nachkriegs.* Stuttgart: Kohlhammer, 1934.

Hundhammer, Alois, *Die Landwirtschaftliche Berufsvertretung in Bayern.* Munich: Pfeiffer, 1926.

Hunt, Richard N. *German Social Democracy, 1918-1933.* New Haven: Yale University Press, 1964.

Jasper, Gotthard. "Zur innerpolitischen Lage in Deutschland im Herbst 1929," *Vierteljahreshefte fuer Zeitgeschichte.* July, 1960.

Juenger, Ernst, ed. *Der Kampf um das Reich.* Essen: Kamp.

Keniston, Kenneth. *Young Radicals, Notes on Committed Youth.* New York: Harcourt, Brace and World, 1968.

Kessler, Harry Graf. *Walter Rathenau, Sein, Leben und Sein Werk.* Wiesbaden: Rheinische Verlagsanstalt, 1962.

Kirkpatrick, Clifford. *Nazi Germany: Its Women and Family Life.* Indianapolis: Bobbs-Merrill, 1938.

Klemperer, Klemens von. *Germany's New Conservatism.* Princeton: Princeton University Press, 1957.

Klose, Werner. *Lebensformen Deutscher Jugend, Vom Wandervogel zur Popgeneration.* Muenchen-Wien: Olzog, 1970.

Kluke, Paul. "Nationalsozialistische Europapolitik," *Vierteljahreshefte fuer Zeitgeschichte.* Volume 3, 1955.

Koeller, Heinz. *Kampfbuendnis an der Seine, Ruhr und Spree.* Berlin: Ruetten and Loening, 1963.

Koennemann, Erwin. *Einwohnerwehren und Zeitfreiwilligenverbaende.* Berlin: Militaerverlag, 1969.

Kornhauser, William. *The Politics of Mass Society.* London: Routledge and Kegan Paul, 1960.

Kracauer, Siegfried. *Die Angestellten aus dem neuesten Deutschland.* Frankfurt: 1930.

Laqueur, Walter Z. *Young Germany.* New York: Basic Books, 1962.

Lasswell, Harold D. and Lerner, Daniel, eds. *World Revolutionary Elites.* Cambridge: MIT Press, 1966.

Lebovics, Herman. *Social Conservation and the Middle Classes, 1914-1933*. Princeton: Princeton University Press, 1969.

Lipset, Seymour M. *Political Man*. New York: Doubleday-Anchor Books, 1963.

Loewenberg, Peter. "The Psycho-Historical Origins of the Nazi Youth Cohort," *American Historical Review*, vol. 76, December 1971.

Lohalm, Ulrich, *Voelkischer Radikalismus*. Hamburg: Leibniz, 1970.

Lowenthal, Leo and Guterman, Norbert. *Prophets of Deceit*. New York: Harper, 1949.

Manvell, Roger and Fraenkel, Heinrich. *The Incomparable Crime*. New York: G. P. Putnam, 1967.

Mattes, Wilhelm. *Die Bayerischen Bauernraete*. Stuttgart: Cotta, 1921.

Merton, Robert et al., eds. *Reader in Bureaucracy*. Glencoe: Free Press, 1952.

Michels, Robert. *Umschichtungen in den herrschenden Klassen nach dem Kriege*. Stuttgart: Kohlhammer, 1934.

Moller, Herbert. "Youth as a Force in the Modern World," *Comparative Studies in Society and History*. Volume 10, October-July 1967-68.

Mosse, George L. *The Crisis of German Ideology*. New York: Grosset and Dunlap, 1964.

Neumann, Franz. *Behemoth, the Structure and Practice of National Socialism, 1933-1944*. New York: Oxford University Press, 1944.

Orlov, Dieter. *The History of the Nazi Party, 1919-1933*. Pittsburgh: University of Pittsburgh Press, 1969.

Ostwald, Hans. *Sittengeschichte der Inflation*. Berlin: Henius, 1931.

Peterson, Edward N. *The Limits of Hitler's Power*. Princeton: Princeton University Press, 1969.

Pinson, Koppel S. *Modern Germany, Its History and Civilization*. Second edition, New York: Macmillan, 1966.

Pross, Harry. *Eros und Politik*. Bern: Scherz, 1964.

Puckett, Hugh Wiley. *Germany's Women Go Forward*. New York: Columbia University Press, 1930.

Pulzer, Peter G. J. *The Rise of Political Anti-Semitism in Germany and Austria*. New York: Wiley, 1964.

Reich, Charles A. *The Greening of America*. New York: Random House-Bantam Books, 1971.

Report of the National Advisory Commission on Civil Disorders. New York: Random House-Bantam Books, 1968.

Roloff, Ernst-August. *Buergertum und Nationalsozialismus, 1930-1933. Brannschweigs Weg ins Dritte Reich*, Hannover: Verlag fuer Literatur und Zeitgeschehen, 1961.

Salomon, Ernst von. *Die Geaechteten*. Berlin: Guetersloh, 1930.

Sauer, Wolfgang. "National Socialism: Totalitarianism or Fascism?" *American Historical Review*, vol. 72, July 1972.

Schaefer, Wolfgang. *NSDAP: Entwicklung und Struktur der Staatspartei des Dritten Reiches*. Frankfurt: Goedel, 1957.

Schelsky, Helmut. *Die Skeptische Generation*. Duesseldorf: Diederich, 1960.

Schleunes, Karl. *The Twisted Road to Auschwitz*. Urbana: University of Illinois Press, 1969.

Schoenbaum, David. *Hitler's Social Revolution, Class and Status in Nazi Germany 1933-1939*. New York: Doubleday, 1966.

Smith, Bradley F. *Adolf Hitler, His Family, Childhood and Youth*. Stanford: Hoover Institute Press, 1969.

Smith, Bradley F. *Heinrich Himmler, A Nazi in the Making 1900-1926*. Stanford: Hoover Institute Press, 1971.

Spethmann, Hans. *Der Ruhrkampf 1923-1925*. Berlin: Hobbing, 1933.

Stern, Fritz. *The Politics of Cultural Despair*. New York: Doubleday-Anchor Books, 1961.

Striefler, Heinrich. *Deutsche Wahlen in Bildern und Zahlen*. Duesseldorf: Wende, 1946.

Sweezy, Maxine B. *The Structure of the Nazi Economy*. Cambridge, Mass: Harvard University Press, 1941.

Thimme, Annelise. *Flucht in den Mythos: die deutschnationale Volks-partei und die Niederlage von 1918*. Goettingen: Vandenhoeck and Ruprecht, 1969.

Uhlemann, Manfred. *Arbeiterjugend gegen Cuno und Poincaré, das Jahr 1923*. Berlin: Neues Leben, 1960.

Volz, Hans. *Daten der Geschichte der NSDAP*. Tenth edition, Berlin: Junker & Duennhaupt, 1939.

Waite, Robert G. L. "Adolf Hitler's Anti-Semitism: A Study in History and Psychoanalysis" in Benjamin B. Wolman, ed. *The Psychoanalytical Interpretation of History*, New York: Basic Books, 1971.

Waite, Robert G. L. "Adolf Hitler's Guilt Feelings: A Problem in History and Psychology," *Journal of Interdisciplinary History*. Issue Two, Winter 1971.

Weigel, Reinhold. *Schicksalsweg des oberschlesischen Volkes*. Berlin: Zentralverlag, 1931.

Wentzke, Paul. *Ruhrkampf, Einbruch und Abwehr im rheinisch-west-faelischen Industriegebiet*. Two Volumes. Berlin: Duncker & Humblot, 1930-1932.

Werner, Andreas. *SA und NSDAP*. Unpublished doctoral dissertation: University of Erlangen-Nuernberg, 1964.

Wunderlich, Frieda. *Farm Labor in Germany 1810-1945*. Princeton: Princeton University Press, 1961.

General Index

(with cross-references to the index
of coded items, appendix A)

Abel, Theodore, vii, 5-6, 8fn, 62-
65, 121, 383n, 528, 578
Agricultural crisis, 77-95 passim,
320, 669; *see also* items 2
and 4
American radical youth, 44, 151,
237, 241, 257-259, 263, 302-
305, 366-367, 428, 436, 536,
589, 610, 677, 714-716
Anti-Marxism, 33, 106, 135, 183,
297, 353, 415, 517, 522-527,
671, 694-695, 702, 707; *see
also* items 27, 34, 35, 40, 43,
47, 56 and 61
Antisemitism, 498-509, 687-694,
715; as an ideology, 448, 455,
516, 477, 498; *see also* item
60; at school, 124, 307, 495,
505; *see also* item 24; genocide,
3, 376-477, 667;
Judenkoller, 33, 128, 169,
271, 377, 418, 494-495, 500-
516, 574; *see also* items 31, 62;
of party members, 33, 498-509;
see also items 60, 61, 62; pre-
1914 movements of, 124, 126,
297, 415, 515, 534; propaganda of, 5, 126, 307, 495,
517, 534, 574; stereotypes of
Weimar leaders, 32, 55, 58,
160, 173-175, 228, 513-518;
see also items 31, 56 and *Jews,
Kunze*, and *Schutz-und-Trutzbund*
Austria (Austrians)
17, 109-110, 115, 134, 143,
168, 248, 388, 456, 460, 663

Authoritarianism
3, 36-37, 43-44, 60, 72, 113,
257, 489-497, 505, 577, 646,
715; *see also* item 72

Bavarian People's Party (BVP)
77, 93, 215, 379, 405, 460
Beerhall putsch (1923)
29, 57, 91, 111, 123, 147, 164,
202, 223-224, 228, 243, 333,
371, 374, 418, 482, 581, 653;
see also item 36
Bolshevism
7, 106, 110, 146, 154, 177-
178, 195, 209-211, 415; *see
also items* 32, 34, 35, 40

Center party
17, 55, 66, 77, 88-89, 93, 97,
110, 120, 132-135, 189, 210,
260, 491, 516, 654
Chamberlain, Houston Stewart
307, 516
Colonial service
107-108, 352, 353
Communist party (KDP)
and Depression, 15n, 627
and Nazi takeover, 470, 644,
646
and political violence, 18n,
79, 260, 270, 334, 374, 376,
399, 404, 414, 420, 426, 603,
606, 625-627, 716
and youth, 13, 53-54, 376;
see also items 13 and *Red Front
Fighters League*
converts from, 211, 271,

Library of Congress Cataloging in Publication Data

Merkl, Peter H
    Political violence under the swastika: 581 early Nazis.

    Bibliography: p.
    1. Nationalsozialistische Deutsche Arbeiter-Partei—History. 2. National socialism—Biography. 3. Germany—Politics and government—1918-1933. I. Title.
DD253.25.M39   329.9'43 [B]   74-12143